Luke Wadding. A Life

Luke Wadding

A Life: Religion, Politics and Culture, 1588–1657

By Benjamin Hazard

PETER LANG
Oxford · Berlin · Bruxelles · Chennai · Lausanne · New York

Library of Congress Cataloging-in-Publication Data
Names: Hazard, Benjamin (Benjamin James Joseph) author
Title: Luke Wadding : a life : religion, politics and culture 1588-1657 / Benjamin Hazard.
Description: Oxford, United Kingdom ; New York : Peter Lang Ltd, [2025] |
Includes bibliographical references and index.
Identifiers: LCCN 2025012389 (print) | LCCN 2025012390 (ebook) | ISBN
9781803747330 hardback | ISBN 9781803747347 ebook | ISBN 9781803747354 epub
Subjects: LCSH: Wadding, Luke, 1588-1657 | Franciscans—Ireland—Biography | LCGFT:
Biographies
Classification: LCC BX4705.W2 H39 2025 (print) | LCC BX4705.W2 (ebook) |
DDC 271/.302—dc23/eng/20250502
LC record available at https://lccn.loc.gov/2025012389
LC ebook record available at https://lccn.loc.gov/2025012390
A catalogue record for this book is available from the British Library.

Bibliographic Information published by the Deutsche Nationalbibliothek
The Deutsche Nationalbibliothek lists this publication in the Deutsche
Nationalbibliografie; detailed bibliographic data is available in the internet at
http://dnb.d-nb.de.

Cover image
Reproduced courtesy of the National Gallery of Ireland.
Cover design by Peter Lang Group AG

ISBN 978-1-80374-733-0 (Print)
ISBN 978-1-80374-734-7 (ePDF)
ISBN 978-1-80374-735-4 (ePUB)
DOI 10.3726/b22821

Published by Peter Lang Ltd, Oxford, United Kingdom

info@peterlang.com www.peterlang.com

This publication has been peer reviewed.

Do mo mháthair, le grá mór.
I gcuimhne ar m'athair.

Contents

Figures

1 A cloak of the same colour as the habit was worn in winter. This painting was once attributed to José de Ribera. However, Lorenzo Salazar, Director of the Biblioteca di San Martino, Naples, identified the portrait as the work of Carlo Maratti; see Lorenzo Salazar, 'Dipinti attribuiti ad artisti Napoletani nella Galleria Nazionale Di Dublino', *Napoli nobilissima*, 13, fasc. 1 (1904), 153–56.

Tables

Glossary

chapter	Regular meeting of the members of a religious order
cismontane family	Franciscan observance in regions south-east of the Alps
confrère	Colleague in one's religious order
consultor	Expert adviser to the Roman curia
conventus nativus	First friary entered by a friar
curia	Administrative institution and Papal court
custos of custodes	Franciscan superior with authority over other superiors
de auxiliis	Theological controversy concerning grace and free will
Franciscan tertiary	Lay man or woman belonging to the Third Order in secular society
Gaelic Irish	Old Irish, often identified by 'O' and 'Mac' prefixes to surnames
incardination	Perpetual enlistment in a province of friars according to canon law
lector jubilatus	Highest academic honour awarded by the Franciscans
legajo	Document bundle
minister general	Head of each branch of the Franciscans: Observants, Conventuals and Capuchins
minister provincial	Head of a province in the various branches of the Franciscan Order
Old English	Descendants of the Anglo-Norman conquest of Ireland
Palesman	Inhabitant of English descent in Dublin, Kildare, Louth and Meath
sacred congregation	Commission composed of cardinals and specialists responsible to the pope for proposing decisions to be taken in the various areas of their competence

Scotism	Franciscan school of thought named after John Duns Scotus
Seraphic family	All Franciscans; men and women, lay and clerical
studium	House of studies and religious formation
socius	Friar assigned to assist another friar in work and travel
ultramontane family	Franciscan observance in regions north-west of the Alps
visitator	Friar appointed to conduct an inspection and report on a province
votum, vota	Detailed written opinion of *consultor*

Preface

I began the research for this book many years ago in an essay on Franciscan historiography at University College Cork, followed by my doctoral thesis at Maynooth University, and further detailed investigation at University College Dublin (UCD) on the Wadding Papers. My debt of obligation to friends and institutions is great. I am much obliged to Thomas O'Connor for supervising my doctorate on Flaithrí Ó Maolchonaire. To the Mícheál Ó Cléirigh Institute at UCD, I owe special gratitude for funding, which permitted me three years' postdoctoral research from 2008 to 2010, before I began teaching with UCD School of History. To John McCafferty and Edel Bhreathnach, I express my thanks. To Séamus Fanning of Waterford for his generosity and words of motivation. To Joseph MacMahon of the Friars Minor of the Irish Province, for his interest in this work at its inception and his encouragement to persevere. To his fellow Franciscan, John O'Keeffe, who permitted me the privilege of staying at St Isidore's College, Rome. To their confrères, Louis Brennan, Ignatius Fennessy, Mícheál Mac Craith, Benignus Millett, Stephen O'Kane and Gearóid Fran Ó Conaire for their guidance and help with sources. To Joseph McDermott and Lar Farrell for organising visits to Assisi and La Verna. To the Irish Pallotines at San Silvestro in Capite for further accommodation in Rome. I am indebted to Pierre Descotes of the Groupe de l'Institut d'Études Augustiniennes at the Université Paris-Sorbonne (Paris IV) for verifying my translations. To Angelo Bottone and Maolsheachlann Ó Ceallaigh for proofreading. I salute my colleagues, Conor Mulvagh and William Mulligan, for facilitating the research and writing since 2023.

The staff of libraries and archives deserve particular thanks for their patience and courtesy. To Kate Manning, Principal Archivist, and the staff at UCD Archives, for unstinting assistance with manuscript materials. To Evelyn Flanagan, Head of UCD Library Special Collections, Eugene Roche, Rachel Daly and Claire Dunne of Cultural Heritage and Special Collections, for all their help with seventeenth-century printed books. To Seamus Helferty for archival supervision of the project to catalogue and digitally preserve five volumes of the UCD-OFM 'D' manuscripts, from

2008 to 2010. At the National Library of Ireland, Gráinne MacLochlainn, Berni Metcalfe, Aoife Murphy and Máire Ní Chonalláin proved supportive and efficient. Caoimhe Ní Ghormáin at the Manuscripts & Archives Research Library, Trinity College Dublin, facilitated the acquisition of images, for which I am grateful. To Jérôme Sirdey, Yves Jocteur Montrozier and Pierre Guinard of the Bibliothèque Municipale de Lyon for their help relating to seventeenth-century Lyonnais booksellers. I am grateful to José María Burrieza Sánchez for assistance with cartographic material at the Archivo General de Simancas. To Rosie Keane of the National Gallery of Ireland for help with the Wadding portrait in Dublin. Further thanks to Maria Flynn for her prayers. To Carla Margarida da Cruz Valente and Margarida Relvão Calmeiro for their help in obtaining relevant material from Coimbra.

To José García Oro and Fray Natalio Saludes for valuable support relating to the Franciscan province of Santiago. To Brian Kirby, Provincial Archivist of Capuchin Archives, Ireland, and Esther Carreño Corchete of Biblioteca Central Capuchinos, Salamanca, for advice on Franciscan sources. My sincere thanks are due to James Kelly and William Murphy of Dublin City University, Hiram Morgan and Larry Walsh. To Kenneth Nicholls for sharing his extensive knowledge, to Julian Walton for kindly allowing me to consult his unpublished work on Waterford, to Donnchadh Ó Ceallacháin and Ben Murtagh for suggesting the Wadding family tree. To Tim O'Neill for the generous supply of relevant books, Kenneth Ferguson for timely information on the history of art and Liam Brockey for insights into Portuguese historiography.

Portions of this work have appeared in earlier form in print: 'Illustration and Ornamentation in the Works of Luke Wadding, Seventeenth-Century Historian and Theologian', in Alexander Wilkinson and Alejandra Ulla Lorenzo, eds, *Typography, Illustration and Ornamentation in the Early Modern Iberian Book World* (Leiden: Brill, 2020), 350–71; 'Irish Franciscans and the Santiago Province of Spain', in Matteo Binasco, ed, *Luke Wadding, the Franciscans and Global Catholicism* (Abingdon: Routledge, 2020), 19–38; 'Luke Wadding and the Breviary of Urban VIII: A Study of the Book Trade between Rome, the Low Countries and the Spanish Empire', *Studia Hib.*, 39 (2014), 87–101; 'Some Unpublished Correspondence of Luke

Wadding OFM to Giovanni Pietro Puricelli, Archpriest of San Lorenzo Maggiore, Milan, and Pietro di Gallarà', *Seanchas Ard Mhacha*, 24 (2012), 29–45; 'Saint Isidore's Franciscan College, Rome: From Centre of Influence to Site of Memory', in Enrique García Hernán and Óscar Recio Morales, eds, *Redes y Espacios de Poder de la Comunidad Irlandesa en España y la América Española, 1600–1825. Power Strategies: Spain and Ireland, 1600–1825* (Valencia: Albatros Ediciones, 2012), 103–14; 'A Manuscript Copy of the Declaration of Arbroath from the Roman Archives of Fr Luke Wadding OFM (1588–1657)', *SHR*, 90 (2011), 296–315; 'Correspondence from Jean-Baptiste Devenet and Claude Prost, Book Merchants of Lyon, to Fr Luke Wadding OFM, 1647–54', *AFH*, 104 (2011), 519–45; 'Luke Wadding's Petition to the Papacy on Behalf of Dutch and Flemish Migrants in Waterford, c.1642–51', *An. Hib.*, 41 (2009), 1–12.

In completing this work, many thanks are due to James McGuire. I also acknowledge the assistance I received from Beatrix Färber and James Egan. To Enrique García Hernán, Igor Pérez Tostado and Óscar Recio Morales for inviting me to participate in their projects. To Eduardo de Mesa Gallego for conversations about early modern times. To Tony Mason, I pay special tribute. For her encouragement and cooperation throughout, I am most grateful to my wife, Hélène, who read every chapter and made many helpful suggestions.

Abbreviations

ACSI	Archives of the College of St Isidore, Rome
AFH	*Archivum Franciscanum Historicum*
AGRB	Archives Générales du Royaume, Brussels/ Algemeen Rijksarchief, Brussel
SEG	Secrétaire d'État et de Guerre/Secretarie van State en Oorlog
AGS	Archivo General de Simancas
GA	Guerra Antigua
AHP	*Archivum Historiae Pontificiae*
An. Hib.	*Analecta Hibernica*
Annales Minorum	Luke Wadding, *Annales Minorum seu trium Ordinum a S. Francisco institutorum, ab anno 1541 continuati a pluribus viris eruditis*, 3rd edn, 32 vols (Quaracchi, 1931–64)
Archiv. Hib.	*Archivium Hibernicum*
BAV	Biblioteca Apostolica Vaticana
Barb. Lat.	Codici Barberini Latini
BnF	Bibliothèque nationale de France, Paris
Bodl.	Bodleian Library, Oxford
BCH	*British Catholic History*
Cal. state papers, Ire.,	*Calendar of State Papers, Ireland*
Cal. Carew MSS.	*Calendar of the Carew manuscripts*, 6 vols (London, 1867–73)
Cal. Ormond Deeds	*Calendar of Ormond Deeds* (Dublin, 1932–43)
Collectanea ord. Cist. Ref.	*Collectanea ordinis Cisterciensium reformatorum*
Coll. Hib.	*Collectanea Hibernica*
Comment. Rinucc.	Richard O'Ferrall and Robert O'Connell, *Commentarius Rinuccinianus de Sedis apostolicae legatione ad Foederatos Hiberniae Catholicos per annos 1645–49*, ed Stanislaus Kavanagh, 6 vols (Dublin, 1932–49)

C.I.É.	Córas Iompair Éireann (Public Transport Company of Ireland)
Cork Hist. Soc. Jn.	*Journal of the Cork Historical and Archaeological Society*
DBe	*Diccionario Biográfico electrónico de la Real Academia de la Historia*
Decies	*Decies: Journal of the Waterford Archaeological & Historical Society* (1976–)
DBI	*Dizionario biografico degli Italiani* (Rome, 1960–2020)
DIB	*The Dictionary of Irish Biography*, eds James McGuire and James Quinn, 9 vols (Cambridge, 2009)
EHR	*English Historical Review*
Fiants Eliz. Ire.	*The Irish fiants of the Tudor sovereigns: during the reigns of Henry VIII, Edward VI, Philip & Mary, and Elizabeth I / with a new introduction by Kenneth Nicholls and preface by Tomás G. Ó Canann* (Dublin, 1994)
Gilbert, *Contemp. Hist.*	J. T. Gilbert, ed, *A Contemporary History of Affairs in Ireland from 1641 to 1652*, 3 vols (Dublin, 1879–80)
Gilbert, *Ir. Confed.*	J. T. Gilbert, ed, *History of the Irish Confederation and the War in Ireland, 1641–3*, 7 vols (Dublin, 1882–91)
HJ	*Historical Journal*
Hist. MSS Comm. rep.	*Historical Manuscripts Commission Report*
IER	*Irish Ecclesiastical Record*
IHS	*Irish Historical Studies*
IJA	Irish Jesuit Archive, Dublin
ITQ	*Irish Theological Quarterly*
JEH	*Journal of Ecclesiastical History*
Jennings, *Wadding Papers*	Brendan Jennings, ed, *Wadding Papers, 1614–38* (Dublin, 1953)

JGAHS	*Journal of the Galway Archaeological and Historical Society*
JRSAI	*Journal of the Royal Society of Antiquaries of Ireland*
leg.	*legajo*
NHI, 3	*A New History of Ireland*, 3, eds, T. W. Moody, F. X. Martin and F. J. Byrne (Oxford, 1976; reprinted with bibliographical supplement, 2009)
ODNB	*The Oxford Dictionary of National Biography*
OFM	Order of Friars Minor
OFM, Cap.	Order of Friars Minor, Capuchin
OFM, Conv.	Order of Friars Minor, Conventual
Ormonde *MSS*	*Manuscripts of the Marquis of Ormonde, Preserved at the Castle, Kilkenny* (London, 1895–99)
PBSR	*Papers of the British School at Rome*
P&P	*Past and Present: A Journal of Historical Studies*
PL	J.- P. Migne, ed, *Patrologia Latina: Patrologiae cursus completus sive bibliotheca universalis [...] omnium ss. patrum, doctorum scriptorumque ecclesiasticorum qui ab aevo apostolico Innocentii III tempora floruerunt: recusio chronologica omnium quae exstitere monumentorum catholicae traditionis per duodecim priora ecclesiae saecula*, 221 vols (Parisiis: Excudebat Migne, 1844–64)
PULC	*Princeton University Library Chronicle*
RHE	*Revue d'histoire ecclésiastique*
RIA Proc.	*Proceedings of the Royal Irish Academy*

Scriptores ordinis minorum	*Scriptores ordinis minorum. Quibus accessit syllabus illorum, qui ex eodem Ordine pro fide Christi fortiter occubuerunt [...] Recensuit Fr. Lucas Waddingus* (*Editio novissima*, Rome, 1906)
SHR	*Scottish Historical Review*
Studia Hib.	*Studia Hibernica*
Studies	*Studies, an Irish quarterly review*
UCD-OFM	Irish Franciscan Manuscripts at University College Dublin
Vita Fratris Lucae Waddingi	Francis Harold, *Vita Fratris Lucae Waddingi*, 3rd edn (Quaracchi, 1931)
Opera omnia	*Opera omnia Ioannis Duns Scot*, eds, Luke Wadding et al., 16 vols (Lyon, 1639)
Wadding, *Opuscula*	Luke Wadding, *Beati Patris Francisci Assisiatis Opuscula* (Antwerp, 1623)
Waterford Arch. Soc. Jn.	*Journal of the Waterford and South-East of Ireland Archaeological Society* (1894–1920)

Note on Conventions

I have aimed to provide the closest possible translation in its historical context. Unless otherwise stated, the translations and figures are my own work. I report the original text in a footnote for citations in languages other than English and have expanded manuscript contractions marked in italics.

In the twentieth century, a second, separate numbering system was recorded on manuscript material in UCD-OFM, D.02 to UCD-OFM, D.04. Both sets are inserted here. I have retained the original orthography wherever possible and designated references to NLI microfilm to indicate that documents can be consulted at the National Library of Ireland.

Footnotes referring to the *Annales Minorum* and the *Scriptores ordinis minorum* relate to the third edition and the new edition respectively, as outlined in the list of abbreviations. However, when discussing Wadding's dedicatory letters and original approbations, the first edition of both these works is cited with the publication details enclosed in parentheses.

The Gregorian Calendar, introduced by Gregory XIII in 1582, became identified as New Style. It was immediately adopted in Italy, the Iberian Peninsula and France. Whereas in England and Ireland, the Julian Calendar, or Old Style, was still in use in 1752. To avoid confusion, all dates are left at the date of the original document.

Introduction

The Franciscan Luke Wadding is rightly regarded as a pivotal player in the seventeenth century. A well-known figure internationally, Wadding was a priest, a scholar, an educator and a mediator who packed into a life of seventy years incessant activity. From his early life in Ireland to his education in Portugal and Spain, from his career in Rome and the civil wars of the 1640s to the compilation and distribution of books, Wadding was not merely a survivor from the sixteenth century. Born in Ireland, he achieved distinction in Mediterranean Europe, which was comparatively unaffected by the Reformation and where Catholicism continued to operate unimpaired. Essay collections tend to survey peripheral events not directly related to the subject. The following monograph seeks to reveal fresh perspectives about Wadding. Since the central relationship between his religious concerns and contemporary politics has hitherto been overlooked, this book begins with a thorough assessment of change in late sixteenth-century Waterford. From the start, the question arises, how did Wadding's upbringing influence his subsequent formation? Before now, his early years have received little attention.

Wadding provides an important framework for understanding Ireland and Europe in the sixteenth and seventeenth centuries. His life, therefore, requires rigorous reassessment because parts have been studied in detail but separately from its continuity as a whole. This book provides an account of early modern authority and obedience. We follow Wadding from his family of origin in Ireland to the taking of vows with the Franciscans in Portugal, followed by the Spanish Habsburg presence in his life and the influence of papal primacy, before finding his own authority challenged at St Isidore's, the first of his three colleges, founded in 1625. Tracing this journey enables us to discern the influence that his own education brought to bear on the faculty and curriculum at the two houses he established in Rome and at the Irish Franciscan noviciate in Capranica.

In his chronicles and correspondence, Wadding approached history at a world level with an interpretation of events from the late Middle Ages until the early sixteenth century. In these terms, Wadding's finest achievement was the *Annales Minorum*. First published in eight volumes, it remains the most valuable source of Franciscan history from the order's origins in Europe to its continuance in the New World. By closing his eighth volume in 1540, Wadding dealt with the Reformation and the organisation of new missions with contrasting effect. An adequate appraisal of his contribution to the Irish presence on the continent and how this related to life in Ireland is essential to our understanding of the seventeenth century.

In response to the Reformation and its consequences, Wadding espoused the Franciscan view that renewal of the Church needed to be continual and, following the example of St Francis of Assisi, that reform began within each individual first. This equates with the tradition of being 'renewed in the spirit of your mind and not to be conformed to this world, that you may prove what is the good and pleasing and perfect will of God'.[1] As reform was closely connected with education and had to keep being intentional, Wadding recognised that the Church required the instruction of teachers at centres of excellence such as St Isidore's. The idea of a universal Christian monarchy under the providential leadership of the Habsburgs and the papacy endured until the 1630s.[2] Until that time, an alliance existed between Spain and the Irish Friars Minor.[3] Therefore, Luke Wadding's early affiliation to the Spanish Habsburgs occurred in the context of their

1 Romans 12:2, 'Et nolite conformari huic saeculo, sed reformamini in novitate sensus vestri, ut probetis quae sit voluntas Dei bona et beneplacens et perfecta'; cited by Robert Karris, *The Admonitions of St Francis. Sources and Meanings* (St Bonaventure, NY: Franciscan Institute Publications, 1999), 64. See also Timothy Johnson, 'Preaching and Praying on the Seine: Minorite Theology and the Prothemes in Bonaventure's *Sermones dominicales*', *The Cord*, 55 (2005), 2–9.

2 H. G. Koenigsberger, *The Habsburgs and Europe, 1516–1660* (Ithaca, N. Y.: Cornell University Press, 1971), xiv, 59, 247–51; Jean Bérenger, *A History of the Habsburg Empire, 1273–1700*, translated by C. A. Simpson (London: Longman, 1994), 219.

3 Óscar Recio Morales, *Ireland and the Spanish Empire, 1600–1825*, translated by Michael White (Dublin: Four Cours Press, 2010), 58–59; Declan Downey, 'A Castilian-Regalist Cradling: Spanish-Habsburg formation of the early Irish Counter Reformation', in Howard Clarke and J. R. S. Phillips, eds, *A Turbulent Priest Essays in Memory of Professor F. X. Martin OSA* (Dublin: University College Dublin Press, 2006), 96–206.

aspiration to re-establish the unity of Christendom. However, political decline ensued for Spain during the reign of Philip IV, which led him to declare: 'All are against us; we are against all'.[4] Once settled in the bosom of Rome, Wadding gravitated towards the papacy. His role in Urban VIII's spiritual endeavours and the pope's reassertion of supreme papal authority are dealt with from Chapter 4 onwards.

As an ecclesiastical historian once stated: 'History should be studied always as a process, not a picture'.[5] This study is divided into ten different stages corresponding to Wadding's experiences in Ireland, the Iberian Peninsula and Italy. Wadding did not spring ready from nowhere. Since no serious account exists of his early years, these will be examined in the first chapter as a necessary background to this study with a description of Wadding's infancy and youth in Waterford, the city of his birth, taking account of the influence that his family had upon his life and the schooling he received. It explains the various crises that occurred in the port city at that time, the relevance of the Anglo-Spanish war in Wadding's early life and the events that led to his departure from Ireland for Portugal. Once informed by Counter-Reformation teachings, religious thinking in Ireland coalesced against the Reformation campaign by 1580.[6] This points to religious beliefs among the laity and indicates how they participated in the early stages of the Counter Reformation in Ireland.

We then follow Wadding to Portugal. The second chapter discusses what he referred to as his 'apprenticeship' as a Franciscan friar, before assessing the progress he made as a scholar from the perspective of places of learning connected with him and his writings about Portugal. This involves tracing the journeys that he made and describing the people he met on the way, based on his own accounts. At twenty-five years of age, Wadding

4 'Todos contra nos, nos contra todos'; cited by Alfred de Reumont, *The Carafas of Maddaloni: Naples under Spanish Dominion* (London: Henry Bohn, 1854), 150.

5 J. P. Whitney, *Reformation Essays* (1st edn, London: SPCK, 1939), 5; cited by Trevor Jalland, *The Church and the Papacy* (repr. London: SPCK, 1946), vii.

6 Brendan Bradshaw, 'The English Reformation and Identity Formation in Ireland and Wales', in Brendan Bradshaw and Peter Robertson, eds, *British Consciousness and Identity: The Making of Britain, 1533–1707* (Cambridge: Cambridge University Press, 2004), 49–50.

left Portugal for Spain where he studied and taught until 1618. The third chapter accompanies him from Salamanca to Madrid as a Franciscan friar of the Santiago province, the friendships he established and the rivalries he encountered with members of other religious orders.

The next chapter describes the first two decades that Wadding spent in Italy from his arrival in Rome as part of the mission to promote the Immaculate Conception, to his research in many regions and cities, such as Umbria and Naples, followed by his return to the Eternal City. Extensive studies and continual pastoral work by mendicant friars required the accumulation of books and the creation of libraries. Wadding played a major role in defending the credentials of St Francis of Assisi and of the Franciscans more broadly. This part of the book concentrates on three of Wadding's first editions which illustrate the links between the Habsburg Netherlands, the Iberian Peninsula and Rome.

The fifth chapter concentrates on the foundation of St Isidore's in 1625 and deals with daily life at the college, and similarities with the Franciscan College of the Immaculate Conception in Prague, as well as the patronage enjoyed by Irish friars in Rome and the reception of students at the seminary for Irish secular clergy. As a censor of the Holy Office and chronicler of the Franciscan family, Wadding actively helped other scholars. Details are given in the following chapter, together with the concerted exchanges between Wadding and the book trade in the French city of Lyon where he brought eleven volumes to print. Handpicked intermediaries worked on his behalf to facilitate the distribution of his Lyonnais works for more than twenty years. These aspects of Wadding's life enable us to follow the progress of his publication programme and reveal his prudent efforts to achieve greater unity within the Franciscan family. This approach also illustrates some of the hurdles that Wadding faced.

The prominent role Wadding fulfilled at the Roman curia included the selection of bishops for Irish dioceses. The many demands on his time reflect the breadth of the Irish Franciscan's experiences as theologian, historian and *consultor* to the papal secretariat. These points, along with the links between empire and print, are described in Chapter 7. Wadding contributed to the revision of the Roman breviary of Urban VIII. Printed in Antwerp, the intended market for new liturgical books included Spanish overseas colonies. Following his studies in the Iberian Peninsula, his work in Rome, and his contacts with the Plantin-Moretus press, Wadding took a keen interest in the evangelisation of the New World.

The narrative then moves back to Ireland in the 1640s. At first sight, a Franciscan's involvement in a military campaign may seem ambiguous and historians have shied away from dealing with Wadding's experiences during the wars of that decade. Nonetheless, early modern Europe was violent, divisive and restive. Wadding was pressed into service by the supreme council of the confederation of Kilkenny to obtain papal sanction and finance for Gaelic and Old English Catholics who took up arms in an uneasy alliance. This chapter measures the tensions and political sensitivities that Wadding encountered in his efforts to obtain support during a difficult decade. Through his diplomacy, his cultural experiences and his intellectual connections, Wadding enables us to reach a better understanding of the great struggle in seventeenth-century Europe between France and Spain.

The penultimate chapter contends with problems that survived the war and spilled over in Wadding's life. This involved the collapse in relations with the papal nuncio, Rinuccini, as well as an imbroglio with the marquis of Ormond, disagreement over Jansen's *Augustinus* and, perhaps worst of all, internal fighting among the Irish Franciscans. Yet, in the last phase of his life, Wadding successfully completed his publications, including the monumental *Annales Minorum*. In his own words, these were 'an immense work' published in eight large folio volumes. This is dealt with in the final chapter as Wadding continued to attend to his other work in Rome despite declining health and remained preoccupied with the running of St Isidore's College until his death. Historical research witnessed significant advances in the seventeenth century when scholars placed an emphasis on the interrogation of original sources. Therefore, along with James Ussher, Sir James Ware and John Colgan, Luke Wadding made a central contribution to 'the new historiography' in Ireland.[7]

7 T. W. Moody, 'Introduction', *NHI*, vol. 3, lxi.

Historiography

Important research undertaken by many historians provides the foundations upon which this book is built. The following section concentrates on sources about Luke Wadding and does not represent an exhaustive list of information. Wadding recorded autobiographical notes in the *Annales Minorum* and compiled the entry for his own writings in the first edition of the *Scriptores ordinis minorum*. He also cooperated with his nephew, Francis Harold, in compiling a Latin biography.[8] First published in 1662, the *Vita Fratris Lucae Waddingi* remains the most authoritative account. Wadding's memory found fortunate expression in the judgement of Harold, whose work benefitted from first-hand information and his own eye-witness descriptions, many of which are unique. The intended legacy for Francis Harold was Wadding's posthumous reputation and veneration. He cast his uncle in the best possible light and the text occasionally lacks a consistent chronology. This exemplifies the fine line between hagiography and history in the seventeenth century.[9]

The *Vita Fratris Lucae Waddingi* lessened the negative effects of the *Commentarius Rinuccinianus*, another contemporary source that repeatedly refers to Wadding, which was completed in manuscript four years later.[10] Begun by Richard O'Ferrall, defender of the papal nuncio, GianBattista Rinuccini, at the Roman court, and completed by Robert O'Connell, the *Commentarius* is recognised as a major source for the period from 1645 to 1649. O'Ferrall aimed concerted criticism at Old English targets.[11] They

8 Francis Harold, *Vita Fratris Lucae Waddingi* (3rd edn, Quaracchi: Ad Claras Aquas, 1931).

9 Simon Ditchfield, '*Historia magistra sanctitatis*? The Relationship between Historiography and Hagiography in Italy after the Council of Trent (*c.*1564–1742)', in Massimo Firpo, ed, *Nunc alia tempora, alii mores. Storici e storia in età postridentina* (Florence: Olschki, 2005), 159–84.

10 Clare Carroll, 'The *Vita Waddingi* and the Memory of Confederate and Cromwellian Ireland', in Matteo Binasco, ed, *Luke Wadding, the Irish Franciscans, and Global Catholicism* (Abingdon: Routledge, 2020), 186.

11 Ian Campbell, 'Truth and Calumny in Baroque Rome: Richard O'Ferrall and the *Commentarius Rinuccinianus*', 1648–67, *IHS*, 38 (2012), 211–29.

accused Wadding of serving his own interests, claiming that he favoured Ormond, lord lieutenant of Ireland, and Old English political concerns.[12] The direct relevance of this source to Wadding is examined in chapters 8 and 9 below.

Both O'Ferrall and O'Connell were Capuchin friars. St Francis of Assisi represented the single unifying presence common to all members of the Franciscan order and Wadding paid tribute to the Capuchins in the *Annales Minorum*, but regarded them as rivals to his own branch the Observants.[13] For this reason, Mícheál Mac Craith has called for Wadding's life to be examined in greater detail.[14] The Order of Friars Minor consisted of three branches by 1525. These were the Observants, the Conventuals and the Capuchins. The Observant movement marked a return to the ideals of the founding saints and also prevailed in Spain among the monastics but especially the mendicants.[15] In Ireland, the Observant reform had advanced in the second half of the fifteenth century and acquired the majority of Irish Conventual friaries before the Henrician Reformation. The Irish Conventuals were formally incorporated with the Observants by 1567.[16] Therefore, the Observants became known as the Irish Franciscans long before the Capuchins established their mission to Ireland.[17] Both Clement VIII and Philip II supported the Franciscan Observance, which prevented

12 *Comment. Rinucc.*, vol. 4, 239–240.

13 F. X. Martin, *Friar Nugent. A Study of Francis Lavallin Nugent (1569–1635). Agent of the Counter-Reformation*, Bibliotheca Seraphico-Capuccina (Rome: Capuchin Historical Institute; London: Methuen, 1962), 246–47.

14 Mícheál Mac Craith, 'Seraphic Sparks: The Irish Franciscan and Capuchin Colleges on the Continent', in Liam Chambers and Thomas O'Connor, eds, *Forming Catholic Communities: Irish, Scots and English College Networks in Europe, 1568–1918* (Leiden: Brill, 2017), 52.

15 A. D. Wright, *Catholicism and Spanish Society under the Reign of Philip II, 1555–98, and Philip III, 1598–1621* (Lampeter: Edwin Mellen Press, 1991), 101.

16 Colmán Ó Clabaigh, *The Friars in Ireland, 1224–1540* (Dublin: Four Courts Press, 2012), 68–70, 192–93; idem, *The Franciscans in Ireland: From Reform to Reformation* (Dublin: Four Courts Press, 2002), 158–180; Francis Cotter, *The Friars Minor in Ireland from Their Arrival to 1400* (St Bonaventure: Franciscan Institute, 1994), 15, 23.

17 For the papal charter of 1608, see Martin, *Friar Nugent*, 301.

the Capuchins from establishing themselves on a strong footing.[18] Chapter 6 of the present work refers to Wadding's attempts to bring calm to his relationship with the Capuchins later in life.

In the eighteenth century, Walter Harris translated the works of Sir James Ware from Latin. The second volume included a history of the writers of Ireland that continued beyond Ware's *De scriptoribus Hiberniae* of 1639, which Harris revised with many additions. Ware respected Wadding's scholarship and his own references to the Irish Franciscan were dispersed through his work.[19] In a detailed description of Wadding's life, Harris wished that he could 'excuse him from the Hand he had in fomenting and aiding the Irish Rebellion, which broke out in 1641, the only Action of his Life that hath tarnished his great Virtues'.[20] However, Wadding stated that he was unaware of the insurrection when it broke out on 22 October 1641 and was only invited to become involved a year later. This point is dealt with at the start of Chapter 8.

The *Árbol Chrónologico de esta Santa Provincia de Santiago* is perhaps the most significant Spanish source for Wadding. Compiled by his confrère, Jacobo de Castro, and published in Salamanca in two volumes, the contents of the first volume note Wadding's life in detail. From his taking of vows in Portugal and his commitments at Salamanca, to the manifold tasks he accomplished in Rome as an official at the curia. Above all, though, the

18 Benjamin Hazard, 'Irish Franciscans and the Santiago Province of Spain', in Matteo Binasco, ed, *Luke Wadding, the Irish Franciscans, and Global Catholicism* (Abingdon: Routledge, 2020), 20.

19 James Ware, *De Scriptoribvs Hiberniae. Libri Dvo Prior continet Scriptores, in Hibernia natos. Posterior, Scriptores alios, qui in Hibernia munera aliqua obierunt* (Dublin: Typographia Societatis Bibliopolarum, 1639), 59–61, 64–65, 71, 76, 96, 124.

20 Walter Harris, ed and trans, *The Whole Works of Sir James Ware concerning Ireland, Revised and improved. The Writers of Ireland in two books [...] Written in Latin by Sir James Ware, Knight; Now Newly Translated into English* (Dublin: Reilly, 1746), Book 1, 138. The *Enciclopedia Italiani* entry on Wadding appeared to follow suit; Nicola Turchi, 'Wadding, Luca, Teologo e storico francescano', *Enciclopedia Italiana di scienze, lettere ed arti* (Rome: Treccani, 1937); <http://156.54.191.164/enciclopedia/luca-wadding_%28Enciclopedia-Italiana%29/> accessed 14 September 2024: 'la cui infelice ribellione antinglese del 1641–49 sostenne con efficacia e con tatto'.

Árbol description refers to Wadding's publications as a theologian and his work as chronicler of the Franciscan family.[21]

From 1731 to 1745, José Maria da Fonseca arranged the reprinting of the *Annales Minorum* in Rome, in nineteen volumes with the addition of new material up to 1564.[22] Interest may have remained limited to readers of Latin within religious orders but, following a period of comparative silence,[23] Irish historians gave renewed attention to his life and consulted manuscripts at St Isidore's. Charles Meehan, a member of the Young Ireland movement, made important findings and, in 1846, published *The Confederation of Kilkenny*.[24] In later decades, this was followed by many editions of *The Rise and Fall of the Irish Franciscan Monasteries*.[25] Wadding was a key protagonist for Meehan, but aspects of his work were prone to overstatement when referring to Donatus Mooney, historian of the Irish province.[26] John T. Gilbert conducted notable research on the years 1641–52, drawn from sources with a Gaelic Irish outlook.[27] Based on documentary evidence from an Old English perspective, Gilbert subsequently described Wadding's

21 Jacobo de Castro, *Árbol Chronólogico de esta Santa Provincia de Santiago*, 2 vols (Salamanca: por Francisco García Onorato y San Miguel, 1722; repr. Madrid: Editorial Cisneros, 1976–77), vol. 1, 126–128.

22 Maria Gabriela Oliveira, 'A reedição dos 'Annales Minorum' de Lucas Wadding e a figura de Fr. Joseph Maria da Fonseca e Évora', in José Adriano Moreira de Freitas Carvalho, ed, *Frei Marcos de Lisboa: cronista franciscano bispo de Lisboa. Actas do Colóquio patrocinado por la Faculdade de Letras do Porto* (Porto: Faculdade de Letras do Porto, 2002), 93–104.

23 Joseph MacMahon, 'The Silent Century, 1698–1829', in Edel Bhreathnach, Joseph, MacMahon and John McCafferty, eds, *The Irish Franciscans 1534–1990* (Dublin: Four Courts, 2009), 77–101.

24 Charles Meehan, *The Confederation of Kilkenny* (Dublin: James Duffy, 1846); cited by Nicholas Canny, *Imagining Ireland's Pasts. Early Modern Ireland Through the Centuries* (Oxford: Oxford University Press, 2021), 237–240.

25 Charles Meehan, *The Rise and Fall of the Irish Franciscan Monasteries and Memoirs of the Irish Hierarchy in the Seventeenth Century* (3rd edn, Dublin: James Duffy, 1870).

26 Brendan Jennings, ed, 'Brussels MS. 3947: *Donatus Moneyus, De Provincia Hiberniae S. Francisci*', *An. Hib.*, 6–7 (1934), 12.

27 Gilbert, *Ir. Confed.*

role in the political progress of the confederation of Kilkenny.[28] Joseph O'Shea's account of Wadding, inspired in part by the romanticism of Irish nationalism, often lacked chronological context and would have benefitted from an organised system of annotation.[29]

Following the unrest of the Risorgimento, ongoing interest from scholars in Ireland led the friars at St Isidore's to obtain permission from the Franciscan minister general to assign Irish manuscripts to Dublin 'in boxes sealed with the seal of the British legation at Rome to ensure their diplomatic immunity'.[30] Contained within were sources relating to Wadding's work as theologian, historian, Irish agent in Rome, and *consultor* to several sacred congregations and papal commissions. Wadding's papers are also to be found in the Vatican Library; Biblioteca Luca Wadding at the Franciscan curia, Rome; Biblioteca Landiana, Piacenza; Biblioteca Nazionale, Naples; Biblioteca Ambrosiana, Milan; the Archives of the Bollandists, Brussels; the Archives Générales du Royaume, Brussels; the Von Harrach Archive, Vienna; and the Franciscan friary of St Jerome in Vienna.[31] Matteo Binasco has recently discovered further material at the Archivio storico del Vicariato di Roma.[32]

By 1886, twenty-five volumes of the *Annales Minorum* were completed by Franciscan friars, up to the year 1622.[33] Twenty years later, an Historical Manuscripts Commission report was begun in Dublin by George Burtchaell, a practising barrister, and completed by James Macmullen Rigg, a legal scholar and translator. The sources they edited included many letters that Wadding wrote and received in Rome. Burtchaell and Rigg

28 Gilbert, *Contemp. Hist.*

29 Joseph O'Shea, *The Life of Father Luke Wadding: Founder of St Isidore's College, Rome* (Dublin: M. H. Gill, 1885).

30 Myles Dillon, Canice Mooney and Pádraig de Brún, eds, *Catalogue of Irish Manuscripts in the Franciscan Library, Killiney* (Dublin: Dublin Institute for Advanced Studies, 1969), xviii.

31 Benignus Millett, 'Luke Wadding (1588–1657), Franciscan Priest, Scholar and Churchman', *DIB*, vol. 9, 680–85.

32 Matteo Binasco, 'Not Only a "Hibernese" in the *Urbs*. Luke Wadding and His Entourage in Seventeenth Century Rome', in idem, ed, *Luke Wadding, the Irish Franciscans and Global Catholicism*, 88.

33 Hubert Jedin and J. P. Dolan, eds, *History of the Church: From the High Middle Ages to the eve of the Reformation* (London: Burns & Oates, 1980), 677.

were assisted by scholars such as the Oxford historian, Charles Plummer, and Michael McEnery of the Public Record Office of Ireland.[34] Their work represented a strong start to twentieth-century scholarship on Wadding and cast new light on his life. Although space constraints limited the report to summaries and translations of documents without recourse to the original languages, the Bollandist Paul Grosjean referred to Burtchaell and Rigg for his own catalogue.[35]

Archivum Franciscanum Historicum, the flagship journal of Franciscan history, has presented readers with peer-reviewed research about Wadding since 1912. The earliest contributions relate to his correspondence, printed work from his later years, and the various editions of the *Annales Minorum* written by Wadding and his continuators.[36] The librarians at Merchants Quay in Dublin, Thomas O'Reilly and E. B. Fitzmaurice, followed long-established Franciscan methods by dividing the manuscripts into sections with alphabetically ordered shelf-marks. O'Reilly also composed a report on matters for his confrères in Rome.[37]

From 1916 to 1920, *The Catholic Bulletin* published a complete translation of diaries by Dionisius Massari, second-in-command to Rinuccini. The anonymous translator stated that the memoirs were written by Massari, or prepared under his direction, for Count Tommaso Rinuccini, the

34 G. D. Burtchaell and J. M. Rigg, eds, *Hist. MSS Comm. rep. on Franciscan Manuscripts Preserved at the Convent, Merchants' Quay, Dublin* (Dublin: Historical Manuscripts Commission, 1906). Raymond Gillespie, 'The Historical Manuscripts Commission and the Franciscan manuscripts', *Irish Archives*, 14 (2007), 22–32.

35 Paul Grosjean, 'Catalogus codicum hagiographicorum latinorum bibliothecarum Dubliniensium', *Analecta Bollandiana*, 46, (1928), 81–82.

36 Apart from other articles mentioned elsewhere in this literature review, see Benvenuto Bughetti, 'Alcune lettere inedite del P. Luca Waddingo OFM a Pier Maria Campi', *AFH*, 5 (1912), 149–53; Livarius Oliger, 'De nova Lucae Waddingi Annalium Minorum editione', *AFH*, 24 (1931), 402–4; Michael Bihl, 'Tabula chronologica variarum editionum Annalium Minorum a Luca Waddingo aliisque conscriptorum', *AFH*, 28 (1935), 579–82; Edith Pasztor, 'Luca Wadding, editore della «Vita Anselmi episcopi Lucensis»', *AFH*, 54 (1961), 303–28; Basilio Pandžić, 'Gli «Annales Minorum» di Luca Wadding', *AFH*, 70 (1977), 656–66.

37 Thomas O'Reilly, 'Manuscripta Franciscana Archivi Conventus Dublinensis OFM', *AFH*, 7 (1914), 749–59; *Duanaire Dháibhidh Uí Bhruadair*, ed John MacErlean (London: Irish Texts Society, 1910), 206.

nuncio's brother, in Florence. The manuscript of 363 pages is preserved at Propaganda Fide Historical Archives.[38] As becomes apparent from 1645 to 1649, Massari's experiences show that Wadding's involvement in the conflict became more peripheral during Rinuccini's nunciature.

To mark the third centenary of St Isidore's, Gregory Cleary published his research on the College and its founder Luke Wadding. In so doing, Cleary provided an essential landmark of lasting value to historians. Notwithstanding the demands of his workload as guardian, he acknowledged that the book was a task that he could only partially finish.[39] Cleary's narrative reflects post-Civil War interests in Ireland. Contemporary concerns concentrated on supporting the fledgling Free State by promoting a favourable image of Ireland's past to show that the country was capable of existing independently. In this setting, Cleary echoed the earlier tradition, with an explanation of Wadding's saintly life and the sanctity of St Isidore's College. Between 1931 and 1964, the third edition of the *Annales Minorum* appeared in print in thirty-two volumes.[40] By then, apart from Luke Wadding, Francis Harold and José Maria da Fonseca, the following Franciscan editors brought the *Annales Minorum* up to the year 1680: Giovanni da Lucca, Giuseppe Maria di Ancona, Gaetano Michelessi and Eusebius Fermendžin, Stanislaus Melchiorri, Aniceto Chiappini and Basilio Pandžić.[41]

38 'My Irish Campaign', in *The Catholic Bulletin*, 6 (1916): 28–35, 82–8, 153–9, 217–22, 302–8, 367–73, 445–9, 502–5, 563–5, 618–20, 655–8; 7 (1917), 111–14, 179–82, 246–9, 295–6; 8 (1918), 140–2, 195–7, 247–9, 300–3, 396–8; 9 (1919), 66–8, 116–17, 200–1, 310–11, 488–90, 538–40, 603–4, 649–52; 10 (1920), 735–44. The original source is *Relazione del viaggio di Dionisio Massari, per servizio della religione cattolica nell'anno 1645, 1646 et 1647 in Ibernia con Mons. Rinuccini* (Archivio della Sacra Congregazione di Propaganda Fide (APF), Miscellanee Varie, vol. 9); NLI Microfilm n.5410, p.5541. The translator was, perhaps, John Hagan, vice-rector of the Pontifical Irish College, Rome, from 1904–19 and rector from 1919–30. Hagan was a trained historian based in Rome and often contributed to *The Catholic Bulletin*.

39 Gregory Cleary, *Father Luke Wadding and St Isidore's College, Rome: Biographical and Historical Notes and Documents* (Rome: Tipografia del senato del G. Bardi, 1925), v.

40 *Annales Minorum seu trium Ordinum a S. Francisco institutorum*, 32 vols (3rd edn, Quaracchi: Collegio San Bonaventura, 1931–64).

41 *Pubblicazioni dei Frati Editori di Quaracchi Fondazione Collegio San Bonaventura* (Grottaferrata: Frati Editori di Quaracchi, 2011), 28–30.

Michael Hynes published the results of his doctoral research on Rinuccini's manuscripts in 1932, and the core of his work remains solid.[42] Two years later, Brendan Jennings printed documents from St Isidore's in *Analecta Hibernica*.[43] At a time of increased interest in history, these sources were vital for those who sought to understand past events. Many manuscript sources and guides to such sources relating to Wadding have been published in *Archivium Hibernicum* since the late 1940s. These include references to Wadding's involvement in the Ludovisian College and also show how the writing of ecclesiastical history is no longer limited to the clergy.[44]

In 1945, Canice Mooney, Joseph Healy and Máire O'Brien documented records of Irish interest at the Archivo General de Simancas, where they compiled a microfilm survey of material for the National Library of Ireland.

42 Michael Hynes, *The Mission of Rinuccini, Nuncio Extraordinary to Ireland, 1645–49* (Dublin: Browne & Nolan, 1932), 9–11, 16, 34, 60, 71, 78, 81, 133, 160, 174, 176, 183, 238, 242, 263–64, 295, 306.

43 Brendan Jennings, ed, 'Documents from the Archives of St Isidore's College', *An. Hib.*, 6 (1934), 203–47.

44 Brendan Jennings, ed, 'Miscellaneous Documents I, 1588–1634', *Archiv. Hib*, 12 (1946), 70–200; idem, ed, 'Miscellaneous Documents II, 1625–40', *Archiv. Hib.*, 14 (1949), 1–49; idem, ed, 'Miscellaneous Documents III, 1602–1715', *Archiv. Hib.*, 15 (1950), 1–73; Cathaldus Giblin, ed, 'Vatican Library: MSS Barberini Latini: A Guide to the Material of Irish Interest on Microfilm in the National Library, Dublin', *Archiv. Hib.*, 18 (1955), 67–144; Brendan Jennings, ed, '*Acta Sacrae Congregationis de Propaganda Fide*, 1622–50', *Archiv. Hib.*, 22 (1959), 28–139; Michael Olden, ed, 'Episcopal Comments on the *Decreta pro Recto Regimine Ecclesiarum Hiberniae*, 1635–36', *Archiv. Hib.*, 27 (1964), 1–12; Benignus Millett, 'The Archives of St Isidore's College, Rome', *Archiv. Hib.*, 40 (1985), 1–13; Tadhg Ó hAnnracháin, 'Vatican Diplomacy and the Mission of Rinuccini to Ireland', *Archiv. Hib.*, 47 (1993), 78–88; Hugh Fenning, ed, 'Documents of Irish Interest in the "Fondo Missioni" of the Vatican Archives', *Archiv. Hib.*, 49 (1995), 3–47; idem, ed, 'Irishmen Ordained at Rome, 1592–1697', *Archiv. Hib.*, 59 (2005), 1–36; Vera Orschel and John Hanly, eds, 'Calendar of Seventeenth- and Eighteenth-Century Documents at the Archives of the Irish College, Rome (with Index)', *Archiv. Hib.*, 63 (2010), 7–263; Matteo Binasco and Vera Orschel, eds, 'Prosopography of Irish Students admitted to the Irish College, Rome, 1628–1798 (with Index)', *Archiv. Hib.*, 66 (2013), 16–62; Matteo Binasco, 'The Irish Community in Rome, 1377–1870: a Historiographical Overview', *Archiv. Hib.*, 71 (2018), 147–57.

Original letters relating to the life of Luke Wadding were among their discoveries.[45] Elsewhere, writing about Luke Wadding's nephew, Bonaventure Barron of Clonmel, Benignus Millett discovered that Wadding received some votes in a conclave for a papal election.[46]

In 1953, the Franciscan Father Brendan Jennings published *Wadding Papers, 1614–38* for the Irish Manuscripts Commission. This provided readers with a series of archival documents in Latin, Italian, Spanish, French and English, thus enabling detailed study of the administrative and religious history of Ireland. These sources were drawn from Wadding's extensive correspondence then preserved at the Dún Mhuire House of Studies in Killiney, Dublin. Two articles subsequently published in the *Irish Ecclesiastical Record* heralded the most concerted period of scholarship relating to Wadding. First, Professor Patrick Corish of St Patrick's College, Maynooth, examined Wadding's diplomacy in its Counter-Reformation setting, taking account of Old English and Gaelic interaction within the Franciscan order, Irish patriotism, relations with the papacy and the war in Ireland during the 1640s.[47] Meanwhile, Canice Mooney presented a number of Wadding's letters and parts of letters written by him, together with a helpful synopsis.[48] Mooney established himself as an authority on Wadding a year later with a further article relating to the numerous

45 *National Library of Ireland Report of the Council of Trustees for 1950–51* (Dublin: National Library of Ireland, 1952).

46 Bonaventure Barron, *Annales Ordinis SS. Trinitatis Redemptionis Captivorum fundatoribus SS. Ioanne de Matha et Felice de Valois tomus primus primam centuriam annorum complexus hoc est ab anno Christi Domini 1198 ad annum 1297* (Rome: Angelo Bernabò, 1684), ii, where he explains: 'qui etiam in Conclavi, aliquot Cardinalium suffragio pro summon Pontificatu accepit; denique Authori nostro avunculus'; Benignus Millett, 'Bonaventure Barron OFM, *Hibernus Clonmeliensis*', in Philip O'Connell and W. C. Darmody, eds, *Siege of Clonmel Commemoration: Tercentenary Souvenir Record* (Clonmel: Nationalist Newspaper Co., 1950), 41–46. See also Edel Bhreathnach, 'Luke Wadding (1588–1657): The Only Irishman to Receive Votes in a Papal Conclave', *History Ireland*, 15 (2007), 12–13.

47 Patrick Corish, 'Father Luke Wadding and the Irish Nation', *IER*, 5th series, 88 (1957), 377–95.

48 Canice Mooney, 'The Letters of Luke Wadding', *IER*, 5th series, 88 (1957), 396–409.

publications his confrère oversaw in the early seventeenth century.[49] Eager to popularise history, Mooney completed important research in publications intended for the general public. As chaplain to C.I.É. bus workers, he published in their magazine *Terminus* for three years from 1954.[50] A detailed article on Wadding's medical history followed in the journal *Assisi* to mark the tercentenary of his death.[51]

Lucius McClean, an Irish friar and regular newspaper columnist, compiled a tercentenary tribute to Wadding, his home country's 'greatest emigrant and exile'.[52] In Dublin, the Department of External Affairs recorded that Augustine Sepinski, minister general, visited Ireland in connection with the tercentenary. He received an honorary doctorate of law from the National University of Ireland and was made a freeman of Waterford.[53] More Wadding commemorations led to events across Ireland. At University College Galway, Síle Ní Chinnéide delivered the Tercentenary Lecture. Her concise account of Wadding's life comprised the early years and his studies followed by his learned endeavours at St Isidore's and at the Roman curia.[54] In commemoration of Wadding's tercentenary, a volume of essays was compiled by recognised experts in their respective fields.[55] Canice Mooney made a systematic defence of Wadding to counter accusations that he was biased against the Gaelic Irish and opposed to the best interests of Ireland.[56] Manuel de Castro investigated Wadding's associations

49 Idem, 'The Writings of Father Luke Wadding OFM', *Franciscan Studies*, 18 (1958), 225–39.

50 Colmán Ó Clabaigh, 'Review: Benedict O'Sullivan OP, edited by Hugh Fenning OP, *Medieval Irish Dominican Studies* (2009)', *JRSAI*, 139 (2009), 135–136.

51 Canice Mooney, 'Father Luke Wadding – The Last Years', *Assisi*, 19 (1957), 89–91.

52 Lucius McClean, *Father Luke Wadding: Irishman and Franciscan* (Dublin: Assisi Press, 1956), 7. See also Mary E. Daly, 'A Second Golden Age: The Irish Franciscans, 1918–1963', in Edel Bhreathnach, Joseph MacMahon and John McCafferty, eds, *The Irish Franciscans, 1534–1990* (Dublin: Four Courts Press, 2009), 144.

53 *Éire Ireland: Weekly Bulletin of the Department of External Affairs*, 363 (1957), 4.

54 Síle Ní Chinnéide, 'Luke Wadding, 1588–1657: Tercentenary Lecture', *JGAHS* 26 (1955), 81–93.

55 Franciscan Fathers, eds, *Father Luke Wadding Commemorative Volume* (Dublin: Clonmore & Reynolds, 1957).

56 Canice Mooney, 'Was Luke Wadding a Patriotic Irishman?', in Franciscan Fathers, eds, *Father Luke Wadding Commemorative Volume*, 15–92.

with Portugal and Spain, from his arrival in the Iberian Peninsula until the Spanish theological mission to Rome more than a decade later. De Castro's contribution to the volume was both scholarly and thorough, but he stated that circumstances prevented him from writing a more complete account.[57] Benignus Millett sought 'to encourage and facilitate' the writing of a comprehensive monograph by presenting scholars with his guide to a biography of Wadding.[58]

In 1628, Luke Wadding and Cardinal Ludovisi established a college in Rome to educate candidates for the Irish diocesan priesthood. Patrick Corish accounted for the Ludovisian College's early years, the difficulties encountered and the circumstances of the college's transfer to the Society of Jesus.[59] More recently, Thomas O'Connor has enhanced the research with his observations on the reorganisation of Catholicism in Ireland and the need for an institution that existed exclusively for the reception of Irish diocesan students in Rome.[60]

In a study of 110 pages, Lucien Ceyssens, the foremost authority on the history of Jansenism, carefully assessed Wadding's role in the debate that took place over the *Augustinus* by Dutch theologian and bishop of Ypres, Cornelius Jansen. Ceyssens recorded his verdict in conjunction with his views on Flaithrí Ó Maolchonaire and Hugh Bourke, Wadding's Irish confrères.[61] Whereas De Castro and Ceyssens often gave only the Latin in

57 Manuel de Castro, 'Wadding and the Iberian Peninsula', in Franciscan Fathers, eds, *Father Luke Wadding Commemorative Volume*, 122.

58 Benignus Millett, 'Guide to Material for a Biography of Father Luke Wadding', in Franciscan Fathers, eds, *Father Luke Wadding Commemorative Volume*, 229.

59 Patrick Corish, 'The Beginnings of the Irish College, Rome', in Franciscan Fathers, eds, *Luke Wadding Commemorative Volume*, 284–294. See also John Hanly, ed, 'Records of the Irish College, Rome, under Jesuit administration', in *Archiv. Hib.*, 27 (1964), 13–75. The Ludovisian College moved twice before reaching its present location near St John Lateran.

60 Thomas O'Connor, 'The Irish College, Rome, in the Age of Religious Renewal, 1625–90', in John Hanly, ed, *Collegium Hibernorum de Urbe, 1628–78. An Early Manuscript Account of the Foundation and Development of the Ludovisian College of the Irish in Rome* (Rome: Pontificio Collegio Irlandese, 2003), 13–32.

61 Lucien Ceyssens, 'Florence Conry, Hugh de Burgo, Luke Wadding, and Jansenism', Franciscan Fathers, eds, *Father Luke Wadding Commemorative Volume*, 295–404.

the text of their essays, I have translated the original sources to facilitate the reader.

The intricacy of Wadding's theological thought deserves an entire book in its own right. He specialised in the life and works of John Duns Scotus, the Subtle Doctor of Franciscan theology who championed the Immaculate Conception of Mary, dealt with in detail by Charles Balić.[62] New research by Matthew Vander Vennet draws our attention to Wadding's role in the history of the dogma during the early seventeenth century.[63] Wadding's most notable accomplishment in theology was the first edition of the *Opera omnia* of Duns Scotus and, although the contents have been superseded, this edition was well-judged and practical.[64] A document in Wadding's own hand, preserved among his papers at University College Dublin, defends Mary and includes his considered opinion on her passing from earthly life, prepared for print with many marginalia and occasional notes in Spanish.[65] To close the 1957 commemorative volume, Cathaldus Giblin transcribed and translated seventeenth-century manuscripts relating to the appointment of bishops to vacant Irish sees. Amongst other matters, he showed that Wadding stood as first witness for Thomas Walsh before his promotion to the archbishopric of Cashel.[66]

The most significant contribution to Wadding studies was made by twentieth-century Franciscans. From 1958 to 2006, the Franciscan Province of Ireland published historical sources and finding aids in *Collectanea Hibernica*, many of them relevant to Wadding.[67] At the outset, Brendan

62 Charles Balić, 'Wadding the Scotist', in Franciscan Fathers, eds, *Luke Wadding Commemorative Volume*, 463–507.

63 Matthew T. Vander Vennet, 'An Early Defender of the Immaculate Conception of the Blessed Virgin Mary: Fr. Luke Wadding, OFM' (Unpublished PhD thesis: The Catholic University of America, 2023).

64 Ibid, 463.

65 *Quaedam quae inservire possunt pro Tractatibus Conceptionis* (UCD-OFM, D.26, folder 1); Cleary, *Father Luke Wadding and St Isidore's College*, 58.

66 Cathaldus Giblin, 'The *Processus Datariae* and the Appointment of Irish Bishops in the Seventeenth Century', in Franciscan Fathers, eds, *Father Luke Wadding Commemorative Volume*, 542–43.

67 Brendan Jennings, ed, 'Ecclesiastical appointments in Ireland, Aug., 1643–Dec., 1649', *Coll. Hib.*, 2 (1959), 18–65; idem, ed, 'Some Correspondence of Father Luke

Jennings highlighted the need for a satisfactory monograph and stated, 'the necessary research work in preparation for it has hardly been begun'.[68] Cathaldus Giblin unearthed sources at the Vatican Library relevant to Wadding and Benignus Millett brought to print manuscript calendars of material preserved in Propaganda Fide Historical Archives in Rome. These include references to Wadding from 1622 onwards in letters, petitions, minutes and memoranda, dispatches, and reports by *consultores* of the curia.[69] As is the case with Giblin's work on the Irish Trinitarians, a number of copies of Propaganda Fide documents are found among the Wadding Papers at University College Dublin.

Based upon his PhD research, Donal Cregan, a Vincentian, improved our knowledge of Wadding's life from the mid-1620s until the late 1640s.[70]

Wadding OFM', *Coll. Hib.*, 2 (1959), 66–94; idem, ed, 'Theses Defended at St Isidore's College, Rome, 1631–49', *Coll. Hib.*, 2 (1959), 95–104; Cathaldus Giblin, ed, 'Documents on the Irish Trinitarians, 1621–71', *Coll. Hib.*, 27/28 (1986), 14, 19–20, 37, 39; Ignatius Fennessy, ed, 'Printed Items among the Wadding Papers', *Coll. Hib.*, 39/40 (1998), 32–95; idem, 'More Printed Items from the Wadding Papers (FLK MSS D 1–2, and others)', *Coll. Hib.*, 41 (1999), 36–57; idem, ed, 'An Alphabetical Index for Some Manuscripts in St Isidore's College, Rome', *Coll. Hib.*, 43 (2001), 50–85; Benignus Millett, ed, 'Copies of Some Decisions from the Missing Discretorial Registers of St Isidore's College, Rome, 1652–1739', *Coll. Hib.*, 43 (2001), 86–89; Ignatius Fennessy, ed, 'Some Post-Incunabula in St Isidore's College, Rome', *Coll. Hib.*, 44/45 (2002/2003), 7–12.

68 Jennings, ed, 'Some Correspondence of Father Luke Wadding OFM', 66.

69 Cathaldus Giblin, ed, 'Catalogue of Material of Irish Interest in the Collection "Nunziatura di Fiandra", Vatican Archives: Part 1, Vols. 1–50', *Coll. Hib.*, 1 (1958), 78; Benignus Millett, ed, 'Catalogue of Volume 294 of the "Scritture originali riferite nelle congregazioni generali" in Propaganda Archives', *Coll. Hib.*, 8 (1965), 9–12, 14, 19–21, 26, 28, 30–31; idem, ed, 'Catalogue of Irish Material in Fourteen Volumes of the "Scritture originali riferite nelle congregazioni generali in Propaganda Archives', *Coll. Hib.*, 10 (1967), 9, 11–13, 17, 23, 27, 40, 55, 58–59; idem, ed, 'Catalogue of Irish Material in Vols. 132–139 of the "Scritture originali riferite nelle congregazioni generali" in Propaganda Archives', *Coll. Hib.*, 12 (1969), 18, 41; idem, ed, 'Calendar of Volume 2 (1669–71) of the "Scritture riferite nei congressi, Irlanda", in Propaganda Archives: Part 1, ff. 1–401', *Coll. Hib.*, 16 (1973), 39. Fr. Luke Wadding OFM (1588–1657) is not to be confused with Bishop Luke Wadding (1628–87).

70 Donal Cregan, 'The Confederate Catholics of Ireland: The Personnel of the Confederation, 1642–9', *IHS*, 29 (1995), 490–512; idem, 'The Social and Cultural

Benignus Millett went on to examine the history of the Irish Franciscans from the Cromwellian conquest until the early years of the Restoration in a book that incorporates an excellent guide to the sources in archives and libraries in many countries.[71] During this period, Wadding's energies were consumed by various issues, from the collapse of the confederation of Kilkenny to the resulting disputes between Old English and Gaelic Irish. In addition, Wadding continued his work for St Isidore's and the Capranica friary, as well as the Prague college, the Wieluń friary in Poland and his own writings. Therefore, Benignus Millett took an interest in the later stages of his confrère's chequered career.[72] Four years later, Giblin and Millett published on the doctrine of Duns Scotus, bringing to the fore Hugh McCaghwell's contribution to the *Opera omnia* of 1639, followed by a prosopography of Wadding's protégés and their teaching record across the continent.[73] Whilst librarian and archivist at Dún Mhuire, Ignatius Fennessy catalogued the 'B' Collection consisting of 166 manuscripts, many of them rare. From the total, the provenance of thirty can be ascribed to Wadding.[74]

Background of a Counter-Reformation Episcopate, 1618–60' in Art Cosgrove and Donal McCartney, *Studies in Irish History presented to R. Dudley Edwards* (Dublin: University College Dublin, 1979), 85–117; idem, 'The Confederation of Kilkenny', in Brian Farrell, ed, *The Irish Parliamentary Tradition* (Dublin: Gill and Macmillan, 1973), 102–115; idem, 'Some members of the Confederation of Kilkenny', in Sylvester O'Brien, ed, *Measgra i gcuimhne Mhichíl Uí Chléirigh. Miscellany of Historical and Linguistic Studies in Honour of Brother Michael Ó Cléirigh, Chief of the Four Masters, 1643–1943* (Dublin: Assisi Press, 1944), 34–44.

71 Benignus Millett, *The Irish Franciscans, 1651–65* (Rome: Gregorian University Press, 1964), xi–xviii, xxviii–xxxiv.

72 Ibid, 9–20, 43–48, 116–27, 128–30, 155–63, 170–172, 195–99, 464–7, 524–25.

73 Cathaldus Giblin, 'Hugh McCaghwell OFM and Scotism at St Anthony's College, Louvain', in *De doctrina Ioannis Duns Scoti. Acta Congressus Scotistici Internationalis Oxonii et Edimburgi 11–17 Septembris 1966 celebrati, cura Commissionis Scotisticae*, 4 vols (Rome: Societas Internationalis Scotistica, 1968), vol. 4, 375–397; Benignus Millett, 'Irish Scotists at St Isidore's College, Rome, in the Seventeenth Century', in *De doctrina Ioannis Duns Scoti*, vol. 4, 399–419. See also Joseph MacMahon, 'Irish Franciscan Scotists of the Seventeenth Century', in Jens Röhrkasten, ed, *Canterbury Studies in Franciscan History*, 2 (2009), 85–112.

74 Ignatius Fennessy, 'The 'B' Manuscripts in the Franciscan Library, Killiney', in Benignus Millett and Anthony Lynch, eds, *Dun Mhuire Killiney, 1945–95: Leann*

Luke Wadding's care for books and his reading habits become apparent from his childhood onwards. Since direct access to manuscripts and printed texts was vital for the completion of studies, the Observant Franciscans were known for gathering significant library collections. John McCafferty and Joseph MacMahon have provided an analysis of the well-stocked library at St Isidore's, which benefitted from Spanish patronage before Wadding's death.[75] Although accessible to a wider readership, until the late twentieth century, historical writings about Wadding were primarily the concern of his religious order. Significant developments have occurred since then with chronologies and studies that assess broader perspectives. In-depth research by Ian Campbell reveals the nuances of early modern thought and explores the integral role that Wadding played in the revival of Scotism in seventeenth-century Rome.[76] Similarly, Raymond Gillespie added to our understanding of St Isidore's where Scotism and Franciscan history found a new home before the disorder witnessed during the Cromwellian conquest.[77]

At the height of Wadding's influence, Catholic prelates expressed ongoing discontent against mendicant activity in Ireland. This is central to an essay by Tadhg Ó hAnnracháin who has frequently referred to Wadding in his writings.[78] In the same volume, John McCafferty states that Englishness

agus Seanchas (Dublin: Lilliput Press, 1995); Clement Schmitt, 'Manuscrits de la "Franciscan Library" de Killiney', *AFH*, 57 (1964), 165–90.

75 John McCafferty, 'A Life in and for Books', in Binasco, ed, *Luke Wadding, the Irish Franciscans and Global Catholicism*, 108–22; Joseph MacMahon and John McCafferty, 'The Wadding Library of Saint Isidore's College, Rome, 1622–1700', *AFH*, 106 (2013), 97–118.

76 Ian Campbell, 'The Wadding Circle and the History of Political Thought', in Binasco, ed, *Luke Wadding, the Irish Franciscans and Global Catholicism*, 145–163; idem, *Renaissance Humanism and Ethnicity Before Race: The Irish and the English in the Seventeenth Century* (Manchester: Manchester University Press, 2013), 153–154.

77 Raymond Gillespie, 'The Irish Franciscans, 1600–1700', in Bhreathnach, MacMahon and McCafferty, eds, *The Irish Franciscans*, 45–76.

78 Tadhg Ó hAnnracháin, 'The Regular Clergy and the Episcopate in Ireland, 1600–50', in Cormac Begadon and James E. Kelly, eds, *British and Irish Religious Orders in Europe, 1560–1800: Conventuals, Mendicants and Monastics in Motion* (Woodbridge: Boydell & Brewer, 2022), 43–59. See also Tadhg Ó hAnnracháin, *Confessionalism and Mobility in Early Modern Ireland* (Oxford: Oxford University Press, 2021); and

was equated with Protestantism in the post-Reformation period. This led Old English Catholics, such as Wadding, to find common cause with Gaelic Irish contemporaries.[79] McCafferty shows how Wadding became a major contributor to the Friars Minor, as seen by the demand for his 1639 edition of the *Opera omnia*, the voluminous *Annales Minorum*, and St Isidore's, 'a vast archive or relic of his life and his preoccupations'.[80] Furthermore, according to McCafferty, Wadding propagated the image of Ireland as the home of saints and scholars. Since 1390, the entire Franciscan order honoured St Patrick on 17 March. Wadding went one better and succeeded in having St Patrick's feast day extended to the universal Church.[81] Work by Clare Carroll features chapters on Wadding's *Annales Minorum* and frescoes painted at St Isidore's after his death, as part of her examination of the Irish presence in Rome and early modern representations of Irish identity.[82]

Generations of Waterford historians have raised awareness of Luke Wadding and his family. The late Niall Byrne completed many scholarly books and articles on early modern Waterford, especially his edition of the *Great Parchment Book* for the Irish Manuscripts Commission, which provides details relevant to Wadding's early years.[83] Many aspects of Julian Walton's research direct us to the civic history of Waterford where members of the Wadding family served in an administrative capacity.[84] In the pages

idem, *Catholic Reformation in Ireland: The Mission of Rinuccini, 1645–49* (Oxford: Oxford University Press, 2002).

79 John McCafferty, 'Recycling an Island's Past for a Global Catholicism: Irish Franciscans in the Seventeenth Century', in Begadon and Kelly, eds, *British and Irish Religious Orders in Europe, 1560–1800: Conventuals, Mendicants and Monastics in Motion*, 68–69.

80 Ibid, 66.

81 Ibid, 77.

82 Clare Carroll, *Exiles in a Global City: The Irish and Early Modern Rome, 1609–1783* (Leiden: Brill, 2017), 11–14, 48–90.

83 Niall Byrne, ed, *The Great Parchment Book of Waterford: Liber Antiquissimus Civitatis Waterfordiae* (Dublin: Irish Manuscripts Commission, 2007); idem, 'Luke Wadding's Waterford', *Decies*, 63 (2007), 34–99; idem, 'Reformation in Elizabethan Waterford', *Decies*, 57 (2001), 43–72.

84 See, for instance, Julian Walton, 'Church, Crown and Corporation in Waterford City, 1520–1620', in William Nolan and Thomas Power, eds, *Waterford: History and*

of his books, the industrious Canon Power often wrote of notables such as the Waddings in the context of Waterford's people and places.[85] *The Story of Waterford* by Edmund Downey provided a well-written chapter on events in Wadding's life during the 1640s, illustrated with a woodcut of the Waterford Franciscan after the portrait by Carlo Maratti.[86]

As shown above, parts of Wadding's life have received due consideration while others have been overlooked. Wadding's Roman career is the best documented in his life, but current writings are characterised by the division of research into Italian and Spanish topics. Paolo Broggio has written on the relevance of religious rivalries to Wadding and how the urgency of ideas indicates the level of competition generated among the orders such as the Franciscans, Dominicans and Jesuits.[87] Drawing upon Francis Harold's *Vita*, Giovan Battista Fidanza brought to light Wadding's tastes in architecture at St Isidore's College, his eye for artistry and how he directed patronage to the production of specific works.[88] Matteo Binasco

---

Society. Interdisciplinary Essays on the History of an Irish County, associate editor Des Cowman (Dublin: Geography Publications, 1992), 177–98; idem, 'Age of Faith', in Eamonn McEneaney, ed, *A History of Waterford and its Mayors from the Twelfth to the Twentieth Century* (Waterford: Waterford Corporation, 1995); idem, ed, 'The Freemen of Waterford, 1542–1650', transcribed by Julian Walton, *Irish Genealogist*, 5 (1978), 560–72.

85 See Patrick Power, *Waterford and Lismore: A Compendious History of the United Dioceses* (Cork: Cork University Press, 1937); idem, *Waterford Saints and Scholars (17th century)* (Waterford: Waterford Press, 1920), 64–66; idem, *The Place Names of Decies* (London: David Nutt, 1907, repr. Cork: Cork University Press, 1952).

86 Edmund Downey, *The Story of Waterford: from the Foundation of the City to the Middle of the Eighteenth Century* (Waterford: Waterford News Printing Works, 1914), 111–28.

87 Paolo Broggio, 'Teologia, Ordini Religiosi e Rapporti Politici: La Questione Dell'Immacolata Concezione di Maria tra Roma e Madrid (1614–63)', *Hispania Sacra*, 61 (2013), Extra I, 255–81; idem, 'Un Teologo Irlandese nella Roma del Seicento: il francescano Luke Wadding', *Roma Moderna e Contemporanea*, 18 (2010), 151–78.

88 Giovan Battista Fidanza, *Luke Wadding's Art. Irish Franciscan Patronage in Seventeenth Century Rome* (St Bonaventure University, NY: Franciscan Institute Publications, 2016), i–vii. See also Giovan Battista Fidanza, 'Being the Court Painter of a Cardinal in Baroque Rome: Chronicle and History of Carlo Maratti for Antonio Barberini the Younger', *Memoirs of the American Academy in Rome*, 69 (2024), 400–464.

has written about Luke Wadding, his part in organising the West Indies mission, Irish Catholicism and Irish experiences in Rome.[89] A collection of essays subsequently edited by Binasco outlines the requirements for a complete study of Wadding's life.[90] Studies by Giulia Spoltore offer insights based upon primary source research, such as Wadding's friendship with the Cistercian abbot, Ilarione Rancati, at the Roman curia, and similarities in the method between the *Annales Minorum* and the historiographical tradition of Cesare Baronius.[91] This recalls a point made by Bernadette Cunningham on the subject of Irish Franciscan historiography.[92]

89 Matteo Binasco, *Breaking and Remaking the Irish Missionary Network: Ireland, Rome and the West Indies in the Seventeenth Century* (Cham: Springer, 2020), 7–10, 47–69, 76–81, 88–95, 151–58; idem, *Rome and Irish Catholicism in the Atlantic World, 1622–1908* (Basingstoke: Palgrave Macmillan, 2019), 1–20; idem, 'Luke Wadding and Irish Diplomatic Activity in Seventeenth-Century Rome', *Studi Irlandesi*, 6 (2016), 193–203; idem, '"A Powerful Hibernese': Luke Wadding and his Diplomatic Role in Seventeenth-Century Rome', *Revue d'Histoire Ecclésiastique*, 112 (2017), 169–84; idem, 'Gli esuli irlandesi nella Roma del seicento', *Bollettino della Società di Studi Valdesi*, 214 (2014), 79–115; idem, 'Few, Uncooperative, and Endangered: The Activity of the Irish Catholic Priests in the West Indies of the Seventeenth Century, 1638–68', in Igor Pérez Tostado and Enrique García Hernán, eds, *Irlanda y el Atlántico Ibérico: Movilidad, Participación e Intercambio Cultural* (Valencia: Albatros, 2010), 211–23.

90 Raymond Gillespie, 'Review: Matteo Binasco, ed, *Luke Wadding, the Irish Franciscans and Global Catholicism* (Abingdon: Routledge, 2020)', *BCH*, 35 (2021), 489.

91 Giulia Spoltore, 'Carlo Maratti, Giovan Pietro Bellori, Luke Wadding e Ilarione Rancati: dibattito teologico e strategie politiche a Roma negli anni di discussion dell'Augustinus di Giansenio', in Francesco Carta, Silvia Omenetto and Giulia Spoltore, eds, *Itinera, Uomini, oggetti e idee in movimento* (Rome: Edizioni Efesto, 2023), 131–62; idem, 'Luke Wadding and scholars for the arts in seventeenth-century Rome', in Binasco, ed, *Luke Wadding, the Irish Franciscans, and Global Catholicism*, 123–44; idem, 'Luke Wadding, Ilarione Rancati e la famiglia Ludovisi per un'impresa editoriale: la *Vita del B. Nicolò Albergati* (1652–54)', forthcoming; cited by Spoltore, 'Luke Wadding and Scholars for the Arts in Seventeenth-Century Rome', 142; idem, 'Luke Wadding e l'Eredità di Cesare Baronio: Storiografia e Arte nel Seicento a Roma', *Annales Oratorii*, 17 (2019), 41–60; idem, ed, 'Una lettera di Luke Wadding ad Ilarione Rancati sull'Immacolata Concezione', *AFH*, 111 (2018), 551–56.

92 Bernadette Cunningham, *The Annals of the Four Masters. Irish History, Kingship and Society in the Early Seventeenth Century* (Dublin: Four Courts Press, 2010), 164–7.

Essays edited by Declan Downey and Julio Crespo MacLennan emphasise the long-standing links between Ireland and Spain. In his contribution, Downey draws attention to the influence that Salamanca exerted upon Wadding and his Irish classmates.[93] This is part of a significant corpus of work created by historians from both countries in recent decades. Cristina Bravo Lozano highlights Wadding's correspondence in tracing the accomplishments of an Irish network during the early years of the Spanish mission that provided for an educated clergy and sent missionaries to Ireland.[94] Placing the focus on the 1640s, Igor Pérez Tostado has emphasised that Wadding was a key figure among the Irish abroad who influenced Spanish foreign policy.[95] Further analysis by Pérez Tostado shows that trust was integral to Wadding's relationship with the Spanish crown.[96] This is consistent with observations by Downey and Recio Morales who have noted that a generation of Irish Franciscan friars actively promoted Spanish Habsburg supremacy over the Church.[97] Nonetheless, an abundant supply of information in Harold's *Vita*, the *Commentarius Rinuccinianus*, Marchant's *Relatio veridica* and Massari's report from 1645 to 1647 has hitherto been overlooked.[98]

93 Declan Downey, 'Archbishop Florence Conry of Tuam', in Declan Downey and Julio Crespo MacLennan, eds, *Spanish-Irish Relations through the Ages* (Dublin: Four Courts Press: 2008), 97.

94 Cristina Bravo Lozano, *Spain and the Irish Mission, 1609–1707* (Abingdon: Routledge, 2018).

95 Igor Pérez Tostado, *Irish Influence at the Court of Spain in the Seventeenth Century* (Dublin: Four Courts Press, 2008), 93–94, 97, 102, 113.

96 Idem, ''Learned, Attached and Reliable': Luke Wadding, Agent of the Spanish Monarchy', in Binasco, ed, *Luke Wadding, the Irish Franciscans, and Global Catholicism*, 40–43, 52–53.

97 Recio Morales, *Ireland and the Spanish Empire*, 58–59; Downey, ''A Castilian-Regalist Cradling': Spanish-Habsburg formation of the early Irish Counter Reformation', 96–206.

98 See Pierre Marchant, *Relatio veridica et sincera status Provinciae Hiberniae ordinis Minorum Regularis Observantiæ sub regimine F. Petri Marchant, Commissarii Generalis Nationalis super provincias Germanioe superioris, Belgii et Britannicas, ad Reverendissimum Patrem totius Ordinis Generalem necnon Rmos ac plurimum Reverendos Patres in Capitulo generali Romae congregatos hoc anno 1651 in festo pentecostes*; UCD Special Collections (1 OFM 0675).

In 2009, Ignatius Fennessy's biographical entry on Wadding was highly commended by the Consultant Editor for all the seventeenth-century lives in the *Oxford Dictionary of National Biography*.[99] Benignus Millett's account of Wadding appeared in *The Dictionary of Irish Biography* that year.[100] In relation to Wadding's enthusiasm for the works of St Augustine, Declan Downey has written on the 'Salvific Question of Grace' at the University of Salamanca in the late sixteenth and early seventeenth centuries.[101] On topic, Thomas O'Connor has opened new avenues for discussion by drawing attention to the connections between Irish Jansenists and the confederate wars of the 1640s.[102] Jansenism fleetingly appealed to leading circles in Irish society because it potentially allowed for Catholic allegiance to the English crown. O'Connor makes the case that Wadding was amenable to the views of Ormond's brother-in-law, Muskerry. A freeman of Waterford, Muskerry was a well-connected political moderate who favoured a formal agreement between royalist and confederate forces. In Rome, Wadding was also in contact with John Callaghan of Cork, a kinsman of Muskerry with Jansenist sympathies.[103]

Wadding's qualities meant that he was well equipped to access generous patronage in Roman society.[104] To O'Connor, Wadding was among the most gifted Irish clergymen who joined the Franciscans before an influential career in papal and Spanish service. His initial success in representing both sets of interests in Rome enabled him to secure St Isidore's College

99 Ignatius Fennessy, personal communication; Ignatius Fennessy, 'Wadding, Luke [name in religion Francis] (1588–1657)', in *ODNB*, vol. 56, 643–49.

100 Benignus Millett, 'Luke Wadding (1588–1657), Franciscan Priest, Scholar and Churchman', *DIB*, vol. 9 vols, 680–85.

101 Declan Downey, 'The Irish Contribution to Counter-Reformation Theology in Continental Europe', in Brendan Bradshaw and Dáire Keogh, eds, *Christianity in Ireland: Revisiting the Story* (Dublin: Veritas, 2002), 96–108.

102 Thomas O'Connor, *Irish Jansenists, 1600–70: Religion and Politics in Flanders, France, Ireland and Rome* (Dublin: Four Courts Press, 2008); idem, *An Irish Jansenist in Seventeenth-Century France: John Callaghan, 1605–54*. The O'Donnell Lecture 2004 (Dublin: National University of Ireland, 2005), 5.

103 O'Connor, *An Irish Jansenist in Seventeenth-Century France*, 7, 10.

104 Thomas O'Connor, 'Luke Wadding's Networks at Home and Abroad', in Dáire Keogh and Albert McDonnell, eds, *The Irish College, Rome and its World* (Dublin: Four Courts Press, 2008), 14–23.

for the Irish Franciscans.[105] O'Connor has judged the merits of Wadding's contribution to the creation of a college network. Along with Mícheál Mac Craith, he concludes that Wadding was, perhaps, the greatest of all the Irish founders on the continent.[106] In recent decades, historiography has drawn attention to the presence of many Irish communities of clergy and laity on the European continent in early modern times. This is particularly apparent in relation to the complex network of colleges established in the sixteenth and seventeenth centuries, as shown in essay collections edited by Liam Chambers and Thomas O'Connor.[107]

Since 2001, a series of volumes from the Irish in Europe Project present a variety of new insights that result from discussion and debate among many historians.[108] A number of the contributors illustrate the range of activities that Wadding pursued in Rome. Hector McDonnell's description of the MacDonnells of Antrim deals with Wadding's criticism of the Scottish mission, its funding and organisation.[109] Tadhg Ó hAnnracháin has dealt with Wadding's involvement in diplomacy between the papacy and the Kilkenny confederacy, with an assessment of the Irish friar's presence at the

105 Idem, 'Prequels: The Irish European Diaspora', in Bettina Migge and Gisela Holfter, eds, *Ireland in the European Eye* (Dublin: Royal Irish Academy, 2019), 11.

106 Idem, 'Exile Movement: Male Institutions, 1568–1640', in John McCafferty and James E. Kelly, eds, *The Oxford History of British and Irish Catholicism*, 203–222 ; Mícheál Mac Craith, 'The Franciscan Continental Colleges and the Doctrine of the Immaculate Conception', in Matteo Binasco, ed, *Rome and Irish Catholicism in the Atlantic World* (Basingstoke: Palgrave MacMillan, 2019), 137–165.

107 Liam Chambers and Thomas O'Connor, eds, *College Communities Abroad: Education, Migration and Catholicism in Early Modern Europe* (Manchester: Manchester University Press, 2017); Liam Chambers and Thomas O'Connor, eds, *Forming Catholic Communities: Irish, Scots and English College networks in Europe, 1568–1918* (Leiden: Brill, 2018).

108 Thomas O'Connor and Mary Ann Lyons, *Strangers to citizens: the Irish in Europe, 1600–1800* (Dublin: National Library of Ireland, 2008); Thomas O'Connor, ed, *The Irish in Europe, 1580–1815* (Dublin: Four Courts Press, 2001).

109 Hector McDonnell, 'The MacDonnell Clan and Change in Early Seventeenth-Century Ulster', in Thomas O'Connor and Mary Ann Lyons, eds, *Irish Migrants in Europe after Kinsale, 1602–1820* (Dublin: Four Courts Press, 2003), 64–87.

time of Rinuccini's appointment as nuncio.[110] In the meantime, Raymond Gillespie has referred to the complexities of the student population at St Isidore's, Wadding's role in the publication of theological works and in the movement of multiple scholars across the European continent.[111] Well-organised and thorough biographies from early modern Ireland are still needed to avoid concealing individual difference.

As part of the UCD-OFM Partnership, the many letters and papers of Luke Wadding and his contemporaries are now in the care of UCD Archives to ensure the preservation of unique historical sources through an extensive programme of conservation. When writing letters in Italian, Wadding occasionally borrowed words from Spanish and Portuguese, which was not unusual in the seventeenth century and reflects the years he spent in the Iberian Peninsula.

Since 2009, the present author has published a series of manuscript studies and research papers. Based on original findings, these relate to the print campaign overseen by Wadding, his correspondence with scholars and booksellers, the preservation of his manuscripts at University College Dublin, his expertise on liturgical texts, his negotiations in political dealings and his links to Spain.[112] This book presents a narrative of Wadding's historical and spiritual journey, with meaning for his personal and institutional life as a Franciscan friar. As such, each of the chapters predominantly concentrates on a geographic region during the intervening period. Within the overall structure, the chapters are arranged in chronological order to provide as much coverage as possible of each decade. Throughout, Wadding maintained allegiances to his extended family. Therefore, the contents deal first with Waterford before moving to Portugal and Spain. Thereafter, Wadding lived and worked in Italy for nearly forty years.

110 Tadhg Ó hAnnracháin, 'Irish Diplomatic Missions to Rome during the 1640s', in Thomas O'Connor and Mary Ann Lyons, eds, *Irish Communities in Early-Modern Europe* (Dublin: Four Courts Press, 2006), 395–408.

111 Raymond Gillespie, 'Contrasting Communities: A Comparative Approach to Irish Communities in Baroque Europe', in Thomas O'Connor and Mary Ann Lyons, eds, *The Ulster Earls and Baroque Europe: Refashioning Irish Identities, 1600–1800* (Dublin: Four Courts Press, 2010), 166–82.

112 See Preface in the present work for full details.

Religion was one of the fundamental communal passions in the sixteenth and seventeenth centuries. This reveals how current perceptions differ from the mediaeval and early modern actuality. We meet Wadding at St Isidore's. Invoking the name of 'the most excellent and high God', the inscription in capitals on his tomb recalls: 'The Reverend Father, Friar Luke Wadding, an Irishman, an erudite man adorned with virtues of church, religion and country', before remembering the 'meritorious, retired lecturer, chronicler of the entire Franciscan order, the best and most loving father and founder'.[113] In mourning, the College placed this monument 'at the expense of Lord Ercole Ronconi, lawyer in the city, his true friend'.[114] 'He died on 18 November 1657 aged 70, to be lamented hereafter, death remains victorious'. The inscription closed: 'His bones are beneath marble; his spirit holds the stars'.[115]

113 Inscription on the tomb of Luke Wadding, St. Isidore's College, Rome, 'D*EO* O*PTIMO* M*AXIMO* / R*EVERENDO* A*DMODUM* P*ATRI,* F*RATRI* LUCAE WADDING HIBERNO / VIRO ERUDITO / VIRTUTIBUS ORNATO / DE ECCLESIA RELIGIONE ET PATRIA / BENEMERITO / LECTORI IUBILATO / TOTIUS ORDIN*IS* MINOR*UM* CHRONOLOGO / PATRI AC FUNDATORI / OPTIMO ET AMANTISSIMO'.

114 Ibid, 'COLLEGIUM MOERENS POSUIT / AERE D*OMINO* HERCULIS RONCONII / IN URBE ADVOCATI / IUS VERI AMICI'.

115 Ibid, 'OBIIT / XVIII NOVEMBRIS MDCLVII / AETATIS LXX / FLEBILIS HINC ABSIS SUBITO MORS VICTOR REMANSIT / OSSA TEGIT MARMOR SPIRITUS ASTRA TENE'.

1 Late Elizabethan Waterford

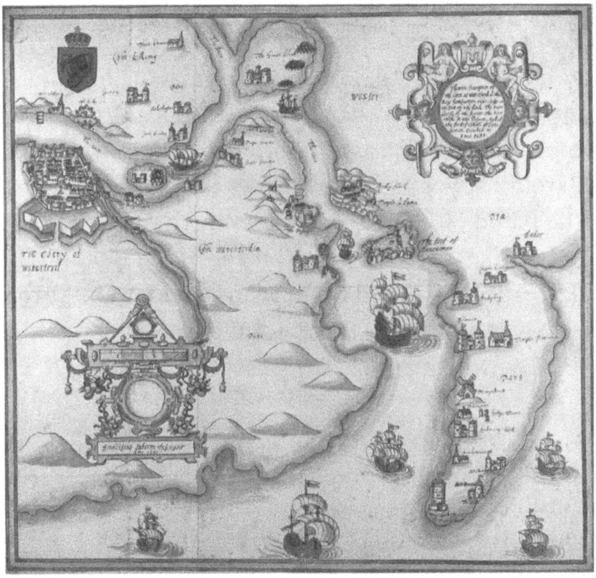

Map 1 Francis Jobson's navigational chart of Waterford Harbour, 1591; IE TCD MS 1209 (64). Reproduced by kind permission of The Board of Trinity College Dublin.

Introduction

Luke Wadding was born in Waterford on 16 October 1588. He described his birthplace as being founded by Norse pirates or Ostmen, stating that it was: 'Famous in the province of Munster for the flowing River Suir, for its opportune port, its wealth and population, for the construction of its buildings'.[1] Wadding was proud of his origins, referring to himself as 'an

1 *Annales Minorum*, 3 vols (1240), 51–52, n. 26: 'in Civitate Waterfordiæ, quæ mihi natale solum fuit, [...] a Norwegis piratis constructa, ut placet Camdeno, sive ut alii

Irishman from Waterford'.[2] He believed that the city deserved its title of *Urbs intacta*, that is, 'unconquered City'.[3] He explained that this was because Waterford 'most consistently maintained Christian piety' and was, therefore, known as Little Rome.[4]

Wadding was baptised on the feast of St Luke the Evangelist.[5] His mother, Anastasia Lombard, refrained from church attendance until the traditional blessing of a woman and her child, which was a cause of celebration in early modern Ireland.[6] This indicates that Luke's father, Walter Wadding, initiated him into the Church. The local priest conducted the baptism, which was regarded as a vital rite of passage where, in the words of Francis Harold, the young Luke was 'torn from the jaws of the Devil and washed in the blood of Christ'.[7] Walter and Anastasia had ten sons and four daughters. Luke was the eighth son and eleventh child. In large and pious families, younger sons were often considered destined for the priesthood in late sixteenth-century Ireland and parts of continental Europe.[8]

---

volunt, a Sitaraco Ostmanno [...] Celebris in Momoniæ Provincia ab adlabente fluvio Surio, a portus opportunitate, ab opulentia, a populi frequentia, ab ædificiorum structura; sed inde celebrior, quod pietatem Christianam, & Catholicam Religionem Romanam constantissime retinuerit; atque hinc sane mihi carior, & æstimabilior quam quod ortum tribuerit'.

2 'Fr. Luca Waddingo Hiberno Menapiensi'; For instance, from 1625–54, on the title pages of volumes one, six and eight of the *Annales Minorum*, Wadding referred to himself in these terms.

3 *Annales Minorum*, vol. 3 (1240), 52: 'illud suum mereatur elogium, *Urbs intacta manens*: inde etiam laudatissima [...] ut gloriose passim res hoc audiat nomine Parva Roma'.

4 Ibid.

5 Harold, *Vita Fratris Lucae Waddingi*, 10.

6 Wadding's cousin, Patrick Comerford, told him that 'in our countrie women fondly esteeminge more the office of churchinge then the baptisinge' (Jennings, ed, *Wadding Papers*, 617). See J. C. Cox, *Churchwardens Accounts from the Fourteenth Century to the Close of the Seventeenth Century* (London: Methuen, 1913), 193–94.

7 Harold, *Vita Fratris Lucae Waddingi*, 10: 'quo quis e Diaboli faucibus eruptus, et Christi sanguine lotus'; Jennings, ed, *Wadding Papers*, 9; John Bossy, 'Blood and Baptism: Kinship, Community and Christianity in Western Europe from the Fourteenth to the Seventeenth Centuries', *Studies in Church History*, 10 (1973), 129–43.

8 Michael Robson, 'The Commemoration of the Living and the Dead at the Friars Minor of Cambridge', in John Lee and Christian Steer, eds, *Commemoration in*

Childhood experiences are foundational and noteworthy because they influence the subsequent development of an adult's life. In the case of Wadding, although records are scarce, it is possible to notice habits and behaviour that endured to the end. Parental expectations and their personal example consciously shaped their son's vocation. The following chapter describes Wadding's upbringing, his early schooling and the social unrest that took place in Waterford before his departure for the continent.

Crisis and Opportunity

1588 was a year made famous by the Great Armada.[9] The *Annales Minorum* recorded that Philip II sent a fleet 'into England against Elizabeth, but it was not successful and only worsened her attacks against many Catholics, men and women, and some priests who underwent death and other punishments at her command'.[10] A number of participants from Waterford were onboard the Great Armada, some of whom survived the expedition.[11]

Medieval Cambridge (Woodbridge: Boydell, 2018), 35, <https://doi.org/10.2307/j.ctv1qv1xc.10>, accessed 21 September 2024; Rodger Charles, *Christian Social Witness and Teaching: From Biblical Times to the Late Nineteenth Century* (Chichester: Gracewing, 1998), 146.

9 Jorge Calvar Gross, José Ignacio González-Aller Hierro, Marcelino de Dueñas Fontán and María del Campo Mérida Valverde, eds, *La Batalla del Mar Océano: corpus documental de las hostilidades entre España e Inglaterra, 1568–1604*, 5 vols (Madrid: Ministerio de Defensa: Secretaría General Técnica: Turner, 1988–2015).

10 *Annales Minorum*, vol. 22 (1588), 198, n. 16: 'Dum Philippus II classem [...] in Angliam contra Elisabetham, et infelici successu, mittebat, ipsa magis contra catholicos, multi eorum utrisque sexus, atque inter eos nonnulli sacerdotes mortem, aliaque supplicia eius mandato subierunt'. On the invention of the term 'Invincible Armada' by William Cecil, Lord Burghley, see Colin Martin and Geoffrey Parker, *The Spanish Armada. Revised Edition* (Manchester: Manchester University Press, 1999), 243, 247n.

11 Among others, a 'gentleman adventurer' from Waterford named Robert Dobbin survived the Armada (AGS, GA, leg. 307, f. 135) and Walter Lee of Waterford was aboard the flagship hulk, *El Gran Grifón* (AGS, GA, leg. 314, f. 178). See <https://irishineurope.maynoothuniversity.ie/records> accessed 12 May 2025. Óscar Recio Morales, ed, *La Presencia Irlandesa en los Ejércitos de la Monarquía Hispánica, 1580–1818* (CD-ROM, Madrid, Ministerio de Defensa, 2007); Waterford merchants

A decisive watershed was fast approaching for Spanish foreign policy. Admittedly no lasting damage was done to their empire, but the 1588 Armada caused a crisis of confidence for Philip II who, thereafter, avoided committing more blood and treasure to an invasion of England that would re-establish Catholicism. In a reversal of opinion, from hubris to humility, the king of Spain's counsellors expressed this sense of doubt and saw the Armada's destruction as a penance.[12]

The post-Armada crisis is of significance to this study of Luke Wadding. Notwithstanding Kinsale and smaller missions to Ireland in the coming years,[13] debate ensued in Spain over military intervention. Faced with persistent pleas from Irish, English and Scottish exiles, the Spanish Habsburgs looked for a more viable strategy. They settled upon support for the formation of Counter-Reformation clergy in their territories when Philip II endorsed and implemented improvements in the education of the priesthood,

---

sent corn and horses to the Spanish fleet in Lisbon in 1588, albeit in small quantities; Sir William FitzWilliam to Lord Burghley, 28 October 1588 (*Cal. SP Ire. 1588–92*, 67); Waterford Corporation completed the fortification of Duncannon in the harbour and the mayor kept the English authorities informed of subsequent developments in Munster; Privy Council to Vice-President of Munster, 21 December 1588 (*Cal. SP Ire. 1588–92*, 89); Paul Kerrigan, 'The fortifications of Waterford, Passage and Duncannon, 1495–1690', *Decies*, 29 (1985), 12–23. Waterford merchants provided the Spanish authorities with news of the expedition's arrival in Ireland; D. Higueras Rodríguez and M. P. San Pío Aladrén, 'Irish Wrecks of the Great Armada', in Don Cruickshank, Patrick Gallagher, eds, *God's Obvious Design: Papers for the Spanish Armada Symposium, Sligo, 1988: with an Edition and Translation of the Account of Francisco de Cuéllar* (London: Tamesis, 1990), 151. In 1586, Waterford was a proposed landing point for Spanish troops. See Francis Kelly, *Captain Francisco de Cuéllar: The Armada, Ireland, and the Wars of the Spanish monarchy, 1578–1606* (Dublin: Four Courts Press, 2020), 107, 148.

12 Pedro de Ribadeneira, *Tratado de la Tribulacion, Repartido en Dos Libros* (Madrid: Pedro Madrigal, 1589); idem, *Tratado de la Religión y Virtudes que debe tener el Príncipe Cristiano* (Madrid: Pedro Madrigal, 1589); cited by Charles O'Neill and José María Domínguez, eds, *Diccionario Histórico de la Compañía de Jesús*, 4 vols (Rome: Institutum Historicum Societatis Iesu–Madrid: Universidad Pontificia de Comillas, 2001), vol. 4, 3345.

13 Patrick Williams, *Philip II* (Basingstoke: Palgrave Macmillan, 2017), 244; Enrique García Hernán, 'Philip II's Forgotten Armada', in Hiram Morgan, ed, *The Battle of Kinsale* (Dublin: Wordwell, 2004), 45–58.

as recommended by the Council of Trent.[14] Within four years, the first such college in the Iberian Peninsula was founded at Salamanca. Wadding was among the many Irish clerical students who benefitted from such measures. Furthermore, through the colleges he later founded and conducted on the continent, Wadding continued to gain from this policy until his death.

Paternal influence

The Waddings, originally from the baronies of Forth and Bargy in Co. Wexford, were part of the Old English community, which traced its ancestry back through five centuries to the Anglo-Norman conquest of Ireland.[15] Luke Wadding attributed his early education to his 'devout father Walter who, in addition to [his] origin, gave such special attention to [his] Christian formation and brought [him] up to be vigilant with regard to [his] education'.[16] Luke came from a merchant family, as did many of the leading clergy from the southern dioceses of Ireland, such as David Rothe of Ossory, Thomas Walsh in Cashel, Patrick Comerford of Waterford, Richard Arthur of Limerick, and William Tirry of Cork and Cloyne.[17]

Luke's father was a merchant at a time when much business in Waterford was conducted overseas with England and the continent. In Ireland, the Counter-Reformation mission was unimaginable without the intervention of merchants and their agents who organised an information network 'at the junction' between the continent and Ireland.[18] Negotiations were part

---

14 On the prelude to the Council and the subsequent relevance of education to its proceedings, see John W. O'Malley, *Trent: What Happened at the Council* (Cambridge MA: Harvard University Press, 2013), 37, 42–45.

15 Cleary, *Father Luke Wadding and St Isidore's College*, 61.

16 *Annales Minorum*, vol. 3 (1240), 53, n. 28: 'Vvalterus pius meus genitor, cui praeter ortum, est quod amplius debeam sedulam in Christiana disciplina curam, & summam circa probe educandum vigilantiam'.

17 Cregan, 'The Confederate Catholics of Ireland: The Personnel of the Confederation, 1642–9', 506.

18 John Bossy, 'The Character of Elizabethan Catholicism', in Trevor Aston, ed, *Crisis in Europe, 1560–1660* (repr. Abingdon: Routledge, 2013), 234.

and parcel of Walter Wadding's work. Appropriately, he handed on these skills to his son, Luke, who became a diplomatic mediator in later years.

Walter Wadding was sworn in as a freeman of Waterford Corporation in 1566 and, as a merchant, was required to pay twenty shillings in return. He secured his status by taking a solemn oath to be 'good and true' to the sovereign and their successors, to the civic body, and to preserve the interests of the city.[19] In addition, he undertook not to declare the goods of non-Waterford merchants as their own without the payment of customs. Finally, within three months of attaining freedom of the city, Walter Wadding was expected to have 'good and able' breastplate and back armour 'to defende the Citie'.[20]

As a merchant freeman of Waterford, he operated in business without impediment, exempt from the dues for markets and fairs, the tolls for bridge crossings and the tariffs levied on merchandise passing into the city for sale or consumption.[21] The continual threat of losing investments in times of political trouble, the risks of fire, floods and bankruptcy meant that merchants held strong religious convictions. To accomplish honourable commerce, piety was an essential attribute.[22] Moreover, from one generation to the next, the Waddings depended upon goodwill and a reputable name. Luke Wadding grew up to value these points in his interactions with an extensive network of contacts.

Waterford was the largest city in Munster and commanded three rivers – the Suir, the Nore and the Barrow – at the point where they entered the sea.[23] Agricultural goods such as 'wool, woollen cloth, hides and fish' were

19 A sixteenth-century example of the freeman's oath is printed in Niall Byrne, ed, *The Great Parchment Book of Waterford* (Dublin: Irish Manuscripts Commission, 2007), 49.

20 Ibid.

21 Byrne, ed, *The Great Parchment Book of Waterford*, xxi–xxiii.

22 Henri Lapeyre, *Une Famille de Marchands: les Ruiz. Contribution à l'Étude du Commerce entre la France et l'Espagne au Temps de Philippe II* (Paris: Armand Colin, 1955), 91, 126-137.

23 J. C. Beckett, *The Making of Modern Ireland, 1603–1923* (New York: Alfred Knopf, 1966), 31.

dispatched down these rivers for export.[24] Waterford merchants imported oil, vinegar, salts, nuts and iron from the Iberian Peninsula. Ships from Waterford also imported wines into Ireland, which were then brought by river to inland towns.[25] Ports such as Waterford faced towards the quayside where ships were moored to load and unload.[26]

Commercial activity provided merchants with the finance to acquire landholdings. Ten years later, Walter Wadding entered into a consortium to acquire all of the lands, tenements and hereditaments of Patrick White in Waterford.[27] At the same time, Walter obtained three dwelling houses with adjacent buildings and lands. The Latin deed located one of these properties adjacent to Boat Street, the bed of the Suir and a dwelling house with land which formerly belonged to Luke's grandfather, Nicholas Wadding.[28] Walter's brother, Thomas, witnessed the deed. Thomas Wadding, head of the extended family, was a lawyer who played an integral part in civic life and held the mayoralty in 1596.[29]

On Ireland's southeast coast, Waterford eagerly received Counter-Reformation ideas. Recusancy, the refusal to conform to Protestantism, was well established in the port city by the end of the 1570s.[30] When Pius V excommunicated Elizabeth I in 1570, it released Catholics from their allegiance to the queen but also provoked repercussions from the authorities and ended any hopes that the papacy would reach an

24 Walton, 'Age of Faith', in McEneaney, ed, *A History of Waterford and its Mayors from the Twelfth to the Twentieth Century*, 96.

25 Byrne, ed, *The Great Parchment Book of Waterford*, 90.

26 Detlev Ellmers, 'Development and Usage of Harbour Cranes', in Christiane Villain-Gandossi et al., eds, *Medieval Ships and the Birth of Technological Societies, 1: Northern Europe* (Valletta: Foundation for International Studies, 1998), 43–69; cited by R. W. H. Miller, *One Firm Anchor: The Church and the Merchant Seafarer, an Introductory History* (Cambridge: Lutterworth Press, 2012), 22, 43.

27 *Calendar of Ormond Deeds, 1172–*, vol. 5, (1547–84), 275–76.

28 Ibid.

29 Benjamin Hazard, 'Thomas Wadding, Waterford Landowner and Lawyer of Gray's Inn, 1562–1613', *Decies*, 77 (2021), 17–42.

30 Gilbert Yorke to Walsingham, 5 December 1579 (*Cal. SP Ire. 1574–85*, 199). For a description of Catholicism in Dungarvan, Waterford and Youghal in 1574 by Captain Diego Ortiz de Urizar, see Enrique García Hernán, *Ireland and Spain in the Reign of Philip II* (Dublin: Four Courts Press, 2009), 87–91.

accommodation with Elizabeth I.[31] A year later, Walter Wadding and twelve others in Waterford were pardoned.[32] Together they were fined 53 shillings and 4 pence.[33] Although their pardon is silent about the actual offence, recusancy provides a possible answer.[34] Measures against recusancy were aimed at the heads of families who were obliged to pay a fine for refusing to enter Sunday service with the state church.[35] In the case of Walter Wadding, there is no recurring record for the same offence. Instead, when an offence was omitted, fines were intended to promote compliance and avoid the trouble of having to appear before a commission.[36] The pardon of Walter Wadding identified the recipients as two aldermen, four gentlemen, a gentlewoman, five merchants and one yeoman, that is, a freeholder or servant in a household. Among them, Patrick Dobbin was a former mayor of the city and Richard Strang fitz Peter a freeman who served as bailiff and sheriff.[37] The lawyer Thomas Wadding, Walter's older brother, also appeared on the list. The name of the gentlewoman was Margaret Keane.[38]

31 See Adriano Prosperi, *Il Concilio di Trento: una introduzione storica* (Turin: Giulio Einaudi, 2001), 95.

32 *Fiants Eliz. Ire.* 1784.

33 This was equivalent to the four merk piece, a silver coin in circulation in late sixteenth-century Ireland. Herbert Grueber, *Handbook of the Coins of Great Britain and Ireland in the British Museum, London* (London: Spink, 1970), liii.

34 Cf. Frederick Smith, 'The Origins of Recusancy in Elizabethan England Reconsidered', *HJ*, 60 (2017), 301–32.

35 Henry Jefferies, 'Why the Reformation failed in Ireland', *IHS*, 40 (2016), 151–70.

36 James Murray, *Enforcing the English Reformation in Ireland: Clerical Resistance and Political Conflict in the Diocese of Dublin, 1534–90* (Cambridge: Cambridge University Press, 2011), 283–84; K. J. Kesselring, *To Pardon and to Punish: Mercy and Authority in Tudor England* (Cambridge: Cambridge University Press, 2000), 30, 44.

37 Byrne, ed, *The Great Parchment Book of Waterford*, 121, 133, 139, 151–52, 156, 166.

38 *Fiants Eliz. Ire.* 1784.

Roman Breviary

In the late sixteenth century, parents provided support to the local priest who was responsible for catechesis in the parish. Indeed, the catechism taught parents that this was among their duties.[39] Luke's nephew, Francis Harold, explained that when Luke learnt to read and recite the principles of Christian teachings from memory, his parents gave him a small book containing the minor offices of the revised breviary.[40] The essential function of the breviary was didactic.[41] Books of devotion belonging to the lay man or woman grew in popularity during the late Middle Ages. Printing subsequently established a consistent standard for the written word and, in 1568, Pius V ordered that all former breviaries were to be set aside for his own. This was the official text of public prayer, published in folio and in octavo in Rome and the Low Countries as the universally valid model. The Pian breviary cut back on the over-abundance of saints, removed unauthenticated tales and re-established the place of Scripture in the Office of Readings.[42]

The new text accentuated devotion to Mary with the inclusion of detailed notes on 8 December, the feast of the Immaculate Conception. Pius V also renewed the Little Office of the Blessed Virgin Mary.[43] Luke

---

39 Lucy Underwood, *Childhood, Youth and Religious Dissent in Post-Reformation England* (Basingstoke: Palgrave Macmillan, 2014), 59; John Bossy, 'The Counter-Reformation and the People of Catholic Europe', in David Martin Luebke, ed, *The Counter-Reformation: The Essential Readings* (Blackwell, Malden MA, 1999), 87; John A. McHugh and Charles Callan, eds, *Catechism of the Council of Trent for Parish Priests Issued by Order of Pius V*, translated into English with notes (New York: Joseph F. Wagner, 1936), 418.

40 Harold, *Vita Fratris Lucae Waddingi*, 10.

41 Hazard, 'Luke Wadding and the Breviary of Urban VIII', 87–102.

42 Robert Swanson, *Religion and Devotion in Europe, c.1215–c.1515* (Cambridge: Cambridge University Press, 1995), 59–69, 96–97.

43 Michael Mullett, *The Catholic Reformation* (repr. Abingdon: Routledge, 2023), 117. On the office of the dead from the office of the Virgin Mary in Franciscan tradition, see Pietro Messa, 'L'Officium mortuorum e l'Officium beate Marie virginis nel Breviarium sancti Francisci', *Franciscana: Bollettino della Società internazionale di studi francescani*, 4 (2002), 111–149.

Wadding's theological awareness began in this well-established context. Appropriately, Mary's portrait was attributed to his namesake, Luke the Evangelist. In the late sixteenth century, children were taught to offer thanksgiving to God for all the gifts he bestowed on Mary.[44] Moreover, according to Niall Byrne, the iconography of the *Great Parchment Book of Waterford* encompassed the city's religious values in a time of great change.[45] The devotion of the people and their mentors to Mary is clearly shown on folio 91, which records events in 1566. Here, Elizabeth I is depicted as a mere mortal without royal emblems, ruling her kingdom under the auspices of the Blessed Virgin who is shown nursing the infant Jesus.[46]

Late sixteenth-century prayer books were comparatively economical to produce and remained in circulation. The timing of the campaign to print Catholic devotional works was opportune. At the same time, newly ordained priests began returning to Ireland.[47] Members of the clergy, therefore, smuggled Latin prayer books home from the continent.[48] In the sixteenth century, the reading of edifying texts was an audible activity.[49]

44 McHugh and Callan, eds, *Catechism of the Council of Trent for Parish Priests Issued by Order of Pius V*, 419.

45 Byrne, ed, *The Great Parchment Book of Waterford*, xvi–xvii.

46 Cf. Caitríona MacLeod, 'A Carved Oak Nursing Madonna from Askeaton, Co. Limerick', in Étienne Rynne, ed, *Figures from the Past: Studies on Figurative Art in Christian Ireland in Honour of Helen M. Roe* (Dún Laoghaire: The Glendale Press for The Royal Society of Antiquaries of Ireland, 1987), 251; Byrne, ed, *The Great Parchment Book of Waterford*, Plates V and VI.

47 For example, James Walsh and Richard Walsh, both from the city of Waterford, graduated from Leuven in 1566. Jeroen Nilis, ed, 'Irish students at Leuven University, 1548–1797 (with index)', *Archiv. Hib.*, 60 (2006/2007), 37–38. See also Eamon Duffy, *Reformation Divided: Catholics, Protestants and the Conversion of England* (London: Bloomsbury, 2017), 208.

48 Mary Ann Lyons, 'Foreign Language Books, 1550–1700', in Raymond Gillespie and Andrew Hadfield, eds, *The History of the Irish Book*, vol. 3: *The Irish Book in English, 1550–1800* (Oxford: Oxford University Press, 2005), 365.

49 John Bossy, *Christianity in the West, 1400–1700* (Oxford: Oxford University Press, 1985), 100. On the Irish context, see Bernadette Cunningham, 'Introduction', in Bernadette Cunningham and Máire Kennedy, eds, *The Experience of Reading: Irish Historical Perspectives* (Dublin: Rare Books Group of the Library Association of Ireland and ESHSI, 1999), 1–9.

Walter Wadding made it a custom at home that his children should say their prayers together in the form of call and response.[50] They also prayed the rosary, and said the morning and evening exercises in common. Further, young Luke recited the Little Office of the Blessed Virgin each day, and twice every week the penitential psalms, with the litany of the saints and accompanying prayers. Frequently each month, he completed the office for the dead. From this, Luke grew in the practice of virtue, became more familiar with the Latin language and with Catholic liturgy.[51] This suggests parental instruction helped by clerical teaching.

The image of a holy infancy followed by divinely ordained deeds later in life originated in mediaeval hagiographical works.[52] As the innocence of young adolescents was regarded as 'the salvation of the world', children received pious instruction.[53] This approach continued to find favour in the seventeenth century, as shown in the *Vita* written by Francis Harold. Nevertheless, at the institutions he founded, Luke Wadding made united prayer a greater priority than book learning. He did so with the same dedication and reverence established in his childhood. Moreover, in later years, Wadding maintained an interest in continued improvements to Divine Office texts when Urban VIII appointed him to serve as an adviser for the revision of the Roman breviary.

---

50 Harold, *Vita Fratris Lucae Waddingi*, 10.

51 Ibid.

52 Underwood, *Childhood, Youth and Religious Dissent in Post-Reformation England*, 59, 193; Simon Ditchfield, '*Historia magistra sanctitatis*? The Relationship between Historiography and Hagiography in Italy after the Council of Trent (*c*.1564–1742)', in Massimo Firpo, ed, *Nunc alia tempora, alii mores. Storici e storia in età postridentina* (Florence: Olschki, 2005), 159–84. Therefore, Protestants were not alone in thinking that a good education was linked to sanctity; see Alex Ryrie, *Being Protestant in Reformation Britain* (Oxford: Oxford University Press, 2013), 262; Andrew Cambers, *Godly Reading: Print, Manuscript and Puritanism in England, 1580–1720* (Cambridge: Cambridge University Press, 2011), 181.

53 Richard Trexler, 'Ritual in Florence: Adolescence and Salvation in the Renaissance', in Charles Trinkaus and Heiko Oberman, eds, *The Pursuit of Holiness in Late Medieval and Renaissance Religion* (Leiden: Brill, 1974), 260.

Waterford Schooldays

As an exceptional and serious-minded young scholar, Luke Wadding was well-prepared for school. Greater prosperity gave merchants such as his father a broader outlook and more interest in education.[54] Young people traditionally studied Latin before university to acquire the skills for law and medicine.[55] Called to promote Catholicism through the sacraments and preaching after the Council of Trent, the clergy were required to have a better education. As such, the priesthood began to develop as a profession.[56] During the later Elizabethan period, recusant parents employed dedicated tutors to ensure that their offspring would be raised in the Catholic faith.[57]

In Francis Harold's words, Luke was 'a character inclined to religion and literature'.[58] His first cousin, Thomas Strange, stated that John Flahy was their schoolmaster in the city of Waterford.[59] Under the tutelage of

54 Brendan Bradshaw, *The Dissolution of the Religious Orders in Ireland under Henry VIII* (repr. Cambridge: Cambridge University Press, 2008), 225.

55 Dick Akerboom, 'Spiritual Leadership in an Age of Uncertainty: Geert Grote and the Modern Devotion', in Doris Nauer, Rein Nauta and Henk Witte, eds, *Religious Leadership and Christian Identity*. Tilburg Theological Studies (Münster: Lit Verlag, 2004), 61.

56 Angelo Turchini, 'La nascita del sacerdozio come professione', in Paolo Prodi, ed, *Disciplina dell'anima, disciplina del corpo e disciplina della società tra medioevo ed età moderna* (Bologna: Il Mulino, 1994), 225–256; Joseph Bergin, 'Between Estate and Profession: the Catholic Parish Clergy of Early Modern Western Europe', in Michael Bush, ed, *Social Orders and Social Classes in Europe Since 1500* (Abingdon: Routledge, 1992), 66–85; John W. O'Malley, 'Priesthood, Ministry, and Religious Life: Some Historical and Historiographical Considerations', *Theological Studies*, 49 (1988), 223–257.

57 Jan Graffius, ''Bullworks against the Furie of Heresie': Identity, Education, and Mission in the English Jesuit College of St Omers', in Chambers and O'Connor, eds, *Forming Catholic Communities: Irish, Scots and English College Networks in Europe*, 95.

58 Harold, *Vita Fratris Lucae Waddingi*, 10: 'indolem in religionem et litteras proclivem'.

59 Thomas Strange to Wadding, Dublin, 20 Nov. 1629 (Jennings, ed, *Wadding Papers*, 319).

Flahy, Wadding 'applied himself to the study of grammar and humanities'.[60] Flahy was a layman married to Anne Walsh, daughter of Patrick Walsh who became bishop of Waterford and Lismore in the brief reign of Edward VI.[61]

At Flahy's school, Wadding enjoyed bookbinding, a practical skill that suggests he studied and compiled books in manuscript.[62] This raises significant questions about book production.[63] He also became proficient at composing Latin in either prose or verse and made so much progress that, in his thirteenth year, whatever topics Flahy gave him, Luke could render Latin successfully and to the great approval of his schoolmaster.[64] Patrick Comerford, another of Wadding's cousins and one of his classmates, referred to 'the very famous and very fortunate Schoolemaster Iohn Flaghie to whom especially the province of Munster is beholding for good breeding, as it was formerly to Master Peter White'.[65] To the seventeenth-century Oxford historian, Anthony Wood, teaching was 'a most excellent employment in Ireland' because it enabled the nobility and gentry to 'be trained up in their religion, and so consequently keep out Protestancy'.[66]

60 Harold, *Vita Fratris Lucae Waddingi*, 10: 'Grammaticis dehinc et humaniorum litterarum studiis applicitus Lucas'.

61 Jennings, ed, *Wadding Papers*, 319; Walton, 'Church, Crown and Corporation in Waterford, 1520–1620', 184.

62 Harold, *Vita Fratris Lucae Waddingi*, 11.

63 On the import of books and the output of Irish presses, see Raymond Gillespie, *Reading Ireland: Print, Reading and Social Change in Early Modern Ireland* (Manchester: Manchester University Press, 2012), 129–56, 186–89.

64 Harold, *Vita Fratris Lucae Waddingi*, 11.

65 Patrick Comerford, *The Inquisition of a Sermon Preached in the Cathedral Church of the City of Waterford in February 1617 etc by Robert Daborne, by P.C.* (Waterford: Thomas Bourke, 1645), 19.

66 Anthony Wood, *Athenæ Oxonienses: An Exact History of all the Writers and Bishops who have had their Education in the University of Oxford. To which are added the Fasti, or Annals of the said University*, ed Philip Bliss, 4 vols (London: Rivington, 1813–20), vol. 1, 575.

This was recusant schooling.[67] One 'John fflahy' was admitted as a freeman of Waterford in 1606 for two half barge stones.[68] Nine years later, the commissioners of a royal visitation of Waterford and Lismore unsuccessfully called upon Flahy to appear before them for non-attendance at Protestant services. Moreover, they objected to him educating candidates for the ecclesiastical state 'beyond the seas'.[69] Pupils from a wide geographical area in the southeast of Ireland studied with Flahy for up to seven years.[70] Endowments to schools were socially altruistic.[71] Flahy received parental support from the citizens of Waterford who paid him £20 per year from 1602 to 1617.[72] The consolidation of Catholicism by the Old English reflected the desire to safeguard their faith by sending their sons to Irish colleges on the continent.[73] In the same period, records show that Flahy educated sixteen scholars who went on to commence studies at Salamanca.[74]

67 Thomas O'Connor, 'Domestic Grammar Schools and Overseas Colleges in the Formation of Irish Catholic Clergy (1560–1620)', in Anja-Silvia Goeing, Glyn Parry and Mordechai Feingold, eds, *Early Modern Universities: Networks of Higher Learning* (Leiden: Brill, 2021), 211; Colm Lennon, 'Education and Religious Identity in Early Modern Ireland', *Paedagogica Historica*, 35 (1999), 67.

68 Byrne, ed, *The Great Parchment Book of Waterford*, 216.

69 'Diocese of Waterford and Lismore in 1615', *Waterford Arch. Soc. Jn.*, 1 (1894–95), 144–45.

70 Denis O'Doherty, ed, 'Students of the Irish College Salamanca (1595–1619)', *Archiv. Hib.*, 2 (1913), 13–33; cited by Timothy Corcoran, 'Early Irish Jesuit Educators (I)', *Studies*, 29 (1940), 556.

71 Bradshaw, *The Dissolution of the Religious Orders in Ireland under Henry VIII*, 223–24.

72 Michael Quane, 'Waterford Corporation Free School', *Cork Hist. Soc. Jn.*, 65 (1959), 85.

73 R. Dudley Edwards, 'Ireland, Elizabeth I and the Counter-Reformation', in Stanley Bindoff, Joel Hurstfield and Charles Williams, eds, *Elizabethan Government and Society. Essays Presented to Sir John Neale* (London: Athlone Press, 1961), 329.

74 O'Doherty, ed, 'Students of the Irish College Salamanca (1595–1619)', 15, 22, 23, 24, 25, 26, 29, 30, 33, 34.

Anglo-Spanish War

During the Anglo-Spanish war of 1585–1604, more than two-thirds of Irish trade with Spain and Portugal was conducted on Irish vessels, most of which were from Waterford.[75] Since England and Spain were at war, their own ships were excluded from maritime trade, whereas Irish merchants operated under Spanish licences as Catholic subjects of the English crown. This was permitted by the English authorities for the duration of the war with Spain, but led to smuggling.[76] Merchants feared war would destroy their trade. They employed shipmasters for the transfer of goods to intermediate ports, which became the base for the clandestine shipment of English goods to Spain and Spanish exports to England.[77]

Although Waterford's political loyalty to Elizabeth I was beyond reproach, the city's merchants continued to maintain commerce with the Iberian Peninsula. In the Nine Years' War, the port became a centre of operations for government troops harboured in Waterford.[78] This followed established practice from earlier times.[79] The city also lent the large sum of £800 sterling in support of Elizabeth I's war effort and attended

75 Susan Flavin, *Consumption and Culture in Sixteenth-century Ireland: Saffron, Stockings and Silk* (Woodbridge: Boydell, 2014), 23, 31; Karin Schüller, 'Special Conditions of the Irish-Iberian Trade during the Spanish-English War, 1585–1604', in Óscar Recio Morales, Bernardo García García, Miguel Ángel de Bunes Ibarra, Enrique García Hernán, eds, *Irlanda y la Monarquía Hispánica. Kinsale 1601–2001: guerra, política, exilio y religion* (Madrid: Consejo Superior de Investigaciones Científicas, 2002), 463.

76 Flavin, *Consumption and Culture in Sixteenth-century Ireland*, 28; Schüller, 'Special Conditions of the Irish-Iberian Trade', 463.

77 W. J. Smith, ed, *Herbert Correspondence: The Sixteenth- and Seventeenth-Century Letters of the Herberts of Chirbury, Powis Castle and Dolguog, formerly at Powis Castle in Montgomeryshire* (Cardiff: University of Wales Press; Dublin: Irish Manuscripts Commission, 1968), 191, 241.

78 Byrne, ed, *The Great Parchment Book of Waterford*, 182.

79 On campaign twice in Ireland in the 1390s, Richard II landed in and sailed home from Waterford with a large army. See Darren McGettigan, *Richard II and the Irish Kings* (Dublin: Four Courts Press, 2016); James Lydon, *Ireland in the Later Middle Ages* (Dublin: Gill, 1973), 109–114.

to the wounded upon direction of the lord deputy.[80] This proof of loyalty enabled the citizens to continue in their refusal to attend Protestant services. Elizabeth I's bishop of Cork acknowledged Luke Wadding's uncle, Thomas, as 'a great lawyer'.[81] Nevertheless, neither Wadding nor his sheriffs ever attended state church whilst he was mayor 'nor sithence this reign, nor none of the citizens, men nor women nor in any town or city throughout this province'.[82]

As mayor, Thomas Wadding wrote regularly to Dublin Castle with reports he received from merchants. Much of this information originated in Portugal, as well as dispatches from the seas around the southern coasts of Ireland. Informed of the capture of Cadiz by the English and Dutch, Thomas Wadding notified Lord Deputy Russell of arrangements 'suddenly made' in Spain upon the news.[83] Russell communicated this to Burghley in Whitehall. In response to messages about Philip III's confidence in Hugh O'Neill, Thomas Wadding advocated the strengthening of defences at Duncannon fort. That year, a new Spanish fleet was assembled, for the most part at Lisbon. It set sail for Ireland in late October but was destroyed by a storm off the northwest coast of Spain.[84]

Munster Plantation

At that time, Wadding's father and uncle were among the Old English claimants who supported the confiscation of FitzGerald estates in Munster and took the opportunity to assert ownership of these assets.[85] The FitzGerald earls of Desmond had owned large tracts of land, until defeated in successive rebellions against the crown.[86] This led to the Munster plantation, a settle-

80 Byrne, ed, *The Great Parchment Book of Waterford*, 182.
81 Hazard, 'Thomas Wadding, Waterford Landowner and Lawyer of Gray's Inn', 39.
82 Ibid.
83 Ibid.
84 Ibid.
85 Hazard, 'Thomas Wadding's Title to Lands at Knockmaon, Co. Waterford, May 1587', *Archiv. Hib.* 76 (2023), 7–12.
86 Anthony McCormack, *The Earldom of Desmond, 1463–1583: the Decline and Crisis of a Feudal Lordship* (Dublin: Four Courts Press, 2005), 196.

ment scheme which began in the southwest of Ireland in 1585.[87] However, a year later, it became clear to local inhabitants that the majority of lands were to go to Elizabethan undertakers.[88]

Thomas Wadding and his brother, Walter, lost out when they tried to establish rightful ownership to Knockmaon Castle and its lands in Co. Waterford.[89] In May 1587, the Irish exchequer of pleas confirmed Thomas Wadding's title to the property, which he purchased from Sir Maurice FitzJohn, a son of Sir John Desmond. Nevertheless, the details of the case were complicated and could not be proven beyond a reasonable doubt. The following year, Walter Wadding was named 'the Recoveror' in the hope that the lands could be conveyed to him and his heirs.[90] On 3 September, he made a bill of complaint in a formal statement accompanied by a petition to obtain relief from the court. In doing so, he enumerated the claim to Knockmaon along with lands at Carriglea, Garryroe, Dunbricky, Coolecromp, Glanavodera, Ballinacourty and Killeshill, Co. Waterford.[91]

However, the privy council had already made title for Elizabeth I. More than a year before the examination of the Waddings' title, Knockmaon was allocated to Sir Christopher Hatton. A courtier and favourite of Elizabeth I, Hatton was vice-chamberlain of the Queen's household before he became lord chancellor.[92] Owing to their land investments and the ruling reached by the exchequer of pleas, the Waddings' holdings were, for a time, in reduced circumstances in Co. Waterford. This may have influenced four of Thomas Wadding's sons in their decision to join the Society of Jesus and take the vow of poverty. As did their first cousin, Ambrose.[93] Meanwhile,

87 Nicholas Canny, *Making Ireland British, 1580–1650* (Oxford: Oxford University Press, 2001), 111, 131.

88 Michael McCarthy Morrogh, *The Munster Plantation: English Migration to Southern Ireland, 1583–1641* (Oxford: Clarendon Press, 1986), 130–131.

89 Hazard, 'Thomas Wadding's Title to Lands at Knockmaon, Co. Waterford, May 1587', 10.

90 Ibid, 9.

91 Ibid.

92 Ibid, 10.

93 Terry Clavin, 'Wadding, Ambrose (1583–1619), Jesuit and university teacher', *Dictionary of Irish Biography*, vol. 9, 680.

his younger brother, Luke, became a Franciscan friar.[94] Economic adversity for a previously well-off family, interpreted through a spiritual lens of experiencing something of the self-emptying of Jesus in his incarnation, would be an incentive to identify with him and lead to an embrace of poverty as a way of life.[95]

A fresh crisis erupted when, following his victory at the battle of Yellow Ford, Hugh O'Neill agitated political unrest in Munster.[96] What ensued illustrates Waterford's involvement in the conflict and the precarious nature of Elizabethan rule in Ireland at the height of the war. Emboldened by O'Neill, the FitzGeralds of Desmond joined together with other leaders to expel English settlers from the Munster plantation. According to Peter Lombard, Catholic archbishop of Armagh and Luke Wadding's cousin, those driven out turned for help to Sir Thomas Norris, governor of Munster. They received no response from him, other than he could only defend himself with difficulty. Therefore, they proceeded towards Waterford where they acquired a fleet of eighteen ships, which carried 1,800 of them to England.[97] This accounted for half of the total number of English settlers in the colony.[98] Thus, the Munster plantation was swept away.

Recusancy Revolt

In an area of approximately 30,000 inhabitants, the Wadding family were related by blood or marriage to many of their Old English neighbours in a

94 Hazard, 'Thomas Wadding's title to lands at Knockmaon, Co. Waterford, May 1587', 7–12.

95 I am grateful to Fr. Gearóid Ó Conaire OFM for this insight.

96 James O'Neill, *The Nine Years War, 1593–1603: O'Neill, Mountjoy and the Military Revolution* (Dublin: Four Courts Press, 2018), 77–78; McCarthy Morrogh, *The Munster Plantation*, 107, 134.

97 Peter Lombard, *De regno Hiberniae sanctorum insula commentarius*, ed Patrick Moran (Dublin: Duffy, 1868), 168: 'progressi ulterius versus civitatem Waterfordiam Anglis'.

98 McCarthy Morrogh, *The Munster Plantation*, 147.

diocese that witnessed major religious change in the sixteenth century.[99] As attorney to the Butlers of Ormond, Thomas Wadding, Luke's uncle, was rewarded with the lands, rents and revenues of the Hospitallers of Saint John of Jerusalem at Kilbarry, within the city liberty of Waterford. This became the Wadding seat.[100] For much of that century, the long-term repercussions of the Reformation remained unclear to the laity and to members of the clergy.[101]

In 1539, Waterford Franciscan friary was suppressed. Even so, the Waddings continued to keep their family tomb in the friary where Luke's father and uncles were buried. According to Wadding, the friary was 'among the numerous and beautiful sacred buildings that Waterford possessed [...] remarkable both for the size of the building and from the number and dignity of the friars'.[102] The friary was part of Waterford's defences. At the same time, the friars were a short walk away from the port, close to local inhabitants and visitors. It was, Wadding explained, 'located in the eastern quarter of the city, within the walls and by the quayside'.[103]

However, the strain caused by many years of war and religious unrest first became apparent in Waterford before spreading to the towns of Munster, Kilkenny, Wexford and Drogheda after the death of Elizabeth I. The news was greeted with relief by Catholics. They assumed that better times were ahead with the accession of James VI of Scotland to the throne. Though raised a Protestant, he was the son of Mary Queen of Scots and baptised a Catholic. Following Hugh O'Neill's defeat and submission, the towns rose up in an attempt to re-establish the public exercise of Catholicism. Fynes Moryson, secretary to Lord Deputy Mountjoy, described these events as

99 Giblin, 'The *Processus Datariae* and the Appointments of Irish Bishops in the Seventeenth Century', 552; Hazard, 'Thomas Wadding, Waterford Landowner and Lawyer of Gray's Inn', 17–42; At the Benedictine priory of St John the Evangelist, Luke's grandfather, Nicholas Wadding, sat on a jury to inquire into the property of the priory before its secularisation in 1536.

100 Hazard, 'Thomas Wadding, Waterford Landowner and Lawyer of Gray's Inn', 31.

101 On the historiographical debate from the writings of Bradshaw to those of Jefferies, see Murray, *Enforcing the English Reformation in Ireland*, 1–19.

102 *Annales Minorum*, vol. 3 (1240), 52, n. 26: 'inter frequentes & speciosas quas possedit sacras aedes, illa nostra fuit spectabilis tum ex aedificij amplitudine, tum ex fratrum numero & dignitate'.

103 Ibid: 'Sita est ad Orientalem plagam civitatis prope, sed intra muros iuxta navale'.

'mutinous disorders'.[104] Protestant ministers were ousted and their books burnt in Waterford, Cork and Clonmel.[105] This became known as the recusancy revolt.

In the latter part of Elizabeth I's reign, representatives of the crown began to reduce the municipal privileges enjoyed by towns and cities in Ireland. Recent historical writing has, therefore, concentrated on the recusancy revolt as a protest against lost civic authority and curbed business interests.[106] Existing accounts have also examined experiences across the towns of Munster during the period that followed Elizabeth I's death.[107] These events marked forty years since the completion of the Council of Trent. Hence, a gap in the research is apparent with regard to the religious significance of the revolt in Waterford. The implementation of its reforms clarified Catholic teaching and led to a resurgence of the Church in response to the upheaval of the Reformation.[108]

No bishops were being appointed to Ireland by Rome at that time. Instead, the papacy granted administrative jurisdiction to vicars apostolic in their dioceses. From 1600 to 1610, James White was vicar apostolic of Waterford where he was closely connected to the Waddings.[109] According to White, the laity and clergy went to the house where he lived in Waterford and called on him to reconsecrate all churches and places of prayer, which

104 Fynes Moryson, *An Itinerary: containing his Ten Yeeres Travell through the Twelve Dominions of Germany, Bohmerland, Sweitzerland, Netherland, Denmarke, Poland, Italy, Turky, France, England, Scotland and Ireland* (London: John Beale, 1617; repr. 4 vols Glasgow: James MacLehose, 1907–8), vol. 3, 314.

105 *The Jesuit Irish Mission: A Calendar of Correspondence, 1566–1752*, ed Vera Moynes (Rome: Institutum Historicum Societatis Iesu: 2017), 380.

106 John Walter, 'The 'Recusancy Revolt' of 1603 Revisited, Popular Politics and Civic Catholicism in Early Modern Ireland', *HJ*, 65 (2022), 249–74; Anthony Sheehan, 'The Recusancy Revolt of 1603: A Reinterpretation', *Archiv. Hib.*, 38 (1983), 3–13.

107 Alan Ford, "Firm Catholics' or 'Loyal Subjects'? Religious and Political Allegiance in Early Seventeenth-Century Ireland', in D. G. Boyce, Robert Eccleshall and Vincent Geoghegan, eds, *Political Discourse in Seventeenth- and Eighteenth-century Ireland* (Basingstoke: Palgrave Macmillan, 2001), 1–31.

108 O'Malley, *Trent: What happened at the Council*, 248–277.

109 Patrick Power, *Waterford and Lismore. A Compendious History of the United Dioceses*, 14, 281; Benjamin Hazard, 'Thomas Wadding's title to lands at Knockmaon, Co. Waterford, May 1587', *Archiv. Hib.*, 76, 7–12.

they regarded as 'the hereditary right' of Catholics.[110] White emphasised the participation of 'all the respectable families, men and women, and the whole population of the city'.[111] He willingly responded and also delegated several of his fellow priests to the task. Apart from Waterford and Lismore, White fulfilled similar requests in the neighbouring dioceses of Ossory, Ferns and Cashel.[112]

On hearing of these developments, Mountjoy immediately ordered the towns to close the churches and suspend the sacraments.[113] He marched south to the gates of Waterford at the head of an army but was refused admission. The mayor, Paul Sherlock, and his sheriffs asked the lord deputy to bring no more troops than they could accommodate with convenience. In response, Mountjoy resolved 'to raze the city of Waterford to the ground and to put all its inhabitants to the sword'.[114] Since towns such as Kilkenny and Wexford had already capitulated, any possibility of open defiance by the local inhabitants had ended.[115] While negotiations continued, White was employed as an agent of Waterford Corporation with Wadding's cousin, the Cistercian Thomas Lombard.[116]

The vicar apostolic offered a robust defence telling Mountjoy that he acted on the authority vested in him by the pope, recounting that he 'had not done injury to any man in the kingdom' and had given 'many undoubted proofs' of allegiance to the crown.[117] Despite the crisis provoked, these events passed off peacefully. Recalled by Mountjoy a second time

110 In Rome, White presented a Latin account of these events. For an English translation published in 1894, see 'A brief summary and true narrative of the affairs of the Catholics, lay and clerical, in the kingdom of Ireland, immediately after the death of Elizabeth, late queen of England. By James White, an Irishman, Doctor of theology and vicar-apostolic of Waterford and Lismore, in said kingdom – Rome, 25 July 1604', in P. M. Egan, *History, Guide & Directory of County and City of Waterford* (Kilkenny: Egan, 1894), 114–42.

111 Egan, *History, Guide & Directory of County and City of Waterford*, 119.

112 Ibid, 121.

113 Ibid.

114 Ibid, 124.

115 Richard Bagwell, *Ireland under the Stuarts and during the interregnum*, 3 vols (London: Longmans, Green & Co., 1909–1916), vol. 1, 2–5.

116 Egan, 125.

117 Ibid, 125, 129–130.

that day, White asked him to allow the free exercise of religion. Mountjoy replied that it was not within his authority and only the king could grant such permission.[118] Instead, he declared that he would allow priests to celebrate Mass in private houses with full liberty, to preach to the people and to fulfil all the other duties of their ministry. Mountjoy also demanded an oath of allegiance to James I from the citizens with a disavowal of any foreign ruler. Despite their adherence to Catholicism, the citizenry cooperated with the lord deputy.[119]

In 1603, the politico-religious debate between White and Mountjoy clearly illustrated the impact of Counter-Reformation policy among the laity and the clergy of Waterford. White's readiness in the city and his advocacy in the presence of the lord deputy demonstrates the level of formation required for effective pastoral ministry after Trent. Moreover, lay men and women understood the tenets of their faith and actively sought spiritual direction from members of the clergy who, in return, offered people religious consolation.

The recusancy revolt caused alarm in official circles and called into question Mountjoy's conciliatory approach towards O'Neill at Mellifont. By then, however, political opinion was probably too divided for any agreement to be reached in Ireland. More was expected of the urban Old English, as emphasised by William Camden who said that Waterford showed 'singular faith and obedience' to the government since the Norman conquest.[120] Crown administrators still saw the corporate towns of Ireland as citadels of English civilisation surrounded by the wild Irish.[121] As a result, urban areas such as Waterford continued to receive official support in return for

118 Ibid, 131.

119 Moryson, *An Itinerary*, vol. 3, 329.

120 William Camden, *Britannia: siue Florentissimorum regnorum Angliae, Scotiae, Hibernia, et insularum adiacentium ex intima antiquitate chorographica descriptio: nunc postremo recognita, plurimis locis magna accessione adaucta, et chartis chorographicis illustrata* (Londini: impensis Georgii Bishop & Ioannis Norton, 1607), 740.

121 Colm Lennon, *Sixteenth-Century Ireland: The Incomplete Conquest* (Dublin: Gill & Macmillan 1994), 29, 190.

their political trust and commercial exchange.[122] Yet, as we shall see, James I's decision to return Catholics to the situation that existed before his reign signified an erosion of religious freedom in the public sphere and signalled his need for a new colonial elite of English and Scottish Protestants.

Plague in Waterford

In November 1603, James White set sail for Bordeaux before departing for Rome where he gave a report to Clement VIII.[123] In the accompanying letter, White compared the Reformation in northern Europe to a 'most pestilential and infectious fever'.[124] He made this metaphor in the context of his times. During the final phase of the war, many Irish towns were hit by an outbreak of plague with devastating effects.[125] At fourteen years of age, Luke Wadding was bereaved of both his parents.[126] A 'vehement' epidemic began in Waterford on 24 October 1603 and lasted until 23 September 1604, with a death toll of 116 per week in the previous month. According to the *Great Parchment Book*, 2,256 lives were lost.[127] Prominent individuals and the broader population were similarly affected. Wadding's mother, Anastasia Lombard, was among the dead. Francis Harold described her as 'equally illustrious among her contemporaries' and related by blood to Peter Lombard.[128] Anastasia's forebears were Italian financiers who collected

122 Anthony Sheehan, 'Irish Towns in a Period of Change, 1558–1625', in Ciaran Brady and Raymond Gillespie, eds, *Natives and Newcomers: Essays on the Making of Irish Colonial Society* (Dublin: Irish Academic Press, 1986), 111.

123 Egan, 141.

124 John Lynch, *Cambrensis eversus, seu potius Historica fides in rebus Hibernicis Giraldo Cambrensi abrogata*, ed Matthew Kelly, 3 vols (Dublin: The Celtic Society, 1848–52), vol. 3, 521: 'Pestilens admodum, et inficiens est febris illa'.

125 Harold, *Vita Fratris Lucae Waddingi*, 10: 'Anno Christi MDCII quo saeva lues plures Hiberniae civitates afflixit'. Beckett, *The Making of Modern Ireland*, 25.

126 Harold, *Vita Fratris Lucae Waddingi*, 9–10.

127 Byrne, ed, *The Great Parchment Book of Waterford*, 210–211; *Cal. Carew MSS. 1589–1600*, 308.

128 Harold, *Vita Fratris Lucae Waddingi*, 9.

crown and papal revenues in Ireland in earlier times.[129] Divided in death from her husband on account of the plague's severity, Anastasia's body was buried in a mass grave outside the walls of the city in the grounds of the former Augustinian priory of St Catherine.[130] Both spouses, 'as they had loved each other in their lifetime, died almost at the same time'. Walter was buried in the Wadding tomb in the Lady Chapel by the south wall of the Franciscan friary.[131]

Meanwhile, Mountjoy's forces were struck by a persistent contagion, which accounted for the death of several thousand soldiers.[132] Nine hundred were garrisoned in Waterford due to the recusancy revolt of 1603. The municipal authorities took deliberate steps to stop them from plundering the houses of the dead for their clothing and possessions, which spread the infection. At night, the inner gates of the city were shut, 'which were not closed many yeeres before', and the garrison was reduced to a minimum.[133]

Conclusion

In the religious and educational currents of his time, Luke Wadding was a child of the recusant movement, which represented a counter-revolution in northern Europe. Amidst the storms of life in the late sixteenth century,

129 Mary D. O'Sullivan, *Italian Merchant Bankers in Ireland in the Thirteenth Century: A Study in the Social and Economic History of Medieval Ireland* (Dublin: Figgis, 1962), 107, 117–118, 126.

130 *Annales Minorum*, vol. 3 (1240), 53, n. 28: 'Diuisit eum in morte à chara coniuge & nostra genitrice Anastasia Lombarda saeua lues pestis, ob quam hanc non licuit viro coniungi, tumulata que est in monasterio S. Catharinae extra ciuitatem'.

131 Harold, *Vita Fratris Lucae Waddingi*, 10: 'Uterque conjugum, ut in vita sua se dilexerunt […] fere simul defuncti'.

132 Letter of Mountjoy and Council of Ireland to the Lords of England, Cork, 15 Feb 1601, cited by Cyril Falls, *Elizabeth's Irish Wars* (Syracuse NY: Syracuse University Press, 1997), 315; Thomas Stafford, *Pacata Hibernia: or, a History of the Wars in Ireland, during the Reign of Queen Elizabeth especially within the Province of Munster under the Government of Sir George Carew*, ed Standish O'Grady (London: Downey, 1896), 112.

133 Byrne, ed, *The Great Parchment Book of Waterford*, 212.

prayer and study provided him with an essential anchor that prepared him for the years ahead. The breviary of Pius V was an emblem of Catholic identity and its presence in late Elizabethan Waterford shows the strength of Walter Wadding's religious convictions. Therefore, from an early age, Luke's reading habits encompassed Catholic Europe, in keeping with his description of Waterford as Little Rome.[134]

Wadding's home life indicates that he was diligent and peaceable. His lifelong interest in books and scholarship, and his devotion to the Virgin Mary began during childhood. Luke's parents recognised the value of education and placed him in the school of John Flahy. From the tragedy of the Great Armada to the outbreak of plague in Waterford, from the Nine Years War to the Munster plantation and the recusancy revolt of 1603, increasingly turbulent times acquainted Wadding with the frailty of human life and the fleeting nature of material wealth. The decision that he and his cousins took to pursue religious life exemplifies the generational change that occurred in youth culture in late sixteenth- and early seventeenth-century Ireland. There remained a possibility that Luke would remain there until the recusancy revolt and the restoration of the *status quo ante* by the government. Faced with ongoing unrest and instability, it became necessary for Wadding to seek further formation overseas. The education he had received in Ireland came to fruition as a Franciscan in the Iberian Peninsula where he developed his tastes as a Latinist and bibliophile. This is dealt with in the next chapter.

134 *Annales Minorum*, vol. 3 (1240), 52, n. 26: 'ut gloriose passim res hoc audiat nomine Parva Roma'.

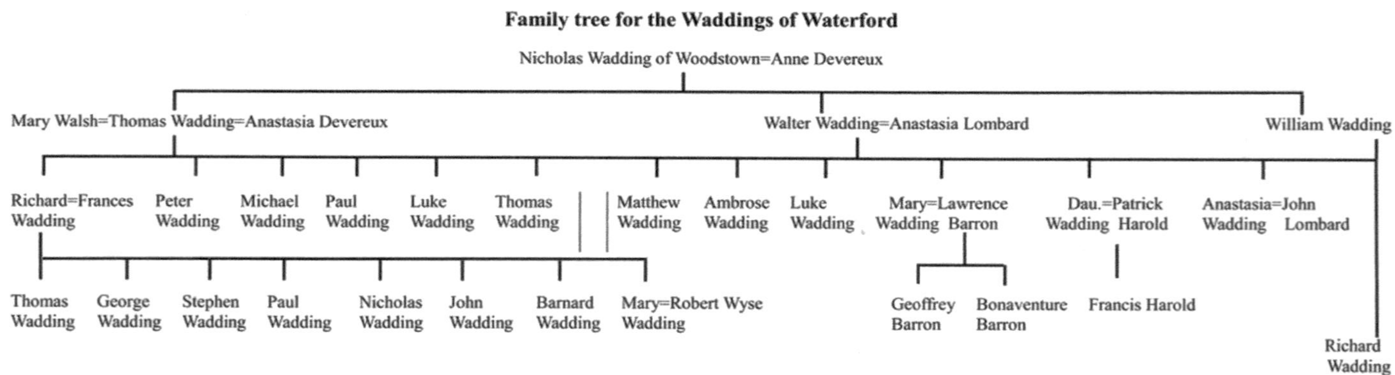

Figure 1.1 Family tree of the Waddings of Waterford

2 Apprenticeship in Portugal

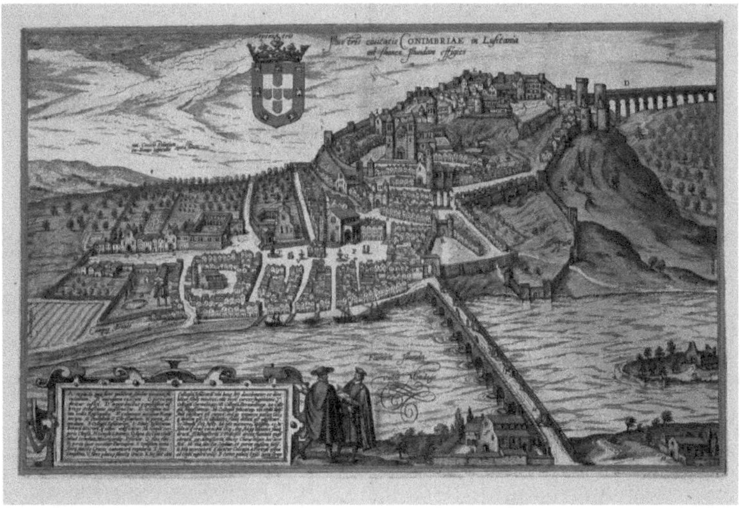

Figure 2.1 *Illustris Civitatis Conimbriae in Lusitania ad flumen Illundam effigies*, Braun & Hogenberg. Engraving of Coimbra on the river Mondego with two scholars in foreground. Reproduced courtesy of Biblioteca de Fundo Antigo da Universidade de Coimbra.

Introduction

At fourteen years of age, after the death of their mother and father, Wadding's brother Matthew took him under his care and protection.[1] Matthew Wadding was a merchant active in Andalusia, Portugal and Galicia.[2] Luke studied logic and physics in Ireland until, in due course,

1 Harold, *Vita Fratris Lucae Waddingi*, 11.

2 Examinations of Matthew Wadding, Peter Strange FitzRichard, and Michell Hore, 9 July 1601, certified by Edward Goeghe, mayor of Waterford (*Cal. SP Ire. 1600–01*, 425, 431).

Matthew sailed out of Waterford and took Luke with him. He, therefore, travelled with someone familiar with the terrain and language who could help along the way. This chapter follows Luke Wadding to Portugal. It discusses what he referred to as his apprenticeship with the Friars Minor, before assessing the significant progress he made as a scholar in the context of the places that were connected with him and his writings about Portugal. This reveals Wadding's own view of his exile on the continent.

In 1604, the end of the Anglo-Spanish war was confirmed in the Treaty of London.[3] This stabilised lawful mercantile activity in the interests of recovery. Since the plague ceased in Waterford, 'plentie of all grayne was such as there were Corn shipps and barks laden with wheate transported owt of this haven to the ports beyond the seas'.[4]

That year, the Wadding brothers dropped anchor in Lisbon where Matthew placed Luke, then fifteen, in the Irish College.[5] The voyage south from Ireland took a fortnight. The seaports of Galicia and Portugal formed a chain stretching from La Coruña to Lisbon, Santa María and beyond.[6] Thus, to shelter from the Bay of Biscay, ships made intervening calls along the way.[7] The best times of the year for sea voyages occurred between the spring and autumn equinox but discomforts such as sea sickness were difficult to reduce, and the rigours of rough waters were familiar to travellers. Guided by the judgement of others on the uncertainties of the sea, the

3 José Pablo Alzina, *Embajadores de España en Londres: Retratos de la Embajada de España* (Madrid: Ministerio de Asuntos Exteriores, 2001), 89–105. Alexandra Gajda, 'War, Peace, Commerce and the Treaty of London (1604)', in *Historical Research*, 96 (2023), 459–72, <https://doi.org/10.1093/hisres/htad011>.

4 Byrne, ed, *The Great Parchment Book of Waterford*, 212.

5 Patricia O Connell, *The Irish College at Lisbon, 1580–1834* (Dublin: Four Courts Press, 2001), 45, 52.

6 Spanish council of state to Don Juan de Cardona, Aranjuez, 27 Jun 1602 (AGS, Estado, leg. 191), NLI Microfilm n.452, p.72. *Merchants Aviso, or Instructions very necessary for their Sonnes and Servants, when they first send them beyond the Sea, as to Spaine and Portingale, or other Countries* (London: John Bill, 1616), 9. The manuscript for this source was completed in the late 1580s.

7 Roger Stalley, 'Sailing to Santiago: Medieval Pilgrimage to Santiago de Compostela and its Artistic Influence in Ireland', in John Bradley, ed, *Settlement and Society in Medieval Ireland: Studies presented to F. X. Martin OSA* (Kilkenny: Boethius Press, 1988), 402–403.

following phrase was much quoted: 'He who knows not how to pray, may learn to sail'.[8] Merchants often provided for spiritual traffic by bringing on board clergymen and students. Therefore, clergy and ships could be seen together on the waterfront.[9]

One-fifth of vessels from Ireland landed in Lisbon.[10] Matthew Wadding made his home there. Merchants in the city also gave the authorities information on conditions in Munster, such as Thomas Comerford who reported that everyone in Waterford was Catholic: 'They heard Mass and received the sacraments, but in secret from the English'.[11] Merchants and factors unable to sell their produce in Lisbon also brought it to San Lucar in Andalusia, travelling overland to Seville and Huelva to participate in domestic Iberian trade.[12]

Catholic students from Ireland had tested education in exile since the 1570s. By the time that Wadding moved to Portugal, the practice was a well-organised endeavour with colleges established on the continent. In 1593, John Howling of Wexford founded the Irish College in Lisbon to cater for an initial intake of thirty scholars. Howling managed the college and taught there for six years.[13] The Lisbon college had an important bearing on events in Ireland, 'determining in a very great measure, the Catholic future of the country'.[14] There, Wadding commenced the philosophy course under the instruction of the Jesuit Fathers and remained

8 'Qui nescit orare, discat navigare' cited by Ernest Bates, *Touring in 1600: A Study in the Development of Travel as a Means of Education* (London, 1911; repr. London: Century, 1987), 71, 76.

9 Miller, *One Firm Anchor: The Church and the Merchant Seafarer*, 22, 43.

10 Thomas O'Connor, *Irish Voices from the Spanish Inquisition: Migrants, Converts and Brokers in Early Modern Iberia* (Basingstoke: Palgrave Macmillan, 2016), 37–38, 43, 214.

11 Report by Comerford, Lisbon, 22 February 1597, 'Que en Guateford son todos Catholicos y oyen misa y reciben los sacramentos pero escondidamente de los ingleses'. (AGS, Estado, 434, fol. 68); cited by Michael E. Williams, 'Alarms and Excursions in Lisbon under Castilian Domination: The Case of Captain Richard Butler', *Portuguese Studies*, 6 (1990), 100.

12 Schüller, 'Special Conditions of the Irish-Iberian Trade', 451, 456–57, 487–98.

13 O'Connor, *Irish Voices from the Spanish Inquisition*, 52–53, 58–62.

14 Edmund Hogan, cited by James B. Stephenson, 'Menology of the Irish Province of the Society of Jesus' (IJA, BKS/41).

in the college for six months. The Society of Jesus provided candidates for the priesthood with preparatory instruction. Records show that from its foundation to 1615, forty-eight students from the Irish College in Lisbon entered the secular priesthood, twenty-eight became Jesuits, twenty-one joined the Franciscans, sixteen the Dominicans, seven the Augustinians, seven the Discalced Carmelites, three the Cistercians and thirty-four died.[15] Wadding was among those who became a Franciscan.

Franciscan formation

Due to the popularity of their mission in Ireland and their continental colleges, the Society of Jesus in Lisbon may have been inundated with Irish hopefuls for the priesthood. Nevertheless, there were clear-cut reasons for Wadding's determination to join the Friars Minor. As the most pastorally active mendicants in Portugal, they concentrated on the towns and cities.[16] At that time, Franciscan texts on preaching were much sought after with multiple editions and translations on 'contempt for the world and the vanities thereof' finding a ready readership.[17] Francis Harold drew upon conversations with his uncle and, in his frequent references to the Franciscan order, stated that Luke's parents were 'singularly devoted' to the Waterford friary. This occurred despite – or perhaps because of – its suppression in April 1541.[18] Indeed, it was 'in his sixteenth year, when he was often reminded of the past suggestions of his parents about the Order of St

15 Thomas Morrissey, 'Review: *A New History of Ireland, Vol. III: Early Modern Ireland, 1534–1691*', edited by T. W. Moody, F. X. Martin, F. J. Byrne, *Studies*, 65 (1976), 349–54; see also Francis Finegan, 'Analysis of Documents relating to the Irish College in Lisbon' (IJA ICOL/LIS/4).

16 José Sebastião da Silva Dias, *Correntes de Sentimento Religioso em Portugal: Séculos XVI a XVIII*, 2 vols (Coimbra: Universidade de Coimbra, 1960), vol. 1, pt 1, 267.

17 Alexander Wilkinson, ed, *Iberian Books / Libros Ibéricos (IB): Books published in Spanish or Portuguese or on the Iberian Peninsula Before 1601 / Libros publicados en español o portugués o en la Península Ibérica antes de 1601* (Leiden: Brill, 2010), 177.

18 Harold, *Vita Fratris Lucae Waddingi*, 10: 'in coenobio Sancti Francisci, cui erant singulariter devoti'.

Francis' that Luke took the decision to become a friar.[19] Wadding recalled the deep impression that a remarkable event made on him in Waterford during his childhood. By chance, he attended the transfer of the remains of a local Franciscan friar, John Luker, who was 'buried in a hidden and sacred place in the same church, as he asked to be done before death'.[20] When the body was exhumed, Wadding heard that the corpse was found incorrupt, 'with his clothes and sandals undamaged'.[21] Younger sons often pursued a religious vocation. The changing circumstances for Wadding's family prepared him to abandon material considerations as they may not have had sufficient means to educate him abroad.

Francis Harold asserted that Wadding was inspired by God in his adolescence to assume the habit of St Francis of Assisi.[22] The Franciscan charism and spirituality appealed to Wadding, as shown by his regular descriptions of the natural world where the love of creation was love of the creator.[23] He chose St Francis as a role model and was an authentic devotee. Both were sons of a merchant father and, just as Pietro di Bernardone was firmly established in the *comune* of Assisi, so was Walter Wadding in Waterford. Moreover, both Francis and Luke shared adverse experiences of warfare early in life. Aware of the Franciscan reputation for scholarship, Wadding wished to pursue university studies and travelled to Portugal for the acquisition of knowledge. Friars enjoyed exemptions from university fees because the mendicant orders developed a system where each province supplied tuition and contributed to the maintenance of their own students.[24]

In later years, Wadding quoted from the second chapter of the Franciscan rule of 1223 to affirm that genuine candidates were motivated by divine inspiration to become friars.[25] The rule recommended that they should be received kindly and, once it was determined that they were constant in

19 Ibid, 11.

20 *Annales Minorum*, vol. 3 (1240), 52, n. 27; Canice Mooney, 'The Franciscans in Waterford', *Cork Hist. Soc. Jn.*, 69 (1964), 79.

21 *Annales Minorum*, vol. 3 (1240), 52, n. 27.

22 Harold, *Vita Fratris Lucae Waddingi*, 11.

23 Among many examples, see *Annales Minorum*, vol. 2 (1268), 322, n. 10; ibid, vol. 9 (1392), 137, n. 23; ibid, vol. 9 (1408), 403, n. 6; ibid, vol. 10 (1419), 32, n. 11.

24 Bert Roest, *A History of Franciscan Education, c.1210–1517* (Leiden: Brill, 2000), 64.

25 Wadding, *Opuscula*, 223.

this purpose, the minister provincial should be told as soon as possible.[26] On meeting together, the provincial should tell the candidate about the tenor of Franciscan life whereupon the spiritually able were expected to sell all their belongings and give everything to the poor. Meanwhile the friars and their ministers were careful not to take any money for themselves, nor through an intermediary.[27] Next, the minister provincial granted the aspirant the clothes for the probationary period, until one year elapsed, namely two tunics without hoods, cord and trousers, and a hood reaching to the cord. Both Franciscan friars and Poor Clare sisters abided by the rule not to appropriate anything for themselves.[28]

Wadding entered the Order of Friars Minor with Richard Synott of Wexford, a classmate from the Irish College in Lisbon.[29] They made the novitiate together a mile north of Porto at the Franciscan Recollect friary of the Immaculate Conception at Matosinhos on the coast, where they were initiated into 'religious apprenticeship' by the minister provincial of Portugal, Pedro da São Francisco, received the habit and made solemn profession in September 1605.[30] Wadding and Synott promised to observe the Gospel by living in obedience, without property and in chastity according to Rule of St Francis.[31] As a reformed branch of the Observant Franciscans, the Recollects at Matosinhos consecrated their lives to prayer and penance in spiritual recollection. Due to their zeal and their reputation for honesty, the Recollects had no need to quest for alms themselves because the people of Porto and the surrounding countryside provided them with the necessities. Harold noted that, in his old age, Wadding

26 Ibid, 223–24.

27 Ibid, 133–34.

28 Ibid, 173, 197.

29 Harold, *Vita Fratris Lucae Waddingi*, 11.

30 *Annales Minorum*, vol. 9 (1392), 137, n. 23.

31 Wadding, *Opuscula*, 133: 'Quod fratres debent vivere in obedientia, sine proprio, et in castitate'. Maintaining chastity was greatly respected during the Counter Reformation. See Isabel Mendes Drummond Braga, 'Poor Relief in Counter Reformation Portugal: The Case of the *Misericórdias*', in Andrew Cunningham, Jon Arrizabalaga and Ole Peter Grell, eds, *Health Care and Poor Relief in Counter-Reformation Europe* (London: Taylor & Francis, 2005), 210.

continued to recall the memory of the Recollects with affection. He took the name Luke of St Francis in religion.[32]

Wadding wrote that he stayed for one and half years. He progressed in virtue and his vocation took deeper root, 'both by instruction through the teaching he received and by example'.[33] The *Vita* by Francis Harold echoes this sentiment.[34] The way of life was strict with fasting, prayer vigils and silence. Nevertheless, according to Wadding, there were compensations. Within the grounds of the friary there were 'very large gardens, well-tended orchards, pleasant greens, green meadows, dark oaks, tall pines, a placid river, and among these are retreats for the devout, and pious oratories, suitable for prayer and meditation'.[35]

Mendicant life

After the novitiate, all Franciscan friars wore poor garments mended from sackcloth and other patches, 'with the blessing of God'.[36] To live the Franciscan rule was to live 'according to the example of Christ Jesus' poverty and cross'.[37] Pedro da São Francisco judged that Wadding and Synott did not require further preparations and had already advanced enough.[38] Therefore, twelve days before Christmas, he took them to Porto

32 Harold, *Vita Fratris Lucae Waddingi*, 12.

33 *Annales Minorum*, vol. 9 (1392), 137, n. 23: 'utinam majori virtutis profectu, altioresque egisset radices, quae illic per sesquianum tum praeceptoris institutione, tum patrum exemplo proposita est disciplina'.

34 Harold, *Vita Fratris Lucae Waddingi*, 12.

35 *Annales Minorum*, vol. 9 (1392), 137, n. 23: 'Intra monasterii ambitum amplissimi habentur horti, refecta pomaria, amoena viridaria, virentia prata, opacae quercus, altissimae pinus, placidum flumen, atque inter haec devoti recessus, et pia oratoria, orationi et meditationi satis opportuna'.

36 Wadding, *Opuscula*, 133–34.

37 Angelo Clareno, *Expositio Regulae Fratrum Minorum* (Ad Claras Aquas, Quaracchi: Typis Collegii S. Bonaventurae, 1912), 15; cited by Giorgio Agamben, *The Highest Poverty: Monastic Rules and Form-of-Life*, translated by Adam Kotsko (Stanford, California: Stanford University Press, 2013), 106.

38 De Castro, 'Wadding and the Iberian Peninsula', 124.

where they received minor orders to progress to the priesthood. While there, Wadding made a presentation on the birth of Jesus in poetry and in prose, and Synott defended a number of conclusions reached by John Duns Scotus, which they had learnt in studying philosophy. Scotus was the foremost Franciscan philosopher and a most noteworthy thinker of the thirteenth century. His teaching ensured him many followers in the late Middle Ages in several religious orders. There was even more enthusiasm for his works in the seventeenth century when theologians such as Wadding organised his arguments into a system known as Scotism.[39] This philosophical school was especially popular among Irish scholars who held that Scotus was an Irishman.

Wadding often returned to visit Porto. Founded by Zacarias and Gualter, two friars sent by St Francis himself, the city's friary was one of the first Franciscan houses in Portugal.[40] This was among the oldest of Portugal's early Gothic buildings.[41] Wadding described the adjoining church of St Francis as very large and, with the observance of the friars, a place of great worship, well located in the busiest part of the city. Within its walls, the chapel of St John the Baptist was built in the Manueline style of Portuguese architecture from the early sixteenth century.[42] In Wadding's view, the whole friary wielded authority and was imposing on all sides.[43] This marked the origins of his religious order in Portugal. His time there reflected the mendicant life of a Franciscan friar. A few months after profession, their spiritual directors sent Wadding with Synott to the friary of St Francis at

39 Alasdair Macintyre, *God, Philosophy, Universities: A Selective History of Catholic Philosophical Tradition* (Lanham MD: Rowman and Littlefield, 2009), 98, 100.

40 António Montes Moreira, 'Implantação e Desenvolvimento da Ordem Franciscana em Portugal – Séculos XIII-XVI', in *I-II Seminário: O Franciscanismo em Portugal* (Lisbon: Fundação Oriente, 1996), 13–27.

41 Pedro Dias, Dalila Rodrigues, Fernando Grilo and Nuno Vassallo e Silva, *The Manueline. Portuguese Art during the Great Discoveries* (Vienna: Museum Ohne Grenzen, 2017), 140.

42 Ibid.

43 *Annales Minorum*, vol. 4 (1268), 322, n. 13: 'Ecclesia amplissima, et promptis fratrum obsequiis, est gravi cultu, et commodissimo situ, ultra omnes totius urbis a creberrimo populi concursu commendata. Magnam universa domus praesefert auctoritatem, undique augusta'.

Leiria in central Portugal, founded in 1232, where they completed a course of philosophy in two years.[44]

The Seraphic Seminary

Wadding and Synott then read theology further south at Lisbon before Wadding continued his studies at Coimbra, the Franciscan seminary in Portugal, from early 1609 until 1613. He remained lifelong friends with Synott who acquitted himself very well in the Franciscan province of Portugal.[45] For the next four years, 'the Coimbra academy of theology' was the fulcrum of Wadding's studies.[46] Between Lisbon and Porto, the memory of Anthony of Padua was still fresh at the Friary of Santo António dos Olivais near Coimbra, where the saint received the Franciscan habit in 1220.[47] On several occasions, Wadding visited the place of initiation and wrote of the church, 'Before entering it, I, as a passer-by, was still permitted to see the inscription partially repaired'.[48] The first Franciscan martyrs, five friars, were beheaded in the lifetime of St Francis of Assisi. Every year, the people of Coimbra made a pilgrimage to the relics, as recorded by Wadding in 1610.[49]

That year, at twenty-two years of age, Luke Wadding nearly died.[50] In addition to other responsibilities, his superiors chose him to defend a

44 *Annales Minorum*, vol. 4 (1268), 321, n. 10.

45 Harold, *Vita Fratris Lucae Waddingi*, 13.

46 *Annales Minorum*, vol. 1 (1217), 304, n. 22: 'adhuc ibi recens memoria, et initiationes locus ostenditur, quem ego saepius invisi, dum per quadriennium ferme in academia Conimbricensi Theologiae operam dedi'.

47 José García Oro, 'Cuándo San Antonio llega a España', *Verdad y vida*, 53 (1995), 425–443.

48 *Annales Minorum*, vol. 1 (1220), 409, n. 73: 'Mihi illac, antequam initiarer, transeunti, adhuc licuit inscriptionem videre ex parte refectam'.

49 De Castro, 'Wadding and the Iberian Peninsula', 126. See also Christopher MacEvitt, *The Martyrdom of the Franciscans: Islam, the Papacy, and an Order in Conflict* (Philadelphia, University of Pennsylvania Press, 2020), 1–14, 73–78.

50 Mooney, 'Father Luke Wadding – the Last Years', 89.

number of theological disputations in a public debate. The night beforehand, finding himself unprepared, Wadding studied in his room with a brazier and some live coals, but fell asleep exhausted. Waking up later, he was choking and nearly overcome by the smoke from the coals. Fortunately, the friar in the next cubicle heard the commotion, raised the alarm and Wadding was dragged into the corridor. The accident caused him chronic asthmatic and bronchial problems that worsened as he grew older.[51]

During his stay in Coimbra, Wadding recounted the professors that he met. At the College of Saint Bonaventure, he was taught by the 'learned and honest' Franciscan, Diogo Limadensis.[52] The University of Coimbra, the oldest in Portugal, was founded in 1290 by Dinis, king of Portugal. As a student, Wadding attended lectures by the Jesuit theologian, philosopher and jurist, Francisco Suárez, whom Philip II sent to Coimbra, and Egidio da Fonseca, an Augustinian professor who succeeded Suárez to the principal chair of theology.[53] Fonseca shared Wadding's scholarly interests in books and Mariology, that is, theological studies relating to the Virgin Mary. Fonseca was a bibliophile who renovated his order's library in Coimbra, which was among the best in the Iberian Peninsula.[54] Moreover, his writings included an extensive theological study of Mary drawn from the teachings of St Augustine.[55] In turn, Suárez was known as 'the Father of modern systematic Mariology', contributing works on Mary's miraculous

51 Ibid.

52 Harold, *Vita Fratris Lucae Waddingi*, 13.

53 *Annales Minorum*, vol. 16 (1530), 341, n. 27.

54 Gian Pietro Soliani, 'Antonio Pérez (1599–1649) on Intentional Identity: A Revisionism of Peter Auriol's Thought', *Patristica et Mediævalia*, 44 (2023), 51. Taddeo Guidelli, *Thaddaei Perusini OSA Registrum viatorium, 1577–81* (Rome: Institutum historicum Augustinianum, 2007), 114.

55 Aegidio a Praesentatione, *De immaculata beatae virginis conceptione ab omni originali peccato immuni libri quatuor, dicati sacrae maiestati Philippi III Hispaniarum regis* (Conimbricae: apud Didacum Gómez de Loureyro, 1617). David Gutiérrez, *Storia dell'ordine di Sant'Agostino: Gli Agostiniani dal protestantesimo alla riforma cattolica* (Rome: Institutum Historicum Ordinis Fratrum S. Augustini, 1972), 187. See also Adolar Zumkeller, 'Aegidius (Fonseca) a Praesentatione, O.E.S.A'. *Lexikon für Marienkunde*, 1 (1957), 45.

virginity and her role in redemption.[56] As such, both can be seen to have influenced Wadding's own writings on the subject of Mary. Although he reckoned Suárez and Fonseca 'among the first Doctors of Europe', he regarded his own conversation as juvenile at that time.[57]

Even so, León de Sancto Thoma, a Benedictine, remembered that Wadding was placed in charge of his fellow students in the Coimbra friary and led by example. The faith and modesty that Wadding showed, his keen wit and the subtlety of his Scotist reasoning surpassed the quickest by a long distance.[58] A chair of Scotism, founded at Coimbra in 1562, countered the primacy of Thomism at the university.[59] The Scotus chair at Coimbra was also held by scholars from the Augustinians, Cistercians and Carmelites.[60] Wadding's cousin, the Augustinian friar Richard Wadding, was a professor of theology at Coimbra where he flourished in the early 1630s. Thus, in comparison with Salamanca, the influence of the Dominicans at Coimbra was counterbalanced with other religious orders.[61]

56 Mark Miravalle, 'Marian Coredemption at the Heart of the Christian Mystery', in Judith Gentle and Robert Fastiggi, eds, *De Maria Numquam Satis. The Significance of the Catholic Doctrines on the Blessed Virgin Mary for All People* (Washington DC: Catholic University of America Press, 2009), 154; Robert Fastiggi, 'Francisco Suárez SJ (1548–1617) on Mary's *Virginitas in Partu* and Subsequent Doctrinal Development', *Marian Studies*, 58 (2007), 26–45.

57 Harold, *Vita Fratris Lucae Waddingi*, 13.

58 Ibid, 173. Leo a Sancto Thoma was historian at the monastery of St Martin of Tibães, the Benedictine mother house in Portugal and Brazil. He published a history of the order in Portugal. Francis Harold mistook him for a Cistercian.

59 Lidia Lanza and Marco Toste, 'The Influence of Salamanca in the Iberian Peninsula: The Case of the Faculties of Theology of Coimbra and Évora', in Thomas Duve, José Luis Egío and Christiane Birr, eds, *The School of Salamanca: A Case of Global Knowledge Production* (Leiden: Brill, 2021), 140.

60 Félix Fernando Lopes, 'O ensino das doutrinas de Escoto na Universidade de Coimbra', in *Itinerarium*, 12 (1966), 193–264; idem, 'As doutrinas escostitas na cultura e escolas de Portugal', in *Revista Portuguese de Filosofia*, 23 (1967), 17–45; Lanza and Toste, 'The Influence of Salamanca in the Iberian Peninsula', 136, 142.

61 Lidia Lanza and Marco Toste, 'The Sentences in sixteenth-century Iberian scholasticism', in Philipp Rosemann, ed, *Mediaeval commentaries on the Sentences of Peter Lombard*, 3 vols (Leiden: Brill, 2002–15), vol. 3, 427.

Suárez took Scotism into account with other major schools of thought and agreed with certain conclusions reached by Scotus. For example, Suárez followed the Scotist view that metaphysical arguments have the demonstrative force to prove God's existence. Suárez also concurred with the Scotist view that the intellect possessed 'the power of forming a direct concept of the individual'.[62] Nonetheless, Coimbra's university had a regional character whereas the influence exerted by the University of Salamanca was exceptional. Although apparent in the philosophy course given by the Society of Jesus from 1592 to 1606,[63] this was most evident in scholastic theology with the introduction of ideas and teaching materials by professors from Spain.[64]

In defence of St Francis

Since the previous century, the secular clergy and prominent Protestant writers such as Luther condemned the elaborate Franciscan memory of St Francis.[65] From the Conventual friar Pietro Ridolfi to the Observant friars Francesco Gonzaga and Luke Wadding, the Franciscans responded to these denouncements with increased scholarship to make a strong defence of their founder. These friars saw themselves as rebuilding Franciscan

62 Maurice De Wulf, *History of Medieval Philosophy*, translated by Peter Coffey, 2 vols (London: Longmans, Green and Company, 1909–26), vol. 1, 495. On the shared views of Suárez and Scotus on grace, will and nature, see Simone Guidi, 'Separated Soul and its Nature: Francisco Suárez in the Scholastic Debate', in Juan Antonio Senent de Frutos and Robert Maryks, eds, *Francisco Suárez (1548–1617): Jesuits and the Complexities of Modernity* (Leiden: Brill, 2019), 365.

63 Mário Santiago de Carvalho, 'Uma "Escola Filosófica de Coimbra"? História, tendências e problemas', *Revista Filosófica de Coimbra*, 32 (2023), 255–78.

64 Lanza and Toste, 'The Influence of Salamanca in the Iberian Peninsula', 126–27, 133–34, 137–8.

65 Giacomo Mariani, *Roberto Caracciolo Da Lecce (1425–1495). Life, Works, and Fame of a Renaissance Preacher* (Leiden: Brill, 2022), 19; Geoffrey Dipple, 'Anti-Franciscanism in the Early Reformation: The Nature and Sources of Criticism', *Franciscan Studies*, 55 (1998), 53–81.

beliefs and practices while upholding a pure and simple observance of the rule.[66] Wadding's first opportunity to write for the press happened during his Coimbra studies when 'the thought of illuminating the universal Franciscan order' occurred to him.[67] Wadding received several discouraging letters from friends 'in the last months of his apprenticeship'.[68] These letters disparaged the character of the Franciscan order, 'in which, as it were, there was neither the adornment of letters, nor any worship of genius'.[69] Therefore, 'immediately after his profession he drew up his pen' to point out 'both that the superfluous ornament of letters was nothing but mere vanity, and that their true use always showed reverence and respect in the Order of St Francis'.[70] Wadding was also motivated by a preacher who cast aspersions on the attitude of St Francis towards learning and literature.[71] In defence of *il Poverello*, Wadding quoted Bonaventure who maintained that Francis was conversant with literary matters. The Waterford friar also asserted that it was clear from the rule that it was incumbent on friars to study.[72]

Holidays

In the summertime, Wadding retreated from his academic work to the neighbouring friary of St Anthony at Figueira da Foz, a Recollect house on the Atlantic coast.[73] He spent several holidays there, consulted the library and began his *Opuscula* on the writings of St Francis.[74]

66 André Vauchez, *Francis of Assisi: The Life and Afterlife of a Medieval Saint*, translated by Michael F. Cusato, (New Haven CT: Yale University Press), 230.

67 Harold, *Vita Fratris Lucae Waddingi*, 14–15. 'Hinc ergo primum suscepit cogitatum Ordinem universum suis lucubrationibus illustrandi'.

68 Ibid, 14.

69 Ibid.

70 Ibid.

71 Mooney, 'The Writings of Father Luke Wadding OFM', 225–39.

72 Harold, *Vita Fratris Lucae Waddingi*, 14.

73 *Annales Minorum*, 16 (1527), 288, n. 20.

74 Harold, *Vita Fratris Lucae Waddingi*, 15; Mooney, 'The Writings of Father Luke Wadding OFM', 225.

For several months, Wadding undertook further studies at Alenquer, regarded in local tradition as the cradle of Franciscan devotion in Portugal.[75] Wadding wrote that the structure of the first Franciscan house there was still intact, supporting his statement by citing Francesco Gonzaga and a genealogy of Sancho I.[76] On their mission to Morocco, the five Franciscan martyrs stopped off at Alenquer where their memory continued to be venerated.[77] Sancha, daughter of Sancho I of Portugal and sister of Afonso II, founded a Franciscan house on a high slope in the village in 1222. Sent by St Francis, Zacarias was the first guardian. The friary was extended from 1280 to 1355 under the patronage of Beatriz, queen of Portugal, and her son Dinis, king of Portugal, who completed the work.[78] The main church has a Gothic portal, a single nave, a broad choir-loft and a Manueline baptismal font on the Gospel side of the altar. Two floors of cloisters were richly decorated with polychrome paintings, Gothic double columns, phytomorphic capitals on double columns and a Manueline portal with zoomorphic and anthromorphic motifs. A Renaissance chapel was built in the midst of the cloisters.[79] While studying at Alenquer, Wadding took time off nearby at Santa Catalina where the many trees, well-kept gardens and statues of saints inspired piety in him.[80]

In his writings, Wadding stated that he could have spent more time on the Franciscan monuments of Portugal but could only present them in a small way. Adjacent to the region of Coimbra, in the diocese of Guarda,

75 De Castro, 'Wadding and the Iberian Peninsula', 131.

76 *Annales Minorum*, I (1217), 305, n. 23; ibid, (1219), 354, n. 52; ibid, II (1222), 60–61, n. 41.

77 John R. H. Moorman, *A History of the Franciscan Order from its Origins to the Year 1517* (Oxford: Clarendon Press, 1968), 71.

78 Inês Olaia, 'Two Sisters, Two Towns, Two Kings', in Munro Price, Fabian Persson and Cinzia Recca, eds, *Resilience and Recovery at Royal Courts, 1200–1840* (Basingstoke: Palgrave Macmillan, 2023), 13; Paula Pinto Costa and Renata Cristina de Sousa Nascimento, *A visibilidade do sagrado: relíquias cristãs na Idade Média* (2nd edn, Curitiba: Editora Appris, 2022), 37–40.

79 Catarina Almeida Marado, *Arquitetura conventual e cidade medieval: a formação e os impactos dos sistemas urbanísticos mendicantes em Portugal: séc. XIII–XV* (Coimbra: Imprensa da Universidade de Coimbra, 2018), 109–112, 117, 135, 165, 167.

80 De Castro, 'Wadding and the Iberian Peninsula', 131–32.

Rodrigo de Castro built a chapel near Valhelhas on land that belonged to him, where he placed a devout image representing Christ. In 1548, his son-in-law, Diogo Lobo, gave the chapel to the Franciscans to establish a friary and the donation was confirmed by Pope Julius III four years later.[81] During his studies in Portugal, Wadding saw for himself this 'devoted and solitary place' where crowds of local people came together to venerate 'a most sacred image'.[82]

Portuguese friaries were usually much larger than their monastic counterparts with up to fifty friars housed in each establishment.[83] Even in his leisure time, Wadding showed unquenchable interest in the Franciscan historical landscape.[84] A clear pattern emerged for him in the north of Portugal, which enjoyed more temperate summers than the south. In 1611, Wadding travelled from Coimbra to visit the friary of St Francis at Guimarães, which was founded in 1217 – one of the earliest in Portugal – where tradition held that St Francis went during his pilgrimage to Santiago.[85] In large part, the growth of Guimarães was connected with the ongoing presence of the Franciscans and Dominicans.[86] A day's journey further east, on a mountain slope near Barcelos, Jaime of Bragança took care to establish a friary named Bom Jesu. Although Wadding's description suggests he was unable to stop there, he considered it 'capable of accommodating twelve friars comfortably'.[87] He found the place quite pleasant, and it made him smile as he passed by. Elsewhere in northern Portugal, two

81 José Osório da Gama e Castro, *Diocese e districto da Guarda: serie de apontamentos históricos e tradicionaes sobre as suas antiguidades, algumas observações respeitantes à actualidade e notas referentes à cathedral egitaniense e respectivos prelados* (Porto: Typographia Universal, 1902), 100.

82 *Annales Minorum*, vol. 15 (1505), 355, n. 40: 'Vidi ipse devotum et solitarium locum, devotissimam imaginem et frequentiam vicinorum populorum eo confluentium'.

83 Anthony Disney, *A History of Portugal and the Portuguese Empire*, 2 vols (Cambridge: Cambridge University Press, 2009), vol. 1, 103.

84 De Castro, 'Wadding and the Iberian Peninsula', 128.

85 *Annales Minorum*, vol. 1 (1217), 305, n. 25, where the placename is given as *Vimaranensium*.

86 Dias, Rodrigues, Grilo and Vassallo e Silva, *The Manueline*, 148.

87 *Annales Minorum*, vol. 15 (1505), 356, n. 41: 'satis amoeno, et quae mihi illac transeunti vehementer arrisit. Capax est et commodum duodecim religiosorum habitaculum'.

houses were founded in the port town of Vila do Conde, dedicated to St Francis and St Clare respectively.[88] After his visit there, Wadding declared: 'I have seen both and they are complete from every side'.[89] The Convent of St Clare was an imposing Gothic structure overlooking the river Ave.[90]

Priesthood

In 1613, the final year of his Coimbra studies, Wadding was ordained to the priesthood in the Cathedral of Viseu by Dom João Manuel, the bishop of that city. Wadding aspired to the highest standards as a clergyman and a scholar worthy of his calling. He gave his first sermon to the people of Viseu there in the local friary church.[91] Located north of Coimbra, Viseu was a prosperous settlement, and the surrounding diocese was among the oldest and most important in Portugal.[92] On completing his studies, Wadding was transferred back to Leiria in order to instruct the people. Commissioned to preach in both Portuguese and Castilian, he read the Church Fathers and methodically compiled two large volumes of material on the finest of paper. The entries are cross-referenced and indexed with alphabetical headings and marginalia, supplemented with selections from both the Old and New Testament.[93] Wadding wrote the entries in a smaller hand than his letters to make space and left some entries blank.

88 *Annales Minorum*, vol. 16 (1526), 275, n. 36. On the Rule of St Clare at Vila do Conde, see *Annales Minorum*, vol. 6 (1318), 373, n. 44: 'Alphonsus Sanctus, Dionysii Portugalliae Regis nothus, et coniux eius Tarrasia, Sancii Castellae Regis ex filio neptis supplices miserunt hoc anno Pontifici litteras vt concederé dignaretur sororibus monasterii Villaecomitis (oppidi haud ignobilis dioecesis Braccaren) ab ipsis constructi, regula Clarisarum per Alexandrum quartum Damianitis praescriptam quorum pecitioni benigne pontifex subscripit'.

89 *Annales Minorum*, vol. 16 (1526), 275, n. 36: 'Utrumoque hoc coenebium ego ipse conspexi undequaque completum'.

90 Dias, Rodrigues, Grilo and Vassallo e Silva, *The Manueline*, 143–46.

91 Harold, *Vita Fratris Lucae Waddingi*, 15.

92 Dias, Rodrigues, Grilo and Vassallo e Silva, *The Manueline*, 124.

93 Luke Wadding 'Ms. Locurum communium collectorum F. Luca Waddingo' (UCD-OFM, B.34 & B.35, volume 3 is bound in with volume 2); Fennessy, 'The B Manuscripts in the Franciscan Library, Killiney', in Millett and Lynch, eds, *Dun*

His devotion to the Blessed Virgin Mary was already noticeable and a significant part of his commonplace book consists of a tribute to her. Wadding detailed Mary's conception in sixteen points relating to her piety and her joy, as well as referring to her birth and presentation, her dedication, the Annunciation, Visitation and Purification.[94] In Leiria on 7 April 1613, he began the third volume, the contents of which relate to the relevance of liturgical feasts to a preacher and writer.[95]

According to Francis Harold, Wadding had 'a sweet love' of Ireland, not merely from natural instinct but, one that 'moved from his heart and from judgment, deliberately cultivated as a Christian virtue'.[96] Writing on the subject in 1613, Wadding stated that it was essential to seek spiritual perfection far from his homeland because 'a prophet is not accepted in his own country'.[97] Perhaps Wadding identified with his source, St Jerome,

---

Mhuire Killiney, 1945–95, 163–64; Cleary, *Father Luke Wadding*, 9–10. Among many other matters, the entries relate to twenty-four points on the order, state and rule of the Friars Minor, events from the life of Jesus until the Ascension; on the glorious name of Jesus; the Passion of the Christ; the Blessed Virgin Mary; the love of God; the Eternal Father; on obedience; on man; fatherhood; the papacy; the priesthood; martyrs and martyrdom; on doctors and doctrine; on the role of the pastor, preachers and preaching; kings and kingdoms; nobility; princes and principalities; on occasions of sin; concupiscence; penance; on the world and idolatry; on temptations; on friendliness; on hospitality; on angels; on peace; modesty and humility; on patience and perseverance; on marriage; on eyesight; impurity and worldliness; the renunciation of these times; on the end of our lives; on science; on sobriety; on the carnal and the spiritual; on luxury; on poverty; and on redemption. Among the saints referred to in the manuscript are Paul of Tarsus and his conversion; John the Baptist and his birth; James the Apostle; Matthew the Apostle; Mary Magdalene; John the Evangelist; Ambrose of Milan; Augustine of Hippo; and Anthony of Padua.

94 Wadding, 'Ms. Locurum communium collectorum F. Luca Waddingo' (UCD-OFM, B.35/281–346).

95 Ibid, 'Quae colligere incaepit author in convent Lyrinensi anno humanae salutis 1613, 7 Idus Aprilis dominica in eo incidente in Albis'.

96 Harold, *Vita Fratris Lucae Waddingi*, 111.

97 Wadding, 'Ms. Locurum communium collectorum F. Luca Waddingo', 96. 'Nemo in patria sua perfectus [...] Nemo Propheta in patria sua honorem habet'. (Luke 4:24).

the ascetic priest, theologian and historian. Quoting from Jerome's letters, Wadding continued:[98]

> Nor did the Lord seek, since he fled away lest he should be appointed king by the multitudes. But where there is no honour, there is contempt. Where there is contempt, there is frequent injury: but where there is injury, there is also indignation: where there is indignation, there is no rest: where there is no rest, there the mind is often diverted from purpose. But when, through restlessness, something is taken away from the study, less is made of that which is taken away: and where there is less, it cannot be said to be perfect.

Jerome withdrew from urban life in Antioch for a life of monastic contemplation.[99] On this understanding, Wadding echoed the words of Jerome in saying that 'it follows that a monk cannot be perfect in his own country [and] not to aim at perfection is itself a sin'.[100]

Francis Harold related that these manuscripts helped Wadding in 'every opportunity of preaching' and 'brought him not a little help in other studies as well'.[101] That year, Wadding's superiors called him to Lisbon. At the provincial chapter, he produced a first-rate intellectual performance that showed an ability to investigate and discuss theological principles 'aptly and acutely'.[102] As a direct consequence, Antonio de Trejo, vicar general of

98 Ibid: 'Neque dominus quaerebat, quippe qui ne a turbis rex constitueretur, aufugit. Sed ubi honor non est, ibi contemptus est. Ubi contemptus, ibi frequens iniuria: ubi autem iniuria, ibi et indignatio: ubi indignatio, ibi quies nulla: ubi quies non est, ibi mens a proposito saepe deducitur. Ubi autem per inquietudinem aliquid aufertur ex studio, minus fit ab eo, quod tollitur: et ubi minus est, perfectum non potest dici. Ex hac supputatione summa illa nascitur'. See *Correspondance de Saint Jérôme: Lettres 1–22*, ed Jérôme Labourt (Paris: Les Belles Lettres, 2003), 40.

99 Stefan Rebenich, *Jerome* (Abingdon: Routledge, 2002), 17.

100 'Ms. Locurum communium collectorum F. Luca Waddingo', 96 (UCD-OFM, B.35/281–346): 'Monachum in patria sua perfectum esse non posse, perfectum autem esse nolle, delinquere est'.

101 Harold, *Vita Fratris Lucae Waddingi*, 16.

102 Ibid. Francis Harold stated that Wadding excelled in 'seven sciences'. This appears to be a reference to the *trivium* and the *quadrivium*, namely grammar, rhetoric, logic, astronomy, music, arithmetic and geometry.

the order and president of the chapter, brought Wadding to the *studium* in Salamanca to continue his studies.

Wadding's tribute to Portugal

Wadding expressed his gratitude to Portugal for introducing him to Franciscan life and for 'the disciplines of sacred theology'.[103] In the *Annales Minorum*, he recognised the country first as the kingdom of Lusitania from the Christian reconquest of the early thirteenth century. He went on to define its territory as Portugal and the Algarve in the same century.[104] In this context, Wadding commented upon 'the surrender and acquisition of the kingdom' in 1581, acknowledging that Castile and Portugal remained 'separated from each other' in his lifetime.[105] Philip II of Spain succeeded to the Aviz inheritance following the death of Sebastian I of Portugal in 1578.[106] Three years later, Portuguese nobles benefitted from a status that made Habsburg rule desirable for the next six decades. In turn, financiers from Portugal supported the Spanish monarchy. Therefore, when Wadding arrived in Lisbon, the crown of Portugal was incorporated into the Spanish Habsburg dominions. In Wadding's times, rulers exercised the princely and royal function, not only in Portugal but throughout Europe, as an earthly representative of Christ in a compact with the Church as guarantor.

103 *Annales Minorum*, 4 vols (1232), 320, n. 9: 'sacrae Theologiae disciplinis'.

104 For instance, Wadding refers to the Algarve (*Algarbiorum*) in the reign of Dinis, see *Annales Minorum*, 3 vols (1228), 239, n. 2.

105 *Annales Minorum*, 1 vol (1214), 227, n. 14: 'quam non uniendum cum Hispanico, seu Castellano Regnum Lusitanieum? Idipsum jam falsum apparuisse dices statim ac Philippus II rerum potitus est in Lusitania. At si ad conditiones, & pacta deditionis & acquisitionis Regni te vertas diligenterque examinanda proponas, etiam sub uno Domino regnum utrumque Castellanum et Lusitanum, utrinque divisum, & ab invicem separatum invenies'.

106 Jean Frédéric Schaub, *Portugal na Monarquia Hispânica, 1560–1640* (Lisbon: Livraria Horizonte, 2001), 9–12, 15–16, 18, 46; Fernando Jesús Bouza Álvarez, *Felipe II y el Portugal dos povos: imágenes de esperanza y de revuelta* (Valladolid: Ediciones Universidad de Valladolid, 2010), 49.

The friars who inhabited Franciscan foundations and the patronage provided to them by illustrious families gave form and spirit to Wadding's chronicles of the religious order's first four centuries. These were key elements in his Franciscan world as shown in the *Annales*. As a matter of course, the sixteenth-century Portuguese Franciscan, Mark of Lisbon, and his *Chronicle of the Friars Minor* was a major source for Wadding.[107] In Portugal, Franciscan influence extended to the upper echelons of society. Whereas political crises affected Portugal in the fourteenth and fifteenth centuries, Wadding emphasised the growth and subsequent stability of Franciscan reform and observance. This arrived in northern Portugal in the early 1390s.[108] Wadding wrote of the support of the nobility who, by establishing strong links with the mendicants, validated their claims to power. For Wadding, union between the crowns of Castile and Portugal was embodied by the Franciscan holiness and generosity of St Elizabeth, a Spanish princess who married King Dinis of Portugal.[109] Dinis reigned from 1279 to 1325 in which time, according to Wadding, he strengthened the kingdom.[110] Emphasising the sacrament of confession, the Irish friar absolved Dinis of indiscretions and chose, instead, to accentuate the positive links to the king's Franciscan confessor, Friar Stephen, who was raised to 'the most noble and wealthiest bishopric of Lisbon' before his promotion to Cuenca in Castile.[111] St Elizabeth belonged to the Franciscan Third Order. Wadding repeatedly referred to her canonisation by Urban VIII and how

107 See, for instance, *Annales Minorum*, vol. 4 (1268), 321, n. 9.

108 Vítor Gomes Teixeira, *O Movimento da Observância Franciscana em Portugal (1392–1517). História, Património e Cultura de Uma Experiência de Reforma Religiosa* (Porto: Centro de Estudos Franciscanos – Editorial Franciscana, 2010).

109 *Annales Minorum*, vol. 6 (1317), 343, n. 66; Bert Roest, *Order and Disorder: The Poor Clares Between Foundation and Reform* (Brill: Leiden, 2013), 103.

110 *Annales Minorum*, vol. 7 (1325), 49, n. 12.

111 *Annales Minorum*, vol. 6 (1310), 197, n. 11: 'Alium etiam Minoritam Fr. Stephanum confessarium Dionysii Regis Lusitaniae non mediocri affecit honore praeficiens eum Ecclesia'; *Annales Minorum*, vol. 6 (1313), 245, n. 17: 'Frater Stephanus Episcopus Portugallensis, de superius praefati sumus, translatus est ad nobilissimum & pinguissimum Episcopatum Vlyssiponensem'. *Annales Minorum*, vol. 6 (1322), 460, n. 72: 'Stephanus Episcopus primo Portugallensis, deinde Vlyssiponensis in Lusitania, ad pinguem Ecclesiam Conchensem in Castella sub Archiepiscopo Toletano, per mortem Paschasii'.

'the most holy queen of Portugal' completed the Poor Clares monastery 'in the city of Coimbra on the left bank of the river Mondego at the foot of the mountain' indicating his familiarity with the actual site.[112] Elizabeth also founded a Cistercian monastery and, on the death of her husband, retired to live near the Poor Clares of Coimbra.[113] Wadding was present at the opening of her tomb in 1612 when, in the presence of 'the most skilled doctors and surgeons', the postulators for her canonisation found her body incorrupt.[114] An official for her cause subsequently gave Wadding several large volumes of the canonisation process to faithfully archive.[115] In the *Annales Minorum*, Wadding showed his appreciation for Elizabeth, queen of Portugal, with a lengthy tribute to her life.[116]

Conclusion

Walter and Anastasia Wadding made a conscious statement of faith by encouraging religious vocations in their sons. Aware that the life of a mendicant friar was more easily endured when borne from youth, Luke Wadding took the decision to join the Franciscans soon after his arrival in Portugal.[117] He was a diligent student who developed his abilities earlier than usually expected. Following the example of St Francis, Wadding cultivated friendships and spent time in nature where he contemplated the divine presence in creation. Wadding's eagerness to unearth the works of St Francis in the

112 *Annales Minorum*, vol. 6 (1317), 343, n. 66: 'Hoc etiam anno vel antecedenti sanctissima regina Portugalliae Elizabetha, de qua saepiùs egimus superiùs, quamque Vrbanus VIII quai hodie sedet, in Sanctorum numerum retulit, egregium extruere vel ab honesta quadam foemina inchoatum, vt quidam volunt, perficere coepit Clarissis coenobium, ad ciuitatem Conimbriae ex alia parte fluminis Mondi ad montis radices'. See also Roest, *Order and Disorder: The Poor Clares Between Foundation and Reform*, 102.

113 *Annales Minorum*, vol. 7 (1325), 50, n. 15.

114 Ibid (1336), 229, n. 26, 'peritissimus medicis, chirurgisque'.

115 De Castro, 'Wadding and the Iberian Peninsula', 126.

116 *Annales Minorum*, vol. 7 (1327), 85, n. 19.

117 Harold, *Vita Fratris Lucae Waddingi*, 11.

defence of his name was awakened in Portugal where discoveries motivated more research and, not to be diverted, Wadding's love of Franciscanism continued during his recreational activities. The oldest Franciscan foundations in Portugal owed their origins to Friars Zacarias and Gualter who Francis sent into the kingdom. Wadding's *Annales* illustrated that the provision of royal funds for the foundation of new mendicant houses and the extension of existing friaries depended upon the mutually conducive stability of interaction between the friars and their patrons. For almost a decade, Wadding earned respect among his superiors, professors and fellow scholars before making an excellent impression on Antonio de Trejo who advanced Wadding's prospects further. He flourished at Coimbra where he devoted himself to theology, not only at the Franciscan house of studies but also at the local university. Yet Wadding considered himself immature and saw this decade as a time of preparation. In the coming years, he became well known among contemporaries at Salamanca where the university's reputation was greater than that of Coimbra. I shall keep this in mind in the following chapter.

3 In the Kingdom of Castile

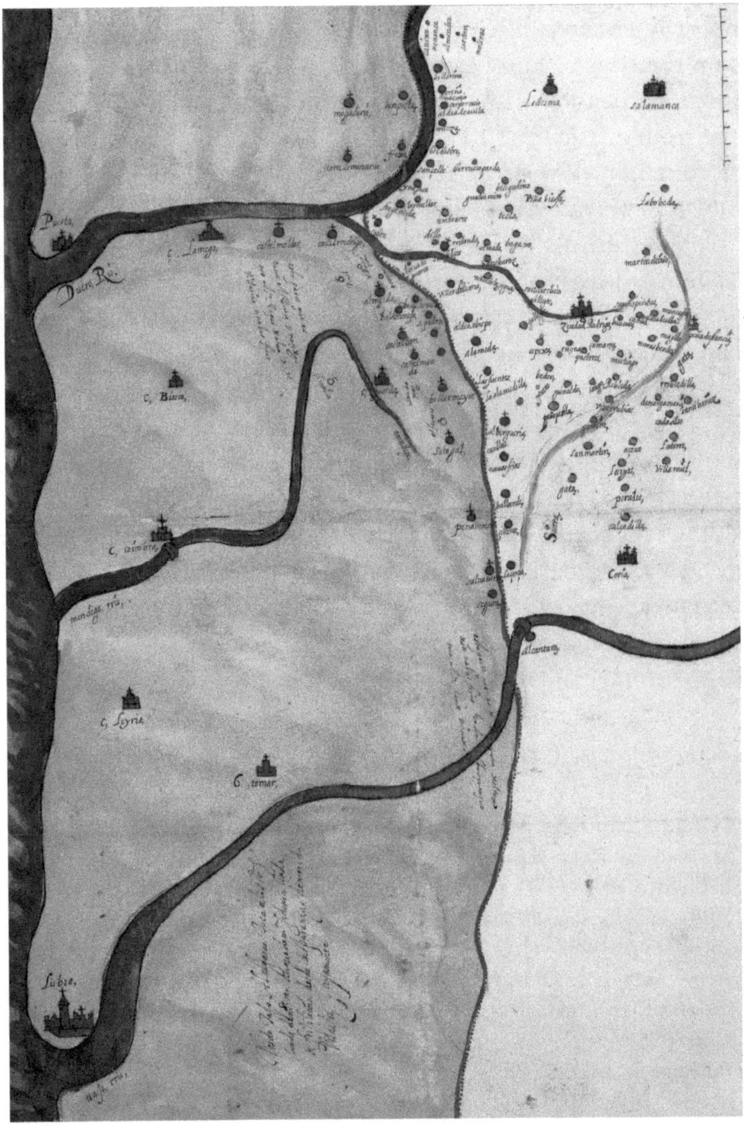

Map 2 The Spanish and Portuguese frontier, between the Duero and Tagus rivers (1641), (AGS, MPD,5,176). Courtesy of the Ministerio de Cultura, Madrid.

Introduction

When writing about his uncle, Francis Harold told the reader that Wadding travelled from Portugal to Castile and Italy.[1] From a geographical viewpoint, early seventeenth-century Portugal was essentially a seafaring nation on the edge of Europe, whereas Castile was landlocked and intent on further expansion.[2] This mirrors Wadding's life on the continent as he moved from one country to another. At twenty-five years of age, shortly after ordination, he went to Salamanca where he studied and taught sacred theology for several years.[3] The proximity of Portugal meant that many Portuguese students congregated in Salamanca, a small city of 20,000 inhabitants with a proportionally high ratio of clergy who lived alongside the laity.[4] As a first-rate centre of studies, almost all of the religious orders gathered there. Each had their own habit and lived an austere life centred upon the cloister and communal table. On arrival, Wadding stayed at the friary of San Francisco el Real where the guardian, Hernando del Campo, built new dormitories, restored the choir, renovated the screen of the main chapel, as well as repairing the friary's other chapels.[5] This chapter traces Wadding's footsteps from Salamanca to Madrid as a friar of the Santiago province and the path he took to a professorship, his friendships with the Cistercians and fellow Franciscans and his increased interest in the doctrine of the Immaculate Conception.

1 Harold, *Vita Fratris Lucae Waddingi*, 9. Part of this chapter is an updated and revised version of my paper, 'Irish Franciscans and the Santiago Province of Spain', in Binasco, ed, *Luke Wadding, the Irish Franciscans, and Global Catholicism*, 19–38.

2 William Atkinson, *A History of Spain and Portugal* (London: Pelican, 1967), 73.

3 *Annales Minorum*, vol. 3 (1238), 17, n. 19.

4 Ángel Marcos de Dios, *Portugueses en la Universidad de Salamanca de la Edad Moderna*, in Luis Enrique Rodríguez-San Pedro Bezares, ed, *Historia de la Universidad de Salamanca*, vol. 3, tome 2, *Saberes y Confluencias* (Salamanca: Ediciones Universidad de Salamanca, 2004), 1101–28.

5 Manuel de Castro, *San Francisco de Salamanca y su studium generale* (Santiago de Compostela: Aldecoa Ediciones, 1998), 112–113.

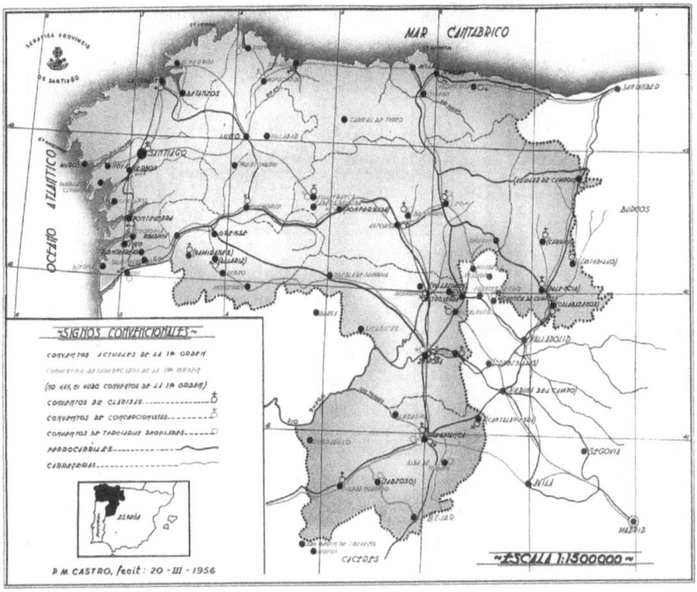

Map 3 Franciscan province of Santiago, Spain; Manuel de Castro, *La Provincia Franciscana de Santiago. Ocho Siglos de Historia* (Santiago de Compostela: Liceo Franciscano, 1984). Reproduced by kind permission of the friars of the Santiago province.

Son of Santiago

Wadding's *conventus nativus* was Matosinhos in Portugal but, once affiliated to the friary of St Francis in Salamanca, he was welcomed into the Franciscan province of Santiago in whose territory the house was situated.[6] Thereafter, Wadding considered himself 'a son of Santiago'.[7] St Francis was believed to have venerated the relics of Santiago and visited Salamanca in

6 On this process, see Lázaro de Aspurz, *Franciscan History: The Three Orders of St Francis of Assisi,* translated by Lawrence Landini (Chicago: Franciscan Herald Press, 1982), 10.

7 De Castro, 'Wadding and the Iberian Peninsula', 133–35.

the second decade of the thirteenth century.[8] The Franciscan province of St James, that is, Santiago de Compostela, was founded in 1232 and occupied the north-west of the Iberian Peninsula. This helps to explain the extent of the province from the north coast to Salamanca, thereby including Galicia, Asturias and León.[9] The province was organised into seven *custodiae* or regions. At one time, Portugal was within the geographical scope of the Santiago province.[10]

Admission to Spanish and Portuguese society required 'purity of blood' – *limpieza de sangre* – that is, freedom from Jewish or Moorish blood, the ancestry prosecuted by the Inquisition.[11] In its first thirty years, the Society of Jesus proved an exception among the religious orders in its refusal to discriminate against Christians of Jewish heritage.[12] The concern for *limpieza de sangre* led the Franciscan province of Santiago to recruit many friars from Ireland. Hugh Ward of Donegal, for example, studied at the Irish College in Salamanca before being admitted to the Santiago province in 1616 with help from Wadding who considered Ward 'very learned, with admirable facility and special skills in the Irish language'.[13] Aside from the contemporary taste for scholasticism, Irish friars regarded Duns Scotus as an Irishman. In 1593, the Franciscans named Scotus 'Doctor of the Order'. By the end of that century, there was a chair in Scotist theology at Salamanca, thereby placing the Order of Friars Minor and the Order of Preachers on a par at the university. This consolidated the authority of Franciscan theology. Nevertheless, while the friary of St Francis

8 See José García Oro, 'Francisco de Asís en la España Medieval', *Liceo franciscano*, 41, *Francisco de Asís en la España Medieval* (1988), 1–558.

9 See Map 3.

10 Hazard, 'Irish Franciscans and the Santiago Province of Spain', 20.

11 O'Connor, *Irish Voices from the Spanish Inquisition*, 76; Stafford Poole, 'The Politics of *Limpieza de Sangre:* Juan de Ovando and his Circle in the Reign of Philip II', *Americas*, 55 (1999), 359–89.

12 Robert Maryks, 'Jesuits of Jewish Ancestry under Francisco de Borja's Generalate', in Enrique García Hernán and María del Pilar Ryan, eds, *Francisco de Borja y su tiempo: Política, religion y cultura en la Edad Moderna* (Valencia: Albatros Ediciones; Rome: Institutum Historicum Societatis Iesu, 2011), 189–98.

13 Wadding, *Scriptores ordinis minorum,* 121: 'Cum admirabili facilitate, et singulari peritia in linguam Hibernicam'.

concentrated on the teaching of Scotism, their Dominican counterparts continued to focus on Thomism.[14]

Clothed in the habit, friars of the Santiago province maintained a visible presence in forty-three houses and three university towns, namely Salamanca, Santiago and Oviedo. Beyond its confines, the province occasionally sent friars to Alcalá de Henares, which was renowned for its theology curriculum and biblical studies, founded by the Observant Franciscan Cardinal Francisco Jiménez de Cisneros in 1509.[15] In later years, Wadding recounted that he attended 'all three of Spain's most noble universities at Coimbra, Salamanca and Alcalá', where he noted Scotist chairs were established with professors assigned to teach the doctrine of Scotus.[16] Indeed, at Alcalá, Scotism took first place among all the universities.[17]

Salamanca – 'most remarkable academy'[18]

Wadding regularly recorded his links with Salamanca on the title pages to his books. In later years, he wrote about the University of Salamanca as this 'most remarkable academy, famous throughout the world'.[19] Lope de Vega, Franciscan tertiary and great dramatist of the Spanish golden age, described the university town as 'the laurel of Spain', a symbol of eternal and triumphant peace.[20] The decision that Irish friars took to join the

14 De Castro, 'Wadding and the Iberian Peninsula', 119–70.

15 Erika Rummel, *Jiménez de Cisneros: On the Threshold of Spain's Golden Age* (Tempe AZ: Arizona Center for Medieval and Renaissance Studies, 1999), 38–40, 53–65.

16 *Authoris vita, a R. P. Fr. Luca Waddingo conscripta; R.P.F. Ioannis Duns Scoti, doctoris subtilis ordinis Minorum Opera omnia, quae hucusque reperiri potuerunt* (Lyon: Laurent Durand, 1639), 26.

17 On see, Isaac Vázquez Janeiro, 'La enseñanza del escotismo en España', in *De doctrina Ioannis Duns Scoti*, 4 vols (Rome: Frati Editori di Quaracchi, 1968), vol. 4, *Scotismus decursu saeculorum*, 207.

18 *Annales Minorum*, vol. 3 (1238), 17, n. 19.

19 Ibid.

20 Manuel Fernández Álvarez et al., *The University of Salamanca. Eight Centuries of Scholarship* (Salamanca: Ediciones Universidad de Salamanca, 1992), 94.

Santiago province can be attributed to its influence at its seat of learning in Salamanca, where the friary of San Francisco el Real was one of the oldest and most important friaries in Spain, founded by Bernardo de Quintavale, a disciple of St Francis, in 1231.[21] Ten years later, the construction of the church began with the support of the infante Don Fadrique, who was buried in the main chapel. The only remains preserved in their original location are the main apse and the Epistle side of the altar.[22] Since the Peninsular war and its consequences for ecclesiastical buildings, little else survives of the friary of San Francisco el Real, a monumental building with a Renaissance cloister. The chapel that was once part of the friary, now disappeared, currently belongs to the Capuchin Friary in Salamanca.[23]

Daily Life

In Spain, Catholic beliefs permeated every aspect of daily life, and these sentiments extended to the university. Approximately 120 friars dwelt in the friary of San Francisco el Real when Wadding arrived, making it one of the largest such houses in Salamanca.[24] Each province provided for the education of its own friars, with the province of Santiago providing access to the friary's library in Salamanca and free lodgings. The rigour of observance had no objection to the acquisition of books and the formation

21 *Crónica de la provincia franciscana de Santiago, 1214–1614. Por un franciscano anónimo del siglo XVII: Introducción, rectificaciones y notas*, ed Manuel de Castro (Madrid: Archivo Ibero Americano, 1971), 43, 98–99; Concepción Abad Castro and María Luisa Martín Ansón, *Estudio histórico-artístico del convento de San Francisco el Real de Salamanca, panteón de la nobleza de Salamanca* (Madrid: Ediciones de la Universidad Autónoma de Madrid: Asociación Hispánica de Estudios Franciscanos, 2013), 9.

22 Abad Castro and Martín Ansón, *Estudio histórico-artístico del convento de San Francisco el Real*, 9–14.

23 Ibid. See Figure 3.1.

24 De Castro, *San Francisco de Salamanca y su studium generale*, 112–113.

of libraries.[25] The care of books was assigned to novices who cleaned and repaired volumes in the library. Novices also completed kitchen tasks and gardening, cleaning and works of charity in the infirmary. In large Franciscan houses, the friars made and repaired their own footwear. In the kitchen, the common pot consisted of soups and stews, a little mutton and pork, turnips, beans and pulses. Bread and water were the main staples. Fish was cooked on fast days. The friars ate almonds and raisins in times of illness. Poultry and biscuits were also served at such times, with wine reserved for its restorative properties and for comfort.[26]

The novice master instructed the young friars on Christian doctrine, all the precepts of the rule, and the declarations of Nicholas III and Clement V on Franciscan regular observance. The friars' studies began each autumn on the feast of St Francis, 4 October, and ran until the solemnity of Pentecost. Lectures could also begin after the feast of the birth of the Virgin Mary, 8 September.[27] From their arrival onwards, those preparing for the priesthood were expected to participate in and, when necessary, start and lead their fellow friars in vocal prayer. Before obtaining the Bachelor of Arts, friars could contribute to the initial teaching of philosophy and theology in their own province. Nevertheless, it is difficult to arrive at a set plan of studies because the statutes relating to education underwent regular changes. Whenever possible, colleges within the Santiago province observed the Salamanca method for the teaching of theology but the recommended reading in dogmatic, moral and scholastic theology varied over the decades.[28]

Lecturers were required to give more than fifty classes per annum and to attend one another's classes. In return, they were allowed five months' leave each year during which time Wadding visited neighbouring friaries. Each

25 Ángel Weruaga Prieto, *Lectores y bibliotecas en la Salamanca moderna, 1600–1789* (Valladolid, Junta de Castilla y León, 2008); Manuel Rodríguez Pazos, 'Las bibliotecas en la Provincia de Santiago', *Archivo Ibero-Americano*, 14 (1954), 456–480.

26 Luis Enrique Rodríguez-San Pedro Bezares, *Estudiantes de Salamanca* (Salamanca: Ediciones Universidad de Salamanca, 2001), 27–28.

27 Hazard, 'Irish Franciscans and the Santiago Province of Spain', 22.

28 Manuel Rodríguez Pazos, *Los Estudios en la Provincia Franciscana de Santiago-Tratado Histórico* (Madrid: Escuelas Profesionales Sagrado Corazón de Jesús, 1967), 91, 95.

Franciscan centre of formation consistently included a chief administrator, graduate instructor, master of the students, biblical graduate, reader in theology, sub-lector and general assistant. In Wadding's case, he was master of the students at the friary of San Francisco el Real. At Salamanca, friars who became doctors or masters of the university had an extra incentive to qualify. While the Franciscan rule of 1223 forbade travel on horseback, Alexander VI lifted the ban in 1500 for the completion of higher degrees by Observant and Conventual Franciscans.[29]

To hold a chair at Salamanca, Wadding was first expected to have taught grammar, logic, philosophy and theology. He also needed to reach 'the master's stage', which required the approval of the Franciscan chapter general. His appointment to a professorship subsequently happened after biblical studies, the supervision of students and 'private study of the Greek and Hebrew languages'.[30] A certain amount of discretion appears to have been shown towards Wadding in meeting the usual criteria. Before taking up their posts, Salamanca professors were expected to contribute to the development of subjects and to have assembled two books per year.[31] Wadding accomplished these conditions in collaboration with Franciscan professors at Salamanca, such as Francisco de Sosa.

At Salamanca, the Dominicans and Augustinians reigned supreme until the Society of Jesus challenged their hegemony in the early seventeenth century.[32] Scholars were admitted via a selective process since advanced studies at Salamanca were seen as preparatory experience for higher office. Student attendance ranged from fourteen to twenty-five years of age. Seventeen or eighteen was the usual limit for access to higher faculties.[33] Wadding arrived in his mid-twenties. Conscious that he was among the

29 Regis Armstrong, William Short and J. A. Wayne Hellmann, eds, *Francis of Assisi: Early Documents*, 6 vols (New York: New City Press, 1999), vol. 1, *The Saint*, 73, 102. Manuel de Castro, *San Francisco de Salamanca y su Studium Generale* (Santiago de Compostela: Aldecoa, 1998), 59.

30 Harold, *Vita Fratris Lucae Waddingi*, 17: 'quem a Graecae, et Hebraicae linguae privato studio retulit'.

31 Pazos, *Los Estudios en la Provincia Franciscana de Santiago*, 116.

32 Rodríguez-San Pedro Bezares, *Estudiantes de Salamanca*, 48–49.

33 Ibid.

mature students in Salamanca, Wadding was fortunate to become protégé of Antonio de Trejo, vicar general of the order.

During the sixteenth century, in opposition to the accumulation of academic degrees and professorial titles, the Friars Minor withdrew from university teaching in Salamanca because they considered it promoted ambition and boastfulness, contrary to the spirit of observance. Their concern was that too much attention could be given to study to the detriment of camaraderie and simplicity of life in the order. As such, they operated their *studium* formation house independently while remaining committed to spiritual direction and preaching on campus.[34] Along with the Dominicans and Augustinians, they retained long-standing concessions to deliver sermons at the university on significant feast days in the varsity calendar. However, Wadding held that functioning separately from university life only marginalised the Observant Franciscans thereby depriving the Church of capable administrators and learned scholars. While keeping this in mind, he echoed the advice of St Francis and placed prayer foremost among the friars' priorities.[35]

The Irishman reached Salamanca in the same year as Ilarione Rancati, a Cistercian who had studied ancient Greek and Hebrew, as well as French and Spanish, at the monastery of Sant'Ambrogio in Milan. Wadding and Rancati became conversant with the theological controversy over grace, *De auxiliis*, and the celebrated Cistercian, Ángel Manrique, was among Rancati's teachers. Manrique was general of the Cistercians throughout Spain where he sat on the council of state and held Salamanca's *Víspera* chair of theology.[36] Since studying in Milan, Rancati understood the possibilities afforded to clergymen skilled in languages with an interest in the liturgy. As such, he may have encouraged Wadding to achieve distinction in oriental languages. Academic disputes were part and parcel of the teaching pedagogy and, since Scripture was a

34 Ibid.

35 Hazard, 'Irish Franciscans and the Santiago Province of Spain', 23.

36 Ceferino García Rodríguez, 'Rememorando al Ilmo. Fr. Ángel Manrique, Obispo de Badajoz (1645–9)', *Cistercium*, 1 (1949), 54–7; idem, 'El Ilmo Fr. Angel Manrique', *Collectanea Ord. Cist. Ref.*, 12 (1950), 195–207; 13 (1951), 128–39.

source of authority, the Bible was among the official texts of continuous reference at Salamanca.[37]

The rejuvenation of theology was the primary objective for the Salamanca School. This school of thought consisted of three generations of theologians and theology professors, all of whom considered the Dominican thinker, Francisco de Vitoria, the chief architect of their movement. Until the early seventeenth century, in their teaching and texts they pursued the theological renewal that he began.[38] Instruction at Salamanca consistently arrived at similar doctrinal conclusions, but the views of professors could differ.[39]

Not content with 'frequent and fervent public debates' at Salamanca, Wadding made the most of wider opportunities in Castile.[40] In 1615, eager to read the Bible in its original language, he studied Hebrew under Francisco Castillo, 'a great expert' at Alba de Tormes where the Franciscan friary was founded at the end of the fifteenth century with a college library intended for the formation of theologians.[41] Ten students dwelt at the college with the teaching staff. Alba de Tormes faced ongoing financial difficulties sustained for the most part by the dukes of Alba who paid the expenses for some of the students. As the province could not sustain the house, it was converted into a place of prayer, penance and contemplation in the following decade.[42] The study of Hebrew was customary in the Santiago

37 Daniel Sánchez y Sánchez, 'Metodología didáctica en la Universidad de Salamanca durante el siglo XVI', paper presented at *15th International Congress of Historical Sciences, Bucharest, 1980. Documents, Information, Testimonies*, 3 vols (1980), vol. 3, 409–52; Águeda Rodríguez Cruz, *Historia de la Universidad de Salamanca* (Salamanca: Fundación Ramón Areces y Congregación de Santo Domingo, 1990), 167.

38 Juan Belda Plans, *La Escuela de Salamanca: La renovación de la teología en el siglo XV* (Madrid: Biblioteca de Autores Cristianos, 2000), 156–57; Prosperi, *Il Concilio di Trento*, 23.

39 Lanza and Toste, 'The Influence of Salamanca in the Iberian Peninsula', 124.

40 Harold, *Vita Fratris Lucae Waddingi*, 16.

41 *Annales Minorum*, vol. 14 (1489), 542, n. 26; Angela Atienza López, *Tiempos de conventos. Una historia social de las fundaciones en la España moderna* (Madrid: Marcial Pons, 2008), 491; De Castro, ed, *Crónica de la provincia franciscana de Santiago, 1214–1614*, 173–74.

42 Manuel de Castro, *La Provincia Franciscana de Santiago. Ocho Siglos de Historia* (Santiago de Compostela: Liceo Franciscano, 1984), 182–83.

province. Wadding subsequently composed an authoritative treatise on the origin, importance and usefulness of Hebrew. Considering his taste for contemplative life, Wadding may have preferred the comparative seclusion of Alba de Tormes. A year later, he was recalled to Salamanca and began his university career, teaching sacred theology for the first time at San Francisco el Real at twenty-seven years of age.

Path to Professorship

Shortly after his appointment in Salamanca, Wadding was made lector of sacred theology at León, once the capital of the kingdom of the same name. Founded with royal patronage and papal protection in the mid-thirteenth century, the León friary was, according to Wadding, a pleasant but humble place located opposite the ancient Benedictine monastery of St Claudius, martyr.[43] During this teaching assignment, Wadding visited the Franciscan friary at Zamora between León and Salamanca to consult seven volumes compiled in the thirteenth century by Juan Gil Zamora, secretary to the king of Castile, Alfonso the Wise.[44] Looking back in later years, Wadding recalled that these sources were read and cited by many, but they were left in a state of disrepair at the friary and subsequently disappeared.[45] Further afield in the province of Zamora, the provincial chapter was held at Benavente in 1614 and 1617. According to Manuel de Castro, Wadding attended the latter event and recorded that Juan Francisco Alfonso de Pimentel Ponce de León, count of Benavente, covered the expenses.[46] As had been the case in Portugal, Wadding was a wandering friar in Castile.

43 *Annales Minorum*, vol. 3 (1240), 47, n. 20.

44 Manuel de Castro, 'Las ideas políticas y la formación del princípe en el *De preconiis Hispaniae* del franciscano Fr. Juan Gil de Zamora (1278)', *Hispania*, 22 (1962), 507–41.

45 De Castro, 'Wadding and the Iberian Peninsula', 136. For recent scholarship, see H. Salvador Martínez, *Alfonso X, the Learned. A Biography*, translated by Odile Cisneros (Leiden: Brill, 2010), 62.

46 De Castro, 'Wadding and the Iberian Peninsula', 134, 137.

He was often admitted to the friary at Toro and 'never entered it without piety and discipline'.[47] Founded near Zamora before 1270 and restored in 1463 after fire damage, the friary at Toro became home to well-known friars a century later, such as Mateo de Oviedo, archbishop of Dublin, and Juan de Rada, archbishop of Patti, both Scotists at Salamanca. Francisco de Sosa also dwelt at Toro and became minister general of the Observant Franciscans from 1600 to 1606. A productive writer, he was commissioned by Philip III to promote the Immaculate Conception.[48]

St Francis of Assisi consecrated his religious vocation to the Blessed Virgin at the Porziuncula in the countryside beneath Assisi and, from the late sixteenth century onwards, the Church made Mary more widely known because of her virtues of humility, obedience and chastity.[49] Consequently, the doctrine – Mary, as the mother of God, was free from original sin from the moment of her conception – grew in importance during the Catholic Reformation. A natural ally for Wadding, Sosa also served as bishop of the Canaries, of Osma, as bishop-elect of Segovia, and as a member of the Spanish council of state.[50]

Wadding held his post at León for a year until his superiors transferred him back to Salamanca, sufficiently impressed by 'his talent, labour, and energy'.[51] Following the Council of Trent, the Church emphasised that

47 *Annales Minorum*, vol. 5 (1290), 276, n. 30: 'Saepius hoc in Conventu hospitio exceptus numquam illum ingressus sum, quin pietam, et disciplinae regularis specimen manifeste prae se ferre mihi videretur'. For further sources on the Toro friary, see De Castro, 'Wadding and the Iberian Peninsula', 137.

48 Sosa published in quarto his *Memorial que dio el Reverendissimo Senor Don Fray Francisco de Sosa Obispo de Osma a la Magestad del Rey Don Felipe III en la materia de la Purissima Concepcion de la Virgen*, 15 October 1617. For his other writings, see Alejandra Ulla Lorenzo and Alexander Wilkinson, eds, *Books published in Spain, Portugal and the New World or elsewhere in Spanish or Portuguese between 1601 and 1650*, 3 vols (Leiden: Brill, 2015), vols 2 & 3, 2228.

49 Peter Damian Fehlner, *Franciscan Mariology – Francis, Clare, and Bonaventure: the Collected Essays*, edited by J. Isaac Goff with an Introduction by Charles Robinson, 4 vols (Eugene: Wipf and Stock, 2023), vol. 3, 40, 80.

50 Antonio Domínguez Ortiz, *Las clases privilegiadas en la España del antiguo régimen* (Madrid: Ediciones ISTMO, 1973), 277.

51 Harold, *Vita Fratris Lucae Waddingi*, 16: 'ejus ingenium, laborem, et industriam satis probaverant'.

ordained ministry required liturgical and theological training at university level and encouraged the clergy to read. This gave rise to works of moral theology.[52] After completing his own theological studies, Wadding's superiors recognised his developing editorial aptitude. As such, they ordered him to produce a concise edition of *Summa de casos de consciencia*. These cases of conscience were popular lessons in morals written by the Portuguese Observant friar, Manuel Rodrigues, who spent much of his life in Salamanca and died in 1613.[53]

Whilst lecturing in theology and as master of Franciscan students at Salamanca, another opportunity was given to Wadding. As the cloisters at both the friaries of St Francis and of St Anthony were decorated with paintings, Wadding's superiors asked him to give details on each of the pictures by contributing verses about them. He performed his task beyond their wishes, so much so that even the painter marvelled at the natural composition of the poems.[54] Wadding entrusted poems on the holy name of Jesus, Franciscan saints and the Immaculate Conception to Francisco de Sosa to accompany a series of his own tracts printed in Salamanca.[55] Wadding's work consisted of a fifty-nine page treatise dedicated to Antonio de Trejo and the Salamanca friars, in honour of 'the most glorious seraphic patriarch, our father Saint Francis'.[56]

52 Pedro Manuel Guibovich Pérez, 'Martín de Azpilcueta in the Andes (16th-17th centuries)', in Manuela Bragagnolo, ed, *The Production of Knowledge of Normativity in the Age of the Printing Press. Martín de Azpilcueta's Manual de Confessores from a Global Perspective* (Leiden: Brill, 2024), 180.

53 Hugh Fenning, 'Some Irish Donors of Books to the Irish College in Rome, 1611–78', in Keogh and McDonnell, eds, *The Irish College, Rome, and its World* (Dublin: Four Courts Press, 2008), 47; Manuel de Castro, *Escritores de la Provincia Franciscana de Santiago, siglos XIII–XIX* (Santiago de Compostela: S. N., 1996), 222–57.

54 Harold, *Vita Fratris Waddingi*, 16.

55 *Tratados del Illustrissimo y Reverendissimo Señor Don Fr. Francisco De Sosa: Hijo De La Santa Provincia De Santiago y del Convento de S. Francisco De Salamanca; General de toda la Orden, Obispo de Canarias, Osma y Segovia, del Consejo de su Magestad, en el Real Supremo de la Sancta General Inquisición* (Salamanca: Antonio Vázquez, 1623).

56 Ibid, 'Tratado nono sanctorale seraphicum gloriosissimi patriarcha seraphici patris nostri Santi Francisci'. Wadding appears to have compiled some of the contents during his studies in Portugal. Amongst other matters, these consist of a Franciscan

The office of confessor and spiritual counsellor to religious sisters was sought after by the priesthood in the seventeenth century.[57] During his time in Salamanca, Wadding was confessor to the local Poor Clare convent. He stated that he often witnessed the holiness of the sisters in the convent where he was frequently summoned to hear their confessions and, on several occasions, was present to help sisters who were sick or dying. The Irish friar reported that the community lived in 'a most spacious and comfortable dwelling' and that he did not see anything unworthy or profane about the place.[58]

Antonio de Trejo

Trejo's influence upon Wadding's early career was clearly apparent in the Irish friar's progress before he was assigned the chair of Franciscan theology in Salamanca. At each turn, the earlier experiences of his Spanish superior prefigured the path that Wadding took to his professorship. Trejo studied theology and arts in Salamanca, completed the noviciate and took the habit of St Francis. After profession, he served as reader of arts at the León friary in 1599, as did Wadding in later years. Trejo was then transferred to teach arts in Zamora and returned to León where, in 1609, he was reader of theology and guardian of the friary.[59]

---

calendar of saints and martyrs such as Beraldus, Petrus, Adiutus, Accursius and Otho who stayed in Portugal before travelling to Morocco, St Anthony of Padua who was born in Lisbon, St Bonaventure, the Portziuncula church in Assisi, St Clare, St Louis IX of France, St Francis and St Pedro of Alcántara, followed by litanies to the Blessed Virgin Mary and a treatise on the Blessed Sacrament.

57 Javier Burrieza Sánchez, 'La monarquía "de los descalzos". Rigores y reformas en las órdenes religiosas', in Consuelo Martínez-Sicluna y Sepúlveda et al., eds, *La configuración de la Monarquía Hispánica* (Madrid: Dykinson, 2023), 233–68; Jodi Bilinkoff, *Related Lives: Confessors and their Female Penitents, 1450–1750* (Ithaca NY: Cornell University Press, 2018), 68–70, 79–80.

58 De Castro, 'Wadding and the Iberian Peninsula', 139: 'Capacissimum et commodum habent Sorores habitaculum, neque quidpiam profanum aut indignum clarissis vidi in interioribus officinis'.

59 Silvano Giordano, *Istruzioni di Filippo III ai suoi ambasciatori a Roma, 1598–1621* (Rome: Dipartimento beni archivistici e librari-Direzione Generale per gli Archivi,

While Wadding's prospects continued to improve in Castile, his patron and advocate Trejo met with obstacles in the upper echelons of the Observant Franciscans. Appointed commissary general of the Indies in 1610, Trejo was obliged to relocate to the royal court in Madrid where he became friends with Philip III. As the Franciscan general chapter approached two years later, the king recommended Trejo to Paul V, Cardinal Borghese and Cardinal Arrigoni in the expectation that the Spanish friar would be elected minister general of the Franciscan observance. This only caused opposition among members of the chapter to be held in Rome where Trejo was present. Juan de Hierro from Cordoba was elected instead but died a year later on 1 November, which led to an extraordinary chapter in Madrid. Trejo's appointment to govern the Order of Friars Minor as vicar general was confirmed on the feast of the Immaculate Conception, 8 December, and Juan de Vivanco, then guardian of the Salamanca friary, became commissary general of the Indies.[60]

Different religious orders often took opposing sides in contentious theological debate. The Franciscans defended teachings on the Immaculate Conception of Mary, mother of Jesus, since the work of their thirteenth-century confrère, Scotus, whereas the Dominican order did not.[61] The seventeenth-century Franciscan campaign in support of the doctrine began at Toledo in 1606.[62] By order of the supreme council of the Inquisition in Madrid, the Franciscan bishop of Osma, Francisco de Sosa, approved two theological discourses on the Immaculate, which were published in 1614.[63] A year later, Franciscan friars affiliated to the

2006), LXVII-LXVIII; Javier Nadal Iniesta, 'Fray Antonio de Trejo: el primer principe contrarreformista de la diócesis de Cartagena', in María Concepción de la Peña Velasco et al., eds, *Congreso Internacional Imagen Apariencia* (Murcia: Universidad de Murcia, 2009), <https://digitum.um.es/digitum/bitstream/10201/44224/1/CongresoImagen125.pdf>, accessed 27 March 2024.

60 Giordano, *Istruzioni di Filippo III ai suoi ambasciatori a Roma, 1598–1621*, LXVIII.

61 Broggio, 'Teologia, ordini religiosi e rapporti politici', 255–81; Jacob Schmutz, 'Bellum scholasticum. Thomisme et antithomisme dans les débats doctrinaux modernes', *Revue thomiste*, 108 (2008), 137, 178–79.

62 Hazard, *Faith and Patronage*, 51.

63 Francisco de Sosa, *Tomo primero de tratados y sermones de la limpia Concepcion de Nuestra Señora, sin mancha de pecado original, con seis tablas copiosas para predicadores y teologos* (Seville: Alfonso Rodriguez Gamarra, 1617).

University of Salamanca vowed to defend the teachings of Scotus and all graduates were called to swear an oath in honour of the Immaculate. Further, the venerable Salamanca joined with its new rival at Alcalá to mark the feast days in honour of Mary at the two universities.[64] The detailed chronicle of the Alcalá festivities emphasised these links by including a letter written by one Salamanca friar, Francisco de Sosa, to another, Antonio de Trejo. Here, Sosa described the commission he received as extraordinary ambassador of Philip III to promote the doctrine in Rome.[65] Sosa acted cautiously and with courage to overcome the opposition expressed in the papal decree *Dominus noster* of August 1610, which prohibited public disputes about the matter. This was relied upon by Philip III's Dominican confessor, Luis de Aliaga, and by the nuncio to Spain, Antonio Caetani, who followed papal instructions to maintain the opposite doctrinal position.[66] These difficulties paralysed the initiative and cast a shadow over the career of Francisco de Sosa who died on 8 January 1618.[67]

64 *Relacion de las famosas fiestas que se hizieron en la Vniuersidad de Alcala de Henares, despues de auer hecho voto de guardar y tener en ella el Sacrosancto Misterio de la Inmaculada Concepcion: lleua al fin tres cartas, la vna del Obispo de Osma, Francisco de Sosa al padre fray Antonio de Trejo, General de toda la orden de San Francisco, donde da cuenta de su viage a Roma* (Alcalá de Henares: Viuda y herederos de Juan Gracián, 1617); *Relacion de las fiestas que la Vniversidad de Salamanca celebro desde el 27 hasta el 31 de octubre del año 1618 al juramento del nuevo estatuto hecho el 2 de mayo de dicho año de que todos los graduados defenderan la pura, y limpia Concepcion de la Virgen nuestra Señora, concebida sin mancha de pecado original. Ordenada por mandado y comission de la mesma Vniuersidad, en su Claustro Pleno* (Salamanca: Antonia Ramirez viuda, 1618). The Salamanca report is attributed to the Augustinian priest, Juan Márquez de Villareal.

65 Ibid.

66 Emilio Callado Estela, 'El confesor regio fray Luis de Aliaga y la controversia inmaculista', *Hispania Sacra*, 68 (2016), 317–26.

67 Broggio, 'Teologia, ordini religiosi e rapporti politici', 275; José García Oro, 'Sosa, Francisco de', *DBe*, 50 vols (Madrid: Real Academia de la Historia, 2009–13), 47, <https://dbe.rah.es/biografias/30662/francisco-de-sosa>, accessed 28 March 2024.

Franciscan General Chapter

For his nephew Francis, Wadding's performance at the Salamanca general chapter of 1618 was prefigured by that held in Lisbon five years earlier.[68] Those who favoured papal definition of the Immaculate Conception argued that their theological mission to Rome must continue.[69] The campaign was strongly supported at the Descalzas Reales Convent, the most important institution for religious sisters in the centre of Madrid where the Infanta Margarita, aunt of Philip III, lived as a Poor Clare nun. She had a great devotion to the Immaculate and promoted its veneration, writing to Paul V in the hope that he would declare it a dogma of the Church.[70]

To break the deadlock in Rome, new crown representatives were required by the king. Until 1618, Wadding served as professor in theology and master of the student friars at Salamanca. At the age of thirty and in the thirteenth year since his profession, the Franciscan general chapter was celebrated in the city, where Trejo fulfilled the office of vicar general and Benigno da Genova was elected minister general.[71] One of Wadding's chief collaborators in defending the cause of Scotus, Hugh McCaghwell of Co. Down, studied at Salamanca and subsequently attended the 1618 general chapter as *custos* of *custodes* in the company of Eugene Field, Irish minister

68 Harold, *Vita Fratris Lucae Waddingi*, 17.

69 See Paolo Broggio, 'Gli ambasciatori straordinari spagnoli a Roma per la definizione del dogma dell'Immacolata tra difesa delle prerogative episcopali, teologia e Ragion di Stato (1616–1661)', in Flavia Tudini, Manfredi Merluzzi and Gaetano Sabatini, eds, *La Vergine contesa. Roma, l'Immacolata Concezione e l'universalismo della Monarchia Cattolica (secc. XVII–xIX)* (Rome: Viella Libreria Editrice, 2022), 237–264.

70 Magdalena Sánchez, 'Where Palace and Convent met: the Descalzas Reales in Madrid', *Sixteenth Century Journal*, 46 (2015), 53–82; Pou y Martí, 'Embajadas de Felipe III a Roma pidiendo la definición de la Inmaculada Concepción de María', *Archivo Ibero-Americano*, 36 (1933), 37–38.

71 *Statuta, constitutiones et decreta generalis pro hac Cismontana, Familia Ordinis Minorum [...] in Generali Capitulo Pentecostes Salmanticae in conventu S. Francisci, Provinciae S. Iacobi celebrato* (Madrid: Ludovicus Sanctius, 1618).

provincial.[72] Field was from Munster and studied at the Irish College in Santiago before joining the Franciscan province of Santiago at Salamanca.[73]

The Immaculate Conception formed the centrepiece of the general chapter that summer. The Friars Minor were ordered to encourage devotion to the Blessed Virgin Mary and Franciscan theses were presented during the proceedings.[74] On 2 June, as domestic reader at the chapter and second to none, Wadding defended theological conclusions concerning the Immaculate Conception in which he proved himself skilled in Mariology, in early Franciscan theology and in the mysteries of the most Holy Trinity.[75] Wadding convinced Trejo once more and won over Benigno da Genova 'so much that for the rest of his life he became the best of Wadding's patrons and friends', indeed 'the promoter of good thoughts'.[76] Thereafter, Wadding was chosen as theologian for the Spanish mission to Rome.

Wadding and Rancati, his Cistercian friend from Milan, both supported the king of Spain who traditionally promoted veneration of this devotion to Mary. Ángel Manrique, was a significant advocate for the cause as was his disciple Rancati.[77] From the Cistercian perspective, Bernard of Clairvaux venerated Mary in his homilies, which thereby influenced the Liturgy

72 Patrick Conlan, 'The Little Brother from Down – Aodh Mac Aingil as a good Franciscan', *Seanchas Ard Mhacha*, 19, Golden Jubilee Issue (2003), 63–70.

73 Hazard, 'Irish Franciscans and the Santiago Province of Spain', 21, 30. Eugene Field served as guardian of St Anthony's College, Leuven, where he taught philosophy and theology. For three years from 1618, he served as Irish minister provincial. Appointed commissary of the Franciscans in Ireland, he became guardian of Sherkin and Timoleague, Co. Cork, where he died a centenarian on 23 November 1668.

74 *Primera Parte de Sermones de la limpisima Concepcion de Nuestra Señora, Salmanticæ, predicados en el real convento de San Francisco de Salamanca y recogidos por el P. Fray Gaspar de Vigachoaca OFM* (Salmanticae: apud Didacum à Cussio anno Domini, 1619).

75 Harold, *Vita Fratris Lucae Waddingi*, 17.

76 Ibid: 'ut reliqua vita ipsum habuerit Patrem optimum, carissimum, amicum, et bonarum cogitationum promotorem'.

77 Fernando Herrero Salas, ed, *Actas Capitulares del Cister en el Monasterio de Palazuelos* (Madrid: Bubok s.l., 2015), 395, 476; Louis Lekai, 'The Cistercians: Ideals and Reality in Early Cistercian Life and Legislation', in J. R. Sommerfeldt, ed, *Cistercian Ideals and Reality* (Kalamazoo: Cistercian Publishing, 1978), 243.

of the Hours. Wadding commented on Franciscan tradition in light St Bernard's praise of Mary's virginity, humility and motherhood as *Stella Maris*, the star of the sea.[78] Theologically, however, Bernard did not affirm Mary's Immaculate Conception.[79] Nonetheless, his sermons did provide the Franciscans with support for a number of themes that were important to Scotist thinking in later centuries.[80] The Blessed Virgin Mary was first commemorated in Cistercian liturgy before the death of Bernard who also composed a breviary entry in her honour.[81]

Madrid

Philip III provided Trejo with a credential bearing the date of 14 September 1618 seeking to obtain papal approval of the doctrine. According to Wadding, when news of the new theological embassy was announced, damaging slurs were made against Trejo in Madrid.[82] Nonetheless, the king presented Trejo with the mitre of Cartagena two days later. He was consecrated at the church of the Descalzas Reales Convent in Madrid.

78 *Annales Minorum*, vol. 6 (1317), 343, n. 66; ibid, 9 (1400), 312–313, *Peroratio*; vol. 15 (1500), 258, *Peroratio*. On this point, see Bernard of Clairvaux, *Sermons for the Autumn Season*, ed Mark Scott (Collegeville MN: Liturgical Press, 2016), xix, xxv–xxvi, 14–15, 84, 185, 269.

79 On the relevance to the Canons of Lyon and Bernard of Clairvaux, see Marie-Bénédicte Dary, 'Saint Bernard et l'Immaculée Conception: La Question Liturgique', *Revue Mabillon*, 13 (2002), 219–36; Charles Balić, 'The Mediaeval Controversy over the Immaculate Conception up to the Death of Scotus', in Edward O'Connor, ed, *The Dogma of the Immaculate Conception, History and Significance* (Notre Dame, IN: University of Notre Dame Press, 1958), 173.

80 Spoltore, ed, 'Una lettera di Luke Wadding ad Ilarione Rancati sull'Immacolata Concezione', 551–56.

81 Frederick Jelly, 'The Christocentric Devotion to Mary in Saint Bernard of Clairvaux', *Cistercian Studies Quarterly*, 34 (1999), 89–99.

82 Lope Pascual Martínez, 'La Embajada a Roma de Fray Antonio de Trejo, Obispo de Cartagena', *Anales de la Universidad de Murcia. Filosofía y letra*, 32 (1973), 24.

Wadding was in attendance with the entire court of Philip III.[83] While in the capital, Wadding stayed in the south-east of Madrid at the Franciscan friary of Jesus and Mary, where the heads of the Franciscan order in Spain lived and also the principal preachers.[84] Aptly, the Irish had settled in the same area. The adjoining Basilica of San Francisco el Grande became the most popular mendicant site for the burial of Irish exiles.[85] At that point, another Irish friar, Archbishop Flaithrí Ó Maolchonaire, also dwelt at the friary. Wadding described him as 'the best student of the Church Fathers' that he had met.[86] They shared an interest in the doctrine of the Immaculate Conception and must have discussed the subject together. In 1619, Ó Maolchonaire arranged the publication of his considered opinion of St Augustine's thoughts on the question of whether Mary was free from original sin from the moment of her conception. Using exegesis in support of the doctrine, Ó Maolchonaire proposed that, while the Immaculate Conception is not found explicitly in Augustine's writings, it is not opposed, and moreover can be deduced from key passages.[87] Thus, he sought to confound opponents of the doctrine who claimed it had not been accepted before the twelfth century. Ó Maolchonaire appears to have been first to nominate his confrère Wadding for the episcopacy.[88]

83 Pou y Martí, 'Embajadas de Felipe III a Roma pidiendo la definición de la Inmaculada Concepción de María', *Archivo Ibero-Americano*, 35 (1932), 88.

84 De Castro, 'Wadding and the Iberian Peninsula', 142. See also Luis Miguel Aparisi Laporta, *El plano de Teixeira, trescientos cincuenta años después* (Madrid: Ayuntarniento de Madrid, 2000), 100.

85 Ciaran O'Scea, 'From Convents to Chapels of Ease: Irish Burial and Funerary Practices in Early Modern Madrid, 1600–80', in Benjamin Hazard, ed, *Path to Salvation: Temporal and Spiritual Journeys by the Mendicant Orders, c.1370–1740* (Lausanne: Peter Lang, 2023), 152, 160–61.

86 Hazard, *Faith and Patronage*, 127.

87 Florentius Conrius, *Tractatus de Augustini sensu circa beatae Mariae Virginis Conceptionem* (Antwerp: Jan van Keerberghen, 1619). An extant copy of this rare work is preserved at the University Library of Nijmegen.

88 Jennings, ed, *Wadding Papers*, 21. This refers to a recommendation by the earl of Tyrconnell from October 1619, which appears to have been written by his mentor, Ó Maolchonaire, who knew Wadding and authored the tract on the Immaculate Conception mentioned above.

To accelerate Trejo's elevation to a bishopric, Philip III had gone against the council of Castile to choose Trejo for the vacant see of Cartagena in Murcia, thereby excluding the transfer of a bishop from either Zamora, Astorga or Ciudad Rodrigo.[89] Having received a dossier from various theological commissions that had discussed the problem, Trejo and his party departed from Madrid for Murcia where Wadding recorded their stay at the Franciscan friary. They continued south to Trejo's seat at Cartagena and intended to embark for Italy, but an illness held the bishop back.[90]

Conclusion

For Wadding, Spain provided a broadening experience both among his immediate superiors and with friends from orders other than the Observant Franciscans. In particular, the strong understanding that he shared with Trejo and Rancati was a foundation stone for Wadding's future. Friaries provided him with a communal life and beneficial social support from Observant Franciscans, based on long-standing arrangements within their own institutions. By 1618, Wadding had emerged as a recognised authority on teaching and theology. Castile made a lasting impression on his work in a variety of ways, from his appreciation of monastic buildings to local Baroque architecture and his early writings, interests that later flowered into new foundations and many printed volumes. The next chapters explore how Wadding's experiences as a scholar in Spain and Portugal resulted in many productive years of scholarship in Italy where the influence of Salamanca was evident at the first college he founded in Rome.

89 Beatriz Comella Gutiérrez, 'Los nombramientos Episcopales para la Corona de Castilla bajo Felipe III, según el Archivo Histórico Nacional: Una Aproximación', *Hispania Sacra*, 60 (2008), 729.

90 De Castro, 'Wadding and the Iberian Peninsula', 143.

4 To the City and the World

Introduction

Wadding's arrival in Rome marked the beginning of a long career at the very centre of Catholicism. As a priest and scholar, he had come to know the Church in Spain at first hand, its internal life and external relations, its liturgy and its sacred music. Yet, Spain's geographical position also contributed to its cultural isolation.[1] The people of Wadding's birthplace regarded their city as Little Rome.[2] As his first cousin, Patrick Comerford, explained, Waterford remained 'constant and firme in the holy and ancient Catholicke Roman beliefe'.[3] Comerford continued: 'Recusancie made Rome so famous and holy [...] Recusancie exanimated & broke the hearts of Diocletian, Maximinian, Nero, Julian the Apostate and other such impious persecutors of Roman Catholickes'.[4]

When Wadding arrived in the early seventeenth century, many remnants of the old Roman world were still in existence. Latin was his preferred means of communication and a language at which he excelled. For early modern scholars, Latin proficiency commanded respect. A sign of authority, the language provided a generous heritage, especially in learned and

1 Ramón Menéndez Pidal, *The Spaniards in Their History* (New York: Norton, 1955), 109.

2 Comerford, *The Inquisition of a Sermon Preached in the Cathedral Church of the City of Waterford*, 197.

3 Ibid.

4 Ibid.

official circles.[5] Closely attached to the life of the Church, its significance was religious more so than cultural or literary in the seventeenth century. In the rhetorical tradition, Wadding's words sought to persuade. The following chapter describes the first eight years that he spent in Italy. It takes account of his first three publications as chronicler of the Franciscan family, which were circulated and shared across the European continent and the New World.

The Immaculate

The legation led by Antonio de Trejo, bishop of Cartagena, weighed anchor on 22 November 1618. Trejo believed that the voyage augured well for his mission. Although the Gulf of Lyon was dangerous, Trejo wrote to Philip III that the crossing from Cartagena to Barcelona, and on to Genoa, was so swift and peaceful the sailors swore that in twenty years of sailing the Gulf of Lyon they had never seen the sea and sky as calm. Instead, they were accustomed to always seeing storms. To reach the papal states, Philip III then ordered the duke of Tursis to lend Trejo one of his galleys.[6] The party reached Civitavecchia on 13 December, entered Rome three days later and was received that day by Paul V.[7] The bishop of Cartagena kept Philip III and Jorge de Tovar, secretary of state, informed of his results. In turn, the king instructed the most influential Spanish cardinal in Rome, Gaspar de Borja, to ensure that Trejo and his party would be well received.[8]

The strong Marian tone to the earliest Franciscan writings makes the order's links to the Immaculate Conception more intelligible.[9] Whereas

5 Jason Harris, 'Catholicism', in Sarah Knight and Stefan Tilg, eds, *The Oxford Handbook of Neo-Latin* (Oxford: Oxford University Press, 2015), 314–15.

6 Luke Wadding, *Presbeia sive legatio Philippi III. et IV. Catholicorum regum Hispaniarum* (Leuven: Henrick van Hastens, 1624), 40.

7 Harold, *Vita Fratris Lucae Waddingi*, 18.

8 Wadding, *Presbeia sive legatio*, 19, 29–30, 446.

9 Pietro Messa, 'Le feste mariane nel Breviarium sancti Francisci', in Stefano Cecchin, ed, *La "Scuola Francescana" e l'Immacolata Concezione: atti del congresso mariologico*

Protestants challenged the view that Mary was preserved free from original sin, early modern Catholicism reasserted its identity by exalting Mary as the mother of Jesus.[10] This was especially the case within Spain where Mary was regarded as the supreme model of holiness due to her faith in and obedience to God.[11] It was believed that prayers made to Mary led to Jesus, the source of all grace. As a sign of their devotion, the Friars Minor, Poor Clares and Franciscan tertiaries recited the 'Crown of the Blessed Virgin' from the early fifteenth century.[12] Wadding traced the origins of the Franciscan Crown to *c.*1422. In so doing, he followed Mark of Lisbon who cited Marianus of Florence as his source. This was a vocal and mental prayer that focused attention on the seven joys in the life of Mary.[13] Moreover, mendicant friars often took Mary's name in religion.

---

francescano, S. Maria degli Angeli, Assisi, 4–8 dicembre 2003 (Città del Vaticano: Pontificia Academia Mariana 2005), 55–85.

10 Stefano Cecchin, 'L'Immacolata Concezione nel "Siglo de oro" spagnolo tra re, papi e francescani', *Annali di Storia Sociale ed Ecclesiastica*, 1 (2017), 7–60; Bridget Heal, *The Cult of the Virgin Mary in Early Modern Germany: Protestant and Catholic Piety, 1500–1648* (Cambridge: Cambridge University Press, 2014), 80–81.

11 On the origins of the Immaculate Conception movement in Spain, see Pérez Tostado, '"Learned, Attached and Reliable': Luke Wadding, Agent of the Spanish Monarchy', 44; Rosilie Hernández, *Immaculate Conceptions: The Power of the Religious Imagination in Early Modern Spain* (Toronto: Toronto University Press, 2019), 23–31.

12 Filippo Sedda, 'John of Capistrano and the Virgin Mary', in Steven McMichael and Katie Wrisley Shelby, eds, *Medieval Franciscan Approaches to the Virgin Mary: Mater Misericordiae Sanctissima et Dolorosa* (Leiden: Brill 2019), 418.

13 Erminia Ardissino, 'Literary and Visual Forms of a Domestic Devotion: The Rosary in Renaissance Italy', in Maya Corry, Marco Faini and Alessia Meneghin, eds, *Domestic devotions in Early Modern Italy* (Brill: Leiden 2019), 346. See also Sergi Doménech García, 'La propaganda concepcionista franciscana en el mundo hispánico. El grabado apologético y la obra de Pedro de Alva y As torga', in Camino Sánchez Oliveira, Alberto Gamarra Gonzalo, Manuel José Pedraza Gracia, eds, *La fisonomía del libro medieval y moderno: entre la funcionalidad, la estética y la información* (Zaragoza: Prensas de la Universidad de Zaragoza, 2019), 367–78; Ellénita de Mol, 'Le culte de la Vierge après le Concile de Trente, perçu à travers trois triptyques flamands de la fin du XVIe siècle et du début du XVIIe siècle', in Wim François and Violet Soen, eds, *The Council of Trent: Reform and Controversy in Europe and Beyond*, vol. 3, 93–116.

The legation formed an integral part of Philip III's pressure groups at the papal court and the king had a special devotion to the Blessed Virgin.[14] In common with Charles V, Ferdinand I and Philip II before him, he wore an image of the Immaculate on the breastplate of his armour.[15] On looking for a team of persuasive communicators capable of dealing with difficult negotiations, the king entrusted the mission to the Franciscan province of Santiago.[16] Wadding and José Vásquez, commissary of the order, served as theological assessors and were accompanied by Benigno da Genova, the recently appointed minister general of the Friars Minor. Wadding and Trejo stayed first at the palace of Cardinal Gabriel de Trejo, the bishop's brother.[17] Finding the surroundings at odds with his vocation, Wadding went from there to reside at the Spanish friary of San Pietro in Montorio, which overlooks the Eternal City.[18]

Proceedings began between the Spanish embassy and the Roman curia in the New Year when Trejo's party presented a memorial at the papal court. In February 1619, while Trejo was preparing his second memorial to Paul V, complaints against Philip III spread throughout Rome. It was publicly stated that the king of Spain exceeded his status by mixing religious matters with temporal, and that he put too much effort into the dogmatic definition of the mystery of the Immaculate Conception. To extinguish these claims, Trejo and Wadding composed a lengthy apology arguing that Philip III was a very Catholic monarch who acted responsibly

14 José-María Pou y Martí, 'Embajadas de Felipe III a Roma, pidiendo la definición de la Inmaculada Concepción de María' *Archivo Ibero-americano*, 34 (1931), 371–417, 508–534; 35 (1932), 72–88, 424–434, 481–525; 36 (1933), 5–48.

15 Carlos Martínez Shaw, ed, *Arte y Saber: la cultura en tiempos de Felipe III y Felipe IV*. Museo Nacional de Escultura, Palacio Villena, Valladolid (Madrid: Ministerio de Educación y Cultura Dirección General de Bellas Artes y Bienes Culturales, 1999), 34.

16 Manuel de Castro, *La Provincia Franciscana de Santiago*, 58.

17 Harold, *Vita Fratris Lucae Waddingi*, 18.

18 On the relevance of San Pietro in Montorio for Wadding, see Mícheál Mac Craith, 'Wadding and the Irish Tombs in San Pietro in Montorio', in Binasco, ed, *Luke Wadding, the Irish Franciscans and Global Catholicism*, 167–84.

to calm the controversy between kingdoms on this matter, and to settle discord among the clergy.[19]

In March and April, Trejo presented the third memorial on Mary's conception.[20] A few days later, he requested an audience with Paul V, but the pope responded that he had examined the subject carefully and did not find it easy or convenient to issue a definition. Upon hearing this, Trejo promised Paul V a paper, which he assigned to Wadding who prepared and presented it to the pope with all brevity.[21] However, as had been the case with the *De auxiliis* controversy, Paul V was opposed to hasty pronouncements and therefore asked for Trejo to be recalled to Spain. Philip III acceded to the request on 22 June, withdrawing Trejo's credentials in a letter brought to Rome by the duke of Alburquerque, newly appointed ambassador. Antonio de Trejo remained in Rome for two more years before returning to his bishopric in Cartagena where he continued to defend the Immaculate Conception. He remained friends with Wadding who stayed in Rome to assist Albuquerque as his theological adviser.[22] Wadding's enduring devotion to the Immaculate reflected his loyalty to the teachings of Scotus and, in later years, the Waterford Franciscan published three tracts about the baptism, death and redemption of Mary. Since his arrival in Rome, Wadding gathered evidence from libraries and archives to compile arguments in favour of the doctrine. These studies served as a basis for future debate on the question.[23]

19 'Apologia pro Rege Catholico', in Wadding, *Presbeia sive legatio*, 56–78.

20 Wadding, *Presbeia sive legatio*, 239, 399, 432.

21 Martínez, 'La Embajada a Roma de Fray Antonio de Trejo, obispo de Cartagena', 37.

22 Igor Pérez Tostado, "Learned, Attached and Reliable': Luke Wadding, Agent of the Spanish Monarchy', 45.

23 Luke Wadding, *De Morte B. Mariae Virginis: Immaculatae Conceptioni B.V.M. non adversari eius mortem corporalem* (Rome: Tinassi, 1655); *De Baptismo B.M. Virginis* (Rome: Tinassi, 1656); *De Redemptione B.M. Virginis* (Rome: Tinassi, 1656).

Chronicler of the Seraphic family

During his studies a decade earlier, Wadding was inspired to defend his religious order and the credentials of its founder from what he saw as unfair attacks and criticism. In support of this ambitious idea, Benigno da Genova wrote to every province of the Friars Minor directing them to transcribe and forward to Rome documents relevant to their history.[24] Wadding dedicated the first volume of the *Annales Minorum* to Benigno da Genova. Consequently, his name is inseparable from the project, which was among the most important initiatives during his term of office.[25]

Following his election as pope two years later, Gregory XV granted Wadding permission to consult the Vatican Archives and Library, which were then a branch of the secretariat of state rather than a resource for historians to consult.[26] Therefore, Wadding's work with Trejo at the papal court provided him with the necessary foundation to consult what was otherwise a closed institution. When he obtained access, the Vatican repositories were deployed as an instrument of cultural policy by the papacy.[27] The Vatican archivist and secretary of apostolic briefs, Cardinal Scipione Cobelluzzi, and the library prefect, *primo custode*, Nicolò Alemanni, supplied much material to Wadding for transcription.[28] Consequently, he 'amassed good-sized volumes of transcripts of

24 Encyclical letter of Benigno da Genova, Rome, 20 April 1619 (ACSI, Rome, W16/13).

25 Francesco Cagnetti, 'Benigno da Genova (al secolo Agostino Rosso)', in *DBI*, <https://www.treccani.it/enciclopedia/benigno-da-genova_(Dizionario-Biografico)/>, accessed 2 November 2024.

26 Luke Wadding to Gregory XV, San Pietro in Montorio, *c.*1622 (UCD-OFM, D.03/1/317–319).

27 Peter Rietbergen, *Power and Religion in Baroque Rome: Barberini* (Leiden: Brill, 2006), 401–404; Francis X. Blouin, 'Introduction', in idem, Claudia Carlen, Leonard Coombs, Katherine Gill and Elizabeth Yakel, eds, *Vatican Archives: An Inventory and Guide to Historical Documents of the Holy See* (Oxford: Oxford University Press, 1998), xx.

28 *Annales Minorum*, vol. 1, Prolegomena, ix–x: 'quae multam subministrarunt materiam'.

papal bulls and briefs'.[29] Wadding called Cobelluzzi 'my singular patron' and dedicated the 1628 edition of his work, *Angeli del Pas, in Lucae Evangelium Commentaria*, to the cardinal in recognition of his assistance.[30] After Cobelluzzi's death, Francesco Barberini held the post of cardinal librarian and was succeeded by Antonio, his brother. Therefore, it was fitting that Wadding's benefactors included the Barberini. St Francis of Assisi was a patron saint of the family and Maffeo Barberini, later Urban VIII, lauded the Franciscan rule.

News of Wadding's archival searches in Rome reached his contemporaries in Ireland, most notably the Protestant archbishop of Armagh, James Ussher. Thomas Strange, a cousin and confrère of Wadding, sent him a list of points that Ussher 'would have you doe for him by searching the Vaticane'.[31] Records for the year 1073 were the starting point for such research: 'The Romaene register having begunne in Gregorius 7 time, [where] you may find in the registers all what may concerne our country scince that time but not before'.[32] Ussher also enlisted the help of David Rothe, Catholic bishop of Ossory, who wrote to Wadding requesting copies of twelfth-century documents from the papacy of Eugenius III and the canonisation process of Archbishop Richard Creagh of Armagh, which Wadding had found in the Vatican.[33] Not to be outdone, Patrick Comerford asked his cousin, Luke, about sources relating to ecclesiastical revenues and ancient endowments for church property. Comerford was 'persuaded that in the records of the Vatican a man might finde in the original letters [...] all the veritie of this matter'.[34]

29 Mooney, 'The Writings of Father Luke Wadding OFM', 236–37.

30 Ibid; Fernand Combaluzier, 'Sacres episcopaux a Rome de 1565 à 1662. Analyse intégrale du Ms. Miscellanea XIII, 33 des Archives Vaticanes', *Sacris Erudiri*, 18 (1967–8), 120–30.

31 Jennings, ed, *Wadding Papers*, 280–1.

32 Ibid.

33 Aubrey Gwynn, 'Archbishop Ussher and Father Brendan O Conor', in *Father Luke Wadding Commemorative Volume*, 271–3.

34 Jennings, ed, *Wadding Papers*, 489–90.

Salvation History

Whilst in Portugal, Wadding began to study the life of St Francis in detail. As the initial impulse for the order came from Assisi, he consulted the library in the birthplace of St Francis and home of the order. The Irish friar's move to Italy paved the way for further investigation and he travelled to various towns and cities with the purpose of studying manuscripts. Consequently, for the first time, Wadding published a detailed edition of the works of St Francis.[35] Two years later, the first volume of the first edition of his *Annales Minorum* treated of events from the birth of the saint to the year 1250. Rather than regarding Francis as just another saint, the Friars Minor saw him 'as a sign of the final age, as one sent by God'.[36] In 1625 and 1628, Wadding demonstrated that Francis had 'a very precisely determined and unexchangeable place within an exactly delimited line of salvation history'.[37] This idea of *angelus ascendens ab ortu solis* formed the basis of the Bonaventurian theology of history. Therefore, Wadding's theological understanding of Francis was from the Book of the Apocalypse, where the Angel 'ascends from the rising of the sun with the seal of the living God'.[38] This stemmed from Bonaventure's *Quaestiones disputatae* of 1255 and from his *Legenda maior*.[39]

The twelfth-century Cistercian abbot, Joachim of Fiore, advocated that an order of barefoot clergy would be the harbingers of a third age of the Holy Spirit in the thirteenth century.[40] This made a deep impression on

35 See Regis Armstrong, J. A. Wayne Hellmann and William Short, *Francis of Assisi. Early Documents*, 3 vols (New York: New City Press, 1999), vol. 1, 37.

36 Joseph Ratzinger, *The Theology of History in St Bonaventure*, translated by Zachary Hayes OFM (repr. Chicago: Franciscan Herald Press, 1989), 33–34, 179–80.

37 Ibid.

38 Ibid, 179. Apoc. 7:2, 'Then I saw another angel come up from the East, holding the seal of the living God. He cried out in a loud voice to the four angels who were given power to damage the land and the sea'.

39 Ibid: 'The angel with the seal of the living God'.

40 William J. Short, 'Early Franciscan Sources and Joachite Prophetic Sources in the Book of Conformities', in Michael F. Cusato, Timothy Johnson, Steven McMichael, eds, *Ordo et Sanctitas: The Franciscan Spiritual Journey in Theology and Hagiography:*

many Franciscan friars and influenced the historical consciousness of the Cistercians. To preserve the unity of the Friars Minor, Bonaventure made Joachim's Old Testament exegesis his own.[41] Wadding regarded Joachim as essential to understanding Franciscan beliefs and practices, a point made clear at intervals in the first four volumes of the *Annales Minorum*.

In 1619, Wadding stayed at the great friary of St Francis in Assisi.[42] The *Laudes Dei* manuscript, dictated by Francis to Friar Leone, was much revered at Assisi's *Sacro Convento* where it was preserved in a reliquary. In the upper margin, Friar Leone had added a note, which clearly dated the source, 'two years before he died in Lent in the place of the mountain La Verna'.[43] Wadding later wrote, 'I saw it myself in 1619, and carefully observed it'.[44] He took the opportunity to transcribe the manuscript. Immediately after the *Laudes Dei*, Francis wrote the blessing of Friar Leone. Wadding published both, albeit separately, in his *Opuscula* four years later.[45] In Assisi, Wadding also examined a papal bull for the confirmation of the Franciscan rule and a copy of the rule written by Francis in his own hand.[46] Thomas of Celano's *First Life of St Francis* was known to Wadding and, during his visit to Assisi, he studied the Legend of the Three Companions, a biography of St Francis written by three of his followers, namely Leone, Rufino and Angelo.[47]

A Festschrift in Honor of J. A. Wayne Hellmann, OFM Conv. (Leiden: Brill, 2017), 251–71.

41 Ibid.

42 Wadding, *Opuscula*, 492; 'quam ego anno 1619 in Conventu Assisiensi'.

43 Ibid, 101: 'Beatus Franciscus duobus annis ante mortem suam fecit quadragesimam in loco montis Alvernae'.

44 Ibid. 'Eam ipse vidi anno 1619, diligentiusque observavi'.

45 Wadding, *Opuscula*, 101, 492. See also Solanus Benfatti, 'The Testimonies of Brother Leo Pertaining to La Verna and the Stigmata of Francis of Assisi', in Mario Panconi and Andreea Chiricheş, eds, *Studi Francescani*, 121 (2024), 395–412: 396–397.

46 *Annales Minorum*, vol. 1 (1223), 78, n. 25.

47 John R. H. Moorman, *The Sources for the Life of S. Francis of Assisi* with a foreword by A. G. Little (Manchester: Manchester University Press, 1940), 3–4.

St Clare of Assisi

In Umbria, popular devotion never separated remembrance of St Francis from that of St Clare.[48] Wadding paid due attention to the life of Clare in his studies. In 1625, he described the life and rule of the Poor Clares at length.[49] Wadding noted the education of Clare and her piety at an early age, her humility and gift for healing, her followers notable for their sanctity and their convent at San Damiano.[50] On a visit to the Poor Clare church of St George in Assisi, Wadding saw a poultice still in use that Clare first made for Francis to relieve the pain of the wound in his side and, 'by the same virgin's industry, shoes so as to cover the upper part of his feet' so that the stigmata were not seen.[51] The lower part of the foot was also raised high enough to ensure that the wounds did not hinder his step at all. In later years, the English Poor Clares at Aire-sur-la-Lys translated extracts from the *Annales*, which they published in the Habsburg Netherlands.[52]

48 Paul Sabatier, *Life of St Francis* (New York: Charles Scribner, 1894), 147.

49 *Annales Minorum*, vol. 1 (1224), 88–96, n. 1–12.

50 For more on the life of St Clare, see *Annales Minorum*, 1 (1221), 26–27, n. 31; *Annales Minorum*, 1 (1226), n. 42; *Annales Minorum*, vol. 1 (1247), 189, n. 43.

51 *Annales Minorum*, vol. 1 (1224), 106, n. 18: 'In Ecclesia Sancti Georgij Clarissarum Assisij vidi adhuc feruari quoddam genus cataplasmatis, seu emplastri vulgo Italico antiquo, camocium dictum, quod ad leniendum lateralis plage dolorem & sanguinem retinendum viro sancto fecit virgo sanctissima Clara; similiter & calceos, eiusdem virginis industria ita factos, vt superiorem pedum partem ne videretur, cooperirent, & inferiorem ita à terra eleuarent, vt prominentes clauorum cuspides greslum non omnino impedirent'.

52 *The history of the angelicall virgin glorious S. Clare dedicated to the Queen's most excellent majesty. Extracted out of the R.F. Luke Wadding his Annalls of the Freer Minors chiefly by Francis Hendricq and now donne into English. By Sister Magdalen Augustine, of the holy order of the Poore Clarcs [sic] in Aire* (Douai: Martin Bocart, 1635). See John McCafferty, 'History of St Clare', in Edel Bhreathnach and Bernadette Cunningham, eds, *Writing Irish History: The Four Masters and their World* (Dublin: Wordwell, 2007), 113.

Further Travels in Italy

Wadding continued along the Umbrian valley – a day's journey at the time – to the nearby town of Perugia where early Franciscan manuscripts were kept at the friary of San Francesco al Prato.[53] St Francis had been held captive in Perugia and, after his conversion, spent time in the hilltop town during the final years of Innocent III's papacy. Blessed Giles, one of Francis' disciples, was buried in the friary where relics of the order were stored in the sacristy: the hood from the habit of Blessed Giles and that of Pascal Baylon, together with Bernardino of Siena's walking stick.[54]

Apart from Umbria, Wadding visited Piceno in the Marche region, Transpadana in northern Lombardy, as well as Tuscany. In doing so, he collected several codices of manuscripts before 'plucking up the strength and courage to investigate the preceding centuries, and bring our whole history together in several volumes'.[55] Returning to central-southern Italy, Wadding found further material at Ara Coeli. In Naples, he discovered the *Vita* of James of the Marches in manuscript.[56] Buried in the Franciscan church of Santa Maria La Nova, James of the Marches was venerated among the patron saints of Naples and beatified in 1624.[57] Wadding subsequently

53 Harold, *Vita Fratris Lucae Waddingi*, 19.

54 Donal Cooper, '"Qui Peruse in Archa Saxea Tumulatus": The Shrine of Beato Egidio in San Francesco Al Prato, Perugia', *PBSR*, 69, Centenary Volume (2001), 223–44.

55 *Annales Minorum* (1st edn, Lyon: Claude Landry, 1625), vol. 1, Address to the Reader, unpaginated: 'Umbriam, Picenum, Tusciam & Lombardiam Transpadanam, collectis pluribus codicibus MSS. et aliunde transmissis aliis, vires et animum assumpsi ad anteriora saecula lustranda, et pluribus voluminibus universam historiam ad nostra'.

56 Francis Harold, ed, *Epitome annalium ordinis minorum* (Romae: Ex typographia Nicolai Angeli Tinassii, 1662), 19; Harold, *Vita Fratris Lucae Waddingi*, 19. For further details, see pages 174–176 of the present work.

57 Jean-Michel Sallman, *Naples et ses saints à l'âge baroque, 1540–1750* (Paris: Presses universitaires de France, 1994), 46. The Capuchin reform began in the Marches province of Italy and led to the sixteenth-century division of the Franciscan order.

Figure 4.1 Frontispiece of *B.P. Francisci assisiatis opuscula: nunc primum collecta, tribus tomis distincta, notis et commentariis asceticis illustrata* (Antwerp, 1623). Reproduced by kind permission of UCD Library Special Collections.

sent Irish friars to preach and study in the city before their return to Rome.[58] Two decades later, he brought the manuscript to print, of which more anon.

On the Writings of St Francis

Wadding began publishing Franciscan works in earnest from 1623.[59] His first books appeared in the Habsburg Netherlands and his experience of new technology shows how various printing techniques facilitated the creation of visual images.[60] Finely engraved illustrations kept printing houses in the Low Countries to the forefront of the book market for Spain and Italy.[61] While living on Rome's Janiculum hill at the friary of San Pietro in Montorio, Wadding commissioned Balthasar Moretus I of Antwerp to print in quarto the writings of St Francis.[62] Wadding needed a trusted corrector at the printing press to consult the text. At that time, an Irish typefounder named 'Thomas Strong' was employed at the Moretus workshop.[63] There is a strong possibility that this was Wadding's cousin and confrère Thomas Strange of Waterford.

58 Luke Wadding, ed, *Vita et res gestae B. Jacobi Piceni, per Johan Baptist Petruccium* (Lyon: Laurent Durand, 1641), 57; Cleary, *Father Luke Wadding and St Isidore's College*, 80, 82–83, 100, 130.

59 Luke Wadding, *B.P. Francisci assisiatis opuscula: nunc primum collecta, tribus tomis distincta, notis et commentariis asceticis illustrata...* (Antwerp: Balthasar Moretus I, 1623).

60 This section of the chapter is an updated and improved version of my essay, 'Illustration and Ornamentation in the Works of Luke Wadding, Seventeenth-Century Historian and Theologian', in Alexander Wilkinson and Alejandra Ulla Lorenzo, eds, *Typography, Illustration and Ornamentation in the Early modern Iberian Book World* (Leiden: Brill, 2020), 350–71.

61 Lucien Febvre and Henri-Jean Martin, *The Coming of the Book: The Impact of Printing, 1450–1800*, translated by David Gerard (London: Verso, 1976), 100–101.

62 Carl Van de Velde, 'Lucas Wadding. *B.P. Francisci Assisiatis opvscvla. Antverpiae, ex officina Plantiniana apud Balthasarem Moretum, et viduam Ioannis Moreti, et Io. Meursium*, 1623', in Karen Lee Bowen and Dirk Imhof, eds, *The Illustration of Books Published by the Moretuses* (Antwerp: Plantin-Moretus Museum, 1997), 142–43.

63 Dermot McGuinne, 'Irish Types in Europe', *Gutenburg Jahrbuch*, 82 (2007), 169–70.

Wadding's *Opuscula* was the first complete and annotated edition. Popular editions without the commentaries were printed at Salamanca, Alessandria della Paglia, Naples, Cologne and elsewhere.[64] As stated earlier, Wadding had started the research for this book in Portugal. The Friars Minor ranked their founder among the Church Fathers because of the influence he exerted on Christian tradition in the Middle Ages.[65] The *Opuscula* honoured the saint. Wadding dedicated the book to Antonio de Trejo, bishop of Cartagena and legate of the embassy, who defrayed the cost of publication on behalf of the Franciscans. The Waterford friar also paid tribute to Cardinal Gabriel de Trejo, a Franciscan tertiary, with a commendatory epistle that depicted Moses with the Israelites in the desert gathering manna from heaven.[66]

The frontispiece of Wadding's *Opuscula* illustrates how architecture influenced the composition of contemporary engravings.[67] The design resembles a stage set for a state entry.[68] The subjects are drawn from the hagiography of Francis and from the rule for his religious order.[69] At the apex of an open pediment, the saint is portrayed half-length in an aureole. He holds a crucifix in his left hand and the palm of martyrdom in his right. Although St Francis did not die a martyr's death, his early biographers equated his mission and stigmatisation with martyrdom.[70] The coat of arms of the Order of Friars Minor is displayed at the centre of the design with garlands suspended in a curve between the scrolls. The visual narrative here appears to be inspired by previous artworks. Two heralds, each with a trumpet of fame, rest upon spiral scrolls at either side. According to current research, Pieter Paul Rubens produced very

64 Cleary, *Father Luke Wadding and St Isidore's College*, 54.

65 Paschal Robinson, *The Writings of Saint Francis of Assisi* (Philadelphia: Dolphin Press, 1905), xi.

66 Wadding, *Opuscula*, iii.

67 Philip Hofer, *Baroque Book Illustration: A Short Survey from the Collection in the Department of Graphic Arts* (Cambridge, MA: Harvard College Library, 1951), 5–9.

68 Van de Velde, 'Lucas Wadding', 142. See Figure 4.1.

69 See William Cook, 'The Early Italian Representations of Francis of Assisi', in Xavier Seubert and Oleg Bychkov, eds, *Beyond the Text: Franciscan Art and the Construction of Religion* (Saint Bonaventure NY: Franciscan Institute, 2013), 1–12.

70 Isabelle Heullant-Donat, 'Martyrdom and identity in the Franciscan order (thirteenth and fourteenth centuries)', *Franciscan Studies*, 70 (2012), 429–453.

similar images of putti in the frontispiece he designed for the *Vita Beati P. Ignatius Loiolae* printed in 1609.[71] Four prominent Franciscans – Saints Anthony of Padua, Bonaventure, Bernardino of Siena and Louis IX – are incorporated into the central space. On either side, the title is bounded by pillars with Corinthian capitals. Illustrations of key events from the life of St Francis are inscribed with biblical verses to demonstrate how the Franciscan order was foreshadowed in scripture.

Frontispieces provided an excellent means to summarise the themes within a book. Although the friars would only have read a small proportion of the existing literature, they could examine the illustrations included in works more easily.[72] Above fluted pillars, on the left, Francis is shown preventing the collapse of the Lateran Basilica: *In vita sua suffulsit domuum* (Eccles. 30). The image here is modelled after examples referencing Giotto. On the right, the saint is supporting the chapel of San Damiano: *Confortabo domum Iuda* (Zach. 10:6). The base of each pillar contains a depiction of Francis after his death. On the left, he looks out from a semicircle of clouds with his hands raised and is revered by humanity: *Omnis terra adoret te* (Psalm 65:4). On the right, the saint is meeting Jesus: *In signaculum similitudinis meae* (Ezekiel 28). Between the bases of the pillars, the Trejo family crest is placed beneath a flat, wide-brimmed episcopal hat with six tassels on each side.

The *Opuscula* revisited several themes from a frontispiece published by Wadding in 1621, that is, the Concordance of Hebrew scriptures of Mario de Calasio.[73] Both feature St Francis, putti and four figures standing before columns with accompanying imagery. Nevertheless, the result

71 Van de Velde, 'Lucas Wadding', 143. *Vita Beati P. Ignatii Loiolae Societatis Iesu fundatoris* (Rome: s.n., 1609). Rubens and Balthasar Moretus I were childhood friends and worked together to ensure that book decoration flourished at the printing works.

72 MacMahon and McCafferty, 'The Wadding Library of Saint Isidore's College Rome, 1622–1700', 113.

73 *Concordantiae Sacrorum Bibliorum Hebraicorum: in quibus Chaldicae, etiam Librorum Esdae, & Danielis suo loco inseruntur: deinde post Thematum seu Radicum omnia derivata & usus latius deducta; ac linguarum Chaldaicae, Syriacae et Arabicae, vocabulorumque Rabbinicorum cum Hebraicis convenientiam: Latina ad verbum versio adiungitur, ad quam Vulgatae, et Septuaginta editionum differentia fideliter expenditur*, 4 vols (Rome: Stefano Paulino, 1621).

is clearer and better organised in the *Opuscula*. Wadding learnt Hebrew at Alba de Tormes and prefixed a treatise on the subject to the Concordance. With permission from Paul V and funding from his superiors in Rome, Wadding obtained Hebrew type.[74] The Concordance explains where given words occur in the Hebrew Bible and presents the earliest extant Greek and Latin translations while noting their relationship to Chaldean, Syriac, and Arabic.[75]

Carl Van de Velde has cited earlier frontispieces as possible sources for Wadding's books. The central figure of the saint with two putti was notably conveyed in 1614 by Cornelis van der Steen in *Commentaria in omnes D. Pauli epistolas*. In common with the 1615 *Vitae patrum* of Heribert Rosweyde, the Concordance and *Opuscula* have pilasters and bases covered with illustrations.[76]

The *Opuscula* design was engraved by Hans Collaert and noted in the account book of Balthasar Moretus I. On 30 December 1622, Collaert received the sum of four guilders 'for the engraving of the print'.[77] The same sum was paid to Ferdinand Arsenius for making the inscriptions. However, the actual design of the frontispiece does not appear to be recorded. The frontispiece of Rosweyde's *Vitae patrum* was engraved by Cornelis Galle after his own drawings. A master engraver, Galle was an accomplished painter who worked with Rubens, perhaps the most famous Baroque artist to produce iconographic frontispieces and title pages.[78] The similarity in style between the *Vitae patrum* of Rosweyde and the *Opuscula* makes it probable that both designs were the work of the same person.[79]

After the first volume of the *Annales Minorum* appeared in 1625, Wadding regularly entered into agreement with Lyonnais printers who

74 Harold, *Vita Fratris Lucae Waddingi*, 25; cited by Mooney, 'The Writings of Father Luke Wadding OFM', 235.

75 James Weinheimer, 'Finding Calasio: Princeton's Library Catalogs, 1760–1966', *PULC*, 58 (1996), 32–56.

76 Van de Velde, 'Lucas Wadding', 143.

77 Ibid.

78 J. Richard Judson and Carl Van de Velde, *Book Illustrations and Title Pages* (Corpus Rubenianum Ludwig Burchard, XXI), 1–2 (London: Miller/Philadelphia: Heyden, 1978), 170–173.

79 Van de Velde, 'Lucas Wadding', 143.

exported to Spain.[80] Between 1628 and 1642, the *Opuscula* design was published with minor changes in volumes two, three, four and five of the *Annales*.[81] As Wadding was on good terms with successive Spanish officials at the papal court, he dedicated the third volume of the *Annales* to Fernando Enríquez de Ribera, duke of Alcalá, the fourth volume to the marquis of Castel Rodrigo, and the eighth to Philip IV.[82] Heraldry was one of Castel Rodrigo's abiding interests and his coat of arms was emblazoned on his dedicatory epistle.[83]

As historian of his religious order, Wadding received the full support of the Friars Minor to bring publications to print.[84] Ornamentation edified the *Opuscula* which consists of more than 600 pages. The main contents are the testament, letters and prayers of the saint, and the Franciscan *regulae*.[85] These are followed by the *Vita Christi* ascribed to St Bonaventure, an anonymous *Fama postuma* of St Francis, and the *Contemplatio Lyrani de gestis B. Francisci*.[86] Wadding introduced each of these writings with his own commentaries. Therefore, we find the advice of St Francis to his friars where he warned them: 'Let us pay attention, all brothers, to the good shepherd, who endured his passion and the cross for the salvation of his sheep. The Lord's sheep followed him in tribulation and persecution and shame, hunger and thirst, in weakness and temptation, and other

80 Hazard, 'Correspondence from Jean-Baptiste Devenet and Claude Prost, Book Merchants of Lyon, to Fr. Luke Wadding OFM', 524.

81 Wadding, *Annales Minorum* (1st edn, Lyon, 1628–42), vols 1–5.

82 Carroll, *Exiles in a global city*, 137.

83 Hazard, 'Saint Isidore's Franciscan College, Rome: from Centre of Influence to Site of Memory', in Recio Morales, ed, *Redes y espacios de poder de la comunidad irlandesa en España y la América Española*, 109.

84 Mary Ann Lyons, 'Foreign Language Books, 1550–1700', in Andrew Hadfield and Raymond Gillespie, eds, *The History of the Irish Book* (Oxford: Oxford University Press, 2005), III, 363.

85 On the daily prayer of St Francis imparted by Wadding in the *Opuscula*, see Benedikt Mertens, 'Philothea's Pilgrimage to Perfection: Vernacular Franciscan Spirituality in a 17th-Century Retreat Manual Written by John Cross', in Michael F. Cusato and Steven McMichael, *"Non enim fuerat Evangelii surdus auditor…" (1 Celano 22): Essays in Honor of Michael W. Blastic OFM on the Occasion of his 70th Birthday* (Leiden: Brill, 2020), 276.

86 Wadding, *Opuscula*, 525–26, 575–76.

things'.[87] This directly reflects the teaching of the great defender of Francis, St Bonaventure, who wrote of the human suffering and weakness that Christ assumed in this life.[88]

The order imposed on the book by Wadding prioritised texts he attributed to the saint, followed by the rule to be observed for religious life, before dealing with the sources by other authors. In turn, Moretus gave the *Opuscula* a recognisable structure that alternates between ornate decoration and minimal adornment. Its historiated woodcuts relate specifically to the Franciscans and the Spanish mission of 1618. The design illustrates scenes from the life of Francis. For example, the testament of St Francis has an initial S for *Sanctus* five lines in depth.[89] It shows a friar carrying a questing sack and leaning on a cross-cut wood saw. This represented a friar-quaestor who begged food and firewood to help sustain a friary.[90] He is positioned facing into the text. Relying on providence was central to the Franciscan charism. The 1223 rule by St Francis stated that the friars were to work for the necessities in life, without taking money in return.[91] For brief discourses about St Clare of Assisi and St Anthony of Padua, Moretus assigned one woodcut initial to each. The vine and branches in the book's tailpieces symbolise Jesus and his disciples (John 15:5).[92]

87 Wadding, *Opuscula*, 74: 'Attendamus, omnes fratres, bonum pastorem qui pro ovibus suis salvandis crucis sustinuit passionem. Oves Domini secutae sunt eum in tribulatione et persecutione et verecundia, fame et siti, in infirmitate et tentatione et ceteris aliis'.

88 Noel Muscat, 'The Life of Saint Francis in the Light of Saint Bonaventure's Theology on the *Verbum crucifixium*', *Studia Antoniana cura Pontificii Athenei Antoniani edita*, 33 (Floriana, Malta: Edizzjoni Tau, 1989), 58–65.

89 Wadding, *Opuscula*, lv.

90 See Michael F. Cusato, 'The Gathering Storm: The Emergence of Evangelical Poverty as the Primary Descriptor for the Franciscan Charism (1220–50)', in Cusato and McMichael, eds, *"Non enim fuerat Evangelii surdus auditor…" (1 Celano 22)*, 119–66; Francis Cotter, *The Friars Minor in Ireland from Their Arrival to 1400* (St Bonaventure NY: Franciscan Institute, 1994), 52.

91 Wadding, *Opuscula*, 16, 138–39.

92 Ibid, 130, 283, 398, 575.

The ornamentation of books presented doctrine in a similar way to the decorative language that orators used in sermons.[93] For Moretus, the cornucopia symbolised abundance and intellect. In a historiated T for Tau at the start of the second section, a Franciscan priest is depicted saying Mass with a group of friars in attendance.[94] Moretus gave ornate initials to the approval of the first rule by Innocent III in 1209, Wadding's praise of the second rule and the life of the friars. The Poor Clares' rule for religious life is illustrated with a basket of flowers.[95] Most notably, perhaps, the first chapter about candidates entering the order shows a capital S with Samson and the lion, four lines in depth.[96] This was an analogy to the spirit of God overcoming sin (Judges 14:6), after Albrecht Dürer's Renaissance woodcut of the 1490s.[97]

A greater quantity of decoration resumes in the third section where the historiated T for Tau represents Jacob's Ladder with angels ascending the ladder to its cross beam.[98] As a hymn of praise, the Canticle of the Creatures, also known as the Canticle of the Sun, has a higher proportion of ornamentation than the more austere second section of the book. Wadding cast doubt on the authenticity of seven brief sermons of St Francis in an appendix to the *Opuscula* where, on page 508, the historiated N of *Nolvi* portrays the nativity of Jesus.

Wadding's collection of aphorisms assigned to St Francis has an historiated initial P. It shows St Paul seated, perusing the text referring to his conversion with a scroll in his lap and a sword resting on the back of his chair.[99] This adhered to the iconographical tradition that compared the experiences of Paul and Francis.[100] After the *finis* for the book, a salutation to Wadding from his superiors, and the approval of the censors, Moretus

93 Mark Morford, *Stoics and Neostoics: Rubens and the Circle of Lipsius* (Princeton: Princeton University Press, 2017), 182–3.

94 Wadding, *Opuscula*, 131.

95 Ibid, 133, 170, 185, 190.

96 Ibid, 223.

97 Sharon Gregory, *Vasari and the Renaissance Print* (Farnham: Ashgate, 2012), 164.

98 Wadding, *Opuscula*, 284.

99 Ibid, 422.

100 Rosalind Brooke, *The Image of St Francis: Responses to Sainthood in the Thirteenth Century* (Cambridge: Cambridge University Press, 2006), 218, 232.

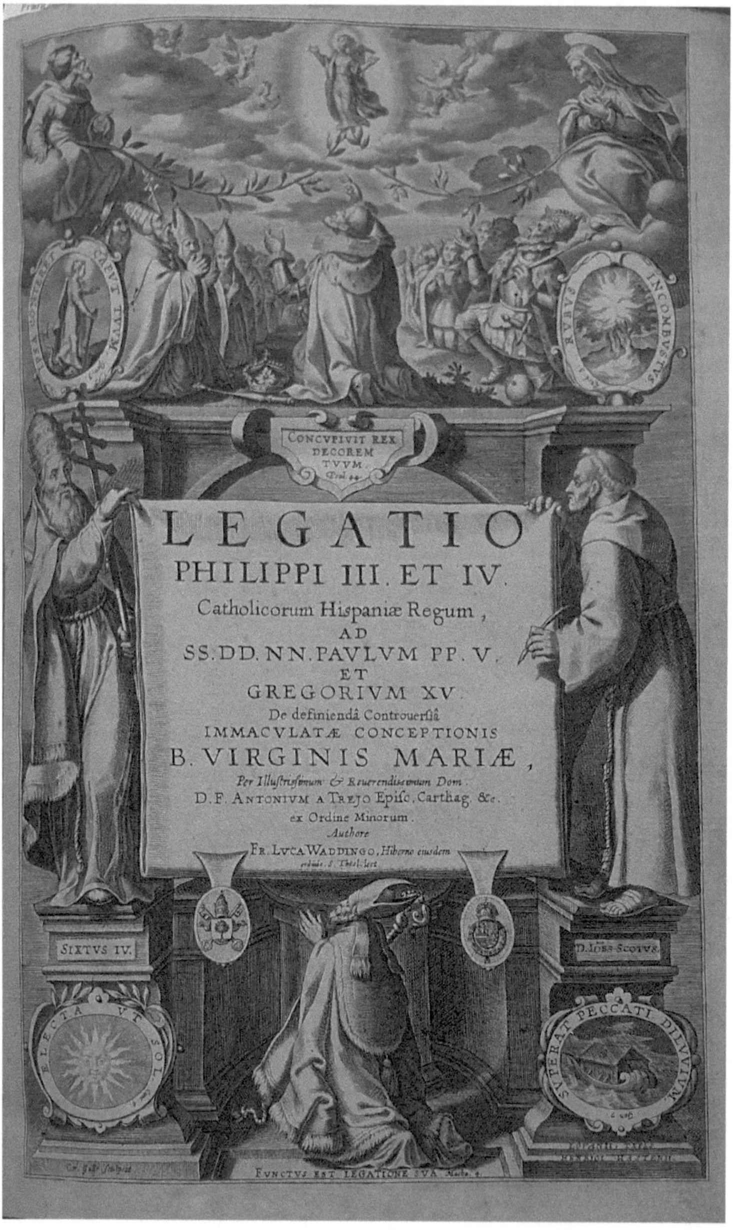

Figure 4.2 Frontispiece of *Presbeia sive legatio Philippi III. et IV.* (Leuven, 1624). Reproduced by kind permission of UCD Library Special Collections.

printed the royal privilege from Philip IV of Spain, followed by a colophon leaf and a large woodcut of the Plantin-Moretus device with their motto for hard work and perseverance, *Labore et Constantia.* In the following year, Wadding's report of the martyrdom of fourteen Franciscan friars in Prague was printed in Vienna. Wadding had sent the manuscript to his confrère, Jerome Strasser, to check the contents but Strasser published under his own name.[101]

On the Spanish legation to Rome

Before leaving Rome, Antonio de Trejo put in order all of his legation papers and entrusted them to Wadding. Their confrère, Flaithrí Ó Maolchonaire, persuaded Wadding to send him his report of the proceedings and the theological questions relating to the Spanish mission to Rome.[102] Therefore, the text appeared in print at Leuven in the Habsburg Netherlands where Ó Maolchonaire arranged to have the first edition printed in folio. Ó Maolchonaire's *Tractatus de statu parvulorum* was also accepted for publication that year. He chose the same printer, Hendrick van Hastens of Leuven, to print Wadding's work.[103] In tribute to the Immaculate and for the reputation of Spain, Count Maximilian Boxhorinckx, a financier and member of the council of Brabant, made it available in print. The design for the frontispiece was engraved by Cornelis Galle of the Antwerp school who signed the foot of the left column: 'Cor. Galle sculpsit'.[104] As stated above, Galle engraved the frontispiece of Rosweyde's *Vitae patrum* and worked with Rubens. Ó Maolchonaire arranged for Wadding's work to

101 Luke Wadding, *Illustre Martyrium XIV Fratrum Minorum ab Haereticis Bohemis Pragae pro Fide Catholica occisorum* (Vienna: Matthäus Formica, 1624); cited by Cleary, *Father Luke Wadding and St Isidore's College*, 13. See also *Scriptores ordinis minorum*, 492.

102 Harold, *Vita Fratris Lucae Waddingi*, 19.

103 Hazard, *Faith and Patronage*, 128.

104 Wadding, *Presbeia sive legatio*, Frontispiece. See Figure 4.2.

be read in St Anthony's College at mealtimes, and also made a gift of the book to the University of Leuven and to the council of Brabant.[105]

The period presided over by Philip III and his son was marked by the bold defence of Spanish monarchy. The doctrine of the Immaculate Conception – that Mary, as the mother of God, was free from original sin from the moment of her conception – was championed by successive Habsburg rulers in the sixteenth and seventeenth centuries. Although contentious, the Franciscans defended the doctrine and actively sought papal support for its definition. In 1616, Philip III assembled an administrative council of theologians in Madrid to consider the doctrine. Two years hence, Philip III sent Wadding with the legation to bring Spanish authority to bear at the Holy See but matters remained unresolved.

Presbeia sive legatio is evidence based, consisting of the collected letters and memorials of the matters discussed by the legation. In the eighth memorial, Wadding recorded that both words and pictures were clearly calculated to instruct.[106] Throughout the book, he referred to visual images and their copies with the following words: *imago*, *tabula*, *tabula picta*, and *effigies*.[107] Wadding explained that the Spanish theological mission proposed having a medal struck, with an image of Mary's conception on one side, surrounded by the inscription, 'From conception without original sin'.[108] They nevertheless decided that no image would appear on any kind of metal, with or without letters affixed to it, without the express permission of the pope. To Wadding's mind, the medals were 'laudable images' but he explained that Spanish hopes for papal approval and an indulgence from Paul V were declined.[109] The papacy refused to grant the concession because approval of the inscription could have been seen as an implicit dogmatic definition by Rome. Wadding narrated the episode of the medals because, during many centuries, it was allowed in churches to represent the Virgin Mary in the mystery of her conception,

105 Downey, 'Archbishop Florence Conry of Tuam', 97.

106 Ibid, 215: 'appositis verbis, vel accommodatis picturis, expresse et clare docet Mariam fuisse sine peccato conceptam'.

107 Ibid, 215, 296–297.

108 Ibid, 295–96: 'ex Concepta sine peccato originali'.

109 Wadding, *Presbeia sive legatio*, 296: 'laudibiles imagines'.

whereas the Spanish embassy was forbidden to set in words what was represented in painting or in stone.[110]

Set within a double border, the typographical title page begins with *πρεσβεία* in Greek capitals,[111] referring to the legation. In the book itself, the word is translated *Presbeia* in Latin. The 'description and elaboration' of the work by Wadding is recorded after the title which incorporates the name of Antonio de Trejo. Below a dividing line, between place and year of publication, Henrick van Hastens of Leuven announced that he was 'typographer to town and university' before referring to the royal privilege obtained from Philip IV.[112]

Engravings were more expensive to produce than woodcuts and often had to be printed separately on a special press.[113] Nevertheless, copper engraving made it possible to include far more detailed illustrations in printed books. The engraved frontispiece for Wadding's book provides an allegory of the Spanish legation. It occupies the whole page, and its contents show the interaction between temporal and spiritual authority. Divided into two levels, the 1624 frontispiece exemplifies how Baroque imagery exalted the absolute sovereign and portrayed Catholicism as triumphant. Two pillars support a celestial stage with Philip III at the centre. In reference to his role as leader of the Church militant, the king is shown in armour with the hilt of his sword showing but also wears ruff collar and fur-edged cloak. He kneels with Habsburg crown and sceptre beside him, in honour of the Virgin Mary. The depiction of the king resembles the bronze statue of Philip II in prayer that Pompeo Leoni produced for El Escorial in 1598.

110 Ibid, 294–308, 325–34.

111 Karl-Wilhelm Welwei, 'Presbeia, Presbeis', *Brill's New Pauly, Antiquity*, edited by Hubert Cancik and Helmuth Schneider, English edition by Christine Salazar, *Classical Tradition*, edited by Manfred Landfester, English edition by Francis Gentry, <http://dx.doi.org/10.1163/1574-9347_bnp_e1008130>, accessed 15 August 2024.

112 Henrick van Hastens also operated a press in Antwerp during the 1620s. His motto was 'Without hesitation I hasten' (*Cunctando proper*). See Els Stronks, *Negotiating Differences: Word, Image and Religion in the Dutch Republic* (Leiden: Brill, 2011), 180.

113 William Pettas, *A History and Bibliography of the Giunti (Junta) Printing Family in Spain 1526–1628* (New Castle DE: Oak Knoll Press, 2005), 82.

The iconography of the Immaculate was well established in the early seventeenth century and among the most popular themes of Spanish art.[114] Nevertheless, the image of Mary produced in the 1624 frontispiece is quite modest in comparison to the other protagonists shown.

Symmetry and winged putti were among the Baroque decorative models of Habsburg tradition.[115] Mary is raised up to heaven and guarded by five angels in the Wadding frontispiece of 1624. Seated on clouds are Joachim and Anna, the parents of Mary. Philip III looks towards the left, thus enabling recognition of his features. In the left foreground, Paul V kneels in approval with pontifical vestments and triple crosier. In his presence are cardinals in mitres, members of the clergy and at his shoulder what appears to be a Swiss Guard. To the right, on one knee, Philip III's grandfather, Charles V, wears the crown of Holy Roman Emperor and holds his sceptre. The emperor's antecedents kneel in the background.

In the introductory epistle to Philip IV of Spain, Wadding asserted that, since the foundation of their dynasty in 1273, the Habsburgs inherited the mantle of Christian rule from Constantine the Great and from Charlemagne.[116] It was also in the late thirteenth century that the Franciscan theologian, John Duns Scotus, known as the Subtle Doctor, defended the teaching of Immaculate Conception. Along with Thomas Aquinas and William of Ockham, he was one of the three most important thinkers in mediaeval philosophy and theology.[117] Scotus understood each person to be *imago Dei*, that is, the image and likeness of God.[118] The implication that the king was God's image, first portrayed in Christian

114 Suzanne Stratton, *The Immaculate Conception in Spanish Art* (Cambridge: Cambridge University Press, 1994), 100–102.

115 Paul Shore, 'A Unique Seventeenth-Century Rusyn Catechism and the Jesuit Connection', in Richard Kirwan and Sophie Mullins, eds, *Specialist Markets in the Early Modern Book World* (Leiden: Brill, 2015), 380.

116 Wadding, *Presbeia sive legatio*, unpaginated.

117 Thomas Williams, 'Introduction: The Life and Works of John Duns the Scot', in idem, ed, *The Cambridge Companion to Duns Scotus* (Cambridge: Cambridge University Press, 2003), 1–14.

118 Mary Beth Ingham, *The Harmony of Goodness: Mutuality and Moral Living according to John Duns Scotus* (New York: Franciscan Publications, 1996), 5–8.

historiography in the Life of Constantine by Eusebius, was preserved in manuscript images.[119]

An inscribed plaque beneath Philip III's feet is held in place by two stone clasps. It commemorates his commitment to the teaching of Immaculate Conception: 'The king has desired thy beauty' (*Concupivit rex decorum tuum*. Psalm 44:12). Ovals on either side continue the theme. Exegetical verses allude to Mary crushing the head of the serpent (*Ipsa Conteret Caput Tuum*. Gen. 3:15); and compare her with the burning bush unconsumed by fire (*Incombustus Rubus*. Exodus 3:2). Before the left column in the frontispiece stands the Franciscan Pope Sixtus IV. It recounts how, in 1476, he approved the feast of the Immaculate Conception.[120] An oval decorated with garlands appears at the base of the plinth bearing Sixtus IV, referring to Mary being as bright as the sun (*Electa ut Sol*) from the text of the breviary prayers. The aforementioned Duns Scotus stands to the right with pen in hand. The words inscribed on an oval below his plinth relate to the grace that abounded in Mary (*Superat Peccati Diluvium*). Both these Franciscan figures hold the title of Wadding's book, which is supported on three half columns. The scroll is sealed with the papal coat of arms and those of the Spanish Habsburgs. In front of the title scroll, Antonio de Trejo kneels with crozier, looking up at his own name. At his feet appears the inscription, *Functa Legatione Sua* (He fulfilled his mission).

An ornamented headpiece occurs at the start of the first section. It shows two-winged sea creatures. Each has a human head and torso, and the tail of a fish. At the centre of the ornament, they hold the Ouroboros symbol of a serpent biting its own tail which contains another sea creature.[121] Here text and image appear to have a parallel with Iberian seafaring and exploration. The text refers to Philip III and his son as 'most glorious monarchs' of a vast empire which encompassed religions, great cities and

119 Jacques Le Goff, 'Le roi dans l'Occident médiéval: caractères originaux', in Anne Duggan, ed, *Kings and kingship in medieval Europe* (London: Centre for Late Antique and Medieval Studies, 1993), 1–40. For later political implications, see Jeremy Larkins, *From Hierarchy to Anarchy: Territory and Politics before Westphalia* (Basingstoke: Palgrave, 2010), 76, 80, 85.

120 Cf. Antonie Vos, *The Theology of John Duns Scotus* (Leiden: Brill, 2018), 27–28.

121 Wadding, *Presbeia sive legatio*, 1.

communities.[122] The book closes with FINIS and a capital M for Mary is the focus of attention in the book's tailpiece.[123]

In keeping with his biblical work three years earlier, Wadding published the *Concordance of St. Anthony of Padua* in April 1624, dedicating it to Urban VIII. The book's contents incorporated the *Promptuarium morale*, assigned to an anonymous Irish friar of the late thirteenth century.[124] This attribution is supported by internal evidence with detailed entries on Irish saints such as Brigid, Columcille, Patrick, Columbanus, Malachy and Laurence O'Toole.[125] Moral concordances were texts that helped in the compilation of sermons with alphabetical listings for Sundays throughout the year and for feast days. Wadding explained that he discovered the source in an old manuscript codex in the library of Ara Coeli and that the edition was primarily intended for theologians and preachers.[126] He completed the book while living at San Pietro in Montorio.[127] The title page was illustrated with an engraving of St Anthony of Padua and the Christ Child in the top centre, watched over by eagles and putti on either side. The text on the title page appears between two pillars. These are decorated with sea creatures and scrolls above two ovals displaying, from left to right, the Franciscan symbol of the cross between the arm of Christ and the arm of St Francis, and the five wounds of Christ. In the lower half, to emphasise his loyalties, Wadding noted the permission of his superiors, next to Urban VIII's coat of arms charged with three Barberini bees, crested with the papal tiara and supported by the Petrine keys. At the foot of the page, the place of

122 Ibid, 1–2.

123 Ibid, 462.

124 Ó Clabaigh, *The Friars in Ireland*, 291.

125 A. B. Scott, 'Latin Learning and Literature in Ireland, 1169–1500', in Dáibhí Ó Cróinín, ed, *A New History of Ireland*. Vol. 1, *Prehistoric and Early Ireland* (Oxford: Oxford University Press, 2005), 973.

126 *S. Antonii de Padua Concordantiae morales sacrorum Bibliorum: miro ingenio, et optimo ordine dispositae: quibus accessit egregium Promptuarium S. Scripturae, anonymi cuiusdam Franciscani Hyberni, ad omnes festiuitates, et materias praedicatoribus, et theologis vtilissimum; nunc primum extracta ex MSS. Bibliothecae FF. Minorum Araecoli in Capitolio* (Romae: ex typographia Alphonsi Ciacconi, 1624).

127 Ibid, Dedicatory epistle, 'Ex Sancti Petri in Ianiculo, Kalendis Aprilis, Anno MDCXXIV'.

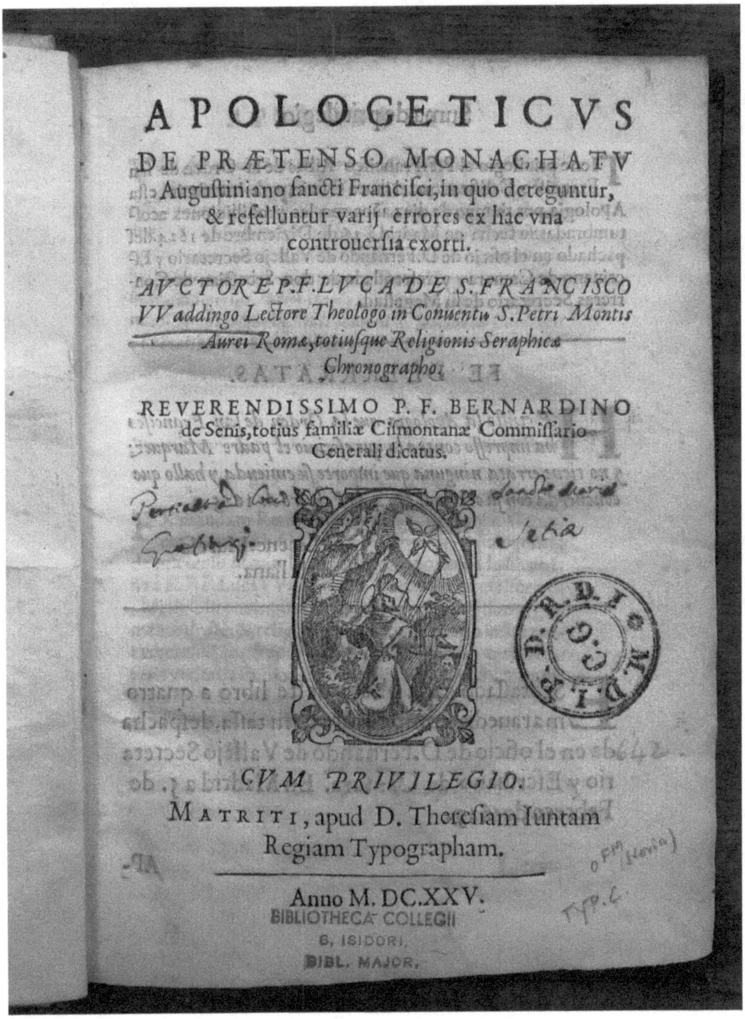

APOLOGETICVS
DE PRÆTENSO MONACHATV
Auguſtiniano ſancti Franciſci, in quo deteguntur, & refelluntur varij errores ex hac vna controuerſia exorti.

AVCTORE P.F. LVCA DE S. FRANCISCO VVaddingo Lectore Theologo in Conuentu S. Petri Montis Aurei Romæ, totiusque Religionis Seraphicæ Chronographo.

REVERENDISSIMO P. F. BERNARDINO de Senis, totius familiæ Ciſmontanæ Commiſſario Generali dicatus.

CVM PRIVILEGIO.

MATRITI, apud D. Thereſiam Iuntam Regiam Typographam.

Anno M. DC.XXV.

Figure 4.3 Title page of *Respuesta apologética contra los que pretenden aver sido N. P. S. Francisco frayle de los Ermitaños de S. Agustín* (Madrid, 1625). Reproduced by kind permission of Collegio S. Isidoro.

composition, Rome, was inscribed above the name of the printer, Alfonso Ciacconi, and the year marked in Roman numerals. The approbations were written in the previous year by Wadding's Franciscan confrères, Benigno da Genova, Hugh McCaghwell and Gaspar de la Fuente. The Irish theologian, John Roche, also gave his approval. Francisco Bivar, the Spanish Cistercian historian, and Nicolò Ridolphi, Dominican master of the sacred palace, provided the *imprimatur*. This combination of backgrounds reflects the intended readership among religious orders and secular clergy. In the same month that Wadding dedicated the book to the pope, Roche was appointed bishop of Ferns by Urban VIII.[128] As was so often the case with his publications, Wadding accompanied the text with his own copious notes.

On claims that St Francis was an Augustinian

We now come to a book produced for Wadding by the Imprenta Real, that is, the royal press in Madrid.[129] At that time, the Imprenta Real was located on the Carrera de San Francisco in the parish of San Andrés. This road connected the Puerta de Moros with the old Franciscan friary.[130] The founder of the royal press, Julio Junti de Modesti, was buried in the Franciscan habit in the adjoining church of San Francisco.[131] From 1618, his nephew, Tomás Junti, became royal typographer and printer to the king. Tomás died in 1624, and, on 26 December, Philip IV granted a *real cédula*

128 Patrick Corish, 'An Irish Counter-Reformation Bishop: John Roche, III', *ITQ*, 25/2 (1958), 118.

129 Alexander Wilkinson and Alejandra Ulla Lorenzo, eds, *Iberian Books Volumes II & III / Libros Ibéricos Volúmenes II y III: Books published in Spain, Portugal and the New World or elsewhere in Spanish or Portuguese between 1601 and 1650 / Libros publicados en España, Portugal y el Nuevo Mundo o impresos en otros lugares en español o portugués entre 1601 y 1650* (Leiden: Brill, 2015), 2404–2405.

130 Consolación Morales Barrero, *La imprenta real de Madrid desde su fundación hasta fines del siglo XVII* (Madrid: Artes Gráficas Municipales, 1976), 7.

131 Pettas, *A History and Bibliography of the Giunti (Junta) Printing Family in Spain*, 72, 76, 178.

to Teresa Junti, daughter and heiress of Julio Junti, widow of Tomás.[132] That year, Tomás Junti's houses were divided and the premises reduced only to the space for the press. Philip IV renewed the exemption first granted to Julio Junti, with the privilege for governmental and church printing in Latin and Spanish. The name Teresa Junta appeared on editions issued by the Imprenta Real for the next three years.[133] Exemplars of her work for the Augustinians, the Obregón Congregation, the Society of Jesus and the Trinitarians demonstrate that the coat of arms of each order was often the only emblem to feature on title pages.[134]

In his 1625 *Apologeticus*, Wadding refuted the erroneous claim that St Francis was originally an Augustinian hermit. This, perhaps, addressed the confusion caused when a direct contemporary of Francis, St Anthony of Padua, joined the Augustinians before becoming a Franciscan. In 1625, Pedro Navarro published a Spanish translation in Madrid.[135] Another work attributed to Navarro, *Apologia sobre que san Francisco no fue fraile Antonio* probably refers to his 1625 translation.[136]

132 Morales Barrero, *La imprenta real de Madrid desde su fundación hasta fines del siglo XVII*, 10.

133 Pettas, *A History and Bibliography of the Giunti (Junta) Printing Family in Spain*, 77. On the use of her own name on the title pages of Imprenta Real works, see Alejandra Ulla Lorenzo, 'Women and the Iberian book trade, 1472–1650', in Alexander Wilkinson and Alejandra Ulla Lorenzo, eds, *A Maturing Market: The Iberian Book World in the First Half of the Seventeenth Century* (Leiden: Brill, 2017), 76.

134 Juan Márquez, *El gobernador cristiano, deducido de las vidas de Moysen y Jesucristo* (Madrid, En la Imprenta Real, Por doña Teresa Junta, impressora del Rey N. S., 1625); Andrés Fernández Truyols, ed, *Instruccion de enfermeros para aplicar los remedios a todo genero de enfermedades y acudir a muchos accidentes que sobreuienen en ausencia de los medicos* (Madrid, por Teresa Junta y en la Imprenta Real, 1625); Bernardino de Villegas, *La esposa de Christo instruida con la vida de santa Lutgarda, virgen, monja de san Bernardo* (Madrid: en la Imprenta Real por Teresa Junta, 1625); Hortensio Félix Paravicino, *Panegyrico Funeral* (Madrid, por Teresa Junta, 1625); Hortensio Félix Parvicino, *Epitafios o Elogios funerales al Rey don Felipe III el Piadoso* (Madrid, Teresa Iunti, 1625).

135 Luke Wadding, *Respuesta apologética contra los que pretenden aver sido N. P. S. Francisco frayle de los Ermitaños de S. Agustín* (Madrid, En la Imprenta Real, Por doña Teresa Junta, impressora del Rey N. S., 1625).

136 *Apologia sobre que san Francisco no fue fraile Antonio* (Madrid, n. d., 1625).

Large friaries kept several book collections for the sacristy, the refectory, the reference collection and the communal library.[137] Printing made gathering books easier and the Imprenta Real found a ready export market in missions to the New World. To provide for demand, book merchants from Seville and the port cities of Spain were based in Madrid, as were representatives from Antwerp, France and Italy.[138] In earlier centuries, the Franciscans regarded excessive decoration as a sign of opulence and idle curiosity. The ornamentation of the *Apologeticus* and its translation was, therefore, in keeping with the Franciscan ideal of 'unadorned simplicity'.[139] The title-page woodcut for these texts relates directly to the subject. After a lengthy Baroque title, both are illustrated with a vignette of St Francis receiving the stigmata from a seraphic angel in flight. Again, the orientation of the image clearly referenced the painting of Giotto. According to Pettas, the woodcut measures 55x40cm.[140] Woodcuts of St Francis marked with the stigmata, that is, the five marks of the Crucifixion, appeared on numerous title pages and became the most recognised image of the saint.[141] Indeed, the visible signs of stigmatisation were understood to instruct and strengthen remembrance of the event. This inspired devotion in readers who recognised a familiar theme and, therefore, felt an affinity with it.[142] Printers made repeated use of woodcut material.[143] The vignette of St

137 K. W. Humphreys, *The Friars' Libraries* (London: British Library, 1990), xix.

138 Cristóbal Pérez Pastor, 'Impresores y libreros de Madrid. Documentos referentes a ellos', *Memorias de la Real Academia Española* (1926), 374, 384, 391.

139 Lotte Hellinga, *Texts in Transit: Manuscript to Proof and Print in the Fifteenth Century* (Leiden: Brill, 2014), 373.

140 Pettas, *A History and Bibliography of the Giunti (Junta) Printing Family in Spain*, 851–853.

141 MacMahon and McCafferty, 'The Wadding Library of Saint Isidore's College Rome, 1622–1700', 114. On the significance of the stigmatisation and other aspects of Franciscan iconography, see Pamela Askew, 'The Angelic Consolation of St Francis of Assisi in Post-Tridentine Italian Painting', *Journal of the Warburg and Courtauld Institutes*, 32 (1969), 280–306.

142 Jill Bennett, 'Stigmata and Sense Memory: St Francis and Affective Memory', *Art History*, 24 (2001), 1–16.

143 José Manuel Aznar Grasa, 'La ilustración del libro impreso en Salamanca: Siglos XV y XVI', in Pedro Manuel Cátedra García and María Luisa López-Vidriero Abello, eds, *El libro antiguo español: actas del Segundo Coloquio Internacional,*

Francis had special significance for the Franciscans at that time. Writing in Wadding's *Opuscula*, Gabriel de Trejo related that the 'feast of the stigmata of St Francis, previously celebrated only by Franciscans, was extended to the universal church' in 1614.[144]

Friends, Romans, Countrymen

Wadding recorded that his confrère, Patrick Fleming, searched 'the chief libraries of Italy, France, the Habsburg Netherlands and Germany' in search of the Lives of Irish Saints.[145] For three years from 1623, Fleming taught in Rome. Whilst there, he compiled historical research with help from Luke Wadding who obtained access to libraries, located source material, transcribed and translated manuscripts for him.[146] Wadding advised Fleming to record where he found each of his sources, 'for the greater credibility of history', as Wadding told him that he did the same in his writings.[147]

From the 1620s, as well as being chronicler of his religious order, Wadding served as *consultor* to several congregations and commissions in the papal bureaucracy, the curia. This experience was fundamental for his future understanding of ecclesiastical office. Through his involvement in these activities, Wadding became more accustomed with Roman ways. First,

---

Madrid (Salamanca & Madrid: Ediciones de la Universidad de Salamanca, Biblioteca Nacional de Madrid, Sociedad Española de Historia del Libro, 1992), 61–95.

144 Wadding, *Opuscula*, xxxix–xl; cited by Mooney, 'The Writings of Father Luke Wadding OFM', 239.

145 *Scriptores ordinis minorum*, 182: 'Lustratis praecipuis Italia, Gallie, Belgij, & Germania Bibliothecis'. This corresponds to Fleming's research in Rome, the province of Piacenza, Wallonia and Bavaria.

146 Fleming to Ward, 24 August 1624 (Jennings, ed, 'Part IV: Documents from the Archives of St Isidore's', 215), 'Lovanium prae aliis locis maxime diligo, praesertim quando pro Sanctis tecum laborandum esset'.

147 Fleming to Ward, Rome, 22 July 1623 (Jennings, ed, 'Part IV: Documents from the Archives of St Isidore's', 204) 'Vide ut notes ex quo loco desumpsisti et ex qua bibliotheca quamlibet vitam, ad majorem historiae fidem, quia multum hoc refert, ut mihi dixit Pater Lucas, et ipse passim in suis scriptis idem facit'.

Paul V appointed him *consultor* to the Holy Office and later Gregory XV made him *consultor* to the Index. In this capacity, he was assigned to be a book censor between both congregations. More importantly, however, ecclesiastical matters relating to Ireland were regulated by the Holy Office before Propaganda Fide was created in 1622. Thus, Wadding was recognised as an expert on the resolution of questions relating to Ireland.[148] Urban VIII then named him *consultor* to Propaganda Fide. He also served as *quaresimalista*, Lenten preacher, for the papal household. This entailed working with the pope's Dominican theologian at the Apostolic Palace. As Wadding's experiences at the Franciscan chapters in Salamanca and Lisbon showed, he was capable of oratory and known for his eloquence. The classics were secondary to his command of scriptural and patristic sources for sermons delivered to the pope and college of cardinals in the papal chapel. The themes propounded by preachers at the curia emphasised Church teaching in relation to the opinions and beliefs of their hearers.[149]

As his role at the curia was to advise and assist the papacy, Wadding's commitment to papal primacy was unquestioned.[150] This was a significant development in his career when one considers his commitment to the Spanish Habsburgs. Since Innocent III gave his approbation to the rule in 1209, the Franciscans established a direct relationship with the pope. Both the Franciscans and Dominicans were protected by the supreme pontiff who they defended as vicar of Christ.[151] During this period, Wadding counted Cardinal Scipio Borghese, Paul V's nephew; Cardinal Giovanni Garzia Mellini, vicar general of Rome; and Scipione Cobelluzzi, the cardinal archivist, among his friends. These were soon followed by Urban VIII's nephews, Francesco and Antonio Barberini, who were both created

148 Jennings, ed, *Wadding Papers*, vii.

149 John W. O'Malley, 'Preaching for the Popes', in Charles Trinkaus and Heiko Oberman, eds, *The Pursuit of Holiness in Late Medieval and Renaissance Religion* (Leiden: Brill, 1974), 408–440.

150 Paolo Broggio, 'Un Teologo Irlandese nella Roma del Seicento: il francescano Luke Wadding', *Roma Moderna e Contemporanea*, 18 (2010), 153–154.

151 Christian Mouchel, *Rome franciscaine: essai sur l'histoire de l'éloquence dans l'Ordre des Frères Mineurs au XVIe siècle* (Paris: Champion, 2001), 324–25; Klaus Schatz, *Papal Primacy: From Its Origins to the Present* (Collegeville MN: Liturgical Press, 1996), 84.

cardinal, and Taddeo Barberini, another of Urban's nephews, who became prince of Palestrina and prefect of Rome; and with the two Ludovisi cardinals, Ludovico and Niccolò, and Prince Ludovisi, Ludovico's brother.[152]

Conclusion

While Spain was the great potentate of the Mediterranean when Wadding travelled to Rome, the Spanish legation taught him the limits of political power. In the record of his life, there is an evident connection between his interaction with long-standing institutions and his mission to safeguard memory. In addition to his loyalty to the papacy, the lasting bonds between Wadding and specific benefactors in Rome furthered the interests of St Isidore's College where he made his home in the coming decades. Wadding's presence in Rome provided him with access to a new network of relationships connected to cultural production. This enabled him to achieve distinction but also involved the demands of patrons who held him in high regard. This aspect of Wadding's everyday life is dealt with in more detail in the next chapter.

152 Jennings, ed, *Wadding Papers*, vii; Harold, *Vita Fratris Lucae Waddingi*, 80, 108, 143.

5 Powerhouse of Learning

Figure 5.1 St Isidore's Franciscan College, Rome. Reproduced by kind permission of Collegio S. Isidoro, Rome.

Introduction

1625 being a jubilee year, Rome was in celebration. In the spring, Benigno da Genova offered Wadding a new unfinished church and small friary on the Pincian hill in the city.[1] Wadding accepted and the college opened for

1 This chapter is a revised and updated version of my essay, 'Saint Isidore's Franciscan College, Rome: From centre of influence to site of memory', published in *Redes y Espacios de Poder de la Nación Irlandesa en España y la América Española, 1600–1825.*

the education of Franciscans for the mission to Ireland on 13 June, the feast of St Anthony of Padua.[2] As the Franciscan rule renounced the ownership of property, *Exiit qui seminat* decreed that the dominion over such property remained in the hands of the papacy.[3] The small church could seat approximately 100 people. Work had begun four years earlier when a group of discalced Spanish Franciscans obtained permission to build a house in Rome. They dedicated the church and friary to Isidore of Madrid who, along with Ignatius Loyola and Francis Xavier of the Society of Jesus, Teresa of Ávila, great reformer of Carmel in Spain, and Philip Neri, founder of the Oratory, was canonised on 12 March 1622 by Gregory XV.[4] This was the most remarkable canonisation celebration of the century, attended by a great multitude from Spain. The events led Romans to remark that 'the pope had canonised four Spaniards and a saint'.[5]

Religiously motivated exile is part of the confessional tradition of Catholics and Protestants across Europe.[6] Unlike their counterparts from Germany, England and Scotland, no institution existed in Rome exclusively for the reception of Irish exiles when Wadding arrived at the papal court.[7] From 1578 until 1689, a total of thirty-one continental colleges were

---

Power Strategies: Spain and Ireland, 1600–1825, ed Óscar Recio Morales (Valencia: Albatros Ediciones, 2012), 103–14.

2 McCafferty, 'Recycling an Island's Past for a Global Catholicism: Irish Franciscans in the Seventeenth Century', 64.

3 Ryan Thornton, *Franciscan Poverty and Franciscan Economic Thought, 1209–1348* (Leiden: Brill, 2023), 128–36; Moorman, *A History of the Franciscan Order*, 317.

4 David García Cueto, *'Seicento' Boloñés y Siglo de Oro Español: El Arte, la Época, los Protagonistas* (Madrid, Centro de Estudios Europa Hispánica, 2006), 81, 91–4, 107, 302.

5 Antonio Sicari, *Il Grande Libro dei Ritratti di Santi* (Milan: Jaca, 1997), 267: 'il Papa aveva canonizzato quattro spagnoli e un santo'.

6 Cf. Heinz Schilling, 'Christliche und Jüdische Minderheitengemeinden im Vergleich: Calvinistische Exulanten und westliche Diaspora der Sephardim im 16. und 17. Jahrhundert', *Zeitschrift für Historische Forschung*, 36/3 (2009), 407–44.

7 O'Connor, 'The Irish College, Rome, in the Age of Religious Renewal', 13–32; Fearghus Ó Fearghail, 'Irish Links with Santa Maria dell'Anima in Rome', *Seanchas Ard Mhacha*, 22 (2009), 25–50.

founded for the mission to Ireland.[8] The *studium* at St Isidore's was to become a major seat of learning.[9] In the mid-1620s, the Catholic mission to Ireland was largely inactive. As such, Wadding's first priority for the new college was the training of friars to serve in Ireland. As a house of regular observance, St. Isidore's sent well-trained preachers to the Irish mission field and served as a first-class school of theology. Benigno da Genova 'wished to live nowhere else [for] as long as it was permitted by the order, and finally to die and be buried there'.[10] In its original setting, therefore, St Isidore's offers the contemporary observer perhaps the best surviving example of these centres for learning and mission activity. Apart from two terms of partial occupation during the Napoleonic period, the college has remained in Franciscan hands.

Since the beatification of Isidore the Ploughman in 1619, he was also patron to the Spanish royal family which had advanced the cause for sainthood with the civil authorities in Madrid since the reign of Philip II.[11] To a certain extent, this was a time of renewal for the Franciscan houses of Rome where noble families earnestly supported ascetic reform. Wadding was directly responsible for such renewal and also for the completion of St Isidore's. The outcome of each papal election brought with it 'family and friends eager to establish their own positions and ready to invest money' in construction.[12] St Isidore's offers a clear example of such benefaction.

8 Enrique García Hernán, 'La Misión de Irlanda (1610–1628). Aproximación a una Nueva Investigación', in Alberto Marcos Martín, ed, *Hacer Historia desde Simancas. Homenaje a José Luis Rodríguez de Diego* (Valladolid, Junta de Castilla y León, 2011), 339–64.

9 Binasco, *Making, Breaking and Remaking the Irish Missionary Network*, 45–70.

10 Harold, *Vita Fratris Lucae Waddingi*, 17: 'Reverendissimus Pater Benignus a Genua [...] quam in Collegio sancti Isidori, deinceps dum per Ordinis gubernandi curam licebat vivere voluerit, ac denique mori et sepeliri'.

11 María José Del Río Barredo, *Madrid, Urbs Regia: La Capital Ceremonial de la Monarquía Católica* (Madrid: Marcial Pons, 2000), 83–118.

12 Giovanni Careri, 'The Artist', in Rosario Villari and Lydia Cochrane, eds, *Baroque Personae* (Chicago: University of Chicago Press, 1995), 300; Giovanni Careri and Ferrante Ferranti, *Baroques* (Paris: Citadelles & Mazenod, 2002), 33.

Ordinations to Holy Orders

On opening in 1625, almost all the staff and students at St Isidore's were from St Anthony's College, Leuven. Four years later, Wadding witnessed the first ordination in Rome of a Franciscan from St Isidore's, Patrick Cournane from Connacht.[13] The two colleges maintained strong links. Anthony Doherty, for instance, was called to Rome from Leuven in 1636 to pursue further studies in theology. He was ordained a priest at Rome the following year and went on to become Irish minister provincial.[14] Fifty-four Franciscans from St Isidore's were ordained in the quarter century from 1629 to 1654. In cases where ordinands can be recognised by their surnames, the numbers are evenly-balanced between Gaelic and Old English, with a slight majority in favour of Gaelic *alumni*. The province of Munster accounted for the largest cohort, followed by Leinster, Connacht and Ulster in that order. On the one hand, the lower numbers from the latter two provinces helps to explain the resentment that Wadding faced from certain quarters in those twenty-five years, but it also suggests a shortage of students from Connacht and Ulster.[15]

Immersed in a milieu of patronage

Patronage of the arts and architecture silently communicated and animated the ideas of the Counter-Reformation movement.[16] From the time of his arrival at the papal court, Wadding initially served the cause of the Immaculate for ten years. He commanded public respect in Rome, where a

13 Hugh Fenning, ed, 'Irishmen Ordained at Rome, 1572–1697', *Archiv. Hib.*, 59 (2005), 1–22; Bartholomew Egan, Cathaldus Giblin and Cuthbert McGrath, eds, 'Irish Students Ordained in Rome (1625–1710)', *IER*, 5th ser., 61 (1945), 116–124.

14 Ibid.

15 Ibid.

16 Francis Haskell, *Patrons and Painters: A Study in the Relations between Italian Art and Society in the Age of the Baroque* (New Haven: Yale University Press, 1980), 120.

good name helped secure an influential following.[17] To this end, collegians such as Antony Hickey emphasised the consistent high standards at St Isidore's.[18] Once established in the city, Wadding's own commissions to the arts made him a patron as well and his reputation increased through benevolence. The perpetuation of memory, culture, authority and tradition are interconnected.[19] In turn, sites of memory represent a symbolic element of heritage thereby serving a commemorative function of culture, such as landscapes and architecture, burial sites and monuments.[20] On this basis, parallels exist between the prominence of specific religious groups which depend on the effective memory of and accounts by their descendants.[21] Immersed as it was in a milieu of patronage, St Isidore's provides a case in point. This is evident both in the construction of the college that Wadding established, its early benefactors and the college's mission to Ireland, as seen from its archival collections.

The papal bull of foundation granted to Luke Wadding and his confrères stated that the discalced friars from Spain started a hospice in 1621 on ground donated by Ottaviano Vestri di Barbiano, a member of the Roman clergy and a knight of Calatrava.[22] Letters to and from Philip IV in the college records, now at University College Dublin, reveal much

17 Fathers of St Isidore's to Philip IV, Rome, 29 November 1628: 'Padre Guardian Fray Lucas de San Francisco [...] Ha servido estos 10 años en la causa de la limpia Concepción de la Virgen Señora'.

18 Antony Hickey, *Expostulates Bzovius; seu Nitela Franciscanae religionis et abstersio sordium quibus earn consfurcare frustra tentavit Abrahamus Bzovius* (Lyon: Claude Landry, 1627), Dedicatory epistle, unpaginated.

19 Aleida Assmann, *Cultural Memory and Western Civilization: Functions, Media, Archives* (Cambridge: Cambridge University Press, 2009), 9; Jan Assmann, *Cultural Memory and Early Civilization: Writing, Remembrance, and Political Imagination* (Cambridge: Cambridge University Press, 2011), 111.

20 Pierre Nora, 'From *Lieux de Mémoire* to Realms of Memory', in Idem, *Realms of Memory*, 3 vols (New York: Columbia University Press, 1996-98), translated by Arthur Goldhammer, edited and with a foreword Lawrence Kritzman, vol. 1, xvii.

21 Heinz Schilling, *Early Modern European Civilization and its Political and Cultural Dynamism* (Waltham MA: Brandeis University Press, 2008), 41–42.

22 Cleary, *Father Luke Wadding and St Isidore's College*, 178. On Italian membership of the Calatrava military order, see Francisco Fernández Izquierdo, *La Orden Militar*

about the early years. In November 1624, amid concerns that the discalced fathers would separate from the Franciscan order, Philip IV instructed his ambassador, Ruy Gómez de Silva, duke of Pastrana, to treat with Urban VIII and Cardinal Barberini.[23] A small group of Observant Spanish friars replaced the discalced but were unable and unwilling to pay the debts already incurred to acquire the site and build on it. Given a month to either settle or sell the house, the minister general of the order resolved to give St Isidore's to the Irish Franciscan province.[24]

Wadding's understanding with his patrons corresponded to a network of trust established over decades of mutual experience, which provided the friars with the means to uphold their vow of poverty. Support from principal elements in the Franciscan order and from influential members of the ecclesiastical hierarchy was vital to the endurance of the Irish Friars Minor.[25] Through his work with the commission on the Immaculate Conception since 1618, Wadding remained on excellent terms with the Trejo brothers and successive Spanish representatives at the papal court: Albuquerque, Monterrey, Pastrana, Alcalá and Oñate.[26] Authorised by Urban VIII, the first Irish friars arrived at St Isidore's seven years later. Cardinal Gabriel de Trejo paid the debts outstanding and supported more building work.[27]

---

de Calatrava en el Siglo XVI: Infraestructura Institucional: Sociología y Prosopografía de sus Caballeros (Madrid, CSIC, 1992), 289.

23 Philip IV to Pastrana, Madrid, 9 November 1624 (UCD-OFM, C.31); Cleary, *Father Luke Wadding and St Isidore's College*, 175.

24 Ibid, 'En este aprieto consulto el Padre General [...] y resolvio que se diese para Colegio de los religiosos yrlandeses Franciscanos [...] y que hallavan quien les pagasse las deudas'.

25 Mary Ann Lyons, 'The Role of St Anthony's College, Louvain in Establishing the Irish Franciscan Network, 1607–60', in Bhreathnach, MacMahon and McCafferty, eds, *The Irish Franciscans, 1534–1990*, 27–44.

26 Fathers of St Isidore's to Philip IV, Rome, 29 November 1628: 'por guardian al Padre Guardian Fray Lucas de San Francisco [...] el año de 1618 por teologo del Obispado de Cartagena. Ha servido estos 10 años en la causa de la limpia Concepción de la Virgen Señora y otras [...] mas a todos los demas embajador de *Vuestra Magestad* al Duque de Albuquerque, al Conde de Monterrey, al Duque de Pastrana, al Duque de Alcalá, y ultimamente al Conde de Oñate como cada uno de ellos testificara'.

27 Ibid, 'el Señor Cardenal de Trejo Presidente del Consejo Real de *Vuestra Magestad* les amparo y favorecio y pago por ellos las deudas'.

According to Francis Harold, in its early years, Andrew Wyse of Ballinacourty, Co. Waterford, visited St Isidore's and contributed generous funds towards the college.[28] The Wyse family were among the leading merchants in Waterford where they were established since the thirteenth century.[29] Wyse was related to Wadding and had been a member of the Collaterale council of Naples, serving Philip II for more than fifty years. A knight of the Order of Malta, he was nominated Grand Prior of England at the behest of Philip II and Mary I.[30] As a sovereign entity, the Order of Malta had a role in the transfer of money deposited with them.[31] The order also accepted pledges as a financial guarantee and made collections for the maintenance of church property.[32] Therefore, it is possible that Wyse gathered incomes in Ireland to contribute to the foundation and upkeep of St Isidore's College. For example, Walter Butler, 11th earl of Ormond, employed his assets in support of the Catholic clergy and was connected to Luke Wadding through Lawrence Barron, Wadding's brother-in-law, who rented land from Butler in Clonmel.[33]

28 Harold, *Vita Fratris Lucae Waddingi*, 80. In 1589, Luke Wadding's father, Walter, enumerated a claim to farmland and fishing grounds at Ballinacourty. On Andrew Wyse, see also Carroll, *Exiles in a Global City*, 54.

29 Fennessy, 'Wadding, Luke [name in religion Francis] (1588–1657)', *ODNB*, vol. 56, 643–49; Walton, 'Church, Crown and Corporation in Waterford, 1520–1620', 190.

30 Declan Downey, 'Continuity, Legitimacy and Strategy: The Titular Priors of Ireland – Romegas, González, Wyse and Brochero, and their Relations with the Spanish Monarchy, 1576–1625', in Martin Browne and Colmán Ó Clabaigh, eds, *Soldiers of Christ: The Knights Hospitaller and the Knights Templar in Medieval Ireland* (Dublin: Four Courts Press, 2015), 61–80.

31 Cf. David Allen, 'The Order of St John as a School for Ambassadors in Counter-Reformation Europe', in Helen Nicholson, ed, *The Military Orders: Welfare and Warfare* (Abingdon: Routledge, 1998), 363–379.

32 Ignacio de la Torre, 'Financial Services for the Kings in the Thirteenth Century', in Helen Nicholson and Malcolm Barber, eds, *The Military Orders: On Land and by Sea* (Aldershot: Variorum, 1994), 126; James Gordon, 'An Inventory of the Effects belonging to the Scotch Mission in Rome, and Confiscated by the French there in February 1798', *Journal and Appendix to Scotichronicon and Monasticon*, 1 (1869), 638.

33 David Edwards, *The Ormond Lordship in County Kilkenny, 1515–1642* (Unpublished PhD thesis, Trinity College Dublin, 1998), 296–97.

Art & Architecture

The building projects at St Isidore's offered Wadding and the Irish friars a framework for cultural engagement in Rome. Giovan Battista Fidanza has done much to reveal Wadding's appreciation of art and how St Isidore's became an integral part of Rome's urban design.[34] The new church handed over to Wadding was only a shell in the shape of a Latin cross with a well-proportioned dome.[35] Wadding's first priority was to settle the building expenses. He then purchased more land, including a portion recovered from the Capuchins, added a processional passage with the agreement of his neighbour, Prince Niccolò Ludovisi, and enclosed the whole site with a solid wall. In the monastic tradition, high walls kept the world outside.[36]

Between the southern and western arms of the church the Spanish friars had placed a small cloister with dormitories above. The church was built to the designs of Felice Antonio Casoni in the early Baroque style. Wadding oversaw the plastering and whitewashing of the church walls, 'ornamenting them here and there with stucco, paving the floor and putting glass in the windows'.[37] The high altar was then erected with inlaid marble and alabaster pillars to designs by the architect Mario Arconio, with Andrea Sacchi's painting of St Isidore as the altarpiece. A reliquary was placed beneath containing the relics of early martyrs.[38] Relics of St Isidore the Ploughman were given to the house by the civic authorities of Madrid.[39]

34 Fidanza, *Luke Wadding's Art*, 43–57, 144–45.

35 Conlan, *St Isidore's*, 11.

36 Ibid, 67.

37 Harold, *Vita Fratris Lucae Waddingi*, 68; cited by Cleary, *Father Luke Wadding and St Isidore's College*, 162.

38 Certificates of Alexander Vittrici, Bishop of Alatri, 20 August 1650 (UCD-OFM, G.18, G.31). For an inventory of sacred relics, see Cleary, *Father Luke Wadding and St Isidore's College*, 221–224.

39 Fathers of St Isidore's to Philip IV, Rome, 29 November 1628: 'la casa tiene por titular al Glorioso S. Isidoro de Madrid, de qien esa villa se ha servido de dar para ella reliquia'. In 1656, the Irish friars received permission to recite a proper office in honour of Santa María Torribia de la Cabeza, wife of St Isidore of Madrid; Conlan, *St Isidore's*, 16.

The funds that great ruling families provided for the completion of St Isidore's exemplify the support for ascetic renewal in Rome during the 1630s. During his papacy, the Francophile Urban VIII assumed control of papal commissions from Paul V and Gregory XV – funding building projects for religious orders or a favourite nephew interested in acquiring a valuable collection of art and artefacts.[40] Wadding's custody of St Isidore's illustrates such patronage. When setting the foundations to the original façade of the church, Wadding determined that they should be set deeper than initially intended. On digging the groundwork, the builders discovered a grotto that held five ancient statues. Providentially for Wadding, these were purchased by Francesco Barberini, Cardinal Protector of the Friars Minor.[41] The statues were five herms. These monuments consisted of squared stone columns with a carved head on top, which marked boundaries such as gateways in antiquity.[42]

The original portico and façade at St Isidore's were undertaken by papal architect, Domenico Castelli. The six side chapels to the church were begun by Wadding who found the necessary patrons to commission architects and painters to build and decorate them. Pietro Pavoni was the original patron of the chapel of St Patrick and St Francis on the Gospel side of the transept. Pavoni was secretary and master of the treasury to Paul V and Gregory XV. As was the case with fellow patron, Ottaviano Vestri di Barbiano, the Pavoni family demonstrates how interlinked Italians were with Spanish institutions in papal Rome.[43] Pavoni also funded an annexe to the convent buildings at St Isidore's and his mortuary monument was placed in the church.[44]

40 Careri, 'The Artist', in Villari and Cochrane, eds, *Baroque Personae*, 300.

41 Aedan Daly, 'S. Isidoro', in Carlo Galassi Paluzzi and Carlo Pietrangeli, eds, *Le Chiese di Roma illustrate. Collana di monografie* (Rome: Marietti, 1971), 5–6.

42 The Italian government intervened to prevent the dispersal abroad of the herms, which are now preserved at the Museo Nazionale Romano. Hubert Quinn, *Saint Isidore's Church and College of the Irish Franciscans, Rome* (Rome: Tipografia Poliglotta Vaticana, 1948), 7.

43 Cesare Clementini, *Trattato de'Lvoghi Pii, e de'Magistrati di Rimino al svo Raccolto Istorico* (Rimini: Giovanni Simbeni, 1617), vi, 58, 113.

44 Cleary, *Father Luke Wadding and St Isidore's College*, 167.

Work on the chapel of St Anthony of Padua was paid for by the prelate Gaetano Gaetani who employed Gian Domenico Cerrini of Perugia to paint the altarpiece and frescoes on the sidewalls.[45] Although his inspiration found expression in literary works, Wadding understood art as a means of instruction to encourage devotion – words could only express what visual images convey in more immediate ways. At Salamanca, he wrote a number of poems to accompany a series of paintings at the friaries of St Francis and St Anthony prior to the Franciscan general chapter held there in 1618.[46] Wadding later wrote that graphic images are no less important than the written word.[47]

Carlo Maratti was commissioned by Ercole Ronconi, a lawyer at the Roman court, to decorate the chapel of St Joseph in 1652.[48] Maratti's work at St Isidore's was his first great project and took six years to complete. His decoration of the chapel of the Holy Cross took place next with patronage from Costanza Pamphili, wife of Nicolò Ludovisi, prince of Piombino, and niece of Innocent X.[49] The peace of the community was frequently disturbed by artists coming to view or copy the paintings at St Isidore's.[50] Maratti's final work at the church was the principal painting for the chapel of the Immaculate Conception on the right transept.[51] The chapel was built by the executors of Alonso de Quiñones, auditor of the Sacra Rota and subsequently Patriarch of Jerusalem,[52] before the right of patronage,

45 Harold, *Vita Fratris Lucae Waddingi*, 70.

46 Ibid, 16; De Castro, 'Wadding and the Iberian Peninsula', 139.

47 Luke Wadding, *Presbeia sive legatio Philippi III et IV*, 294–305.

48 Giulia Spoltore, 'Luke Wadding and Scholars for the Arts in Seventeenth-Century Rome', 124, 126–28; Millett, *The Irish Franciscans*, 129. Ercole Ronconi also paid for Wadding's funeral monument at St Isidore's.

49 Catherine Legrand, 'Some Drawings by Carlo Maratti', *The Burlington Magazine*, 136 (1994), 348.

50 Fidanza, *Luke Wadding's Art*, 110.

51 Alessandro Zuccari, 'l'Immacolata a Roma dal Quattrocento al Settecento', in Giovanni Morello, Vincenzo Francia and Roberto Fusco, eds, *Una Donna vestita di Sole: l'Immacolata Concezione nelle Opere dei Grandi Maestri* (Milan, Motta, 2005), 71; Alessandra Anselmi, *L'Immacolata nei Rapporti tra l'Italia e la Spagna* (Rome: De Luca Editori, 2008), 54.

52 Hazard, 'Saint Isidore's Franciscan College, Rome: from Centre of Influence to Site of Memory', in García Hernán and Recio Morales, eds, *Redes y espacios de poder*, 108.

Ius patronus, passed to the family of Rodrigo López de Silva.[53] As Giulia Spoltore points out, this work was completed after Wadding's death.[54]

The surround to the altarpiece is attributed to Gian Lorenzo Bernini as are the sepulchral monuments on either side. Bernini had already completed work for his mentor, Urban VIII, and was in charge of building in St Peter's Basilica.[55] The chapel of St Anne was built by Domenico Castelli who also erected the portico-façade and the stairs to St Isidore's church. Castelli bequeathed the chapel to Cardinal Francesco Barberini who completed its construction.[56] The third storey of the convent was funded by Cardinal Trejo. Among other works, he provided for a room in the house reserved for Spanish royal officials.[57] Wadding noted that this was well-established practice for patrons visiting Franciscan houses.[58] The ambassador often went to St Isidore's. The duke of Pastrana, Gómez de Silva, would go there to compile letters and conduct secret negotiations.[59] In recognition of his devotion to the friars and their gratitude to him for completing the Spanish cloister at St Isidore's, they set a tribute in stone to his memory.[60] Fernando Enríquez de Ribera, duke of Alcalá, offset the

53 Ludwig von Pastor, *History of the Popes from the Close of the Middle Ages drawn from the secret Archives of the Vatican and other original sources*, 40 vols, translated and edited by Frederick Ignatius Antrobus and Francis Kerr (repr. Wilmington NC, Consortium, 1978), vol. 31, 312; Stanislao Fraschetti, *Il Bernini. La sua Vita, la sua Opera, il suo Tempo* (Milan, Ulrico Hoepli, 1900), 441.

54 Spoltore, 'Luke Wadding and Scholars for the Arts in Seventeenth-Century Rome', 125.

55 Bruce Boucher, *Italian Baroque Sculpture* (London: Thames and Hudson, 1998), 46, 63, 106.

56 Millett, *The Irish Franciscans*, 129.

57 Fathers of St Isidore's to Philip IV, Rome (UCD-OFM, C.31): 'El Señor Cardenal de Trejo afuera otras fabricas que hizo en la Casa labro para si un quarto que esta siempre para el servicio de los ministros de *Vuestra Magestad*'.

58 Ó Clabaigh, *The Friars in Ireland*, 113.

59 Fathers of St Isidore's to Philip IV, Rome (UCD-OFM, C.31): 'Ademas la tienen los embajadores de *Vuestra Magestad* la Casa por tan suya que vienen a ella muy a menudo, el Duque de Pastrana en ella se retiraba para despachar los correos y para las negociaciones secretas de servicio de *Vuestra Magestad*'.

60 Ibid: 'y por la devoción que tenia a los que viven en ella les acabo el claustro de que ay memoria y inscripcion en piedra'. The inscription was made in 1626; Cleary, *Father Luke Wadding and St Isidore's College*, 167.

cost of renovating the Spanish cloister where a well bears his coat of arms. Wadding dedicated his third volume of the *Annales Minorum* to the duke of Alcalá.[61]

At the end of May 1632, Manuel de Moura, y Corte Real, marquis of Castel Rodrigo, arrived in Rome as envoy extraordinary of Spain.[62] Castel Rodrigo subsequently served as ambassador to the Holy See until February 1641.[63] Noted for his deep and sincere religious convictions, recognition of Castel Rodrigo's patronage was copper fastened in scholarship and in print.[64] One of several theology theses defended at St Isidore's by Eugene O'Cahan was printed and dedicated to Castel Rodrigo in the year of his arrival in Rome. O'Cahan was later 'martyred on the mission to Ireland'.[65] Among the St Isidore's theses printed in the 1630s and 1640s, others were dedicated to Cardinal Alonso de la Cueva, marquis of Bedmar, and Cardinals Francesco and Antonio Barberini.[66]

Through Castel Rodrigo's generosity the main wing of the new college was built, including the chapter-hall and refectory, one side of a new cloister named after Wadding, and the main dormitory.[67] Heraldry was one of Castel Rodrigo's abiding interests.[68] In its first edition, Wadding

61 Fathers of St Isidore's to Philip IV, Rome: 'y el Duque de Alcalá hizo la cisterna como lo muestran sus armas'.

62 *Annales Minorum* (1st edn, Lyon, 1635), vol. 3, Dedicatory epistle, i–v.

63 Pastor, *History of the Popes*, vol. 28, 308.

64 Santiago Manuel Hernández, 'Don Manuel de Moura Corte Real, Marqués de Castelo Rodrigo: Propaganda, Mecenazgo y Representación en la Monarquía Hispánica de Felipe IV', in Olivier Noble Wood, Jeremy Lawrance and Jeremy Roe, eds, *Poder y Saber Bibliotecas y Bibliofilia en la Época del Conde-Duque de Olivares* (Madrid: Olivier Centro de Estudios Europa Hispánica, 2011), 97–120. I am grateful to Roberto Quirós Rosado for referring me to this article.

65 Jennings, ed, 'Theses Defended at St Isidore's College, Rome, 1631–49', 97.

66 Ibid: 'Una all'eccellentissimo signor ambasciatore di Spagna, Castel Rodrigo, del P. fr. Eugenio Cahanus, di numero 105. 1632'.

67 Paolo Varela Gomes, 'Damnatio Memoriae. A arquitectura dos marqueses de Castelo Rodrigo', in José Luis Colomer, ed, *Arte y Diplomacia de la Monarquía Hispánica en el Siglo XVII* (Madrid: Fernando Villaverde Ediciones, 2003), 358, 373.

68 Joseph Connors, 'Borromini and the Marchese di Castel Rodrigo', *The Burlington Magazine*, 133 (1991), 437.

dedicated the fourth volume of the *Annales Minorum* to the ambassador, emblazoning Castel Rodrigo's coat of arms on the opening page.[69] It is easy to appreciate their mutual understanding when one recalls the formative decade that Wadding spent in Portugal. Three of the artists referred to above were commissioned for work on behalf of Philip IV by Castel Rodrigo. José de Ribera was employed in Naples, while Andrea Sacchi and Giovanni Domenico Cerrini worked in Rome, together producing a series of at least five square paintings with half figures of hermit saints for the Buen Retiro.[70] These paintings were dispatched to Spain in at least two voyages made between 1639 and 1641. The *aula magna* at St Isidore's was completed before Wadding's death but was not decorated until 1672.[71]

Sites of burial are an example of *loci memoriae* that recall specific times. Large slabs forming the floor of the church are inscribed with the details of noted exiles from Ireland, clergy and laypeople, who are interred in the crypt at St Isidore's – the church of the Irish nation in Rome which also contains many nameless Irish graves. Sepulchral monuments to Spanish and Italian patrons of the college line the lateral walls. The mortal remains of Hugh McCaghwell are here, for instance. The lapidary at St Isidore's in McCaghwell's memory was paid for by his confidant John O'Neill, earl of Tyrone. McCaghwell taught theology at the *studium generale* of Ara Coeli, the Franciscan headquarters in Rome, from 1623. Three years later, he was consecrated Primate of Ireland by Cardinal Gabriel de Trejo

69 Wadding, *Annales Minorum* (1st edn, Lyon, 1637), vol. 4, Dedicatory epistle, 1.

70 Andrés Úbeda de Los Cobos, 'The Pictorial Decoration of the Buen Retiro Palace', in Idem, ed, *Paintings for the Planet King, Philip IV and the Buen Retiro Palace* (Madrid: Museo Nacional del Prado, 2005), 21.

71 In 1672, Fra Emanuele da Como painted a series of frescoes in honour of the Immaculate Conception and the Scotist school of thought. These works, especially the large fresco at the end of the hall, are said by art historians to have been worthy of the Cinquecento rather than the late seventeenth century. From 1701–06, Fra Giovanni Antonio Sgaury of the Province of San Francesco a Ripa, an autodidact, frescoed the Wadding Cloister depicting distinguished members of the three Franciscan orders and lunettes with events from the life of St Francis. See Carroll, *Exiles in a Global City*, 89–143.

on 7 June in the church of St Isidore's College.[72] According to Nicholas Vernulz, a jurist at the archducal court and the most dependable authority on McCaghwell's activities, McCaghwell helped to procure St Isidore's for the Irish, and also played a part in establishing the Ludovisian College.[73]

Archives of the College

When Francis Harold returned to St Isidore's to help his uncle complete the *Annales Minorum* in 1651, his first task was to organise and catalogue the many handwritten records that Wadding had assembled at great expense to the college.[74] Benignus Millett provided a detailed synopsis of the archives in 1985.[75] In Wadding's lifetime, some of the manuscripts were arranged according to the history of pontificates, such as the original papal bulls for the Franciscans from Gregory IX to Alexander VII inclusive. However, Harold revealed the confused state of other records before his return and explained that Alexander VII, pope from 1655 to 1667, forbade the removal of any manuscripts or bound volumes from St Isidore's. Moreover, friars were required to obtain written permission from the resident archivist to consult records within the archives and sign a register on arrival. Otherwise, the penalty of automatic excommunication was to be imposed.[76] This may have been a response to the circulation of the lord lieutenant's 1649 letter, of which more is said later.

Wadding's archives were a repository not merely for documentary memory, but also for sacred relics. The combined contents were subsequently recorded in an inventory at the college. Paintings in storage and bundles of printed material that defended Franciscan teachings were also kept in

72 Cathaldus Giblin, 'Hugh McCaghwell OFM, Archbishop of Armagh (†1626): Aspects of his Life', *Seanchas Ard Mhacha*, 11 (1985), 258–290. McCaghwell died of fever before he could set out for Ireland.

73 Ibid, 283.

74 Harold, *Vita Fratris Lucae Waddingi*, 79.

75 Millett, 'The Archives of St Isidore's College, Rome', 1–13.

76 Ibid.

the archives.[77] The 'Primo Archivio' contained five cupboards for storing documents, with many tables and chairs, and paintings on the walls. In the 'Archivio Secundo', a wooden chest held thirty leather-covered wooden plates for bookbinding.[78]

Archives are, to quote Pierre Nora, 'a functional, material, symbolic site' which reinforce memory.[79] Yet, as Óscar Recio Morales has stated, original sources relating to early modern networks represent a challenge when limited to administrative-judicial records and financial transactions, rather than more personal material such as correspondence or diaries.[80] St Isidore's provided Wadding and the friars with a place to keep a repository for documents. For example, Wadding kept an authentic copy of the list of alleged disputes, sent to Rome by the bishop of Meath, vicars general and vicars apostolic in Ireland.[81] This was compiled at the college by Hugh McCaghwell who advised the Congregation of Propaganda Fide on the resolution of disputes among the Catholic clergy in Ireland. Replying to Ludovisi, McCaghwell stated the disputes were no greater than those to be found in any other country, emphasising that they applied in particular instances rather than to all of the clergy in Ireland.

Wadding's Library

Cardinal Francesco Barberini expressed high regard for the library of 5,000 volumes and the manuscript archive prudently assembled by Luke Wadding. Since books were a luxury product, the library at St Isidore's avoided keeping duplicate copies of its acquisitions.[82] An inspection of the

77 Cleary, *Father Luke Wadding and St Isidore's College*, 224, 243.

78 Ibid, 253–54.

79 Pierre Nora, 'Between Memory and History: Les Lieux de Mémoire', in *Representations*, 26 (1989), 14.

80 Hazard, 'A Manuscript of the Declaration of Arbroath from the Roman Archives of Fr. Luke Wadding OFM', 296–315.

81 Giblin, 'Hugh McCaghwell OFM', 260–1.

82 Harold, *Vita Fratris Lucae Waddingi*, 78.

holdings by John McCafferty and Joseph MacMahon indicates that the view at St Isidore's was Mediterranean and shaped by the internal dynamics of the Counter Reformation in Rome.[83] Wadding gave the sixteenth-century Jesuit theologians, Robert Bellarmine, Francisco Suárez, Tomás Sánchez, Gabriel Vásquez and Francisco de Toledo 'an honoured place' on his bookshelves.[84] The holdings were predominantly historical, which reflected almost forty years of preparation for Wadding's *Annales Minorum*. The original collections also consisted of theology and philosophy, patristics, sacred writing, canon law and art. The books were carefully organised and classified with catalogues of the names of authors and works.[85] By the standards of the day, this was a new type of library design with a comparatively small reading room and shelving lining the walls.[86] In 1638, Urban VIII reserved excommunication for anyone who removed, defaced or lost any book or manuscript from the library at St Isidore's, without absolution until such objects were returned unharmed.[87] This points toward the threat of punishment against book thieves at Salamanca,[88] where Wadding's experiences were subsequently instrumental to the training of students, to Scotist research and the dissemination of knowledge.

Scholars at St Isidore's devoted much of their time to studying the works of Duns Scotus. Between 1625 and 1660, the college supplied more than

83 McCafferty and MacMahon, 'The Wadding Library of Saint Isidore's College, Rome, 1622–1700', 97–118.

84 Harold, *Vita Fratris Lucae Waddingi*, 78; Cregan, 'The Social and Cultural Background of a Counter-Reformation Episcopate', 114.

85 Donatella Bellardini and Claudia Costacurta, 'The Development of Libraries in the Seventeenth Century. Luke Wadding's Library', in Binasco, ed, *Luke Wadding, the Irish Franciscans, and Global Catholicism*, 96.

86 Cf. Andrew Hopkins, *Italian Architecture: From Michelangelo to Borromini* (London: Thames and Hudson, 2002), 88, 184.

87 Bellardini and Costacurta, 'The Development of Libraries in the Seventeenth Century. Luke Wadding's Library', in Binasco, ed, *Luke Wadding, the Irish Franciscans, and Global Catholicism*, 98, 102.

88 Ángel Weruaga Prieto, *Los universitarios y el libro en la Salamanca clásica (ss. XVI–XVIII). Estado de la cuestión, fuentes, retos. «Fuentes, archivos y bibliotecas para una historia de las universidades hispánicas»* (Salamanca: Ediciones Universidad de Salamanca, 2016), 298.

seventy professors of philosophy and theology to teaching posts.[89] During the reign of Philip II six chairs of theology were endowed to the University of Salamanca, one of which was assigned to the study of Scotism.[90] Duns Scotus was honoured at the Salamanca friary of San Francisco el Real where Wadding and McCaghwell studied. Francisco de Herrera, one of the university's Franciscan lectors in theology during that time, kept a portrait entitled *Beatus Scotus*. Herrera later became procurator general of the order and participated in the *De auxiliis* debate concerning divine grace and free will. Both Wadding and McCaghwell knew of the *Beatus Scotus* portrait at their Salamanca friary where they were influenced by the Scotistic atmosphere of their surroundings. It is recorded that as early as 1350 an image of Duns Scotus was publicly venerated in the city of Salamanca itself. Exiled Irish students would have noticed the homage paid in Salamanca to, as they thought, one of their own.[91]

First and foremost a Franciscan foundation, St Isidore's remains part of a global body corporate which, in past centuries, maintained links with other Irish colleges in the Iberian Peninsula, the Low Countries, Prague and Poland.[92] Since they resided there, the friars' correspondence with family and friends was preserved in the college archives, which show that family networks operated at St Isidore's where students were drawn from one generation to the next.[93] This exemplifies intergenerational memory

89 Millett, 'Irish Scotists at St Isidore's College, Rome, in the Seventeenth Century', *Studia scholastico Scotistica*, vol. 4, 399–419.

90 José García Oro and María José Porteia Silva, 'Felipe II y la Universidad de Salamanca', in Manuel de Castro ed, *San Francisco de Salamanca y su Studium Generale* (Santiago de Compostela, Imprenta Aldecoa de Burgos, 1998), 337–40.

91 Giblin, 'Hugh MacCaghwell OFM and Scotism at St Anthony's College, Louvain', 380.

92 On 6 July 1645, the Irish province of Observant Franciscans was entrusted with a friary in south-east Poland at Wieluń, but the Polish friars asked them to vacate the friary nine years later. See Brendan Jennings, ed, 'The Irish Franciscans in Poland', *Archiv. Hib.*, 20 (1956), 38–56.

93 See, for instance, Geoffrey Barron of Clonmel to his uncle, Luke Wadding, with news of Lawrence Barron's death and the early studies of Geoffrey's brother, Bartholomew, Dublin, 2 December 1626 (UCD-OFM, D.03/719). See also the letter of Cormac Hickey to his brother Antony Hickey with family news, Dunmoylan, 16 January 1626 (UCD-OFM, D.03/602).

at an individual level. Important papers of specific interest to the mission to Ireland were also accumulated at the college where they were written and received. This, in turn, offers an instance of political memory which contributes to communal identity.

The documents forwarded to Rome by each province of the Friars Minor were preserved at St Isidore's.[94] By reason of his office as *consultor* to the Holy See, many other papers passed through Wadding's hands. From the 1620s, petitions and recommendations were sent to Wadding for appointments to the Irish episcopacy, especially those completed at Propaganda Fide. These dossiers exemplify the concerns involved. Philip IV realised that an Irish bishop educated under his protection in Flanders could help exert influence and 'maintain the bonds with Spain which already existed'.[95] Writing from the first session of the parliament of Aragon in 1626, for instance, the king instructed his ambassador Pastrana to petition for a member of Ireland's regular clergy as successor to the recently deceased Catholic primate, Peter Lombard. The Isidorian presence in Rome also enabled Wadding's administration of Irish parochial and non-episcopal benefices. He compiled his notes for this purpose at the college and preserved them in the archives.

Daily Life

Juan de Riera, a friar from Mallorca, served as interim superior of St Isidore's until Wadding officially took up his functions as guardian on 2 May 1627 and assumed responsibility for the college.[96] Wadding called upon the community to follow an ascetical routine. To this end, he wrote the constitutions of St Isidore's, stating that the guardian 'should be tenacious

94 Hazard, '*In Novi Orbis amplitudine*: Irish Franciscan Views of the Americas, 1610–83', 193–210.

95 Jennings, ed, *Wadding Papers*, 164.

96 Cleary, *Father Luke Wadding and St Isidore's College*, 79–80.

in discipline, in diet, and amenable to the rest of the community'.[97] The friars were categorised as priests, clerics and lay brothers. Wadding forbade the community from seeking or accepting privileges or gifts.[98] Silence was observed in the dormitory, the refectory, the sacristy, the church and in the cloister. The guardian and his advisers at the college designated certain hours for discussion and conversation. According to the statutes of tuition, professors were expected to lecture for two hours each day, with a further hour for debate. Twice a week, more debates followed. These were attended by theologians and philosophers who were expected to keep abreast of one another's work. Every month, a public debate was held at the college and open to the laity. On feast days, studies ceased.[99]

In the same vein as Francesco Gonzaga, Wadding set high standards for students and warned: 'Ignorance is a dangerous thing, and also relegates one into oblivion'.[100] While students were expected to devote themselves to their studies, Wadding reminded them to place prayer above the time allocated to book work. Supervised by their lectors, the students were required to practice preaching and praying publicly in the refectory and school. The official prayers marking the hours of each day were consistent with those held at the college of St Anthony of Padua, Leuven. On a daily basis, devotional material was read aloud to the priests and friars in the refectory. Religious houses honoured the memory of their dead and the dedication they showed towards the ideals of their religious order. In the same way, the friars collected and compiled manuscript material for the praise of specific saints on their feast days.

97 Luke Wadding's Constitutions for St Isidore's, 16 October 1625: 'De Guardiano [...] disciplina, tenax, in victu et reliquis Communitati conformis', cited by Cleary, *Father Luke Wadding and St Isidore's College*, 185.

98 Ibid, 186: 'Sive Guardianus, sive Praeses nec munera nec donationes admittant pro se [...] nihil ad particularem usum accipere possint, sive libros, sive alia alicujus momenti'.

99 Ibid, 186.

100 Heribert Holzapfel, *History of the Franciscan Order*. Translated into English by Antonine Tibesar and Gervase Brinkmann, with an Introduction by Noel Muscat, 372, <https://franciscanstudies.com/wp-content/uploads/2018/10/hol_hist_final.pdf>, accessed 30 September 2024.

On the staff, an instructor was appointed for the young friars.[101] A calm and sensible friar was to be chosen as doorkeeper and porter of the college. Laypeople were not allowed in the house without the guardian's permission, and this was not to be granted except for the distinguished. Wadding held that places that were too accessible were derided and where everything was open to all, it showed a lack of holiness and respect. The sacristan was responsible for keeping both church and sacristy clean. He and the priests celebrating Mass were expected to maintain the peace and quiet of both places to preserve a holy atmosphere.[102] A place was set aside in the friary for the repair of friars' clothing. The laundry was in the same workshop, where items were kept for common use.[103]

The priests at the college were each allocated a small room for their own use, similar to a monastic cell, with sufficient space to pray, study and sleep. In keeping with the vow of poverty, the friars slept on sacks filled with straw. Wadding made provisions for an annual inspection. This was conducted by superiors from outside the college for up to three days. His college statutes were approved by the minister general, Bernardino de Sena, at Ara Coeli on 16 October 1625.[104]

These unaltered constitutions were implemented at the Irish Franciscans' third foundation on the continent, the College of the Immaculate Conception, which opened in Prague four years later.[105] Jan Pařez has suggested that Wadding provided the inspiration for such a centre of learning in the capital of Bohemia.[106] His first cousin, Peter Wadding, taught theology in Prague and became chancellor of the city's Charles University from

101 Cleary, *Father Luke Wadding and St Isidore's College*, 190: 'De Magistro seu Instructore Juvenum'.

102 Ibid, 191.

103 Ibid, 192.

104 Ibid, 194.

105 *Statua domestica pro religio regimine fratrum Minorum strictoris observantiae provinciae Hiberniae, collegii Immaculate conceptionis B.V. Mariae Pragae*; cited by Jan Pařez and Hedvika Kuchařová, *The Irish Franciscans in Prague, 1629–1786. History of the Franciscan College of the Immaculate Conception of the Virgin Mary in Prague* (Prague: Karolinum Press, 2015), 168.

106 Jan Pařez, 'The Irish Franciscans in seventeenth- and eighteenth-century Prague', O'Connor and Lyons, eds, *Irish Migrants in Europe after Kinsale*, 105.

1629 to 1641.[107] Building upon their existing connections to the House of Habsburg, Malachy Fallon prevailed upon the Emperor Ferdinand II for support.[108] Wadding was kept up to date and, three years later, petitioned the emperor and his wife, Eleonora Gonzaga, Adalbert von Harrach, cardinal of Prague, and the papal nuncio in Vienna, on behalf of the new college.[109] In comparable terms, theology was taught at both colleges according to the professors' own methods, but they were expected to honour Duns Scotus. Those who failed to do so were relieved of their post.[110]

Clear evidence of Wadding's authority among peers and students is apparent in the Scotist theses defended at St Isidore's in its early decades. While building work continued, these dissertations were presented before many guests gathered in the church, which included dignitaries and college patrons. Thereafter, the theses were defended in Wadding's recently completed *aula maxima*.[111]

Ludovisian College

At that time and with support from Ludovico Ludovisi, Cardinal Protector of Ireland, Wadding petitioned the papacy for a new Irish diocesan college. The students were accommodated at a house directly opposite St Isidore's.[112] From 1628, the Ludovisian College became the only institution

107 Thomas O'Connor, 'Irish Collegians in Spanish Service (1560–1603)', in Chambers and O'Connor, eds, *Forming Catholic Communities: Irish, Scots and English College Networks in Europe*, 19–20.

108 Pařez and Kuchařová, *The Irish Franciscans in Prague*, 31–32.

109 O'Connor, 'Exile Movement: Male Institutions, 1568–1640', in McCafferty and Kelly, eds, *The Oxford History of British and Irish Catholicism*, 219; Binasco, *Rome and Irish Catholicism in the Atlantic World*, 155–56.

110 Pařez and Kuchařová, *The Irish Franciscans in Prague*, 55.

111 Brendan Jennings, ed, 'Theses Defended at St Isidore's College, Rome, 1631–49', *Coll. Hib.*, 2 (1959), 95.

112 Harold, *Vita Fratris Lucae Waddingi*, 106–111.

for the Irish secular clergy in Rome.[113] The requisites for the college stated that novices should be healthy in mind and body, born of a legitimate marriage and held in good repute.[114] In addition, students were expected to be baptised and confirmed, good-natured and adaptable, accustomed to humanities and letters, frequently receiving the sacraments and ready to return to Ireland after their studies 'to reap the rewards in the vineyard of the Lord'.[115] Those seeking admission were required to bring letters of recommendation. Guardians or lectors customarily provided students with written testimonials of their intellectual qualities, but each candidate had to look after their own letters.[116]

Wadding undertook the supervision of the diocesan college until Eugene Callinan was appointed first rector, followed by Martin Walsh and John Punch, Wadding's confrères.[117] Specific places could become a space of strength and representation which provided a ready means of discourse.[118] Wadding's neighbourhood became the main focal point for the Irish in Rome, so much so that Patrick Comerford referred to it as 'the Irish plantation in Capo le Case'.[119] A year before Wadding's death in 1657, he founded

113 Matteo Binasco and Hannah Thomas, 'Missionary Activity and Religious Houses', in Kelly and McCafferty, eds, *The Oxford History of British and Irish Catholicism*, vol. 2, 120.

114 Jennings, ed, *Wadding Papers, 1624–38*, 281–282.

115 Ibid, 282: 'suo tempore votum emitter adeundi post studia Hiberniam ad fructificandum in vinea Domini'.

116 Ibid.

117 Cleary, *Father Luke Wadding and St Isidore's College*, 42–43. See Corish, 'The Beginnings of the Irish College, Rome', in Keogh and McDonnell, eds, *The Irish College, Rome and its World*, 3–12; O'Connor, 'Luke Wadding's Networks at Home and Abroad', 14–23.

118 Cf. Daniel Nexon, *The Struggle for Power in Early Modern Europe: Religious Conflict, Dynastic Empires and International Change* (Princeton: Princeton University Press, 2009), 25–48. On post-Trent networks, see Justyna Kiliańczyk-Zięba and Magdalena Komorowska, eds, *Early Modern Catholicism and the Printed Book. Agents-Networks-Responses* (Leiden: Brill, 2024).

119 Charles Meehan, *The Rise and Fall of the Franciscan Monasteries in Ireland and Memoirs of the Irish Hierarchy in the Seventeenth Century, with Appendices containing Original Documents from the Rinuccini Manuscripts, Public Records, and the*

a third house, this time for the noviciate at the friary of Our Lady of the Plain, Capranica, of which more shall be said later.[120]

Conclusion

The network of colleges on the continent was the most exceptional characteristic of the Irish Church in exile.[121] At St Isidore's, Wadding brought to the fore the stability instilled by patronage based on personal ties in the commissioning of art and architecture. The college's endurance ensured the continued formation of friars for many generations. This makes the foundation's religious and political significance a monument of abiding interest, which enhances the memory of the early modern past. Wadding was uniquely well placed to pursue his research in the Roman congregations. As shown in the next two chapters, we see the full expansion of his abilities in Rome where Wadding's various curial offices increased the respect held for his country.

There had long been an Irish presence in Rome but, for several centuries, exiles travelled back and forth without a foundation to call their own. After 1625, from the secure vantage point of St Isidore's College, Luke Wadding worked within his own religious order and the Roman curia for decades to establish a clearly recognisable Irish identity among different groups that competed for attention at that time. In doing so, he had to contend with the claims of many others who were eager to advance their cause at the papal court. Through his continued presence in Rome, Wadding contributed to the perception that early modern Irishness was synonymous with Catholicism.

Archives of the Franciscan Convent, Dublin (Dublin: Duffy & Sons, Fifth edition, 1877), 430.

120 Patrick Conlan, *St Isidore's, Rome* (Rome: Tipografia Salesiana, 1982), 103–24.

121 O'Connor, 'Exile Movement: Male Institutions, 1568–1640', in Kelly and McCafferty, eds, *The Oxford History of British and Irish Catholicism*, vol. 1: *Endings and New Beginnings, 1530–1640*, 203–222.

6 Forum of Books

Introduction

Settled in at St Isidore's, Wadding conducted a concerted print campaign to defend the Friars Minor and promote Franciscan scholarship. The majority of volumes in his corpus consisted of folio editions intended for libraries. His first editions were otherwise printed in more portable sizes with seven in quarto, four in octavo and one duodecimo. In his lifetime, Wadding oversaw the publication of works at nine locations in France, the Habsburg Netherlands, Italy, Spain and Austria.[1] These writings clearly acted as a forum for the exchange of ideas and views.

The bindings on many early seventeenth-century books from St Isidore's, now preserved at University College Dublin, are durable and comparatively simple in design. To offset the costs of transport, printers sent new books unbound in bales to friaries and monasteries.[2] To this end, St Isidore's College maintained a workshop for bookbinding. It was equipped with finishing presses and an iron to tighten the book press, an iron rule, large scissors, a compass, a flat iron to smooth books, a knife to cut papers, a large hammer for beating books, a marble column, knives, copper and three

1 Gillespie, 'Contrasting Communities: A Comparative Approach to Irish Communities in Baroque Europe', in O'Connor and Lyons, eds, *The Ulster Earls and Baroque Europe*, 177. In chronological order, these were Douai, Rome, Antwerp, Leuven, Vienna, Mons, Lyon, Madrid, and Viterbo. See Hazard, 'Illustration and Ornamentation in the Works of Luke Wadding, Seventeenth-Century Historian and Theologian', 350–71.

2 Hazard, 'Correspondence from Jean-Baptiste Devenet and Claude Prost, Book Merchants of Lyon, to Fr. Luke Wadding OFM', 524.

pairs of boards for binding books, a pincer, two metal files with a rough blade for shaping material, two small irons for tightening, two hand saws, two needles, a drill and four binding needles.[3]

Throughout the 1640s, Wadding made the necessary arrangements to continue bringing works to print in Lyon, where he regularly published his writings.[4] In that decade, these consisted of a Life of the fifteenth-century Observant Franciscan, James of the Marches; a refutation of claims that St Francis was originally an Augustinian hermit; and three volumes of his *Annales Minorum*. Though not a university seat, Lyon was a city of print recognised by seventeenth-century theologians, biblical scholars and ecclesiastical historians for high-quality works, more competitively priced than Paris and neighbouring countries.[5]

1641 was a busy year in Wadding's literary pursuits.[6] On 1 March, he dedicated the third edition of his *Apologeticus de Praetenso Monachatu Augustinano Sancti Francisci* to Giovanni Battista Pallotto, Cardinal Protector of the Augustinian order.[7] This was diplomatic on Wadding's part because the text rebuffed the

3 Cleary, *Father Luke Wadding and St Isidore's College*, 253. The Franciscan order delegated a commissary and a discreet to inspect St Isidore's and avert any fraud or negligence that could happen. Cleary, *Father Luke Wadding and St Isidore's College*, 256.

4 *Vita et Res Gestae B. Jacobi Piceni, Per Johan Baptist Petruccium Scripta Notis et Commentariis Illustravit L. Waddingus* (Lyon: Laurent Durand, 1641); Wadding, *Apologeticus de Praetenso Monachatu Augustinano Sancti Francisci in Quo Deleguntur, et Rebelluntur Varii Errares Ex Hoc una Controversia Exanti* (1641 edn, Lyon: Laurent Durand); *Annales Minorum* (1st edn, Lyon: Claude Dufour, 1642), vol. 5 (1400–50); *Annales Minorum* (1st edn, Lyon: Devenet & Prost, 1647), vol. 6 (1450–75); *Annales Minorum* (1st edn, Lyon: Prost & Devenet, 1648), vol. 7 (1475–1500).

5 Andrew Pettegree, *The French Book and the European Book World* (Leiden: Brill, 2007), 227; Joseph Bergin, *The Politics of Religion in Early Modern France* (New Haven CT: Yale University Press, 2014), 233.

6 Hazard, ed, 'Some Unpublished Correspondence of Luke Wadding OFM to Giovanni Pietro Puricelli', 29–45.

7 Wadding, *Apologeticus de Praetenso Monachatu Augustinano Sancti Francisci*, Dedicatory epistle; 'Loosely bound pages written in Wadding's hand, numbered pp 439–90, refuting the claim that St Francis of Assisi was once an Augustinian, opening with Epistle to the reader', 19 July 1639 (UCD-OFM, D.26, Folder 6).

idea that St Francis began his religious life as an Augustinian. The first and second editions of 1625 had led an Augustinian historian, Tomás de Herrera, to answer Wadding's *apologia*. The Franciscan replied to Herrera with a new edition published by Laurent Durand in Lyon.[8] The involvement of Wadding's confrère, Louis Cavalli, is apparent. He composed a Latin stanza of eight lines to make peace with the Augustinians and inserted it after the index to attest 'Wadding's work is patent and clear'.[9]

For an intellectual community, the successful production and consumption of books relied upon an efficient communication network. This chapter describes Wadding's literary activities at St Isidore's from the mid-1620s until the late 1640s when the Observant friars, Louis Cavalli and John Tyrell, and a French Capuchin, Benoît de Montbrison, facilitated the Lyonnais works. In particular, Wadding acknowledged the contribution that Cavalli made to the Franciscan scheme. Yet, apart from brief references to date, the efforts of Wadding's associates have remained unsung.

Booksellers invested in the printing and ordering of books. Some were also printers with their own press.[10] Detailed information is presented here on the patronage that Wadding received, his discussions with scholars linked by shared interests, as well as the support he gave to fellow historians and theologians. These aspects of Wadding's life enable us to follow the progress of the publication programme and reveal his prudent efforts to achieve greater unity within the Franciscan family. This approach also shows some of the attendant difficulties that these protagonists faced and how Wadding's immediate circle retained support from influential members of the ecclesiastical hierarchy and from local nobles.

His first readers were the scribes who transcribed his texts, his proofreaders and the censors who authorised the books, the booksellers who

8 Mooney, 'The Writings of Father Luke Wadding OFM', 233; Jennings, ed, 'Some Correspondence of Father Luke Wadding OFM', 74. A close relation of Durand's was an Augustinian friar who delivered letters for him.

9 Wadding, *Apologeticus de Praetenso Monachatu Augustinano Sancti Francisci*, unpaginated: 'Vera reteta patent VVaddingi clara labore'.

10 Frédéric Barbier, *Gutenberg's Europe: The Book and the Invention of Western Modernity*, translated by Jean Birrell (Cambridge: Polity Press, 2017), 15, 101, 131, 147, 156; Hazard, 'Luke Wadding and the Breviary of Urban VIII', 87–101.

published them, the copy editors who prepared for the press and the typesetters who composed the text for printing.[11] Wadding carefully chose each person to achieve the smooth running of this process and counted them among his friends, from the copyist, Jean-Claude Thierry, to Wadding's fellow theologians at St Isidore's and the Cistercian abbot, Ilarione Rancati, the Franciscan scholar, Louis Cavalli, and the printer-publisher, Laurent Durand, for example.

Annales Minorum

In the early 1620s, Wadding told Michele Misserotti, minister general of the Friars Minor Conventual, that he readied himself to write the annals of the Franciscans because of 'not one, but many errors and the heavy loss of our name'.[12] He hastened to this work after Baronius' continuator of the *Annales Ecclesiastici*, Abraham Bzowski, condemned the opinions of John Duns Scotus and severely criticised the Order of Friars Minor.[13] In the spring of 1625, Wadding confirmed these objectives in the preface to his first volume of the *Annales Minorum*, much of which treats of St Francis up to his death on 3 October 1226 and beyond.[14] Wadding aimed to rival the style and method of Baronius, 'prince of Christian historians'.[15] To do

11 Cf. Roger Chartier, *The Author's Hand and the Printer's Mind: Transformations of the Written Word in Early Modern Europe*, translated by Lydia G. Cochrane (Cambridge: Polity Press, 2014), ix, 17, 78–79.

12 Jennings, ed, 'Some Correspondence of Father Luke Wadding OFM', 69: 'accintum stimulo non uno sed frequenti multorum errorum gravique nostri nominis'.

13 Carroll, *Exiles in a Global City*, 57–58, 71, 123. For a description of Bzowski's criticisms, see Balić, 'Wadding the Scotist', 506.

14 See *Annales Minorum* (1st edn, Lyon: Claude Landry, 1625), vol. 1, Address to the reader, unpaginated.

15 Jennings, ed, 'Some Correspondence of Father Luke Wadding OFM', 69, 'Stylum et methodum christianorum historicorum principis Baronii mihi, quantum licuerit, aemulandam proposui, in collectione et collatione authorum (quos omnes meo muneri necessarios quorundam benevolorum munificentia multo aere comparavi) eius laborem et solertiam prae oculis habituris'. For similarities in the method between the *Annales Minorum* and the tradition of Baronius, see Giulia Spoltore, 'Luke Wadding e l'Eredità di Cesare Baronio: Storiografia e Arte nel Seicento a

so, Wadding proposed to collect and collate documents to rebut Bzowski firmly and in a Christian manner. The papal records subsequently printed in each volume of the *Annales Minorum* were directly to hand and easier to reference than had hitherto been the case.[16]

The most significant development in ecclesiastical history since the *Magdeburg Centuries* and Baronius, Wadding's *Annales* marked him out as the best of Franciscan chroniclers.[17] This set the standard for the history of a religious order, accounting for the foundation and development of Franciscan friaries over four centuries; the contacts between friars and their benefactors; and the activities of religious superiors. Wadding endorsed his fellow Franciscan historian, Donatus Mooney, who held that mendicant friaries belonged to their founders and patrons buried within their walls.[18] Wadding based his account on many Franciscan authors. Among others, he followed Bartholomew of Pisa, Marianus of Florence, Mark of Lisbon, Francesco Gonzaga, Pietro Ridolfi, as well as documents of the order, especially the general chapters.[19] However, Wadding's research was not limited to the Friars Minor. He also read the works of those outside the order, such as the Benedictine Matthew Paris, the Cistercian Francisco Bivar, the Dominican Leandro Alberti, Raffaele Maffei of the Servite order, and the Italian humanist, Francesco Sansovino.[20] Wadding showed

---

Roma', 41–60. This was the case with other Irish chroniclers of the early seventeenth century. See Cunningham, *The Annals of the Four Masters*, 164–7.

16 Ó Clabaigh, *The Friars in Ireland*, xx.

17 Lázaro Iriarte, *Historia franciscana. Nueva edición* (Valencia: Editorial Asis, 1979), 20–23. The other three works are Domenico de Gubernatis, *Orbis Seraphicus*, 4 vols (vol. 1, Rome: Typis Stephani Caballi, 1682; vol. 2, Lyon: Annisson, Jean Posuel & Claude Rigaud, 1685; vol. 3 Rome: Nicolò Angelo Tinassi, 1684; vol. 4, Ibid, 1685); Giovanni Giacinto Sbaraglia, ed, *Bullarium franciscanum*, 4 vols (Rome: De Propaganda Fide, 1759–68); and Marcellino de Civezza, *Storia universale delle missioni francescane*, 11 vols (Rome: Tibernia; Prato: Guasti; Florence: Ariana, 1857–95).

18 *Annales Minorum*, vol. 3 (1242), n. 31.

19 See, for instance, *Annales Minorum*, vol. 4 (1268), 321, n. 9; ibid, vol. 5 (1278), n. 13; ibid, vol. 5 (1291), n. 20; ibid, vol. 7 (1343), 361, n. 33; vol. 10 (1432), n. 27; Harold, *Vita Fratris Lucae Waddingi*, 41–42.

20 Ibid, vol. 10 (1432), n. 27; Letter of Luke Wadding to Francisco Bivar, San Pietro in Montorio, 16 February 1625 (*PL*, vol. 31, 0013–0013, col. 1846).

great interest in the monastic past, the histories of other mendicant orders, and of comparatively new religious institutes, above all, the Society of Jesus.[21]

On the title page to every volume of the *Annales Minorum*, Wadding stated that he was an Irishman.[22] Each tome was eagerly awaited by readers, such as the Father General, Juan Merinero, Christopher Davenport, minister provincial of the English Franciscans, and Fr Augustine de Witte in Brussels, who 'greedily anticipated' reading the contents.[23] The first edition was printed in eight volumes by four publishing houses.[24] This distribution of resources helped to avoid the exhaustion of equipment and supplies. Early modern publishers were similar to business start-ups that completed a number of projects in a limited timeframe.[25] The Lyon workshop of Claude Landry yielded first fruits for Wadding's *Annales* when volumes one and two went to press in 1625 and 1628 with funding from Franciscan major superiors.[26] Landry was a stationer who published works in Latin. The motto around his printer's mark read *Hilaris cum pondere virtus*, that is, 'Cheerful with a dose of courage'. In 1627, he printed Antony Hickey's lengthy treatise on Franciscan integrity and Scotism. This text took apart Bzowski chronologically to correct him by objection, censure and moral response.[27]

Wadding assigned Hickey to the works of Scotus with John Punch of Cork who taught philosophy and theology at Lyon. Hickey edited volumes

21 MacMahon and McCafferty, 'The Wadding Library of Saint Isidore's College, Rome, 1622–1700', 109.

22 Each inscription referred to 'Luca Waddingo Hiberno'.

23 Jennings, ed, 'Some Correspondence of Father Luke Wadding OFM', 71, 76, 80.

24 *Scriptores ordinis minorum*, 161.

25 Barbier, *Gutenberg's Europe*, 84.

26 Marie-Jeanne Merland and Guy Parguez, eds, *Répertoire bibliographique des livres imprimés en France au XVIIe siècle*, XXVI: *Lyon, 5e partie: Justet-Pieldouce* (Baden-Baden: Koerner, 2004), 50. I owe this reference to Jérôme Sirdey, Conservateur des bibliothèques, at the Département des collections anciennes et spécialisées, in the Bibliothèque municipale de Lyon.

27 Hickey, *Expostulates Bzovius*. On Bzowski in the Irish milieu and the assembly of libraries, see Salvador Ryan, 'Steadfast Saints or Malleable Models? Seventeenth-century Irish hagiography revisited', *CHR*, 91 (2005), 264; Liam Chambers, 'The Library of an Irish Catholic Émigré: Michael Moore's Bibliothèque, 1726', *Archiv. Hib.*, 58 (2004), 210–242.

eight, nine and ten for the 1639 edition, while Punch edited volumes five and seven.[28] Meanwhile, the dedicatees of Wadding's scholarly circle were acknowledged for their religious and political leadership, for patronage hitherto received and as pledge of continued loyalty, as much as their funding for specific books. From the *Nitela* of Antony Hickey to the fifth volume of the *Annales Minorum*, dedications to Francesco Barberini bookended the Franciscan programme. Hickey placed an emphasis on piety and the pursuit of the truth, which were combined at St Isidore's.[29] He addressed Barberini as papal legate to France, dedicating the *Nitela* to him as Cardinal Protector of the Franciscans.

In Rome, Wadding drew upon a network that included papal families, Spanish officials and Roman nobles. This depth and breadth of contacts represented a strong suit for him because the extent of Wadding's connections meant he could tactfully avoid promoting one side more than another. Indeed, the powerful Barberini family searched for allies and 'competed for the opportunity' to be associated with scholars.[30] The Francophile Cardinal, Francesco Barberini, financed the printing of books on subjects related to his ecclesiastical interests.[31] Wadding indicated that they met on his arrival in the Eternal City and that he was the beneficiary of Barberini patronage for 'twenty years since [he] set foot in Rome'.[32] This points to the

28 Ignatius Fennessy, 'A Select Prosopography of Some Franciscans', in Bhreathnach, MacMahon and McCafferty, eds, *The Irish Franciscans, 1534–1990*, 342. On Punch's writings, see Ian Campbell, 'The Wadding Circle and the History of Political Thought', 149–60.

29 Hickey, *Expostulates Bzovius*, Dedicatory epistle, unpaginated: 'Veritati pietas accedit, iustitia causam souet [...] neque enim inter omnes eius instituti præclaros defensores & Patronos per orbem vniuersum Christianos Principes, qui se suaque eidem gentilitia pietate nunc [...] sed rem & pietatem agnoscens parentum'. Benignus Millett, *The Irish Franciscans, 1651–55*, 116–33. On the origins of the office, see Arnold Witte, 'Cardinal Protectors of Religious Institutions', in Mary Hollingsworth, Miles Pattenden and Arnold Witte, eds, *A Companion to the Early Modern Cardinal* (Leiden: Brill, 2017), 124–43.

30 Haskell, *Patrons and Painters*, 42–43, 50, 62.

31 Franca Petrucci Nardelli, 'Il Cardinale Francesco Barberini senior e la stampa a Roma', *Archivio della Società romana di storia patria*, 108 (1985), 133–198.

32 *Annales Minorum*, vol. 9, p. xi, 'Viginti anni sunt, ex quo pedem in Vrbem intuli; totidem, quo me perpetua gratia prosequeris'.

foundation of St Isidore's College. In accordance with contemporary ideas, Wadding saw Francesco Barberini's generosity as *pietas*, that is, motivated by virtue.[33] Wadding offered him the fifth volume in return as a 'small literary gift to the Prince of letters'.[34] Wadding noted that Barberini had 'built a library abounding in an abundance of all kinds of monuments', and the Franciscan considered himself fortunate if his codex was to be considered among them.[35] The Wadding gift to Francesco Barberini eventually amounted to eighteen books on his library shelves.[36]

Collegiality was an important element of Luke Wadding's network. When composing the eulogy for Hickey after his untimely death, Wadding wrote of their great friendship.[37] The erudition of fellow scholars earned the respect of Wadding. This is apparent from his Spanish confrère, Gaspar de la Fuente, 'a learned man, a most respected friend' who Wadding invited to lecture in Scotism at St Isidore's. He prevailed upon De la Fuente to publish. As a result, a course of lectures by De la Fuente was printed at Lyon by Jacques and André Prost in 1631.[38]

As well as new writings, Franciscan superiors conserved and developed existing resources for the order's publishing scheme. According to Wadding, a Portuguese friar named Luiz de la Cruz discharged his administrative duties to the letter and persevered in his studies when his other

33 *Annales Minorum*, vol. 9, xi: 'reponendi monumenti, quod dignitas et splendor tuus vndequaque attrahat, qui pietati student, vel rem literariam exornant'. On the concept of *pietas*, see Peter Rietbergen, *Power and religion in Baroque Rome: Barberini cultural policies*, 392.

34 *Annales Minorum*, vol. 9, xi: 'Principi literis inclyto literarium afferam munusculum'. For the primacy of *pietas* in Francesco Barberini's patronage, see Karen Lloyd, *Art, patronage and nepotism in early modern Rome* (Abingdon: Routledge, 2022); On Wadding's *Annales* and Renaissance ecclesiastical history, see Carroll, *Exiles in a global city*, 56–58.

35 *Annales Minorum*, vol. 9, xi: 'Bibliothecam instruxisti, omni genere monumentorum copiosissime adfluentem: inter haec si meus iste codex censeatur, felicem reputabo'.

36 *Index Bibliothecae qua Franciscus Barberinus S. R. E. Cardinalis Vicecancellarius magnificentiores reddidit*, 3 vols (Rome: Typis Barberinis 1681), vol. 2, 569.

37 Cleary, *Father Luke Wadding and St Isidore's College*, 84.

38 *Scriptores ordinis minorum*, 98; Gaspar de la Fuente, *Quaestiones dialecticae & physicae ad mentem syiubtilissimi doctorum Ioannis Duns Scoti, quas Roma legit* (Lyon: Jacques & André Prost, 1631).

work permitted.[39] When he died in 1633, De la Cruz left in manuscript his disputations on three papal bulls that dealt with the Crucifixion, Mass for the dead, and theological compositions.[40] Originally assembled on behalf of the Observant province of Naples, Wadding supervised its publication. As lector in sacred theology, Roman inquisitor and qualificator, he approved the text together with Rancati, Cistercian *consultor* to the Holy Office and Sacred Rites. Further endorsements were provided by faculty at St Isidore's including Martin Walsh, guardian of the college, Francis Tully and John Punch. A further endorsement from Claude Cochet, several times Dominican prior of Lyon and Doctor of theology at the Faculty of Paris, provides evidence of Wadding's cordial understanding with religious orders other than his own. Again, the De La Cruz commentaries were completed under the auspices of Francesco Barberini who the Franciscan Fathers praised as a providential gift, for 'just as Francis supported the shoulders of the tottering Lateran, so another powerful Francis supported the leaning edifice of the same'.[41]

Although produced by a variety of booksellers in the Rhône city, the title pages for Wadding's *Annales* enable the year of each volume to be determined with certainty. From 1633, Claude Landry's business was acquired by Claude Dufour and the silk maker, Claude Gapaillon, trading under the name of *Officina Landriana*. Dufour operated in business for twelve years and specialised in theological publications, many of them for the Society of Jesus.[42] The dedicatee of volume three of the *Annales Minorum* was Fernando Enríquez de Ribera, Spanish governor of Sicily. Printed for Dufour in 1635, the measurements of the binding are consistent with the earlier volumes.[43] Dufour retained Landry's typographical device with

39 *Scriptores ordinis minorum*, 163.

40 Luiz de la Cruz, *Disputationes Morales in Tres Bullas Apostolicas, Cruciatae Defunctorum et Compositiones*, ed Luke Wadding (Lyon: Jacques Prost, 1634).

41 Ibid, Dedicatory epistle, unpaginated: 'vt sicut labanti Ecclesiae Lateranensi Franciscus humeros supposuit, ita eiusdem ædificio inclinanti Franciscus alter potenti virtute ferat subsidium'.

42 Merland and Parguez, eds, *Répertoire bibliographique des livres imprimés en France au XVIIe siècle*, XXVI: *Lyon, 5e partie: Justet-Pieldouce*, 50.

43 *Annales Minorum* (1st edn, Lyon: Devenet & Prost, 1647), vol. 6, Dedicatory epistle, xii.

some minor changes. The engraving on the title page depicted Minerva and Mercury, patrons of the printing trades,[44] seated either side of an oak tree. At their feet was a black swan, in a shield beneath a star. The motto *Mature Cunctandis* appeared around the tree in Dufour's editions, meaning a timely delay, an apparent reference to restrained decision making from the Roman historian, Suetonius.[45]

Two years later, Claude Dufour promised to perform point by point everything promised to Wadding in his previous agreement.[46] Volume four was dedicated to Manuel de Moura, Spanish ambassador to Rome.[47] An initial delivery of 200 exemplars was standard for large-scale ventures from Lyon. The journey south to Rome took twelve days via Florence for letters and three weeks for heavier goods.[48] Nevertheless, Dufour told Wadding it was 'impossible for him to provide 200 tomes of the fourth volume of his *Annales* for less than sixteen *jules* a piece because of its size and other costs that must be paid'.[49] Due to the debt incurred, Dufour's Lyon banker, Lazaro Costa, had sent a bill of exchange for 320 ducats to Signori Acciaroli and Martelli who conducted business for the publisher in Italy.

44 On printers' marks, see Lea Hagedorn, 'Minerva in the Printshop: Publisher's Advertising in Frontispieces and the Media Presence of Early Modern Printer-Publishers', in Gitta Bertram, Nils Büttner and Claus Zittel, eds, *Gateways to the Book: Frontispieces and Title Pages in Early Modern Europe* (Leiden: Brill, 2021), 92–123.

45 Suetonius, *De Vita Caesarum, Lib.III Tiberius*, 25.1 cited by Mark Hebblewhite, *The Emperor and the Army in the Later Roman Empire, AD 235–395* (Abingdon: Routledge, 2016), 215.

46 Letter of Claude Dufour to Luke Wadding, Lyon, undated, 1637 (UCD-OFM, D.11/4/290).

47 *Annales Minorum* (1st edn, Lyon, 1647), vol. 6, Dedicatory epistle, xii.

48 Jean Delumeau, *Rome au XVI siècle* (Paris: Hachette, 1975), 14, 16–17.

49 Dufour to Wadding, Lyon, 1637 (UCD-OFM, D.11/4/290), 'il est impossible que ie vous puisse donner les 200 tomes de v*otr*e 4e des Annales moings de seize julles piece pour cause de sa grosseur et autres frais'. The *giulio* was a silver Roman coin weighing 3 grams. It was minted at Avignon during the pontificate of Urban VIII. Since the previous century, instead of gold, bills of exchange were honoured in 'no lesser currency than the giulio', which was prized in the monetary system. See Carlo Cipolla, *Money in Sixteenth-Century Florence* (Berkeley CA: University of California Press, 1989, repr. 2023), 7, 22, 48.

Wadding's contacts successfully connected publishers with readers. It was, nonetheless, demanding to complete each volume and unfeasible to dispose of large print runs locally.[50] Therefore, as travel was necessary to distribute his products, in 1637 Dufour asked Wadding to reimburse Acciaroli and Martelli in Rome, enclosing ten printed first sheets of the volume so that Wadding could see that there would not be any mistakes.[51] Dufour reported that he had hired 'another Printer, and one of the most famous', stating that he had placed Wadding's copy 'in the hands of a proof-reader for the press to read first before work on it', which cost him 'at least a hundred pounds of extra expenses'.[52] Dufour stated his preference 'for finer paper for your honour and mine' and assured Wadding that the paper to be used would be 'splendid high-quality as the enclosed sheets will testify for you'.[53] He continued:[54]

> I am happy you have finished the fifth and that you are working on the final volumes as I would be very contented to reach the end in a few years because, without them, your other volumes will not sell until then. I have spoken to several of your religious who say that the friaries do not want to take charge of your *Annales* as they are not complete. You believe all that you will but, please, I assure you that I do not sell one tome of them.

50 For the adversity faced by Laurent Durand in later years, see Jennings, ed, 'Some Correspondence of Father Luke Wadding OFM', 84–88.

51 Dufour to Wadding, Lyon, 1637.

52 Ibid: 'c'est un autre Imprimeur et des plus fameux iay mis vre coppie entre les mains d'un correcteur pour la press*e* lire premier que je travailler dessus ce qui me coustera pour le moings cent livres d'extraordinaire'.

53 Ibid: 'mais i'aimee mieux vre honneur et le mien que plus de bien pour le papier il sera tres bean et bon les feuilles cy jointe vous le tesmoigneront'. Mashed linen was often used for paper. Scribes could make their own ink, which needed to be thick and adhesive for a quill, but this was acidic and burnt the writing surface over time.

54 Ibid: 'ie me resjonis de ce que vous avez fini le cinquieme et que vous travaillez aux autres derniers car ie serois bien ayse dans quelques années d'envoyer la fin car sans cella vous autres tomes ne ce vendront poin iay parle à plusieurs de vous relligieux qui disent que ses couvents ne ce veulent charger de vous Annales quelles ne soient achevez vous en croire tout ce qu'il vous plairra ie vous assure que ie n'en vend pas un tome'.

Dufour's task was made difficult by the outbreak of hostilities between France and Spain two years earlier. He told Wadding he wanted to believe this war was the cause of all his trouble before stating that it was 'very regrettable to make great advances in the printing of a book only to find that one is not able to withdraw one's money for a long time'.[55] We do not know how Wadding reacted to this letter, but Dufour proved mistaken in thinking he would print the remaining four volumes of the *Annales Minorum*.

In 1642, Claude Dufour replied to a letter he received from Wadding through Nemesius Trichet who financed publication of the Observant friars' *Disputationes morales* eight years earlier and undertook to sell the book.[56] Dufour announced to Wadding that he had started printing the fifth volume of the *Annales Minorum*, with the intention of continuing until completion. Nevertheless, he informed Wadding that Cavalli and Montbrison had found another bookseller who would print all of Wadding's works.[57]

Dufour, therefore, appealed to Wadding's kindness, stating that he only wished to serve and not for the profit that he made in printing his volumes. If Wadding's book could be printed on better terms, Dufour declared that he would not regret seeing another bookseller take on the work, in Lyon or elsewhere.[58] He was ready to return the manuscript for the volume to whomever Wadding ordered. For the sheets that he had already printed, Dufour awaited Wadding's answer before consigning them to whoever Wadding wanted. In return, Dufour asked to be reimbursed at face value because he did not want to serve Wadding with regret. On this occasion, Dufour employed a good friend to represent him in Rome, Signor Tartagna, and hired a printer in Lyon to whom he consigned the manuscript so that he could work on it.[59]

55 Dufour to Wadding, Lyon, 1637: 'il est bien fascheux de faire de grands advances à l'Impression d'un livre pour n'en pouvoir retirer son argent de longtemps'.

56 Letter of Claude Dufour to Luke Wadding, with seal, Lyon, undated, 1642 (UCD-OFM, D.11/11/04).

57 Ibid.

58 Ibid.

59 Ibid.

Dufour expressed his hopes that Wadding would be happy with the printed sheets that he enclosed, noting 'the beauty of the paper, the quality of the print and the standard of correction' that he asked of Louis Cavalli, 'even more than usual'.[60] The paper was 'very expensive, just as Cavalli would confirm' and Dufour also had to deal with a scarcity of print-workers.[61] His petition to Wadding evidently worked in the short-term as he succeeded in completing the fifth volume. Thereafter, the first edition of volumes six and seven, and the contract for volume eight, were assigned to Jean-Baptiste Devenet of Lyon in collaboration with Claude Prost.[62] All the earlier volumes were also given to Devenet, so that scholars who worked on them found them more conveniently with only one bookseller.[63] For the first edition, the eighth volume of the *Annales Minorum* was eventually published in Rome in 1654. According to the editors of the third edition of the *Annales Minorum*, printed in 1931, there is no evidence that a Lyon edition of volume eight went to press.[64]

Opera omnia

Wadding was among the continental scholars who provided for demand from religious houses for editions of approved theologians and philosophers.[65] A decade after the first two volumes of the *Annales Minorum* appeared in print, Wadding and his associates produced the first critical

60 Ibid: 'la beaute du papier et bonte de l'Impresse la bonne correction s'en suis iay prie le P. Cavaly'.

61 Ibid: 'le papier en cherit fort come le P. Cavali le peut assearer [...] davantage du passe L'Impression n'en est pas de moings pour cause de la disette des ouvriers'.

62 Hazard, ed, 'Correspondence from Jean-Baptiste Devenet and Claude Prost, book merchants of Lyon, to Fr. Luke Wadding OFM', 519–45.

63 Benoît de Montbrison to Luke Wadding, Lyon, 10 July 1652 (UCD-OFM, D.11/01/01).

64 *Annales Minorum*, vol. 1, 'Prolegomena seu Apparatus criticus ad tertiam "Annalium" editionem', xix.

65 Ian MacLean, *Learning and the Marketplace: Essays in the History of the Early Modern Book* (Leiden: Brill, 2009), 157.

edition of all works by Duns Scotus.[66] This represented his chief accomplishment as a theologian.

After printing the third edition of *Beati Patris Francisci Assisiensis Opuscula* at Lyon, Wadding commissioned Laurent Durand to publish the *Opera omnia* of Scotus.[67] The Observant general chapter of Toledo declared that provinces of the order were to be furnished with sufficient numbers of copies.[68] Durand, a native of Grenoble, established himself among the booksellers of Lyon who specialised in publishing Spanish authors and opened a branch in Spain. His longevity in business, from 1610 to 1651, made him an exception among printer-publishers.[69] For the *Opera omnia*, Durand prefixed the dedication to Alphonse-Louis du Plessis de Richelieu, Cardinal of Lyon.[70] He was the elder brother of the chief minister of Louis XIII.[71] The publisher alluded to Duns Scotus by comparing the dedicatee's life to 'a subtle kind of theology', praising him for not leaving Lyon during plague the previous year and for his courage against political adversaries.[72] Durand wished to 'to testify to all this in lasting characters'.[73]

66 *Opera Omnia*, ed Luke Wadding et al., 16 vols (1st edn, Lyon: Laurent Durand, 1639).

67 *Opera omnia* (1st edn, Lyon: Laurent Durand, 1639), vol. 1, Frontispiece. The printer's mark for Durand was the goddess Aurora in a chariot drawn by winged horse.

68 MacMahon, 'Irish Franciscan Scotists of the Seventeenth Century', 106.

69 Merland and Parguez, eds, *Répertoire bibliographique des livres imprimés en France au XVIIe siècle*, XXII: *Lyon, 3e partie: Carret-Durelle*, 305.

70 *Opera omnia* (1st edn, Lyon: Laurent Durand, 1639), vol. 1, Dedicatory epistle, unpaginated.

71 Joseph Bergin, *The Rise of Richelieu* (Manchester: Manchester University Press, 1997), 60–62, 67–68.

72 *Opera omnia*, (1st edn, Lyon: Laurent Durand, 1639), vol. 1, Dedicatory epistle, unpaginated: 'Vita tua subtilis quaedam Theologia est'. See also Alison Forrestal, *Fathers, Pastors and Kings: Visions of the Episcopacy in Seventeenth-Century France* (Manchester: Manchester University Press, 2004), 201.

73 *Opera omnia* (1st edn, Lyon: Laurent Durand, 1639), vol. 1, Dedicatory epistle: 'id totum duraturis characteribus testari voluit'. On the Richelieu brothers, see David Parrott, *Richelieu's Army: War, Government and Society in France 1624–42* (Cambridge: Cambridge University Press, 2001), 96.

Considering his ongoing links with the Iberian Peninsula,[74] it seems unlikely that Wadding could have compiled such a dedication himself. This illustrates the fine line that he walked between French and Spanish contacts in Rome. Volume one of the Lyon *Opera omnia* opens with a portrait of Duns Scotus engraved by Cornelis Bloemaert, a Dutch painter and printmaker. Pen in hand, Scotus contemplates the Immaculate Conception in a painting above his bookcase. Light enters through the open window to his right with two friars on the path to St Isidore's in the background.[75]

The *Opera omnia* was a major undertaking that required a trusted corrector of the Latin press. When an author or editor could not consult the text themselves, the role was usually fulfilled by the printer. However, as Wadding's earlier experience shows, printers charged more for proof-reading.[76] On the other hand, his work in Rome made his presence in Lyon unfeasible. Wadding served four terms of office as guardian of St Isidore's from 1634 until 1643.[77] This occurred while he completed work as theologian, historian, Irish representative at the Vatican, and *consultor* to congregations and commissions at the papal secretariat. To overcome the challenge, he sent Cavalli and Tyrell to complete these duties for him. Wadding placed Cavalli at Laurent Durand's Lyon atelier where he worked continuously for four years to proof-read and correct the *Opera omnia* before publication.[78] This was bound for libraries in either eight, twelve or sixteen volumes.[79]

Born in the village of Rodelinghem, near the town of Ardres in Normandy, Louis Cavalli descended from an Italian family that settled in France.[80] In 1607, he went to the nearby port of Boulogne-sur-Mer where

74 Hazard, 'Irish Franciscans and the Santiago Province of Spain', 19–38.

75 *Opera omnia* (1st edn, Lyon: Laurent Durand, 1639), vol. 1, Frontispiece.

76 Dufour to Wadding, Lyon, 1637.

77 Millett, 'Luke Wadding (1588–1657), Franciscan Priest, Scholar and Churchman', *DIB*, vol. 9, 680–85.

78 *Scriptores ordinis minorum*, 162; Cavalli, *Scala Parnassi seu syllabarum quantitas*, Preface, unpaginated.

79 Merland and Parguez, eds, *Répertoire bibliographique des livres imprimés en France au XVIIe siècle*, XXII: *Lyon, 3e partie: Carret-Durelle*, 315.

80 *Scriptores ordinis minorum*, 162. On the Italian presence in early modern Normandy, see Jean-François Dubost, 'La Normandie italienne à l'époque modern XVIe et

he was professed in the Observant Franciscans. For more than a decade, he taught Classics at the Franciscan friary in Nancy and in the cathedral city of Rouen. By the early 1630s, Cavalli held the office of lector in the Franciscan province of Paris. At that point, the minister general, Giovanni Battista de Campania, called him to teach at St Isidore's. He was popular with students, 'collaborating with pristine persistence' in Wadding's writings.[81] All the works of Duns Scotus that could be found, were collated and reviewed with annotations at St Isidore's. For the most part, the contents were edited by Wadding's confrère, Hugh McCaghwell, who set the precedent for Irish Scotists at the Landry atelier in 1625.[82]

The Durand workshop was organised around the press with press-workers, the compositor who arranged the movable type and the corrector at the end of the work chain. According to a diary of St Isidore's College, John Tyrell, a theologian from Westmeath, was assigned to help Cavalli in Lyon on 24 March 1636.[83] Once the proofs were verified, Tyrell arranged the indexes. In the first volume, to honour the memory of 'arduous and troublesome work', Luke Wadding wrote of Cavalli as 'a Frenchman of Boulogne, a learned and humane man, Professor of Letters and Humanities'

XVIIe siècles', *Annales de Normandie*, 29 (2000), 163–177. Normandy received Spanish influence through its ports and from the Catholic Netherlands. For a description of the political and religious context, see Joseph Bergin, 'The Europe that the Earls Encountered', in O'Connor and Lyons, eds, *The Ulster Earls and Baroque Europe*, 8.

81 *Scriptores ordinis minorum*, 162: 'assiduitate pristina collaborans'.

82 Giblin, 'Hugh McCaghwell OFM, Archbishop of Armagh (†1626)', 286; *Doctoris subtilis Johannes Duns Scoti, Quaestiones super libris Aristotelis de anima illustrate atque discussae per R. P. F. Hugonem Cavellum* (Lyon: Claude Landry, 1625). McCaghwell obtained the royal privilege from Louis XIII to print this work which was approved in Lyon by Bishop Robert Berthelot of Damasco, 3 January 1625.

83 Jennings, ed, 'Miscellaneous Documents II 1625–40', *Archiv. Hib.*, 14 (1949), 5; Cavalli, *Scala Parnassi seu syllabarum quantitas*, Preface, unpaginated: 'in typographiis Lugdunen sibus, pro noua operum Scoti nostri editione, versarer, vna cum P.F. loanne Tyrello Hiberno (qui mihi Roma asignatus fuerat comes itineris, facius laboris in dictis operibus emendandis, quo Tum Indices ipse disposuit)'. Once he had completed his work on the *Opera omnia*, John Tyrell asked to return to Ireland as a preacher and confessor.

who diligently ensured that the edition should appear from the press unblemished.[84] Cavalli implied that he accomplished his task without difficulty, stating that he re-read poetry by Virgil at the same time.[85] He also delivered letters in Lyon on Wadding's behalf.[86]

Following the successful publication of the *Opera omnia* in Lyon, Wadding noted the minister general, Giovanni Battista de Campania, was in good spirits. The Irish friar told Laurent Durand that he would 'not exchange [Durand's] grace for anyone'.[87] While continuing to print the *Opera omnia* after 1639, Durand supplied another three books for Wadding in more portable sizes. Among his readers, Wadding exchanged letters with Jerónimo de San José, chronicler of the Discalced Carmelites, who praised the *Annales Minorum* and wrote of his happiness to be counted among Wadding's friends.[88] Collecting hagiographical texts was a priority for the Irish Franciscans. As such, Wadding endeavoured to publish the Lives of Saints. At the Vatican, he transcribed a large number of manuscripts relating to the Life of the Carmelite St Peter Thomas of Aquitaine believing, at first, that they referred to a Franciscan namesake and predecessor as bishop of Patti. So as not to waste his work, Wadding proceeded with publication as a sign of his regard for the Carmelites.[89] He submitted the text to the press in Lyon and, thus, extended the Franciscans' association with Durand.[90]

84 *Opera omnia* (1st edn, Lyon: Laurent Durand, 1639), vol. 1, Preface to the Reader, unpaginated.

85 Cavalli, *Scala Parnassi seu syllabarum quantitas*, Preface, unpaginated.

86 Claude Dufour to Luke Wadding, Lyon, 1637.

87 Jennings, ed, 'Some Correspondence of Father Luke Wadding OFM', 77: '[...] no le trocará a vuestra merced por nadie'. In the same letter, Wadding reminded Durand to send a collection of chained books to be attached to the bookcases at St Isidore's Library.

88 Atanasio López, ed, 'Correspondencia epistolar de Waddingo con el P. Fr. Jerónimo de San José, Carmelita', in *Archivo Ibero-Americano*, 15 (1921), 219–225; cited by De Castro, 'Wadding and the Iberian Peninsula', 157.

89 Mooney, 'The writings of Father Luke Wadding OFM', *Franciscan Studies*, 18 (1958), 235.

90 Wadding, ed, *Vita et res gestae. B. Petri Thomae aquitani, ex ordine B. Mariae Virginis a Monte Carmelo patriarchae constantinopolitani et sedis apostolicae legati* (Lyon: Laurent Durand, 1637); Harold, *Vita Fratris Lucae Waddingi*, 28.

Pillar of Franciscan Observance

In Naples two decades earlier, Luke Wadding had found the *Vita* of James of the Marches in manuscript by Giovanni Battista Petrucci, archbishop of Taranto.[91] Known as one of the 'four pillars' of the Franciscan Observance, James of the Marches was the fifteenth-century preacher, superior and inquisitor beatified in 1624.[92] Illustrated with his own notes and commentaries, Wadding retained Durand's services in Lyon to print the Life of St James of the Marches.[93]

This reflects Wadding's close connections with Spain. Philip IV was also king of Naples where the administration was in the hands of a governor named from Madrid, and local nobles.[94] Wadding knew that this was the traditional source of patronage for the Observant Franciscans in what was a much larger city than Rome in the seventeenth century. Sovereignty over Naples gave Spain influence across the Italian Peninsula, except for Venice and the papal states. However, the Spanish encountered widespread dissatisfaction in Naples where, for nearly a century, the cardinal archbishop had led the local inquisition.[95] This was exceptional in Italy but met with objections in Rome.[96] Since the archbishop and the secular authorities in

91 Francis Harold, ed, *Epitome annalium ordinis minorum*, 19. See also Chapter 4 of the present work.

92 Robert Karris, 'Giacomo della Marca's Sunday Sermon 52 on the ineffable mercy of God', *Franciscan Studies*, 63 (2005), 443–60; Fennessy, 'An Alphabetical Index for Some Manuscripts in St Isidore's College, Rome', *Coll. Hib.*, 43 (2001), 50–85. Capuchin reform began in the Marches of Italy.

93 Wadding, ed, *Vita et res gestae B. Jacobi Piceni*, Frontispiece.

94 On the background, see Luigi De Rosa, 'Naples, a Capital', *Journal of European Economic History*, 26 (1997), 349–373; H. G. Koenigsberger, *The Government of Sicily under Philip II of Spain: A Study in the Practice of Empire*; Foreword by J. M. Batista i Roca (London: Staples Press, 1951), 45, 59.

95 Céline Dauverd, *Church and State in Spanish Italy: Rituals and Legitimacy in the Kingdom of Naples* (Cambridge: Cambridge University Press, 2020), 151, 179; Domenico Sella, *Italy in the Seventeenth Century* (Abingdon: Routledge, 2014), 168.

96 Giovanni Romero, 'Inquisition and Church in Early Modern Naples', in Tommaso Astarita, ed, *A Companion to Early Modern Naples* (Leiden: Brill, 2013), 245; Prosperi, *Il Concilio di Trento*, 150.

Naples maintained strong links, the viceregal administrators of the kingdom were opposed to the presence of a delegate of the Roman Inquisition. In 1630, they voiced their objections to Philip IV and his ambassador to Rome, Don Manuel de Zuñiga, count of Monterrey. Philip IV responded the following year by ordering that no papal pronouncement should be implemented in Naples without authorisation from the Spanish viceroy. Since Urban VIII denied the need for viceregal approval, wrangles ensued between Madrid and the papal court. While the Spanish in Rome defended Philip IV's jurisdiction, the pope appealed to him for clarification. Eventually, the Roman Inquisition was officially instituted in Naples.[97]

James of the Marches was well known in Naples for his role as an inquisitor and for his strict observance. As an official to the Holy Office, which administered to the Roman Inquisition,[98] Wadding was aware of the developments that preceded the publication of his book. Therefore, he wrote a prose composition for the viceroy, Ramiro Núñez Felípez de Guzmán, duke of Medina de las Torres, as well as the senate and the Neapolitan people, 'most devout followers of Blessed James'.[99] Medina de las Torres took great interest in the acquisition of books and manuscripts, which he often forwarded to Philip IV. Therefore, Wadding sent the viceroy copy of the *Vita* as a gift for his library. Louis Cavalli participated in its production and recorded his presence between the theological approbations and the dedication to Innocent VIII with an anagram for Wadding's name and, at the end of the book, a lengthy poem in praise of James of the Marches.

Wadding became regarded as something of an authority on the history of Naples. He corresponded with Bartolomeo Chioccarello, a Neapolitan legal expert who chronicled the Spanish administration of the kingdom for Philip IV of Spain. Wadding and Chioccarello exchanged letters about the Cistercian order in the late fifteenth century and a work of three volumes

97 Henry Charles Lea, *The Inquisition in the Spanish Dependencies: Sicily, Naples, Sardinia, Milan, the Canaries, Mexico, Peru, New Granada* (New York: Macmillan, 1908), 95.

98 Wadding to the Roman Inquisition, St Isidore's, 8 May 1626 (TCD, MS. 1245, 36r).

99 *Encomium Neapolitanum*, written by Luke Wadding in praise and thanksgiving to the Spanish governor, the senate and nobility of Naples, 1641 (UCD-OFM, D.01/39–40).

on the kingdom, published at Rome in 1586.[100] Chioccarello subsequently cited the first four volumes of Wadding's *Annales* in his catalogue of Neapolitan clergy.[101]

Cavalli's reward

Cavalli appears to have completed his work as Wadding's proof-reader in Lyon after two decades.[102] Throughout this time, Cavalli also brought his own writings to print. He saw through the press a small edition of the *Opuscula* of St Francis, omitting Wadding's commentaries for more convenient use and dedicated the text to the minister general, Giovanni Battista de Campania.[103] Cavalli concentrated most on the correct method of Latin versification, collected from the best authors, arranged in an easy and clear manner. This was relevant to preaching skills, poetry and music. The book first appeared in Paris.[104] This was followed by an enlarged edition in Rouen, the well-developed centre of print in Normandy.[105] The

100 Chioccarello to Wadding, Naples, 17 May 1643 (UCD-OFM, D.11/17).

101 Bartolomeo Chioccarello, *Antistitum praeclarissimae Neapolitanae ecclesiae catalogus* (Naples: Pietro Agnelli, 1643).

102 Francis Harold, ed, *Epitome annalium ordinis minorum* (Romae: Ex typographia Nicolai Angeli Tinassii, 1662), Dedicatory epistle and Preface to the Reader; Hazard, ed, 'Correspondence from Jean-Baptiste Devenet and Claude Prost, book merchants of Lyon, to Fr. Luke Wadding OFM', 528.

103 *Scriptores ordinis minorum*, 162–63.

104 Louis Cavalli, *Prosodia, seu Versificandi ratio, ex optimis quibusque hujus artis auctoribus collecta, & facili ac perspicua methodo, in quatuor libros digesta* (Paris: Cottard, 1630).

105 *Scriptores ordinis minorum*, 162–63; Louis Cavalli, *Scala Parnassi seu syllabarum quantitas* (Rouen: Romain de Beauvais, 1633; repr. 1634). This was followed by *Franciscias: seu, D. Francisci Assisiatis vita* (Rouen: Laurent Maurry, 1634), a late sixteenth-century epic poem on Francis of Assisi and the foundation of the order. Cavalli accompanied the text with a life of the Franciscan poet Francesco Mauri. On Rouen printers and Paris, see Jean-Dominique Mellot, *L'édition rouennaise et ses marchés (vers 1600–vers 1730): dynamisme provincial et centralisme parisien*. Préface de Henri-Jean Martin (Paris-Geneva, École des Chartes-Droz, 1998), 110–122; Pablo

source was later reissued by Laurent Durand of Lyon and his nephew, Laurent Arnaud,[106] thereby maintaining Franciscan links to the publisher. John Tyrell, Cavalli's Irish associate, Luigi Marracci of Lucca,[107] and the Jesuit author, Gabriel Pilverderius, each provided epigrams on how Cavalli helped the reader to scale Mount Parnassus, the home of classical poetry. The patron of this work was Louis XIII's governor of Lyon, Charles de Neuville, marquis of Halincourt.[108] Cavalli recounted Neuville's donations to the Observants in France, from founding the friary at Magny-en-Vexin, to conferring patronage on both the Basilica of St Bonaventure and the church of Sainte-Marie-des-Anges.[109]

The Lyon edition shows the conciliatory nature that made Louis Cavalli a mediator for Luke Wadding. While based in the city, Cavalli met Pierre Labbé of the Society of Jesus, professor of sacred theology in the College of Lyon. The arrangement of Cavalli's book was suggested to him by Labbé, 'a man gifted with singular dexterity in the delivery of eulogies'.[110] When asked by Cavalli, Labbé commended Scotus, the Subtle Doctor, with a eulogy in print.[111] Labbé also received a positive reception at St Isidore's.

Sánchez León, 'European Provincial Towns: Demographic and Institutional Trends in Regional Networks, 1400–1600', in Benito Rial Costas, ed, *Print Culture and Peripheries in Early Modern Europe: A Contribution to the History of Printing and the Book Trade in Small European and Spanish cities* (Leiden: Brill, 2012), 13–14; Malcolm Walsby, *Booksellers and printers in provincial France, 1470–1600* (Leiden: Brill, 2020), 71–73, 171–73, 235–36.

106 Louis Cavalli, *Scala Parnassi omnibus gradibus suis absoluta [...] opera et labore P. F. Ludovici Cavalli Minoritae Observantini Bolonien* (Lyon: Durand & Arnaud, 1640).

107 Luigi Marracci (Ludovicus Marracius) was a noted Orientalist who taught in Rome; Jean Delisle and Judith Woodsworth, eds, *Translators through History*, revised edition (Amsterdam: John Benjamins Publishing, 2012), 174.

108 Cavalli, *Scala Parnassi omnibus gradibus suis absoluta*, Dedicatory epistle, unpaginated. On Halincourt, see Yann Lignereux, *Lyon et le roi de la bonne ville à l'absolutisme municipal, 1594–1654* (Seyssel: Champ Vallon, 2003), 262, 359–60; Bergin, *The Rise of Richelieu*, 72–75.

109 Cavalli, *Scala Parnassi omnibus gradibus suis absoluta*, Dedicatory epistle, unpaginated.

110 Ibid, Preface, unpaginated: 'vir pangendis Elogiis dexteritate singulari praditus'.

111 Ibid: 'rogatus à mes, Doctorem nostrum Subtilem, velut alter subtilis egregio commendauit encomio'. For the elegy, see Philippe Labbé, *Elogia sacra, theologica et*

When the *Opera omnia* appeared in print a year earlier, Wadding asked Laurent Durand to send him all the Labbé eulogies.[112] Before presenting his own work to the public, Cavalli shared it first with the Jesuit fathers Philibert Monet and Pierre le Gras, 'the wisest and most learned Prefect of the Lyon College'.[113]

The opportunity to publish these works may have been Wadding's reward for Cavalli's invaluable help. At the same time, Cavalli made the most of a favourable situation while it lasted. This ensured the wider distribution of Franciscan literature in France. Two years later, he edited *Breviloquium S. Bonaventura*, a work intended for students of the saint's philosophy and theology.[114] While based at St Bonaventure's friary, he also completed a new edition of Francisco de Herrera's *Manuale theologicum*.[115] It contained an epistle that Herrera wrote at Ara Coeli in Rome to Pompeio Arrigoni, Cardinal Protector of the Franciscans.[116] Cavalli's edition was subsequently printed on the rue Mercière in Lyon where many typographic workshops were located. He followed up a year later with the Scotist teachings of Eleutherius Albergoni in octavo.[117]

Called back by the fathers of his own province, Cavalli was appointed guardian of the friary at Bologne-sur-Mer. Yet, at Wadding's request, the minister general sent Cavalli back to St Isidore's again, to work 'with the

philosophica, regia, eminentia, illustria, historica, poetica, miscellanea (Grenoble: Balleonius, 1674), 67–68. Both Cavalli and Labbé lauded the city of Lyon and dedicated their writings to Halincourt. See Lignereux, *Lyon et le roi de la bonne ville*, 395.

112 Jennings, ed, 'Some Correspondence of Father Luke Wadding OFM', 77.

113 Cavalli, *Scala Parnassi omnibus gradibus suis absoluta*, Preface, unpaginated.

114 Fabienne Henryot, 'Les Lyonnais et Saint Bonaventure (fin du XVe–XVIIIe siècles)', *Revue Historique*, 682 (2017), 267–296.

115 *Scriptores ordinis minorum*, 163.

116 Francisco de Herrera, *Manuale theologicum et resolutissimo dilucidatio principalium quaestionem, quae communiter in quatuor libros sententiarum disputantur […] ab innumerius quibus expurgatum per Ludovicum Cavalli Minoritam* (Lyon: Jérôme Delagarde, 1642). See Forrestal, *Fathers, Pastors and Kings*, 40, 171–72, 195 for the popularity of these manuals in seventeenth-century France.

117 *Scriptores ordinis minorum*, 72, 163; Eleutherius Albergonius, *Resolutio doctrinae Scoticae, io qua quid Doctor subtilis circa singulas, quas exagitat quaestiones sentiat, et si oppositum alii opinentur, brevibus ostenditur* (Lyon: Jean-Aimé Candy, 1634).

same diligence as before'.[118] In the intervening time, Wadding was preoccupied by his work as agent and procurator in Rome for the confederation of Kilkenny.[119] This helps to explain Cavalli's renewed presence at St Isidore's. He joined the Apostolic College of Confessors at St John Lateran and continued to exchange letters with the Jesuit Fr. Philippe Labbé.

Benoît de Montbrison OFM Cap.

Another correspondent of Labbé contributed to Luke Wadding's literary endeavours in Lyon.[120] His name was Benoît de Montbrison, a local superior of Capuchin communities in the province of Lyon. His birthplace, Montbrison, was at the heart of Forez where handmade rag-paper of lasting quality was manufactured for printers and publishers.[121] The papermills of Forez were closer to Lyon and less expensive than their counterparts in Angoulême.[122]

Two Italian Capuchins and a French historian related a miracle story from Montbrison's life. In 1631, he was seized with a continuous fever for three weeks and given up for dead. The Capuchin vowed to say a certain number of Masses nearby at Le Puy-en-Velay. He promptly recovered, celebrated the Masses the following day and attributed his revival to the

118 *Scriptores ordinis minorum*, 162.

119 Fennessy, 'Wadding, Luke [name in religion Francis] (1588–1657)', *ODNB*, vol. 56, 643–49.

120 Carlos Sommervogel, ed, *Bibliothèque de la Compagnie de Jésus*, 12 vols; vols 1–10 (Brussels: Schepens, 1890–1909; repr. Louvain: Éditions de la Bibliothèque S.J., 1960); vol. 11 (Paris: Picard, 1932); vol. 12 (Louvain: Éditions de la Bibliothèque S.J., 1960), vol. 4, 1307–08; Jacques-Charles Brunet, *Catalogue des livres de la bibliothèque du cabinet de feu M. Parison* (Paris: Henri Labitte, 1856), 24.

121 Bernard Dompnier, *Enquête au pays des frères des anges: les Capucins de la province de Lyon aux XVIIe et XVIIIe siècles* (Saint Étienne: presses universitaires de Saint-Étienne, 1993), 34–35; Michel Boy and Jean-Louis Boithias, *Moulins, papiers et papetiers d'Auvergne, Livradois-Forez, Ambert, Richard-de-Bas* (Champétières: Éditions des Monts d'Auvergne, 2013), 120–25.

122 Henri-Jean Martin, *Livre, pouvoirs et société à Paris au XVIIe siècle: 1598–1701*, 2 vols (Geneva: Librairie Droz, 1999), vol. 2, 584.

Blessed Virgin. Directly afterwards, Montbrison set out for a provincial chapter where he arrived before his travelling companion, who was not a little surprised at his sudden presence.[123]

Montbrison's agreement with Wadding may seem puzzling in view of his broils with the Capuchins. In the mid-1620s, the Irish Capuchin superior, Francis Nugent, believed that Wadding was opposed to their mission in Ireland.[124] Wadding exercised vigilance in the examination of books for the Congregation of the Index. In February 1630, fellow bibliophile, Francisco de Eraso, informed him of Capuchin writings which he perceived to be objectionable.[125] That month, Patrick Comerford, Wadding's first cousin, noted that 'dealing with your brothers the Capuchins' was one of his priorities in Rome.[126] Even after Nugent's death, Wadding was opposed to Capuchin interests.[127] Nevertheless, the Irish friar needed an ally because he detected misrepresentations in Capuchin publications. Wadding justified this more conciliatory approach after Zacharia Boverio, official chronicler of the Capuchin order, published the *Annales Capuccinorum* at Lyon in two volumes in 1632 and 1639.[128] According to Wadding, Boverio was 'an erudite man' but the first volume claimed the Capuchins adhered more closely to the rule of St Francis than the Observants. Edoardo d'Alençon

123 Zaccaria Boverio, *Annali de frati minori, tradotti in volgare da F. Benedetto Sanbenedetti*, 2 vols (Venice: Apresso I Giunti, 1643–45), vol. 2, 180; Benedetto Palocci, *Frutti serafici, ouero Laconismo delle vite dell'huomini piu illustri in santita, e dottrina. De' frati minori Capuccini, dall'anno 1525. Fino all'anno 1612* (Rome: Angelo Bernabò dal Verme, 1656), 401; François Saron Campigny, *Histoire de l'eglise angelique de Nôtre Dame de Puy* (Au Puy: Antoine Delagarde, 1693), 447. The Cathedral of Notre Dame in Puy-en-Velay was the start of the *Via Podensis* from France to the tomb of St James in Spain.

124 Mícheál Mac Craith, 'Seraphic Sparks: Irish Franciscan and Capuchin Colleges on the Continent', in Chambers and O'Connor, eds, *Forming Catholic Communities*, 39–61.

125 Francisco de Eraso Carrillo y Pacheco, count of Humanes, to Luke Wadding, Madrid, 10 February 1630 (UCD-OFM, D.02/114–115).

126 Jennings, ed, *Wadding Papers*, 344, 'ora lidiando con sus hermanos Capuchinos'.

127 Martin, *Friar Nugent*, 258.

128 Alejandra Concha Sahli, '"The True Habit of St Francis': the Capuchins and the Construction of a New Franciscan Identity', *Collectanea Francescana*, 87 (2017), 513–52.

concluded that Boverio and Wadding neither agreed with each other nor with the authentic sources.[129] Wadding regretted division among the three branches of the Franciscan order. Rather than representing just the Observants or Conventuals, he was in his own words, 'General Annalist of the Seraphic family'.[130]

In 1652, Montbrison wrote that he was very happy to hear that Wadding had finished the eighth volume of the *Annales Minorum*.[131] Montbrison promised Wadding that he would diligently work from manuscript 'in the correctness of the press' for years.[132] Intriguingly, the Capuchin closed by saying: 'From the *Annales Capuccinorum*, I took away everything that Your Reverence told me are acidic opinions'.[133] This raises, perhaps, more questions than answers because there appears too great a gap between Boverio's *Annales* and Montbrison's letter. Nevertheless, Montbrison was fluent in Italian. It is possible that he removed everything that appeared injurious to Wadding while production continued at the printing press, which was usual practice with large-scale productions for religious orders. When the Italian translation appeared, changes were made to the two volumes from independent sources.[134]

129 *Tribulationes Ordinis Fratrum Miroum Capuccinorum primis annis Pontificatus Pauli III (1534–1541). Haec Brevis Illustratio Monumentorum, editorum vel ineditorum, quae ad dicti Ordinis historiam spectant, correcta et ampliata secundo prodit, cura P. Eduardi Alenconiensis, Romae, Apud Curiam Generalitiam O.M.Cap. cura P. Eduardi Alenconiensis* (Romae: apud Curiam generalitiam O.M.Cap., 1914), <https://www.capdox.capuchin.org.au/studies/edoardo-dalencon-troubles-of-capuchins-under-paul-iii/>, accessed 15 August 2024.

130 Luke Wadding to Gaspar de la Fuente, Rome, 9 January 1631; Gaspar de la Fuente, *Quaestiones dialecticae & physicae ad mentem subtilissimi doctorum Ioannis Duns Scoti, quas Roma legit*, Preface: 'Seraphicæque familiæ Generalis Annalistæ'.

131 Montbrison to Wadding, Lyon, 10 July 1652 (UCD-OFM, D.11/01/01).

132 Ibid: 'Io pigliarlo agora gran differencia della correctione della stampa, conforme alla promesa, ch'io ho fatto a V*ostra* P*aternità* R*everendissima* e faro ogni diligeroza anni quella opera riesa a sodiffatione sua'.

133 Ibid: 'd'Annales Capuccinorum, que tu cosè, che V*ostra* P*aternità* R*everendissi*ma mi mando sono parerrhi aroni'.

134 Father Cuthbert OSFC, *The Capuchins: A Contribution to the History of the Counter-Reformation*, 2 vols (London: Longmans, Green, 1928–1929), vol. 2, 433.

'True and real correspondence' [135]

As Patrick Fleming's experiences showed in the early 1620s, Wadding supported his fellow scholars.[136] He did not limit his help to the Friars Minor and, paying attention to literary pursuits, drew upon correspondence for his historical writings. For example, he often wrote to Pietro Maria Campi, a historian and canon of Piacenza cathedral. Commissioned to revise the local breviary by his bishop, Campi compiled a series of saints' lives as a result.[137] Eight of Wadding's letters to Campi are preserved at Piacenza, Biblioteca Landiana.[138] While vice-procurator general from 19 February 1633 to 24 April 1634, Wadding resided at Ara Coeli.[139] During that time, he responded to comments by Campi about the Roman martyr Cyprian and the relocation of his decapitated skull from Rome to Piacenza in the year 1001. Wadding was familiar with the Life of Cyprian as Duns Scotus had commented upon the subject and the martyr's homilies were assigned to Wadding at the papal curia. He advised Campi to accept the opinion of Baronius whose authority Wadding cited for the *Opera omnia*.[140]

Updating Campi on the *Annales Minorum*, Wadding told him the third volume was being printed in Lyon. The fourth volume was ready and additions for the earlier volumes would be included in its contents. The Irish historian notified Campi he would write again in relation to the dioceses of Pavia and Piacenza.[141] Campi replied without delay by sending

135 Luke Wadding to Pietro Maria Campi, Ara Coeli, 29 October 1633; cited by Benvenuto Bughetti, ed, 'Alcune lettere inedite del Luca Waddingo OFM a Pier Maria Campi', *AFH*, 5 (1912), 153: 'una vera e propria corrispondenza tra amici'.

136 See page 129 of the present work.

137 Simon Ditchfield, *Liturgy, Sanctity and History in Tridentine Italy: Pietro Maria Campi and the Preservation of the Particular* (Cambridge: Cambridge University Press, 2002), 186.

138 Bughetti, ed, 'Alcune lettere inedite del Luca Waddingo OFM a Pier Maria Campi', 149–53. See also Andrea Corna, ed, 'Alcune lettere inedite del P. Luca Vadingo OFM a Pier Maria Campi', *Bollettino Storico Piacentino*, 5 (1910), 208–16.

139 Ibid, 150. See also Ditchfield, *Liturgy, Sanctity and History in Tridentine Italy*, 111.

140 Bughetti, ed, 'Alcune lettere inedite del Luca Waddingo OFM a Pier Maria Campi', 150.

141 Ibid.

Wadding a large quantity of historical data, which the Franciscan gratefully acknowledged on 25 June. After Campi promised to send a catalogue of Piacenza bishops, Wadding looked to him for twelfth-century hagiographical sources about the diocese for the *Annales Minorum*. In return, Wadding was able to identify a late fourteenth-century Augustinian bishop of Piacenza, Andrea Serazoni, as the immediate predecessor of a Franciscan named Guglielmo Centuaria.[142]

Writing on 6 August, Wadding revealed perhaps the real reason for his letters to Piacenza. The Irish friar complained to Campi that he had been 'harshly criticised' by Pico Ranuccio, secretary to the duke of Parma, for stating that St Louis IX of France was a professed member of the Franciscan Third Order.[143] Campi was friends with Ranuccio who, in the previous year, had published a life of the saint in Piacenza.[144] According to Wadding, Ranuccio's work fell under the remit of Francesco de Rossi, whose job it was to inspect hagiographies at the papal court. The book by Ranuccio then found its way into the hands of Urban VIII who relished it so much he had it read at his table.[145] Although Ranuccio respected the authority of the *Annales Minorum*, he could not find any proof that Louis IX took vows in the Third Order. Instead, Ranuccio carefully argued that Louis only wore the Franciscan habit out of devotion. The duke of Parma's secretary avoided mentioning Wadding, but the Franciscan took offence at Ranuccio's argument. As a consequence, Wadding told Campi that he hoped Ranuccio's book would be revised and updated.[146]

Benvenuto Bughetti, the historian, expressed surprise at Wadding's annoyance since he was accustomed to much fiercer adversaries.[147] Wadding believed that his work had not been treated properly, but later changed his mind and did not insist on defending himself following the intervention

142 Ibid, 151.

143 Ibid, 152: 'L'amico poi Pico tratta molto male gli amici e me scrive gagliardamente contro intorno al essere S. Luigi del Terz'Ordine'.

144 Ditchfield, *Liturgy, Sanctity and History in Tridentine Italy*, 169, 265.

145 Bughetti, ed, 'Alcune lettere inedite del Luca Waddingo OFM a Pier Maria Campi', 152.

146 Ibid: 'si che spero verrà molto notiziato et ingrandito; estimarollo come devo, massime essendo tanto commendato dal purgato intelletto di lui'.

147 Ibid.

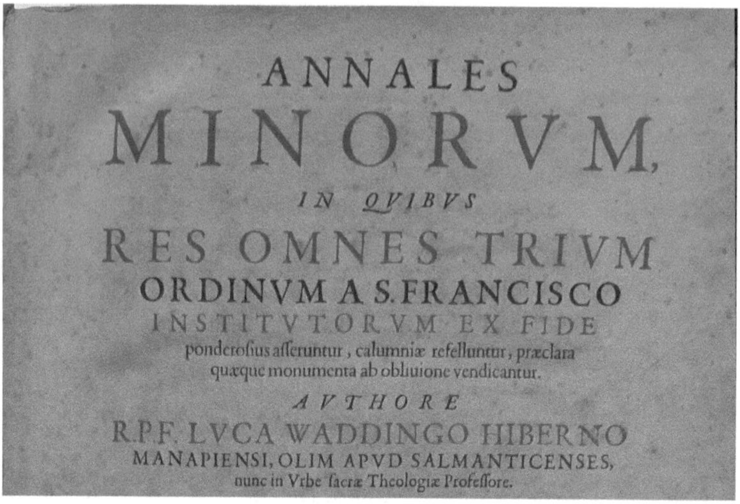
ANNALES
MINORVM,
IN QVIBVS
RES OMNES TRIVM
ORDINVM A S. FRANCISCO
INSTITVTORVM EX FIDE
ponderosius asseruntur, calumniæ refelluntur, præclara
quæque monumenta ab obliuione vendicantur.
AVTHORE
R.P.F. LVCA WADDINGO HIBERNO
MANAPIENSI, OLIM APVD SALMANTICENSES,
nunc in Vrbe sacræ Theologiæ Professore.

Figure 6.1 Detail of title page of *Annales Minorum seu trium ordinum a S. Francisco institutorum* (1st edn, Lyon, 1625), vol. 1. Reproduced by kind permission of UCD Library Special Collections.

of Pietro Maria Campi.[148] Wadding wrote the final extant letter between them from St Isidore's on 23 July 1639 but, according to Bughetti, their correspondence did not end there.[149]

Motivator and Mentor

To conduct business in Latin and candidly present one's case before the cardinals, Roman censorship required an ability to calmly assess, delegate and select in a balanced way.[150] Wadding met these obligations as a censor for the Index and a *consultor* to the Holy Office. This involved assigning tasks to trusted assistants, such as Antony Hickey, and paving the way

148 Ibid, 153.
149 Ibid.
150 Peter Godman, *The Saint as Censor: Robert Bellarmine between Inquisition and Index* (Leiden: Brill, 2000), 52–53.

for confrères to succeed him. One such example from St Isidore's is John Heslenan who served with the Holy Office.[151] The mind of the censor was 'wide-ranging and versatile, rational and sober'.[152] A twentieth-century Capuchin historian described Wadding as 'generous and impartial' in his work.[153]

Wadding explained that historical works had to compete with his administrative duties: 'Only in the course of the night was it possible to complete the work, the whole day being preoccupied by annoying cares'.[154] Francis Harold recalled that his uncle would begin his studies at one o'clock in the afternoon and was so absorbed that he was often awakened at midnight by the great bell of the Most Holy Trinity on the Pincian hill, above the Spanish Steps.[155] Wadding's research and writing were no sinecure. He explained that, since an ecclesiastical historian must be complete and uncorrupted:[156]

> He should not dare to say anything false, let him dare to tell the truth [...] to speak against our own where it is necessary and also for strangers, and when the matter demands, to remind both of wrongdoings in their own person, modestly, however.

It was in this capacity that scholars contacted Wadding seeking his assistance. While preparing the *Opera omnia*, he exchanged letters with Christopher Davenport, the English minister provincial, who was known as Francis à Sancta Clara in religion. Davenport was a Puritan convert to Catholicism who studied at Salamanca and read theology at Douai before

151 Millett, 'Catalogue of Irish Material in Fourteen Volumes of the "Scritture originali riferite nelle congregazioni generali" in Propaganda Archives', *Coll. Hib.*, 10 (1967), 11; Jennings, ed, 'Some Correspondence of Father Luke Wadding OFM', 91.

152 Godman, *The Saint as Censor*, 206.

153 Father Cuthbert OSFC, *The Capuchins*, vol. 2, 439.

154 *Annales Minorum*, vol. 1, 'Prolegomena seu Apparatus criticus ad tertiam "Annalium" editionem' lxiii; ibid, vol. 12, xvii.

155 Harold, *Vita Fratris Lucae Waddingi*, 43.

156 *Annales Minorum*, vol. 1, lxvii: 'cum historicum ecclesiasticum, integrum et incorruptum esse oporteat; ut ne quid falsi dicere audeat, ne quid veri non audeat, [...] contra nostros ubi oportet, et pro alienis etiam dicere, et cum res postulat, utrosque nullius accepta persona sui errata, modeste tamen admonere'. Cf. Canice Mooney, 'The Writings of Father Luke Wadding OFM', 239.

becoming chaplain to Charles I's wife, Henrietta Maria.[157] Davenport eagerly awaited each new volume of the *Annales Minorum* and encouraged Wadding to look forward to a time when England would be reconciled to the Catholic Church.[158] For his work, *Deus, Natura, Gratia*, Davenport drew upon Scotist thinking, but caused offence in England and on the continent by interpreting Anglican beliefs and practices from a Catholic viewpoint. Nonetheless, on his Irish confrère's birthday in 1635, Davenport thanked Wadding for his 'charitable offices' in bringing the book to print in Lyon.[159] We can look to earlier events for an explanation. In October 1628, John Roche wrote to Wadding pleased to know that the Irish friar had found a way to avoid a formal Roman enquiry into writings by the Dublin Jesuit, William Malone, who had argued against Anglicanism. Roche held that, on hearing of such an enquiry, Whitehall would have enforced penalties against English Catholics.[160] Wadding sought, perhaps, to avoid similar measures by facilitating Davenport's work.

Wadding also corresponded with Giovanni Pietro Puricelli, a significant figure in the study of Christian archaeology and ecclesiastical history.[161] When Puricelli compiled a Latin treatise on the basilica and monastery of Sant'Ambrogio in Milan, he asked for Wadding's support in overcoming possible obstacles. The canons at Sant'Ambrogio regarded Puricelli's book as an attempt to reopen a dispute between the canons and monks at the monastery which had been settled by a *Concordia* ratified by Urban VIII

157 *Scriptores ordinis minorum*, 79; John Berchmans Dockery, *Christopher Davenport, Friar and Diplomat* (London: Burns and Oates, 1960), 25.

158 Hazard, ed, 'Correspondence from Jean-Baptiste Devenet and Claude Prost, book merchants of Lyon, to Fr. Luke Wadding OFM, 526; Mertens, 'Philothea's Pilgrimage to Perfection: Vernacular Franciscan Spirituality in a 17th-Century Retreat Manual Written by John Cross', 258–80.

159 Davenport to Wadding, 18 November 1635 (*Cal. SP Domestic: Charles I, 1635* (London: HMSO, 1865), 488). See Anne Ashley Davenport, *Suspicious Moderate. The Life and Writings of Francis à Sancta Clara (1598–1680)* (Notre Dame: University of Notre Dame Press, 2017), 173–246.

160 Patrick Corish, 'An Irish Counter-Reformation Bishop: John Roche, VII', *ITQ*, 26/4 (1959), 103.

161 Hazard, ed, 'Some Unpublished Correspondence of Luke Wadding OFM to Giovanni Pietro Puricelli', 29–45.

in 1630.[162] Consequently, the canons denounced Puricelli and his book. Before it could be printed, the Congregation of the Index prescribed some minor amendments, ordering Puricelli to precede the final edition with the complete text of the 1630 *Concordia* and a *Protestatio* which declared the controversy closed.[163]

A substantial part of Puricelli's narrative concerned the history of the Cistercian order in northern Italy. The Cistercians dwelt in the monastery of Sant'Ambrogio in the early seventeenth century and their understanding was, therefore, essential.[164] Prior to publication, Puricelli sent Wadding advance copy of the prefatory material directed to the Congregation of the Index for approval. Wadding recognised Puricelli's book as 'most learned' and 'erudite' – a book 'adorned with study and diligence'.[165] Apart from works by St Bernard of Clairvaux, the Irishman collected a number of Cistercian histories for the library of St Isidore's College.[166]

162 The canons and monks at Sant'Ambrogio argued over the use of the belltower in the first half of the twelfth century. Papal pronouncements were made in favour of the canons. The civil authorities in Milan supported the case of the monks, as did Puricelli who brought to print documents relating to the discord at the basilica. See Puricelli, *Ambrosianae Mediolani Basilicae ac Monasterii hodie Cisterciensis Monumenta*, cap. 335, cap. 398. Pietro Zerbi, 'La chiesa ambrosiana di fronte alla chiesa romana dal 1120 al 1135, Excursus I: la controversia fra monaci e i canonici di S. Ambrogio nella storiografia milanese dei secoli XVII e XVIII', *Studi Medievali*, 3 (1963), 185–6.

163 Annamaria Ambrosioni, 'Per una storia del monastero di S. Ambrogio', in Maria Pia Alberzoni and Alfredo Lucioni, eds, *Milano, papato e impero in età medievale: raccolta di studi* (Milan: Vita e Pensiero, 2003), 181–2.

164 Elena Maria Gagliardi, 'Giovanni Pietro Puricelli e l'erudizione ecclesiastica nella Milano del Seicento', (Unpublished Doctoral thesis, Università Cattolica del Sacro Cuore, 2010); Monica Mazza, 'Giovanni Pietro Puricelli storico degli Umiliati, tesi di laurea discussa presso la facoltà di Lettere e Filosofia dell'Università Cattolica del Sacro Cuore di Milano' (Unpublished MA thesis, Università Cattolica del Sacro Cuore, 1989/90).

165 Hazard, ed, 'Some Unpublished Correspondence of Luke Wadding OFM to Giovanni Pietro Puricelli', 45: 'il libro è degno parto dell'authore e ornato col studio e particolare diligenza di *Vostra Signoria* al quale deve il pubblico questo singoiar beneficio'.

166 There are two copies of *Privilegia congregationis S. Maria de Alcobatia cisterciensis* (Venice: Imberti, 1593); Roberto Rusca, *Origine del sacro ordine Cisterciense* (Milan:

To help Puricelli, he turned to Rancati who was born in Milan, studied at the monastery of Sant'Ambrogio and was among the Roman censors. In the summer of 1645, the text was approved, whereupon the city of Milan congratulated Puricelli for his work. Happy at the news, Wadding pronounced himself ready to serve in every occasion.[167] Puricelli's nephew, Pietro di Gallarà, was a Franciscan student of theology with the Observant Reformed friars in Milan. At Puricelli's request, Wadding arranged Gallarà's licence to preach.[168]

After founding St Isidore's, Wadding was unwilling to be seen far from Rome. In return for his help, he made several requests of Puricelli. First, he sought a book on behalf of Augustinian clergymen who asked if Augustine and Simpliciano had written about one another. Simpliciano succeeded Ambrose as bishop of Milan in 397 and knew Augustine well.[169] Wadding then enquired whether the text of an early life by a contemporary of Augustine and Simpliciano was available in Milan. Wadding also asked Puricelli for the name of the abbot of Sant'Ambrogio who presided over the Franciscan chapter general at Assisi by papal order of Callistus III in

---

Paganello, 1598); Aubert le Mire, *Chronicon cisterciensis ordinis* (Cologne: Bernard Gualther, 1614); two other works are bound in with this volume: idem, *Origines ac progressus* (Cologne: Bernard Gualther, 1614) and idem, *De collegiis canonicorum* (Cologne: Bernard Gualther, 1615). The other works are Crisóstomo Henríquez, *Fasciculus sanctorum ordinis cisterciensis* (Cologne: Ex officina Coliniana, 1631); Ángel Manrique, *Cisterciensium seu Verius Ecclesiasticorum Annalium a condito Cistercio*, 4 vols (Lyon: Boissat, Anisson & Devenet, 1642–59); and Ippolito Marracci, ed, *Adae abbatis Perseniae, sacri ordinis cisterciensis alumni, natione Galli, viri doctissimi as disertissimi, Mariale Quo eiusdem Adae de Mariae Deiparae Virginis laudibus sermones aurei, ac fragmenta pretiosa ad posteritatis notitiam transmittuntur: opus hactenus eneditum ex per antiquo codice pergameno m. s. olim bibliothecae monasterij casamarij erutum, notisque illustratum a P. Hippolyto marraccio Lucensi* (Rome: Ignazio Lazzari, 1652).

167 Hazard, ed, 'Some Unpublished Correspondence of Luke Wadding OFM to Giovanni Pietro Puricelli', 44.

168 Ibid, 44.

169 Henry Chadwick, ed and trans, *Saint Augustine. Confessions* (Oxford: Oxford University Press, 1991), 133–6; R. P. H. Green, ed and trans, *Saint Augustine. On Christian Teaching* (Oxford: Oxford University Press, 1997), x, 65, 154. St. Augustine was baptised in Milan.

1455. Wadding related that the pope praised this abbot, though young in years, for his learning and wisdom.[170] The answer, Biagio Ghilini, was relevant to the sixth volume of the *Annales Minorum*. Whether Wadding received a reply to this particular enquiry is unclear since his description of the 1455 general chapter occurs without mentioning the abbot by name. On behalf of Augustino di Merato, lector of Santa Maria del Giardino, Wadding then asked for details of St Bonaventure's *Corpore Christi* from the Biblioteca Ambrosiana.[171] Santa Maria del Giardino was an imposing friary at the centre of Milan, built for the Franciscans in 1456.[172] To overcome contemporary considerations of long-distance journeys and terrain, he asked Puricelli for the wording of the title, together with the first and last words of the text doubting that this was to be found among those by Bonaventure already in print.[173]

Turning now to the Cistercians, Wadding saw the need for new ecclesiastical histories in their Counter-Reformation context. As such, he called upon scholars to address the gap in publications and research. Ángel Manrique held the most renowned chair of theology at Salamanca, where Ilarione Rancati was his disciple.[174] From 1642 to 1659, Manrique published the Cistercian annals, dealing with the period from 1098 to 1236.[175] His background illustrates how key individuals served as historians of their respective orders at that time. In doing so, Manrique paid tribute to Wadding's *Annales Minorum*, the first volume of which appeared in print more than three decades earlier.[176] Evidence based and organised chronologically, it set the standard for others to follow. In this context, the Flemish

170 Hazard, ed, 'Some Unpublished Correspondence of Luke Wadding OFM to Giovanni Pietro Puricelli', 41.

171 Ibid, 42.

172 Ibid, 39.

173 Ibid, 42.

174 García Rodríguez, 'Rememorando al Ilmo. Fr. Ángel Manrique, Obispo de Badajoz (1645–9)', *Cistercium*, 1 (1949), 54–57; idem, 'El Ilmo Fr. Ángel Manrique', *Collectanea Ord. Cist. Ref.*, 12 (1950), 195–207; 13 (1951), 128–139.

175 Ángel Manrique, *Cisterciensium seu Verius Ecclesiasticorum Annalium a condito Cistercio*, 4 vols (Lyon: Boissat, Anisson & Devenet, 1642–59).

176 Harold, *Vita Fratris Lucae Waddingi*, 170.

abbot and historian, Gaspar Jonghelincx, paid tribute to Wadding for the 'learned and painstaking manner' that he prepared his publications.[177]

As a scholar, the Irishman was something of a troubleshooter in Rome during the early 1630s when the work of Alphonsus Ciacconius on Roman pontiffs and cardinals was published under the authority of Urban VIII. The original text was enlarged with recourse to studies by the Florentine Cistercian, Ferdinando Ughelli. Before the book went to print, however, Urban VIII appointed Wadding to correct any historical errors and ensure its accuracy.[178] Ughelli and Wadding shared similar experiences in Rome. Both were friends of Francesco Barberini, they also served as *consultores* to the Index and declined promotion to the episcopacy. This enabled Wadding to cultivate his connection with the Cistercian order further and Ughelli wrote the official approval to print volume six of the *Annales Minorum*.[179]

The *Italia sacra* of Ughelli was published from 1644 to 1662 and categorised by bishoprics.[180] To accomplish his work, Ughelli merged a series of regional histories, such as *Sicilia sacra* and *Napoli sacra*, in a lengthy process.[181] This protected local privileges against lay encroachment, becoming an exemplar for the *Gallia christiana* and Gerbert's *Germania sacra*. According to Ughelli, Wadding anticipated the need for such a study and helped bring it to press in Rome. As the first Church history of its kind in nine folio volumes, the contents were occasionally prone to error but its

177 Ibid, 171: 'quos aliquot voluminibus eruditissime ac laborissime descripsit'.

178 Alfonsus Ciacconi, *Vita; et res gestae pontificum Romanorum et S.R.E. cardinalium* (Romae: Philippi et Antonii de Rubeis, 1630).

179 'Approbatio pro Magistro Sacri Palatis'. 1647 (UCD-OFM, D.14/6); *Annales Minorum* (1st edn, Lyon: Prost & Devenet, 1648), vol. 7, Imprimatur, unpaginated.

180 Ferdinando Ughelli, *Italia sacra siue De episcopis Italiae et insularum adiacentium rebusque ab ijs praeclare gestis deducta serie ad nostram vsque aetatem*, 9 vols (Rome: 1644–62), Bernardo Tani printed the first three volumes from 1644–47. Volumes four and five were published at the expense of Biagio Deversin and Zanobio Masotti, appearing from the presses of Vitale Mascardi from 1652–43. Typographia rev. camerae apostolicae, printed volume 6 in 1659. Deversin and Mascardi collaborated again to print volumes 7–9 from 1659–62.

181 Simon Ditchfield, *Liturgy, Sanctity and History in Tridentine Italy*, 290, 350–51, 368.

praise outweighed any criticism.[182] Referring to the Franciscan friar as his 'friend, the learned Irishman', Ughelli stated that Wadding compelled the *Italia sacra* to come to light earlier than anticipated, both by his annotations and by encouragement.[183]

Conclusion

A more human side of Luke Wadding becomes apparent from the assistance he gave to fellow scholars. His contacts in Lyon were the link between his booksellers and readers. Later in life, he sought to heal divisions between branches of the Franciscan order. On the one hand, the mediation of the Capuchin priest, Benoît de Montbrison, maintained the links begun by Louis Cavalli at the Latin press. On the other, the understanding shared by Cavalli, Montbrison and Wadding aimed at improving relations between the Capuchins and Observants. The extant letters of Laurent Durand, Claude Dufour and their contemporaries in the book trade provide a valuable insight into the relationship between an editor and his publishers in the early seventeenth century. These sources give us a clear impression of the influence exerted by Wadding's contacts when making enquiries among booksellers on his behalf. These writings underline Wadding's significance as a culturally and politically engaged scholar who worked with facility between Italy, France and Spain. The approbations printed in Lyon provide evidence of Wadding's friendly relations with the Cistercians, while also building bridges with fellow mendicants in the Dominicans and Augustinians. Third, the dedicatees for publications from St Isidore's show how Wadding managed competing interests to balance his networks, both within the Franciscan family and further afield in Church and state.

182 Denys Hay, 'Scholars and Ecclesiastical History in the Early Modern Period: The Influence of Ferdinando Ughelli', in Phyllis Mack and Margaret C. Jacob, eds, *Politics and Culture in Early Modern Europe: Essays in Honour of H. G. Koenigsberger* (Cambridge: Cambridge University Press, 1987), 215–229.

183 Harold, *Vita Fratris Lucae Waddingi*, 38, 171.

Figure 6.2 Fra Emanuele da Como, Fresco of Luke Wadding and associates: Antony Hickey, Bonaventure Barron and John Punch, Aula Maxima, St Isidore's College, Rome. One of a series of frescoes painted in 1672, in honour of the Immaculate Conception and the Scotist school of thought. Reproduced by kind permission of Collegio S. Isidoro, Rome.

7 At the Papal Curia

Introduction

The following chapter focuses on Wadding's experiences in Rome during the reign of Urban VIII when the papacy reasserted its supremacy over the whole Church. It describes Wadding's role in the selection of bishops for Irish dioceses, his liturgical work on the revision of the Roman breviary, the promotion of St Patrick to the universal calendar and Wadding's direct interest in the overseas book market. These developments occurred during a decline in Spanish influence.[1] Details are given on Wadding's contribution to the defence of Santiago, patron saint of Spain, which occurred in the context of skirmishes between Spanish and Italian interest groups, before considering the first signs of discontent against the Waterford Franciscan.

Wadding's Bishops?

For sixteen years, Wadding helped to shape the Catholic episcopacy of Ireland responding to requests from Irish dioceses for guidance and intervention. While F. X. Martin suggested it was an exaggeration to say that Wadding nominated the Irish bishops from 1624 to 1646, Brendan Jennings concluded that the part played by Wadding 'seems to have been practically of final importance, and his approbation almost invariably led

1 Thomas Dandelet, *Spanish Rome, 1500–1700* (New Haven: Yale University Press, 2001), 188–201.

to promotion'.[2] On close examination, Wadding was the gatekeeper who coordinated recommendations prepared by others ahead of time. This could take repeated efforts before a candidate was successful. Two examples suffice from the selection process for the primacy of Ireland in 1625. Edmund Dungan of Co. Down was recommended in the following terms: doctor in theology, of the most impeccable character and held in utmost regard by the nobility, clergy and people, proposed by the papal nuncios to Brussels and to Paris; the queen of France; the Infanta Isabel, governor of the Habsburg Netherlands; the province of Armagh; the clergy of Ulster; John O'Neill and Albert Hugh O'Donnell.[3] At that time, Bonaventure Magennis was a confessor at St John Lateran. The recommendation in his favour stated that he was 'of noble birth and a good life, manners and doctrine', proposed by the papal nuncio to Paris, John O'Neill and Albert Hugh O'Donnell, the clergy and people of Ulster, the Church of Armagh and the vicar apostolic of Down.[4] Note the subtle distinction that described Dungan in more laudatory terms than Magennis before the recommendations reached Wadding's hands in Rome. Neither party was promoted on that occasion.

Renewal and reform of the bishop's office and of the diocese were central concerns at the Council of Trent.[5] The prudent selection of worthy candidates was seen as essential to ensure the decrees of Trent reached every part of the Church. Strict implementation from within was the council's answer. Moreover, the bishop would have to be accountable in a detailed and immediate way to Rome. As such the ideal type of bishop, as apostle

2 Martin, *Friar Nugent*, 246; Jennings, ed, 'Ecclesiastical Appointments in Ireland', 18–19.

3 Burtchaell and Rigg, eds, *Hist. MSS Comm. rep. on Franciscan Manuscripts*, 83. See also Eduardo De Mesa, 'Un noble irlandés al servicio de Felipe IV: John O'Neill, Conde de Tyrone', in Ricardo Franch Benavent, Fernando Andrés Robres and Rafael Benítez Sánchez-Blanco, eds, *Cambios y resistencias sociales en la edad moderna. Un análisis comparativo entre el centro y la periferia mediterránea de la monarquía hispánica* (Madrid: Sílex, 2014), 339–48.

4 Ibid.

5 Ronnie Po-chia Hsia, *The World of Catholic Renewal, 1540–1770* (Cambridge: Cambridge University Press, 1998), 24, 98, 106–108.

and shepherd, became an essential element of reorganisation within the Church.[6]

Among the council's main priorities, great importance was placed on the need for bishops to live in their dioceses.[7] The Counter Reformation was fully established in Italy by 1555. From the outset, the preservation of Catholicism in Italy was the priority.[8] When Gregory XV established Propaganda Fide, Ireland was placed within its jurisdiction.[9] Nonetheless, the provincial councils envisioned by Trent never transpired.[10] Thus, the presence of an Irish adviser in Rome remained vital since the authorities did not fully understand conditions in Ireland where Catholic bishops relied on Wadding's assistance.

Before his arrival in Rome, appointments to vacant Irish bishoprics were influenced by another of his cousins, Peter Lombard, Catholic archbishop of Armagh.[11] In the five years from 1620 onwards, bishops were appointed to Limerick, Emly, Cork, Ferns, Down and Connor, Raphoe, Kilmore, and Elphin.[12] Following Lombard's demise on 5 September 1625, Wadding succeeded him as Irish bishops' agent in Rome.[13] Wadding was sensitive to episcopal authority. However, the mendicants' apostolic privileges to preach and exercise pastoral ministry remained relevant. As such, Wadding

6 Francesco Cesareo, 'The Episcopacy in Sixteenth Century Italy', in Kathleen Comerford and Hilmar Pabel, eds, *Early Modern Catholicism: Essays in Honour of John W. O'Malley S.J.* (Toronto: University of Toronto Press, 2001), 72–74, 78–79. On the succeeding century, see Alison Forrestal, *Fathers, Pastors and Kings*.

7 Vincenzo Lavenia, 'Bishops', in Nelson Minnich, ed, *The Cambridge Companion to the Council of Trent* (Cambridge: Cambridge University Press, 2023), 180–208.

8 Dermot Fenlon, *Heresy and Obedience in Tridentine Italy: Cardinal Pole and the Counter Reformation* (Cambridge: Cambridge University Press, 1972), 45–62, 79, 101.

9 Ó hAnnracháin, *Catholic Reformation in Ireland*, 6.

10 Robert Bireley, *The Refashioning of Catholicism, 1450–1700. A Reassessment of the Counter-Reformation* (London: Macmillan, 2015), 56, 59–60.

11 Lombard, *De regno Hiberniae*, ed, Patrick Moran, lxiii-lxvi.

12 Ó hAnnracháin, *Confessionalism and Mobility in Early Modern Ireland*, 18–55; Cregan, 'The Social and Cultural Background of a Counter-Reformation Episcopate', 112.

13 Tadhg Ó hAnnracháin, 'The Early Stuarts', in Kelly and McCafferty, eds, *Oxford History of British and Irish Catholicism*, 94.

also defended the interests of his own religious order.[14] Consequently, diocesan clergy recently returned to Ireland questioned his work in the early 1630s, but Wadding's strong suit was that he knew Rome from within and brought to bear his experience on behalf of the Irish hierarchy.[15]

After 1622, Irish bishops learnt to submit their correspondence to both the Holy Office and Propaganda Fide whereupon Wadding interceded on their behalf.[16] To obtain the promotion of their nominees to episcopal office, and of others to ecclesiastical benefices, the priests and people of Ireland petitioned Rome before Wadding's advice was acted upon at the Vatican.[17] This point was not lost on the bishop of Waterford and Lismore, Patrick Comerford, who asked Wadding, 'out of zele towards your countrie', to obtain a settlement from the Holy Office and Propaganda Fide 'otherwise our church in Ireland will become worsse than any that ever hath beene'.[18]

Ireland had thirty-two dioceses, more than half of which were in Gaelic regions at a distance from Crown control.[19] From 1626 to 1642, Wadding was actively involved in the appointment of sixteen bishops. His contacts in the Holy Office, the Index and Propaganda Fide facilitated this work with the Irish Church.[20] As the table below shows, clerics from a Gaelic background were well represented, along with seven bishops of the habit – four Franciscans, two Dominicans and one Augustinian – to offset appointments from the secular clergy. This counteracts claims that Wadding prioritised the promotion of Old English candidates.

His advice to the papacy on the Irish hierarchy first became apparent in the appointment of his fellow Franciscan and Salamanca *alumnus*, Hugh McCaghwell of Co. Down, who may have advised Wadding to address Ulster concerns by advancing Gaelic candidates. Soon after his consecration

14 Hazard, *Faith and Patronage*, 92–93.

15 O'Connor, 'Luke Wadding's Networks at Home and Abroad', 14–23.

16 Jennings, ed, *Wadding Papers*, 295, 324.

17 Ibid, 499, 517–18, 540.

18 Ibid, 324.

19 Peter Marshall, 'The Break with Rome and the Early Reformation', in Kelly and McCafferty, eds, *Oxford History of British and Irish Catholicism*, 18.

20 Binasco, 'Not Only a "Hibernese" in the *Urbs*', 79.

Table 7.1 Dates of nominations, appointments and consecrations to the Irish episcopate during Wadding's tenure as the Irish bishops' agent in Rome, 1626–42.

Name	Type of Clergy	Office	Date
1. Hugh McCaghwell	Observant Franciscan	Archbishop of Armagh	Appointed 27 April 1626
2. Thomas Walsh	Diocesan	Archbishop of Cashel	Appointed 27 April 1626
3. Edmund Dungan	Diocesan	Bishop of Down and Connor	Appointed 19 July 1626
4. Hugh O'Reilly	Diocesan	Archbishop of Armagh	Appointed 21 August 1628
5. Ross MacGeoghegan	Dominican	Bishop of Kildare	Nominated 29 January 1629
6. Patrick Comerford	Augustinian	Bishop of Waterford and Lismore	Nominated 29 January 1629
7. Eugene MacSweeney	Diocesan	Bishop of Kilmore	Appointed 18 September 1629
8. John O'Cullenan	Diocesan	Bishop of Raphoe	Appointed 9 June 1625 Consecrated bishop 1629
9. Malachy O'Queely	Diocesan	Archbishop of Tuam	Appointed 28 June 1630
10. Bonaventure Magennis	Observant Franciscan	Bishop of Down and Connor	Appointed 22 April 1630
11. John O'Molony	Diocesan	Bishop of Killaloe	Appointed 12 August 1630
12. Richard O'Connell	Diocesan	Bishop of Ardfert and Aghadoe	Appointed 16 September 1641
13. Louis Dillon	Observant Franciscan	Bishop of Achonry	Appointed 16 September 1641
14. Heber MacMahon	Observant Franciscan	Bishop of Down and Connor	Nominated 10 February 1642
15. Edmund O'Dempsey	Dominican	Bishop of Leighlin	Appointed 10 March 1642
16. John Bourke	Diocesan	Bishop of Clonfert	Consecrated 28 May 1642

Source: Cregan, 'The Social and Cultural Background of a Counter-Reformation Episcopate'.

as archbishop of Armagh, McCaghwell died of a fever. He was succeeded by Hugh O'Reilly who discouraged the promotion of Old English clergy in Connacht and Ulster, remaining in the primatial see until 1653.[21]

In keeping with established practice at the Roman curia, Wadding did not necessarily act on recommendations immediately. Following an eleven-year hiatus that drew criticism from various quarters in Ireland for being too slow, Wadding supported Richard O'Connell's appointment to the diocese of Ardfert and Aghadoe on 16 September 1641.[22] In a further example, many years after Thomas Strange sent him good report of Louis Dillon's suitability for higher office, Wadding approved Dillon's elevation to the see of Achonry.[23] In early 1642, the Dominican priest, Edmund O'Dempsey, acquired the diocese of Leighlin, a strategic move that further protected mendicant interests. That year another mendicant, the Franciscan Heber MacMahon, was made bishop-elect of Down and Connor.

On 7 December 1642, the supreme council in Kilkenny addressed a letter to Wadding asking that no Irish bishop should be appointed without first consulting the local Catholic archbishop and the supreme council.[24] Wadding acceded to their request. Heber MacMahon's subsequent career path benefitted from this move when the supreme council successfully petitioned to have their adherent, MacMahon, translated to his home diocese of Clogher.[25] The papal nuncio Rinuccini further illustrates the machinations involved. He vied for control of the selection process from 1645 to 1647, making recommendations to Rome, whereupon twelve bishops were appointed to vacant sees during those years. As an archbishop, Rinuccini had an added advantage over Wadding by being able to consecrate prelates, such as Terence Albert O'Brien, bishop of Emly.

21 Giblin, 'Hugh McCaghwell OFM, Archbishop of Armagh (†1626)', 258–90.

22 Millett, ed, 'Catalogue of Irish Material in Vols. 140–3 of the "Scritture originali riferite nelle congresazioni generali" in Propaganda Archives', 28.

23 Jennings, ed, *Wadding Papers*, 350.

24 Letters patent of the supreme council appointing Wadding agent and proctor in Italy, Kilkenny, 7 December 1642 (UCD-OFM, D.04/3/1157–60, formerly 586–90).

25 Séamus Ó Mórdha, 'Heber MacMahon, Soldier-Bishop of the Confederation of Kilkenny', *Clogher Record*, 3 (1975), 50.

Wadding maintained regular contact with senior clergymen in Ireland. His correspondence reflects a considerable network in the clergy and these extended beyond the nominations he oversaw himself. For example, Thomas Fleming, archbishop of Dublin, and Boethius MacEgan, bishop of Elphin, were among Wadding's Franciscan allies in the 1630s. Family relationships accounted for further connections within the hierarchy. John Roche was appointed bishop of Ferns in 1624 and referred to Wadding as his 'most lovinge coussen'.[26] They worked in close cooperation until Roche's death twelve years later. Another two of Wadding's cousins, Thomas Walsh of Cashel and Patrick Comerford of Waterford and Lismore, addressed him in comparable terms to Roche.[27] As part of a much older tradition in the Church, relatives were regarded as trustworthy associates in the early seventeenth century, but nepotism also gave rise to factions.[28] In return for preferential treatment, the loyalty instilled in recipients called upon them to support their patron.[29] Similarly, Wadding chose friars from his own province of Munster for the team he assembled to publish Franciscan works, with Antony Hickey from Thomond and John Punch from Cork, while Wadding's nephews, Bonaventure Barron and Francis Harold, were from Tipperary and Limerick respectively. From the early 1620s to the mid-1640s, this combined approach strengthened Wadding's position at St Isidore's and, by his own account, safeguarded the college in Irish hands.[30] Reciprocal nepotism was distinct from the practice of giving for the accumulation of private profit, which was contrary to Franciscan poverty.[31] Moreover, from 1625, Wadding helped to sustain the Irish bishops

26 Jennings, ed, *Wadding Papers*, 336.

27 Ibid, 343, 419, 542, 611.

28 Wolfgang Reinhard, 'Papal Power and Family Strategy in the Sixteenth and Seventeenth Centuries', in Ronald G. Asch and Adolf M. Birke, eds, *Princes, Patronage, and the Nobility: The Court at the Beginning of the Modern Age c.1450–1650* (Oxford: Oxford University Press, 1991), 329–56.

29 Miles Pattenden, *Pius V and the Fall of the Carafa: Nepotism and Papal Authority in Counter-Reformation Rome* (Oxford: Oxford University Press, 2013), 11–12, 81.

30 Luke Wadding to Pedro Manero, St Isidore's, 24 June 1655 (UCD-OFM, D.12/04); Jennings, ed, 'Some Correspondence of Father Luke Wadding OFM', 91–92.

31 Reinhard, 'Papal Power and Family Strategy in the Sixteenth and Seventeenth Centuries', 332–333, 339–340.

'on utterly insufficient resources'.[32] Newly appointed bishops were often greeted with obstacles on their return to Ireland. Patrick Comerford, for instance, experienced severe financial hardship and was obliged to live in his brother's house.[33]

While Wadding facilitated Irish causes in Rome, he did not give his full support in every case. From 1645, Hugh Bourke emerged as the central figure in Madrid for the Kilkenny confederates.[34] Two years hence, he became bishop of Kilmacduagh and subsequently gave his support to the Ormond peace. According to a formal defence of Bourke's conduct, as his influence increased, Wadding denied him access to the papal court and opposed his presence in Rome.[35]

Books for 'men fit to be bishops'

Wadding's research on the office of bishop extended beyond their historical significance. Most of his reading material on post-Tridentine bishops and cardinals was published after 1620. This indicates he only took a direct interest in the subject after he settled in Rome and began being consulted on Irish bishoprics. His reading material was distributed between French, Italian and German sources, with the majority published in Rome. Wadding obtained an early sixteenth-century Venice edition by Bartolomé Carranza who attended the Council, compiled instructions for episcopal office and advocated the need for bishops and clergymen to live in their dioceses.[36]

32 Corish, 'An Irish Counter-Reformation Bishop: John Roche, VII', *ITQ*, 26/4 (1959), 123.

33 Michael Olden, *The Life and Times of Patrick Comerford OSA (1586–1652): Counter-Reformation Bishop of Waterford and Lismore, 1629–52* (Waterford: Intacta, 2013), 41; Jennings, ed, *Wadding Papers*, 345.

34 Enrique García Hernán, 'Clérigos irlandeses en la corte de Madrid', in Downey and Crespo MacLennan, eds, *Spanish-Irish Relations through the Ages* (Dublin: Four Courts Press: 2008), 62.

35 *Contemp. Hist.*, vol. 2, 143.

36 Bartolomé Carranza, *Controversia de necessaria residentia personali episcoporum et aliorum inferiorum pastorum Tridenti* (Venice: Ad Signum Spei, 1547).

According to Carranza, personal presence was a divine law whereas absence from one's diocese was a serious disorder. In this context, Carranza also recognised the importance of preaching and teaching by suitable candidates for the office of bishop.[37] In residence, works of true charity by the bishop and the completion of his apostolic tasks took primacy.[38] At Salamanca, familiar territory for Wadding, theologians echoed the need for virtuous prelates who, invested with the responsibility of spiritual authority, required personal sanctity, prudence, strength, diligence and care for their flock.[39]

In the *Regestum Pontificium*, which he published as a supplement to the *Annales Minorum*, Wadding kept in mind the reform of Church discipline and gave historical examples of exceptional Franciscan bishops in earlier centuries.[40] Pietro di Anversa, for instance, held office as bishop of Sulmona-Valva in Abruzzi for three years. Wadding recorded that his fourteenth-century confrère presided over the diocese, exercising himself 'laudably and prudently in the pastoral office' where he understood and was able 'by the Lord's authority, to govern the Church serviceably and govern it effectively'.[41] In a list of Franciscan friars appointed bishop in 1344, Wadding described the

37 Dermot Fenlon, 'Pole, Carranza, and the Pulpit', in John Edwards and Ronald Truman, eds, *Reforming Catholicism in the England of Mary Tudor: The Achievement of Friar Bartolomé Carranza* (Aldershot: Ashgate, 2005), 81–98.

38 José Ignacio Tellechea Idígoras, *El obispo ideal en el siglo de la Reforma* (Rome: Instituto Español de Historia Eclesiástica, 1963), 187, 215–35.

39 Ibid, 69–112, 197–212. Joseph Bergin has described exemplary works on pastoral qualities as inert and theoretical. This raises the possibility that such literature had lost momentum in early seventeenth-century Italy. See Joseph Bergin, *The Making of the French Episcopate, 1589–1661* (New Haven: Yale University Press, 1996), 209; Idem, 'The Counter-Reformation Church and its Bishops', *P&P*, 165 (November 1999), 48.

40 On the origins of pastoral reform in the late Middle Ages, see Nicole Lemaitre, 'L'idéal pastoral de réforme et le Concile de Trente (XIVe–XVIe siècle)', in Wim François and Violet Soen, eds, *Council of Trent. Reform and Controversy in Europe and Beyond (1545–1700)*, 3 vols (Göttingen: Vandenhoeck & Ruprecht, 2018), 2, 9–32.

41 *Annales Minorum*, vol. 7 (1330), 494, n. 2: 'Ecclesiæ hactenus utiliter præsuisti, teque alias exercuisti laudabiliter & prudenter in officio Pastorali, dictam Valven. Ecclesiam scies & poteris, auctore Domino, utiliter regere, & feliciter gubernare, noftrum animum duximus dirigendum'.

Venerable Guglielmo Isnardi in comparable terms. After serving as bishop of Alba and as archbishop of Brindisi, Isnardi was appointed to the diocese of Benevento in 1344. Again, Wadding recorded that Isnardi exercised himself 'worthily and cautiously' as bishop of his diocese, 'knowing how and being able, by the Lord's authority, to rule usefully and successfully'.[42] Moreover, in Wadding's narrative, attentive bishops were efficient administrators who oversaw prosperous dioceses.[43] This implies the bishop's responsibility to live in the diocese under his care, a recurring topic for debate at Trent, which became a vital priority. In Wadding's view, these were 'men fit to be bishops' who governed favourably and were, therefore, 'of happy memory'.[44]

Wadding eschews the mitre

Wadding avoided accepting a bishop's mitre for himself. By the mid-1620s, his reputation for holiness, his extensive contacts on the continent and his skills as a communicator led contemporaries to nominate him for the episcopate himself. A year after the Irish Franciscan's arrival in Rome, Albert Hugh O'Donnell, earl of Tyrconnell, recommended Wadding for the vacant see of Waterford since he possessed the required 'nobility, discipline, talent, dexterity, knowledge, maturity, experience and behaviour'.[45] Hence, O'Donnell earnestly asked that Wadding be promoted. Similarly, after the death of Hugh McCaghwell, Wadding was among the names of Irish

42 *Annales Minorum*, vol. 7 (1344), 638, *Regestum Pontificium*: 'teque alias exercuisti laudabiliter & prudenter in officio Pastorali, dictam Beneventan. Ecclesiam scies & poteris, auctore Domino, utiliter regere ac feliciter gubernare, nostrum animum duximus dirigendum'.

43 *Annales Minorum*, vol. 6 (1301), 467, *Regestum Pontificium*: 'proficiant incrementis'.

44 Ibid, vol. 6 (1320), 620, *Regestum Pontificium*; ibid, vol. 7 (1345), 657, *Regestum Pontificium*: 'viros idoneos in pastores […] felicis memoriae'.

45 Albert Hugh O'Donnell to the Cardinal Protector of Ireland, Leuven, 7 October 1619 (UCD-OFM, D.03/208): 'nobilitas, disciplina, ingenium, in rebus agendis dexteritas, scientia, maturitas aetatis, vitae et morum opinio […] Quapropter illustrissimam amplitudinem vestram quam enixe rogamus ut eundem patrem, in quo nulla apparet exceptio, ad sedem Waterfordiensem'. Jennings, ed, *Wadding Papers*, 20. This letter appears to have been written by Flaithrí Ó Maolchonaire.

churchmen suggested for the archbishopric of Armagh and the primacy of Ireland.[46] Patrick Corish regarded it as normal for the Irish bishops' agent in Rome to be the first candidate considered,[47] but the matter ended there.

Once more, in 1644 the supreme council of the confederation of Kilkenny wrote to Urban VIII and the Barberini cardinals, Antonio and Francesco, asking for a cardinal's red hat to be conferred on Wadding, but somehow he intercepted the documents and concealed them in the archives at St Isidore's.[48] There are a number of possible explanations for Wadding's avoidance of further advancement. First, St Francis of Assisi issued instructions on preserving one's humility and the love of poverty rather than accepting honours.[49] Second, Wadding had witnessed the difficulties encountered by two friends when elevated to the office of bishop namely Francisco de Sosa and Antonio de Trejo. Indeed, to have accepted such promotion would have diverted Wadding from his projects within the Franciscan order. This question remained relevant to Wadding and, as such, is discussed further in the next chapter.

Urban VIII's Breviary

The Order of Friars Minor well understood the content and history of liturgical books, particularly the breviary.[50] The friars traditionally prayed

46 Jennings, ed, *Wadding Papers*, 174–75.

47 Patrick Corish, 'An Irish Counter-Reformation Bishop: John Roche, part 3', *ITQ*, 26 (1959), 118.

48 Supreme council of the confederation of Kilkenny to Cardinal Antonio Barberini and Cardinal Francesco Barberini, Kilkenny, 14 June 1644 (UCD-OFM, D.12); *Hist. Ir. Confed.*, vol. 3, 186–94; Meehan, *The Rise and Fall of the Irish Franciscan Monasteries*, 97–98.

49 Armstrong, Hellmann and Short, *Francis of Assisi. Early Documents*, vol. 3, 389. Through John Flahy's classical school in Waterford, Wadding may have been familiar with the ideas of Horace who warned against the dangers of ambition and higher office. Cf. Stanford Lehmberg, 'Sir Thomas More's Life of Pico della Mirandola', in *Studies in the Renaissance*, 3 (1956), 61–74.

50 S. J. P. van Dijk and J. Hazleden Walker, *The Origins of the Modern Roman Liturgy: The Liturgy of the Papal Court and the Franciscans in the Thirteenth Century* (London: Newman Press, 1960), 37.

the canonical hours together according to the rising and setting of the sun, beginning with vigils after midnight, matins in the early hours of the morning and lauds at dawn, followed by prime, terce, sext, none, vespers through the day and compline before retiring to sleep.[51] In 1629, Urban VIII assigned Wadding to the revision of the Roman breviary and, in 1631, to the revision of the Roman missal.[52] This made him part of a small but significant commission of nine *consultores* assembled from the Congregation of Rites. Cardinal Luigi Gaetani presided with Tegrimio Tegrimi, bishop of Assisi, appointed secretary. Wadding's fellow *consultores* were Ilarione Rancati, Cistercian abbot; the Barnabite liturgist, Bartolommeo Gavantus; the Jesuit Father Terenzio Alciati, prefect of studies at the Collegio Romano; Girolamo Lanuvio of the Signatura tribunals; the Augustinian Fortunato Scacchi, papal sacristan; the Dominican Niccolò Riccardi, master of the sacred palace; and Giacomo Volponi, an Oratorian theologian.[53] In his work on the liturgy, Wadding corresponded with the Theatine order, the essential aim of which was to recall the clergy to edification and, through them, to reach the lay faithful.[54]

51 Ó Clabaigh, *The Friars in Ireland*, 170–171.

52 *Scriptores ordinis minorum*, 162–63. Wadding acknowledged the assistance he received from his French confrère, Louis Cavalli. See also Pierre Batiffol, *History of the Roman Breviary,* translated by Atwell Baylay (London: Longmans, Green & Co., 1912), 281–3.

53 Hazard, 'Some Unpublished Correspondence of Luke Wadding OFM to Giovanni Pietro Puricelli', 29–45. Gavantus was first appointed to the commission for the reform of the breviary by Clement VIII to advise Cesare Baronius. The Barnabites, like the Theatines, were a comparatively new religious order. See A. G. Dickens, *The Counter-Reformation* (London: Thames & Hudson, 1968), 70–1, 96. Alciati prepared the history of the Council of Trent, published after his death by Cardinal Pietro Sforza Pallavicino. When Alciati became ill in the summer of 1629, his place was taken by a fellow Jesuit, Girolamo Petrucci: see Pastor, *History of the Popes,* vol. 29, 12–14.

54 Millett, 'The Archives of St Isidore's College, Rome', 10. On the Theatines, see Ditchfield, *Liturgy, Sanctity and history in Tridentine Italy*, 25–31, 74; Dickens, *The Counter-Reformation*, 68–71, 165.

The breviary is a compendium of daily prayers, psalms, and readings divided into four parts corresponding to the seasons of the year.[55] Before the Reformation, the provision of liturgical books was the responsibility of individual bishops and religious orders.[56] Almost every diocese and monastery had its own breviary, with more than one hundred and fifty different versions in circulation in the West.[57] Compact and convenient to carry for missionary orders, the Roman breviary was popularised for centuries by the Franciscans.[58]

Much of the writing on the subject of Urban VIII's breviary has concentrated on the attempts to bring its hymns closer to classical Latin poetry.[59] Wadding's contribution to liturgical books reveals that was only part of the narrative. The 'world of the breviary', precise and to-the-point, was familiar to Wadding from an early age.[60] As soon as he could read, his parents gave him a prayer-book containing the minor offices of the breviary of Pius V so that he could join his siblings in the daily recital of the liturgical prayers.

The advent of print helped to ensure that a standardised approach could be adopted for liturgical books, while remaining true to the original. The papal bull of approval, *Quod a nobis,* published in 1568, resolved to settle on an official text of public prayer – the Roman breviary – as the only universally valid model except for pre-existing rites over two hundred

55 E. J. Quigley, *The Divine Office: A Study of the Roman Breviary* (Dublin: Gill, 1920), 1–5.

56 Ditchfield, *Liturgy, Sanctity and History in Tridentine Italy*, 25–31, 74.

57 On the production of liturgical manuscripts in thirteenth- and fourteenth-century Umbria, and the relevance of various texts to communal identity, see Anna Welch, *Liturgy, Books and Franciscan Identity in Medieval Umbria* (Leiden: Brill, 2015), 87–91, 204–213.

58 The Franciscan order adapted the liturgical custom of the Lateran Palace in the thirteenth century. See S. J. P. van Dijk and J. Hazleden Walker, *The Origins of the Modern Roman Liturgy*, 217–37; Ó Clabaigh, *The Friars in Ireland*, 173–74.

59 Aemilius Springhetti, 'Urbanus VIII PM poeta latinus et hymnorum Brevarii emendator', *AHP*, 6 (1968), 163–90; Kevin Maguire, 'The Revision of the Breviary Hymnal under Urban VIII', in Francis Caims, ed, *Papers of the Liverpool Latin Seminar 1976* (Liverpool: Cairns Publishing, 1977), 203–205; Vincent Lenti, 'Urban VIII and the revision of the Latin hymnal', *Sacred Music,* 120 (1993), 30–33 at note 7.

60 Ditchfield, *Liturgy, Sanctity and History in Tridentine Italy*, 130.

years old.[61] Considered 'the minimum library of a working parish priest',[62] the essential purpose of the revised breviary was didactic, maintaining an adequate level of education among the clergy and as a result, the practice of virtue by the laity. Exceptions to the liturgical calendar led to the addition of supplements: one for countries and one for the religious orders. In the old world and the new, however, plans for ecclesiastical and pastoral renewal had to take account of the Roman breviary, its contents, structure and purpose.[63]

The major post-Tridentine breviaries were those of Pius V, Clement VIII, and Urban VIII. Pius V was noted for amending the Roman breviary, Clement VIII for the revision of the liturgical instructions, and Urban VIII for amending the hymns. Thus the text was not definitively set before 1632.[64] The commission for liturgical reform sat sixty-six times between 12 July 1629 and 18 December 1631.[65] The revision of many offices of the breviary was entrusted to Wadding – above all the lessons of the second nocturns of matins.[66] In *Scriptores ordinis minorum*, Wadding stated that he either compiled or revised according to more dependable sources the lives of saints for churches in Italy, Spain, Germany, Bohemia, Hungary and other countries. He was also assigned the texts of homilies from the Church Fathers, from St Cyprian and Pope St Leo for the new breviary.[67]

Wadding was in much demand during this period in his life. In 1632, he was called, with Rancati and Riccardi, to join a commission that examined

61 Suitbert Bäumer, *Histoire du Bréviaire,* translated by Réginald Biron, 2 vols (Paris: Letouzey et Ané, 1905).

62 Ditchfield, *Liturgy, Sanctity and History in Tridentine Italy,* 10–11, 33–5, 66, 319.

63 Thomas Steele, *Santos and Saints: The Religious Folk Art of Hispanic New Mexico* (Santa Fé, NM: Ancient City Press, 1994), 198.

64 Wadding's notes on this work are extant in papers at a number of archives.

65 'Varia S. Congregationis Rituum de Breviario, Missali, [...] tempore Urbani VIII, consultore P. L. Waddingo' (Rome: Archivio Generale at the General Curia of Friars Minor, Ms. 2/22); cited by Millett, 'The Archives of St Isidore's', 10. In 1635, Francesco Ingoli consulted Wadding with regard to the Greek and Armenian liturgy: Millett, 'Guide to Material for a Biography of Father Luke Wadding', 248.

66 Mooney, 'The Writings of Father Luke Wadding OFM', 237.

67 Millett, 'The Archives of St Isidore's', 10; see also Harold, *Vita Fratris Lucae Waddingi,* 132.

doubts arising from the missions in Japan.[68] Wadding participated as a specialist in eastern languages. Accustomed to working on publications intended for the Orient, he was tasked with drafting an instruction intended for Catholic missionaries. Together with his confrère, Filippo Guadagnoli, Wadding insisted on the need to revise and print the profession of faith in various languages, so that missionaries could avoid making mistakes. On the presence of Christ in the Eucharist, Wadding agreed with Francesco Ingoli, secretary of Propaganda Fide – 'a stickler for the letter of the law'[69] – who recommended the insertion of an article in the profession of faith.[70] They did so on the understanding that the article already existed in previous confessions of faith. Nonetheless, the issue at stake was controversial for Protestant thinkers. At the same time, Wadding and Guadagnoli disapproved of missionaries demanding a profession of undefined dogmatic questions, such as the Immaculate Conception.[71] The following year, Wadding was raised to the office of vice-procurator general for the Franciscans at Ara Coeli in Rome.[72]

Feast of St Patrick

During the reign of Philip IV, scholars claimed that the Gospel was first preached in Ireland by the Apostle Santiago and his father Zebedee who remained there after him as first bishop.[73] This idea gave Ireland a

68 Aurélien Girard, 'Comment reconnaître un chrétien oriental vraiment catholique? Élaboration et usages de la profession de foi', in Marie-Hélène Blanchet and Frédéric Gabriel, eds, *L'union à l'épreuve du formulaire. Professions de foi entre Églises d'Orient et d'Occident (XIIIe–XVIIIe siècle)* (Leuven: Peeters, 2016), 235–58.

69 Pastor, *History of the Popes*, vol. 29, 28.

70 Girard, 'Comment reconnaître un chrétien oriental vraiment catholique?' 247.

71 Ibid, 246.

72 Silvano Giordano, 'Uomini e apparati della politica internazionale del papato', in Maria Antonietta Visceglia, ed, *Papato e politica internazionale nella prima età moderna* (Rome: Viella, 2013), 131–48.

73 Salvador Ryan, 'Reconstructing Irish Catholic History after the Reformation', in Katherine Van Liere, Simon Ditchfield and Howard Louthan, eds, *Sacred History:*

Roman pedigree and was supported by Juan Gil Zamora, the Franciscan hagiographer and historian with whose works Wadding was familiar since studying in Spain.[74] Even so, Wadding's organised mind saw the need for greater clarity and understood that the proposition conflicted with well-established Irish beliefs in St Patrick.

In the early 1630s, the Irish bishops wished to adapt the image of St Patrick according to seventeenth-century liturgical requirements.[75] Finding a suitable way to enter the saint's feast day on 17 March in the universal calendar was central to their project.[76] The Franciscans were well accustomed with the subject. In 1390, the feast of St Patrick was approved for the entire order at the General Chapter in Assisi.[77] Patrick Comerford emphasised to Wadding that Ireland's patron saint warranted at least a semidouble office in the new breviary.[78] Wadding used his influence on the commission to implement Comerford's directions and when the new breviary appeared in print, John Roche, bishop of Ferns, praised Wadding for the incorporation of St Patrick in the text. Roche wrote of his gratitude:[79]

> God reward you for procuring his feast to be put in ye Romaine calendar. The himnes, antiphons, responsories, be them that weare in the ancient office. Ye legend of the saint is moderne, drawen out of ye best writers, more seemly to be read then the ancient legend.

Thereafter, to quote John McCafferty, 'Muirchú's seventh-century Moses of Armagh became a Tridentine Moses for a seventeenth-century Catholic

Uses of the Christian Past in the Renaissance (Oxford: Oxford University Press, 2012), 197; María del Henar Velasco López, 'Divus Iacobus in Ibernia', in Jesús María Nieto Ibañez, ed, *Lógos Hellenikós: Homeaje al Profesor Gaspar Morocho Gayo*, 2 vols (León: Universidad de León, 2003), vol. 2, 783–95.

74 See page 87 of the present work.

75 For the contemporary context, see Kelly and McCafferty, 'Introduction', in idem, eds, *Oxford History of British and Irish Catholicism*, 7.

76 Bernadette Cunningham and Raymond Gillespie, '"The Most Adaptable of Saints': The Cult of St Patrick in the seventeenth century', *Archiv. Hib.*, 49 (1995), 82–104.

77 *Annales Minorum*, vol. 9 (1390), 114, n. 16.

78 Jennings, ed, *Wadding papers*, 344.

79 Ibid, 544.

nation'.[80] The Life of Patrick by Jocelyn of Furness, an early thirteenth-century English Cistercian, furnished Wadding's peers with an appropriate narrative to adapt. Irish Franciscan descriptions of past events provide an example of how applicable texts were to the adaptation of ideas and actions for a key group. This was similar to the objectives of another Irish Franciscan, Robert Rochford, whose work was intended for an Irish audience faithful to the papacy while, at the same time, comfortable with the political interests of the Stuarts.[81] Alternatively, Gaelic friars, such as John Colgan, attributed the causes of upheaval in Ireland to temporary influences before native exertions restored harmony.[82]

Santiago, Apostle of Spain

At the same time as Irish calls for the recognition of St Patrick in the universal calendar, various Spanish parties complained that Santiago had been deleted from the Roman breviary, which 'diminished the splendour of so great a work'.[83] They vehemently called for a return to the breviary of Pius V, which Wadding had learnt as a child. Spanish churchmen appealed to the commission by quoting a battery of popes, saints, cardinals, patriarchs, archbishops and bishops in their favour. This demonstrates Wadding's role in jurisdictional battles between the Spanish and Italian authorities.

80 John McCafferty, *The Reconstruction of the Church of Ireland: Bishop Bramhall and the Laudian reforms, 1633–41* (Cambridge: Cambridge University Press, 2007), 9.

81 Robert Rochford, *The Life of the Glorious Bishop S. Patricke Apostle and Primate of Ireland, Together with the Lives of the Holy Virgin S. Bridgit and of the Glorious Abbot Saint Columbe Patrons of Ireland* (Saint-Omer: for Iohn Heigham, 1625); cited by Ryan, 'Steadfast Saints or Malleable Models?', 261.

82 John McCafferty, 'The Communion of Saints and Catholic Reformation in Early Seventeenth-Century Ireland', in Tadhg Ó hAnnracháin and Robert Armstrong, eds, *Community in Early Modern Ireland* (Dublin: Four Courts Press, 2006), 199–214; Cunningham and Gillespie, "The Most Adaptable of Saints", 93.

83 Zacarías García Villada, *Historia eclesiástica de España*, 3 vols (Madrid: Compañía Ibero-americana de Publicaciones, 1929–1936), vol. 1, 38.

Confronted with the Spanish Habsburg presence, the Church became a vehicle for Italian patriotism. On the subject of Santiago, the Italian Cardinals Baronius and Bellarmine both denied that the saint had ever gone to Spain as a missionary.[84] Baronius and Bellarmine were on the commission revising the breviary under Clement VIII. As a result, the text printed in 1602 merely recorded the mission of Santiago as a widespread tradition in the Spanish Church. At the same time, Cardinal Federico Borromeo contested Spain's claim to Southern Italy. As Federico was influenced by Baronius and became a friend of the Oratory, the Spanish authorities regarded them both as the main source of ecclesiastical opposition to Spain's involvement in Italy.[85] This caused considerable anxiety at court in Madrid and among Spanish representatives to the Holy See.[86] These matters remained unresolved, until prolonged discussions in 1631, when corrections to the text were made at a meeting attended by Wadding on 18 September.[87] Documents at the Vatican Library record the unanimous decision to remove the reference to Santiago's mission being merely a tradition within the Spanish Church.[88] Wadding was among the signatories of the amendment, which declared that 'the Spanish tradition, sustained by so many authors, seemed to carry more weight that everything Baronius alleged'.[89] This represented something of an exception for Wadding who otherwise respected the views and historical methods of Baronius. The

84 Ditchfield, *Liturgy, Sanctity and History in Tridentine Italy*, 56–57. In terms of insight, illustration, intelligibility and regard for the scriptures, the Benedictine Dom Matthew Britt considered it doubtful whether Bellarmine's *Explanatio in Psalmos* (Rome: Bartolomeo Zannetti, 1611) and Bishop Agellius' *Commentarii in Psalmos et in divinii Officii Cantica* (Rome: Typographia Vaticana, 1606) 'have been excelled by any commentators ancient or modern'. See Britt, ed, *A Dictionary of the Psalter containing the Vocabulary of the Psalms, Hymns, Canticles, and the Miscellaneous Prayers of the Breviary Psalter* (New York: Benziger, 1928), xii.

85 A. D. Wright, *The Counter-Reformation: Catholic Europe and the Non-Christian World* (Farnham: Ashgate, 2005), 55, 168–69.

86 Richard Kagan, *Clio and the Crown: The Politics of History in Medieval and Early modern Spain* (Baltimore MD: The Johns Hopkins University Press, 2009), 258.

87 *García Villada, Historia eclesiástica de España*, vol. 1, 40.

88 Ibid, vol. 1, 366–7.

89 'Ratio decreti fuit, quia tradition quae in Hispania uiget, recepta a plurimus auctoribus, videtur habere plus ponderis, quam quae in contrarium afferentur a Baronio

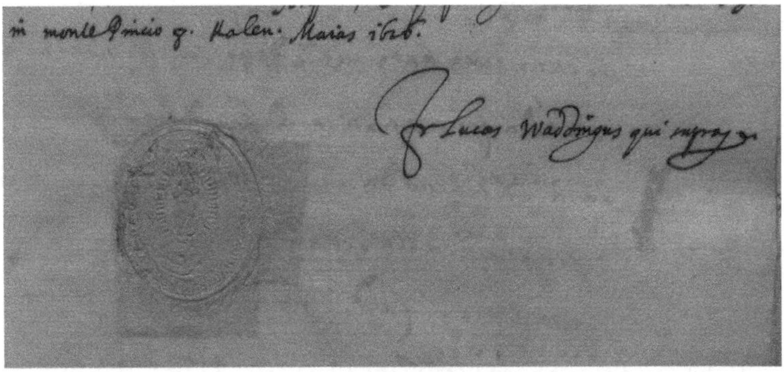

Figure 7.1 Signature and personal seal of Luke Wadding, dated 8 May 1626, showing the Virgin Mary above the Franciscan symbol of a cross between the arms of Jesus and St Francis crossed over, both bearing the nail marks of the Crucifixion on their hands; with the inscription 'Lucas Waddingus'; IE TCD MS 1245, folio 36r. Reproduced by kind permission of The Board of Trinity College Dublin.

commission's decision followed the canonisation of several Spanish saints during the previous decade and was part of a well-organised campaign to counter the diminishing influence of Philip IV in Rome.

Wadding and the Empire of Print

For four decades, Wadding steered a course between Spanish patronage and the increasing pressure represented by French competition. The ecclesiastical, economic and political links between Wadding and the Plantin-Moretus press in Antwerp represent an intriguing episode in early modern history.[90] From an early age, Wadding was well acquainted with prayer books published in the Flemish city and, six years before he began

etc'. BAV, Barb. Lat., 1185, A.; cited by *García Villada, Historia eclesiástica de España*, vol. 1, 377.

90 Christian Péligry, 'La oficina Plantiniana, el monasterio de El Escorial y los libros litúrgicos en España durante el siglo XVII', *Cuadernos bibliográficos*, 37 (1978), 74.

assisting in the reform of the breviary, he commissioned Balthasar I Moretus to print his first edition of St Francis' writings.[91] The frontispiece incorporates various saints of the Franciscan order.[92] As his experiences in Lyon show, Wadding sent friars to see his books safely through the press.[93] At Antwerp, there is a distinct likelihood that this role was fulfilled by Thomas Strange, his cousin and confrère from Waterford.[94] In later years, Balthasar II Moretus corresponded with Wadding to seek his advice on liturgical works.

As observed by Febvre and Martin, New World exploration and the development of printing occurred concurrently.[95] Books were an important commodity among goods of European origin in high demand in the Spanish empire. Inventories and catalogues for the consignment of books to the New World show that overseas territories constituted an active market. Thus, a large quantity of works found a ready sale there with a wider public than that of Spain alone.[96] 'Universities, schools, catechising missionaries and private citizens alike imported their books from Spain'.[97]

To a significant extent, the demands of the Spanish market were met by the presses of Antwerp, the centre of publishing to the Spanish empire.[98] Amid the extensive literature of *apologia* and studies produced in this Counter-Reformation setting,[99] Irish historical and theological texts also featured. These date back to the first edition of Stanihurst's *De Rebus in*

91 See pages 111–119 of the present work.

92 De Castro, 'Wadding and the Iberian Peninsula', 134.

93 See Chapter 6.

94 Dermot McGuinne, 'Irish types in Europe', *Gutenburg Jahrbuch*, 82 (2007), 169–70.

95 Febvre and Martin, *The Coming of the Book: The Impact of Printing*, 206–8.

96 Irving Leonard, 'Pérez de Montalbán, Tomás Gutiérrez, and two book lists', *Hispanic Review*, 12 (1944), 275–287.

97 J. H. Parry, *The Spanish Seaborne Empire* (London: Hutchinson, 1966), 123, 239: see also Peter Bakewell, 'Conquest after the Conquest: The Rise of Spanish Domination in America', in Richard Kagan and Geoffrey Parker eds, *Spain, Europe and the Atlantic: Essays in Honour of John H. Elliott* (Cambridge: Cambridge University Press, 2003), 308; Stafford Poole, *Juan de Ovando: Governing the Spanish Empire in the Reign of Philip II* (Norman OK, University of Oklahoma Press: 2004), 187.

98 Febvre and Martin, *The Coming of the Book*, 190–1.

99 León Voet, *The Golden Compasses. The History of the House of Plantin-Moretus*, 2 vols (Amsterdam: Van Gendt, 1969–72), vol. 1, 226.

Hibernia Gestis, which Plantin undertook to publish in the city in 1584.[100] Thereafter, imprints by Irish members of the Society of Jesus and of the Order of Friars Minor regularly appeared at Antwerp.[101]

From 1568, the exclusive rights to print breviaries, missals, psalters, books of hours and antiphonies for Spain and its overseas territories belonged to the Plantin press.[102] War in the Netherlands interrupted the book trade at which point the printing presses of Burgos, León, Madrid and Salamanca ably dealt with orders for liturgical works in Iberia.[103] Nevertheless, a great commercial emporium such as Antwerp enabled Spain to extend its political and religious influence. Therefore, in keeping with their resolve to safeguard the Catholic Netherlands, the Spanish sought to protect Antwerp's

100 When Antwerp was besieged from July 1584 to August 1585, Plantin moved his presses to Leiden. See *Great Deeds in Ireland: Richard Stanihurst's De Rebus in Hibernia Gestis*, ed, John Barry and Hiram Morgan (Cork: Cork University Press, 2013), 42–43.

101 The following texts and editions also appeared in the capital of Flanders: Christopher Holywood's *Defensio decreti Tridentini et sententiae Roberti Bellarmini* (Antwerp: Jan van Keerberghen, 1604); Bonaventure O'Hussey, *An Teagasg Críosdaidhe* (Antwerp: Jacob Mesius, 1611); Florentius Conrius, *Tractatus de Augustini sensu circa beatae Mariae Virginis Conceptionem* (Antwerp: Jan van Keerberghen, 1619); Hugh McCaghwell, *In quatuor libros sententiarum*, 2 vols (Antwerp: Jan van Keerberghen, 1620); Luke Wadding, *Beati Patris Francisci Assisiensis opuscula* (Antwerp: Jan Moretus, 1623); Peter Wadding, *Tractatus de Incarnatione Rev. P. Petri Wadingi, Waterfordiensis Hiberi S.J., S. Theologiae Doctoris, olim in Lovainensi nunc in Pragensi Academia Professoris* (Antwerp: Martinus Nutius, 1635); John Colgan, *Tractatus de Ioannis Scoti, Doctoris Subtilis theologorumque principis, vita, patria, elogiis encomiasticis, scriptis* (Antwerp: Marcel Parys, 1655). For the cultural background, see Susannah B. Monta and Salvador Ryan, 'Catholic Written Cultures', in Kelly and McCafferty, eds, *Oxford History of British and Irish Catholicism*, 260–79.

102 For 250 years from the late thirteenth until the early sixteenth century the book of hours was the best-seller, more so than the Bible: see Roger Wieck, *Time Sanctified: The Book of Hours in Medieval Art and Life* (London: George Braziller, 1988), 39–40.

103 Cristóbal Pérez Pastor, 'Impresores y libreros de Madrid. Documentos referentes a ellos', *Memorias de la Real Academia Española* (1926), 202–7, 211. In the late 1570s, to meet the demands of fifty bishops in Spain for 1,500 breviaries each, forty presses in Castile produced 40,000 missals and 40,000 breviaries: see Henri Lapeyre, *Une famille de marchands: les Ruiz* (Paris: Armand Colin, 1955), 572–3.

claims to this business and the city was allowed to grow at the expense of urban centres in Castile.[104] This helps to contextualise Wadding's role.

Renowned for their consistent high standards, Plantin's Moretus heirs regained the imperial concessions for new prayer books and supplied the Spanish-American markets again after the ceasefire of 1607.[105] The Moretus family, abiding by the precedent set by Plantin, continued to publish the classical authors and scientific dissertations but, since the market for religious editions guaranteed frequent reprints, liturgical texts were their most profitable export.[106] On average, gaps of a decade in duration occur in the demand for these works.[107] As shown by Stijn van Rossem in recent studies, after 1635, the Plantin-Moretus press supplied religious books in conjunction with the Verdussen firm of printers.[108]

Baroque title pages and frontispieces by Rubens assisted the recovery of the Moretus workshop from 1613 to 1637, including eleven illustrations and a title page for a new edition of the Roman breviary.[109] After the death of Balthasar I Moretus, management of the *Officina Plantiniana* passed to his

104 Geoffrey Parker, *The Dutch Revolt* (repr. Harmondsworth: Penguin, 1981), 260–1; Carla Rahn Phillips, *Ciudad Real, 1500–1750. Growth, Crisis and Readjustment in the Spanish Economy* (Cambridge MA: Harvard University Press, 1979), 16.

105 Ludo Simons and Pierre Delsaerdt, *Plantin and the Typographical Tradition in Flanders* (London: Wynkyn De Worde Society, 2001), 9–10; Karen Bowen and Dirk Imhof, *Christopher Plantin and Engraved Book Illustrations in Sixteenth-Century Europe* (Cambridge: Cambridge University Press, 2008), 125.

106 Voet, *The Golden Compasses*, vol. 1, 216–27.

107 Pérez Pastor, 'Impresores y Libreros de Madrid', 247–79, 295–331. A decline in orders recorded for the period 1624–86 reflects the economic downturn experienced in the printing industry later in the seventeenth century.

108 Stijn van Rossem, 'The Bookshop of the Counter-Reformation Revisited: the Verdussen Company and the Trade in Catholic Publications, Antwerp, 1585–1648', *Quaerendo*, 38 (2008), 306–21; idem, 'Books and the City. The Urban Networks of the Verdussen family (1585–1700)' in Renaud Adam, Ann Kelders, Claude Sorgeloos and David Shaw, eds, *Urban Networks and the Printing Trade in Early Modern Europe (15th-18th Century)* (Brussels: Consortium of European Research Libraries and Royal Library of Belgium, 2010), 39–52.

109 The original drawings were executed by Rubens and subsequently engraved in copperplate: see Frans Baudouin and León Voet, 'The Moretuses', *Antwerp's Golden Age: The Metropolis of the West in the Sixteenth and Seventeenth Centuries* (Washington: Smithsonian Institute, 1973), 177–8, 182–3.

nephew Balthasar II in 1642.[110] Printers were the first to read new works from the initial stages at press.[111] This ensured that they kept abreast of new developments.[112] As official publisher of new prayer books for Spain and its empire, Balthasar II made evident his command of Latin.[113] When organising publication Moretus consulted Luke Wadding who, during the same decade, was asked to intercede with the papacy on behalf of Dutch-speaking Catholics in Waterford.[114] By his own account, this was otherwise a difficult time for the Irish friar. Made commissary general of the ultramontane family at the papal court in 1648, he encountered sharp criticism in Rome and internal strife among Irish Franciscans.[115]

The Plantin-Moretus press supplied large print runs of liturgical books as widely as possible.[116] Apart from dispersing his publications among other book merchants, Moretus relied upon patrons of the family business, such as Wadding, who arranged methods of further distribution for most of the breviaries. Due to Wadding's role as a *consultor* to the Congregation of Rites, Moretus made requests of him about the Roman breviary, the psalter and episcopal ceremonies in the late 1640s and early 1650s. As stated earlier, the modifications which liturgical books underwent meant that with each revision earlier editions became invalid.[117] Neglecting to consult the Roman curia first meant that any publisher who started the imprint of a liturgical book risked making a financial loss when, at the moment of

110 Voet, *The Golden Compasses,* vol. 1, 216–27; idem, *Museum Plantin-Moretus* (Antwerp, 1965), 13–15.

111 Febvre and Martin, *The Coming of the Book,* 149–50.

112 Alfonse Willems, *Les Elzevier: Histoire et Annales Typographiques* (Brussels: G. A. van Trigt, 1880), lxxx–i, ccxxxviii, ccxlvii.

113 Balthasar II Moretus to Wadding, Plantin printing house, Antwerp, 20 Nov. 1649 (UCD-OFM, D.11/16).

114 Hazard, 'Luke Wadding's Petition to the Papacy on Behalf of Dutch and Flemish Migrants in Waterford', 11–10. See *Comment. Rinucc.*, vol. 2, 269, where it is shown that the request was made in 1645.

115 Wadding to Rinuccini, 16 May 1649; see Mooney, 'Was Luke Wadding a Patriotic Irishman?', 31, 53. See also O'Connor, *Irish Jansenists,* 226–7, 295–301.

116 Robert Kingdon, 'Patronage, Piety and Printing in Sixteenth-Century Europe', in David Pinkney and Theodor Ropp, eds, *A Festschrift for Frederick B. Artz* (Durham NC: Duke University Press, 1964), 34.

117 Péligry, 'La oficina Plantiniana', 65.

sale, they learnt of new changes to the text. The preparations for a complete edition took time, often several years in the best of conditions.

Referring to their earlier correspondence in November 1649 and his desire to serve the Catholic Church, Moretus told Wadding that he planned to reprint the Roman breviary in folio, the Roman psalter for choral practice and the *Manuale Episcoporum by* Bartolommeo Gavantus, Wadding's fellow *consultor*.[118] With regard to the breviary, Moretus asked Wadding to send him details of additions and corrections made by the Congregation of Rites.[119] The Antwerp publisher then proposed reprinting the Roman psalter 'in the same character and form which my grandfather Joannes Moretus printed in the year 1609'.[120] Before doing so, Balthasar II wished to know whether he ought to make use of the Gregorian chant for hymns such as the *Te Deum* and the *Salvae Regina*. Once more, Moretus asked Wadding to send him a copy of any changes which he ought to follow.[121]

Operating up to eleven presses in his workshop, Moretus printed 1,968 breviaries of various sizes, 1,280 diurnals, 726 missals and 165 books of hours in 1650.[122] His trade to Spain accounted for almost half of the books he sent worldwide while new liturgical works represented more than 25 per

118 Moretus to Wadding, Plantin printing house, Antwerp, 20 November 1649: 'cogito recudere Breviarium Romanum in folio, quod hactenus cum Hymnis à Papa Urbano VIII. Correctis non prodiit: item Psalterium Romanum pro Choris maiori charactere: ac praetereà Barth. Gavanti Manuale Episcoporum et Praxim Visitationis'. The first edition referred to here is: Bartolommeo Gavantus, *Enchiridion, seu Manuale Episcoporum, pro decretis* (Venetiis: apud haeredes Thomae Iunta, 1644).

119 Moretus to Wadding, 20 November 1649: 'Quod ad Breviarium attinet, dubia quaedam occurrunt, qua inclusa Schedulâ proponuntur, ad quae Sacrae Ritium Congregationis responsum et resolutionem mihi transmitti rogo; et praetereà si quid aliud in eodem Breviario addendum aut emendandium sit; et si quae novia Officia prodierint'.

120 Ibid: 'Psalterium cogito recudere eo charactere et formâ, quibus ab ano meo Ioani Moreto olim anno 1609. excusum est'. This refers to Jan I Moretus (1543–1610), son-in-law and successor of Plantin.

121 Ibid. See *Psalterivm Davidis, cum canticis sacris & selectis aliquot orationibvs* (Antverpiæ: ex officina Plantiniana Balthasaris Moreti, 1657), <http://www.vlaamse-erfgoedbibliotheek.be/en/database/stcv>, accessed 15 August 2024.

122 Péligry, 'La oficina Plantiniana', 71–2.

cent of that total.[123] The following year, Balthasar II reprinted the work of Gavantus at Antwerp. From 1635 until Wadding's death in November 1657, seventeen editions of the Roman breviary were published at the Plantin-Moretus press, including one specifically intended for the Friars Minor.[124]

Marked with the seal of the Counter-Reformation, 'breviaries of the new prayers' as they were known, were delivered by the Plantin-Moretus family to Italy, Spain and it overseas dominions.[125] The Atlantic trade offered Flemish merchants recompense for declining commerce in northern Europe.[126] After the outbreak of war with France in 1635, instead of travelling overland, bales of books were sent via the Bay of Biscay and the English Channel.[127]

Indeed, according to Claude Dufour of Lyon, the internal unrest in France known as the Fronde delayed the printing and distribution of the *Annales Minorum*.[128] The sea-route was an itinerary familiar to merchants and soldiers from Ireland.[129] Delivered in comparatively small consignments, prayer books from Antwerp were sent aboard ships protected by

123 Ibid, 70, 74.

124 Hans Bohatta, *Bibliographie de Breviére, 1501–1850* (2nd edn, Leipzig: Karl Hiersemann, 1937), 46–9, 139.

125 Teodoro Hampe Martínez, 'La biblioteca del virrey Don Martín Enríquez. Aficiones intelectuales de un gobernante colonial', *Historia Mexicana*, 36 (1986), 251–71.

126 The Schelde river gave Antwerp its access to the sea. On the economic damage caused by the Dutch blockade and efforts to divert trade, see Jonathan Israel, *Empires and Entrepots: The Dutch, the Spanish Monarchy and the Jews, 1585–1713* (London: Bloomsbury, 1990), 4, 23, 107, 356–7; idem, *Dutch primacy in World Trade, 1585–1740* (Oxford: Oxford University Press, 1989), 30, 41, 113, 359; José Alcalá-Zamora y Queipo de Llano, *España, Flandes, y el Mar del Norte (1618–39): la última ofensiva europea de los Austrias madrileños* (repr. Madrid: Centro de Estudios Políticos y Constitucionales, 2001), 99–101.

127 See Robert Stradling, *The Armada of Flanders: Spanish Maritime Policy and European War, 1568–1668* (Cambridge: Cambridge University Press, 1992), 77, 125.

128 Letter of Claude Dufour to Luke Wadding, Lyon, undated, 1637 (UCD-OFM, D.11/4/290). As a result, the transfer of books could take nine months from Antwerp to Rome, and more than a year to Spain: see Ian Maclean, *Scholarship, Commerce, Religion: The Learned Book in the Age of Confessions, 1560–1630* (Cambridge MA: Harvard University Press, 2012), 300.

129 Hazard, *Faith and Patronage*, 111.

convoys which sailed from Ostend, Dunkirk, Calais and, from time to time, Amsterdam.[130] In San Sebastián and Bilbao the factors of Moretus received the goods. They checked the quality and exact quantity, of which they were already notified, before setting the books on the road to Madrid.[131] Book orders from Spanish America were processed at the monastery of San Lorenzo at El Escorial before being dispatched to the ports of Seville or Cadiz.[132]

Wadding's work on the reform of the breviary served as a source for his historical writings for the Franciscan order.[133] By the second half of the seventeenth century, accounts of *terra incognita* and its exploration were impressed upon the consciousness of Europe.[134] Wadding was a mendicant friar more immediately concerned with detachment from the world. While based in Rome and as part of a body corporate fulfilling a key role in the missions, his attention was drawn to pastoral activity in Latin America.[135] Wadding's papers contain a manuscript account of the Amazon, its ethnography and natural history. This *relación geográfica* records the successive journeys made by Ecuadorian Franciscans from the headwaters of the

130 Febvre and Martin, *The Coming of the Book,* 222–4.

131 Péligry, 'La oficina Plantiniana', 66.

132 Baudouin and Voet, 'The Moretuses', *Antwerp's Golden Age,* 177–8. These book orders were made in job lots by bishops and abbots; Pérez Pastor, 'Impresores y Libreros de Madrid', 215, 221, 227.

133 Severino Gori, 'Le lettere inedite di Luca Wadding ad Antonio Caracciolo e la riforma liturgica di Urbano VIII', *AFH,* 66 (1973), 118–19. For more recent work see Pádraig A. Breathnach, 'An Irish Bollandus: Fr. Hugh Ward and the Louvain Hagiographical Enterprise', *Éigse,* 31 (1999), 1–30. See also Ditchfield, *Liturgy, Sanctity and History in Tridentine Italy,* 10–11, 18–20.

134 Hazard, '*In Novi Orbis Amplitudine:* Irish Franciscan Views of the Americas, 1610–83', in Pérez Tostado, ed, *Irlanda y el Atlántico Ibérico,* 193–210.

135 Wadding's cousin, Michael, spent thirty-four years as a Jesuit missionary to New Spain where he served among the Mayos, the Tephanes, the Comicaris and the Basiroas. A theologian, he also taught for several years in various colleges in Mexico: see Benjamin Hazard, 'On mission to Mexico: Michael Wadding SJ of Waterford (1587–1644)', in Salvador Ryan (ed.), *Treasures of Irish Christianity: to the ends of the earth* (Dublin: Veritas, 2015), 70–72; J. J. Silke, 'Irish Scholarship and the Renaissance, 1580–1673', *Studies in the Renaissance,* 20 (1973), 169–206.

Amazon to the mouth of the river at Pará.[136] Such methodology enabled Wadding to document the work of Franciscan missionaries whose expeditions, in his words, 'filled the earth with the seed of sound doctrine'.[137]

Seeds of discontent

In the early 1630s, an extensive letter to Ludovico Ludovisi, Cardinal Protector of Ireland, made a sustained attack on Wadding.[138] The author concealed his identity but the level of detail, combined with concerted opposition to Munster interests, indicates that Wadding's detractor was from Connacht or Ulster. Internal evidence suggests that Francis Tully, a Franciscan friar from Connacht and an ally of the O'Neills, composed the document, which is kept at the archives of Propaganda Fide. According to Brendan Jennings, the other papers in this volume date from 1632 to 1634.[139]

More than once, the letter mentions that Wadding deliberately hindered the promotion of Tully. Instead, Wadding took care 'to promote the advancement of another priest in the hope of money', which he could not obtain from Tully.[140] Thus, Wadding was accused of being 'partial and partisan'.[141] However, accounts kept by Wadding showed that he incurred

136 Hazard, '*In novi orbis amplitudine*', 205–9.

137 Ibid, 204: 'in vastissimis Asiae et Americae provinciis, in novi Orbis amplitudine [...] vidi quod etiam super omnes aquas seminaverunt'.

138 Brendan Jennings, ed, 'To the Cardinal Protector of Ireland concerning Fr. Luke Wadding', undated, *Archiv. Hib.*, 12 (1946), 184–87. For Canice Mooney's discussion of the allegations of partiality against Wadding, see 'Was Luke Wadding a patriotic Irishman', 64–74.

139 'To the Cardinal Protector of Ireland concerning Fr. Luke Wadding', 184.

140 Ibid: 'Dictus frater Lucas, ut unum religiosum Franciscanum ex suis possit commodius promovere, praedicti fratris Francisci a Sancta Maria promotionem impedit, et alterius sacerdotis spe pecuniarum, quas a fratre Francisco obtinere non potest, promoveri curat, de quo etiam testes sunt Romae'.

141 Ibid: 'Adeo dictus frater Lucas est partialis et factiosus'.

expenses related to ecclesiastical appointments, such as scribal work for official papal documents.[142]

The criticism became more personal stating that Wadding lacked 'sufficient knowledge of the kingdom of Ireland, because he has been outside the kingdom almost from childhood'.[143] That said, when in Spain, Wadding reached a better understanding of Connacht and Ulster from the friendships he established with Hugh Ward, Flaithrí Ó Maolchonaire and Hugh McCaghwell.

Rather than being a passive bystander who relayed information on behalf of others, Wadding was denounced by the well-informed author for 'busying himself here in Rome for about four years with the business and promotions of all things done in Ireland'.[144] Hence, the accuser sharply criticised Wadding as the only source of privileged information 'for the whole kingdom of Ireland'.[145] Placing 'the open letters of the princes, nobles, or provinces of that kingdom' in Wadding's hands was 'the greatest inconvenience thus far'.[146] The unnamed correspondent then accused Wadding of suppressing and manipulating nominations to the archdioceses of Cashel in 1626 and Tuam in 1630. In Waterford, he alleged, Wadding overlooked his own cousin, the Franciscan preacher Thomas Strange, in favour of a less capable candidate. Strange corresponded frequently with Wadding on behalf of whom he completed various projects.[147] Strange was nominated for Waterford, but Wadding may have been reluctant to lose his help.[148]

Next, despite being 'the principal princes of the royal race' who took up arms in defence of Catholicism, the Ulster earls' nominees were 'always

142 Jennings, ed, 'Ecclesiastical Appointments in Ireland, Aug. 1643–Dec. 1649', 59, 61.

143 'To the Cardinal Protector of Ireland concerning Fr. Luke Wadding': 'Dictus frater Lucas nullam notitiam sufficientem habet de regno Hiberniae, quia ab infantia fere est extra regnum'.

144 Ibid: 'fratris Lucae Wadding, se semper ingerentis a iv circiter annis hic Romae negotiis et promotionibus omnibus in Hibernia factis; fuit quasi solus informator'.

145 Ibid: 'qualiter omnino inprimis expediat ut nullius particularis personae informatio accipiatur pro toto regno Hiberniae'

146 Ibid: 'nisi illius regni principum, nobilium, aut provinciarum patentes litteras in ordine ad hoc habeat. Hujus rei defectus maxima incommoda evenerunt hactenus'.

147 Hazard, 'Irish Franciscans and the Santiago Province of Spain', 29.

148 Jennings, ed, *Wadding Papers*, 235, 248.

resisted' by Wadding, as was Tully's nomination to Killala. This, it was claimed, was also apparent in the election of both the archbishop of Armagh and the bishop of Down.[149] The consistent approach taken by both Lombard and Wadding, however, was 'to give as little offence as possible' to the government.[150] Moreover, John Roche of Ferns told Wadding there were too many Irish bishops, a view shared by Thomas Messingham, partly because of the shortage of church livings to support the clergy.[151] These combined factors help to explain why the Ulster earls' candidates were ignored.

Although the Roman curia was responsible for eventual appointments, the letter repeatedly stated that Wadding 'managed to promote' candidates himself and often from his extended family.[152] For example, it claimed that 'in [Wadding's] own province of Munster alone, he promoted five or six bishops from among the sons of merchants, thereby leaving aside the nobility'.[153] This appears to be imprecise on the part of the accuser, as early seventeenth-century appointments to the ecclesiastical province of Cashel began before Wadding started his work with the curia.

Supported with examples, these accusations were not limited to the selection of bishops. In the diocesan seminary which Wadding established for six scholars in Rome, 'the most eminent Cardinal Ludovisi' allowed four from

149 'To the Cardinal Protector of Ireland concerning Fr. Luke Wadding': 'Quoties videt promovendum ex parte principum Tyrconalliae et Tyroniae, qui sunt principales principes ex regia stirpe, qui summorum pontificum brevibus et catholicorum regum litteris, fama orbi nota, contra reginam Angliae Isabellam 20 circiter annis pugnarunt, cum effusione sanguinis et perditione suorum statuum, dictus frater Lucas semper hujusmodi promovendis restitit, ut patuit in electione utriusque Armacani ultimi, et in electione episcopi Dunensis'.

150 Cregan, 'The Social and Cultural Background of a Counter-Reformation Episcopate', 89.

151 Roche to Wadding, 7 February 1630, cited by Thomas O'Connor, 'Thomas Messingham (*c.*1575–1638?) and the Seventeenth-Century Church', *Riocht na Midhe*, 11 (2000), 93; Patrick Corish, 'An Irish Counter-Reformation Bishop: John Roche, III', *ITQ*, 25/2 (1958), 115.

152 'To the Cardinal Protector of Ireland concerning Fr. Luke Wadding': 'promoveri curavit ex suis'.

153 Ibid: 'Dictus frater Lucas in sola sua provinciae Momoniae quinque vel sex episcopos promoveri curavit ex suis mercatorum filiis, nobilibus relictis'.

the province of Munster with one from Ulster. A well-deserving Ulster student was, nonetheless, expelled.[154] To prevent his return to Ireland, Wadding reportedly gave him nothing for the journey.[155] Consequently, the said student remained in Rome, where there were 'many witnesses of this matter'.[156] Canice Mooney contended that the student was excluded because he was unsuitable, not because he was from Ulster.[157]

Next, the complainant turned his attention to St Isidore's College, 'which was built by the alms of the pious and supported by them to the effect that the religious, equipped with Catholic doctrines and virtues, should return to the aforesaid kingdom to spread the Gospel'.[158] Yet, the College had no Ulster students:[159]

> the most important in the kingdom of Ireland, in which more and more powerful heretics are found occupying the property of natural princes, who for the defence of the faith are exiled, robbed of honours and wealth, to sojourn in foreign countries.

Very few students from provinces other than Munster were found at the college. Consequently, almost all were from Wadding's province alone. As with other grievances, the writer concluded: 'here in Rome are witnesses of this matter'.[160]

154 Ibid: 'in seminario quod pro sex scholasticis instituit eminentissimus Cardinalis Ludovisius, sint quatuor ex sola sua provincia, et unus qui erat ex provincia Ultoniae, sacerdos, et de studiis optime meritus, illinc sit expulsus'.

155 Ibid: 'patriam peteret nec obulum ex expensis collegii dari fecerit'.

156 Ibid: 'ex quo dictus sacerdos nec iter arripere potest [...] dictus sacerdos est in Urbe, et plures hujus rei testes'.

157 Mooney, 'Was Luke Wadding a Patriotic Irishman?', 66.

158 'To the Cardinal Protector of Ireland concerning Fr. Luke Wadding': 'Praeterea neque in collegio S. Isidori, quod piorum eleemosinis aedificatum, iisdem sustentatur, ad effectum ut religiosi doctrinis Catholicis et virtutibus instructi, in praedictum regnum ad disseminandum evangelium revertantur'.

159 Ibid: 'nullum habet ex praedicta Ultoniae provincia, quae praecipua est in regno Hiberniae, et in qua plures et potentiores reperiuntur haeretici occupantes bona principum naturalium, qui ob defensionem fidei exules, ac honoribus et fortunis spoliati, peregrinantur in alienis regionibus'.

160 Ibid: 'Ex aliis autem regni provinciis valde pauci in praedicto collegio reperiuntur, ita ut fere omnes ex sola ipsius provincia sint; hujus rei testes sunt hie Romae'.

Towards the end, the writer claimed that Wadding had persuaded the Roman authorities that, with few exceptions, no further appointments to Irish dioceses were necessary. This was consistent with the earlier strategy employed by Lombard.[161] The letter complained that Richard O'Connell had petitions 'from almost all the nobles, bishops, and archbishops' of Munster.[162] Moreover, O'Connell enjoyed Wadding's support.[163] In Leinster, Ulster and Connacht, the demand for the promotion of bishops could be clearly seen by the appeals sent to Rome. In summing up, the letter writer stated that several important clergymen and some priests, worthy in piety and learning from all the provinces of Ireland, were able to report in full on the state of the whole kingdom.[164]

Revealingly, an Irish Dominican named Terence O'Connell corroborated Wadding's anonymous critic. Writing from London in December 1639, O'Connell informed Francesco Ingoli, first secretary of Propaganda Fide, that Wadding ruled the Church in Ireland, controlled news and made recommendations on appointments to vacant Irish dioceses. Moreover, O'Connell added, Wadding was not politically neutral.[165]

However, despite being directed to Ludovisi and Ingoli, these accusations appear to have made no impression on this occasion.[166] Instead, on Wadding's watch, promotions to the episcopacy in Ireland successfully met the requirement to reside in one's diocese. Moreover, Wadding's active response met the required standard for Urban VIII who added surveys

161 On unfulfilled requests for the appointment of Irish bishops, see Thomas McCoog, 'Mission or Church, 1570–1640?', in McCafferty and Kelly, eds, *The Oxford History of British and Irish Catholicism*, vol. 1, 109–10; J. J. Silke, 'The Irish Peter Lombard', *Studies*, 64 (1975), 150.

162 'To the Cardinal Protector of Ireland concerning Fr. Luke Wadding', 184: 'constat de contrario, nam germanus frater doctoris Conalli, vicarii apostolici, promovendi ad episcopatum, habet omnium fere nobilium, episcoporum, et archiepiscopi illius provinciae postulationes'.

163 Jennings, ed, *Wadding Papers*, 484.

164 'To the Cardinal Protector of Ireland concerning Fr. Luke Wadding', 184.

165 Millett, ed, 'Catalogue of Irish Material in Vols. 132–139 of the "Scritture originali riferite nelle congregazioni generali" in Propaganda Archives', 41.

166 'To the Cardinal Protector of Ireland concerning Fr. Luke Wadding', 184.

of nominees and dioceses in the 1627 bull, *Si Processus*.[167] The papal nuncio to each respective country provided this information to the curia, in much the same way that Wadding represented the Irish cause. In the long pontificate of Urban VIII, the consistent limitation of appointments to bishoprics bears fair comparison with his close examination of the canonisation process for saints.[168]

Blessed Raymond Llull

Evidence of Wadding's reputation is apparent from his involvement in the cause for the canonisation of Raymond Llull, a thirteenth-century Franciscan philosopher, theologian and poet who influenced mysticism in the seventeenth century.[169] Juan de Riera, from the Franciscan province of Mallorca, spent sixteen years as postulator to the cause of Llull. At St Isidore's where Riera resided, Wadding assisted him after he faced difficulties from Roman congregations opposed to the cause, especially the Holy Office. Riera published a formal defence of Llull in 1627 but died six years later. Consequently, the archives at St Isidore's acquired many manuscript-works and over 1,000 documents and papers relating to the cause of Llull. These included treatises by Llull and one of only two known versions in Catalan of the *Liber de affatu*.[170]

In his third volume of the *Annales Minorum*, Wadding paid ample tribute to Llull.[171] However, Lorenzo Carreras, archdean at the cathedral of Mallorca, feared that Riera's work would be in vain. Therefore, he

167 See Massimo Faggioli, 'Urbano VIII e la riforma del procedimento di nomina dei vescovi', *Cristianesimo nella storia*, 23 (2002), 79–121.

168 Ibid.

169 Llorenç Pérez Martínez, 'Fray Lucas Wadding, postulador de la causa de Beatificación de Ramón Llull (1638)', *Studia lulliana*, 1 (1957), 262–68. See *Doctor Illuminatus: A Ramon Llull Reader*, edited and translated by Anthony Bonner with a new translation of *The Book of the Lover and the Beloved* by Eve Bonner (Princeton NJ: Princeton University Press, 1993).

170 Millett, 'The Archives of St Isidore's College', 9.

171 *Annales Minorum* (1st edn, Lyon: Claude Dufour, 1636), vol. 3, 136, 156, 160–61.

nominated Wadding, whereupon the Irish friar undertook the cause for seven years from 1638. Although the civil authorities in Mallorca supported Wadding's appointment and expected that he would finish off matters, there appears to be no mention of the work Wadding conducted on the cause.[172] Nonetheless, twelve years later, he drew attention to Llull's many writings with a lengthy entry in the *Scriptores ordinis minorum*.[173]

Kith and Kin

While based in Rome, frequent letters from multiple sources provided Wadding with constant information. In the case of Ireland, he often heard from members of the clergy recently returned from the continent and from the laity. His correspondence indicates that he held in high regard well-established kin groups, related by blood or marriage. Ties of allegiance were the basis of authority where people remained faithful to their own districts and local elites. These ties were, perhaps, more easily formed in Ireland than in larger countries such as Spain and France.[174] The comparative weakness of the state meant that the control of civic authority and finance was in the hands of a number of influential families. Apart from occasional bouts of pressure, a 'period of partial toleration for Irish Catholics' occurred with accession of Charles I in 1625.[175] Nevertheless, efforts to introduce renewal in the Catholic Church met with difficulties for the remainder of the decade in Ireland.

172 Pérez Martínez, 'Fray Lucas Wadding, postulador de la causa de Beatificación de Ramón Llull', 262–68.

173 *Scriptores ordinis minorum*, 197–202.

174 Benjamin Hazard, '"An Ark in the Deluge': Multyfarnham Abbey and the Nugents of Delvin, 1607–41', *Ríocht na Mídhe: Journal of Meath Archaeological and Historical Society*, 22 (2011), 113–23; Cf. Henry Kamen, 'The Statesman', in Rosari Villari, ed, *Baroque Personae*, translated by Lydia G. Cochrane (Chicago: Chicago University Press, 1995), 9–31.

175 R. Dudley Edwards, 'Church and State in the Ireland of Míchél Ó Cléirigh, 1626–41', in Sylvester O'Brien, ed, *Measgra i gCuimhne Mhíchíl Uí Chléirigh* (Dublin: Assisi Press, 1944), 1–20.

Writing to Wadding from Waterford, the Franciscan guardian Thomas Strange explained that, prevented from obtaining a house: 'Wee live all everyone in his frind and kinsman's house'.[176] Later that month, however, Strange made clear to his cousin Luke that they were accommodated 'at the charges of the said kinsman or friend, which are by no means slight'.[177] Wadding kept abreast of events in Waterford as they unfolded. In February 1628, for example, Thomas Walsh informed him that a nephew of Laurence Lea, vicar general of Waterford, was travelling to Rome to study with Wadding.[178] In 1630, Fr. Thomas Lea was part of the community of friars at St Isidore's and Wadding stayed up to date with news about the family.[179] Some of Wadding's correspondents had an eye to personal advantage in maintaining the link. The relationship in such cases was between patron and clients. Eager for employment, a cousin of Patrick Comerford asked him to obtain the deanery of the Cathedral Church and the priorate of St John's Abbey, which Laurence Lea had previously held in Waterford.[180]

Further, in seventeenth-century Ireland, it was often necessary to find nobles powerful enough to protect senior clergymen. With this in mind before his return to Ireland, Hugh Bourke assured Wadding that he was a kinsman of 'all the lords of Connacht and Munster'.[181] The Ulster earls' absence from Ireland may explain why Wadding did not give serious consideration to candidates proposed by the exiled O'Neills and O'Donnells of Ulster.

Lawrence Barron of Clonmel married Wadding's sister, Mary. On 2 December 1626, Lawrence's son, Geoffrey, sent news of his father's sudden death to Luke, his 'Right reverend and deerly respected uncull'.[182] Before dying, Geoffrey Barron's father appointed John White FitzLaurence and Luke Wadding's first cousin, Richard, to assist the widow and five young

176 Jennings, ed, *Wadding Papers*, 440–41.

177 Burtchaell and Rigg, eds, *Hist. MSS Comm. rep. on Franciscan Manuscripts Preserved at the Convent, Merchants' Quay, Dublin*, 34.

178 Ibid, 4.

179 Jennings, ed, 'Miscellaneous Documents II', 1–49.

180 Burtchaell and Rigg, eds, *Hist. MSS Comm. rep. on Franciscan Manuscripts Preserved at the Convent, Merchants' Quay, Dublin*, 21.

181 Ibid, 132.

182 Jennings, ed, *Wadding Papers*, 239.

children. Aged fifteen, Geoffrey was the eldest. He paid for the schooling of Bartholomew, his brother, who later joined the Franciscan friars, took the name Bonaventure in religion and became an illustrious scholar.[183]

Richard Wadding helped rear the children for four years until his own death on Wednesday, 24 May 1628.[184] He was survived by his wife Frances.[185] Thomas Walsh, archbishop of Cashel, wrote to Luke Wadding with the 'sad news of our dearest cousin' but struggled to bring himself to write about the death.[186] The loss of 'our good cousin Richard' continued to occupy the extended family's thoughts and they commended him to God in further letters.[187] By 1630, the tone had changed when Thomas Strange signed off to Luke from London: 'Your cousin is here, Mr. Thomas Wadding, son and heir to Richard, may he be in heaven. He is studying law here again and entrusts himself to your paternity'.[188]

Conclusion

As noted by Tadhg Ó hAnnracháin, seventeenth-century appointments to Irish bishoprics occurred with little involvement of the laity and none on the part of the early Stuarts.[189] Although the level of influence he exerted caused resentment among some contemporaries, Wadding's Roman agency for Irish bishops turned him into a national figure. His personal influence

183 Ibid. See also Millett, 'Bonaventure Barron OFM, *Hibernus Clonmeliensis*', 41–46.

184 Jennings, ed, *Wadding Papers*, 239.

185 Dublin, Royal Irish Academy, Ordnance Survey Collection, Inquisition 5 Charles I. I am grateful to Julian Walton for this reference.

186 Jennings, ed, *Wadding Papers*, 259: 'Tristes nuevas me han escrito de my charíssimo Richard Wadding; no me basta el ánimo de escriverles a vuestra paternidad'.

187 Ibid, 273: 'nuestro buen primo Richard Wadding'.

188 Ibid, 365: 'Aquí está su primo el señor Thomas Wading, hijo y heredero de Richardo que está en gloria. Estudia aquí las leyes de nuevo, y se encomienda a vuestra paternidad'.

189 Tadhg Ó hAnnracháin, 'Conflicting Loyalties, Conflicted Rebels: Political and Religious Allegiance among the Confederate Catholics of Ireland', *EHR*, 119 (2004), 851.

was pivotal to the development of a Church capable of withstanding the seventeenth century in Ireland. Constraints on appointments to Irish dioceses reflected Urban VIII's requirements. The amiable and prudent Wadding spoke in person on behalf of the bishops. This remained the hallmark of his diplomacy in Rome. Further, by successfully placing St Patrick in the universal calendar, Wadding avoided confusion with purported opinion. This met with the same pope's more exacting rules for a clearer definition and understanding of sainthood. Despite any pressure from French competition, Spain reversed thirty years of discomfort when Urban VIII reconfirmed Santiago's mission. Wadding's accord with the verdict and his efforts for the cause of Raymond Llull echoed his time in the Iberian Peninsula and his place in the Santiago province of the Franciscan order.

The correspondence that Wadding received from his kin group casts light on the bonds between them. In keeping with Roman patronage, Wadding offered support to specific followers who owed him loyalty and service. On returning to Ireland, they could be trusted to provide reliable information. His detractor's decision to remain anonymous indicates Wadding's unchallenged authority at that time, but animosity had begun to develop against him. His apparent preference for Munster causes and the first signs of trouble at St Isidore's combined in the coming years.

8 War in Ireland

Introduction

The strength of Catholic resentment against their exclusion from public office in Ireland and the confiscation of their lands was evident since the mid-1630s.[1] Sir Phelim O'Neill and others took up arms on 22 October 1641 maintaining they promoted rebellion for the defence of the native Irish, but many Protestants were stripped naked and killed, others were jailed or expelled and almost all were robbed of their belongings.[2] The war in Ireland was subsequently characterised by ruthless brutality on both sides.[3]

During this decade, the majority of Wadding's correspondence related to wartime in Ireland.[4] The following chapter relates to his work on behalf of the parliament that assembled at Kilkenny from 1642 to 1649, clarifying the

1 John Morrill and Liam Temple, 'Introduction', in Kelly and McCafferty, eds, *Oxford History of British and Irish Catholicism*, vol. 2, 1–2; Eamon Darcy, *The Irish Rebellion of 1641 and the Wars of the Three Kingdoms* (Woodbridge: Boydell, 2015), 81; Pádraig Lenihan, *Confederate Catholics at War, 1641–49* (Cork: Cork University Press, 2001), 16–18; John McCavitt, 'The Political Background to the Ulster Plantation, 1607–20', in Brian Mac Cuarta, ed, *Ulster 1641: Aspects of the Rising* (Belfast: Institute for Irish Studies, 1997), 11.

2 Proclamation by Sir Phelim O'Neill, Dungannon, 24 October 1641; Gilbert, *Contemp. Hist.*, vol. 1, 363.

3 Micheál Ó Siochrú, *Confederate Ireland, 1642–49: A Constitutional and Political Analysis* (Dublin: Four Courts Press, 2005), 11, 23–24; Francis Harold reiterated Sir Richard Bellings' view that Irish Catholics lacked weapons, acted in self-defence and in support of Charles I; Harold, *Vita Fratris Lucae Waddingi*, 117–118. See Carroll, 'The *Vita Waddingi* and the Memory of Confederate and Cromwellian Ireland', 191–92. Micheál Ó Siochrú, 'Bellings (Bealing), Richard', *DIB*, vol. 1, 441–443.

4 Mooney, 'The Letters of Luke Wadding', 406.

facts and sorting out the intricacies of Wadding's experiences. It examines threats to his endeavours and the relevance of the conflict to his own family before revealing the potential tensions between Wadding's religious life and political activity. Preparations for the *Annales Minorum* continued unabated, as did his conciliary work within the Franciscan order. For example, in Provence and Aquitaine, Recollect Fathers in the province of St Bernardine argued against the legitimacy of their 1644 provincial chapter. Wadding was appointed advocate at the Franciscan curia to resolve this dispute. Three years later, Innocent X issued an apostolic brief confirming the chapter. He ordered that Fathers of the province divested of their voting rights should have them restored, in keeping with the practice of other ultramontane provinces in the Franciscan order.[5]

'Tumults in the country'[6]

The war in Ireland occurred in the context of conflict in England and Scotland from 1639 to 1652, and the long-running Thirty Years War on the European continent.[7] When the Irish insurrection began, Wadding had no plans to deal with war. In a letter he delivered by hand to Cardinal Francesco Barberini, Wadding wrote that the uprising was more deep-rooted than he first thought.[8] As war ensued and the need for information

5 José Maria Pou y Martí, *Index Regestorum Familiae Ultramontanae, Saec. XVI et XVII* (Quaracchi: Ex Typographia S. Bonaventurae, 1927), 80–81; cited by Canice Mooney, *Irish Franciscans and France* (Dublin: Clonmore and Reynolds, 1964), 35–36.

6 John Colgan to Luke Wadding, Leuven, 2 April 1642 (UCD-OFM, D.04/1/325, formerly 204); Gilbert, *Contemp. Hist.*, vol. 1, 407: 'tumultuum Patria'.

7 Peter Wilson, *Thirty Years War: Europe's Tragedy* (Cambridge MA: Belknap Press, 2011); Norman Housley, *Religious Warfare in Europe, 1400–1536* (Oxford: Oxford University Press, 2002), 11–12, 20–24, 112; Jane Ohlmeyer, 'The Civil Wars in Ireland', in Peter Kenyon and Jane Ohlmeyer, eds, *The Civil Wars, a Military History of England, Scotland and Ireland, 1638–60* (Oxford: Oxford University Press, 1998), 73–102.

8 Luke Wadding to Francesco Barberini, Rome, 14 January 1642 (BAV, Barb. Lat., 6483, f. 3r.); Giblin, ed, 'Vatican Library: MSS. Barberini Latini: A Guide to the Material of Irish Interest on Microfilm in the National Library, Dublin', 67–144.

escalated, Wadding relied upon his confrères at St Anthony's College, Leuven. Under normal circumstances, the college served as a listening post where there were 'but few things done in the court of Ireland, be it ever so secret, but it will be heard or else sought out by them'.[9] In war time, however, Wadding discovered that communications from Ireland were intercepted in England before reaching their intended recipients.[10]

Working of his own accord, Wadding obtained an expression of support for the war from Urban VIII,[11] who also wrote to the 'Happy Lord O'Neill' in a letter that reveals the pope's reserved nature.[12] As Urban VIII and the Roman curia looked to Wadding for advice about Ireland since the 1620s, it is likely that the Irish friar influenced the composition of this letter. While Phelim O'Neill's plans to prosecute the war may have been 'the bulwark of the true faith and the defence of Catholics', his fervour led Urban VIII to think 'there should be room for commendation rather than encouragement'.[13] He also called upon Phelim O'Neill 'with ardour of mind, to take care of the best of all the faithful inhabitants of Christ in such a critical situation'.[14]

The Donegal Franciscan, John Colgan, had contacted Wadding 'at the beginning of the tumults', but received no reply.[15] Colgan persisted, chiefly with what he learnt from others. He also shared news with Hugh Bourke, commissary general for the Irish Friars Minor in the German states and

9 Hazard, *Faith and Patronage*, 95.

10 Hugh Bourke to Luke Wadding, Leuven, 29 November 1641 (UCD-OFM, D.04/1/5, formerly 53).

11 Brief of Urban VIII in support of the Catholic cause in Ireland, 2 February 1642 (UCD-OFM, D.04/1/281, formerly 182).

12 'Domino Felicio O'Neill'; Urban VIII to Phelim O'Neill, Rome, 2 February 1642 (UCD-OFM, D.04/1/185–88, formerly 138–41); Gilbert, *Contemp. Hist.*, vol. 1, 521.

13 Ibid: 'Ea consilia assidue meditari solet Dominatio tua, quæ in isto regno propugnaculum veræ fidei et Catholicis præsidium esse possint… commendationi potius quam hortatibus locum esse arbitratur'.

14 Ibid: 'quonam animi ardore in tanto rerum discrimine de vniuersis Christi fidelibus isthic degentibus optime mereri curaturus sis'.

15 Colgan to Wadding, 2 April 1642 (UCD-OFM, D.04/1/325, formerly 204); Gilbert, *Contemp. Hist.*, vol. 1, 407–408: 'Iam secundo vel tertio sub initio tumultuum Patria scripsi ad Vestram Paternitatem quæ de iisdem offerebantur certiora noua. Responsum tamen vestrum interea nullum vidi'.

the Southern Netherlands. Thereafter, Colgan sent Wadding charters and instruments issued by Catholic nobles about 'that war of faith'.[16] These reports were printed. Colgan posted a supply to Wadding, carrying news that almost all the Catholic leaders of Ireland were up in arms. According to Colgan, they occupied 'all the cities, towns, castles and fortified places except for Dublin, Londonderry, Coleraine and Knockfergus', as well as other fortifications in the hands of their enemies.[17] It was also certain that 'Dublin was not captured, or even formally besieged' by Catholic forces, before 20 March 1642, as confirmed in a letter written by a certain merchant at Antwerp.[18]

The Catholic Irish in the field numbered 'eighty, or nearly a hundred thousand'.[19] Nonetheless, they suffered from 'scarcity of arms, of gunpowder, of cannon, and of the like equipment necessary for such a war'.[20] In the event they were sufficiently armed, it was widely thought 'that the war would be short-lived'.[21] Here, Colgan hinted at the support that Wadding could provide in Rome by obtaining military materials. Colgan considered that the Irish were 'no doubt to be feared'.[22] Thus, according to English sources, 'by numerous letters and newspapers', it was 'hopeless to bring back the Irish except by way of convention and concord'.[23] 'All things in

16 Ibid: 'Nec tamen idcirco destiti Paternitati Vestræ abinde scriber; sed præcipue quod sciuerim ab aliis. Ac inprimis mitto constitutiones et ordinationes procerum regni de bello illo fidei vel potius de regno tempore illius belli administrando: constitutiones sane pernecessarias'.

17 Ibid: 'de facto occupant omnes ciuitates, oppida, castella, arces aliaque munita regni loca, exceptis Dublinio, Londonderia, Culrania, et Cnocfergus, aliisque quibusdam fortalitiis quæ jacent in manibus hæreticorum'.

18 Ibid: 'Certum tamen est Dublinium non esse interceptum, vel etiam formaliter obsessum ante 20 Martii vt litteræ inde a quodam mercatore Belga Antwerpiam scriptæ testantur'.

19 Ibid: 'Exercitus Catholicorum ascendit octaginta vel iuxta multos centum millia'.

20 Ibid: 'sed laborant penuria armorum, pulveris tormentarii, tormentorum et similium apparatuum ad tale bellum necessariorum'.

21 Ibid: 'quæ si in sufficientia adessent, omnes existimant bellum illud breui habiturum intentum'.

22 Ibid: 'Hibernis dubio procul metuenda'.

23 Ibid: 'quin et Angli plurimis litteris et gazetis de facto indicant esse desperandum de Hibernis reducendis nisi per viam conventionis et concordiæ, Hibernis'.

England are very disturbed', Colgan concluded, 'on account of the differences and dissensions between the king and parliament', as testified in the gazettes he sent to Wadding.[24]

A month later, Catholic prelates and clergy gathered in Kilkenny for three days.[25] They agreed the war was a justified defence of Catholicism and of the powers that belonged to the king; that councils should be created to govern the parts of Ireland taken by the insurgents; that strength was unity and weakness division.[26] In June 1642, the lords and gentry of Ireland joined them and made common cause. The first Catholic confederate assembly was duly established, bringing the Gaelic Irish and Old English into an uneasy alliance. Together, they selected twenty-four members for the supreme council of Ireland, evenly distributed among the four provinces, and drafted an oath of association to be sworn by all Catholics in the country. The rights of the Catholic Church were to be upheld, and taxes were levied.[27] Wadding himself noted that letters from the Kilkenny assembly were sent by 'the Parliament'.[28] Nevertheless, a lack of preparedness persisted, and no representative was sent to Rome at that time. Defending itself against criticism, the supreme council explained that the war was a localised conflict that broke out in different parts at different times, before spreading everywhere.[29]

24 Ibid: 'Omnia in Anglia sunt turbatissima propter differentias et dissensiones inter Regem et Parliamentum provt gazettæ quæ vobis mittuntur, testantur'.

25 Ó hAnnracháin, *Catholic Reformation in Ireland*, 25; Ó Siochrú, *Confederate Ireland*, 207.

26 Aidan Clarke, *The Old English in Ireland, 1625–42* (Dublin: Four Courts Press, 2000), 214.

27 Edmund Curtis and R. B. McDowell, eds, *Irish Historical Documents: 1172–1922* (London: Methuen, 1943), 148; Charles O'Conor, *Bibliotheca ms. Stowensis. A Descriptive Catalogue of the Manuscripts in the Stowe Library* (Buckingham: John Seeley, 1818), 240.

28 See, for instance, Wadding's note on the letter from the supreme council to Urban VIII, 28 November 1642 (UCD-OFM, D.04/3/1089–92, formerly 547–48), 'Lra. Parliamenti ad Beatissime 28 novembris 1642'. See also Wadding's note on his copy of the letter sent by the Kilkenny parliament to Francesco Barberini notifying him of Wadding's appointment as their agent and proctor at the papal court, 28 November 1642 (UCD-OFM, D.04/3/1045, formerly 530), 'Parliamenti ad Cardinalem Barberini, 28 novembris 1642'.

29 Gilbert, *Ir. Confed.*, vol. 2, 100.

In marked contrast to more deferential correspondence that Wadding received, Owen Roe O'Neill wrote in more forceful terms. Eager to stake his claims to his family chieftaincy instead of Phelim O'Neill, Owen Roe asked Wadding to secure assistance from Urban VIII. Acknowledging receipt of Wadding's letters, O'Neill described them as 'witnesses of your zeal for the homeland known by many other proofs'.[30] Notwithstanding Wadding's words of support, however, Owen Roe called upon him to take decisive action because, despite assurances, 'the foreign assistance long hoped for and expected' had not appeared.[31]

Wadding foresaw that, in the absence of help from the Catholic rulers of Europe, the Apostolic See in Rome 'with its usual piety, would lend a helping hand [...] for the defence of the Catholic faith and for justice'.[32] In response, O'Neill stated that this was because the Apostolic See was 'entrusted with the duty to restore the same faith and preserve it from destruction'.[33] 'Time slips by', O'Neill warned and, 'groaning under so great a burden [he] wondered and grieved at the slowness'.[34]

In what appears to be a veiled threat to Wadding, O'Neill then raised the possibility that a similar task could be committed to Hugh Bourke as supervisor: 'who, out of his zeal and prudence, would not allow it to be expended in any other way than the common gain required, and he would like to contribute the support himself'. [35] Aware that Wadding was apprehensive about missing out on such decisions, O'Neill closed

30 Owen Roe O'Neill to Luke Wadding, Brussels, 18 May 1642 (UCD-OFM, D.03/239), Gilbert, ed, *Contemp. Hist.*, vol. 1, 449, 'Accepi Vestræ Paternitatis litteras, zeli vestri in patriam aliis multis argumentis noti, testes'.

31 Ibid: 'sed longa spe et expectatione externi succursûs, quem maturè affuturum non dubitauit, et appropinquantem non videt'.

32 Ibid: 'si omnes Principes Catholici sua hac in parte denegarent auxilia, quin Sedes Apostolica solita sua pietate adjutricem porrigeret manum, vbi ipsa tam arduum attentaret negotium pro fidei Catholicæ et æquitatis defensione'.

33 Ibid: 'ex officio incumbere eandem fidem refouere, et ab interitu preseruare'.

34 Ibid: 'Tempus labitur [...] licet sub tam graui onere ingemiscens miretur et doleat eius tarditatem'.

35 Ibid: 'Sed hoc et quæ hactenus significaui Vestræ Paternitatis zelo et prudentiæ committo: a qua non aliud in similibus expecto quam quod ad bonum commune patriæ et gloriam Dei promovendam melius judicabit expedire'.

by reassuring him that he entrusted matters to Wadding's 'zeal and prudence' and expected nothing less than his judgement 'in the country's best interests and for the glory of God'.[36] In the meantime, however, O'Neill declared that he and his country were afflicted.[37] He addressed his letter to St Isidore's and noted Wadding's role as qualificator to the Holy Office where he represented the Irish cause. Alarmed by serious tensions between the O'Neills, Wadding believed that Owen Roe's rivalry with Phelim O'Neill would prevent him from following his cousin's orders in Ireland. That later proved to be the case.[38]

By 22 March 1642, Wadding had convinced the Roman authorities to support the war as a spiritual defence, securing the assistance they could offer and bringing to bear diplomatic pressure in the capitals of Europe. He confided in Bourke his fears of Owen Roe's departure and went as far to ask his fellow Franciscan to delay matters in Flanders. This was complicated by the fact that Wadding had secured 10,000 scudi from Urban VIII for Owen Roe to buy arms and ammunition.[39] In turn, another dynastic dispute became apparent among Irish exiles after Con O'Neill, the leading member of his family in Spain, departed for Ireland. As a result, Wadding also expected disagreements between Con and his cousin, Owen Roe, over their competing interests.[40]

Matters were complicated further by ongoing war between France and Spain. Consequently, Philip IV kept up appearances with England to avoid making another enemy. At the same time, Francis O'Sullivan, a Franciscan, and James Talbot, an Augustinian priest, received Spanish silver, 4,000 muskets, four pieces of cannon and other supplies purchased with 20,000 ducats from Philip IV.[41] However, Francisco de Melo, governor-general of the Habsburg Netherlands, did not permit Irish soldiers to return home

36 Ibid.

37 Ibid: 'Interim me et afflictum patriæ mihi'.

38 Gilbert, *Contemp Hist.*, vol. 3, xxxiii.

39 Wadding to Bourke, Rome, 22 March 1642 (UCD-OFM, D.04/1/301–4, formerly 192–93).

40 Mooney, 'The Letters of Luke Wadding', 408.

41 Bagwell, *Ireland under the Stuarts and during the Interregnum*, vol. 2 (1642–60), 78–79.

and closely monitored sea traffic in the ports of Spanish Flanders. In an attempt, perhaps, to disarm the new Spanish governor before asking for his help, Wadding told Melo that he was obliged to pray for him.[42] A month later, the nuncio at Brussels sought authorisation for Owen Roe O'Neill to go to Ireland, at which point the governor suspected this was due to interference from Francesco Barberini.[43] In O'Neill's case, however, being prohibited from leaving did not prevent him from setting sail.[44] Seeing Irish units return home to fight, the great powers of Europe attempted to recruit Irish soldiers in Ireland and on the continent but did not encounter much success in doing so.[45]

Owen Roe O'Neill earned his reputation as a leader long before 1641. He was among the most experienced soldiers of his generation, serving Spain from 1607 to 1642.[46] Forced to wait on events, he notified Wadding in June that he and some of his relations were about to leave the Low Countries.[47] Expressing his gratitude, O'Neill asked Wadding to continue his business with Urban VIII 'in case the evidence for his eagerness was

42 Luke Wadding to Francisco de Melo, Rome, 30 January 1642 (AGRB, SEG, 574); Brendan Jennings, ed, *Wild Geese in Spanish Flanders, 1582–1700: Documents Relating Chiefly to Irish Regiments, from the Archives Générales du Royaume, Bruxelles, and Other Sources* (Dublin: Irish Manuscripts Commission, 1964), 355–56.

43 Jerrold Casway, 'Owen Roe O'Neill's Return to Ireland in 1642: The Diplomatic Background', *Studia Hib.*, 9 (1969), 53–54.

44 Eduardo de Mesa, *The Irish in the Spanish Armies in the Seventeenth Century* (Woodbridge: Boydell, 2014), 91.

45 Ibid, 37–39, 60–62, 131–133; Gilbert, *Ir. Confed.*, vol. 3, 165–66. Luke Wadding the Franciscan is not to be confused with his Jesuit cousin and namesake who, at that time, was in Spain hoping to raise Irish troops for Philip IV in exchange for weapons and equipment. See Robert Stradling, *The Spanish Monarchy and Irish Mercenaries: The Wild Geese in Spain, 1618–68* (Dublin: Irish Academic Press, 1994), 43–45, 54.

46 Eduardo de Mesa, 'The Career of Owen Roe O'Neill in the Spanish Army of Flanders (1606–42): Documentation held in Spanish archives', *Archiv. Hib.*, 67 (2014), 7–24.

47 Owen Roe O'Neill to Luke Wadding, Brussels, 7 June 1642 (UCD-OFM, D.04/2/479–80, formerly 275); Gilbert, *Contemp. Hist.*, vol. 1, 476, 'Post varias vias partim frustra expectatas, partim frustra attentatas quibus spes visxderi posset afflictæ patriæ succurendi [...] Vnde statui terræ et maris periculis me committere vt patriæ, qua possum per meam presentiam non videar deesse. Nunc sum accinctus ad nauem cum aliquot meæ gentis nobilibus'.

called into question'.[48] Arms and explosives were still required in Ireland, O'Neill advised. He entrusted some letters to Wadding and requested that he bring them to Urban VIII, which O'Neill regarded as a blessing. Signing off as 'a humble and devoted servant', he bid Wadding farewell, commending himself and the state of Ireland to the Franciscan's prayers.[49] Wadding informed Francesco Barberini that Owen Roe left Flanders for Ireland on 29 June 1642 with two hundred troops, eight captains and other officers. Escorted by the Flanders armada, O'Neill sailed in the *St Francis*, a fully rigged frigate that Wadding obtained for him.[50] Thomas Preston, a Palesman, also served as a senior officer in the Spanish army of Flanders but refused to take ship with O'Neill the Gael in 1642. Preston was jealous of the preferment shown to his rival in the Habsburg Netherlands for many years. The lack of cooperation only worsened once they reached Ireland, and this badly affected morale.[51]

The Holy See consulted Wadding on issues concerning Ireland since his work as official agent of the Irish archbishops and bishops a decade earlier. On the same understanding, he told Urban VIII about Owen Roe O'Neill's departure. In reply, the pope greeted Owen Roe as his 'beloved son'.[52] Praising him, Urban VIII expected evidence of his great qualities as a soldier, which had secured him a singular reputation. Recommending the advice of those indicated in Owen Roe's letters, such as Wadding, the pope prayed 'that the efforts of the adversaries may be reduced to nothing' but

48 Ibid: 'Non duxi Vestram Reuerentiam multum rogandam vt in sua erga patriam zelo pergat eius negotia apud Suam Sanctitatem vrgendo, ne videar vestrum zelum multis argumentis testatissimum in dubium vocare'.

49 Ibid: 'Vestræ Paternitatis humilis et deuotus seruus [...] Quod inter prima recommendandum erat rogo Vestra Paternitas dignetur Suæ Sanctitati porrigere has adjunctas litteras quibus benedictionem mihi'.

50 Wadding to Francesco Barberini, Rome, 26 July 1642 (BAV, Barb. Lat., 6483, f. 33rv).

51 Jerrold Casway, *Owen Roe O'Neill and the Struggle for Catholic Ireland* (Philadelphia: University of Pennsylvania Press, 1984), 74, 145.

52 'Dilecte fili salutem'. Urban VIII to Owen Roe O'Neill, Rome, 8 October 1642; Gilbert, *Contemp. Hist.*, vol. 1, 524. See also Burtchaell and Rigg, eds, *Hist. MSS Comm. rep. on Franciscan manuscripts*, 208, 240.

avoided further commitment.[53] Conscious of Owen Roe's 'long-standing piety', Urban VIII closed by granting him full remission of his sins.[54] All those who followed him, 'if they have truly repented, and duly refreshed with Holy Communion, if possible', also received full pardon.[55]

Liberty of conscience

The freedom to openly profess Catholicism in Ireland was of direct interest to Wadding, as shown by contemporary evidence at St Isidore's.[56] Despite the religious divide, the freedom of worship achieved by Scottish Covenanters from 1638 to 1640 encouraged Irish Catholics.[57] After the outbreak of war, Hugh Bourke wrote to Wadding stating that 'the kingdom [of Ireland] had enjoyed liberty of conscience for a millennium and hundreds of years'.[58] The Irish, he said, 'knew of antiquity, power and riches superior to the Scots who with their revolt have attained from the king absolute liberty of their conscience as it is'.[59] Consequently, Irish Catholics 'would not be content with less than their neighbours had accomplished'.[60]

53 Ibid: 'nos diuinam clementiam indesinenter orantes, vt aduersariorum conatus in nihilum redigat'.

54 Ibid: 'tuæque iampridem pietatis conscij à te'.

55 Ibid: 'si verè poenitentes confessi fuerint, et Sacra Communione (si fieri possit) debite refecti, plenariam suorum peccatorum veniam et remissionem; atque in mortis articulo indulgentiam etiam plenariam elargimur'.

56 See Burtchaell and Rigg, eds, *Hist. MSS Comm. rep. on Franciscan Manuscripts*, 57–107 and 108–247.

57 Darcy, *The Irish Rebellion of 1641 and the Wars of the Three Kingdoms*, 8; David Stevenson, *Scottish Covenanters and Irish Confederates: Scottish-Irish Relations in the Mid-Seventeenth Century* (Belfast: UHF, 1981; repr. 2004), 87–93; John Morrill, 'The Covenant in its British Context', in idem, ed, *The Scottish National Covenant in its British Context* (Edinburgh: Edinburgh University Press, 1990), 1–30.

58 Bourke to Wadding, Brussels, 10 May 1642 (UCD-OFM, D.04/1/377–80, formerly 230–1).

59 Ibid: 'la Libertad de Conciencia, que el Reyno ha gozado mil y centenares de años, q ellos se conoçian de antiguedad, poder, y riquezas superiores a los escoçeses, q*ue* con su solevamiento han alcançado del Rey, absoluta Libertad de su (tal qual) conçiencia'.

60 Ibid: 'no se contentarion con menos de lo q*ue* alcancaron sus vezinos'.

A manuscript copy of the Declaration of Arbroath was preserved at St Isidore's College.[61] A diplomatic appeal written by the Scottish political elite in 1320, the Declaration of Arbroath petitioned the papacy to persuade Edward II to make peace.[62] The history of 'Scotland's struggle for independence under the Bruce offered a prior example of a successful repudiation of English domination'.[63] This prefigured the seventeenth-century Scottish challenge to royal authority which provided inspiration for the insurrection that began in Dublin and Ulster in October 1641.[64]

There are a series of comparisons between the substance of the Declaration of Arbroath, the context in which it was written, and the experiences of Irish confederates during the 1640s. As was the case with the landed wealth of fourteenth-century Scotland,[65] Old English and Gaelic Catholic nobles maintained an uncomfortable political agreement.[66] The Declaration represented part of Robert Bruce's quest for help from overseas,[67] in the same way that the confederation of Kilkenny would invite as protector of Ireland the pope, or France or Spain.[68] The 'careful, even cautious, patriots' of 1320 reflected the moderate political stance of the Kilkenny confederates, as defined by Micheál Ó Siochrú.[69] The Declaration portrays Robert I as

61 Hazard, 'A manuscript copy of the Declaration of Arbroath from the Roman archives of Fr. Luke Wadding', 296–315.

62 A. A. M. Duncan, *The Nation of Scots and the Declaration of Arbroath (1320)* (London: The Historical Association, 1970), 26; Edward Cowan, *'For Freedom Alone': The Declaration of Arbroath, 1320* (East Linton: Tuckwell Press, 2003), 3–4.

63 Hiram Morgan, 'Policy and propaganda in Hugh O'Neill's connection with Europe', in O'Connor and Lyons, eds, *The Ulster Earls and Baroque Europe*, 30.

64 Ó Siochrú, *Confederate Ireland*, 21–2.

65 Duncan, *The Nation of Scots and the Declaration of Arbroath*, 30.

66 Jane Ohlmeyer, *Civil War and Restoration in the Three Stuart Kingdoms: the Career of Randal MacDonnell, Marquis of Antrim* (Dublin: Four Courts Press, 2001), 201–5.

67 Duncan, *The Nation of Scots and the Declaration of Arbroath*, 30.

68 Tadhg Ó hAnnracháin, 'Disrupted and Disruptive: Continental Influence on the Confederate Catholics of Ireland' in Allan Macinnes and Jane Ohlmeyer, eds, *The Stuart Kingdoms in the Seventeenth Century* (Dublin: Four Courts Press, 2002), 135–46. On Charles IV of Lorraine, another prospective protector of Ireland, see Micheál Ó Siochrú, 'The Duke of Lorraine and the International Struggle for Ireland, 1649–53', *HJ*, 48 (2005), 905–932.

69 Duncan, *The Nation of Scots and the Declaration of Arbroath*, 31; Ó Siochrú, *Confederate Ireland*, 175, 247.

'another Maccabaeus or Joshua'. Exiled Irish Catholics identified with the ancient Israelites throughout the early seventeenth century.[70] At Lyon, for example, Peter Reade of Meath published almost 800 folio pages of his Commentary on the Books of the Maccabees.[71]

Without the assurance of civil and religious liberty, Irish Catholic thinkers espoused the view that, since Charles I was not a Catholic, he could justifiably be deposed as ruler of Ireland.[72] Likewise, the government of Robert I avowed that, if he exposed Scotland to Edward II, they should expel him at once as their enemy and make another their king. In November 1642, Anthony Geoghegan, minister provincial of the Irish Observant Franciscans, wrote to Wadding. He announced, 'as we must urge Catholic princes to sustain us, we send two agents from here, Fr Peter Darcy to the French court, and to Rome our Fr Everard, with letters patent'.[73] He notified Wadding that there was 'not an army or regiment, not a province

70 Jerrold Casway, 'Gaelic Maccabeanism: The Politics of Reconciliation' in Jane Ohlmeyer, ed, *Political Thought in Seventeenth-Century Ireland: Kingdom or Colony* (Cambridge: Cambridge University Press, 2000), 176–88; Allan Macinnes, 'Covenanting Ideology in Seventeenth-century Scotland', in Ohlmeyer, ed, *Political Thought in Seventeenth-Century Ireland,* 191–220.

71 John Hennig, 'The Machabees and the Irish', *The Irish Monthly*, 75 (1947), 1–8. Reade's second volume in manuscript was kept at the library of the Irish College in Salamanca. Referred to as *Hibernus Medensis* on the title page of his first volume, Reade was professor of controversies at the Irish College before becoming professor of sacred scripture at the university. He died in 1651 at forty-four years of his age, 'leaving behind him the reputation of a good religious, and an excellent Greek and Hebrew scholar'.

72 Tadhg Ó hAnnracháin, "Though hereticks and politicians should misinterpret their goode zeal': political ideology and Catholicism in early-modern Ireland', in Ohlmeyer, ed, *Political Thought in Seventeenth-Century Ireland,* 155–175. On the relevance of Suárez and Bellarmine to this development in political thought, see Hazard, *Faith and Patronage*, 100–104.

73 Geoghegan to Wadding, Kilkenny, 13 November 1642 (UCD-OFM, D.04/3/1003, formerly 509–10), 'Quare ut apud exteros Catholicos principes continua instituatur procuratio res est pernecessaria. Hinc ob id dimittendi errant ad Gallicam curiam P*ater* Petrus Darci, ad Romanam P*ater* Everardus nostro, cum patentibus litteris'. See also O'Connor, 'The Irish College, Rome, in the Age of Religious Renewal', 13–32; Fearghus Ó Fearghail, 'Irish Links with Santa Maria dell'Anima in Rome', *Seanchas Ard Mhacha*, 22 (2009), 25–50.

or a county, not an angle of land, not a camp or a meeting, not a single expedition or a battle, that the friars are not in the midst of it'.[74]

For Wadding and the friars at St Isidore's, freedom of Catholic worship was a prerequisite for peace in the early 1640s. Despite their motivation to transcribe the Declaration and the support that the Kilkenny confederates sent to the Scottish royalists, there is little evidence to show that the Irish friars made direct use of the text. Their ambiguous attitude towards the anti-royal revolt of the Scots, the depth of religious divisions and the Declaration's radical threat to oust the king may have influenced matters in this regard.[75]

Hesitancy in Kilkenny

Believing the papacy to be 'founded on rock and unity', the supreme council in Kilkenny regarded it as unlawful and improper to approach Rome with divided or different opinions.[76] In a letter to Urban VIII they reported that, although slow to participate at the outbreak of war, the Catholics of Ireland were unanimous a year later. As such, the confederation of Kilkenny notified the pope that they were appointing Wadding their agent and manager. This enabled him to formally present their case at the papal court, faithfully disclosing the present state of affairs. The supreme council reported that Wadding was fully committed to them and humbly proposed their demands, which they hoped would result in positive action.[77] Asking for Urban VIII's blessing 'with one voice and one mind', they explained that Catholics in Ireland had no access to running the

74 Geoghegan to Wadding, 13 November 1642; Canice Mooney, 'The Golden Age of the Irish Franciscans, 1615–50', in O'Brien, ed, *Measgra i gcuimhne Mhichíl Uí Chléirigh*, 24, 30.

75 Cf. Christopher Hill, *The Century of Revolution, 1603–1714* (Abingdon: Routledge, 1974), 86, 104, 117; Stevenson, *Scottish Covenanters and Irish Confederates*, 83–4; Broun, 'The Declaration of Arbroath', 1.

76 Supreme council to Urban VIII, 28 November 1642 (UCD-OFM, D.04/3/1089–92, formerly 547–48); Gilbert, *Ir. Confed.*, vol. 2, 100–101, 'petram et unitatem'.

77 Ibid: 'quem actorem et procuratorem nostrum apud Sanctitatem vestram constituimus Admodum Reverend*us* P*ater* Lucas Waddingus'.

government, or receiving honours.[78] Having ascertained that Protestant settlers 'resolved to uproot and extirpate' them, the Catholic Irish sustained the war with weapons taken from the enemy.[79] Lacking supplies since the start, the supreme council now asked to be 'sufficiently furnished with all the equipment of war' so that, relying on aid from Urban VIII, they need not be afraid of their foes' strength at arms.[80]

Owing to their great confidence in Wadding's 'integrity, zeal, and prudence',[81] the supreme council of the Irish confederation appointed him their agent to manage their affairs in Italy. Wadding was familiar with the signatories before their appointment to each respective diocese. His principal instructions were to petition the papacy for the remission of sins for those engaged in the war, as well as the excommunication of their opponents and neutrals in Ireland.[82] In a direct echo of Wadding's earlier experience at the Roman court, the supreme council directed him to request letters, papal bulls or other means to restrain 'the undue ambition of some ecclesiastics' and that no claim was to be heard for any of Ireland's dioceses when vacant, without first consulting the local archbishop and the supreme council.[83] Many Irish Franciscan friars became directly involved in the ensuing war as preachers and confessors to Irish troops.[84]

78 Ibid: 'uno ore, uno animo'.

79 Ibid: 'At cum satis compertum haberemus Puritanos hostes decrevisse religionem Catholicam radicitus apud nos evellere et extirpare [...] nudi licet inermes contraivimus et ex ipsis hostium manibus arma extorsimus pauca, quibus hactenus bellum sustinuimus adversus crudelissimos hostes'.

80 Ibid: 'omni belli apparatu satis instructos, qu[orum] neque capiemur promissis, nec veremur vires et arma, vestris freti auxiliis'.

81 Letters patent of the supreme council appointing Wadding agent and proctor in Italy, Kilkenny, 7 December 1642 (UCD-OFM, D.04/3/1157–60, formerly 586–90); Gilbert, *Ir. Confed.*, vol. 2, 116: 'Scias, quod nos, de integritate, zelo et prudentia tua plurimum confidentes'.

82 Instructions to be followed by Wadding (UCD-OFM, D.04/3/1161–64, formerly 583–84); Gilbert, *Ir. Confed.*, vol. 2, 119–22: 'Obtineantur Indulgentiæ pro assertoribus præsentis Belli. Excommunicentur adversantes directe vel indirecte, et etiam negative se tenentes, præcipue Hiberni et alii incolæ soli Hibernici, et specialiter neutrales'.

83 Ibid. Wadding's confrères at St Anthony's College, Leuven, were told to bring Gaelic and Latin type, and books to open a school in Tipperary; Hynes, *The Mission of Rinuccini*, 9.

84 See Hazard, *Faith and Patronage*, 33–34, and idem, 'A New Company of Crusaders like that of St John Capistran: interaction between Irish military units and their

The supreme council also asked Wadding to obtain letters from the pope and Propaganda Fide to the German-speaking lands, France, Spain, Portugal, Poland, the state of Genoa and Dutch Catholics. Letters from the pope and cardinals to Cardinal Richelieu, the Count-Duke Olivares, and the clergy of the above-named countries were also required. This was intended to gain assistance for the Irish by sea and land. For this reason, Wadding employed 'a trusty messenger, [his] nephy, Mr. Barron, going over seas' to visit the French court.[85] The eldest son of Wadding's sister, Mary, Geoffrey Barron was a gifted lawyer and treasurer of the Catholic confederation who went on to become diplomatic agent to France.[86]

Letters to Henrietta Maria, Charles I's Catholic queen, were also required. In Rome, Wadding was to emphasise that the success of the war in Ireland would benefit Catholicism in northern Europe as a whole. Likewise, Ireland could then represent 'a haven in mid-ocean for the warships and merchant vessels of Catholics'.[87] In keeping with this observation, Wadding was asked to obtain safe-conducts from France, Spain and the Netherlands for Irish merchants and others to freely transport merchandise, especially war supplies, and to receive other goods in barter.[88] To avoid difficulties over the ownership of former church lands in late 1642, the supreme council also asked Wadding for copy of Cardinal Reginald Pole's dispensation of 1554. As a result, a copy of the papal brief given Pole is now preserved in a fine, neat hand amongst Wadding's papers in Dublin.[89]

Franciscan chaplains, 1579–1654', in Óscar Recio Morales and Enrique García Hernán, eds, *La Nación Irlandesa en el Ejército y la Sociedad Española*, 181–197.

85 Hugh O'Reilly to Luke Wadding, Kilkenny, 9 December 1642 (UCD-OFM, D.04/3/1165, formerly 585); Gilbert, *Ir. Confed.*, vol. 2, 118119.

86 Micheál Ó Siochrú, 'Barron (Baron), Geoffrey, (1606–51), Lawyer, Politician and Diplomat', *DIB*, vol. 1, 315–316, <https://www.dib.ie/biography/barron-baron-geoffrey-a0429>, accessed 20 August 2024; Bagwell, *Ireland under the Stuarts and during the Interregnum*, vol. 1 (1603–42), 315–316; ibid, vol. 2 (1642–60), 103.

87 Gilbert, *Ir. Confed.*, vol. 2, 119.

88 Ibid.

89 *Breve. Julii iii ad Raynaldus Cardinalem Polus sed: Aplice. in Anglia Legatus qua dat illi auctoritatem dispensandi cum detensoribus honorus ecclicorum. Julius Epicopus. Reginaldo Card: Polo Legato. MDLIV. An. V.* (UCD-OFM, D.01, vol. 1, 7–10).

Waterford and the War at Sea

Luke Wadding fully understood the significance of Ireland's ports in times of peace and war. Born into a merchant family, he appreciated the value of trade to his home city of Waterford.[90] Indicatively, he explained to Urban VIII that 'many Dutch and Flemish Catholics' had settled in Waterford bringing 'great profit and wellbeing to the said city with their commerce'.[91] Waterford maintained close connections with the Low Countries in wool, leather and other merchandise. The re-victualling of ships yielded high earnings for merchants.[92] Every vessel carrying freight from the Waterford to Flanders 'had to pay God's penny for the maintenance of Christ Church, the merchant being bound to personally deliver the tax to Christ Church before he sailed'.[93] Thus, Flemish merchants may have traded with south Munster, in ways similar to Irish traders who brought prosperity to parts of Brittany and the Low Countries during the second half of the seventeenth century.[94] The Dutch and Flemish also specialised in the book trade, working closely with engravers and printers. Although a considerable portion of paper was manufactured in France, most of it was bought from Dutch wholesalers. It may not be just coincidental that the first official printing press outside Dublin was founded in Waterford in 1643. Irish friars used good quality, handmade rag-paper shipped to Ireland from Antwerp and Amsterdam.[95] During the early seventeenth century, Dutch merchants gained the upper hand over their English counterparts in Ireland.[96] By then

90 Hazard, 'Luke Wadding's Petition to the Papacy on Behalf of Dutch and Flemish Migrants in Waterford', 5.

91 Ibid.

92 George O'Brien, *The Economic History of Ireland in the Seventeenth Century* (London and Dublin: Maunsell, 1919), 163.

93 Byrne, ed, *The Great Parchment Book of Waterford*, xix–xx. I owe this reference to Dr Edel Bhreathnach.

94 Hazard, 'Luke Wadding's Petition to the Papacy on Behalf of Dutch and Flemish Migrants in Waterford', 5.

95 Bernadette Cunningham, *The Annals of the Four Masters*, 74.

96 Rolf Loeber, 'English and Irish sources for the history of Dutch economic activity in Ireland, 1600–89', *Irish Economic and Social History*, 8 (1981), 70–85.

an Irish military and religious community had emerged in the Habsburg Netherlands. Students from Waterford studied at Leuven and their home city was one of several seaports for the transport of soldiers to and from the Low Countries.[97]

Against the wishes of the mayor, Thomas White, Geoffrey Barron co-operated with Edmund Butler to bring Waterford into the war in 1642.[98] Whether Barron acted upon his uncle's advice is unclear. In Flanders, from December that year to February 1643, agents of the confederation of Kilkenny 'issued at least twenty blank letters of marque to captains of foreign frigates willing to patrol Irish waters in return for freedom to rove the seas'.[99] Flemish privateers were plying a lucrative trade all over Europe.[100] Established on the southeast coast of Ireland by the middle of that decade, these were seen as 'confederate ships'.[101] Although initially centred upon Wexford, Waterford featured prominently throughout this period and, after the fall of Wexford to Cromwell, 'the corsairs maintained a presence at Waterford' until 1651. Giovanni Giustiniani, Venetian ambassador in England, calculated that the Kilkenny parliament kept a fleet of '30 well-armed ships at sea' in the early stages of the war.[102]

Amongst the Flemings associated with privateering in the port city were Joseph Constant, who skippered the *St Peter*; Antonio Vandezipen, whose business was based in Waterford; Daniel Van Vooren, commander of the *St John*; and Francis Oliver, master of the *Patrick*.[103] In line with Wadding's

97 Jennings, ed, *Wild Geese in Spanish Flanders*, 346, 516.

98 Ó hAnnracháin, *Catholic Reformation in Ireland*, 270.

99 Jane Ohlmeyer, 'The Dunkirk of Ireland: Wexford Privateers during the 1640s', *Journal of the Wexford Historical Society*, 12 (1988–9), 23–48; Idem, 'Irish Privateers during the Civil War, 1642–50', *Mariner's Mirror*, 76 (1990), 119–34.

100 Roland Baetens, 'The Organization and Effects of Flemish Privateering in the Seventeenth Century', *Acta historiae neerlandicae. Studies on the History of the Netherlands*, 9 (1977), 54–62.

101 Elaine Murphy, *Ireland and the War at Sea, 1641–53* (Woodbridge: Boydell & Brewer, 2012), 82, 111.

102 Pat McCarthy, '"Waterford and Wexford Swarm with Dunkirkers': Waterford and the War at Sea, 1642–50', *Decies*, 71 (2017), 3.

103 Murphy, *Ireland and the War at Sea*, 111; Ohlmeyer, '"The Dunkirk of Ireland"', 33–43.

mediation on behalf of Flemish Catholics, he arranged for the *St Francis* to take Owen Roe O'Neill to Ireland. A frigate of 200 tonnes with the same name and armed with eighteen guns was part of the Vandezipen fleet.[104]

The recently settled Dutch and Flemish community sought Wadding's help to obtain and renovate a church for their own use in 1645.[105] They expressed a preference for a 'neglected and partly derelict' parish church in the city. This was the church of Olaf the Big, patron saint of Norway, established in the late eleventh or early twelfth century.[106] Olaf II Haraldsson, king of Norway, was born *c.*995 AD and died 29 July 1030. He oversaw the conversion of Norway, and, after his death, devotion to him spread to Viking colonies overseas such as Dublin, Waterford and Wexford.[107]

The eagerness of the petitioners to secure the mediaeval church is attested by their willingness to re-roof and repair the building and to offer a stipend for a priest from Flanders.[108] An early fifteenth-century memorandum deemed it worthy 'to be recorded and kept in memorye' that one Maurice Wadding was a tenant of Waterford Corporation 'in the weste, within the citie, and in the paroche of Saynte Olave'.[109] This is the earliest surviving evidence 'of a member of the Wadding family in Waterford'.[110]

104 Murphy, *Ireland and the War at Sea*, 120; Ohlmeyer, "The Dunkirk of Ireland", 39.

105 Hazard, 'Luke Wadding's Petition to the Papacy on Behalf of Dutch and Flemish Migrants in Waterford', 3; *Comment. Rinucc.*, vol. 2, 269.

106 Michael Byrne, ed, *Waterford 1470: Dean John Collyn and the Chantry of St Saviour* (Drogheda, Choice Publishing, 2013), 87. See also *The Register of St Saviour's Chantry of Waterford: Registrum Cantariae S. Salvatoris Waterfordensis, British Library, Harleian MS 3765*, translated and edited by Niall Byrne with Michael Byrne; revised by Kenneth Nicholls (Dublin: Irish Manuscripts Commission, 2013).

107 Richard Haworth, 'The Site of St Olave's Church, Dublin', in Bradley, ed, *Settlement and Society in Medieval Ireland: Studies presented to F. X. Martin, OSA*, 178.

108 Hazard, 'Luke Wadding's Petition to the Papacy on Behalf of Dutch and Flemish Migrants in Waterford', 4.

109 *Archives of the Municipal Corporation of Waterford*, ed J. T. Gilbert, *Report 10* (London: Historical Manuscripts Commission, 1885), Appendix v, 329: The memorandum related to the loss of lands for non-payment of 'the King's chief rent called Longable' by Richard Bristoll and John Guyere. The extent of the lands measured from Boat Street, in the north, to the lands of St John of Jerusalem in the south and in breadth from William Symcok in the east, to Maurice Wadding's in the west.

110 Byrne, 'Luke Wadding's Waterford', *Decies*, 63 (2004), 35.

The guardian of Waterford's Franciscan friary, Thomas Strange, was Wadding's source on the Dutch and Flemish presence in the port city. Referring to Waterford as Little Rome, Strange told Wadding that as the city that had declared most strongly for the Catholic cause in Ireland.[111] The Stranges lived in the parish of St Olaf and were related to the Waddings by marriage. Like his kinsman, Thomas Strange left Ireland for the Iberian Peninsula, joined the Santiago province of the Friars Minor and trained for the priesthood. He subsequently taught theology in Spain and was once taken captive at sea by the Turks.[112] Wadding may have regarded Dutch and Flemish Catholics as a prospective source of patronage in Ireland where, according to Strange, the confederate war 'impoverished all the benefactors'.[113] We hear of Waterford's Flemish settlers again two years later, when the French ambassador in London wrote to Louis XIV's minister of foreign affairs. He reported that Flemish privateers at Waterford were selling goods captured at sea, 'prized' from the French. Meanwhile, he noted, the Flemish held nothing but contempt for the Irish and that James Butler, 3rd marquis of Ormond, was prepared to come to terms with the confederates.[114]

Well-chosen patrons

Wadding's first task for the supreme council was to express their gratitude to Urban VIII's nephews, Cardinals Antonio and Francesco Barberini.[115]

111 Thomas Strange to Wadding, Waterford, 26 December 1642 (UCD-OFM, D.04/1199–1204, formerly 608–610).

112 Hazard, 'Luke Wadding's Petition to the Papacy on Behalf of Dutch and Flemish Migrants in Waterford', 6.

113 Ibid, 7.

114 Pompone II de Bellièvre, Sieur de Grignon, to Henri-Auguste de Loménie, Comte de Brienne, London, 3 January 1647 (BnF, Paris, fonds français (Registers of Pompone II de Bellièvre), Ms. 15996, ff. 89–91): 'la vente faite par des Flamands à Waterfort de marchandises prises sur les Français et de la haine des Flamands pour les Irlandais; et où le Marquis d'Ormont se serait accommodé avec les confédérés'. James Butler was also 12th earl of Ormond.

115 Supreme council to Wadding, Kilkenny, 6 December 1642 (UCD-OFM, D.04/3/1157–60, formerly 586–90); Gilbert, *Ir. Confed.*, vol. 2 , 117.

This was facilitated by friendship. On his arrival in Rome many years before, Wadding met Francesco Barberini and subsequently became a regular recipient of Barberini patronage.[116] Sir Richard Bellings, secretary to the supreme council, acknowledged the gifts they received from the Barberini nephews describing them as 'the firstlings of the oblations given to our sacred cause'.[117] He thanked Wadding for acquainting 'those well-chosen patrons of ours with our affairs and distress'.[118] Bellings added a postscript: 'The Protestant Bishop Ussher hath often spoken of you unto me, and at all times with great approbation of your ability'.[119]

From February 1643, the pope's nephews sent multiple letters of support to the hierarchy in Ireland, the deputies of the supreme council and all commanders of their forces in Leinster, Munster, Connacht and Ulster.[120] At St Isidore's, Wadding kept annotated copies of those written by Francesco Barberini.[121] A month later, he and his brother Antonio donated 12,000 Roman scudi to buy ordnance for the Irish.[122] Finally on this point and in tandem with Wadding's efforts, the supreme council addressed a letter to Antonio Barberini, Cardinal Protector of Ireland, recommending the translation of Heber MacMahon from the diocese of Down to Clogher.[123]

In keeping with the instructions he received, Wadding secured letters from Urban VIII to Louis XIV, his chief minister, Cardinal Mazarin, who succeeded

116 Wadding, *Annales Minorum*, vol. 9, 'Prolegomena', xi: 'Viginti anni sunt, ex quo pedem in Vrbem intuli; totidem, quo me perpetua gratia prosequeris'. See also 'F*rater* P*ater* Lucae Waddingi ordinis Minorum ad sequentia opuscula praemonitio'. (*PL*, vol. 31, 0013–0013, col. 1846).

117 Bellings to Wadding, Kilkenny, 9 December 1642 (UCD-OFM, D.04/3/1169–72, formerly 579–80); Gilbert, *Ir. Confed.*, vol. 2, 122–23.

118 Ibid.

119 Ibid.

120 Giblin, ed, 'Vatican Library: MSS. Barberini Latini', 73.

121 'Brevia ad G*ene*rales exercitum edit Franc*isc*us Card*ina*lis Barberinus an 1643' (UCD-OFM, D.04/2/875–883, formerly 462–66).

122 Binasco, 'Not Only a "Hibernese" in the *Urbs*', in idem, ed, *Luke Wadding, the Irish Franciscans and Global Catholicism*, 84.

123 Benignus Millett, 'Heber MacMahon, Bishop of Clogher (d.1650)', *Clogher Record*, 16 (1997), 136–144; Gilbert, *Contemp. Hist.*, vol. 3, 156.

Richelieu, and the papal nuncio to France.[124] From 1641 to 1646, the Jesuit Father Matthew O'Hartegan was commissioned as Irish envoy to Paris.[125] He corresponded with Wadding in a clear hand, relayed information from Wadding's nephew, Geoffrey Barron, and endeavoured to see him secretary of state in Ireland.[126] Notwithstanding Irish hopes of help from Henrietta Maria, however, her influence made French intervention unlikely. Nevertheless, France donated financial support and two pieces of 24-pounder artillery, which the Irish forces lacked.[127] O'Hartegan was also convinced that passports were available for Irish soldiers wishing to travel through French ports. Writing with news of weapons and victuals, Hugh Bourke told Wadding that such passports lent a helping hand to the war effort.[128] The supreme council appealed to O'Hartegan for funding. Blaming Ireland's parlous finances on the avarice of Lords Deputy in earlier decades, they petitioned Wadding for 'a speedy supply of mony' in the following year.[129]

124 Supreme council to Wadding, Kilkenny, 21 February 1643 (UCD-OFM, D.04/1/221, formerly 153). The nuncio at that time appears to have been Cardinal Grimaldi-Cavalleroni.

125 Gilbert, *Ir. Confed.*, vol. 2, 67; Thomas Morrissey 'The Career of Matthew O'Hartegan SJ (–1665). Irish Envoy to the Court of France 1641–1646' (IJA, OLD/44).

126 Matthew O'Hartegan to Wadding, Paris, 14 February 1643 (UCD-OFM, D.01/2/425–26); O'Hartegan to Wadding, Paris, 19 August 1643 (UCD-OFM, D.01/2/349–50); O'Hartegan to Wadding, 21 August 1643 (UCD-OFM, D.01/2/417–418); Jennings, ed, 'Ecclesiastical appointments in Ireland, Aug. 1643–Dec. 1649', 19–20.

127 William Carrigan, *The History and Antiquities of the Diocese of Ossory* (Dublin: Sealy, Bryers & Walker, 1905), 25; Murphy, *Ireland and the War at Sea*, 18.

128 Bourke to Wadding, Brussels, 29 November 1642 (UCD-OFM, D.04/3/1099–1102, formerly 552–53).

129 Supreme council to Wadding, Kilkenny, 21 February 1643 (UCD-OFM, D.04/1/221, formerly 153); Gilbert, *Ir. Confed.*, vol. 2, 206.

Pierfrancesco Scarampi and Thomas Wadding

At first, the war went in the confederates' favour with victories in Munster and Leinster, but a lack of leadership hampered their progress from 1643 onwards.[130] The most significant development that year occurred after Wadding proposed that a papal envoy was needed in Ireland with arms, ammunition and money. To that end, Urban VIII appointed Pierfrancesco Scarampi apostolic delegate to the confederation of Kilkenny on 18 April.[131] Matthew O'Hartegan gave Wadding an account of Scarampi's journey to Ireland.[132] He arrived in Wexford in late June with money that Wadding had collected from the Spada, Barberini, Pamphili and other ruling families in Rome. Wadding also gathered powder, bullets and match proportionable for muskets, together with firelocks, pikes, swords, jacks for lifting and other supplies.[133]

Thomas Wadding, Luke's cousin, provided Scarampi with a townhouse and a farm in the Waterford countryside 'together with horses, money, the goods of his house and splendid banquets'.[134] As a Catholic confederate, Thomas was described as 'Senator, knight and civil lawyer of Waterford'.[135] He had followed his father and grandfather into the legal profession becoming a member of the Middle Temple, one of the four Inns of Court in

130 Scott Wheeler, 'Four Armies in Ireland', in Jane Ohlmeyer, ed, *Ireland from Independence to Occupation, 1641–60* (Cambridge: Cambridge University Press, 2002), 65.

131 Binasco, 'Luke Wadding and his entourage', 84; Paolo Aringhi, *Memorie istoriche della vita del venerabile servo di Dio Pier Francesco Scarampi* (Rome: Stamperia Pietro Rosati, 1744), 36; cited by Cleary, *Father Luke Wadding and St Isidore's College*, 27.

132 O'Hartegan to Wadding, Paris, 23 May 1643 (UCD-OFM, D.02, vol. 4, 371/986–87). According to a manuscript life of Scarampi at the Biblioteca Vallecelliana, Rome, Wadding told the Oratorians he would not call Scarampi 'by any other name than that of Apostle of Ireland, for he truly deserves this title'; Patrick Moran, *Memoirs of the Most Rev. Oliver Plunket: Archbishop of Armagh and Primate of all Ireland* (1st edn, Dublin: James Duffy, 1861), 4.

133 Meehan, *History of the Confederation of Kilkenny*, 91.

134 Harold, *Vita Fratris Lucae Waddingi*, 8: 'Petrus Franciscus Scarampus, nobilis & religiosissimus presbyter Oratorii Romani [...] quos cum fui muneris exequendi causa Waterfordiam trahebat, apertam sibi paratamque habebant urbanam domum, & villam ruralem, equos insuper & pecunias Thomae Waddingi, Lucae nostri patruelis'.

135 *Comment. Rinucc.*, vol. 3, 352.

London, on 31 May 1613 before holding office in Waterford as Alderman and Recorder of the city.[136]

During the crisis that began in 1641, Thomas Wadding did 'compose Rebellion and commit high treason'.[137] He enrolled as a signatory of the oath of association and attended proceedings where members of the supreme council were elected.[138] In this context, the confederates compared the taking of the oath to a public sacrament.[139]

As was the case with his immediate forebears, Thomas Wadding was a landed magnate with many tenants in the county. In the records of landownership after 1640, commissioners found that his estate amounted to approximately 4,700 acres, that is, 7,613 acres statute measure.[140] Part of that property consisted of the impropriate rectory at Kilbarry and the lands adjoining, which had been in Wadding hands since the sixteenth century. Thomas Wadding also held lands in the neighbouring diocese of Cloyne,

136 Sturgess, ed and trans, *Register of Admissions to the Honourable Society of the Middle Temple*, 100.

137 Inquisition taken on 9 February 1662 for lands forfeited in the county of Waterford, Ordnance Survey Collection for the County of Waterford, Royal Irish Academy.

138 'Mrs. Briver's account of proceedings at Waterford, 1642'; Gilbert, *Ir. Confed.*, vol. 2, 21, 219. See also Naomi McAreavey, 'This is that I may remember what passings that happened in Waterford: Inscribing the 1641 Rising in the Letters of the Wife of the Mayor of Waterford', *Early Modern Women*, 5 (2010), 77–109.

139 *Comment. Rinucc.*, vol. 2, 168. John Morrill, 'An Irish Protestation? Oaths and the Confederation of Kilkenny', in Michael Braddick and Phil Whithington, eds, *Popular Culture and Political Agency in Early Modern England* (Manchester: Manchester University Press, 2006), 181–95; Raymond Gillespie, 'The Social Thought of Richard Bellings', in Micheál Ó Siochrú, ed, *Kingdoms in Crisis: Ireland in the 1640s* (Dublin: Four Courts Press, 2001), 212–28. On the oaths of association and of supremacy, see *Comment. Rinucc.*, vol. 1, 536, 730.

140 Dublin, Royal Irish Academy, Taylor set of Books of Survey and Distribution, Waterford, 11, I.i.2. Thomas Wadding also held lands at Palmerstown, Co. Dublin, where, according to a bond of 26 November 1637, he received an annuity of £40 sterling per annum. See Brian Donovan and David Edwards, eds, *British Sources for Irish History, 1485–1641* (Dublin: Irish Manuscripts Commission, 1997), 83.

as lay impropriator of Clondulane and Leitrim parishes, in the baronies of Condons and Clangibbon, Co. Cork.[141]

In 1642, Thomas Wadding was appointed 'by the Common Council of the City to be an overseer of a Mint House and that the stamps were made to that purpose by his order'.[142] On 23 July, as Recorder of the city council, Thomas Wadding made an order for the reception of Scarampi, 'then coming into Waterford, with discharge of artillery for him and providing wine, saffron bread, and other necessaries for his accommodations'.[143] According to Thomas Wadding, while Scarampi dwelt in Ireland, everything went well, with victory in battle and 'the flourishing of true Roman Catholic faith without any disturbance'.[144] Despite a warm reception from the Irish people, Scarampi noted serious discord between members of the supreme council and tried to encourage agreement between the competing parties. He also became aware of divisions among the regular orders and secular clergy.[145]

Former church lands and livings

Since Luke Wadding was recognised as the Catholic confederates' representative in Rome, they gave him authority to endorse ecclesiastical appointments after the first general assembly met in Kilkenny.[146] In

141 William Maziere Brady, ed, *Clerical and Parochial Records of Cork, Cloyne and Ross. Taken from Diocesan and Parish Registries, Mss. in the Principal Libraries and Public Offices of Oxford, Dublin, and London, and from private or family papers*, 2 vols (London: Longman, Roberts and Green, 1864), vol. 2, 125, 304, 318. Leitrim civil parish straddled the county bounds between Waterford and Cork, near Imokilly.

142 Cleary, *Father Luke Wadding and St Isidore's College*, 66.

143 Ibid.

144 Aringhi, *Memorie istoriche della vita del venerabile servo di Dio Pier Francesco Scarampi*, 43: 'Nam, dum residebat Vestra Paternitas in Hibernia omnia prospere succedebant incolis [...] victoriae contra inimicos nostros [...] vera Catholica Romana Religio vigebat et floruit absque ulla perturbatione'.

145 Ibid.

146 Jennings, ed, 'Ecclesiastical appointments in Ireland, Aug., 1643–Dec., 1649', *Coll. Hib.*, 2 (1959), 18–65.

the following six years, Wadding received the particulars of vacancies for clerical office and church administration, such as parish priest and chancellor, many of them forwarded to him by Edmund O'Dwyer and Matthew O'Hartegan.[147] The names of those recommended were evenly balanced between candidates from Gaelic and Old English backgrounds. Wadding kept these records together with documents relating to the eventual appointment of nominees, such as papal bulls which proclaimed their selection.[148] Wadding's role in this regard included the promotion of candidates to Cistercian foundations.[149] In doing so, he was advised and assisted by Scarampi who petitioned for certain candidates and obtained official documents via Carlo Francesco Invernizi at the Holy See. This demonstrates that, as long as the confederation exerted its authority, appointments by the papacy, even to parochial and lesser benefices, were once more acknowledged as standard practice in Ireland, as it had been before the Reformation.[150] Nevertheless, matters were made difficult by the loss of Invernizi at sea with official documents that Wadding had entrusted to him for Scarampi.[151]

Before long, Scarampi addressed the problem of ecclesiastical lands and lay ownership, helping Catholic confederates exercise restraint against the restitution of such property.[152] This was done in the belief that depriving the current owners was not the answer, a point that was directly relevant to Thomas Wadding and his family at Kilbarry. According to long-established practice, bishops and abbots in Ireland often farmed out church lands and tithes to Catholic laymen.[153] These revenues were otherwise allocated to the maintenance of buildings and the upkeep of clergy. In the sixteenth

147 Ibid.

148 Ibid, 60.

149 Ibid.

150 Ibid, 18.

151 Ibid, 60.

152 O'Connor, *Irish Jansenists*, 244, 246.

153 Brian Mac Cuarta, *Catholic Revival in the North of Ireland, 1603–41* (Dublin: Four Courts Press, 2007), 91–92, 125; Colm Lennon, *Sixteenth-Century Ireland: The Incomplete Conquest* (Dublin: Gill & Macmillan, 1994), 122, 314, 321.

century, the religious orders resorted to this practice to prevent ecclesiastical property being acquired by Protestants.[154]

Among the orders 'to be observed as the modell of their Government',[155] the general assembly at Kilkenny declared that such property and income was to remain in the hands of the Catholic laity.[156] This was complicated and contentious. Most complaints related to the Cistercian order. Keen to recover old foundations in Ireland that had come into the hands of laypeople, the Cistercians were at odds with members of the gentry and the Irish bishops.[157] In 1626, curia officials instructed the Cistercians not to pursue the restoration of monasteries in Ireland. Furthermore, though small in number, the Cistercian order claimed jurisdiction over its communities, free from episcopal authority. This was a cause for concern for the bishops. Consequently, Wadding's ally, John Roche, wrote to the Roman office that examined the suitability of candidates for benefices. Roche advised against any further titular appointments to Irish Cistercian monasteries.[158]

Before the war, Patrick Comerford wrote to Wadding contesting local Cistercian claims in Waterford and Lismore but the monks, with the full cooperation of their lay impropriator, repeatedly ignored Comerford's instructions.[159] The Italian Cistercian Rancati also called for full restoration to pre-Suppression level.[160] In 1648, the procurator general of the Irish Cistercians, Robert Nugent, appealed for the recovery of twenty-one

154 Brian Mac Cuarta, ed, 'Select document: Catholic ownership of tithes: a County Wexford widow's dispensation, 1595', *IHS*, 42 (2018), 336–344; McCafferty, *The Reconstruction of the Church of Ireland*, 37–38; Kenneth Nicholls, 'A List of the Monasteries in Connacht 1577', *JGAHS*, 33 (1972–73), 28–43.

155 Gilbert, *Ir. Confed.*, vol. 1, 87, 112.

156 Ibid, vol. 2, 81.

157 Giblin, 'Hugh McCaghwell', 263.

158 Corish, 'An Irish Counter-Reformation Bishop: John Roche, VII', *ITQ*, 26/4 (1959), 114–115.

159 'Information provided by the Catholic bishop of Waterford and Lismore concerning the Cistercians in Ireland', *c.*1630 (UCD-OFM, D.01/2/357–60).

160 Colmcille Ó Conbhuidhe, *Studies in Irish Cistercian History, edited by Finbarr Donovan and with a foreword by Roger Stalley* (Dublin: Four Courts Press, 1998), 189–90.

benefices linked to monastic property in Ireland.[161] Nevertheless, his calls appear to have gone unanswered. Impartiality was required of Wadding, but as the bishops' agent in Rome, he does not appear to have accelerated Cistercian claims for the return of lands.

Cessation of hostilities

Ormond commanded the royalist army in Ireland.[162] Acting on behalf of Charles I, he offered the confederation a year's truce intending to offset the expense of war and take as many Irish soldiers as possible to England.[163] This led to a severe rift within the confederation and, in an attempt to convince Scarampi of their case, Bellings addressed a statement of reasons in favour of ceasefire.[164] Gaelic leaders and the clergy refused their support unless Ireland and its parliament were safe, with freedom of worship throughout the country. Their stance was fully backed by Scarampi. Maintaining he did not bring weapons and gold in return for a single year of unstable peace, he issued a statement against the cessation of hostilities, which was followed by similar objections from Rome.[165] Nevertheless, a chronic lack of funds drove the supreme council to the negotiating table, and on 15 September, they signed an agreement with Ormond.

Despite Scarampi's objections to a truce, the supreme council petitioned Urban VIII to appoint him nuncio to Ireland.[166] Writing from Cashel on 1 October, they notified the pope that Wadding would communicate their reasons for concluding hostilities and sought to reassure Urban VIII that Catholic worship was restored in most parts of Ireland, including many

161 O'Connor, *Irish Jansenists*, 136; Jennings, ed, 'Ecclesiastical Appointments in Ireland', 64.

162 Jane Ohlmeyer, 'Introduction', in idem, ed, *Ireland from Independence to Occupation*, 6.

163 Raymond Gillespie, 'The Irish Economy at War, 1641–52', in Ohlmeyer, ed, *Ireland from Independence to Occupation*, 170–73, 180.

164 Gilbert, *Ir. Confed.*, vol. 2, 319–21.

165 Ibid, vol. 2, 320–27.

166 Ibid, vol. 3, 21–22.

of its towns and cities. On the same day, the supreme council informed Wadding they had ceased all conflict, stating their intentions to observe their promises to God of maintaining the exercise of Catholicism. They enclosed the reasons written by Bellings.[167] These were that the cessation met with the wishes of Charles I, whose interests the confederation had sworn to defend since the start, and that his forces in Ireland needed to go to England to assist in the war there. In Ireland, they maintained, greater attention needed to be paid to Sir Robert Monro and the Scots in Ulster who would not accept that hostilities had concluded. All Catholic rulers could see the confederation took up arms for the free exercise of religion, which the supreme council would make 'appere to be the grounds' of their quarrel.[168] They then returned to a familiar cause for concern, calling for their possession of church property and church livings to remain in their hands. Finally, due to the unrest and constant military manoeuvres, the confederation had not had time 'to settle the government' in a regular manner as they had hoped. Therefore, royalists and confederates saw the 1643 cessation as the best way to achieve unity.[169]

After travelling from Ireland to report on the war and surviving a period of imprisonment in Morocco, Edmund O'Dwyer of Tipperary was commissioned by the supreme council to assist Wadding in his work with the papacy in 1642.[170] While the cessation was in place, the supreme council went to considerable lengths to see Wadding promoted to the cardinalate.[171] On 14 June 1644, they wrote to Urban VIII, Cardinal Francesco Barberini and his brother Antonio in Rome. The following day, the supreme council notified Wadding of their intentions.[172] Edmund O'Dwyer was entrusted to bring a memorial to Urban VIII, but the pope died on 29 July before

167 Ibid, 22; *Comment. Rinucc.*, vol. 1, 429.

168 Ibid.

169 Ibid. *Comment. Rinucc.*, vol. 2, 110.

170 Supreme council to Luke Wadding with credentials for Edmund O'Dwyer, 13 June 1644; Gilbert, *Ir. Confed.*, vol. 3, 182.

171 Ibid, 186–89, 194.

172 Supreme council to Wadding, 15 June 1644; Gilbert, *Ir. Confed.*, vol. 3, 194.

the letters reached him. These papers fell into Wadding's hands who kept them at St Isidore's College and the proposals went no further.[173]

Nuncio Rinuccini and Dionisius Massari

Urban VIII was succeeded by Innocent X on 15 September, whereupon the supreme council repeated their calls for Wadding to be made a cardinal. They alerted Innocent X to 'the extremely perilous state' of Ireland and notified him that Richard Bellings would visit Rome to give an eye-witness account.[174] Meanwhile, in response to calls from the Kilkenny confederates, Wadding prevailed upon Innocent X for an apostolic nuncio to be sent to Ireland. At first, Luigi Omodei, clerk of the papal chamber, was mooted for the post. However, Cardinal Mazarin raised objections on behalf of France because Omodei was a Spanish subject from Milan.[175] More shall be said of Omodei below.

As a result, GianBattista Rinuccini, archbishop of Fermo, was nominated for the position. On learning of the news in Florence, as an Ormondist, Bellings took umbrage but remained diplomatic. At a papal audience, Wadding subsequently presented Bellings to Innocent X as accredited envoy of the confederate parliament in February 1645.[176] Caught unawares by Rinuccini's selection, Francesco Albizzi, assessor to the Holy Office, was happy on learning the news, a sentiment shared with Rancati.

173 Supreme council of the confederation of Kilkenny to Cardinal Antonio Barberini and Cardinal Francesco Barberini, Kilkenny, 14 June 1644 (UCD-OFM, D.12); Gilbert, *Ir. Confed.*, vol. 3, 186–94; Meehan, *The Rise and Fall of the Irish Franciscan Monasteries*, 97–8.

174 Gilbert, ed, *Ir. Confed.*, vol. 4, 71–72: 'hujus Regni extreme periclitantis statum [...] Nunc vero oculatum mittimus testem præfatum Dominum Richardum Bellings, qui et rerum nostrarum statum clarius aperiet, et quid nobis in ejusmodi condicione redactis facto opus sit, fideliter referet'.

175 Meehan, *The Confederation of Kilkenny*, 99; Giuseppe Aiazza, ed, *The Embassy in Ireland of Monsignor G. B. Rinuccini, Archbishop of Fermo, in the years 1645–49*, translated by Annie Hutton (Dublin: Alexander Thom, 1873), ix.

176 Gilbert, *Ir. Confed.*, vol. 4, xxii.

Both regarded the appointment as providential for the reestablishment of Catholicism in Ireland.[177] Following confirmation of the Rinuccini appointment, Wadding's role in the conflict waned thereby drawing attention to the advantages of personal presence for the nuncio.

During that time, a majority of supreme council members accepted political overtures from Ormond, and on 28 March 1646 a peace agreement was signed.[178] In Rome, Invernizi had drawn up an official account of the confederation of Kilkenny for Innocent X. This report resulted in the confirmation of Rinuccini as nuncio. In its pages, James Hagan detected traces of Wadding's hand.[179] However, the instructions for Rinuccini's mission were written by Albizzi, who became the nuncio's principal advocate at the papal court.[180] A decade earlier, when Urban VIII appointed the congregation of Ireland within Propaganda Fide, Francesco Barberini chaired its meetings with Albizzi as secretary. Albizzi was, therefore, well acquainted with the state of affairs in Ireland and sent letters to Owen Roe O'Neill during the war.[181] To avoid unnecessary opposition in Ireland, Rinuccini was advised not to disturb Catholic laymen who held lands secularised by Cardinal Pole.[182]

In April, Rinuccini departed for Ireland, accompanied by his secretary, Dionisio Massari, dean of Fermo, travelling via Lyon and Paris, where he was met by Bellings. They sailed from La Rochelle and landed at Kenmare,

177 Tadhg Ó hAnnracháin, 'Vatican Diplomacy and the Mission of Rinuccini to Ireland', *Archiv. Hib.*, 47 (1993), 78–88.

178 Ó hAnnracháin, *Catholic Reformation in Ireland*, 78.

179 James Hagan, ed, 'Rerum hibernicarum ab initio postremi belli gestarum et praesentis status epitome ad innocentium decimum pontificem Optimum Maximum, auctore Carolo Francesco Invernitio Mediolanensi, Sacrae theologiae et iuris utriusque doctore, archipresbytero sancti Ambrosii maioris Mediolanensis, 1645', *Archiv. Hib.*, 6 (1917), 94–129.

180 Ó hAnnracháin, *Catholic Reformation in Ireland*, 77; See 'Instructions from Innocent X to Rinuccini', in Aiazza, ed, *The Embassy in Ireland of Monsignor G. B. Rinuccini*, xxvii–xlix.

181 Mooney, 'Was Luke Wadding a Patriotic Irishman?', 30.

182 Hynes, *The Mission of Rinuccini*, 18.

Co. Kerry, in October.[183] This ensured the rejection of the first Ormond peace. Consorting with a Protestant, such as Ormond, was unacceptable to Rinuccini. However, at their first meeting, Viscount Mountgarrett, president of the supreme council, extended an indifferent reception to the nuncio. Rinuccini regarded this as tactless and mentioned it to Rome, but Cardinal Pamphili downplayed matters, whereupon Wadding was instructed to warn Mountgarrett about the observances required on such occasions.[184]

Wadding's role as an intermediary at the papal court can be seen in opposing opinions towards secret negotiations conducted by Edward Somerset, earl of Glamorgan, on behalf of the king. These raised the possibility of religious concessions for the Kilkenny confederates.[185] By then, however, the cause of Charles I was bleak and the chances of fulfilling an agreement were slim. While Pamphili told Rinuccini to keep to Glamorgan's proposed treaty, Wadding reported that Innocent X was happy to hear of Rinuccini's insistence on papal peace terms instead.[186]

Rinuccini made the collapse of the Ormond peace a priority. Due to the resulting internal conflict, the confederation of Kilkenny split into two opposing factions.[187] Political and cultural loyalties were nuanced in seventeenth-century Ireland.[188] Nevertheless, one side, led for the most part by the Old English laity, placed political loyalty to the king first. On the other, a predominantly Old Irish faction led by the clergy made Catholic beliefs their priority, with the support of Rinuccini. During this period, Wadding kept a collection of codes for ciphers in English, Italian, Spanish and Latin, some written in his own hand. The recipients included

183 *Comment. Rinucc.*, vol. 1, 473; Before his return to France, Bellings visited Florence, Genoa and Venice to raise support but, apart from sympathetic words, no aid was forthcoming.
184 Hynes, *The Mission of Rinuccini*, 34.
185 Ó hAnnracháin, *Catholic Reformation in Ireland*, 12430, 134.
186 Wadding to Rinuccini, 22 April 1646; cited by Hynes, *The Mission of Rinuccini*, 71.
187 Ó hAnnracháin, *Catholic Reformation in Ireland*, 123–165.
188 Cecile O'Rahilly, ed, *Five Seventeenth-Century Political Poems* (Dublin: Dublin Institute for Advanced Studies, 1977), 110, 114, 129, 145.

Scarampi and Bellings, Massari and Comerford, as well as different ciphers for Wadding himself in a variety of languages.[189]

The arrival of Rinuccini gave momentum to the Catholic campaign.[190] Wadding contributed 26,000 Roman scudi, which he himself collected. A year later, he sent Rinuccini and Massari a further sum for the war in Ireland.[191] These combined resources provided the nuncio with the means to equip three armies: his own in Limerick, another led by Thomas Preston in Leinster, and the third for Ulster under the orders of Owen Roe O'Neill who replenished his ranks in the spring of 1646. Dionisio Massari met O'Neill and noted his requirements for 5,000 infantry and 2,500 cavalry. These were '2,000 muskets, 200 brace of pistols, 2,000 pikeheads and 4,000 swords, together with a sum of 16,000 crowns to provide half-pay for his soldiers, and another thousand to purchase corn'.[192] On learning of these details, Rinuccini acceded to O'Neill's request, which the nuncio regarded as 'very moderate'.[193] The money and arms were provided to O'Neill at Kilkenny, whereupon he set off for Ulster. Owen Roe's forces consisted of seven infantry units and an equivalent number of cavalrymen. Many were veterans and better paid than their fellow countrymen in the army of Leinster. Experience of military life in Flanders meant that discipline and training were watchwords for soldiers under O'Neill's command. By the early summer, they were ready for a major battle.[194]

On 5 June, Owen Roe O'Neill inflicted heavy defeat on superior numbers led by the Scottish general, Robert Munro, at Benburb in Co. Tyrone. Innocent X sent his blessing through Wadding for the most remarkable

189 'Variae cifrae P. Wadingi' 1642–49 (UCD-OFM, D.15).

190 Giuseppe Aiazzi, *Nunziatura in Irlanda di Monsignor Gio. Baptista Rinucccini arcivescovo di Fermo negli anni 1645 à 1649* (Florence: Piatti, 1844), xv.

191 Harold, *Vita Fratris Lucae Waddingi*, 126: 'curavit Lucas tradi viginti sex millia scutorum ex illa collecta, quam ipse pro pia causa faciebat, & post annum redeunti ex Hibernia Dionysio Massario, Decano Firmano & Archiepiscopi in Hiberniæ Nunciatura Auditori, dedit aliam summam in belli Catholici subsidium ad Nuncium deferendam'.

192 Massari, 'My Irish Campaign', *The Catholic Bulletin*, 9 (1919), 505.

193 Ibid.

194 Gerard Hayes-McCoy, *Irish Battles* (Belfast: Appletree Press, 1990), 182.

victory won by an Irish army in Ireland.[195] Nevertheless, this was eclipsed by the collapse of the confederation. O'Neill captured substantial spoils after the battle but was unable to consolidate his gains in the coming months.[196] After Benburb, Wadding's close friend Rancati addressed a letter to O'Neill encouraging him to future victories in the field, sending him a small silver reliquary with a fragment of the True Cross from the Santa Croce monastery in Rome. Moreover, Rancati assured Rinuccini of the Cistercian order's continued prayers for O'Neill.[197]

Rinuccini's strength of conviction continued to grow with a victory that he oversaw himself at the siege of Bunratty, Co. Clare.[198] On 27 August, in reply to a letter he received from the nuncio that day, Wadding wrote:[199]

> The most illustrious Lord Rinuccini in the camp! In a hut made of turf and clay! – Rinuccini turned into a soldier and leader! Who would have ever believed it? Who would ever have thought of it? Anyone who wanted to convince themselves of this two years ago would have had their head examined.

Next Wadding compared the nuncio to Moses in Exodus: 'But he did it for God – the finger of God is here. With such a leader (I believe) and such a holy commander-in-chief, the Lord will give courage and strength to

195 Micheál Ó Siochrú, 'O'Neill, Owen Roe (Ó Néill, Eoghan Rua)', *DIB*, vol. 7, 786–92, <https://www.dib.ie/biography/oneill-owen-roe-o-neill-eoghan-rua-a6936>, accessed 28 August 2022.

196 *Contemp. Hist.*, vol. 1, 679.

197 Ó Conbhuidhe, *Studies in Irish Cistercian History*, 189–90.

198 Ó hAnnracháinn, *Catholic Reformation in Ireland*, 138–39, 281–282. For Massari's recollections of the siege, see 'My Irish Campaign', in *The Catholic Bulletin*, 8 (1918), 140–42.

199 *Comment. Rinucc.*, vol. 2, 253: 'Quando Waddingdus iisdem diebus a nuncio accepisset litteras ex tugurio castrensi, et obsidione Bunratensi datas, replicans præfatæ epistolæ, Italice: Illustrissimus (inquit) Dominus Rinuccinus in castris! In tugurio castrensi ex gleba et cespite! – Rinuccinus in militem et ducem conversus! Quis unquam id credidisset futurum et quando ipse id unquam potuisset cogitare? Quisquis id ipsi ante biennium voluissit persuadere, ipsum habuisset mente captum. Sed Dei causa id egit – digitus Dei est hic. Cum tali duce (credo) et tam sancto Præfecto Generali Dominus dabit virtutem et fortitudinem plebi suæ. Benedictus Deus'.

his people'.[200] In summary, Wadding reported that Innocent X was most contented. Everything being said of Rinuccini was now happy:[201]

> [...] of whom previously only lamentations were heard, as though he did nothing, said nothing, wrote nothing and it was not known whether he was alive or dead. But now, having seen what he writes, what he says and how gloriously he conducts things, the thoughts are different, and the language is another, and we shall quickly obtain supplies.

Rinuccini anticipated that he needed half the amount of matériel that Wadding thought necessary to continue the campaign. In response, Innocent X promised that he would give the nuncio what he required.[202] In November, Massari returned to Rome on behalf of the bishops to encourage new contributions from the papal court.[203] Wadding accompanied him to the Quirinal where Innocent X accorded Massari 'a long audience' of three hours, but the pope gave orders that he was to receive Massari alone.[204] Later, Massari recorded that, to guard against vanity, he then went to the residence of Luigi Omodei and made a vow before a crucifix in the presence of Omodei and Wadding.[205]

In total, 50,000 crowns were obtained from the papacy on this occasion. According to Massari, Wadding received another 10,000 crowns from Cardinals Roma, Sacchetti and other members of the college of cardinals, while Rancati contributed another five hundred. Innocent X believed the funds 'should be made payable' to Massari in Paris with 'the balance to

200 Wadding's reference to 'the finger of God' is from Exodus 8:19.

201 Ibid: 'In summa est contentissimus, et nunc omnia dicuntur fausta de Illustrissimo Domino Rinuccino, de quo antea non audiebantur nisi lamentationes, quasi nihil faceret, nihil diceret, nihil scriberet, nec sciretur vivus esset an mortuus? Nunc autem viso quod scribit, quod dicit quod res gerit gloriose, cogitationes aliae sunt, et lingua altera, et obtinebimus cito suppetias'.

202 Ibid: 'sed minores illis quas ego praetendebam, urgens ut suppeditarentur saltem triginta scutorum millia. Sed mihi allegavit Papa Dominationis Vestrae Illustrissimae litteras quindena tantum scutorum millia. Quibus cum legendas curasset, mihi obstruxit buccam. Seque dicit daturum id quod Dominatio Vestra Illustrissima petiit'.

203 Ó hAnnracháin, *Catholic Reformation in Ireland*, 274.

204 Massari, 'My Irish Campaign', in *The Catholic Bulletin*, 9 (1919), 488.

205 Ibid, 539.

remain there' at Rinuccini's discretion.[206] Wadding also sent the sword of Hugh O'Neill as a gift to be given to Owen Roe O'Neill.[207] The resentment that this caused in Old English circles typified Wadding's predicament of dealing with competition between Irish rivals.

Ormond's agreement censured

That year, the supreme council signed a peace settlement with Ormond and the Protestant royalists. On discovering their agreement, Rinuccini left for Waterford where Thomas Wadding welcomed the nuncio at his Kilbarry estate. At an assembly of Catholic bishops, Rinuccini excommunicated all who supported the truce, until they exculpated themselves at the earliest opportunity. Together, the clergy gathered in Waterford and declared that the Ormond Peace broke the oath of association. Rather than face the consequences, the Catholic confederates complied with the nuncio's wishes and rejected the first Ormond Peace on 2 February 1647. Whereas the Ormond party blamed all dissensions on the nuncio, in the following month Rinuccini attributed every disturbance in Ireland to the Ormondists.[208]

Ormond soon reached a withdrawal agreement with the parliamentarians. A year later, Inchiquin, the parliamentary commander, agreed a truce with the supreme council. Once more, Rinuccini censured all those who adhered to, defended, or approved the peace.[209] On this occasion, however, the supreme council appealed to the Holy See against the nuncio's sanctions. To achieve this aim, Nicholas French, Catholic bishop of Ferns, and the lawyer, Sir Nicholas Plunkett, went as envoys

206 Ibid, 738; see also Hynes, *The Mission of Rinuccini*, 160.

207 Patrick Corish, 'Ormond, Rinuccini and the Confederates, 1645–49', *NHI*, 3, 328.

208 'Relazione del Regno d'Irlanda', Kilkenny, 1 March 1646 (o.s.); cited in Aiazzi, *Nunziatura in Irlanda*, 113.

209 Patrick Corish, 'Rinuccini's Censure of 27 May 1648', *ITQ*, 18 (1951), 322–337.

to Rome where Wadding helped to make the confederates' case at the papal court.[210] This is dealt with in the next chapter.

Among his papers at St Isidore's, Wadding kept a draft letter to Innocent X. Written in his own hand in 1648, it appealed for more effective support.[211] Wadding told the pope he feared Catholicism was about to be extinguished in 'the kingdom and holy island of Ireland' where 'the Catholic confederates' sustained the war against what Wadding termed 'the heretics'.[212] However, the Kilkenny confederates disbanded that year after false starts, an irresolute supreme council, inadequate support from France and Spain, followed by Ormond's machinations and internal divisions between the Irish themselves. Following the nuncio's departure from Ireland in February 1649, Wadding wrote in Italian to commiserate with him:[213]

> As soon as I had heard of the landing (on the continent) of your Most Illustrious Lordship, I congratulated him on his successful return in a letter by Parisien courier, being glad to see that you had left that unfortunate island and escaped the hands of those whose ingratitude has been so great that they could not recognise the favours they had received from God.

Emphasising the gravity of the situation, Wadding told Rinuccini: 'I confess that whenever I hear about that infamous peace and the way of proceeding of that nation, or its subject comes to my mind, I feel embarrassed and wish that I had never been born into that nation.[214]

210 Idem, 'The Crisis in Ireland in 1648: The Nuncio and the Supreme Council: Conclusions', *ITQ*, 22 (1955), 231–57.

211 Wadding to Innocent X, Rome, 1648 (UCD-OFM, D.04/1/69–73, formerly 85–86).

212 Ibid: 'Hibernia regnum, sanctorum insula [...] Catholici confederati Hiberni [...] unde heretici'.

213 Wadding to Rinuccini, Rome, 17 May 1649; *Comment. Rinucc.* vol. 4, 235–36. Wadding addressed the nuncio in the third person, which was customary in Italian and Spanish. The *Commentarius* rendered Wadding's letter into Latin: 'Mox atque de Dominationis vestrae Illustrissimae appulsu (in continentem) audiveram, per litteras cum tabellione Parisiensi scriptas ipsi prosperum regressum congratulatus sum, gavisus quod eam videam exiisse illa infortunata Insula, et evasisse illorum manus, quorum tanta fuerat ingratitudo ut beneficia a Deo accepta haud agnoscere norint'.

214 Ibid, 236: 'Fateor me quoties de illa infami pace et illius nationis procedendi ratione audio, vel ejus rei mihi in mentem venit, erubescere, et cupere quod nunquam in ea gente natus fuissem'.

Conclusion

Wadding was able to judge opinion in Rome, Madrid and Paris in 1642, and reached the understanding that the rulers of Europe would not be seen to openly support proceedings in Ireland. Nonetheless, Wadding could see the potential that the uprising offered for achieving Catholic aims. Entrusted with the gathering of information and support for the Irish cause, he commanded confidence to take a central role in organising the war from his vantage point in Rome. His diligence was rewarded with the appointment of Scarampi and financial support from the Barberini family, both of which were heralded a success.[215] Nonetheless, early hopes that the confederation of Kilkenny would finish the war quickly evaporated. Wadding's cousin, Thomas, promoted the rebellion. Although the confederation sought guarantees for the owners of land, the religious orders proceeded with their attempts to recover property, and Thomas Wadding was among those who feared the uncertainty that these times brought. Luke Wadding understood that promotions to the Irish episcopacy could pose a real and present danger to their families. In 1627, for example, Flaithrí Ó Maolchonaire told Wadding that Viscount Magennis, 'a gentleman of such quality and Christianity, could not escape total ruin', if his nephew Fr. Hugh was raised to the Catholic primacy and further repercussions would follow.[216] Wadding knew that promotion may have led to his departure from Rome, but the scale of his own family's investments may provide the best explanation for his reluctance to accept higher office as a bishop or cardinal.

The timing of Rinuccini's nomination for the nunciature disrupted Richard Bellings' plans and ended calls for Wadding to be made a cardinal. While Bellings may have eschewed more papal interest in resolving the war, this course of events excluded the possibility that Wadding could

215 Harold, *Vita Fratris Lucae Waddingi*, 122.

216 Jennings, ed, *Wadding Papers*, 253: 'veer que si el padre fray Hugo fuesse allá agora primado, en mi opinión no pudiera su tyo, el señor visconde MaGenis, cavallero de tanta calidad y christianidad, escaper total ruyna, y también que si empeçassen a perseguir al padre fray Hugo'.

be promoted and sent back to Ireland. Nevertheless, Wadding did not subscribe to the view that a cardinal's red hat was beneficial to the recipient, his order or country of origin. It is important to note that his extant correspondence to and from the Kilkenny confederates, his Franciscan confrères and Owen Roe O'Neill decreased after Rinuccini's nomination. From then on, Wadding kept up with events in Ireland while maintaining direct contact with Rinuccini who, in turn, provided regular reports to the Roman curia.[217] Wadding's letters indicate that he and the nuncio were well acquainted before Rinuccini's departure for Ireland and that the Irishman held the Italian in high regard.

Peace and warfare were complimentary elements of a balanced world in early modern times. Among his books at St Isidore's College, Wadding kept works by St Bernard of Clairvaux and Francisco Suárez, two authors who disdained an excessive preoccupation with temporal affairs, which they believed led to less concern for the needs of the soul.[218] Wadding's involvement in the politico-religious sphere made him aware of the tensions between these two priorities. In the next chapters, the account of his experiences will continue with the breakdown in communication with Rinuccini and internal strife between Irish Franciscans, leading up to Wadding's final illness and death in 1657.

217 See, for example, Gilbert, *Contemp. Hist.*, vol. 1, 680–83.

218 Wadding obtained copies of Bernard of Clairvaux, *Devotissimi Bernardi liber de consideratione ad Eugenium papam explicit* (Rome: Facciotti, 1594), and Francisco Suárez, *Opera omnia* (Madrid: Typ. Regia, 1599). I am grateful to John McCafferty for this information.

9 Troubled Waters on the Tiber

Introduction

As the 1650s approached, Wadding had known no serious challenge to his authority at St Isidore's but, in his final decade, he encountered a series of troubles and had to defend himself against bitter criticism that had first become apparent twenty years earlier. This chapter describes his initial difficulties, followed by the help he received from his nephew, Francis. Details are given on the abiding appeal of books in Wadding's life, the unsettled state of affairs for his family after Waterford's capture, his role in theological debate and the attention he paid to political matters.

Wadding's decline has rightly attracted the attention of historians. In a series of important contributions, Patrick Corish explained the relevance of Rinuccini's sanctions to the Kilkenny confederates and Wadding's efforts during the ensuing fallout.[1] Canice Mooney subsequently published a meticulous investigation into the case as it unfolded in Rome and Madrid.[2] In more recent years, Clare Carroll, Matteo Binasco, Igor Pérez Tostado and Thomas O'Connor have revisited these events with new analysis that adds to our understanding.[3] Among other matters, Ian

1 Patrick Corish, 'Ormond, Rinuccini and the Confederates, 1645–49', in *NHI*, 3, 317–35; 'The Crisis in Ireland in 1648', *ITQ*, 22 (1955), 231–57; idem, 'Two Contemporary Historians of the Confederation of Kilkenny', *IHS*, 8 (1953), 217–36; idem, 'Rinuccini's Censure of 27 May 1648', *ITQ*, 18 (1951), 322–37; idem, 'Bishop Nicholas French and the Second Ormond Peace, 1648–9', *IHS*, 6 (1948), 83–100.

2 Mooney, 'Was Luke Wadding a Patriotic Irishman?', 15–92.

3 Carroll, 'The *Vita Waddingi* and the Memory of Confederate and Cromwellian Ireland', 186–88, 193–94; Binasco, 'Luke Wadding and Irish Diplomatic Activity in Seventeenth Century Rome', 197–201, <http://dx.doi.org/10.13128/SIJIS

Campbell has concentrated on the role of Richard O'Ferrall, Rinuccini's advocate in Rome.[4] However, the *Relatio veridica et sincera* of 1651 merits further investigation because of its relevance to Wadding.[5] This rare work by Pierre Marchant, the Flemish commissary general with responsibility for Ireland, survives in only a few copies.

Entrenchment

The lack of evidence makes it difficult to account for Wadding's involvement in the complete separation that took place between Rinuccini and the Kilkenny confederates. The situation clearly deteriorated from 24 August 1648 when Cardinal Giulio Roma, a good friend of Wadding, wrote to Rinuccini in Italian 'with much humanity and earnestness'.[6] He told the nuncio that further papal support would not be forthcoming unless he reconciled with those he had excommunicated and suggested that he 'should withdraw or suspend the censures, absolutely or conditionally'.[7] Nevertheless, as nuncio, Rinuccini held that he was under orders from the pope. The compilers of the *Commentarius*, O'Ferrall and O'Connell, emphasised the nuncio's noble birth in Florence and stated that he was

---

-2239-3978-18462>, accessed 28 August 2024; Pérez Tostado, *Irish Influence at the Court of Spain in the Seventeenth Century*, 98–99, 107–108; O'Connor, 'Luke Wadding's Networks at Home and Abroad', 18–20.

4 Campbell, *Renaissance Humanism and Ethnicity Before Race. The Irish and the English in the Seventeenth Century* (Manchester: Manchester University Press, 2015), 83–84, 106–12, 113–23; idem, 'Truth and Calumny in Baroque Rome: Richard O'Ferrall and the *Commentarius Rinuccinianus*, 1648–67', *IHS*, 38 (2012), 211–29. See also Nienke Tjoelker and Ian Campbell, 'Transcription and Translation of London version of Richard O'Ferrall's Report to Propaganda Fide (1658)', *Archiv. Hib.*, 61 (2008), 7–61.

5 Marchant, *Relatio veridica et sincera*; UCD Special Collections (1 OFM 0675).

6 *Comment. Rinucc.*, vol. 3, 687: 'D. Cardinalis mihi scribit multa cum humanitate et animi studio'. See also *Comment. Rinucc.*, vol. 4, 247.

7 Ó hAnnracháin, *Catholic Reformation in Ireland*, 209; Mooney, 'Was Luke Wadding a Patriotic Irishman?', 49.

shaken by the likelihood that Innocent X disapproved of his actions.[8] On receiving Roma's letter, Rinuccini looked upon it with suspicion and doubted that Roma had conceived the idea by himself. As Wadding lacked the authority of a cardinal, Rinuccini believed that he had hatched the plan instead and resorted to Roma for help. Consequently, the nuncio wrote back from Galway the following January, telling Roma that the censures remained in place.[9] In doing so, Rinuccini entrusted his reply to his Theatine confessor, Giuseppe Arcamoni, to ensure the letter did not find its way 'into the hands of Luke Wadding'.[10] Taking these points into consideration, the nuncio's censures were, perhaps, a face-saving exercise.

Arcamoni fulfilled his instructions to the letter and was so suspicious of Wadding that he confided nothing in him and also refused to communicate with the Franciscan's associates in Rome, believing Wadding to be 'the secret patron of the parties opposed to the nuncio'.[11] Nevertheless, in the interests of fairness, the compilers of the *Commentarius* examined Wadding's correspondence to Rinuccini while the nuncio was in Ireland and on the continent, as well as Wadding's Italian letters to Rinuccini's brother in Florence. In these sources, Wadding professed his obedience to the nuncio, especially in 1646 when he approved the rejection of the Ormond peace. Indeed, Wadding went as far to say that 'he always abhorred the Ormondist plans'.[12] This was frequent correspondence delivered to Rinuccini in packets sent from Rome.[13]

8 *Comment. Rinucc.*, vol. 4, 184.

9 Mooney, 'Was Luke Wadding a Patriotic Irishman?', 50–51. Carroll, 'The *Vita Waddingi* and the Memory of Confederate and Cromwellian Ireland', 186. On Wadding's friendship with Roma, see Binasco, 'Luke Wadding and his Entourage', 84–85.

10 *Comment. Rinucc.*, vol. 3, 235.

11 Ibid, vol. 3, 235: 'Verum idem Josephus Waddingum tanquam partibus Nuncio, adversantibus occultissime patrocinantem ita suspectum habuit, ut nec ipsi, nec iis, qui eo familiater uterentur, sua consilia communicaret'.

12 Ibid, vol. 3, 235, 'seque ab Ormonistarum molitionibus semper abhorruisse significaverat'.

13 Ibid.

Lord Lieutenant's Letter

In the meantime, the Second Ormond Peace was concluded between the Kilkenny confederates and Ormond, lord lieutenant of Ireland, on 17 January 1649.[14] The two sides agreed to an alliance and elegies were quickly composed for 'the Great Ormonde'.[15] The supreme council then asked the nuncio to depart from Ireland and go to Rome where the general assembly had prepared an appeal against him.[16]

The Irish Friars Minor represented the largest and most effective source of opposition to both peace treaties brokered by Ormond.[17] Thus, the Ormondists stood to gain from a more compliant Irish Franciscan province. Aware of his own authority, the lord lieutenant wrote to Wadding in a letter that points towards the rival influence that the Observant Franciscans exerted in the country at that time. The only known copy is preserved at the Bodleian Library, Oxford. On 20 May, Ormond proposed that Wadding: 'imploy the power [he had] in the Court of Rome', to only select men reputed for loyalty to the Crown to lead the Friars Minor in Ireland.[18] In doing so, Ormond trusted that he and Wadding 'shared affections to his Majesties service, and the bond of alegiance'.[19] Unnamed sources had given Ormond 'good report' of Wadding's 'desires to have this kingdome settled under his Majesties obedience'.[20] Ahead of the next provincial chapter, the marquis of Ormond entreated Wadding to promote the advancement of 'discreet men such as have good affections for his Majestie' instead of those 'in love with rapine and confusion'.[21] Turning his attention to Rinuccini, Ormond stated that the nuncio had done 'iniury and dishonour to his master [Innocent X], by fomenting devisions in the nation, and endeavoring

14 Ó hAnnracháin, *Catholic Reformation in Ireland*, 211.
15 *Ormonde MSS.*, part 1, 105–106.
16 O'Connor, *Irish Jansenists, 1600–70*, 15.
17 Mooney, 'Was Luke Wadding a Patriotic Irishman?', 36.
18 Ormond to Wadding, Kilkenny, 20 May 1649, Bodl. Ms. Carte, 24, f. 461. For a summary, see *Comment. Rinucc.*, vol. 4, 184.
19 Ibid.
20 Ibid.
21 Ibid.

again to imbroyle this kingdome, miserably wasted by a seaven years warr, in perpetuall distraction'.[22]

To demonstrate the preferred type of candidate, Ormond told of an Irish friar named Raymond Carron of Westmeath, recently arrived in Ireland. Carron studied at the Franciscan friary in Drogheda, before further studies at Salzburg and Leuven. He subsequently taught philosophy and theology at St Anthony's College.[23] Believing Carron to be loyal to the king and a zealous Franciscan, the lord lieutenant asked Wadding to approve aspirants similar to Carron and to give no credence to anyone who defamed him.[24] Ormond's hopes appear to have been misplaced, however. In response to pressure from Charles I's wife, Henrietta Maria, and the Ormondist party, Marchant appointed Carron to conduct an inspection visit of the Irish Franciscan province that year. Carron went on to preside over a provincial chapter at Kilkenny in July 1649 where, at the behest of Ormond, he punished friars opposed to the alliance between Ormond and the confederates. In the aftermath, Wadding used his influence and wrote to Daniel à Dongo, vicar general of the Friars Minor, describing Carron as 'an inexperienced and daring young man'.[25] Consequently, Carron was removed from office and summoned back to the Low Countries leaving behind a failed mission.[26]

A week after Wadding wrote to Dongo, Arcamoni informed the nuncio that the lord lieutenant's letter recommended Carron as Franciscan commissary. On investigation, Arcamoni discovered that Carron was an Ormondist who intended punishing all those who had defended the nuncio.[27] Therefore, Arcamoni went to Wadding and asked him to arrange Carron's recall. In reply, Wadding confirmed that Ormond had written such a letter to him. Indeed, Henrietta Maria, Charles I's wife,

22 Ibid.

23 Terry Clavin, 'Carron (Caron), Raymond (Redmond) (*c.*1605–1666), Franciscan visitor apostolic and theologian', in *DIB*, vol. 2, 38082.

24 Ibid.

25 Wadding to Daniel à Dongo, St Isidore's, 2 October 1649, 'juvenum inexpertum et audecem'.

26 Mooney, 'Was Luke Wadding a Patriotic Irishman?', 37–48, 60; *Comment. Rinucc*, vol. 4, 245–46.

27 *Comment. Rinucc.*, vol. 4, 241.

had also written to Wadding recommending Carron. However, Wadding told Arcamoni that he had already obtained Carron's recall from Ireland and awaited news from Rinuccini before appointing someone according to his wishes. The Irishman reassured Arcamoni that he was very much committed to the nuncio and that he refused to answer the letters from Ormond and the queen.[28]

Notwithstanding Wadding's attempts to defuse the situation, pro-nuncio Franciscans such as Francis Bermingham of Galway already resided in Rome where they represented their own interests.[29] The pro-nuncio party became convinced that Wadding had achieved Ormond's objectives by secret schemes.[30] Consequently, they weighed in against the Irish Franciscan to have him removed from positions of influence in Rome. In spite of Wadding's words of support for Rinuccini in 1646, the pro-nuncio party called into question the Waterford friar's origins because his home city only entered into armed conflict when it became clear that the war was being waged for the English Crown. Due to contrasting opinions among the people of the city, the Ormondists prevailed in Waterford two years later.[31] Wadding's critics claimed that he was no different from his ancestors who were loyal to England since mediaeval times and that he merely seized upon his position in Rome to secretly serve his own interests. They said this was widely known before the outbreak of war and led to many complaints against him, such as his distribution of ecclesiastical benefices in Ireland.[32] The pro-nuncio party also argued that Wadding's *Annales* showed a preference for the Old English of Ireland, rather than the Gaelic population.[33] However, the English Franciscan Christopher Davenport stated that any such favouritism on Wadding's part did not extend across the Irish Sea. In

28 Ibid.

29 Ibid, vol. 4, 235.

30 Ibid, vol. 4, 236.

31 Ibid. See also Ormond to Antrim, Waterford, 28 February 1649; Gilbert, *Ir. Confed.*, vol. 7, 268.

32 Ibid, vol. 4, 236.

33 Ibid.

the 1640s, Davenport often corrected 'not without reprimand' the works of Wadding for looking upon the English province 'with an evil eye'.[34]

Worse was to follow. O'Ferrall and O'Connell recalled that Wadding gave Richard Bellings an entrée at the papal court. Moreover, on his return to Kilkenny at the beginning of 1647, Bellings told the general assembly that Wadding witnessed the pope saying that the Irish, bearing in mind Charles I's difficulties, should be content 'with secret assurances for religion from him'.[35] Bellings used this comment to defend the peace agreement of 1646 on Ormond's terms. Summoned to the papal court, Wadding testified to Dr Walter Enos, rector of the Irish College in Leuven, that Innocent X never expressed such a view in his presence.[36] Enos concluded that this was 'a distorted falsity' on Wadding's part.[37]

Bellings was subsequently unable to provide evidence of his speech to the assembly in Kilkenny after his return from Rome but continued to stand over his statement in later years.[38] The Ormondist faction prevailed on the supreme council and recruited Wadding as their agent in Rome.[39] At the beginning of the same year, Nicholas French, Catholic bishop of Ferns, and Sir Nicholas Plunkett, an Old English lawyer from the Pale, were sent to Rome to appeal for the suspension of the nuncio's censures in Ireland. The supreme council ordered French and Plunkett to confer with Wadding in all matters.[40]

A serious disagreement must have taken place in Rome after that point.[41] In this case, Wadding and the envoys, French and Plunkett, were set against the court of Rome. As Wadding was acting in the appeal against the censures, he and the two envoys are likely to have received an indecisive and adverse response from Innocent X. Patrick Corish deduced that the envoys

34 Dockery, *Christopher Davenport, Friar and Diplomat*, 98.

35 Michael Hynes, *The Mission of Rinuccini*, 133.

36 *Comment. Rinucc.*, vol. 4, 237; Hynes, *The Mission of Rinuccini*, 133; Aiazzi, *The Embassy in Ireland of Monsignor G. B. Rinuccini*, 251–52.

37 *Comment. Rinucc.*, vol. 4, 237: 'perversa falsitas, teste ipso R*everenduus* P*ater* Waddingo'.

38 Hynes, *The Mission of Rinuccini*, 133.

39 *Comment. Rinucc.*, vol. 4, 238.

40 Ibid.

41 Corish, 'Bishop Nicholas French and the second Ormond Peace, 1648–9', 90.

were told to bring their concerns to the nuncio's attention and follow his directives.[42] However, on returning to Ireland, the envoys showed 'that they were not prepared to obey the nuncio to the extent of dividing the confederates'.[43] The denouement for Wadding can be seen in this course of action by French and Plunkett. In a major turning point, Innocent X ordered that Wadding's advice should no longer be sought on matters relating to Ireland. In addition, the pope warned Wadding not to make petitions in the name of Irish causes and he ceased to be admitted to the congregations in which Irish matters were discussed.[44] Wadding's accusers had eventually succeeded in landing a punch by claiming that he favoured the Old English in Ireland and at St Isidore's.[45] Apart from Wadding, they said, 'no one well-affected to the public good of Ireland had crept into the favour of the Roman court for so many years'.[46]

Proposal to divide Irish province

The lord lieutenant's letter of 1649 ignited a long-running dispute involving St Isidore's, Wadding and his religious superiors. Ormond acknowledged that he and Wadding did not profess 'the same religion'.[47] Historians have discovered no extant letters from Wadding himself to Ormond and the Irish friar assured Arcamoni that he did not write back.[48] This is understandable in the context of the times when, to avoid accusations of heresy, members of the Catholic clergy sought permission to correspond with

42 Ibid.
43 Ibid.
44 *Comment. Rinucc.*, vol. 4, 247.
45 Ibid, vol. 3, 157–58.
46 Ibid, vol. 4, 248: 'non alius in publicum Iberniae bonum atque in Ecclesiae fautores citra controversiam bene affectus Waddingus in tantum Aulae Romanae favorem et per tot annos irrepserit'.
47 Ormond to Wadding, Kilkenny, 20 May 1649 (Bodl. Ms. Carte 24, f. 461).
48 *Comment. Rinucc.*, vol. 4, 241.

Protestants. Wadding, for instance, only communicated with James Ussher, Protestant archbishop of Armagh, through an intermediary.[49]

Significantly, however, friars at St Isidore's concluded that Wadding was not against the course of action that Ormond proposed. It is not clear who disclosed the document's contents but there are a number of possibilities. The pro-nuncio Gaelic friar, Paul King, was elected to succeed Wadding as guardian of St Isidore's on 21 November 1649 and held office for three years.[50] King gathered information for Rinuccini and became prominent among Wadding's opponents. That year, King composed a letter stating that the nuncio's censures were accepted by 'every Catholic archbishop and bishop in Ireland, as well as all the Capuchins, all Dominicans apart from one, and universally by the Benedictines, Cistercians, Augustinians, the Society of Jesus, the Carmelites and all of the Franciscans besides a few'.[51] While based at Ara Coeli, King worked with the definitor general Francis Bermingham to force Wadding out of the college. This was a betrayal in Wadding's eyes because, when King was captured by Moorish pirates in earlier years, he was set free after Wadding intervened to help.[52]

On the other hand, Massari, second-in-command and auditor to Rinuccini, subsequently served as secretary of Propaganda Fide from

49 Guido Bentivoglio to Maurice Ultach, Brussels, 29 January 1612 (UCD-OFM, D.22). See also Nicholas Canny, *Imagining Ireland's Pasts. Early Modern Ireland Through the Centuries* (Oxford: Oxford University Press, 2021), 76; Alan Ford, 'The Irish Historical Renaissance and the Shaping of Protestant History', in Alan Ford and John McCafferty, eds, *The Origins of Sectarianism in Early Modern Ireland* (Cambridge: Cambridge University Press, 2005), 151; John Silke, 'The Irish abroad, 1534–1691', *NHI*, vol. 3, 620. In earlier centuries, it was standard practice for members of different religious orders to communicate through intermediaries.

50 King, whose surname in Irish was Ó Cingeadh, belonged to the nuncio's party and that of Owen Roe O'Neill. He was appointed guardian of the Kilkenny friary on 4 February 1648; Mooney, 'Was Luke Wadding a Patriotic Irishman?', 15–92.

51 This was *Epistola nobilis Hiberni ad amicum Belgam*, 4 May 1649, printed a year later by Bellings in his *Vindiciae*; see Gilbert, ed, *Contemp. Hist.*, vol. 2, 211–215: 'Paruere mandato Apostolico præter Archiepiscopos, et Episcopos, Patres Capucini omnes, Dominicani præter unum, et alterum refractarium, Omnes Benedictini et Bernardini, Augustiniani, si duos excipias, uniuersi, Patres Societatis, Carmelitani, et Franciscani omnes præter nonnullos malè feriatos'.

52 Jennings, ed, 'Some Correspondence of Father Luke Wadding OFM', 67.

August 1649 to April 1657, at Albizzi's suggestion.[53] This role enabled Massari to obtain all letters and reports on Irish affairs. O'Ferrall and O'Connell stated that Ormond's letter to Wadding was leaked to a few unnamed individuals at the papal court. It is, therefore, tempting to argue but difficult to prove that Rinuccini supporters learnt of Ormond's letter and deliberately used it against Wadding.

As stated in Chapter 7, doubts about Wadding first emerged at the college during the 1630s when an anonymous letter was sent to Ludovico Ludovisi, Cardinal Protector of Ireland, claiming that Wadding ignored the needs of Connacht and Ulster.[54] This was, however, a perennial complaint amongst the Irish clergy and one that predated Wadding's career in Rome.[55] Since the early fourteenth century, fraught relations between Observant Franciscans from Gaelic and Old English backgrounds demonstrated broader differences between the two communities in Irish society.[56] That said, the population of Ireland was most numerous in the towns and cities of Munster and Leinster, which comprised the south and east, compared to the predominantly rural regions of Gaelic Ireland, which comprised the north and west.

The prominent Ormondist, Sir Richard Bellings, expressed his dissatisfaction at the Observant Franciscans' presence in the pulpit, on the battlefield and in the marketplace. In 1646, he told Francis Magruairk, a Franciscan from Ulster, that the supreme council would replace the Observant Franciscans in Ireland with the Capuchins, 'unless the Friars of the Strict Observance lived in accordance with their name and changed their habit of conversation' to benefit Ormond.[57] Magruairk had studied philosophy at St Isidore's in the late 1630s before returning to Ireland as a

53 Benignus Millett, 'Irish Literature in Latin, 1550–1700', in *NHI*, vol. 3, 571.

54 Jennings, ed, 'To the Cardinal Protector of Ireland concerning Fr. Luke Wadding', undated, 184–87.

55 Hazard, *Faith and Patronage*, 52.

56 Anne Müller, 'Conflicting Loyalties: The Irish Franciscans and the English Crown in the High Middle Ages', *RIA Proc.*, 107C (2007), 87–106.

57 Marchant, *Relatio veridica et sincera status Provinciae Hiberniae* (UCD Special Collections, 1 OFM 0675), 31: 'Inter quos (inquit) erat illustrissimus Richardus Bellinge [...] qui mihi licet indigno, tamen tamquam zelum Religionis habenti, dixit necessarium fore, quòd Concilium Catholicum nostrum introducat Capucinos, nisi

confessor and preacher during the confederate wars. He sided with the pro-nuncio party and met Bellings while tasked with Franciscan duties in Paris.[58]

The dilution of Observant Franciscan influence appeared to be close at hand when Irish friars drew up proposals to divide their province in two, with Munster and Leinster on the one side and Ulster and Connacht on the other.[59] To that end, the provincial chapter at Ross Errily, Co. Galway, delegated Magruairk and another friar, Anthony Hally, to advocate the division and reform of the Irish Franciscan province. In Ghent, they met Marchant. He sent them on to Rome and commended matters to Wadding.[60]

After receiving Magruairk and Hally at St Isidore's, Wadding advised Marchant that it was better to 'prudently execute what [was] prescribed at a more convenient time'.[61] As Franciscan commissary general at the papal court, Wadding recommended considering the alternatives before reaching a decision and explained that everything in Ireland was 'in the midst of a great crisis, so that nothing either political or ecclesiastical can be reformed or established'.[62] Instead, he recommended that it would be 'easy to see how things tend by the summer, or what [was] to be expected of the affairs of the Catholic confederates'.[63]

Strictoris Observantiæ Fratres secundùm nomen suum vivant, & conversationis consuetudinem mutarent'.

58 Mooney, 'Father Francis Magruairk, OFM', *Seanchas Ard Mhacha*, 2 (1957), 229.

59 'Friars who petitioned division', 8 September 1647 (UCD-OFM, D.01/898–899); cited by Cathaldus Giblin, 'A Seventeenth-Century Idea: Two Franciscan Provinces in Ireland', *Franciscan College Annual* (Multyfarnham, 1951), 55–67.

60 Marchant, *Relatio veridica et sincera status Provinciae Hiberniae*, 27: 'Omnes porrò suscepi, omnes benignè audivi, quæ exhibuerunt recollegi, & re maturiùs deliberata Patres Antonium Halleum & Franciscum Marguairck Romam dimisi, & negotium Provinciæ indifferenter R.A.P. Luce [sic] Wadingo commendavi'.

61 Wadding to Marchant, Rome, 21 August 1648; *Relatio veridica et sincera status Provinciae Hiberniae*, 27, UCD Special Collections (1 OFM 0675): 'destinan dumque illuc Commissarum qui prudenter præscribenda exequatur tempore opportuniori'.

62 Ibid: 'Etenim nunc omniasusque deque aguntur, versaturque Regnum in summo discrimine, ita ut nihil sive Politicum sive Ecclesiasticum reformari possit, sive stabiliri'.

63 Ibid: 'Hac estate quonam res tendant, aut quid sperandum sit de rebus Catholicorum Confederatorum facilè conspicietur'.

Pierre Marchant wrote that he did not intend to move anything forward unless the friars' difficulties were further aggravated.[64] Instead, he turned to Wadding for advice again as 'a father of the order and chronicler, whose authority and prudence seemed of no average importance'.[65] Replying to Marchant a month later, Wadding reiterated: 'the remedy of the evils had been postponed to a more convenient time'.[66] He himself had witnessed Innocent X express his grief at the 'most miserable state' of Ireland more than once, in the congregation before the cardinals.[67] Nevertheless, the pope 'did not want anything to be innovated or tried about the present' because he vehemently feared for the survival of the kingdom of Ireland and for Catholicism.[68]

A year later, the supreme council intervened and, 'using threats, asked for an official visitator to be appointed to inspect all the Franciscan houses of Ireland', while sending letters from the general assembly to Wadding directly appealing for his help.[69] Wadding replied on 10 April 1649 acknowledging that there was 'a present and great necessity of sending a particular commissioner to Ireland, and that the matter [had] become such that there are greater evils to be feared, and therefore to be early prepared'.[70] Wadding

64 Marchant, *Relatio veridica et sincera status Provinciae Hiberniae*, 27: 'Nec quicquam deinceps movere intendebam, nisi difficultates recruduissent'.

65 Ibid, 36: 'de remediis cum R.A.P. Luca Wadingo, Ordinis Patre, & Chronologo, (cujus auctoritas, & prudentia non mediocris momenti videbatur) consulere, ut Patriæ suæ Hiberniæ compateretur'.

66 Wadding to Marchant, Rome, 19 September 1648: *Relatio veridica et sincera status Provinciae Hiberniae*, 37, UCD Special Collections (1 OFM 0675): 'sed malorum remedium in aliud tempus magis oportunum fuisse dilatum'.

67 Ibid: 'Ita ad hæc adeò dolet Summus Pontifex, vt id etiam lacrymarum profluvio non semel in Congregationibus pro hac recoactis quibus soleo interesse, coram Cardinalibus expresserit'.

68 Ibid: 'timetque vehementer, nè Regnum & Religio Catholica pessumdetur, & propterea nihil vult illic innovari aut tentari de præsenti'.

69 Ibid, 38: 'Comitia Catholica Regni se negotiis immiscerent, & minis adhibitis [...] Commissario in Hiberniam mittendo agebant, cùm & Litteræ Comitiorum Generalium ad ipsum R. P. Lucam Wadingum directe ipsus auxilium'.

70 Ibid: 'video præsentem summamque necessitatem transmittendi Commissarium particularem in Hiberniam, eoque res devenisse, vt majora timenda sint mala, ac propterea maturè præcavenda'.

believed that a friar at St Isidore's, 'prudent, quiet, not presumptuous or impatient and agreeable to all', was best suited as visitator. The name of Wadding's nominee is suppressed in Marchant's source.[71] Wadding was prepared 'as soon as possible to see to all the expeditions [...] so that he may soon depart'.[72] However, Marchant had already appointed Raymond Carron at the suggestion of Thomas Fleming, Franciscan archbishop of Dublin.[73]

Significantly, the authors of the *Commentarius* made claims that Wadding favoured the division of the Irish Franciscan province.[74] Relying on conjecture, they claimed that Wadding changed his mind about supporting Ormond after the lord lieutenant's defeat to English parliamentarians in Dublin on 2 August 1649 and, with that, 'the hope of Ormond and the Ormondists had vanished'.[75] Hence, they thought, Wadding could justify his decision because Ormond was undermined by defeat. This allegedly raised expectations that the chastened Ormond would unite forces with Owen Roe O'Neill to overturn the parliamentary army.[76] Since O'Ferrall and O'Connell lacked conclusive evidence, they pointed indirectly towards Wadding's letter to Dongo in October to account for the change of attitude. Tellingly, the *Commentarius* authors admitted their narrative was sometimes based upon speculation, which could prove deceptive.[77]

71 Ibid: 'Discussâ re cum aliis & Patribus Discretis hujus Collegii in eam itum est sententiam, vt mittatur [N.] Vir prudens, quietus, ne quicquam præceps aut impatiens, nulli parti aut Provinciæ plus æquo addictus, omnibus gratus'. UCD Special Collections (1 OFM 0675).

72 Ibid: 'Ego quamprimùm curabo expeditiones omnes [...] præsentiam abeat ab ea recepturus pleniorem rerum'.

73 Jennings, ed, 'Sint-Truiden: Irish Franciscan Documents', 152.

74 *Comment. Rinucc.*, vol. 4, 240.

75 Ibid, vol. 4, 244: 'Deus permisit ut Ormonii atque Ormonistarum exercitus a Parliamentariis in obsidione Dubliniensi 2 Augusti 1649 [...] adeo ut nemo tunc non viderit Ormonii et Ormonistarum spem evanuisse'.

76 Ibid.

77 Ibid, 249.

Siege and capture of Waterford

Wadding showed the discernment to avoid hasty decisions in a time of crisis. He fully understood the existing conditions in Ireland, especially among the people he himself knew.[78] After landing at Ringsend in Dublin in August 1649, Oliver Cromwell overran the ports and garrisons of Leinster and Munster inflicting military defeat on the Catholic confederates.[79] Richard Synott, who had entered the Friars Minor in Portugal with Wadding and served as guardian of St Isidore's, was killed in 1649 when Cromwell seized Wexford. Six other Franciscan friars were killed in Wexford that year.[80]

On reaching Waterford, Cromwell based himself at Kilbarry, the Wadding seat to the south of the city, where a good house was occupied by Major Edward Aston, an English Protestant. Aston was a tenant of Luke's cousin, Thomas Wadding.[81] Cromwell came upon Waterford on 24 November 1649 and laid siege to the city for eight days but had to withdraw on 2 December to find winter quarters for his troops.[82] Among his books at St Isidore's College, Wadding kept a copy of the *Fasciculus*

78 Jennings, ed, 'Sint-Truiden: Irish Franciscan Documents', 152.

79 Ohlmeyer, *Civil War and Restoration in the Three Stuart Kingdoms*, 204–5.

80 John Morrill, 'Civil Wars and Interregnum', in Kelly and McCafferty, eds, *The Oxford History of British and Irish Catholicism*, vol. 2, 13–14, 29; Cleary, *Father Luke Wadding and St Isidore's College*, 152–53. The minister provincial, Francis O'Sullivan, was decapitated in 1653.

81 Oliver Cromwell to the Mayor and Aldermen of Waterford, Kilbarry, 21 November 1649 (Oliver Cromwell, *Letters and Speeches*, ed Thomas Carlyle, 2 vols (New York: Harper, 1855), vol. 2, 566). For the new edition, see Andrew Barclay, David Smith, Elaine Murphy, Jason Peacey, Joel Halcomb, John Morrill, Micheál Ó Siochrú, Patrick Little and Tim Wales, eds, *Letters, Writings and Speeches of Oliver Cromwell*, 3 vols (Oxford: Oxford University Press, 2022–23), vol. 2: 1 February 1649 to 12 December 1653. See also J. G. Simms, *War and Politics in Ireland, 1649–1730* (London: Bloomsbury, 1986), 16.

82 Patrick Egan, *History, Guide and Directory of County and City of Waterford* (Kilkenny: P. M. Egan, 1895), 73–82; R. H. Ryland, *The History, Topography and Antiquities of Waterford* (London: John Murray, 1824), 74–75; Charles Smith, *The Ancient and Present State of the County and City of Waterford* (Dublin: A. Reilly, 1746), 86–88.

sanctorum ordinis Cisterciensis by Crisóstomo Henríquez.[83] In its pages appeared the name of Nicholas Fagan of Waterford, regarded as venerable in the Cistercian order.[84] Fagan had a strong devotion to the Blessed Virgin and brought a reproduction of her image to Waterford from the Colegio de Nuestra Señora del Destierro in Salamanca.[85] During the siege of the city in 1649, a Spanish statue of Our Lady of the same kind was placed in the city walls. The people of Waterford believed that Cromwell's soldiers were unable to enter the city as a result.[86]

Waterford was besieged again at the beginning of June 1650 before reaching honourable terms with Henry Ireton two months later. Following the capture of Waterford, Luke's cousins, Thomas Wadding and the local bishop, Patrick Comerford, fled to Nantes in France. They were among the many Irish confederates who found themselves exiled during that decade.[87]

83 Crisóstomo Henríquez, *Fasciculus sanctorum ordinis Cisterciensis* (Cologne: Officina Choliniana, 1631), 321–24.

84 Fagan received the Cistercian habit and was professed at the monastery of Santa María de Herrera in the province of Burgos before studying at the University of Salamanca where he applied himself to dogmatic theology. Appointed abbot of St Mary's Abbey at Inishlounaght on the River Suir in Co. Tipperary, he became Cistercian commissary general throughout Ireland. Fagan was elected bishop of Waterford but died on 8 May 1617, the feast of Corpus Christi, before taking office and was buried on the epistle side of the altar in the church of St John the Evangelist. See Colmcille Ó Conbhuidhe, *The Cistercian Abbeys of Tipperary* (Dublin: Four Courts Press, 1999), 145; Malachy Hartry, *Triumphalia chronologica Monasterii Sanctae Crucis in Hibernia*, ed Denis Murphy (Dublin: Fallon, 1891), 128–29.

85 Bernardo Álvarez, *Lustro primero del pulpito consagrado a las gloriosas fatigas de Maria Santissima, desterrada y vencedora* (Salamanca: Gregorio Ortiz Gallardo, 1692), VI; Ángel Manrique, *Cisterciensium seu verius ecclesiasticorum annalium a condito Cistercio Philippo Magno hispaniarum regi. Auctore fratre Angelo Manrique, Burgensi, eiusdem regis à sacris concionibus [...] & in Salmanticensi Academia, scientiarum omnnium principe, sacrae theologiae primario antecessore*, 4 vols (Lyon: Boissat, & Anisson, 1659), vol. 4, 79/691.

86 Catriona McLeod, 'Mediaeval Figure Sculpture in Ireland Statues in the Holy Ghost Hospital, Waterford', *JRSAI*, 76 (1946), 89–100.

87 John Cunningham, 'Lay Catholicism and Religious Policy in Cromwellian Ireland', *JEH*, 64 (2013), 769–86.

Comerford died two years later.[88] The entire estate of Thomas Wadding was confiscated in 1652 before being assigned to John Cooke, one of the Justices of Munster, in the Adventurers Act a year later.[89] Thereafter, all church lands and tithes, including Kilbarry, Co. Waterford, were reserved for the government.[90]

In 1656, Pierfrancesco Scarampi, the former papal envoy to Ireland, consoled Thomas Wadding with the knowledge that his sufferings would count towards his salvation. Unexpectedly, a merchant in Nantes brought a gift of ten Spanish gold coins to Thomas, which he regarded as alms from Scarampi.[91] Thomas Wadding compared the Irish plight to the Trojans at the fall of Troy in Virgil's epic, *Aeneid*: 'We have been, but are no more'.[92] Cromwell had overturned everything. 'Now', Thomas Wadding continued, 'most truly I believe, that he is the second Attila'.[93] All Rome was disturbed by news of the Cromwellian invasion in Ireland. Consequently, the papacy exerted pressure on the continental powers to avoid conciliatory policies towards England.[94]

88 Egan, *History, Guide and Directory of County and City of Waterford*, 100. On 3 July 1651, Comerford wrote to Wadding with news of the siege and capture of Waterford.

89 Robert Simington, ed, *Civil Survey A.D. 1654–56, County of Waterford*, vol. 6, with appendices (Dublin: Irish Manuscripts, 1942), 21, 141, 152, 185, 192, 195, 199, 212, 216, 225–27, 230–3, 255, 259, 261, 263–65, 270, 287.

90 Cleary, *Father Luke Wadding and St Isidore's College*, 66; J. P. Prendergast, *The Cromwellian Settlement of Ireland* (London: Longman, 1865), 23; *Calendar of the State Papers Relating to Ireland Preserved in the Public Record Office, 1625–70*, xxiv.

91 Thomas Wadding to Pierfrancesco Scarampi, Nantes, 21 October 1656 (Aringhi, *Memorie istoriche della vita del venerabile servo di Dio Pier Francesco Scarampi*, 42–43), 'Recepi etiam ex dono Paternitatis vestrae a quodam mercatore hic residente decem pistolas Hispanicas: et mirabar, quod nulla mentio fuerit facta de iis in vestris litteris [...] Sed causam eius omissionis credo esse, ut Paternitas vestra observaret regulam, quam Salvator noster docet et praescripsit datoribus eleemosynarum'.

92 Thomas Wadding to Scarampi, 21 October 1656, 'Fuimus Troes, fuit Ilium, et ingens gloria Dardanidum'. That is, they were Trojans and once held the authority to govern themselves but are no more. *Aeneid*, ii, 325.

93 Ibid, 'Sed nunc ferus omnia Cromwell transtulit [...] Et verissime credo, quod sit secundus Attilas'. See also Sarah Covington, *The Devil from Over the Sea. Remembering and Forgetting Oliver Cromwell in Ireland* (Oxford: Oxford University Press, 2022), 52.

94 Manuel Herrero Sánchez, 'La perduración de la cuestión irlandesa. Un obstáculo en las relaciones anglo-españolas durante la segunda mitad del siglo XVII', in Óscar

Scriptores ordinis minorum

Aware of such events, Wadding took solace from bringing research to print in his final years and, in 1650, published in folio his Franciscan bibliography, *Scriptores ordinis minorum*. He secured the patronage of Cardinal Marcantonio Franciotti for the book, calling upon his help for further publication.[95] Thaddeus Daly, retired theology professor, and Bonaventure Barron, Wadding's nephew, provided the approbations. The book appeared from the presses of Francesco Alberto Tani in Rome, which represented a significant change for Wadding. Many of his publications were otherwise completed outside of Italy, for the most part in France and in the Habsburg Netherlands where the standards of production were consistently high. During the 1650s, however, delays in the distribution of books made the proximity of Italian printers more inviting and, until his death, Wadding's subsequent writings were printed in the Peninsula.

His *Scriptores ordinis minorum* quickly became an essential reference for Franciscan history and theology whilst also providing funds for St Isidore's College in the coming years.[96] As historian of the Seraphic Family, Wadding recorded the details of writers from the three branches of the Franciscan order: Observants, Conventuals and Capuchins, complete with indexes by surname, country, subject matter and topography. The book amounts to more than a bibliography. Early modern sources relating

---

Recio Morales, Bernardo García García, Miguel Ángel de Bunes Ibarra, Enrique García Hernán, eds, *Irlanda y la Monarquía Hispánica. Kinsale 1601–2001: Guerra, Política, Exilio y Religion* (Madrid: CSIC, 2002), 410.

95 *Scriptores ordinis minorum* (Rome: Francesco Alberto Tani, 1650), Dedicatory epistle, unpaginated. The printer, Francesco Alberto Tani, otherwise related to Jesuit writings, early Christian martyrdom, guidebooks on Rome, drama studies, Roman ecclesiastical history, tragicomedy and poetry.

96 Certificate in return for copies of *Epitome annalium ordinis minorum* and *Scriptores ordinis minorum*, provided by the guardian of the Bazati Friary in the Franciscan province of Aquitaine, 20 December 1662 (UCD-OFM, D.17/02/06); A series of twelve receipts, relating to deliveries of the *Annales Minorum* and *Scriptores ordinis minorum*, January, April, July, August and September 1663 (UCD-OFM, D.17/01/subfolder 2).

to martyrdom are complex.[97] Enriched with hagiography, one section of the *Scriptores* contains a martyrology that exclusively lists the Franciscan custom. Furthermore, when recording the works of friends and acquaintances, Wadding provided a pen portrait of their lives.

Ever since 1650, the *Scriptores* remains in constant circulation and, together with Wadding's *Annales*, is a valued authority on the earliest times in Franciscan history. Indeed, these two works represent 'the first scholarly history of the religious orders'.[98] Although concise and minimal, the information they contain is more reliable than other sources which are often incorrect and misleading.[99] The organisation of Wadding's *Scriptores* gives the impression that he gleaned the contents from many contributions, in a similar way to the *Annales*, which depended upon each Franciscan province sending historical material to St Isidore's.[100]

Wadding was not overly scrupulous in completing the *Scriptores*. In keeping with his times, every cited work was not directly to hand, and this could lead to misquoted sources. For example, Wadding expressly recommends not confusing one source with another but seems to have referred to one of William of Ockham's philosophical works, *Summa Logicae*, under separate titles.[101] Similarly, he appears to have given a different title to a

97 Alan Ford, 'Martyrdom, History and Memory in Early Modern Ireland', in Ian McBride, ed, *History and Memory in Modern Ireland* (Cambridge: Cambridge University Press, 2001), 43–66.

98 Wolfgang Müller, Quintín Aldea, Johannes Beckmann, Louis Cognet, Patrick Corish, Oskar Köhler, Heribert Raab, Burkhart Schneider and Bernhard Stasiewski, in, *History of the Church*, vol. 6, *The Church in The Age of Absolutism and Enlightenment*, translated by Gunther Holst, ed Hubert Jedin and John Dolan (London: Burns and Oates, 1981), 532.

99 Millett, 'Wadding, Luke (1588–1657), Franciscan Priest, Scholar and Churchman', in *DIB*, vol. 9, 680–85; Marcellus Pasiecznik, 'John de Bassolis OFM', *Franciscan Studies*, 13 (1953), 61.

100 Encyclical letter of Benigno da Genova, Rome, 20 April 1619 (ACSI, W16/13).

101 *Scriptores ordinis minorum*, 106–107; Philotheus Boehner, 'Three sums of logic attributed to William of Ockham', *Franciscan Studies*, 11 (1951), 173–193; Jean-Barthélemy Hauréau, 'Occam ou Ockam (Guillaume d')', in *Nouvelle biographie universelle depuis les temps les plus reculés jusqu'a nos jours* (Paris: Firmin-Didot Frères, 1862), vol. 38, Nicolle-Ozerof, col. 423–24; Honoré Jean Pierre Fisquet, 'Oderic de Pordenone', in *Nouvelle biographie universelle*, vol. 38, Nicolle-Ozerof, col. 471.

treatise by Oderic of Pordenone, *Historiam suae peregrinationis sexdecim annorum*, to that recorded by the Bollandists, *Odorici Peregrinatio, ab ipsomet descripta*.[102]

Francis Harold

In 1651, Wadding suffered a debilitating fever. Although feeble, he continued to attend meetings of the Roman curia.[103] On Wadding's birthday that year, Pedro Manero, the recently elected minister general, wrote to him in recognition of his many years of service, which Manero described as 'fortunate [and] admirable'.[104] Wadding 'rendered unceasing obedience to [their] most learned order' but had had a prolonged illness since the previous year, Manero commented, before adding that the Irish friar 'always fulfilled his duties in an exemplary manner, such as [their] *Annales* with great effort and great judgment'.[105] This assured Wadding of 'security and veneration' from his religious order.[106]

In addition, he had diligently compiled many other volumes and served on congregations at the Roman curia. For the good of Wadding's health and his 'venerable grey hair', therefore, Manero instructed him to refrain from taking part in daily activities with the rest of the community at St

102 *Scriptores ordinis minorum*, 181; *Acta Sanctorvm quotquot toto orbe coluntur, vel a Catholicis Scriptoribus celebrantur, Quæ ex Latinis & Græcis, aliarumque gentium antiquis monumentis collegit, digessit* [...] (Antwerp: Jan van Meurs, 1643), Januarii Tomus I, 983–92; Honoré Jean Pierre Fisquet, 'Oderic de Pordenone', in *Nouvelle biographie universelle*, vol. 38, Nicolle-Ozerof, col. 471.

103 Mooney, 'Father Luke Wadding – The Last Years', 90.

104 Manero to Wadding, Rome, 18 October 1651; Jennings, ed, 'Some Correspondence of Father Luke Wadding OFM', 67: 'Cum igitur Paternitas Vestra, per longam annorum seriem, fausta, plausabilia atque doctissima Ordini nostro incessanter praestiterit obsequia'.

105 Manero to Wadding, Rome, 18 October 1651: 'cumque etiam nostrae Religionis Annales summo labore summoque iudicio ac studio quampluribus voluminibus exaraverit'.

106 Ibid: 'in magnam semper securitatem ac venerationem devexerit'.

Isidore's.[107] Instead, the minister general recommended more convenient works for Wadding, calling upon the friars at the college to show him deep respect and render all the service he deserved. This appears to have been a reference to established practice in Catholic mendicant orders where, as a mark of continual charity, elderly friars and those with infirmities were assigned the help of a *socius* to assist them. When Bonaventure Barron's sight failed, for instance, he was granted the help of a scribe.[108]

Wadding chose his nephew, Francis Harold, to help him.[109] They were related through one of Luke's sisters who married a Limerick merchant surnamed Harold.[110] Francis had studied at St Isidore's before ordination and went on to teach philosophy and theology in Prague, Vienna and Graz.[111] Since Wadding feared a negative response at first, Manero wrote to Harold in Graz and called him back to Rome where the procurator general was to inform him of his new role.[112] In obedience to the minister general, Harold fulfilled Wadding's wishes returning to Rome in 1651 where he lectured in theology at St Isidore's. On his uncle's recommendation, he was appointed librarian of the college three years later and succeeded Wadding as annalist of the order on 12 April 1655. Harold provided Wadding with vital support in his final years and assisted him in bringing the *Annales Minorum* to successful completion.[113]

Trusted counsel

Wadding's position in Rome was admittedly weaker by 1651 but by no means hopeless since he retained the support of Observant Franciscan confrères

107 Ibid: 'tuaeque venerandae canitiei'.

108 Millett, 'Irish Literature in Latin, 1550–1700', *NHI*, vol. 3, 583.

109 Harold, *Vita Fratris Lucae Waddingi*, 49.

110 Cleary, *Father Luke Wadding and St Isidore's College*, 3.

111 Colmán Ó Clabaigh, 'Harold, Francis (*c.*1617–85), Franciscan Priest and Historian', *DIB*, vol. 4, 469–70, <https://www.dib.ie/biography/harold-francis-a3812>, accessed 28 August 2024.

112 Harold, *Vita Fratris Lucae Waddingi*, 49.

113 Cleary, *Father Luke Wadding and St Isidore's College*, 108–109.

and the respect of contemporaries from Ireland. When Ormond sent the Viscount Taaffe to Brussels with Sir Nicholas Plunkett and Geoffrey Browne, Taaffe sought Wadding's advice.[114] Although not directly involved, Wadding kept up with their talks with Charles IV, duke of Lorraine, for assistance against the English parliamentary army in Ireland. Taaffe informed Antonio Bichi, apostolic nuncio to Brussels, that the duke had donated 60,000 florins for the purchase of arms and had sent frigates to Ireland. He had also sent an abbot to the country, who was to send back news on the conditions there.[115]

The exchange between Taaffe and Bichi provides evidence of Wadding's political contacts at that point. Bichi learnt that Taaffe was against Rinuccini who recommended Colonel Patrick O'Donnell to Bichi. O'Donnell was opposed to Taaffe but supported his negotiations with the duke of Lorraine. Since the Catholic Irish were unified and as Ormond was in France with the earl of Inchiquin, there was a possibility that the army of an English parliament could soon be forced out of Ireland. Bichi believed that Innocent X should be notified, particularly because Taaffe told Bichi that he was writing to Wadding on the subject.[116]

During this time, Manero entrusted certain business of the order in Portugal to Wadding who, for a short period in the 1650s, also administered to the province of St John the Evangelist, Azores.[117] Wadding brought an understanding of both subjects to this work from the knowledge he had hitherto gathered on the friars and Poor Clares,[118] and from the decade

114 Giblin, ed, 'Catalogue of Material of Irish Interest in the Collection "Nunziatura di Fiandra", Vatican Archives: Part 1, vols. 1–50', 78; *Comment. Rinucc.*, vol. 4, 409–10, 460, 480.

115 Ibid.

116 Giblin, ed, 'Catalogue of Material of Irish Interest in the Collection "Nunziatura di Fiandra", Vatican Archives: Part 1, vols. 1–50', 78.

117 Documents relating to Fr. Pedro Manero, minister general (UCD-OFM, D.08/135–164); Draft letter by Wadding concerning difficulties in the province of St John the Evangelist, Azores, *c.*1654 (UCD-OFM/D.08/173); Millett, 'Guide to Material for a Biography of Father Luke Wadding', 251, 257–8.

118 George Boehrer, 'The Franciscans and Portuguese Colonization in Africa and the Atlantic Islands, 1415–99', *The Americas*, 11 (January 1955), 393, 395, 402. On the context, see Jean Frédéric Schaub, 'Maritime Archipelago, Political Archipelago: The

he spent in Portugal.[119] In Ponta Delgada, the capital of the Azores archipelago, the Franciscans acquired copies of Wadding's books from the 1620s onwards.[120]

Finally on this point, Wadding also mediated between Observant and Reformed Franciscans in northern Italy. Their dispute concerned the friary of Sant'Antonio in the town of Casale, diocese of Casale Monferrato, in 1652–53. Wadding's Observant Franciscan confrère and fellow historian, Cardinal Francesco Gonzaga, belonged to the local ruling family and served as archbishop of Mantua from 1593 to 1620.[121] Consequently, Wadding maintained an interest in the duchy and sent Irish friars to teach there.[122] The Observants called upon his help through one of their former provincials, Padre Angelo. Carlo II, duke of Mantua, defended the petition, and on their behalf, Wadding acquired the friary for the Irish province thereby preserving it for the Observants. Although Propaganda Fide responded favourably, Wadding did not pursue matters any further, perhaps because the Observants of Casale had resolved their problems. Benignus Millett asserted that this could have become another Irish seat of learning for Wadding to oversee.[123]

Azores under the Habsburgs (1581–1640)', in Pedro Cardim, Tamar Herzog, José Javier Ruiz Ibáñez, Gaetano Sabatini, eds, *Polycentric Monarchies: How Did Early Modern Spain and Portugal Achieve and maintain a global hegemony?* (Eastbourne: Sussex Academic Press, 2012), 11–26.

119 See Chapter 2 of the present work.

120 Hazard, 'Illustration and Ornamentation in the Works of Luke Wadding, Seventeenth-Century Historian and Theologian', 368. See also Vítor Rui Gomes Teixeira, 'Os Frades Menores em Portugal desde 1217', *Archivo Ibero-Americano*, 77 (2017), 161–220.

121 Carroll, *Exiles in a Global City*, 54.

122 On the Basilica di Santa Barbara of the House of Gonzaga in Mantua (UCD-OFM, D.26, 'Unnumbered papers', Folder 1); Brendan Jennings, ed, 'Some Correspondence of Father Luke Wadding OFM', *Coll. Hib.*, 2 (1959), 73; Idem, ed, 'Theses Defended at St Isidore's College, Rome, 1631–49', 98; idem, ed, 'Miscellaneous Documents II, 1625–40', 8, 11. Post from Rome to Milan travelled along the road to Mantua.

123 'Information on dispute between the Osservanti and Riformati in the town of Casale' (UCD-OFM, D.09/103–106; Millett, 'Guide to Material for a Biography of Father Luke Wadding', 245.

Jansen's *Augustinus*

Education provided the means to reach an in-depth, critical understanding of doctrine. In this context, theological debate contributed to the development of political systems that contended with religious discord.[124] Wadding and Rancati played an integral part in the political culture of Rome during the discussion that took place over the *Augustinus* of Cornelius Jansen, which was first published in Leuven in 1640.[125] The Paris edition appeared a year later, followed by an edition printed in Rouen in 1643. This work concerned the live contemporary issues of grace and free will.[126] Jansen opposed Richelieu's antagonism towards the Habsburgs and owed his promotion to the episcopacy to Philip IV of Spain.[127]

The profound theological influence of Augustine is best understood in the context of the Scotist school, the most significant in scholastic thought from the fourteenth to the seventeenth century.[128] St Augustine's teachings on Plato and Aristotle became foundational for many Scotist positions on theology and philosophy.[129] As Wadding brought to print the first edition of the *Opera omnia* of Duns Scotus, his reputation as a theologian was assured. Two years later, Jansen's *Augustinus* was published posthumously, defending his views on grace and free will. The book quickly became

124 O'Connor, *Irish Jansenists*, 21.

125 Cornelius Jansen, *Augustinus, seu Doctrina S. Augustini de humana nature sanitate, agritudine, medicina, aduersus Pelagianos et Massilienses*, 3 vols (Leuven: Iaocobi Zegeri, 1640).

126 Giulia Spoltore, 'Carlo Maratti, Giovan Pietro Bellori, Luke Wadding e Ilarione Rancati: dibattito teologico e strategie politiche a Roma negli anni di discussion dell'Augustinus di Giansenio', in Carta, Omenetto and Spoltore, eds, *Itinera, Uomini, oggetti e idee in movimento*, 131–62.

127 Mathieu G. Spiertz, 'Anti-jansenisme en jansenisme in de Nederlanden in de achttiende en negentiende eeuw', *Trajecta*, 1 (1992), 233–51; cited by Downey, 'Archbishop Florence Conry of Tuam', 97.

128 Ulrich Leinsle, *Introduction to Scholastic Theology* (Washington DC: Catholic University of America Press, 2010), 291–92.

129 Dominic Keech, *The Anti-Pelagian Christology of Augustine of Hippo, 396–430* (Oxford: Oxford University Press, 2012), 2, 96.

popular in northern Europe and especially in France.[130] Among the clergy, the Society of Jesus emerged as implacable opponents of the Jansenists in the Habsburg Netherlands and in Rome.[131]

Since their studies at Salamanca, Wadding and Rancati were up to date with the complexities of the *De auxiliis* debate on divine grace. In turn, Irish Franciscans on the continent maintained a scholarly interest in grace and free will. Their rigorous interpretation was opposed to the allegedly lax doctrine of grace propagated by members of the Jesuit order. For example, amidst his dispatches on the war in Ireland, Hugh Bourke defended Jansen's *Augustinus* as a 'faithful reproduction' of Augustine's doctrine and asked Wadding to further its cause in Rome.[132] Bourke reported that the *Augustinus* enjoyed widespread support among the bishops and clergy of France and Flanders, with few exceptions.

From the outset, however, matters did not go smoothly. When John Sinnich of Cork, a delegate of the University of Leuven, went to Rome in 1643, Rancati was confined to bed with gout and could not receive Sinnich. The French theologian and philosopher, Antoine Arnauld, led the Jansenists by 1645. That year, Jean Bourgeois, a Sorbonne doctor, arrived in Rome on a mission to defend Arnauld's book, *De la fréquente communion*, against censure. Bourgeois went on behalf of the French bishops who had approved the text.[133] He stated that Wadding showed him kindness and 'always defended every cause in which [he] had an interest with so much zeal and through the unique love he had for the truth, that my memory will always hold him in singular veneration'. Nonetheless, Bourgeois mistook

130 Angela Berlis and Dick Schoon, 'Jansenism Across the Border: The interaction in the seventeenth and eighteenth century between Catholic theologians in France and in the Dutch Republic', *Internationale Kirchliche Zeitschrift*, 99 (2009), 145–69.

131 On the spread of Jansenist ideas in the public sphere, see Pietro Stella, *Il giansenismo in Italia*, 3 vols (Rome: Edizioni di storia e letteratura, 2006), vol. 1. For Picardy and Bordeaux, see T. J. Saxby, *The Quest for the New Jerusalem, Jean de Labadie and the Labadists, 1610–1744* (Dordrecht: Martinus Nijhoff, 2012), 19–40.

132 Bourke to Wadding, Brussels, 6 March 1642; cited by O'Connor, *Irish Jansenists*, 100, 354.

133 O'Connor, *Irish Jansenists*, 208, 353.

the name of St Isidore's College and mistakenly thought that Wadding was many years older than he actually was.[134]

The spread of Jansenism in its various phases over a lengthy period makes it difficult to apply a single term to describe it at any one point in its development.[135] The many and varied works on the subject by Lucien Ceyssens illustrate the complications and wealth of sources.[136] For many years at the curia, the votes of Wadding and Rancati counted in decisions reached by various Roman congregations. Francesco Albizzi of the Holy Office led the Jansenist controversy at the papal court.[137] In 1649, he called upon Rancati and three other qualifiers to consider propositions attributed

134 *Oeuvres de Messire Antoine Arnauld, Docteur de la Maison et Société de Sorbonne*, ed Gabriel Du Pac de Bellegarde and Jean Hautefage (Paris-Lausanne: Sigismond d'Arnay, 1779), 28, 723; cited by Ruth Clark, *Strangers & Sojourners at Port Royal: Being an Account of the Connections between British Isles and the Jansenists of France and Holland* (repr. Cambridge: Cambridge University Press, 2014), 201: 'Il ne me reste qu'un mot à dire de mes autres amis de Rome. Le *Révérend Pére* Luc Wading, Religieux de S. François, Irlandois âgé de quatre–vingts ans, Fondateur à Rome du Monastere de S. Joseph pour les Religieux de son Ordre & de sa Nation, & l'un de mes Juges, m' a témoigné toujours tant de bienveillance, & défendu par-tout toutes les causes où j'avois intérêt avec tant de amis, zele, & par le seul amour qu'il avoit pour la vérité, que sa mémoire me sera toujours en singuliere vénération'.

135 Joseph Bergin, *Church, Society and Religious Change in France, 1580–1730* (New Haven, CT: Yale University Press, 2009), 422.

136 On the period relevant to Wadding, see Lucien Ceyssens, 'Que penser finalement de l'histoire du jansenisme et de l'anti-jansenisme?', *RHE*, 88 (1993), 108–30; idem, *Le cardinal François Albizzi, 1593–1684, un cas important dans l' histoire du jansénisme* (Rome: Pontificium athenaeum Antonianum, 1977); idem, *La première bulle contre Jansénius. Sources relatives à son histoire 1644–53*, 2 vols (Brussels-Rome: Bibliothèque de l'Institut historique belge de Rome, 1961), I: 1644–49, II: 1650–53; idem, *Jansenistica: studiën in verband met de geschiedenis van het Jansenisme*, 4 vols (Mechelen: St Franciscus Drukkerij, 1950–62); idem, 'Florence Conry, Hugh de Burgo, Luke Wadding and Jansenism', 382–400; idem, 'Sources relatives aux débuts du jansénisme et de l'antijansénisme 1640–43', *Bibliothèque de la Revue d'histoire ecclésiastique*, fasc. 31 (1957); idem, 'Jean Recht en mission à Madrid pour l'Augustinus et l'Augustinisme, 1649–53', *Augustiniana*, 1, *Jansenistica minora*, 2/12 (Leuven: Nova et vetera, 1951).

137 Mario Rosa, *La curia romana nell'età moderna. Instituzioni, cultura, carriere* (Rome: Viella, 2013), 77.

to Jansen's *Augustinus*. Rancati was joined by Raffaele Aversa, a philosopher and theologian with the Clerics Regular Minor; Domenico Campanella, a Carmelite friar; and Tommaso Delbene, a Theatine moral theologian.[138]

In the early 1650s, Wadding's time was increasingly occupied by the *Augustinus*. At the start of the decade, he was aware that Philip IV of Spain instructed his ambassador to Rome, Cardinal Trivulzio, to apply for a revision of Jansen's book or, 'if necessary, its correction, so that it could be freely read'.[139] Ceyssens surmised that Philip IV's representatives asked the Hispanophile Wadding to smooth the way for a successful outcome.[140] In the intervening time, Louis Gorin de Saint-Amour, a leading exponent of Jansenist views and deputy of thirteen French bishops, travelled to Rome. Saint-Amour paid special attention to scholars of St Augustine in an attempt to win their support. In doing so, he noted Wadding's persistent character and consulted him 'like an oracle' on multiple occasions.[141] At the same time, Saint-Amour received assurances from Wadding's close ally, Cardinal Roma.[142]

On 20 April 1651, following an appeal by the French bishops for further clarification, Innocent X nominated cardinals and advisers to examine five propositions assigned to Jansen. The pope's decision to appoint a special commission signalled his resolve to uphold established doctrine while, at the same time, showing the extent to which the papacy was attacked.[143] The initial diffusion and early stages of Jansenism in Italy were essentially curial or ecclesiastical. In this setting, the formidable Albizzi feared the immediate threat of religious individualism that Jansenism represented.[144]

138 *Memoires du P. Rene Rapin de la Compagnie de Jesus sur l'Église et la Societe, la Cour, la Ville, et le Jansenisme, 1644–69*, 3 vols (Paris: Gaume frères et J. Duprey, 1865), 1 vol, 328; cited by Ceyssens, 'Conry, De Burgo, Wadding and Jansenism', 372; O'Connor, *Irish Jansenists*, 226.

139 Ceyssens, 'Conry, De Burgo, Wadding and Jansenism', 376.

140 Ibid.

141 Ibid, 372: 'il le consultait comme un oracle'.

142 Ibid, 378.

143 Ó hAnnracháin, *Catholic Reformation in Ireland*, 222.

144 Mario Rosa, 'Spiritualità mistica e insegnamento popolare. L'Oratorio e le Scuole pie', in Gabriele de Rosa, Tullio Gregory and André Vauchez, eds, *Storia dell'Italia religiosa* 3 vols (Rome-Bari: Laterza, 1994), vol. 2: *L'età moderna*, 296.

He supported the Society of Jesus and the Capuchins, counted Jesuit theologians among his friends and was advised by French Jesuits on the ideas of Jansen.[145] Moreover, Albizzi was familiar with Wadding's work at the Holy Office since the early 1630s, but did not look upon him favourably.[146] Albizzi may have disagreed with Wadding limiting the number of appointments to Irish bishoprics and was, perhaps, suspicious of Wadding's repeated reluctance to accept promotion to the hierarchy himself.

The five cardinals who sat on the commission were Domenico Cecchini, Fabio Chigi, Marzio Ginetti, Giulio Roma and Bernardino Spada. Following Roma's death, he was succeeded by Camillo Astalli-Pamphili.[147] Innocent X then appointed theologians to serve with Aversa, Campanella and Delbene. Wadding was among those who judged the five propositions,[148] along with Sforza Pallavicino, a Jesuit;[149] Marcantonio da Carpenedolo, a Capuchin; Angelo Maria Ciria Panvini, a Servite; Modesto Gavazzi da Ferrara, a Conventual Franciscan; Vincenzo Preti, a Dominican; Filippo Visconti, an Augustinian; Vincenzo Candido, a Dominican; Giovanni Agostino Tartaglia della Natività, a Discalced Carmelite; and Celestino Bruni, an Augustinian hermit.[150] However, Albizzi temporarily suspended both Wadding and Rancati as advisers, after 'they let slip a few words that were a little favourable to the doctrine of the bishop of Ypres'.[151] This took place while Wadding was excused from other duties due to illness. Although Pallavicino was the only Jesuit

145 Stefania Tutino, *Uncertainty in Post-Reformation Catholicism. A History of Probabilism* (Oxford: Oxford University Press, 2018), 195, 262; Broggio, 'Un Teologo Irlandese nella Roma del Seicento', 177.

146 O'Connor, *Irish Jansenists*, 227; Ceyssens, 'Conry, De Burgo, Wadding and Jansenism', 381.

147 Chiara Catalano, 'Sforza Pallavicino and the Condemnation of Jansenius' Five Propositions', 254.

148 Stella, *Il giansenismo in Italia*, vol. 1, 1–37.

149 Prosperi, *Il Concilio di Trento*, 167–68.

150 Catalano, 'Sforza Pallavicino and the Condemnation of Jansenius' Five Propositions', 254; Alberto Monticone, 'Albizzi, Francesco', *DBI*, <https://www.treccani.it/enciclopedia/francesco-albizzi_%28Dizionario-Biografico%29/>, accessed 28 August 2024.

151 *Memoires du P. Rene Rapin de la Compagnie de Jesus*, vol. 1, 328; O'Connor, *Irish Jansenists*, 226.

on the commission, Delbene's order, the Theatines, were often compared to the Society of Jesus. More specifically, their theology on free will drew upon Ignatian thought.[152]

The commission examined matters for some months in meetings before the cardinals and before the pope. Wadding showed thoroughness and prudence in his work. He dictated to a scribe the *vota* that he later presented, adding improvements to the text in a less legible hand.[153] This extensive source belongs to the material that Wadding compiled on the *Auxilia* question. Ceyssens therefore deduced that it contains the draft which became the final version that Wadding read to the congregation.[154] The following account of Wadding's part in the proceedings consists of his opinion of the five propositions, based upon papers now preserved at University College Dublin. Ceyssens deciphered the hand but often presented only the Latin, whereas I have translated Wadding's opinions here.

The first proposition was that: 'Some commandments of God are impossible even for the righteous who desire and strive to observe them, given the strengths they currently have, for they lack the grace that would make them possible'.[155] Wadding believed that propositions made by an author were not to be denounced without first confirming their veracity in the correct context.[156] Before the cardinals on 8 October 1652, he declared that this statement was 'heretical, reckless and condemned by the holy

152 William Hudson, ed and trans, *Theatine Spirituality: Selected Writings with an Introduction and Notes*. Preface by Gigliola Fragnito (New York: Paulist Press, 1996), 43, 54–55; John W. O'Malley, *The First Jesuits* (Cambridge MA: Harvard University Press, 1995), 81, 306. See also Andrea Vanni, 'The Order of the Theatines between Carafa's Inquisition and Borromeo's Diocesan Reform', in Wim François and Violet Soen, eds, *Council of Trent. Reform and Controversy in Europe and Beyond (1545–1700)*, 3 vols (Göttingen: Vandenhoeck & Ruprecht, 2018), vol. 2, 173–90.

153 'Documents in manuscript and print concerning the teaching of Cornelius Jansen' (UCD-OFM, D.10).

154 Ceyssens, 'Conry, De Burgo, Wadding and Jansenism', 383.

155 'Documents in manuscript and print concerning the teaching of Cornelius Jansen' (UCD-OFM, D.10/101–112): 'Aliaqua Dei praecepta hominibus iustis volentibus et conantibus, secundum praesentes quas habent vires, sunt impossibilia; deest quoque iis gratia qua possibilia fiant'.

156 Ceyssens, 'Conry, De Burgo, Wadding and Jansenism', 382.

fathers, scandalous, offensive to God, and destructive of men'.[157] Yet, when Wadding submitted his *votum* before the pope on 10 March 1653, he found it difficult to consider that this was the sense in which it was intended: 'For if the proposition is understood in relation to venial sin [...] it deserves no censure'.[158] Instead, Wadding said, St Augustine proved that 'sometimes grace is wanting, many are presumptuous of their own strength of will, and that, as God sometimes withdraws his grace, the will is weak'.[159]

The second proposition considered by the commission was that: 'Interior grace is never resisted in the state of fallen nature'.[160] In giving his opinion before the five cardinals, Wadding stated that 'this proposition under these terms is nowhere to be found in Jansen, nor in the Fathers of the Society in their Leuven theses on whatever seemed worthy of notice in Jansen's work'.[161] Therefore, Wadding drew the meaning of the proposition from the teaching of Jansen, which frequently repeated and strongly emphasised 'that all the grace of Christ is efficacious for healing'.[162] Jansen consequently affirmed 'that in the state of fallen, weak and corrupt nature, which needs the medicine of the Saviour, this grace cannot be resisted'.[163]

In Wadding's judgement, Jansen's main fault was, perhaps, that he pursued his war with the Jesuits too fiercely.[164] This was a recurring theme in

157 Ibid, 384: 'haeretica, sit temeraria, a SS. Patribus damnata, scandalosa, Deo iniuriosa, et homnibus perniciosa'.

158 'Si vero intelligatur de praeceptis respectu peccatorum venialium [...] nullam meretur censuram'. (UCD-OFM, D.10/113–15).

159 Ceyssens, 'Conry, De Burgo, Wadding and Jansenism', 383–85.

160 'Interiori gratiae in statu naturae lapsae nunquam resistitur' (UCD-OFM, D.10/119–128).

161 Ceyssens, 'Conry, De Burgo, Wadding and Jansenism', 385–86: 'Ista propositio sub his terminis quibus nobis discutienda proponitur nusquam reperitur apud Jansenium, neque Patres Societatis, qui exactissime et fideliter in suis Thesibus Lovaniensibus quidquid animaadversione aut nota dignum in opere Jansenii videbatur exposuerunt'.

162 Ceyssens, 'Conry, De Burgo, Wadding and Jansenism', 386: 'quam omnem Christi gratiam medicinalem esse efficacem'.

163 Ibid: 'unde consequenter affirmat in statu naturae lapsae, infirmae et corruptae, quae medicina indiget Salvatoris, huic gratiae non resisti'.

164 Ibid: 'Totum ei bellum cum Patribus Jesuitis, quos nimis acriter insequitur'. On the Jesuit defence of papal authority, see Pietro Stella, *Il giansenismo in Italia*, vol. 1,

Wadding's contributions to the commission. Moreover, he added, Jansen always understood 'Christ's healing and victorious grace as the grace by which God effectively heals the sick', just as Augustine expressly declared in his treatise on nature and grace.[165] From the same source, Jansen inferred that this grace, which Christ brought as physician to the weak, is that which acts and achieves its effect. However, according to Wadding, neither Jansen nor any other theologian would always say that grace should be given to all people equally. Jansen's defenders proceeded in a different way, saying that they did not assert that divine grace is simply, and in itself, never resisted. This was expressed in the *Augustinus* on the grace of Christ the Saviour.[166]

Wadding's verdict on the proposition was that, 'if it is understood as efficacious grace, whether helping or stimulating, it is true and Catholic, but if indeed it is sufficient grace and of any interior grace, according to all the breadth of grace, it is reckless and smacks of heresy'.[167] Wadding's vocabulary is significant. It serves as a reminder of the unresolved *De auxiliis* commission that investigated Molina's writings on prevenient grace and the prevailing belief that interior grace was unnecessary for the salvation of each individual.[168] Delbene submitted his *votum* before Innocent X followed by Wadding on 22 March 1653. The Irish friar began by reiterating

85–86. See also Marc Fumaroli, 'The Fertility and the Shortcomings of Renaissance Rhetoric: The Jesuit Case', in *The Jesuits: Cultures, Sciences, and the Arts*, ed John W. O'Malley, Gauvin Alexander Bailey and Steven J. Harris, 2 vols (Toronto: University of Toronto Press, 1999–2006), vol. 1, 97–99.

165 'Addo insuper Jansenium per gratiam medicinalem Christi et victricem intelligere semper eam gratiam qua Deus vult efficaciter et voluntate consequenti hominem infirmum sanare, sicuti expresse declaravit Augustinus *De Natura et Gratia*, c. 67 [...] et c. 53'. (UCD-OFM, D.10/119); Ceyssens, 'Conry, De Burgo, Wadding and Jansenism', 386.

166 Jansen, *Augustinus, seu doctrina S. Augustini de humanae naturae sanitate*, 347–77.

167 Ceyssens, 'Conry, De Burgo, Wadding and Jansenism', 387: 'si intelligatur de gratia efficaci sive adiuvante sive excitante, sit vera et catholica; si vero de sufficienti, et de quacumque gratia interiori, secundum omnem gratiae latitudinem, sit temeraria et sapiat haeresim'.

168 Kirk MacGregor, *Luis de Molina: The Life and Theology of the Founder of Middle Knowledge* (Grand Rapids, MI: Zondervan, 2015), 64–5, 167–9; Yves Congar, *Tradition and Traditions. An Historical and a Theological Essay*, translated by Michael Naseby and Thomas Rainborough (London: Macmillan, 1967), 240.

that the second proposition was never found under these terms in Jansen and that the Jesuits did not present it in their theses.[169] As long as Jansen did not have this statement as it stood in the proposition, Wadding believed it should not be judged.

The third proposition was that: 'To be worthy or unworthy in the state of fallen nature, it is unnecessary for a man to have freedom from necessity; but freedom from all coercion suffices'.[170] According to Wadding, this was acknowledged to be a difficult question since the time of Augustine.[171] As many of the most authoritative theologians had discussed the proposal, Wadding judged that it was 'probable and not worthy of theological criticism'.[172] Indeed, he asserted, the *Augustinus* 'did not have a single word about merit or demerit in 75 chapters and three books'.[173]

Having carefully read the contents and compared them with the Jesuits' Leuven theses, Wadding raised four objections against Jansen in this regard.[174] However, the proposal was not to be found in the printed works of Michel Baius who influenced Jansen. That made it very difficult to ascertain the real meaning. Thus, Wadding said the third proposition deserved no theological censure, nor should Jansen be condemned because of it.[175]

Understanding the fourth proposition perplexed Wadding for several days, namely: 'The Semi-Pelagians taught the need for interior grace in each particular action, even for the principle of faith; and they were heretics precisely because they considered that this grace was of such a nature that the human will could either obey or resist'.[176] Semi-Pelagianism became

169 Ceyssens, 'Conry, De Burgo, Wadding and Jansenism', 387–88.

170 'Ad merendum et demerendum in statu naturae lapsae non requiritur in homine libertas a necessitate, sed sufficit libertas a coactione'. (UCD-OFM, D.10/139–148).

171 Ceyssens, 'Conry, De Burgo, Wadding and Jansenism', 389.

172 Ibid: 'iudico illam esse probabilem et nulla dignam censura theologica'.

173 Ibid: 'dum neque verbum quidem ex professo de merit ovel demerit habet Jansenius per 75 capitula in tribus integris libris'.

174 Ibid, 390.

175 Ibid, 391.

176 'Semi-pelagini admittebant praevenientis gratiae interioris necessitatem ad singulos actus, etiam ad initium fidei, et in hoc erant haeretici, quod vellent eam gratiam talem esse, cui posset humana voluntas resistere vel obtemperare'. (UCD-OFM, D.10/167–177).

popular in the south of France in the fifth century and represented an attempted compromise between Augustine's teachings on grace and those of Pelagius.[177] These ideas were officially denounced at the Council of Orange in 529. The decision was endorsed by Boniface II two years later and once more at the Council of Trent in 1546.[178]

Wadding declared that 'the wisest of teachers' among his colleagues advised him to divide this question into two parts.[179] The first related to history and the second, doctrine. In the first part, Wadding referred to the irrefutable witness of letters from Prosper of Aquitaine and Hilary of Poitiers. They both warned Augustine of Semi-Pelagian errors. Finally, Boniface II's letter of 531 condemned Semi-Pelagianism and confirmed the Council of Orange decrees in favour of Augustine.[180]

Wadding stated that the second part of the fourth statement was produced from Jansen's *Augustinus*. In his submission before the cardinals, Wadding asserted that Jansen did not condemn the people of Marseille because they established a necessary grace for each individual action, as 'the true grace of Christ was necessary for every good act' and this represented 'the most certain and Catholic dogma'.[181] The Irish Franciscan saw the great ambiguity or obscurity of the fourth proposal. 'The will does not govern grace', he continued, 'but is governed by grace'.[182] In summing up, Wadding thought the fourth proposition 'ill-conceived and, moreover, that Jansen's

177 *Cornelii Jansenii, Episcopi Yprensis, Augustinus, seu doctrina S. Augustini de humanae naturae sanitate, aegritudine, medicina, adversus Pelagianos et Massilienses tribus tomis comprehensa* (Paris: Soly & Guillemot, 1641), 459–92.

178 Rebecca Harden Weaver, *Divine Grace and Human Agency. A Study of the Semi-Pelagian Controversy* (Washington DC: Catholic University of America Press, 1998), 225–232; R. W. Dyson, *The Pilgrim City: Social and Political Ideas in the Writings of St Augustine of Hippo* (Woodbridge: Boydell, 2001), 8–9.

179 Ceyssens, 'Conry, De Burgo, Wadding and Jansenism', 391: 'Hactenus a sapientissimis magistris meis collegis dictum est eam dividi in duas partes, quarum prima sit facti seu historiae, secunda iuris seu doctrinae'.

180 Ibid.

181 Ibid, 393: 'Non propterea Jansenius condemnavit Massiliensis quod veram Christi gratiam admiserint necessariam esse ad singulos actus bonos, quod certissimum est et catholicorum dogma'.

182 Ibid, 'Voluntas non regit gratiam sed regitur a gratia'.

book was scandalous and reckless for defending his opinion too strongly and attacking others, especially the Jesuit Fathers'.[183]

Before the pope on 3 April 1653, Wadding explained that Jansen's doctrine was free from error on the one hand for its condemnation of Semi-Pelagianism but, on the other, it was reckless in that it would prompt the probable judgement of 'the most serious school of the Jesuit Fathers'.[184] This appears to be a reference to *In eminenti*, composed by Albizzi for Urban VIII, forbidding discussion of Jesuit teachings concerning salvation. Therefore, Wadding held that the fourth proposal was ill-conceived.

In response to the fifth proposition that '[i]t is a Semi-Pelagian error to assert that Jesus died or shed his blood for all men, without exception',[185] Wadding described this error as 'hateful and offensive to pious ears'.[186] As Jansen regarded the difference between the two as very serious, 'he proposed to challenge and discuss sufficient grace according to the teaching of the Jesuit Fathers'.[187] Wadding humbly told the cardinals that Jansen's explanation applied 'to the passages of Holy Scripture concerning the death of Jesus for the faithful alone, especially for the predestined, is sound and Catholic as it conforms to the same scriptures'.[188] Wadding based this statement on the authority of Augustine as well as 'other holy fathers and the most important teachers'.[189]

183 Ibid: 'Coeterum in libro Jansenii censeo scandalosum esse et temerarium, nimis vehementem illum modum propugnandi sententiam propriam et impugnandi alienas, prasertim Patrem Jesuitarum'.

184 'Gravissimae scholae Patrum Jesuitarum. Propositionem vero censeo fuisse male conceptam'. Ceyssens, 'Conry, De Burgo, Wadding and Jansenism', 394.

185 'Semi-pelagianum est dicere Christum pro omnibus omnino hominibus mortuum esse aut Sanguinem fudisse'. (UCD-OFM, D.10/187–204).

186 Ibid, 'Odiosam valde et pias aures offendentem'

187 Ceyssens, 'Conry, De Burgo, Wadding and Jansenism', 395: 'Isto illo libro proposuit sibi discutiendam et impugnandam gratiam sufficientem secundum doctrinam Patrum Jesuitarum'.

188 Ibid, 397: 'explicatio autem quam adhibuit locis Sacrae Scripturae de morte Christi pro solis fidelibus, praesertim pro praedestinatis, sana est et catholica, utpote conformis eidem Sacrae Scripturae'.

189 Ibid: 'et quae habetur apud Augustinum et alios Sanctos Patres ac gravissimos doctores'.

Before Innocent X on 7 April, Wadding stated that some had already subjected this proposal on the death and redemption of Jesus to many censures. Yet, according to the Irish friar, the whole stumbling block was that Jansen never said it was a Semi-Pelagian error to assert that Jesus died for absolutely all men. Again, Wadding 'wished that Jansen acted more gently and modestly in reporting and refuting this subject and with less offence to the Society of Jesus'.[190]

Wadding concluded: 'Blessed Father Augustine, without any doubt of all the most learned from anywhere, is most agreeable to the authority of the Holy Scriptures in all things'.[191] Moreover, Wadding continued, Augustine 'held more faithfully, defended more robustly [and] disseminated more effusively'.[192] Having therefore considered matters carefully, Wadding humbly and respectfully said that the fifth proposition, together with that well-known or censured error of Semi-Pelagianism was nowhere to be seen in the *Augustinus*.[193]

In defence of Jansen, Wadding was joined by the two Dominicans, Vincenzo Preti, commissary of the Holy Office, and Vincenzo Candido, master of the sacred palace, Filippo Visconti, procurator general of the Augustinians, and five others. After much thought on the matter, Wadding showed himself ready to accept the decision reached by the papacy.[194] Nevertheless, Innocent X was unmoved by Augustinianism and, as the majority of the advisers on the commission adhered to Albizzi's guidelines, the five propositions were condemned.[195]

Consequently, Innocent X assigned Albizzi to prepare the decree *Cum occasione*, issued 31 May and published 9 June. Considering the downturn in Wadding's circumstances and his family's losses in Waterford, it is worth

190 Ibid, 398: 'Cuperem quidem ego, ut in hoc ipso argumento referent et refellendo mitius et modestius egisset Jansenius et cum minori offensione Patrum Jesuitarum'.

191 Ibid, 399: 'doctrinam Beatissimi Patris Augustini omnium absque ulla dubitatione undecumque doctissimi, Sanctarum Scripturarum auctoritati in omnibus concordissimam'.

192 Ibid: 'fidelius tenuerit, robustius defenderit, effusius disseminaverit'.

193 Ibid.

194 O'Connor, *Irish Jansenists*, 228; Ceyssens, 'Conry, De Burgo, Wadding and Jansenism', 402–403.

195 Broggio, 'Un Teologo Irlandese nella Roma del Seicento', 177.

bearing in mind that Jansenism appealed to a class at risk of political powerlessness.[196] Wadding's ability to accept Innocent X's condemnation of the five propositions clearly shows his view of authority in its early modern context.[197] To Ceyssens, the first statement was unreliable, the ascription to Jansen implausible, and the other four statements unconvincing. Later scholars disagree and argue that the first is to be found in the *Augustinus*, while the other four directly reflect Jansenist thought.[198]

Conclusion

Wadding suffered serious ongoing consequences as a result of the split between Rinuccini and the Kilkenny confederates. The nuncio was sensitive to his position in society and believed he acted upon the authority invested in him. Excommunication turned out to be his last line of defence against the confederates. Aside from its many valuable contemporary sources, the interpretation of events in the *Commentarius* was, at times, speculative. This compounded the problem for Wadding. Hitherto covert, his adversaries were to become increasingly open in their opposition.

The marquis of Ormond's letter of 20 May 1649 reveals his need to neutralise Franciscan opposition in Ireland. In spite of encouragement from Ormondist friars, combined with his agreement with the confederates; the marquis appears to have overreached his authority in a show of excessive confidence. Promoting candidates in line with Ormond's wishes was a bridge too far and would have run counter to Wadding's recognition of papal primacy. Wadding blocked the proposed partition of the Irish

196 Peter Brown, *Augustine of Hippo: A Biography*. Revised Edition with a New Epilogue (Berkeley: University of California Press, 2000), 349; Ceyssens, 'Conry, De Burgo, Wadding and Jansenism', 297.

197 O'Connor, *Irish Jansenists*, 368–69.

198 Ceyssens, 'L'authenticite des cinq propositions condamnées de Jansenius', *Antonianum*, 55 (1980), 368–424; Gert Partoens, 'The Earliest Phase of the Jansenist Controversy among the Flemish Capuchins: Part I: Hildebrand's interpretation and the case of Eugenius of Bruges', *Augustiniana*, 61 (2011), 155–85.

Franciscan province and called instead for caution, as shown in letters to his confrères Pierre Marchant and Daniel à Dongo.[199] In this context, Wadding maintained a clear distance between the Franciscans and the secular authority of Ormond.

The *Scriptores* was the last book that Wadding brought to print before Francis Harold's return to Rome. Chronicles and hagiographical works compiled by religious orders, such as Wadding's *Scriptores*, offer an abundant supply of information on the polemical intent of martyrology.[200] Rather than being viewed uncritically, these are literary compositions that need to be examined and explained in context. Harold's dedication is apparent from his uncle's final literary endeavours and Wadding came to regard him as his son.[201]

The scale of Wadding's scholarship and loyal service to his religious order were much admired by superiors, such as the minister general, but this was about to change as a result of the pro- and anti-nuncio split. Wadding found himself beleaguered during the Cromwellian regime, a time when Irish friars needed stability more than ever. Although he remained a source of counsel for Viscount Taaffe, no letters from the Irish friar substantiate matters further and his direct participation in politics ended with the demise of the supreme council and general assembly in Kilkenny.

Jesuit theologians were opposed to Scotist thought.[202] Nonetheless, Wadding the Scotist avoided making enemies in the Society of Jesus. The Jesuit Irish mission was well received in his birthplace of Waterford. His elder brother, Ambrose, and four first cousins joined the order. Moreover, the Jesuits and Franciscans were allies in advancing the Immaculate Conception, a favourite cause for Wadding.

The position that he reached on Jansen's *Augustinus* was based on a number of factors. First, his predilection for the teachings of Augustine,

199 Giblin, 'A Seventeenth-Century Idea: Two Franciscan Provinces in Ireland', 63.

200 Simon Ditchfield, 'Endnote', in Hazard, ed, *Path to Salvation: Temporal and Spiritual Journeys by the Mendicant Orders, c.1370–1740*, 225.

201 Harold, *Vita Fratris Lucae Waddingi*, 139.

202 Ian Campbell, 'John Punch, Scotist Holy War, and the Irish Catholic Revolutionary Tradition in the Seventeenth Century', *Journal of the History of Ideas*, 77 (2016), 401–21.

which began during his time at Salamanca where he was strongly influenced by the saint's writings and thus became part of a rigorist tradition. Second, he intervened on behalf of others who appealed for him to offer a fair representation of their views on grace and free will. Third, prudence was a watchword for Wadding. He subjected the text to a diligent reading so as to interrogate the statements presented to the commission. Next, he showed the strength of character not to react to others and follow their lead. Since Jansen died before the commission sat and the *Augustinus* was printed posthumously, Wadding's doubts about the five propositions indicate that anti-Jansenists used the *Augustinus* as a convenient basis to criticise Jansen's followers. Moreover, Wadding repeatedly emphasised that Jansen could have avoided disagreement with the Society of Jesus by expressing his views more diplomatically. Finally, Wadding acknowledged the authority of Innocent X's decision against the *Augustinus* and showed exemplary Franciscan obedience. While the foundational virtue of humility inspired Augustine, obedience was a clear signal of humility for Bonaventure. Rooted in Christ, who was 'obedient unto death',[203] this was an essential element of community life, connected with poverty and the denial of one's own will.[204]

203 Philippians 2:8.

204 Raniero Cantalamessa, OFM Cap., *Obedience: The Authority of the Word*, translated by Frances Villa Lonergan (New York: St Pauls, 2018), 5, 10–11, 40. The obligation to obey did not apply when required to do something unjust or wrong. Christopher Bellitto, *Humility: The Secret History of a Lost Virtue* (Washington, DC: Georgetown University Pres, 2023), 70.

10 'I lay down my pen'[1]

Introduction

Luke Wadding was reluctant to spend time sitting for a portrait, believing it to be egotistical, but was won over by the lawyer Ercole Ronconi, who was Carlo Maratti's patron at St Isidore's.[2] The seriousness of Wadding's facial expression in his best-known portraits reflects the gravity of his responsibilities in the latter stages of his life.[3] This style is reminiscent of Veristic statues, which depicted the moral rigour of ancient Roman leaders by accentuating every aspect of ageing, such as a furrowed brow, a frown or wrinkled hands.[4] In concluding his eighth volume of the *Annales Minorum*, Wadding compared its compilation to a long voyage, 'buffetted by the tempests of the vast ocean', stating that he had followed his confrères 'across the seas to India, the Orient, and the countries to the west'.[5] This was written on the feast of the Assumption 1652, five years before his death.

1 *Annales Minorum*, vol. 16, Peroratio, 548: 'Suspenso que calamo'.

2 McCafferty, 'Luke Wadding. A Life in and for Books', 118.

3 Portraits of Wadding can be found in St Isidore's Library, Rome, at the National Gallery of Ireland, Dublin, and at Dún Mhuire, Killiney, Co. Dublin.

4 On the Veristic art of the Late Roman Republic, see Steven Tuck, *A History of Roman Art* (2nd edn, Hoboken NJ: Wiley, 2021), 118–19. On Carlo Maratti's portrayal of Wadding, see Stella Rudolph, 'Carlo Maratti e l'Inghilterra', in Liliana Barroero, Simonetta Prosperi, Valenti Rodinò and Sebastian Schütze, eds, *Maratti e l'Europa* (Rome: Campisano, 2015), 127–43.

5 *Annales Minorum*, vol. 16, Peroratio, 548: 'Tandem post tot annorum velificationes, vastissimi maris agitatus procellis [...] Longum istud iter hactenus emensus, demum veni in altitudinem maris, et Cancri Tropicum, lineamque Aequinoctialem per vastissimum Oceanum praetergressus, Indias, Orientales, et Occidentales per maris Australis, et Septentrionalis littora perlustrans'; Mooney, 'Father Luke Wadding – The Last Years', 89–91.

Compelled 'to gather in the sails of my shivering boat, and having cast anchor, to come to rest in port', Wadding consigned himself 'to the safe harbour of tranquility of mind'.[6] Thereafter, Wadding wished to dedicate his life entirely to the salvation of his soul.[7] This chapter concentrates on the ongoing efforts by Wadding's enemies to damage his influence in the Roman curia, the Spanish court and his own order, before assessing the final publications that he brought to print, taking account of the alliances he maintained with other churchmen and his continued interest in Franciscan education, before his final illness and death.

Mutiny

Wadding's writings were not always to the forefront of his mind in the early 1650s. The internal rift among Irish Observant Franciscans epitomised the conflict between Ormondists and the pro-nuncio party. Notwithstanding the friars' efforts to resolve matters, the split only worsened after the signing of the Second Ormond Peace.[8] Wadding found himself in the eye of the storm and his refusal to cooperate with dividing up the Irish province appears to have intensified these differences. At St Isidore's, the disagreements among staff and students were most concentrated from June 1652 until April 1654.[9] Francis Magruairk subsequently became chief spokesman in a concerted campaign against Wadding. To this end, Magruairk brought his grievances to Innocent X, to Philip IV of Spain and to major superiors in the Franciscan order. Francis Harold alluded to this episode

6 *Annales Minorum*, vol. 16, Peroratio, 548: 'quassatae navis cogor vela colligere, et projecta anchora in portu requiescere […] tempus itaque est ut ab omnibus me prorsus expediam, suspensoque calamo, illud unam agam, quod potissime necessarium est; animae scilicet procurandae totus incumbam, ab aerumnosae vitae procellis ad portum religiosae quietis accedam, pacatique animi fidae me stationi committam'.

7 Ibid: 'quot potissime necessarium est; animae scilicet procurandae totus incumbam'.

8 Patrick Corish, 'Two Contemporary Historians of the Confederation of Kilkenny', *IHS*, 8 (1953), 217–36.

9 Binasco, *Making, Breaking and Remaking the Irish Missionary Network*, 152.

in Wadding's life referring to it as 'obnoxious business' but avoided naming names and stated that his elderly uncle deserved more respect.[10]

Knowledge of Ormond's letter to Wadding was a gift to the pro-nuncio party. In the prolonged assault that followed, Magruairk reacted by claiming that Wadding was 'a correspondent with English hereticks [and] patron of apostates'.[11] At a public audience with Innocent X, a group of Irish friars led by Magruairk knelt in the street before the pope and gave him a report accusing Wadding of mishandling his responsibilities in Rome. Magruairk subsequently shuttled between Ireland, Flanders, Italy and Spain on official business for pro-nuncio bishops and was involved in attempts to convince Charles IV, duke of Lorraine, to send aid to the Irish.[12]

The geography of this controversy reflected both its seriousness and the extent of Irish exile at that time. John Punch of Cork was *lector jubilatus* at St Isidore's and, from 1648, lived in Paris and Lyon where he published theological works and taught. Although his background was Old English, Punch sided with the pro-nuncio party and, while in France, took part in acrimonious debates between Irish exiles after the Kilkenny confederation collapsed.[13] In reply to John Callaghan, Punch defended Wadding against erroneous allegations that he aspired to become a bishop.[14] This rare text was printed at the Grand Couvent in the French capital. Punch's riposte

10 Harold, *Vita Fratris Lucae Waddingi*, 137: 'negotiis obnoxius'.

11 Peter Walsh, *The History and Vindication of the Loyal Formulary, Or Irish Remonstrance, So Graciously Received by His Majesty Anno 1661* (London: n. p., 1674), 592.

12 Mooney, 'Father Francis Magruairk OFM', 240–47.

13 Christopher Gillett, 'Political Theology', in Kelly and McCafferty, eds, *Oxford History of British and Irish Catholicism*, vol. 2, 197; Ian Campbell, 'John Punch, Scotist Holy War, and the Irish Catholic Revolutionary Tradition in the Seventeenth Century', *Journal of the History of Ideas*, 77 (2016), 401–421.

14 On Wadding's reluctance to accept promotion to a bishopric or cardinalate, See pages 203 and 265 of the current work. For John Callaghan's claims, see *Vindiciarum Catholicorum Hiberniae Authore Philopatro Irenaeo ad Alitophilum Libri duo quorum primus Rerum in Hibernia gestarum Synopsim, Secundus Libelli famosi in Catholicos Hiberniæ Proceres accuratam confutationem continet* (Paris: chez la Veuve Jean Camusat, et Pierre le Petit, 1650), 20–21. See also O'Connor, *An Irish Jansenist in Seventeenth Century France: John Callaghan*, 27.

to Callaghan showed his commitment to Catholic doctrine and accused Callaghan of Jansenistic tendencies.[15]

Magruairk appears to have started his anti-Wadding moves in Spain in 1654.[16] His claims reached the ears of the Franciscan minister general, Pedro Manero, in Madrid. Fearing an alliance between the papacy and France, Manero expressed his concerns to Philip IV about Wadding, 'agent for those dispossessed Irish nobles'.[17] Moreover, according to Manero, the Francophile Francesco Barberini, Cardinal Protector of the Franciscans, planned to see Wadding elected ultramontane commissary general at the order's next chapter in Rome.[18] This was a sign of Spanish anxieties about the transfer of hegemony from the Habsburgs to the Bourbons of France. Manero accused Wadding of being artful and cunning, claiming that Oñate, Spanish ambassador to Rome in 1647, was well acquainted with Wadding's tricks and sleight of hand.[19] Further, at Wadding's behest, Barberini had recommended Bernardine Barry, another Old English friar, for the post of vicar provincial. This was contrary to the advice of Manero who had been told by Irish friars on the continent that Barry was to blame for all of Ireland's ills. Whereas Wadding and Barry were claimed to be avowed foes of Spain,[20] Manero wrote that all Gaelic friars were loyal to Philip IV. This suggests that Francis Magruairk was well received by Manero when sent to Madrid by Gaelic interests in the Irish Franciscan province.

15 *D. Richardi Bellingi Vindiciae eversae per R. P. Fr. Ioannem Poncium, Ordinis Minorum [...] Et denique Doctoris Callaghani correctoratus Corisopitanus contra duas ipsius gallicas Epistolas, et Authorem libri gallici: l'Innocence & Verité défendues confirmatur* (Pariis: apud Franciscum Piot, in Conuentu majori Fratrum Minorum, 1653), 185, 190, 192; O'Connor, *Irish Jansenists*, 27; Patrick Corish, 'John Callaghan and the Controversies among the Irish in Paris, 1648–54', *ITQ*, 21 (1954), 32–50.

16 Millett, *The Irish Franciscans*, 11–12.

17 Pedro Manero to Philip IV, 1654 (AGS, Estado, Roma, leg. 3026) NLI Microfilm, n.461, p.81; cited by Mooney, 'Was Luke Wadding a Patriotic Irishman?', 15–16.

18 Ibid.

19 Mooney, 'Was Luke Wadding a Patriotic Irishman?', 15.

20 Ibid, 16–17.

Hugh O'Reilly, Catholic archbishop of Armagh and primate of Ireland, held Francis Magruairk in high regard.[21] Notwithstanding this support, Magruairk was denied further authorisation to represent Irish interests abroad after a serious disagreement took place over the Irish request for aid from the duke of Lorraine. Nonetheless, Magruairk continued to condemn Wadding. In the autumn of 1656, he was in Madrid to present a report to Philip IV stating that Wadding, founder of St Isidore's College, was actually an enemy of Spain who conspired against Irish interests and showed preferential treatment to Munster.[22] Magruairk also claimed that Wadding was Jewish and had demonic powers.[23]

The Spanish council of state was familiar with the details of the case and realised that this was a serious attack on Wadding. Nevertheless, they attributed the Franciscans' difficulties to their own prejudices and preferences. It was difficult for the council of state to arrive at an accurate understanding because the dispute involved not only the Irish province but also Julián Pérez, procurator general of the order to the Roman curia.[24] The council of state examined Magruairk's memorial on 17 November. They remembered Wadding's good name and his sincere affection for Spain. Consequently, they proposed to the king that no further action be taken, apart from referring matters to Julián Pérez.[25] In his reply, Pérez stated that he had no specific proof for the allegations and, although unconfirmed,

21 Mooney, 'Father Francis Magruairk OFM', 239–40, 243.

22 AGS, Estado, Roma, leg. 3030 (1656–7), NLI Microfilm, n.461, p.81: 'Points contained in the memorial of Fr. Francis Magruairk'; Pérez Tostado, "Learned, Attached and Reliable': Luke Wadding, Agent of the Spanish Monarchy', 53; Mooney, 'Was Luke Wadding a Patriotic Irishman?', 27.

23 Ian Campbell, 'The Wadding Circle and the History of Political Thought', in Binasco, ed, *Luke Wadding, the Irish Franciscans, and Global Catholicism*, 146; Pérez Tostado, "Learned, Attached and Reliable': Luke Wadding, Agent of the Spanish Monarchy', 46; Mooney, 'Was Luke Wadding a Patriotic Irishman?', 30.

24 Manuel de Castro, 'El Analista P. Lucas Wadding OFM y sus relaciones con la Peninsula Ibérica', *Salmanticensis*, 5, Fasc. 1 (1958), 147.

25 Fernando Rodríguez de la Torre, 'Pérez García, Julián. Iniesta (Cuenca), 31.I.1598 – Murcia, 4.III.1657. Religioso franciscano (OFM)', *DBe*, <https://dbe.rah.es/biografias/66296/julian-perez-garcia>, accessed 4 June 2024.

the reports against Wadding in Rome were worse than the contents of Magruairk's memorial.[26]

Wadding did not honour Magruairk with a reply but defended himself in a letter to Pedro Manero on 23 August 1654.[27] At the head of the attacks against Wadding stood Julián Pérez at Ara Coeli with support from Paul King who was, by then, at St Isidore's. In response, Wadding maintained he had done nothing but defend himself and the College against the insinuations of Pérez while his confrère, King, waged war on him. Wadding knew that many malicious claims about him had reached Manero's hands from 'the antics of friars and ill-served subjects' but hoped that the minister general would 'judge and weigh-up' such calumny.[28]

Acknowledging past favours from Manero, Wadding reminded him of his own work on Manero's behalf, 'in public and in secret'.[29] The Irish friar stated that he had reposed in the greatest trust at the papal court since 1618. Therefore, Wadding believed his reputation was sufficient to convince the minister general to keep him in his service as had all his predecessors. Indeed, he said, 'the works I have done bear witness to me'.[30] Seeing Manero 'so inclined to promote the glory of his religious order',[31] Wadding expected more from him than anyone else and thanked God that 'no matter how much they spread their slanders, they had made no dent upon his person, nor denigrated his good name'.[32] Tellingly, however,

26 Julián Pérez to Pedro Coloma, secretary of the Spanish council of state, 12 December 1656 (AGS, Estado, Roma, leg. 3030 (1656–7), NLI Microfilm, n.461, p.81; cited by Pérez Tostado, ''Learned, Attached and Reliable': Luke Wadding, Agent of the Spanish Monarchy', 58.

27 Wadding to Manero, St Isidore's College, 23 August 1654; Jennings, ed, 'Some Correspondence of Father Luke Wadding OFM', 89–91.

28 Ibid, 90: 'traversias de frayles y mal contentos de súbitos'.

29 Ibid: 'Yo he servido a Vuestra R*everendisi*ma en lo público y secreto'.

30 Ibid, 'Opera quae ego feci testimonium perhibent me'.

31 Ibid, 'veéndole tan inclinado a promover la gloria y resplendlor de la religion'.

32 Ibid, 'por más que las han esparcido, non han hecho mella en min persona, ni denigrado la fama'.

Wadding asked Manero to cooperate in allowing him to spend his 'few remaining days in peace and quiet before death'.[33]

In an attempt to resolve matters, Wadding selected four suitable candidates to succeed Bernadine Barry as guardian of St Isidore's and sent the details to Pedro Manero.[34] Though signed by Wadding, the letter was penned in another hand, which suggests declining health and old age. He set the following criteria: The successful candidate had to be qualified and authoritative to command the respect of staff and students. He had to speak Italian to deal with the laity and manage the house at St Isidore's, which was maintained for the most part by Italians. The guardian must deal with prelates, lords and cardinals who continually came to the house.[35] Speaking Spanish would help a lot due to the cooperation and communication that existed with Spain. To know the customs of the house, it would help to be a former student. The candidates were Daniel Broder, 50, *lector jubilatus* in Sicily and Prague, born in Connacht; Edmund Bray, 44, taught theology in Germany for many years, had been guardian in the main houses of Ireland, born in Munster and 'raised in this school';[36] John Heslenan, 40, a theology lector in Palermo for many years and *consultor* to the Holy Office, educated at Alcalá de Henares, spoke Spanish and Italian, serious and highly regarded, born in Connacht; Maurus Matthews, 38, taught theology at St Isidore's, read law at Bologna and theology with the reformed Franciscan province of Rome, 'a peaceful and composed character, well regarded by all', born in Munster.[37]

Wadding insisted that his nominations were preferable to a selection process that worked on a revolving basis or from a circle of candidates. Otherwise, the school could be closed, as had happened elsewhere in other Franciscan provinces. He hoped to see either Heslenan or Broder chosen as

33 Ibid, 'Una sola me queda, de passer con paz y quietud los pocos dias que me quedan la vida, y que con ella me dexan morir'.

34 Wadding to Manero, St Isidore's, 24 June 1655 (UCD-OFM, D.12/04); Jennings, ed, 'Some Correspondence of Father Luke Wadding OFM', 91–92. This was a jubilee year in Rome but, unlike that of 1625, St Isidore's was disturbed by various troubles.

35 Ibid, 91.

36 Ibid: 'criado en casa'.

37 Ibid.

no Connacht candidate had been selected before. Two autograph letters of Philip IV state that Heslenan was a naturalised Spanish citizen descended from 'an ancient Irish family', who was educated in Spain before lecturing for twelve years in Palermo where he was employed by the viceroy.[38] Heslenan's appointment was approved by the order, but hostilities persisted.

Julián Pérez was elected vicar general of the Friars Minor on 28 June 1656 after Pedro Manero stepped down from the generalship.[39] Having received the news, Wadding attempted to defuse the dispute among Irish Franciscans by writing to Pérez as his 'humble son and servant'.[40] Congratulating him and the Friars Minor on a well-deserved appointment, Wadding praised the virtue, zeal and authority of Pérez, wishing him a long life and the strength to fulfil his office, especially during the plague which affected Italy at that time. Wadding stated that he continued his work despite old age and his usual ailments. He had heard that a vice-procurator's licence had been sought for someone opposed to his interests and those of St Isidore's. Consequently, Wadding petitioned Pérez to ensure the selection of a 'religious and sane' friar who would not bring trouble to the house as 'some of the past procurators had'.[41] This appears to be a reference to the Magruairk controversy. Wadding did not think it presumptuous to say he deserved such a benefit and repeated his request for 'some peace in these few remaining days' of his life.[42]

In later years, Peter Walsh, former guardian of the Franciscan friary at Kilkenny, came to Wadding's defence against his detractors. Known as 'the stormy petrel of the Irish Franciscan province of the seventeenth century', Walsh strongly sympathised with Ormond and advised him on ecclesiastical matters.[43] Walsh wrote that Wadding's age, his renown for

38 Cleary, *Father Luke Wadding and St Isidore's College*, 113.

39 Mooney, 'Was Luke Wadding a Patriotic Irishman?', 23.

40 Wadding to Pérez, 28 July 1656; Jennings, ed, 'Some Correspondence of Father Luke Wadding OFM', 92–93: 'su humilde hijo y siervo'.

41 Ibid: 'que sea hombre religioso y cuerdo, y no nos metta en degustos y ruydos, como algunos de los procuradores passados'.

42 Ibid, 'gozar una religiosa paz estos pocos dias que me quedan de vida'.

43 Mark Williams, *The King's Irishmen: The Irish in the Exiled Court of Charles II, 1649–1660* (Woodbridge: Boydell, 2014), 44; Millett, *The Irish Franciscans,* 418–19; Thomas O'Connor, 'Marsh's Library and the Irish Catholic tradition', in Muriel

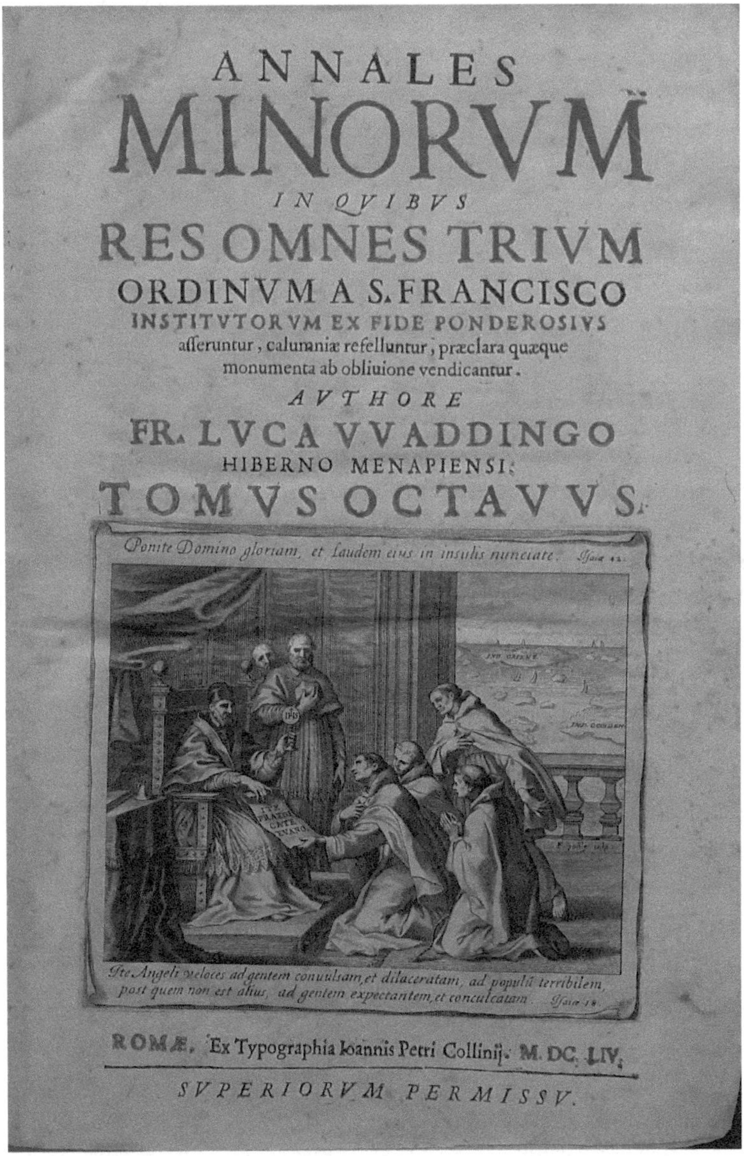

ANNALES
MINORVM
IN QVIBVS
RES OMNES TRIVM
ORDINVM A S. FRANCISCO
INSTITVTORVM EX FIDE PONDEROSIVS
asseruntur, calumniæ refelluntur, præclara quæque
monumenta ab obliuione vendicantur.
AVTHORE
FR. LVCA VVADDINGO
HIBERNO MENAPIENSI.
TOMVS OCTAVVS.

Ponite Domino gloriam, et laudem eius in insulis nunciate. Isaiæ 42.

Ite Angeli veloces ad gentem conuulsam, et dilaceratam, ad populũ terribilem, post quem non est alius, ad gentem expectantem, et conculcatam. Isaiæ 18.

ROMÆ, Ex Typographia Ioannis Petri Collinij. M.DC.LIV.

SVPERIORVM PERMISSV.

Figure 10.1 Title page of *Annales Minorum seu trium ordinum a S. Francisco institutorum* (1st edn, Rome, 1654), vol. 8. Reproduced by kind permission of UCD Library Special Collections.

'almost unrivalled scholarship [and] the past career of the great Franciscan, could not protect him from their insults'.[44] Indeed, Walsh stated, Wadding 'took this procedure of his Countreymen so to heart, that he carried the grief thereof with him not long after to his grave'.[45] Contrary to Walsh's assertion, however, it was Wadding's erudition and influence at the papal court that contributed to the antipathy against him.

Wadding's *Annales*, volume 8 (Rome, 1654)[46]

Luke Wadding and his closest associates at St Isidore's maintained their links with Lyon and its printers. Between 1650 and 1657, he prepared for print and forwarded to the Rhône city an in-quarto manuscript, *Joannis à Cathagená, libri duo, destatu pontificio et cardinalitio.* This unpublished work was supportive of the ultramontane family and its assertions of papal authority, as opposed to the Gallican doctrine that related to the Church in France.[47] In the intervening time, the second enlarged edition of *Panegyrici sacro-prophani* by Bonaventure Barron, Wadding's nephew, appeared at Lyon.[48]

Jean-Baptiste Devenet and Claude Prost had collaborated to print volumes six and seven of the *Annales* in Lyon from 1647 to 1648.[49] Satisfied with their work, Wadding made plans for volume eight when Devenet went on to publish on his own. On 2 January 1650, Devenet said he was

McCarthy and Ann Simmons, eds, *The Making of Marsh's Library: Learning, Politics and Religion in Ireland, 1650–1750* (Dublin: Four Courts Press, 2004), 235–55.

44 Walsh, *The History et Vindication of the Loyal Formulary*, 592–93.

45 Ibid.

46 On the three editions of this work, see Basilio Pandžić, 'Gli *Annales Minorum* di Luca Wadding', *AFH*, 70 (1977), 656–66.

47 Lyon, Bibliothèque Municipale, Ms. 357 (formerly 285), cited by Millett 'Guide to Material for a Biography of Father Luke Wadding', 235; Antoine François Delandin, *Manuscrits de la Bibliothèque de Lyon* (Paris: Jules Renouard, 1812), 250–51.

48 Millett, *The Irish Franciscans*, 366, 473.

49 Hazard, ed, 'Correspondence from Jean-Baptiste Devenet and Claude Prost, Book Merchants of Lyon, to Fr. Luke Wadding OFM', 519–45.

happy that Wadding's health allowed him to finish the eighth volume and asked him to give the manuscript to the Pizzenti, the publisher's agents in Rome.[50] Devenet was prepared to start printing but repeatedly referred to delays in the coming months. Habitually, the high costs of transport had a serious effect on the price of books which were dispatched accordingly unbound in packs.[51] These volumes were later bound at St Isidore's.[52]

The delay in producing volume eight demonstrates the slow and irregular pace of communications in the seventeenth century.[53] Travel times during the reign of Louis XIV remained comparable with those during the first half of the fifteenth century. Prompt dispatches on the road between Lyon and Rome could take three weeks. The loss of postal deliveries en route to their destination was a frequent occurrence. The Franciscan Father General, Juan Merinero, reported that a bale of the *Opera omnia* of Scotus, 'work so lucid', was lost at sea on the way to Barcelona in 1640.[54] Produce travelled along 'the French isthmus', a corridor running from Marseille to Lyon, through Burgundy to Paris and beyond to Rouen.[55] Crucially for Jean-Baptiste Devenet, this route was interrupted in 1649 when he was unable to correspond with his representative in Marseille due to the outbreak of plague in the port city. For this reason, the transfer of volume seven in three bales for Wadding took ten months.[56]

In April 1651, Devenet sent Wadding propositions for his agreement assuring him that he would be pleased with the fine quality of the volume, requesting that Wadding give his permission to proceed via the Pizzenti.[57] As he had not heard from Wadding by the following year, Devenet notified him that he instructed the Pizzenti to withdraw the conditions of the contract. On Wadding's behalf, the Capuchin father Benoît de Montbrison

50 Ibid, 528.
51 Ibid, 524.
52 See Chapter 6 of the present work.
53 Ibid.
54 Jennings, ed, 'Some Correspondence of Father Luke Wadding OFM', 80–1.
55 Fernand Braudel, *The Mediterranean and the Mediterranean World in the Age of Philip II*, 2 vols (Berkeley CA, University of California Press, 1995), vol. 2, 1107.
56 Hazard, ed, 'Correspondence from Jean-Baptiste Devenet and Claude Prost, Book Merchants of Lyon, to Fr. Luke Wadding OFM', 524.
57 Ibid, 525.

restored Devenet's confidence, and he was therefore ready to proceed with publication. To overcome the difficulties of distance, Devenet retained the services of several representatives. Signori Piatti and Pizzenti conducted much of his business in Rome. Monsieur de Gartine took delivery of books in Marseille, while folios from volume seven of the *Annales* were forwarded to Wadding through a Roman courier named Signor Leymi. Devenet also acknowledged the help of a correspondent called Signor Ferrari Coro.[58]

The prefatory material of volume eight records that Pedro Manero gave permission at Ara Coeli to proceed with the final volume on 20 September 1651. The approbations by Bonaventure Barron and Francis Harold are dated 9 September that year and 21 August 1653. The Carmelite theologian, Juan Bautista de Lezana, provided the licence to print on behalf of Vincenzo Candido, master of the sacred palace, on 2 August 1653. Wadding and his associates in Rome were, therefore, ready much sooner than Devenet.[59]

According to a remark by Wadding, he wrote to Devenet on 9 May 1653.[60] In this letter, Wadding accepted the terms of the contract with the proviso that he did not want it printed like that of Claude Dufour, but in the same way as volumes six and seven. Wadding's notification must have crossed in the post with Devenet's letter of 15 May. This stated that the Lyonnais publisher had written to Wadding twice to know his decision about publication of volume eight but had received no reply. On 4 July, Devenet acknowledged receipt of Wadding's letter and said that he had sent the Pizzenti his terms for the contract, the same terms that Wadding had agreed to already. If Wadding was happy with the terms sent to the Pizzenti, Devenet requested that he reimburse them and, as was the case with volumes six and seven, volume eight would be published in eighteen months.[61]

The terms of this contract for publication stated that Wadding agreed to hand a clearly copied manuscript of the volume to Signor Pizzenti and at the same time, to make an advance payment of 200 Roman scudi.[62] He

58 Ibid, 528.
59 Ibid, 526.
60 Ibid, 525.
61 Ibid, 526.
62 Ibid.

agreed to take 200 copies of the volume, settling the remaining costs on receipt of them, paying for all customs expenses at Civitavecchia and Rome and the transport costs from Civitavecchia. Devenet was required to complete the printing within eighteen months, with the same paper, type and layout as volumes six and seven, to pay for delivery to Civitavecchia, to send forty copies as a gift to the author and, during the printing process, to send Wadding proofs for correction either by packet or by courier. Volume eight was, however, produced in folio by a Roman publisher, Giovanni Pietro Collini, in 1654. Printing offices depended on a small staff that often produced only a few books before going out of business. Collini published works from 1651 to 1656.[63]

Reflecting the recovery of Spanish influence at the papal court since 1650,[64] Wadding sought and obtained the approval of Philip IV, to dedicate the final volume to the 'Catholic King of Spain and Monarch of the New World, the most powerful leader of the world'.[65] Wadding's letter to Philip IV is printed at the beginning of the tome. The Franciscan chronicler and theologian recalled the historical memory of the king's forebears Ferdinand and Isabel, Manuel I of Portugal, Charles V and Philip II.[66] This reaffirmed the philosophical principle that monarchical authority should be supreme, with the ruler holding the right to revoke and issue all law, with the support of the nobility.[67] In doing so, Wadding encouraged the view that the most favoured were inspired by fear, love and worship

63 Ibid, 523.

64 Dandelet, *Spanish Rome, 1500–1700*, 202–214.

65 Wadding to Philip IV, St Isidore's, 9 August 1653 (UCD-OFM, D.26, folder 3), 'Philippo IV Catholico Regi Hispaniarum Novi Orbis Monarche In utro que orbe potentissime princeps'.

66 Wadding to Philip IV, 'Ferdinandi, Isabellae, Emanueles, Philippi, Caroli passim hic memorantur è maioribus tuis qui historiam istam'.

67 Allan Wolter, *John Duns Scotus' Political and Economic Philosophy* (New York: Franciscan Institute, St Bonaventure University, 2001), 14, 16; John Leddy Phelan, *The Millennial Kingdom of the Franciscans in the New World: A Study of the Writings of Gerónimo de Mendieta, 1524–1604* (Berkeley CA: University of California Press, 1956), 61.

to increase the kingdom of God by placing their authority at his service.[68] The Franciscan role in New World exploration and settlement during the reign of Charles V and the early sixteenth-century Reformation in Europe predominate in Wadding's eighth volume of his *Annales*, which dealt with the period from 1500 to 1540. Indeed, the New World leads the contents from the prefatory material onwards.

New World

On the authority of Francesco Gonzaga, Wadding stated that Christopher Columbus – 'a sharp-witted man' – navigated the West Indies with the help of a Franciscan friar named Juan Pérez who had once been confessor to Isabel I.[69] To encompass volume eight, Wadding chose two quotes from the prophet Isaiah for the title page: 'Sing a new song to the Lord and announce his praise in the islands', followed by 'Go swift angels to a people scattered and torn to pieces, to a terrible people after which there is no other, to a people expectant and trodden under foot'.[70] The title-page engraving shows Pope Alexander VI giving the Franciscans permission to preach the Gospel in the New World. When endorsed by the Crown, mendicant friars were capable of curbing human weakness among colonial

68 Wadding to Philip IV, 9 August 1653: 'Felix illos reges, qui suam potestatem ad Dei cultum maxime dilatandum, maiestati eius famulam faciunt: Deum timent, diligunt, colunt; et plus amant illud regnum, ubi non timebunt habere consortes'. This is a direct quote from St Augustine, *De Civitate Dei*, Lib. 5, Cap. 24; cf. Samuel Brandon, *History, Time and Deity: A Historical and Comparative Study of the Conception of Time in Religious Thought and Practice* (Manchester: Manchester University Press, 1965), 125.

69 *Annales Minorum* (1st edn, Lyon: Devenet & Prost, 1648), vol. 7, 278–279: 'vir acris ingeni'.

70 The former is from Isa. 42:10 (*Ponite Domine gloriam et laudam eius in insulis nunciate*), and the latter Isa. 18:2 (*Ite Angeli veloces ad gentem convulsam, et dilaceratam, ad populu terribilem, post quem non est alius, ad gentem expectantem, et conculcatam*).

administrators and represented the principal source of local opposition.[71] Wadding made it clear that candidates were selected carefully in the early days of missions to the Indies. Over a twenty-five-year period, Charles V of Spain repeatedly took an active role in ordering the friars to resolve difficulties and discord among the governors of the provinces, and remove the difficult burdens exacted upon the indigenous people.[72]

While his work on the liturgy depended upon a knowledge of Latin, Wadding specifically acknowledged the effort to teach and preach in local languages. When the Franciscans went to the New World, they were often involved in disputes with governors appointed by the king of Spain. Articulate, well-educated friars were, therefore, required by the order. Fr Jan Dekkers and Friar Peter of Ghent, a relative of Charles V, for example, learnt the language of the former Aztec empire before embarking on the provision of primary and secondary education. Besides the courses of study taught in each Franciscan province, a decree of the general chapter of 1633 provided for the foundation of language schools for the missions: one in Spain, another in Italy, a third in France, and a fourth for Germany and the Low Countries. Wadding's source appears to have been Gaspar de la Fuente, a friar who dwelt at St Isidore's College.[73] Teaching of the Immaculate Conception was endorsed at the 1633 general chapter. The uniformity of Scotist teaching was also preserved and, for this purpose,

71 David Lantigua, *Infidels and Empires in a New World Order. Early Modern Spanish Contributions to International Legal Thought* (Cambridge: Cambridge University Press, 2020), 84; Wadding's Castilian confrères of the Santiago province were responsible for missionary territory in South America.

72 Ibid, 52. For a specific example, see Juan Juárez and Zephyrin Engelhardt, 'Florida's First Bishop', *CHR*, 4:4 (1919), 475–485. See also Inga Clendinne, *Ambivalent Conquests: Maya and Spaniard in Yucatan, 1517–70* (2nd edn, Cambridge: Cambridge University Press, 2003), cited by Ethan Shagan, 'Early Modern Violence from Memory to History', in Micheál Ó Siochrú and Jane Ohlmeyer, eds, *Ireland: 1641. Contexts and Reactions* (Manchester: Manchester University Press, 2013), 25–26.

73 *Annales Minorum*, vol. 28 (1633), 35–36; Gaspar de la Fuente, *Historia del capitulo general, que celebro la religion serafica en la imperial Toledo este año de 1633 y accion de gracias de la religion a Dios* (Madrid: Imprenta Real, 1633), 73. On the significance of contemporary Franciscan translations, see John McCafferty, 'Franciscan Rules Printed in the Spanish Netherlands in the Seventeenth Century', *Canterbury Studies in Franciscan History*, 3 (2011), 199–226.

Wadding was entrusted with producing a complete edition of the *Opera omnia* of Scotus. The Immaculate Conception of the Blessed Virgin Mary was chosen as patron of the Franciscan order eight years later.[74]

Catherine of Aragon

As Henry VIII's first wife, Catherine of Aragon, was a Franciscan tertiary, Wadding discussed their divorce from a Franciscan perspective at some length. 'Tertiaries' were lay men and women who belonged to congregations of 'the Third Order' directed by a religious order in secular society.[75] Referring to 'Queen Catherine, the most well read and pious woman, Charles V's aunt',[76] Wadding cited Nicolas Herborn, Franciscan minister provincial of Cologne, who brought to print a book he compiled on the doubt and controversy raised by Henry VIII.[77] Wadding stated that Catherine was intact before her marriage to Henry and attributed the English schism to the 'amorous fury' of the king, to whom few learned men adhered.[78] On the contrary, Herborn 'constantly taught that [Henry's] marriage with Catharine was firm and legitimate, approved by the authority

74 Claus Andersen, 'Short introduction to a Long Tradition - and to This Volume', in Daniel Heider and Claus Andersen, eds, *Cognitive Issues in the Long Scotist Tradition* (Basel: Schwabe Verlag, 2022), 14.

75 See Alison More, 'Canonical Change and the Orders of the Franciscan Tertiaries', in Bert Roest and Johanneke Uphoeff, eds, *Religious Orders and Religious Identity Formation, ca.1420– 1620: Discourses and Strategies of Observance and Pastoral Engagement* (Leiden: Brill, 2016), 69–85.

76 *Annales Minorum*, vol. 16 (1531) 352, n. 9: 'Catharina Regina lectissima & piissima foemina, Caroli V amita'.

77 Ibid, 'Nicolaus Herbornus Minister Coloniae ad Pisottum missit librum a se compositum, & tunc impresum circa dubium & controversia ab Henrico VIII Anglorum Rege motam contra matrimonium'. This is a reference to Nicolaus Herborn, *Locorum Communium Adversus Huius Temporis Haereses Enchiridion* [Cologne: Peter Quentel, 1529], ed Patricius Schlager, *Corpus Catholicorum*, 12 (Münster: Aschendorff, 1927).

78 *Annales Minorum*, vol. 16 (1531), 352, n. 9: 'sui fratris Arthuri primum conjuge, sed intacta [...] Sed pauci viri docti eius amatorio furori adhaeserunt'.

of the Apostle [Julius II], after so many years of conviction, received by offspring, applauded by the whole world, without any protest, confirmed'.[79] Wadding reminded the reader that he enumerated Herborn's works in the *Scriptores ordinis minorum*.[80]

In a comparable way to his tribute for another Franciscan tertiary, St Elizabeth of Portugal, Wadding described the piety of Catherine of Aragon. He recorded that each day at the Franciscan friary next to Greenwich Palace, she got up at midnight to attend the choral prayers of the religious. The queen dedicated her first hours each day to devotion.

Wadding continued:[81]

> Under her royal robes, she wore the habit of the Third Order of St Francis. Every Friday and Saturday she fasted. On every Vigil of the feasts of Mary, she ate only bread and water, and every Wednesday and Friday she went to confession. She received Holy Communion every Sunday and feast day; prayed the Daily Office of the Blessed Virgin Mary [...] After dinner, she often read the lives of the saints for two hours and with her maids also present. Towards evening she went to church again and stayed there until her frugal supper. She always prayed kneeling without a pillow or any other thing between her and the bare floor.

Wadding closed his tribute: 'Who should wonder that this holy woman had to be tried by even greater tribulations, in order to spread the fragrance of her virtue throughout the entire world'.[82] The Franciscan chronicler then

79 Ibid, vol. 16 (1531), 352, n. 9: 'Herbornus, qui constanter docuit ratum firmum & legitimum fuisse eius cum Catharina matrimonium, auctoritate Apost probatum, tot annorum convictu, suscepta prole, orbe universo applaudente, nullo reclamante, confirmatum'.

80 Ibid: 'uti testantur varii illi tractus, quos in libro de Scriptoribus recensui'.

81 *Annales Minorum*, vol. 16 (1535), 447, n. 7: 'Sub regio vestitu, Divi Francisci habitu, ad cujus Tertium Ordinem sese adscripserat, utebatur. Omnibus sextis feriis & Sabbatis jejunabat, omnibus vigiliis beatæ Mariæ Virginis solo pane & aqua vivebat, quartis & sextis feriis peccata sacerdoti confitebatur. Dominicis etiam sumebat Eucharistiam; Officium beatæ Virginis quotidie recitabat [...] a prandio autem Sanctorum vitas, ancillis etiam adstantibus, ad duas sere horas legebat; inde templum repetens, ibi sere manebat usque ad horam cœnæ, quam sumebat longe parcissimam. Orabat semper flexis genibus, absque pulvinali, aut alia quampiam re inter ipsam & pavimentum interjecta'.

82 Ibid: 'Quis jam miretur, si tam sancta foemina, majori quodam tribulationis igne probanda fuit, ut virtutum odor in totum orbem Christianum facilius diffunderetur?'

shared letters exchanged between Catherine of Aragon, John Forrest, the queen's Franciscan confessor, one of her ladies in waiting, and Thomas Abel, her chaplain.[83] Among the religious orders, Wadding compared the English Franciscans to the Carthusians and Bridgettines for preserving the spirit of their founders.[84]

Ecclesiastical Exempla

Apart from historical writings, Wadding concentrated on hagiographical works in the 1650s. According to Francis Harold, Wadding treated Ilarione Rancati 'like a brother and willingly shared everything with him in confidence'.[85] For two years, they collaborated on publishing the Life of Blessed Nicolò Albergati in Italian, recently completed by Bonaventura Cavallo, Franciscan commissary general.[86] Albergati was a fifteenth-century Carthusian monk and cardinal archbishop of Bologna. Praised for his sanctity, he was regarded as a prince of the Church.[87] Since the Albergati were kinsmen of the Ludovisi family and Gregory XV, the book was dedicated to Niccolò I Ludovisi, prince of Piombino, a brother of Cardinal Ludovico Ludovisi.

Rancati's interest in the Life stemmed from the fact that Albergati's titular church from 1426 to 1443 was Santa Croce in Gerusalemme, where

83 Ibid, vol. 16 (1535), 451–454, n. 19–23.

84 Ibid, vol. 16 (1535), 445, n. 1. On the essential role of lay patrons in the much slower dissolution of the religious orders in Ireland, see John McCafferty, '*A mundo valde alieni*: Irish Franciscan Responses to the Dissolution of the Monasteries, 1540–1640', *Reformation and Renaissance Review*, 19 (2017), 50–63.

85 Harold, *Vita Fratris Lucae Waddingi*: 'neque cum alio libentius aut fidentius omnia sua communicabat'.

86 Giulia Spoltore, 'Luke Wadding, Ilarione Rancati e la famiglia Ludovisi per un'impresa editoriale: la *Vita del B. Nicolò Albergati* (1652–54)', forthcoming; cited by Spoltore, 'Luke Wadding and Scholars for the Arts in seventeenth-century Rome', in Binasco, ed, *Luke Wadding, the Irish Franciscans, and Global Catholicism*, 142.

87 *Historia vitae Beati viri Nicolai Albergati* (UCD-OFM, B.41, section IX).

Rancati served as Cistercian abbot in Rome.[88] Wadding wrote the *imprimatur*, the official licence authorising publication, on 10 January 1653, in conjunction with the Dominican, Vincenzo Candido, who wrote the accompanying licence. Innocent X consulted all three men on Jansen's *Augustinus*.

Candido commissioned Wadding to assess 'the holy life and heroic deeds of the great Cardinal and admirable Nicolò Albergati of the Holy Carthusian Order' by Cavallo, Wadding's fellow Franciscan.[89] Although Carthusian, Albergati was affiliated to the Franciscan order and, in 1322, the Albergati family dedicated a chapel to St Anthony of Padua in Bologna. The saint subsequently appeared on the coat of arms of Antonio Albergati, apostolic nuncio to Portugal, in the early seventeenth century.[90] For Wadding, Nicolò Albergati's involvement in politics and diplomacy was similar to his own. Reflecting the Irish friar's work for the hierarchy in Ireland, Albergati was also the ideal model of the pastor of souls who possessed the necessary attributes to care for his flock in keeping with Trent. In so doing, Wadding cooperated in bringing to print an exemplary work about the behaviour that bishops ought to adopt. From his perspective, abstract descriptions were inadequate compared to exemplary lives.

Wadding read the work 'with great pleasure' and considered 'that the propriety of the style corresponds to the dignity of the subject'.[91] Wadding continued: 'Nothing in this work is contrary to the faith, or contrary to

88 Bonaventura Cavallo, *Vita del B. Nicolò Albergati Card. di Santa Croce* (Rome: Vitale Mascardi, 1654), 14.

89 Ibid, Imprimatur by Wadding, unpaginated, 'Ex commissione Reuerendissimi P. Magistri Sacri Palaty Apostolici legi magna quidem voluptate vitam sanctam, & facta heroica magni Cardinalis & admirabilis serui Dei Nicolai Albergati sacri Ordinis Carthusiensis'.

90 Frater Petrus Manero, Minister Generalis, et Servus totius Ordinis Fratrum Minorum Seraphici P.N. Francisci. Eminentissimo Domino Dom Nicolao tit. S. Mariae Angelorum Card. Albergato S.R.E. Maiori Paenitentiario, 1651 (UCD-OFM, D.09, f. 397); *Annales Minorum*, vol. 6 (1301–22), 121–22, n. 53.

91 Ibid, 'Atque, ut ingenue proferam quod sentio, reputo argumenti dignitati respondere styli proprietatem'.

good morals'.[92] According to the Irish friar, Albergati was 'adorned with piety, sanctity, knowledge in government, prudent counsel, dexterity in business, integrity in his judgments, and endorsement of the Apostolic See by his zeal and piety'.[93] Indeed, Albergati compared well with the most distinguished of men for his 'integrity of life, eminence in doctrine, and illustrious skill in action'.[94] Wadding therefore judged the work most worthy.

From 1655 to 1657, the printer-bookseller, Nicolò Angelo Tinassi, worked in the service of Wadding. As the Irish friar neared the end of his life, the government of the Church continued to hold his attention. He often saved research for subsequent use and, on this occasion, had material relating to Anselm, bishop of Lucca.[95] This resulted from Wadding's studies concerning Gregory VII, the eleventh-century Church reformer.[96] According to Canice Mooney, Wadding may have identified with Anselm of Lucca as a fellow scholar and diplomat.[97] Anselm espoused the idea of Roman primacy in his diocese and Wadding may have seen him as a model for the clergy in the seventeenth century.

While preparing the text, Wadding mentioned codex manuscripts kept at 'the library of the Benedictine monastery of Mantua', which appears to be a reference to the monastery of San Benedetto di Polirone.[98] Here, Wadding recognised 'the most eminent Lord Francesco Cardinal Barberini, protector of the Benedictine order, 'for his old and special kindness' towards

92 Ibid, 'Parum itaque vel minimum dixero, si testimonium dumtaxat perbibuero, nihil in hoc opere contineri fidei, aut bonis moribus contrarium'.

93 Ibid, 'fuit ornatus, pitesanctimonia, in regimine scientia, in consilijs prudentia, in periculis conslantia, in negotijs dexteritate, in iudicijs integritate, & demumin promouenda, & sustinenda Sedis Apostolice authoritate Zelo, & pietate'.

94 Ibid, 'viri insignes, vita probitate, doctrine eminentia, rei agende peritia illustres'.

95 Edith Pásztor, 'Luca Wadding, editore della "Vita Anselmi episcopi Lucensis"', *AFH*, 54 (1961), 303–28.

96 Harold, *Vita Fratris Lucae Waddingi*, 29–30.

97 Mooney, 'The Writings of Father Luke Wadding OFM', 235–36.

98 'F.P. Lucae Waddingi ordinis Minorum ad sequentia opuscula praemonitio': 'Quae vero sequuntur opuscula, Arnoldus Uvion tribuit S. Anselmo (UVION in notis ad diem 18 Martii), eaque exstare, et Anselmo ascribi in codicibus praegrandibus membraneis bibliothecae coenobii S. Benedicti Mantuani testatur Possevinus' (*PL*, vol. 149, 567–569, col. 1853).

Figure 10.2 Altar-piece of the Immaculate Conception by Carlo Maratti, St Isidore's College, Rome. This work was completed six years after the death of Luke Wadding. Reproduced by kind permission of Collegio S. Isidoro, Rome.

him.[99] Following the exile in France of Antonio, Francesco and Taddeo Barberini from 1645 to 1647, the family's patronage in Rome was much diminished.[100]

Thus, on 13 April 1657, Wadding dedicated this, his final publication, to Marcantonio Franciotti. As bishop of Lucca from 1637 to 1645, Franciotti

99 Ibid: 'Eminentisimus dominus Franciscus cardinalis Barberinus, Benedictini ordinis protector, pro sua erga me veteri ac peculiari benignitate'. (*PL*, vol. 149, 567–569, col. 1853).

100 Haskell, *Patrons and Painters*, 59–60.

conducted a busy schedule of pastoral visits in his diocese. In line with the Irish Franciscan's interests and those of his friends in Rome, Franciotti consistently consulted with the Barberini cardinals and protected the Cistercian order.[101] After Francis Harold and Bernardine Barry examined the text at St Isidore's, Bartolomé de Villalba the Franciscan general procurator gave his approbation, and the book was published.[102]

Blessed Virgin Mary

Luke Wadding went to print with a set of three volumes in octavo on the baptism, death and redemption of Mary.[103] These were a concerted effort on Wadding's part, as shown by a letter he wrote to Ilarione Rancati on the subject.[104] All three volumes were produced in the workshop of Niccolò Angelo Tinassi. Together they illustrate how books were used by specific interest groups to further their objectives. The cause of the Immaculate Conception was characterised by periods of advocacy

101 Giulia Spoltore, 'Luke Wadding and Scholars for the Arts in Seventeenth Century Rome', 134, 143–44; Kathleen Comerford, *Reforming Priests and Parishes. Tuscan Dioceses in the First Century of Seminary Education* (Leiden: Brill, 2006), 94; Dario Busolini, 'Franciotti, Marco Antonio', in *DBI*, <https://www.treccani.it/enciclopedia/marco-antonio-franciotti_(Dizionario-Biografico)/>, accessed 23 September 2024; Kathleen Cushing, *Papacy and Law in the Gregorian Revolution: The Canonistic Work of Anselm of Lucca* (Oxford: Oxford University Press, 1998), 103–21.

102 Luke Wadding, *Vita S. Anselmi episcopi Lucensis* (Rome: Nicolò Angelo Tinassi, 1657).

103 Luke Wadding, *Immaculatae Conceptioni B. Mariae Virginis Non Adversari eius mortem corporalem. Opusculum* (Rome: Niccolò Angelo Tinassi, 1655); Idem, *De Baptismo B. Mariae Virginis* (Rome: Niccolò Angelo Tinassi, 1656); idem, *De Redemptione B. M. Virginis* (Rome: Niccolò Angelo Tinassi, 1655).

104 Spoltore, 'Una lettera di Luke Wadding ad I. R. sull'Immacolata concenzione', 551–556. See also Franca Trasselli, 'Ilarione Rancati "milanese dell ordine cisterciense", il collegio di studi e la biblioteca Romana di S. Croce in Gerusalemme', *Aevum*, 81 (2007), 793–876.

followed by periods of inactivity.[105] In this case, Spanish influence in Rome had begun to recover after a period of increasing French pressure. Thereafter, Wadding made a significant contribution to the Spanish campaign that led to *Sollicitudo Omnium Pastoralis*, Alexander VII's Apostolic Constitution, which expressed support for the Immaculate Conception and renewed the cause four years after Wadding's demise.[106]

This occurred after the duke of Terranova, Spanish ambassador to the Holy See, sent Wadding's *Immaculatae Conceptioni B. Mariae Virginis Non Adversari Eius Mortem Corporalem Opusculum* to Philip IV. Wadding had dedicated this volume to the king and referred the reader to the patronage of Antonio de Trejo nearly four decades earlier. The master of the sacred palace, Raimondo Capizucchi, had given the text immediate approval for publication. Terranova praised the book as 'written piously and eruditely in answer to an argument that the opponents used against the Immaculate Conception'.[107] Philip IV wrote to Wadding in appreciation of his zeal. In Madrid, the royal commission of the Immaculate Conception pointed out to the king how valuable Wadding's book was to obtain a declaration in favour of the doctrine. As such, they wrote to the Holy See asking Capizucchi not to impede its printing.[108]

105 Pérez Tostado, "Learned, Attached and Reliable': Luke Wadding, Agent of the Spanish Monarchy', 42; Broggio, 'Teologia, Ordini Religiosi e Rapporti Politici', 255–81.

106 See Broggio, 'Gli ambasciatori straordinari spagnoli a Roma per la definizione del dogma dell'Immacolata tra difesa delle prerogative episcopali, teologia e Ragion di Stato (1616–1661)', 247–254; Constancio Gutiérrez, 'España por el dogma de la Inmaculada: la embajada a Roma de 1659 y la bula *Sollicitudo* de Alejandro VII', *Miscelánea Comillas*, 24 (1955), 48.

107 Massimo Bergonzini, *Il culto mariano e immaculista della Monarchia di Spagna: l'ambasciata romana di D. Luis Crespi de Borja, 1659–61* (Porto: CITCEM Transdisciplinary Research Centre, Culture, Space and Memory, 2015), 93.

108 Ibid.

On the Moral Eye

In 1655 and again in 1656, Wadding organised the publication of a small duodecimo volume, *De oculi morali*, which he assigned to John of Wales, a thirteenth-century master at the Franciscan schools of Oxford.[109] John of Wales composed preaching aids,[110] and this may have led Wadding to his conclusion. The book was printed by Tinassi, this time in Viterbo. Wadding dedicated his tome to Archbishop Giulio Rospigliosi, future Pope Clement IX, which historians take as a sign of 'Wadding's own eye for influential contacts'.[111] Intended for the preparation of sermons by priests and bishops, this scientific treatise presented readers with up-to-date optical theories.[112] This was a popular book that sold in large numbers. The text has also been attributed to John Peckham, Duns Scotus and others, but is now ascribed to the Franciscan Peter of Limoges, a pupil of the natural philosopher Roger Bacon.[113]

109 Luke Wadding, ed, *De oculo morali, aureus libellus Joannis Gualensis Anglicii* (Viterbo: Niccolò Angelo Tinassi, 1655). This work was reprinted in 1656. A. G. Little, *The Grey Friars in Oxford. Part I: A History of the Convent, Part II: Biographical Notices of the Friars, Together with Appendices of Original Documents* (Oxford: Clarendon Press, 1892), 175.

110 Jenny Swanson, *John of Wales: a Study of the Works and Ideas of a Thirteenth-century Friar* (Cambridge: Cambridge University Press, 1989), 2–3, 227–28.

111 John McCafferty and Bernadette Cunningham, '*De Oculo Morali* – A Moral Treatise on the Eye', in Edel Bhreathnach and Bernadette Cunningham, eds, *Writing Irish History: The Four Masters and Their World* (Dublin: Wordwell, 2007), 125.

112 Jacques Berlioz, 'Eyes in the Back of the Head: Exempla and Vision in The Moral Treatise on the Eye by Peter of Limoges', in Herbert Kessler and Richard Newhauser, eds, *Optics, Ethics, and Art in the Thirteenth and Fourteenth Centuries: Looking into Peter of Limoges' Moral Treatise on the Eye* (Toronto: Pontifical Institute of Mediaeval Studies, 2018), 65–84.

113 Peter of Limoges, *The Moral Treatise on the Eye*. Translated with an Introduction by Richard Newhauser (Toronto: Pontifical Institute of Mediaeval Studies, 2012).

Our Lady of the Plain, Capranica

Near Viterbo, where a number of his books were printed, Wadding opened a new foundation for the Irish Franciscan province in the village of Capranica, which was the property of the Barberini family.[114] It was in May 1656, under the pontificate of Alexander VII, that Wadding obtained permission for a house of formation.[115] He was on friendly terms with the pope both before and after his elevation to the papacy.[116] Wadding saw the need for this noviciate because the profession of friars could not take place in Ireland since the disruption caused by the Cromwellian conquest.[117] Several places near Rome were offered to Wadding. Keeping in mind young Irish friars who had already gone to the continent and found the climate too inclement to study, the weather in Capranica was more temperate than Rome at certain times of the year.[118]

As a result, a church and unfinished buildings were granted to Wadding outside the western gate of Capranica.[119] These were previously in the hands of Italian Augustinian friars. In his new endeavour, Wadding benefitted from patronage provided by senior churchmen, such as the local bishop, Marcello Anania, Cardinal Archbishop Brancaccio and Prospero Fagnani.[120] Wadding placed the friary of Our Lady of the Plain, Capranica, under the immediate authority of the Franciscan minister general, on the understanding that half a dozen novices were to be received at first.

114 Harold, *Vita Fratris Lucae Waddingi*, 101. On the educational context, see Mary Ann Lyons, 'The Role of St Anthony's College, Louvain, in establishing the Irish Franciscan College Network, 1607–60', in Bhreathnach, MacMahon and McCafferty, eds, *The Irish Franciscans, 1534–1990*, 27–44.

115 Harold, *Vita Fratris Lucae Waddingi*, 101.

116 John McCafferty, 'Luke Wadding: A Life in and for Books', 115; Cleary, *Father Luke Wadding and St Isidore's College*, 46.

117 Harold, *Vita Fratris Lucae Waddingi*, 101.

118 Hazard, *Faith and Patronage*, 53. See also Thomas Flynn, *The Irish Dominicans* (Dublin: Four Courts Press, 1993), 106–7.

119 Giovanni Battista Balducci, *Cenni storici sul Santuario e Convento della Madonna del Piano in Capranica* (Rome: tip. del Senato di Giovanni Bardi, 1924), 15–16.

120 Binasco, *Making, Breaking and Remaking the Irish Missionary Network*, 155–56.

Aspirants from Ireland were to be prioritised and the appointment of guardian was to remain in the hands of the superiors at St Isidore's. Entrants at Capranica do not appear to have been governed by the same rules as friars at St Isidore's.[121] Maurus Matthews of Munster, a lector of theology who sat on the advisory council at St Isidore's, was appointed first guardian and re-elected for a second term of office.[122]

'Welcome, my Sister Death'[123]

On learning of his final illness, St Francis added the following words to his Canticle of the Sun: 'Welcome, my Sister Death'.[124] In keeping with this view of the soul's journey from the earthly life to eternal life, Wadding was aware of his own mortality.[125] Although in poor health for seven years, he dedicated himself to sedentary activities and remained vigorous in mind, governing St Isidore's for a year during the great plague of 1656, and attended all the community's meetings at that time.[126] Despite the epidemic in Rome, the college was unaffected under his direction. Seeing that his uncle did not have long left to live, Francis Harold feared 'the winter months, the equinoxes and all the changes the seasons'.[127] He spoke highly of a lay brother named Thomas of St Anthony who helped his uncle.[128]

121 Harold, *Vita Fratris Lucae Waddingi*, 101.

122 Cleary, *Father Luke Wadding and St Isidore's College*, 113, 216.

123 'Bene, veniat soror mea mors'; cited by Moorman, *The Sources for the Life of S. Francis of Assisi*, 19.

124 Wadding, *Opuscula*, 397–98; Augustine Thompson, *Francis of Assisi. The Life* (Ithaca, NY: Cornell University Press, 2013), 170.

125 Harold, *Vita Fratris Lucae Waddingi*, 139: 'Mortis praeparatio [...] semper quidem, sed peculiari attentione per septem prius annos dietim expectabat'.

126 Ibid, 138. See also Domenico Rocciolo, '*Cum suspicione morbi contagiosi obierunt.* Società, religione e peste a Roma nel 1656–57', in Irene Fosi, ed, *La peste a Roma* (Rome: Università Roma Tre-CROMA, 2006), 111–34.

127 Harold, *Vita Fratris Lucae Waddingi*, 138: 'imo menses omnes, praesertim hyemales, et aequinoctiales, et omnes mutationes temporum ipsi timesemo versabatur'.

128 Ibid, 138.

In Wadding's seventieth year of age, Rome was free from pestilence and, months before, he had handed over the administration of St Isidore's to John Heslenan as guardian with all necessary conditions in place. On 19 October 1657, Wadding attended a sermon at the Basilica of Santa Maria in Ara Coeli on the Capitoline hill. He did so out of respect for the preacher who had invited him, but caught a cold that became worse because he did not rest.[129]

As a consequence, Wadding developed symptoms of bronchitis and catarrh. Two days before death, 'a sudden and most violent tremor shook Wadding's entire body'.[130] Terrified, Francis Harold, who was attending to him, called out to the infirmary for help. Returning to himself, Wadding was exhausted. He had prayed for the grace to die with his senses intact and did manage to receive guests – friends, secular priests, prelates and cardinals – who visited him. Although weak, his voice was clear.[131] He asked his nephew to place an image of Mary, Mother of Jesus, before him for the purposes of prayer and contemplation.[132] Wadding then received confession, before calling together the college superiors to bid them farewell. After that, he received holy communion 'to set out for the unexplored journey' followed by anointing and his prayers.[133]

Ever the diplomat, Wadding remembered Francesco Barberini, who held office as Cardinal Protector of the Franciscan order. The college received his support during the pontificate of Urban VIII and the dedicated support of Cardinal Antonio Barberini. Thus, Wadding recommended that Francesco Barberini receive special consideration.[134] Nevertheless, Wadding commended St Isidore's to the patronage of Cardinal Marcantonio Franciotti and the Ludovisi family, entrusting the college to Alexander VII. Wadding then gave the names of those who would have responsibility for the college's interests at the Roman curia. These were the three Cardinals Giulio

129 Ibid, 139.

130 Ibid, 139: 'duobus ante mortem diebus, dum ego solus ipsi assissterem, invasit illum subitaneus et vehementissimus totius corporis tremor'.

131 Ibid, 138–39, 141.

132 Ibid, 141.

133 Ibid, 141: 'Post haec petit inexperti itineris Viaticum SS. Eucharistiae Sacramentum'.

134 Ibid, 142.

Rospigliosi, Prospero Fagano and Sforza Pallavicino, assisted by Wadding's loyal friend, the Cistercian abbot Ilarione Rancati, and the Oratorian Father Virgilio Spada, papal almoner. Finally, Wadding asked for the return of one or two books he had received to their rightful owners.[135]

Wadding's strength kept failing until Sunday morning, 18 November. He continued to recognise people and took in what they said to him but gradually stopped breathing and passed away peacefully.[136] When the physician opened Wadding's body about five hours after death, he found a stone in one of the kidneys which was significantly damaged. Inside the gallbladder, a stone the size of a hazelnut had caused Wadding stomach ailments. The neck of the bladder was corroded by acid.[137] Both lungs were 'in great part eaten away'.[138] In 1957, Dr Patrick Logan, a chest physician and medical historian, examined the post-mortem details recorded by Francis Harold. Logan confirmed that the final cause of death was 'a failing and enlarged heart' still full of liquid blood.[139]

Wadding was laid to rest in the common vault of the friars at St Isidore's. Clothed in the Franciscan habit, his body was visible in an open space at the friary during which time passers-by visited to pay their respects. On the Tuesday, he was brought to the church and buried the following day after Requiem Mass sung by the Dominican Giacinto Libelli, secretary of the Index and theologian at the papal court. The Master of the Dominicans, Gianbattista Marini, preached the eulogy at the funeral. Marini and Wadding had both studied at Salamanca and Alcalá in the 1610s.[140]

135 Ibid, 142–43.

136 Ibid, 143.

137 Ibid.

138 Mooney, 'Father Luke Wadding – The Last Years', 90; Patrick Logan, 'Medical History of Father Luke Wadding', *Journal of the Irish Medical Association*, 40 (1957), 175–78.

139 Mooney, 'Father Luke Wadding – The Last Years', 90.

140 Harold, *Vita Fratris Lucae Waddingi*, 143.

Conclusion

Rinuccini, Massari and Albizzi wielded considerable influence at the court of Innocent X and acted as the catalyst for open conflict between Wadding and his fellow friars. In the highly competitive surroundings of Rome, Albizzi and his ally Rinuccini shared an aversion for Protestantism. The links between Wadding and the Jansenists raised Albizzi's suspicions that Wadding was sympathetic to their cause and that the Irish friar showed, perhaps, a willingness to compromise with Ormond. Although Francis Magruairk was Wadding's most prominent opponent, he did not act alone and found particular support among his Irish confrères in Rome. Despite sympathising with the papal nuncio, however, Magruairk's activities played into the hands of the lord lieutenant, Ormond, by accentuating the disunity between the Irish Friars Minor. Wadding did not support the division of the Irish Franciscan province and, in accordance with his training, he recognised divine will in obedience to the authority of his superiors. This proved crucial to his survival because, combined with his persistence against bitter criticism, efforts to oust him from the college ultimately ended in failure. His death after Magruairk submitted his report in Madrid reveals the toll that these events took on the founder of St Isidore's.

The coming together of Wadding's eighth volume of the *Annales* and his works on the Blessed Virgin Mary echoed the resurgence of Spanish pressure groups in Rome during the early 1650s. Bringing the *Annales* narrative up to 1540 enabled Wadding to examine the Reformation from a Franciscan perspective, whilst also recording the organisation of the order's provinces in the New World, together with the institution of their Atlantic expeditions. Intervening events had delayed the completion of Wadding's work on the Immaculate Conception, but he retained a strong devotion to Our Lady and dealt with the subject decisively. In his last days, Wadding published books that would be helpful or necessary for readers, often due to a lack of supply.[141] This approach was apparent in the way Wadding catered for bishops' patterns of study in three volumes from

141 Ibid, 142.

1654 to 1657. Despite ill health, his role in providing a novitiate house at Our Lady of the Plain, Capranica, emphasises his lasting concern for the education of Franciscan friars in favourable surroundings. Additionally, Wadding retained his judgement to the end, as shown by the priority he gave to naming those who administered to St Isidore's future interests in accordance with his wishes.

Wadding's library holdings at St Isidore's contained seventeenth-century editions of Robert Bellarmine's work and among them, *The Art of Dying Well*.[142] As St Francis indicated, this was part of much older Franciscan thinking that helped Wadding to observe the priority he set himself in 1654, namely preparing his soul to live well and die holy. Wadding's conciliatory approach with the Dominican order typifies this development, thereby reducing the number of potential foes. Setting aside their view of excessive Franciscan zeal for the doctrine of the Immaculate Conception, leading Dominican friars celebrated the Requiem Mass and preached at Wadding's funeral.

142 See Robert Bellarmine, *Arte de bien morir* (Barcelona: Sebastian y Iayme Matevad, 1624).

General Conclusion

At the ordination of a Catholic priest, after the promise of obedience, the presiding bishop speaks these words: 'May God who has begun the good work in you bring it to fulfilment'.[1] In 1613, the bishop of Viseu, Dom João Manuel, spoke these words to Luke Wadding. In the ten preceding chapters, I have explored the depth and breadth of Wadding's life. In sharing the Franciscan inspiration to rebuild the chapel at San Damiano and save the Lateran from collapse,[2] Wadding fulfilled his office of building up the Church through the projects he initiated and managed.

Early influences precipitated Wadding's ability to relate to the outer world intellectually. From the Anglo-Spanish War to the recusancy revolt, Wadding was schooled in the upheavals that marked the political conditions of his day. Religious belief was central to the formation of his character and ambitions. From joining the friars, Wadding dedicated himself to his religious order. He first showed signs of leadership in Portugal when he was placed in charge of his fellow students at the Coimbra friary. From one area of interest to the next, Wadding remained attentive to his life as a Franciscan. In this view, from his education and the Franciscan institutions that he founded, to his many publications and the level of influence he achieved, Wadding owed his life's work to the religious order he loved and served for more than half a century.

1 'Qui coepit in te opus bonum, Deus ipse perficiat'. (Philippians 1:6); Erwin Iserloh, 'Martin Luther: The Early Years', in Hubert Jedin and J. P. Dolan, eds, *History of the Church: Reformation and Counter Reformation* (London: Burns & Oates, 1980), 14.

2 Armstrong, Short and Hellmann, eds, *Francis of Assisi. Early Documents*, 2, 249–50, 548.

In Waterford, at the end of an age, Wadding's literary gift and love of books, already apparent during his upbringing, prepared him for profound scholarship on the continent. He held that his departure from Ireland was essential for his spiritual growth and found refuge in the Seraphic Family. His enthusiasm to research St Francis' life and defend his name began in Portugal. It was there that he applied himself to the system of theology and philosophy he subsequently taught in Spain and Italy. While completing his formation as a friar, Wadding revealed the potential he went on to fulfil in many ways and, from that time, we notice how he himself saw his journey through life.

His training continued in Spain where the confidence and support of Antonio de Trejo helped to form Wadding in the Franciscan province of Santiago at Salamanca. There, he showed a capacity to build friendships and influence his peers in the exchange of ideas and information. This confirms the influence of Wadding's own formation on the four colleges in Italy and Prague, most notably in the primacy he gave to Scotus.

After acquiring St Isidore's in Rome, Wadding flourished as an educator and editor with an ability to organise a loyal following among prominent benefactors. At home in St Isidore's and in his work with the Holy Office, we see his humanity towards fellow scholars in the manuscripts he transcribed and translated, and the advice that he gave on historical and theological sources. Human excellence was a distinguishing feature of Scotist thought.[3] In the Baroque art and architecture that Wadding chose for St Isidore's, there was no place for mediocrity. The college became symbolic of reform and renewal, confidently announcing Wadding's authority among the Irish in Rome. Despite persistent claims that he favoured Old English and Munster interests, Wadding did not support the division of the Irish Franciscan province in two.

Wadding's contribution to papal administration led him to develop a significant interest in appointments to Irish dioceses. Bishops promoted to dioceses in Ireland from 1626 to 1642 were balanced between appointees from Gaelic and Old English backgrounds, as were the ordinations in Rome of Franciscans from St Isidore's during Wadding's tenure. Indeed, an analysis of

3 Campbell, *Renaissance Humanism and Ethnicity Before Race*, 31–33.

Wadding's role shows that he gave consistent support to Gaelic candidates in key positions. Moreover, a significant number of these episcopal assignments consisted of either regular or pro-regular clergy.[4] His influence as founder and patron in Rome, combined with the potential threat to his family's lands, explains his own reluctance to opt for either a bishopric in Ireland or an appointment as cardinal. He made extensive use of the printing press, not only for pedagogy but also to promote the interests of his religious order in the wider world. As was often the case, he benefitted from collaborating with confrères and many other scholars, such as Ilarione Rancati.

The organisation of the Franciscan publishing project and Wadding's selection of material to be produced reflects the two principal movements that took place in ecclesiastical history before and after the Council of Trent. First, Wadding nourished his research with works on faith and morals from the fifteenth century. Second, his own chronicles helped to defend Catholicism against external attack in the seventeenth century.[5] By securing a place for St Patrick in the universal calendar, Wadding successfully combined Gaelic and Old English interests in Ireland, within his own religious order and among the Irish abroad. Nevertheless, this unity was vulnerable and happened before the setbacks he experienced later in life.

Wadding's path as a friar was less travelled than that of his forebears but his decision to lead a religious life made a greater impact on history than the lawyers, landowners and merchants in his own family. By the 1630s, opponents of Wadding objected to his influence in Rome because he was a hindrance to their ambitions. Following the pro- and anti- nuncio split, matters worsened for him when he refused to comply with Ormond's wishes. Wadding's control of the office of guardian at St Isidore's ensured the college thrived in its first three decades. As other institutes of learning showed, the alternative was a lottery of guardians and inconsistent results that could have led to the college's demise. Wadding showed his wider

4 See John Bossy, 'The Counter-Reformation and the People of Catholic Ireland, 1596–1641', in T. D. Williams, ed, *Historical Studies VIII: Papers Read Before the Irish Conference of Historians, Dublin, 27–30 May 1969* (Dublin: Gill and Macmillan, 1971), 166.

5 Cf. Hubert Jedin, *A History of the Council of Trent*, translated by Ernest Graf, 2 vols (St Louis, MO: Herder Book Co., 1957–61), vol. 2, 58, 74, 144, 399.

allegiances on the commission revising the breviary of Urban VIII. The Irish friar certainly respected Cardinal Baronius as 'prince of Christian historians'.[6] Yet, far from sharing the cardinal's doubts about the Spanish Habsburg presence in Italy, Wadding underlined his abiding commitment to Spanish interests by supporting the full restoration of Santiago to the Roman breviary.

While taken up with the running of St Isidore's, the Franciscan publication scheme and his duties in the curia, Wadding still found time for Ireland. Across mid-seventeenth-century Europe, turmoil occurred between rulers and those they ruled.[7] From the 1641 uprising to the difficulties he faced at St Isidore's, Wadding witnessed the forces of provincialism at work, both in Ireland and among the Irish overseas. He was never simply a spokesman for confederate proposals.[8] Moreover, from the time of his appointment in 1642 onwards, a close examination of the correspondence indicates that Wadding only involved himself when asked to do so and that he participated less after the appointment of Rinuccini as nuncio. Considering Wadding's other commitments in Rome, this is understandable.

Wadding may well have encouraged Nicholas French and Nicholas Plunkett in their work, but they earned the rancour of Rinuccini by taking their case to Rome, as did Wadding by representing them.[9] In turn, Rinuccini provoked resentment by not acknowledging the traditional Old English role in the government of Ireland. By the end of the decade, Wadding had become preoccupied by these events. The handling of Ormond's letter at St Isidore's epitomised the distraction caused by eight years of war. The pro-Rinuccini party sought to discredit Wadding because the influence he exerted was an obstacle to their own intentions. Francis Harold's return to the college two years later helped to steady the ship. Wadding's life as a friar may have elevated him above politics, but it

6 Jennings, ed, 'Some Correspondence of Father Luke Wadding OFM', 69: 'christianorum historicorum principis Baronii'.

7 Geoffrey Parker, *Spain and the Netherlands, 1559–1659: Ten Studies* (London: Collins, 1979), 176.

8 Ó hAnnracháin, *Confessionalism and Mobility in Early Modern Ireland*, 58.

9 *Comment. Rinucc.*, vol. 4, 138.

did not make him immune to criticism or controversy. Acting on behalf of competing interests may have given him leverage in Rome, but therein lies the main political weakness in his commitments. Seventeenth-century thinkers attempted to balance contemplation with an active life and the authority that they held in office. This reflected Wadding's own conception of his role. In common with contemporaries such as Federico Borromeo,[10] he ventured to keep these two lives in equilibrium.

Wadding's attitude towards the Capuchins occurred in this setting and first emerged in relation to the Capuchin mission to Ireland. Despite their shared origins, the problems that Wadding encountered had lasting consequences. Following his initial decline, he made concerted efforts to improve relations but, by the 1650s, his most vocal critics were the Capuchin fathers, Richard O'Ferrall and Robert O'Connell. In comparative terms, Wadding reached an understanding with the Dominican order that led to meaningful expressions of support for the Immaculate Conception four years after his death.

In his theological studies, Wadding applied himself to three dogmatic debates from the time of his arrival on the continent. He experienced the famous Congregation of *De auxiliis* somewhat vicariously at the turn of the century, but learning its complicated lessons on grace and free will prepared him for the Jansenist controversy many years later. In the intervening time, his role in the doctrine of the Immaculate taught him that the papacy was not in the habit of making premature dogmatic declarations.

Towards the end of his life, Wadding narrowed his terrain and skilfully maintained influential patrons. He impressed upon them the significance of his educational establishments and employed his contacts to convince the papacy to secure the future of his colleges. In earlier decades, Wadding had willingly accepted Barberini patronage but did not allow himself to be defined by this relationship. As shown by Cardinal Marcantonio Franciotti, the provision of institutional patronage was intrinsically linked to the funds that Wadding raised for his publications. Wadding deferred to his superiors

10 Federico Borromeo, *Pro suis studiis*, Milan, Biblioteca Ambrosiana, Ms. G310inf, no. 8, 1628; cited by Pamela M. Jones, *Federico Borromeo and the Ambrosiana. Art Patronage and Reform in Seventeenth-Century Milan* (Cambridge: Cambridge University Press, 1993), 19.

to safeguard his position at St Isidore's. This was the case with regard to papal authority at the end of the *Augustinus* dispute and, later, when his Franciscan superiors cast doubt on his motives. In his last moments, he kept the Virgin Mary before his eyes and aimed at stability with a respect for tradition. His death marked the passing of a towering intellect in the field of theology and history. The Counter-Reformation infrastructure provided by his colleges, the successful completion of many written works, and his role in shaping the episcopacy of seventeenth-century Ireland contain the form and substance of all that Luke Wadding accomplished.

Select Bibliography

Guides

Bohatta, Hans, *Bibliographie de Breviére, 1501–1850* (2nd edn. Leipzig: Karl Hiersemann, 1937).

Burtchaell, G. D., and J. M. Rigg, eds, *Hist. MSS Comm. rep. on Franciscan Manuscripts Preserved at the Convent, Merchants' Quay, Dublin* (Dublin: Historical Manuscripts Commission, 1906).

Cappelli, Adriano, *Dizionario di abbreviature latine ed italiane* (repr. Milan: Ulrico Hoepli, 1990).

Donovan, Brian, and David Edwards, eds, *British Sources for Irish History, 1485–1641* (Dublin: Irish Manuscripts Commission, 1997).

Giblin, Cathaldus, ed, 'Vatican Library: MSS Barberini Latini: A Guide to the Material of Irish Interest on Microfilm in the National Library, Dublin', *Archiv. Hib.*, 18 (1955), 67–144.

Gilbert, J. T., ed, *Archives of the Municipal Corporation of Waterford, Report 10* (London: Historical Manuscripts Commission, 1885), Appendix v.

Grosjean, Paul, 'Catalogus codicum hagiographicorum latinorum bibliothecarum Dubliniensium', *Analecta Bollandiana*, 46, (1928), 81–149.

Lewis, C. T., and Charles Short, *A Latin dictionary founded on Ethan Allen Andrews' edition of William Freund's Latin dictionary* (Oxford: Oxford University Press, 1966).

Manuscripts of the Marquis of Ormonde, Preserved at the Castle, Kilkenny (London: HMSO, 1895–1899).

McGuire, James, and James Quinn, *Dictionary of Irish Biography*, 9 vols (Cambridge: Cambridge University Press, 2009).

Merland, Marie-Anne, with the collaboration of Guy Parguez, *Répertoire bibliographique des livres imprimés en France au XVIIe siècle*, XXVI: *Lyon, 5e partie: Justet-Pieldouce* (Baden-Baden: Valentin Koerner, 2004).

——— *Répertoire bibliographique des livres imprimés en France au XVIIe siècle*, XXII: *Lyon, 3e partie: Carret-Durelle* (Baden-Baden: Valentin Koerner, 1997).

Millett, Benignus, 'Guide to Material for a Biography of Father Luke Wadding', in Franciscan Fathers, eds, *Father Luke Wadding Commemorative Volume* (Dublin: Clonmore & Reynolds, 1957), 229–262.

National Library of Ireland Report of the Council of Trustees for 1950–51 (Dublin: National Library of Ireland, 1952).

Pou y Martí, José-María, and Luciano Serrano, eds, *Archivo de la Embajada de España cerca de la Santa Sede*, 4 vols (Rome: Palacio de España, 1915), 2 vols, *Indice analítico de los documentos del siglo XVII*.

Pubblicazioni dei Frati Editori di Quaracchi Fondazione Collegio San Bonaventura (Grottaferrata: Frati Editori di Quaracchi, 2011).

Manuscript Sources

France

Bibliothèque national de France, Paris

Fonds français (Pompone II de Bellièvre), MS. 15996.

Ireland

Irish Jesuit Archive, Dublin

- IJA/LIS/4; IJA/OLD/44; IJA/BKS/41.

National Library of Ireland, Dublin

- NLI Microfilm n.452, p.72.
- NLI Microfilm, n.461, p.81.
- NLI Microfilm n.5410, p.5541.

Royal Irish Academy, Dublin

- Ordnance Survey Collection for the County of Waterford, Inquisition, 9 February 1662, for lands forfeited in the county of Waterford.
- Taylor set of Books of Survey and Distribution, Waterford, 11, I.i.2.

Trinity College, Dublin

- TCD, MS. 1245.

Manuscript Sources (continued)

University College, Dublin

- UCD-OFM, MSS. volumes B.34–B.35; B.41; C.31; D.01; D.02; D.03; D.04; D.08; D.09; D.10; D.11; D.12; D.14; D.15; D.17; D.22; D.26; G.18; G.31.

Italy

Archives of College of Saint Isidore, Rome

MS. W16/13.

Biblioteca Apostolica Vaticana, Rome

- Barberini Latini, volume 1185, A.
- Barberini Latini, volume 6483.

Spain

Archivo General de Simancas

- Estado, legajos 191, 434.
- Estado Roma, legajos 3026, 3030.

Printed Primary Sources

[Published Documents and Correspondence]

A Praesentatione, Aegidio, *De immaculata beatae virginis conceptione ab omni originali peccato immuni libri quatuor, dicati sacrae maiestati Philippi III Hispaniarum regis* (Conimbricae: apud Didacum Gómez de Loureyro, 1617).

Aiazza, Giuseppe, ed, *The Embassy in Ireland of Monsignor G. B. Rinuccini, Archbishop of Fermo, in the years 1645–49*, translated by Annie Hutton (Dublin: Alexander Thom, 1873).

Aringhi, Paolo, *Memorie istoriche della vita del venerabile servo di Dio Pier Francesco Scarampi* (Rome: Stamperia Pietro Rosati, 1744).

Armstrong, Regis, William Short and J. A. Wayne Hellmann, eds, *Francis of Assisi: Early Documents*, 6 vols (New York: New City Press, 1999).

Barclay, Andrew, David Smith, Elaine Murphy, Jason Peacey, Joel Halcomb, John Morrill, Micheál Ó Siochrú, Patrick Little and Tim Wales, eds, *Letters, Writings and Speeches of Oliver Cromwell*, 3 vols (Oxford: Oxford University Press, 2022–23).

Barron, Bonaventure, *Annales Ordinis SS. Trinitatis Redemptionis Captivorum fundatoribus SS. Ioanne de Matha et Felice de Valois tomus primus primam centuriam annorum complexus hoc est ab anno Christi Domini 1198 ad annum 1297* (Rome: Angelo Bernabò, 1684).

Barry, John, and Hiram Morgan, eds, *Great Deeds in Ireland: Richard Stanihurst's De Rebus in Hibernia Gestis* (Cork: Cork University Press, 2013).

Bellarmine, Robert, *Arte de bien morir* (Barcelona: Sebastian y Iayme Matevad, 1624).

——— *Explanatio in Psalmos* (Rome: Bartolomeo Zannetti, 1611).

Bernard of Clairvaux, *Sermons for the Autumn Season*, ed Mark Scott (Collegeville MN: Liturgical Press, 2016).

——— *Devotissimi Bernardi liber de consideratione ad Eugenium papam explicit* (Rome: Facciotti, 1594).

Boverio, Zaccaria, *Annali de frati minori, tradotti in volgare da F. Benedetto Sanbenedetti*, 2 vols (Venice: Apresso I Giunti, 1643–1645).

Brewer, J. S., and William Bullen, eds, *Calendar of the Carew Manuscripts, Preserved in the Archi-episcopal Library at Lambeth*, 6 vols (London: Longmans, Green, Reader, & Dyer, 1867–73).

Britt, Matthew, ed, *A Dictionary of the Psalter containing the Vocabulary of the Psalms, Hymns, Canticles, and the Miscellaneous Prayers of the Breviary Psalter* (New York: Benziger, 1928).

Byrne, Niall, ed, *The Great Parchment Book of Waterford: Liber Antiquissimus Civitatis Waterfordiae* (Dublin: Irish Manuscripts Commission, 2007).

Callaghan, John, *Vindiciarum Catholicorum Hiberniae Authore Philopatro Irenaeo ad Alitophilum Libri duo quorum primus Rerum in Hibernia gestarum Synopsim, Secundus Libelli famosi in Catholicos Hiberniæ Proceres accuratam confutationem continet* (Paris: chez la Veuve Jean Camusat, et Pierre le Petit, 1650).

Calvar Gross, Jorge, José Ignacio González-Aller Hierro, Marcelino de Dueñas Fontán and María del Campo Mérida Valverde, eds, *La Batalla del Mar Océano: corpus documental de las hostilidades entre España e Inglaterra, 1568–1604*, 5 vols (Madrid: Ministerio de Defensa: Secretaría General Técnica: Turner, 1988–2015).

Camden, William, *Britannia: siue Florentissimorum regnorum Angliae, Scotiae, Hibernia, et insularum adiacentium ex intima antiquitate chorographica descriptio: nunc postremo recognita, plurimis locis magna accessione adaucta, et chartis *chorographicis illustrata* (Londini: impensis Georgii Bishop & Ioannis Norton, 1607).

Carranza, Bartolomé, *Controversia de necessaria residentia personali episcoporum et aliorum inferiorum pastorum Tridenti* (Venice: Ad Signum Spei, 1547).

Cavalli, Louis, *Scala Parnassi omnibus gradibus suis absoluta [...] opera et labore P. F. Ludovici Cavalli Minoritae Observantini Bolonien* (Lyon: Durand & Arnaud, 1640).

——— *Franciscias seu, D. Francisci Assisiatis vita* (Rouen: Laurent Maurry, 1634).

——— *Scala Parnassi seu syllabarum quantitas* (Rouen: Romain de Beauvais, 1633; repr. 1634).

Cavallo, Bonaventura, *Vita del B. Nicolò Albergati Card. di Santa Croce* (Rome: Vitale Mascardi, 1654).

Chadwick, Henry, ed and trans, *Saint Augustine. Confessions* (Oxford: Oxford University Press, 1991).

Clareno, Angelo, *Expositio Regulae Fratrum Minorum* (Ad Claras Aquas, Quaracchi: Typis Collegii S. Bonaventurae, 1912).

Comerford, Patrick, *The Inquisition of a Sermon Preached in the Cathedral Church of the City of Waterford in February 1617 etc. by Robert Daborne, by P.C.* (Waterford: Thomas Bourke, 1645).

Conrius, Florentius, *Tractatus de Augustini sensu circa beatae Mariae Virginis Conceptionem* (Antwerp: Jan van Keerberghen, 1619).

Corna, Andrea, ed, 'Alcune lettere inedite del P. Luca Vadingo OFM a Pier Maria Campi', *Bollettino Storico Piacentino*, 5 (1910), 208–16.

Cornelii Jansenii, Episcopi Yprensis, Augustinus, seu doctrina S. Augustini de humanae naturae sanitate, aegritudine, medicina, adversus Pelagianos et Massilienses tribus tomis comprehensa (Paris: Soly & Guillemot, 1641).

Cromwell, Oliver, *Letters and Speeches*, ed Thomas Carlyle, 2 vols (New York: Harper, 1855).

Curtis, Edmund, ed, *Calendar of Ormond Deeds, 1172–*, 6 vols (2nd ed, Dublin: Irish Manuscripts Commission, 1970).

Curtis, Edmund, and R. B. McDowell, eds, *Irish Historical Documents: 1172–1922* (London: Methuen, 1943).

D. Richardi Bellingi Vindiciae eversae per RP Fr. Ioannem Poncium, Ordinis Minorum [...] Et denique Doctoris Callaghani correctoratus Corisopitanus contra duas ipsius gallicas Epistolas, et Authorem libri gallici: l'Innocence & Verité défendues confirmatur (Pariis: apud Franciscum Piot, in Conuentu majori Fratrum Minorum, 1653).

De Bellegarde, Gabriel Du Pac, and Jean Hautefage, eds, *Oeuvres de Messire Antoine Arnauld, Docteur de la Maison et Société de Sorbonne* (Paris-Lausanne: Sigismond d'Arnay, 1779).

De Castro, Jacobo, *Árbol Chronólogico de esta Santa Provincia de Santiago*, 2 vols (Salamanca: por Francisco García Onorato y San Miguel, 1722; repr. Madrid: Editorial Cisneros, 1976–77).

De Castro, Manuel, *Crónica de la provincia franciscana de Santiago, 1214–1614. Por un franciscano anónimo del siglo XVII: Introducción, rectificaciones y notas* (Madrid: Archivo Ibero Americano, 1971).

De Civezza, Marcellino, *Storia universale delle missioni francescane*, 11 vols (Rome: Tibernia; Prato: Guasti; Florence: Ariana, 1857–95).

De Gubernatis, Domenico, *Orbis Seraphicus*, 4 vols (vol. 1, Rome: Typis Stephani Caballi, 1682; vol. 2, Lyon: Annisson, Jean Posuel & Claude Rigaud, 1685; vol. 3 Rome: Nicolò Angelo Tinassi, 1684; vol. 4, Ibid, 1685).

De Herrera, Francisco, *Manuale theologicum et resolutissimo dilucidatio principalium quaestionem, quae communiter in quatuor libros sententiarum disputantur [...] ab innumerius quibus expurgatum per Ludovicum Cavalli Minoritam* (Lyon: Jérôme Delagarde, 1642).

De la Cruz, Luiz, *Disputationes Morales in Tres Bullas Apostolicas, Cruciatae Defunctorum et Compositiones*, ed Luke Wadding (Lyon: Jacques Prost, 1634).

De la Fuente, Gaspar, *Historia del capitulo general, que celebro la religion serafica en la imperial Toledo este año de 1633 y accion de gracias de la religion a Dios* (Madrid: Imprenta Real, 1633).

———*Quaestiones dialecticae & physicae ad mentem syiubtilissimi doctorum Ioannis Duns Scoti, quas Roma legit* (Lyon: Jacques & André Prost, 1631).

De Ribadeneira, Pedro, *Tratado de la Religión y Virtudes que debe tener el Príncipe Cristiano* (Madrid: Pedro Madrigal, 1589).

———*Tratado de la Tribulacion, Repartido en Dos Libros* (Madrid: Pedro Madrigal, 1589).

De Sosa, Francisco, *Tomo primero de tratados y sermones de la limpia Concepcion de Nuestra Señora, sin mancha de pecado original, con seis tablas copiosas para predicadores y teologos* (Seville: Alfonso Rodriguez Gamarra, 1617).

Doctoris subtilis Johannes Duns Scoti, Quaestiones super libris Aristotelis de anima illustrate atque discussae per R.P.F. Hugonem Cavellum (Lyon: Claude Landry, 1625).

Enríquez, Crisóstomo, *Fasciculus sanctorum ordinis cisterciensis* (Cologne: Ex officina Coliniana, 1631).

Gavantus, Bartolommeo, *Enchiridion, seu Manuale Episcoporum, pro decretis* (Venetiis: apud haeredes Thomae Iunta, 1644).

Giblin, Cathaldus, ed, 'Documents on the Irish Trinitarians, 1621–71', *Coll. Hib.*, 27/28 (1986), 11–43.

Gilbert, J. T., ed, *History of the Irish Confederation and the War in Ireland, 1641–3*, 7 vols (Dublin: Irish Archaeological Society, 1882–91).

——— ed, *A Contemporary History of Affairs in Ireland from 1641 to 1652*, 3 vols (Dublin: Irish Archaeological Society, 1879–80).

Gordon, James, 'An Inventory of the Effects belonging to the Scotch Mission in Rome, and Confiscated by the French there in February 1798', *Journal and Appendix to Scotichronicon and Monasticon*, 1 (1869), 638.

Gori, Severino, 'Le lettere inedite di Luca Wadding ad Antonio Caracciolo e la riforma liturgica di Urbano VIII', *AFH*, 66 (1973), 118–19.

Green, R. P. H., ed and trans, *Saint Augustine. On Christian Teaching* (Oxford: Oxford University Press, 1997).

Hamilton, H. C., E. G. Atkinson and R. P. Mahaffy, eds, *Calendar of State Papers, Ireland*, 24 vols (London: Longman, Green, Longman, & Roberts, 1860–1912).

Harold, Francis, *Vita Fratris Lucae Waddingi*, 3rd edn. (Quaracchi: Ad Claras Aquas, 1931).

———ed, *Epitome annalium ordinis minorum* (Rome: Niccolò Angelo Tinassi, 1662).

Hartry, Malachy, *Triumphalia chronologica Monasterii Sanctae Crucis in Hibernia*, ed Denis Murphy (Dublin: Fallon, 1891).

Hazard, Benjamin, ed, 'Some Unpublished Correspondence of Luke Wadding OFM to Giovanni Pietro Puricelli, Archpriest of San Lorenzo Maggiore, Milan, and Pietro di Gallarà', *Seanchas Ard Mhacha*, 24 (2012), 29–45.

——— ed, 'A Manuscript Copy of the Declaration of Arbroath from the Roman Archives of Fr Luke Wadding OFM (1588–1657)', *SHR*, 90 (2011), 296–315.

——— ed, 'Correspondence from Jean-Baptiste Devenet and Claude Prost, Book Merchants of Lyon, to Fr Luke Wadding OFM, 1647–54', *AFH*, 104 (2011), 519–45.

———ed, 'Luke Wadding's Petition to the Papacy on Behalf of Dutch and Flemish Migrants in Waterford, c.1642–51', *An. Hib.*, 41 (2009), 1–12.

Herborn, Nicholas, *Locorum Communium Adversus Huius Temporis Haereses Enchiridion* [Cologne: Peter Quentel, 1529], ed. Patricius Schlager, *Corpus Catholicorum*, 12 (Münster: Aschendorff, 1927).

Hickey, Antony, *Expostulates Bzovius; seu Nitela Franciscanae religionis et abstersio sordium quibus earn consfurcare frustra tentavit Abrahamus Bzovius* (Lyon: Claude Landry, 1627).

Holywood, Christopher, *Defensio decreti Tridentini et sententiae Roberti Bellarmini* (Antwerp: Jan van Keerberghen, 1604).

Hudson, William, ed and trans, *Theatine Spirituality: Selected Writings with an Introduction and Notes*. Preface by Gigliola Fragnito (New York: Paulist Press, 1996).

Jennings, Brendan, ed, 'Some Correspondence of Father Luke Wadding OFM', *Coll. Hib.*, 2 (1959), 66–94.

——— ed, 'Ecclesiastical appointments in Ireland, Aug., 1643–Dec., 1649', *Coll. Hib.*, 2 (1959), 18–65.

——— ed, 'Theses Defended at St Isidore's College, Rome, 1631–49', *Coll. Hib.*, 2 (1959), 95–104.

———ed, *Wadding Papers, 1614–38* (Dublin: Irish Manuscripts Commission, 1953).

———ed, 'Miscellaneous Documents III, 1602–1715', *Archiv. Hib.*, 15 (1950), 1–73.

———ed, 'Miscellaneous Documents II, 1625–1640', *Archiv. Hib.*, 14 (1949), 1–49.

———ed, 'Miscellaneous Documents I, 1588–1634', *Archiv. Hib*, 12 (1946), 70–200.

———ed, 'Brussels MS. 3947: *Donatus Moneyus, De Provincia Hiberniae S. Francisci*', *An. Hib.*, 6–7 (1934), 139–186.

———ed, 'Documents from the Archives of St Isidore's College, Rome', *An. Hib.*, 6 (1934), 203–247.

Labbé, Philippe, *Elogia sacra, theologica et philosophica, regia, eminentia, illustria, historica, poetica, miscellanea* (Grenoble: Balleonius, 1674).

Labourt, Jérôme, ed, *Correspondance de Saint Jérôme: Lettres 1–22* (Paris: Les Belles Lettres, 2003).

Le Mire, Aubert, *Chronicon cisterciensis ordinis* (Cologne: Bernard Gualther, 1614).

Lombard, Peter, *De regno Hiberniae sanctorum insula commentarius*, ed Patrick Moran (Dublin: Duffy, 1868).

Lynch, John, *Cambrensis eversus, seu potius Historica fides in rebus Hibernicis Giraldo Cambrensi abrogata*, ed Matthew Kelly, 3 vols (Dublin: The Celtic Society, 1848–52).

Mac Cuarta, Brian, ed, 'Select document: Catholic ownership of tithes: a County Wexford widow's dispensation, 1595', *IHS*, 42 (2018), 336–344.

Manrique, Ángel, *Cisterciensium seu verius ecclesiasticorum annalium a condito Cistercio Philippo Magno hispaniarum regi. Auctore fratre Angelo Manrique, Burgensi, eiusdem regis à sacris concionibus [...] & in Salmanticensi Academia, scientiarum omnnium principe, sacrae theologiae primario antecessore*, 4 vols (Lyon: Boissat, Anisson & Devenet, 1642–59).

Marchant, Pierre, *Relatio veridica et sincera status Provinciae Hiberniae ordinis Minorum Regularis Observantiæ sub regimine F. Petri Marchant, Commissarii Generalis Nationalis super provincias Germanioe superioris, Belgii et Britannicas, ad Reverendissimum Patrem totius Ordinis Generalem necnon Rmos ac plurimum Reverendos Patres in Capitulo generali Romae congregatos hoc anno 1651 in festo pentecostes.*

Maziere Brady, William, ed, *Clerical and Parochial Records of Cork, Cloyne and Ross. Taken from Diocesan and Parish Registries, Mss. in the Principal Libraries and Public Offices of Oxford, Dublin, and London, and from private or family papers*, 2 vols (London: Longman, Roberts and Green, 1864).

McCaghwell, Hugh, *In quatuor libros sententiarum*, 2 vols (Antwerp: Jan van Keerberghen, 1620).

Memoires du P. Rene Rapin de la Compagnie de Jesus sur l'Église et la Societe, la Cour, la Ville, et le Jansenisme, 1644–69, 3 vols (Paris: Gaume frères et J. Duprey, 1865).

Merchants Aviso, or Instructions very necessary for their Sonnes and Servants, when they first send them beyond the Sea, as to Spaine and Portingale, or other Countries (London: John Bill, 1616).

Moryson, Fynes, *An Itinerary: containing his Ten Yeeres Travell through the Twelve Dominions of Germany, Bohmerland, Sweitzerland, Netherland, Denmarke, Poland, Italy, Turky, France, England, Scotland and Ireland* (London: J. Beale, 1617; repr. 4 vols Glasgow: J. MacLehose, 1907–8).

Moynes, Vera, ed, *The Jesuit Irish Mission: A Calendar of Correspondence, 1566–1752* (Rome: Institutum Historicum Societatis Iesu: 2017).

O'Ferrall, Richard and Robert O'Connell, *Commentarius Rinuccinianus de Sedis apostolicae legatione ad Foederatos Hiberniae Catholicos per annos 1645–49*, ed Stanislaus Kavanagh, 6 vols (Dublin: Irish Manuscripts Commission, 1932–49).

O'Rahilly, Cecile, ed, *Five Seventeenth-Century Political Poems* (Dublin: Dublin Institute for Advanced Studies, 1977).

Palocci, Benedetto, *Frutti serafici, ouero Laconismo delle vite dell' huomini piu illustri in santita, e dottrina. De' frati minori Capuccini, dall'anno 1525. Fino all'anno 1612* (Rome: Angelo Bernabò dal Verme, 1656).

Primera Parte de Sermones de la limpisima Concepcion de Nuestra Señora, Salmanticæ, predicados en el real convento de San Francisco de Salamanca y recogidos por el P. Fray Gaspar de Vigachoaca OFM (Salmanticae: apud Didacum à Cussio anno Domini, 1619).

Privilegia congregationis S. Maria de Alcobatia cisterciensis (Venice: Imberti, 1593).

Psalterivm Davidis, cum canticis sacris & selectis aliquot orationibvs (Antverpiæ: ex officina Plantiniana Balthasaris Moreti, 1657).

Puricelli, Giovanni Pietro, *Ambrosianae Mediolani Basilicae ac Monasterii hodie Cisterciensis Monumenta: quibus Historia Mediolanensis mireficè illustrata, multis ab erroribus vindicatur: Volumen Primum. Auctore Joanne Petro Puricello, Sacrae Theologia Doctore, Laurentianae Archipresbytero* (Milan: Typis J. P. Ramellati, 1645).

Relacion de las fiestas que la Vniversidad de Salamanca celebro desde el 27 hasta el 31 de octubre del año 1618 al juramento del nuevo estatuto hecho el 2 de mayo de dicho año de que todos los graduados defenderan la pura, y limpia Concepcion de la Virgen nuestra Señora, concebida sin mancha de pecado original. Ordenada por mandado y comission de la mesma Vniuersidad, en su Claustro Pleno (Salamanca: Antonia Ramirez viuda, 1618).

Relacion de las famosas fiestas que se hizieron en la Vniuersidad de Alcala de Henares, despues de auer hecho voto de guardar y tener en ella el Sacrosancto Misterio de la Inmaculada Concepcion: lleua al fin tres cartas, la vna del Obispo de Osma, Francisco de Sosa al padre fray Antonio de Trejo, General de toda la orden de San Francisco, donde da cuenta de su viage a Roma (Alcalá de Henares: Viuda y herederos de Juan Gracián, 1617).

Rochford, Robert, *The Life of the Glorious Bishop S. Patricke Apostle and Primate of Ireland, Together With the Lives of the Holy Virgin S. Bridgit and of the Glorious Abbot Saint Columbe Patrons of Ireland* (Saint-Omer: for Iohn Heigham, 1625).

Rusca, Roberto, *Origine del sacro ordine Cisterciense* (Milan: Paganello, 1598).

Salas, Fernando Herrero, ed, *Actas Capitulares del Cister en el Monasterio de Palazuelos*, (Madrid: Bubok s.l., 2015).

Sbaraglia, Giovanni Giacinto, ed, *Bullarium franciscanum*, 4 vols (Rome: De Propaganda Fide, 1759–68).

Simington, Robert, ed, *Civil Survey A.D. 1654–56, County of Waterford*, 6 vols, with appendices (Dublin: Irish Manuscripts, 1942).

Spoltore, Giulia, ed, 'Una lettera di Luke Wadding ad Ilarione Rancati sull'Immacolata Concezione', *AFH*, 111 (2018), 551–556.

Stafford, Thomas, *Pacata Hibernia: or, a History of the Wars in Ireland, during the Reign of Queen Elizabeth especially within the Province of Munster under the Government of Sir George Carew*, edited with an introduction and notes by Standish O'Grady (London: Downey, 1896).

Statuta, constitutiones et decreta generalis pro hac Cismontana, Familia Ordinis Minorum [...] in Generali Capitulo Pentecostes Salmanticae in conventu S. Francisci, Provinciae S. Iacobi celebrato (Madrid: Ludovicus Sanctius, 1618).

Suárez, Francisco, *Opera omnia* (Madrid: Typ. Regia, 1599).

The history of the angelicall virgin glorious S. Clare dedicated to the Queen's most excellent majesty. Extracted out of the R.F. Luke Wadding his Annalls of the Freer Minors chiefly by Francis Hendricq and now donne into English. By Sister Magdalen Augustine, of the holy order of the Poore Clarcs [sic] in Aire (Douai: Martin Bocart, 1635).

The Irish fiants of the Tudor sovereigns: during the reigns of Henry VIII, Edward VI, Philip & Mary, and Elizabeth I / with a new introduction by Kenneth Nicholls and preface by Tomás G. Ó Canann (Dublin: De Burca, 1994).

The Register of St Saviour's Chantry of Waterford: Registrum Cantariae S. Salvatoris Waterfordensis, British Library, Harleian MS 3765, translated and edited by Niall Byrne with Michael Byrne; revised by Kenneth Nicholls (Dublin: Irish Manuscripts Commission, 2013).

Tratados del Illustrissimo y Reverendissimo Señor Don Fr. Francisco De Sosa: Hijo De La Santa Provincia De Santiago y del Convento de S. Francisco De Salamanca; General de toda la Orden, Obispo de Canarias, Osma y Segovia, del Consejo de su Magestad, en el Real Supremo de la Sancta General Inquisición (Salamanca: Antonio Vázquez, 1623).

Wadding, Luke, *Annales Minorum seu trium Ordinum a S. Francisco institutorum, ab anno 1541 continuati a pluribus viris eruditis*, 3rd edn. 32 vols (Quaracchi, 1931–64).

——— *Scriptores ordinis minorum. Quibus accessit syllabus illorum, qui ex eodem Ordine pro fide Christi fortiter occubuerunt [...]* (*Editio novissima*, Rome: Attilio Nardecchia, 1906).

——— *Vita S. Anselmi episcopi Lucensis* (Rome: Nicolò Angelo Tinassi, 1657).

———*De Baptismo B.M. Virginis* (Rome: Niccolò Angelo Tinassi, 1656).

———*De Redemptione B.M. Virginis* (Rome: Niccolò Angelo Tinassi, 1656).

———*De Morte B. Mariae Virginis: Immaculatae Conceptioni B.V.M. non adversari eius mortem corporalem* (Rome: Niccolò Angelo Tinassi, 1655).

———ed, *De oculo morali, aureus libellus Joannis Gualensis Anglicii* (Viterbo: Niccolò Angelo Tinassi, 1655).

——— ed, *Vita et res gestae B. Jacobi Piceni, per Johan Baptist Petruccium* (Lyon: Laurent Durand, 1641).

——— *Apologeticus de Praetenso Monachatu Augustinano Sancti Francisci in Quo Deleguntur, et Rebelluntur Varii Errares Ex Hoc una Controversia Exanti* (1641 edn, Lyon: Laurent Durand).

——— *Vita et Res Gestae B. Jacobi Piceni, Per Johan Baptist Petruccium Scripta Notis et Commentariis Illustravit L. Waddingus* (Lyon: Laurent Durand, 1641).

——— *Respuesta apologética contra los que pretenden aver sido N. P. S. Francisco frayle de los Ermitaños de S. Agustín* (Madrid: En la Imprenta Real, Por doña Teresa Junta, impressora del Rey N. S., 1625).

——— *Presbeia sive legatio Philippi III. et IV. Catholicorum regum Hispaniarum ad SS. DD. NN. Paulum PP. V. et Gregorium XV. de definienda controversia immaculatae conceptionis B. Virginis Mariae, per illustriss. et reverendiss. Dom. D. Fr. Antonium a Trejo [...] Descripta ac concinnata per P. Fr. Lucam Waddingum [...]* (Leuven: Henrick van Hastens, 1624).

——— *Illustre Martyrium XIV Fratrum Minorum ab Haereticis Bohemis Pragae pro Fide Catholica occisorum* (Vienna: Matthäus Formica, 1624).

——— *Beati Patris Francisci Assisiatis Opuscula* (Antwerp: Balthasar Moretus I, 1623).

——— *De Hebraicae linguae origine, praestantia et utilitate ad sacrarum literarum studiosos interpretes, opusculum* (Rome: Stefano Paolino, 1621).

Wadding, Peter, *Tractatus de Incarnatione Rev. P. Petri Wadingi, Waterfordiensis Hiberi S.J., S. Theologiae Doctoris, olim in Lovainensi nunc in Pragensi Academia Professoris* (Antwerp: Martinus Nutius, 1635).

Walsh, Peter, *The History and Vindication of the Loyal Formulary, Or Irish Remonstrance, So Graciously Received by His Majesty Anno 1661* (London: n. p., 1674).

Ware, James, *De Scriptoribvs Hiberniae. Libri Dvo Prior continet Scriptores, in Hibernia natos. Posterior, Scriptores alios, qui in Hibernia munera aliqua obierunt* (Dublin: Typographia Societatis Bibliopolarum, 1639).

Wood, Anthony, *Athenæ Oxonienses: An Exact History of all the Writers and Bishops who have had their Education in the University of Oxford. To which are added the Fasti, or Annals of the said University*, ed Philip Bliss, 4 vols (London: Rivington, 1813–20).

Secondary Works

Abad Castro, Concepción, and María Luisa Martín Ansón, *Estudio histórico-artístico del convento de San Francisco el Real de Salamanca, panteón de la nobleza de*

Salamanca (Madrid: Ediciones de la Universidad Autónoma de Madrid: Asociación Hispánica de Estudios Franciscanos, 2013).

Adam, Renaud, Ann Kelders, Claude Sorgeloos and David Shaw, eds, *Urban Networks and the Printing Trade in Early Modern Europe (15th-18th Century)* (Brussels: Consortium of European Research Libraries and Royal Library of Belgium, 2010).

Agamben, Giorgio, *The Highest Poverty: Monastic Rules and Form-of-Life*, translated by Adam Kotsko (Stanford, California: Stanford University Press, 2013).

Alberzoni, Maria Pia, and Alfredo Lucioni, eds, *Milano, papato e impero in età medievale: raccolta di studi* (Milan: Vita e Pensiero, 2003).

Almeida Marado, Catarina, *Arquitetura conventual e cidade medieval: a formação e os impactos dos sistemas urbanísticos mendicantes em Portugal: séc. XIII-XV* (Coimbra: Imprensa da Universidade de Coimbra, 2018).

Alzina, José Pablo, *Embajadores de España en Londres: Retratos de la Embajada de España* (Madrid: Ministerio de Asuntos Exteriores, 2001).

Anselmi, Alessandra, *L'Immacolta nei Rapporti tra l'Italia e la Spagna* (Rome: De Luca Editori, 2008).

Asch, Ronald G., and Adolf M. Birke, eds, *Princes, Patronage, and the Nobility: The Court at the Beginning of the Modern Age c.1450–1650* (Oxford: Oxford University Press, 1991).

Askew, Pamela, 'The Angelic Consolation of St Francis of Assisi in Post-Tridentine Italian Painting', *Journal of the Warburg and Courtauld Institutes*, 32 (1969), 280–306.

Assmann, Aleida, *Cultural Memory and Western Civilization: Functions, Media, Archives* (Cambridge: Cambridge University Press, 2009).

Assmann, Jan, *Cultural Memory and Early Civilization: Writing, Remembrance, and Political Imagination* (Cambridge: Cambridge University Press, 2011).

Aznar Grasa, José Manuel, 'La ilustración del libro impreso en Salamanca: Siglos XV y XVI. Análisis cuantitativo y temático', in Pedro Manuel Cátedra García and María Luisa López-Vidriero Abello, eds, *El libro antiguo español: actas del Segundo Coloquio Internacional, Madrid* (Salamanca & Madrid: Ediciones de la Universidad de Salamanca, Biblioteca Nacional de Madrid, Sociedad Española de Historia del Libro, 1992), 61–95.

Baetens, Roland, 'The organization and effects of Flemish privateering in the seventeenth century', *Acta historiae neerlandicae*, 9 (1977), 54–62.

Bagwell, Richard, *Ireland under the Stuarts and during the Interregnum*, 3 vols (London: Longmans, Green & Co., 1909–1916).

Balducci, Giovanni Battista, *Cenni storici sul Santuario e Convento della Madonna del Piano in Capranica* (Rome: tip. del Senato di Giovanni Bardi, 1924).

Balić, Charles, 'The Mediaeval Controversy over the Immaculate Conception up to the Death of Scotus', in Edward O'Connor, ed, *The Dogma of the Immaculate Conception, History and Significance* (Notre Dame, IN: University of Notre Dame Press, 1958), 161–211.

——— 'Wadding the Scotist', in Franciscan Fathers, eds, *Luke Wadding Commemorative Volume* (Dublin: Clonmore & Reynolds, 1957), 463–507.

Barbier, Frédéric, *Gutenberg's Europe: the Book and the Invention of Western Modernity*, translated by Jean Birrell (Cambridge: Polity Press, 2017).

Bates, Ernest, *Touring in 1600: A Study in the Development of Travel as a Means of Education* (London: Houghton Mifflin, 1911; repr. London: Century, 1987).

Batiffol, Pierre, *History of the Roman Breviary,* translated by Atwell Baylay (London: Longmans, Green & Co., 1912).

Bäumer, Suitbert, *Histoire du Bréviaire,* translated by Réginald Biron, 2 vols (Paris: Letouzey et Ané, 1905).

Beckett, J. C., *The Making of Modern Ireland, 1603–1923* (New York: Alfred Knopf, 1966).

Belda Plans, Juan, *La Escuela de Salamanca: La renovación de la teología en el siglo XV* (Madrid: Biblioteca de Autores Cristianos, 2000).

Bellardini, Donatella, and Claudia Costacurta, 'The Development of Libraries in the Seventeenth Century. Luke Wadding's Library', in Matteo Binasco, ed, *Luke Wadding, the Irish Franciscans, and Global Catholicism* (Abingdon: Routledge, 2020), 95–107.

Benfatti, Solanus, 'The Testimonies of Brother Leo Pertaining to La Verna and the Stigmata of Francis of Assisi', in Mario Panconi and Andreea Chiricheş, eds, *Studi Francescani*, 121 (2024), 395–412.

Bennett, Jill, 'Stigmata and Sense Memory: St Francis and the Affective Memory', *Art History*, 24 (2001), 1–16.

Bérenger, Jean, *A History of the Habsburg Empire, 1273–1700*, translated by C. A. Simpson (London: Longman, 1994).

Bergin, Joseph, *The Politics of Religion in Early Modern France* (New Haven CT: Yale University Press, 2014).

——— 'The Europe that the Earls Encountered', in Thomas O'Connor and Mary Ann Lyons, eds, *The Ulster Earls and Baroque Europe* (Dublin: Four Courts Press, 2010), 5–17.

——— *Church, Society and Religious Change in France, 1580–1730* (New Haven, CT: Yale University Press, 2009).

——— 'The Counter-Reformation Church and its Bishops', *P&P*, 165 (1999), 30–73.

——— *The Rise of Richelieu* (Manchester: Manchester University Press, 1997).

——— *The Making of the French Episcopate, 1589–1661* (New Haven CT: Yale University Press, 1996).

——— 'Between Estate and Profession: the Catholic Parish Clergy of Early Modern Western Europe', in Michael Bush, ed, *Social Orders and Social Classes in Europe Since 1500* (Abingdon: Routledge, 1992), 66–85.

Bergonzini, Massimo, *Il culto mariano e immaculista della Monarchia di Spagna: l'ambasciata romana di D. Luis Crespi de Borja, 1659–61* (Porto: CITCEM Transdisciplinary Research Centre, Culture, Space and Memory, 2015).

Berlioz, Jacques, 'Eyes in the Back of the Head: Exempla and Vision in The Moral Treatise on the Eye by Peter of Limoges', in Herbert Kessler and Richard Newhauser, eds, *Optics, Ethics, and Art in the Thirteenth and Fourteenth Centuries: Looking into Peter of Limoges' Moral Treatise on the Eye* (Toronto: Pontifical Institute of Mediaeval Studies, 2018), 65–84.

Berlis, Angela, and Dick Schoon, 'Jansenism Across the Border: The interaction in the seventeenth and eighteenth century between Catholic theologians in France and in the Dutch Republic', *Internationale Kirchliche Zeitschrift*, 99 (2009), 145–69.

Bhreathnach, Edel, 'Luke Wadding (1588–1657): The Only Irishman to Receive Votes in a Papal Conclave', *History Ireland*, 15 (2007), 12–13.

Bihl, Michael, 'Tabula chronologica variarum editionum Annalium Minorum a Luca Waddingo aliisque conscriptorum', *AFH*, 28 (1935), 579–82.

Bilinkoff, Jodi, *Related Lives: Confessors and their Female Penitents, 1450–1750* (Ithaca NY: Cornell University Press, 2018).

Binasco, Matteo, and Hannah Thomas, 'Missionary Activity and Religious Houses', in James E. Kelly and John McCafferty, eds, *The Oxford History of British and Irish Catholicism*, 5 vols (Oxford: Oxford University Press, 2023), vol. 2, *Uncertainty and Change, 1641–1745*, 17–35.

——— ed, *Luke Wadding, the Franciscans and Global Catholicism* (Abingdon: Routledge, 2020).

——— 'Not Only a "Hibernese" in the *Urbs*. Luke Wadding and His Entourage in Seventeenth Century Rome', in idem, ed, *Luke Wadding, the Irish Franciscans and Global Catholicism* (Abingdon: Routledge, 2020), 77–92.

——— *Breaking and Remaking the Irish Missionary Network: Ireland, Rome and the West Indies in the Seventeenth Century* (Cham: Springer, 2020).

——— ed, *Rome and Irish Catholicism in the Atlantic World, 1622–1908* (Basingstoke: Palgrave Macmillan, 2019).

——— 'The Irish Community in Rome, 1377–1870: a Historiographical Overview', *Archiv. Hib.*, 71 (2018), 147–57.

——— '"A powerful Hibernese": Luke Wadding and his Diplomatic Role in Seventeenth-Century Rome', *Revue d'Histoire Ecclésiastique*, 112 (2017), 169–184.

——— 'Luke Wadding and Irish Diplomatic Activity in Seventeenth-Century Rome', *Studi Irlandesi*, 6 (2016), 193–203.

——— 'Gli esuli irlandesi nella Roma del seicento', *Bollettino della Società di Studi Valdesi*, 214 (2014), 79–115.

——— 'Few, Uncooperative, and Endangered: The Activity of the Irish Catholic Priests in the West Indies of the Seventeenth Century, 1638–68', in Igor Pérez Tostado and Enrique García Hernán, eds, *Irlanda y el Atlántico Ibérico: Movilidad, Participación e Intercambio Cultural* (Valencia: Albatros, 2010), 211–223.

Binasco, Matteo, and Vera Orschel, eds, 'Prosopography of Irish Students admitted to the Irish College, Rome, 1628–1798 (with Index)', *Archiv. Hib.*, 66 (2013), 16–62.

Bireley, Robert, *The Refashioning of Catholicism, 1450–1700. A Reassessment of the Counter-Reformation* (London: Macmillan, 2015).

Boehner, Philotheus, 'Three sums of logic attributed to William of Ockham', *Franciscan Studies*, 11 (1951), 173–193.

Bonner, Anthony, ed and trans, *Doctor Illuminatus: A Ramon Llull Reader*, with a new translation of *The Book of the Lover and the Beloved* by Eve Bonner (Princeton NJ: Princeton University Press, 1993).

Bossy, John, 'The Character of Elizabethan Catholicism', in Trevor Aston, ed, *Crisis in Europe, 1560–1660* (repr. Abingdon: Routledge, 2013), 223–246.

——— 'The Counter-Reformation and the People of Catholic Europe', in David Martin Luebke, ed, *The Counter-Reformation: The Essential Readings* (Malden MA: Blackwell, 1999), 86–104.

——— *Christianity in the West, 1400–1700* (Oxford: Oxford University Press, 1985).

——— 'Blood and Baptism: Kinship, Community and Christianity in Western Europe from the Fourteenth to the Seventeenth Centuries', *Studies in Church History*, 10 (1973), 129–143.

——'The Counter-Reformation and the People of Catholic Ireland, 1596–1641', in T. D. Williams, ed, *Historical Studies VIII: Papers Read Before the Irish Conference of Historians, Dublin, 27–30 May 1969* (Dublin: Gill and Macmillan, 1971), 155–169.

Boucher, Bruce, *Italian Baroque Sculpture* (London: Thames and Hudson, 1998).

Bouza Álvarez, Fernando Jesús, *Felipe II y el Portugal dos povos: imágenes de esperanza y de revuelta* (Valladolid: Ediciones Universidad de Valladolid, 2010).

Bowen, Karen Lee, and Dirk Imhof, eds, *The Illustration of Books Published by the Moretuses* (Antwerp: Plantin-Moretus Museum, 1997).

—— *Christopher Plantin and Engraved Book Illustrations in Sixteenth-Century Europe* (Cambridge: Cambridge University Press, 2008).

Boy, Michel, and Jean-Louis Boithias, *Moulins, papiers et papetiers d'Auvergne, Livradois-Forez, Ambert, Richard-de-Bas* (Champétières: Éditions des Monts d'Auvergne, 2013).

Bradshaw, Brendan, 'The English Reformation and Identity Formation in Ireland and Wales', in Brendan Bradshaw and Peter Robertson, eds, *British Consciousness and Identity: The Making of Britain, 1533–1707* (Cambridge: Cambridge University Press, 2004), 43–65.

—— *The Dissolution of the Religious Orders in Ireland under Henry VIII* (repr. Cambridge: Cambridge University Press, 2008).

Braudel, Fernand, *The Mediterranean and the Mediterranean world in the Age of Philip II*, 2 vols (Berkeley CA, University of California Press, 1995).

Bravo Lozano, Cristina, *Spain and the Irish Mission, 1609–1707* (Abingdon: Routledge, 2018).

Breathnach, Pádraig A., 'An Irish Bollandus: Fr Hugh Ward and the Louvain Hagiographical Enterprise', *Éigse*, 31 (1999), 1–30.

Broggio, 'Teologia, Ordini Religiosi e Rapporti Politici: La Questione Dell'Immacolata Concezione di Maria tra Roma e Madrid (1614–63)', *Hispania Sacra*, 61 (2013), Extra I, 255–281.

——'Gli ambasciatori straordinari spagnoli a Roma per la definizione del dogma dell'Immacolata tra difesa delle prerogative episcopali, teologia e Ragion di Stato (1616–1661)', in Flavia Tudini, Manfredi Merluzzi and Gaetano Sabatini, eds, *La Vergine contesa. Roma, l'Immacolata Concezione e l'universalismo della Monarchia Cattolica* (secc. XVII-XIX) (Rome: Viella Libreria Editrice, 2022), 237–264.

——'Un Teologo Irlandese nella Roma del Seicento: il francescano Luke Wadding', *Roma Moderna e Contemporanea*, 18 (2010), 151–178.

Brooke, Rosalind, *The Image of St Francis: Responses to Sainthood in the Thirteenth Century* (Cambridge: Cambridge University Press, 2006).

Brown, Peter, *Augustine of Hippo: A Biography*. Revised Edition with a New Epilogue (Berkeley: University of California Press, 2000).

Bughetti, Benvenuto, 'Alcune lettere inedite del P. Luca Waddingo OFM a Pier Maria Campi', *AFH*, 5 (1912), 149–53.

Burke, William P., *History of Clonmel* (Waterford: Harvey & Co. for the Clonmel Library Committee, 1907).

Burrieza Sánchez, Javier, 'La monarquía "de los descalzos". Rigores y reformas en las órdenes religiosas', in Consuelo Martínez-Sicluna y Sepúlveda et al., eds, *La configuración de la Monarquía Hispánica* (Madrid: Dykinson, 2023), 233–268.

Byrne, Michael, ed, *Waterford 1470: Dean John Collyn and the Chantry of St Saviour* (Drogheda, Choice Publishing, 2013).

Byrne, Niall, 'Luke Wadding's Waterford', *Decies*, 63 (2007), 34–99.

——— 'Reformation in Elizabethan Waterford', *Decies*, 57 (2001), 43–72.

Callado Estela, Emilio, 'El confesor regio fray Luis de Aliaga y la controversia inmaculista', *Hispania Sacra*, 68 (2016), 317–26.

Campbell, Ian, 'The Wadding Circle and the History of Political Thought', in Matteo Binasco, ed, *Luke Wadding, the Irish Franciscans and Global Catholicism* (Abingdon: Routledge, 2020), 145–163.

——— 'John Punch, Scotist Holy War, and the Irish Catholic Revolutionary Tradition in the Seventeenth Century', *Journal of the History of Ideas*, 77 (2016), 401–21.

——— *Renaissance Humanism and Ethnicity Before Race: The Irish and the English in the Seventeenth Century* (Manchester: Manchester University Press, 2013).

——— 'Truth and Calumny in Baroque Rome: Richard O'Ferrall and the *Commentarius Rinuccinianus*', 1648–1667, *IHS*, 38 (2012), 211–229.

Canny, Nicholas, *Imagining Ireland's Pasts. Early Modern Ireland Through the Centuries* (Oxford: Oxford University Press, 2021).

——— *Imagining Ireland's Pasts. Early Modern Ireland Through the Centuries* (Oxford: Oxford University Press, 2021).

——— *Making Ireland British, 1580–1650* (Oxford: Oxford University Press, 2001).

Cantalamessa, Raniero, *Obedience: the authority of the word*, translated by Frances Villa Lonergan (New York: St Pauls, 2018).

Careri, Giovanni, and Ferrante Ferranti, *Baroques* (Paris: Citadelles & Mazenod, 2002).

Carrigan, William, *The History and Antiquities of the Diocese of Ossory* (Dublin: Sealy, Bryers & Walker, 1905).

Carroll, Clare, 'The *Vita Waddingi* and the Memory of Confederate and Cromwellian Ireland', in Matteo Binasco, ed, *Luke Wadding, the Irish Franciscans, and Global Catholicism* (Abingdon: Routledge, 2020), 185–199.

——— *Exiles in a Global City: The Irish and Early Modern Rome, 1609–1783* (Leiden: Brill, 2017).

Casway, Jerrold, 'Gaelic Maccabeanism: The Politics of Reconciliation' in Jane Ohlmeyer, ed, *Political Thought in Seventeenth-Century Ireland: Kingdom or Colony* (Cambridge: Cambridge University Press, 2000), 176–188.

——— *Owen Roe O'Neill and the Struggle for Catholic Ireland* (Philadelphia: University of Pennsylvania Press, 1984).

——— 'Owen Roe O'Neill's return to Ireland in 1642: The Diplomatic Background', *Studia Hib.*, 9 (1969), 53–54.

Catalano, Chiara, 'Sforza Pallavicino and the Condemnation of Jansenius' Five Propositions', in Maarten Delbeke, ed, *Sforza Pallavicino. A Jesuit Life in Baroque Rome* (Leiden: Brill, 2022), 253–274.

Cecchin, Stefano, 'L'Immacolata Concezione nel "Siglo de oro" spagnolo tra re, papi e francescani', *Annali di Storia Sociale ed Ecclesiastica*, 1 (2017), 7–60.

Cesareo, Francesco, 'The Episcopacy in Sixteenth Century Italy', in Kathleen Comerford and Hilmar Pabel, eds, *Early Modern Catholicism: Essays in Honour of John W. O'Malley S.J.* (Toronto: University of Toronto Press), 67–83.

Ceyssens, Lucien, 'Florence Conry, Hugh de Burgo, Luke Wadding, and Jansenism', Franciscan Fathers, eds, *Father Luke Wadding Commemorative Volume* (Dublin: Clonmore & Reynolds, 1957), 295–404.

Chambers, Liam, 'The Library of an Irish Catholic Émigré: Michael Moore's Bibliothèque, 1726', *Archiv. Hib.*, 58 (2004), 210–42.

Chambers, Liam, and Thomas O'Connor, eds, *College Communities Abroad: Education, Migration and Catholicism in Early Modern Europe* (Manchester: Manchester University Press, 2017).

——— eds, *Forming Catholic Communities: Irish, Scots and English College networks in Europe, 1568–1918* (Leiden: Brill, 2018).

Chartier, Roger, *The Author's Hand and the Printer's Mind: Transformations of the Written Word in Early Modern Europe*, translated by Lydia G. Cochrane (Cambridge: Polity Press, 2014).

Cipolla, Carlo, *Money in Sixteenth-Century Florence* (Berkeley CA: University of California Press, 1989, repr. 2023).

Clark, Ruth, *Strangers & Sojourners at Port Royal: Being an Account of the Connections between British Isles and the Jansenists of France and Holland* (repr. Cambridge: Cambridge University Press, 2014).

Clarke, Aidan, *The Old English in Ireland, 1625–42* (Dublin: Four Courts Press, 2000).

Cleary, Gregory, *Father Luke Wadding and St Isidore's College, Rome: Biographical and Historical Notes and Documents* (Rome: Tipografia del senato del G. Bardi, 1925).

Combaluzier, Fernand, 'Sacres episcopaux a Rome de 1565 à 1662. Analyse intégrale du Ms. Miscellanea XIII, 33 des Archives Vaticanes', *Sacris Erudiri*, 18 (1967–8), 120–30.

Comella Gutiérrez, Beatriz, 'Los nombramientos Episcopales para la Corona de Castilla bajo Felipe III, según el Archivo Histórico Nacional: Una Aproximación', *Hispania Sacra*, 60 (2008), 703–733. <https://doi.org/10.3989/hs.2008.v60.i122.74>

Concha Sahli, Alejandra, '"The true habit of St Francis": the Capuchins and the Construction of a New Franciscan Identity', *Collectanea Francescana*, 87 (2017), 513–52.

Conlan, Patrick, *St Isidore's, Rome* (Rome: Tipografia Salesiana, 1982).

Connors, Joseph, 'Borromini and the Marchese di Castel Rodrigo', *The Burlington Magazine*, 133 (1991), 434–440.

Cooper, Donal, '"Qui Peruse in Archa Saxea Tumulatus': The Shrine of Beato Egidio in San Francesco Al Prato, Perugia', *PBSR*, 69, Centenary Volume (2001), 223–44.

Corish, Patrick, 'Ormond, Rinuccini and the Confederates, 1645–49', in T. W. Moody, F. X. Martin and F. J. Byrne, eds, *A New History of Ireland* ((Oxford: Oxford University Press, 1976; reprinted with bibliographical supplement, 2009), vol. 3, *Early Modern Ireland, 1534–1691*, 317–335.

——— 'An Irish Counter-Reformation Bishop: John Roche, III', *ITQ*, 25/2 (1958), 101–123.

——— 'The Beginnings of the Irish College, Rome', in Franciscan Fathers, eds, *Luke Wadding Commemorative Volume* (Dublin: Clonmore & Reynolds, 1957), 284–294; reprinted in Dáire Keogh and Albert McDonnell, eds, *The Irish College, Rome and its World*, 3–12.

——— 'Father Luke Wadding and the Irish Nation', *IER*, 5th series, 88 (1957), 377–395.

——— 'The Crisis in Ireland in 1648', *ITQ*, 22 (1955), 231–257.

——— 'Two Contemporary Historians of the Confederation of Kilkenny', *IHS*, 8 (1953), 217–236.

——— 'Rinuccini's Censure of 27 May 1648', *ITQ*, 18 (1951), 322–337.

——— 'Bishop Nicholas French and the Second Ormond Peace, 1648–9', *IHS*, 6 (1948), 83–100.

Corry, Maya, Marco Faini and Alessia Meneghin, eds, *Domestic devotions in Early Modern Italy* (Brill: Leiden 2019).

Cotter, Francis, *The Friars Minor in Ireland from Their Arrival to 1400* (St Bonaventure NY: Franciscan Institute, 1994).

Covington, Sarah, *The Devil from Over the Sea. Remembering and Forgetting Oliver Cromwell in Ireland* (Oxford: Oxford University Press, 2022).

Cowan, Edward, *'For Freedom Alone': the Declaration of Arbroath, 1320* (East Linton: Tuckwell Press, 2003).

Cox, J. C., ed, *Churchwardens Accounts from the Fourteenth Century to the Close of the Seventeenth Century* (London: Methuen, 1913).

Cregan, Donal, 'The Confederate Catholics of Ireland: The Personnel of the Confederation, 1642–9', *IHS*, 29 (1995), 490–512.

——— 'The Social and Cultural Background of a Counter-Reformation Episcopate, 1618–60' in Art Cosgrove and Donal McCartney, *Studies in Irish History presented to R. Dudley Edwards* (Dublin: University College Dublin, 1979), 85–117.

——— 'The Confederation of Kilkenny', in Brian Farrell, ed, *The Irish Parliamentary Tradition* (Dublin: Gill and Macmillan, 1973), 102–115.

——— 'Some members of the Confederation of Kilkenny', in Sylvester O'Brien, ed, *Measgra i gcuimhne Mhichíl Uí Chléirigh. Miscellany of Historical and Linguistic Studies in Honour of Brother Michael Ó Cléirigh, Chief of the Four Masters, 1643–1943* (Dublin: Assisi Press, 1944), 34–44.

Cunningham, Bernadette, *The Annals of the Four Masters. Irish History, Kingship and Society in the Early Seventeenth Century* (Dublin: Four Courts Press, 2010).

Cunningham, Bernadette, and Máire Kennedy, eds, *The Experience of Reading: Irish Historical Perspectives* (Dublin: Rare Books Group of the Library Association of Ireland and ESHSI, 1999).

Cunningham, Bernadette, and Raymond Gillespie, "The Most Adaptable of Saints': The Cult of St Patrick in the seventeenth century', *Archiv. Hib.*, 49 (1995), 82–104.

Cunningham, John, 'Lay Catholicism and Religious Policy in Cromwellian Ireland', *JEH*, 64 (2013), 769–86.

Cusato, Michael F., 'The Gathering Storm: The Emergence of Evangelical Poverty as the Primary Descriptor for the Franciscan Charism (1220–50)', in Cusato and McMichael, eds, *"Non enim fuerat Evangelii surdus auditor..." (1 Celano 22)*, 119–66.

Cushing, Kathleen, *Papacy and Law in the Gregorian Revolution: The Canonistic Work of Anselm of Lucca* (Oxford: Oxford University Press, 1998).

Da Silva Dias, José Sebastião, *Correntes de Sentimento Religioso em Portugal: Séculos XVI a XVIII*, 2 vols (Coimbra: Universidade de Coimbra, 1960).

Dandelet, Thomas, *Spanish Rome, 1500–1700* (New Haven: Yale University Press, 2001).

Darcy, Eamon, *The Irish Rebellion of 1641 and the Wars of the Three Kingdoms* (Woodbridge: Boydell, 2015).

Dary, Marie-Bénédicte, 'Saint Bernard et l'Immaculée Conception: La Question Liturgique', *Revue Mabillon*, 13 (2002), 219–36.

Davenport, Anne Ashley, *Suspicious Moderate. The Life and Writings of Francis à Sancta Clara (1598–1680)* (Notre Dame, 2017).

De Aspurz, Lázaro, *Franciscan History: The Three Orders of St Francis of Assisi*, translated by Lawrence Landini (Chicago: Franciscan Herald Press, 1982).

De Carvalho, Mário Santiago, 'Uma "Escola Filosófica de Coimbra"? História, tendências e problemas', *Revista Filosófica de Coimbra*, 32 (2023), 255–278.

De Castro, Manuel, *San Francisco de Salamanca y su studium generale* (Santiago de Compostela: Aldecoa Ediciones, 1998).

——— *Escritores de la Provincia Franciscana de Santiago, siglos XIII-XIX* (Santiago de Compostela: S. N., 1996).

——— *La Provincia Franciscana de Santiago. Ocho Siglos de Historia* (Santiago de Compostela: Liceo Franciscano, 1984).

——— 'Las ideas políticas y la formación del princípe en el *De preconiis Hispaniae* del franciscano Fr. Juan Gil de Zamora (1278)', *Hispania*, 22 (1962), 507–541.

——— 'El Analista P. Lucas Wadding OFM y sus relaciones con la Peninsula Ibérica', *Salmanticensis*, 5, Fasc. 1 (1958), 107–62.

——— 'Wadding and the Iberian Peninsula', in Franciscan Fathers, eds, *Luke Wadding Commemorative Volume* (Dublin: Clonmore & Reynolds, 1957), 119–170.

Delumeau, Jean, *Rome au XVI siècle* (Paris: Hachette, 1975).

De Mesa Gallego, Eduardo, *The Irish in the Spanish Armies in the Seventeenth Century* (Woodbridge: Boydell, 2014).

——— 'Un noble irlandés al servicio de Felipe IV: John O'Neill, Conde de Tyrone', in Ricardo Franch Benavent, Fernando Andrés Robres and Rafael Benítez Sánchez-Blanco, eds, *Cambios y resistencias sociales en la edad moderna. Un análisis comparativo entre el centro y la periferia mediterránea de la monarquía hispánica* (Madrid: Sílex, 2014), 339–48.

——— 'The Career of Owen Roe O'Neill in the Spanish Army of Flanders (1606–42): Documentation held in Spanish archives', *Archiv. Hib.*, 67 (2014), 7–24.

De Mol, Ellénita, 'Le culte de la Vierge après le Concile de Trente, perçu à travers trois triptyques flamands de la fin du XVIe siècle et du début du XVIIe siècle', in Wim François and Violet Soen, eds, *Council of Trent. Reform and Controversy in Europe and Beyond (1545–1700)*, 3 vols (Göttingen: Vandenhoeck & Ruprecht, 2018), vol. 3, 93–116.

De Reumont, Alfred, *The Carafas of Maddaloni: Naples under Spanish Dominion* (London: Henry Bohn, 1854).

De Rosa, Gabriele, Tullio Gregory and André Vauchez, eds, *Storia dell'Italia religiosa* 3 vols (Rome-Bari: Laterza, 1994).

De Wulf, Maurice, *History of Medieval Philosophy*, translated by Peter Coffey, 2 vols (London: Longmans, Green and Company, 1909–26).

Del Río Barredo, María José, *Madrid, Urbs Regia: La Capital Ceremonial de la Monarquía* Católica (Madrid: Marcial Pons, 2000).

Delisle, Jean, and Judith Woodsworth, eds, *Translators through History*, revised edition (Amsterdam: John Benjamins Publishing, 2012).

Dias, Pedro, Dalila Rodrigues, Fernando Grilo and Nuno Vassallo e Silva, *The Manueline. Portuguese Art during the Great Discoveries* (Vienna: Museum Ohne Grenzen, 2017).

Dickens, A. G., *The Counter-Reformation* (London: Thames & Hudson, 1968).

Disney, Anthony, *A History of Portugal and the Portuguese Empire*, 2 vols (Cambridge: Cambridge University Press, 2009).

Ditchfield, Simon, 'Endnote', in Benjamin Hazard, ed, *Path to Salvation: Temporal and Spiritual Journeys by the Mendicant Orders, c.1370–1740* (Lausanne: Peter Lang, 2023), 221–228.

——— '*Historia magistra sanctitatis*? The Relationship between Historiography and Hagiography in Italy after the Council of Trent (*c.*1564–1742)', in Massimo Firpo, ed, *Nunc alia tempora, alii mores. Storici e storia in età postridentina* (Florence: Olschki, 2005), 159–184.

——— *Liturgy, Sanctity and History in Tridentine Italy: Pietro Maria Campi and the Preservation of the Particular* (Cambridge: Cambridge University Press, 2002).

Doménech García, Sergi, 'La propaganda concepcionista franciscana en el mundo hispánico. El grabado apologético y la obra de Pedro de Alva y As torga', in Camino Sánchez Oliveira, Alberto Gamarra Gonzalo, Manuel José Pedraza Gracia, eds, *La fisonomía del libro medieval y moderno: entre la funcionalidad, la estética y la información* (Zaragoza: Prensas de la Universidad de Zaragoza, 2019), 367–78.

Dompnier, Bernard, *Enquête au pays des frères des anges: les Capucins de la province de Lyon aux XVIIe et XVIIIe siècles* (St Étienne: presses universitaires de Saint-Étienne, 1993).

Downey, Declan, 'Continuity, Legitimacy and Strategy: The Titular Priors of Ireland – Romegas, González, Wyse and Brochero, and their Relations with the Spanish Monarchy, 1576–1625', in Martin Browne and Colmán Ó Clabaigh, eds, *Soldiers of Christ: The Knights Hospitaller and the Knights Templar in Medieval Ireland* (Dublin: Four Courts Press, 2015), 61–80.

Downey, Declan M., and Julio Crespo MacLennan, eds, *Spanish-Irish Relations through the Ages* (Dublin: Four Courts Press: 2008).

——— 'A Castilian-Regalist Cradling: Spanish-Habsburg Formation of the early Irish Counter Reformation', in Howard Clarke and J. R. S. Phillips, eds, *A Turbulent Priest Essays in Memory of Professor F. X. Martin OSA* (Dublin: University College Dublin Press, 2006), 96–206.

——— 'The Irish Contribution to Counter-Reformation Theology in Continental Europe', in Brendan Bradshaw and Dáire Keogh, eds, *Christianity in Ireland: Revisiting the Story* (Dublin: Veritas, 2002), 96–108.

Downey, Edmund, *The Story of Waterford: from the Foundation of the City to the middle of the Eighteenth Century* (Waterford: Waterford News Printing Works, 1914).

Dubost, Jean-François, 'La Normandie italienne à l'époque modern XVIe et XVIIe siècles', *Annales de Normandie*, 29 (2000), 163–177.

Dudley Edwards, R., 'Ireland, Elizabeth I and the Counter-Reformation', in Stanley Bindoff, Joel Hurstfield and Charles Williams, eds, *Elizabethan Government and Society. Essays Presented to Sir John Neale* (London: Athlone Press, 1961), 315–339.

Duffy, Eamon, *Reformation Divided: Catholics, Protestants and the Conversion of England* (London: Bloomsbury, 2017).

Duncan, A. A. M., *The Nation of Scots and the Declaration of Arbroath (1320)* (London: The Historical Association, 1970).

Duve, Thomas, José Luis Egío and Christiane Birr, eds, *The School of Salamanca: A Case of Global Knowledge Production* (Leiden: Brill, 2021).

Dyson, R. W., *The Pilgrim City: Social and Political Ideas in the Writings of St Augustine of Hippo* (Woodbridge: Boydell, 2001).

Egan, Bartholomew, Cathaldus Giblin and Cuthbert McGrath, eds, 'Irish Students Ordained in Rome (1625–1710)', *IER*, 5th ser., 61 (1945), 116–124.

Egan, Patrick, *History, Guide & Directory of County and City of Waterford* (Kilkenny: P. M. Egan, 1894).

Faggioli, Massimo, 'Urbano VIII e la riforma del procedimento di nomina dei vescovi', *Cristianesimo nella storia*, 23 (2002), 79–121.

Falls, Cyril, *Elizabeth's Irish Wars* (Syracuse NY: Syracuse University Press, 1997).

Fastiggi, Robert, 'Francisco Suárez SJ (1548–1617) on Mary's *Virginitas in Partu* and Subsequent Doctrinal Development', *Marian Studies*, 58 (2007), 26–45.

Father Cuthbert OSFC, *The Capuchins: A Contribution to the History of the Counter-Reformation*, 2 vols (London: Longmans, Green & Co., 1928–1929).

Febvre, Lucien, and Henri-Jean Martin, *The Coming of the Book: The Impact of Printing, 1450–1800*, translated by David Gerard (London: Verso, 1976).

Fehlner, Peter Damian, *Franciscan Mariology – Francis, Clare, and Bonaventure: the Collected Essays*, edited by J. Isaac Goff with an Introduction by Charles Robinson, 4 vols (Eugene OR: Wipf and Stock, 2023).

Fenlon, Dermot, 'Pole, Carranza, and the Pulpit', in John Edwards and Ronald Truman, eds, *Reforming Catholicism in the England of Mary Tudor: The Achievement of Friar Bartolomé Carranza* (Aldershot: Ashgate, 2005), 81–98.

——— *Heresy and Obedience in Tridentine Italy: Cardinal Pole and the Counter Reformation* (Cambridge: Cambridge University Press, 1972).

Fennessy, Ignatius, 'A Select Prosopography of Some Franciscans', in Bhreathnach, MacMahon and McCafferty, eds, *The Irish Franciscans, 1534–1990* (Dublin: Four Courts Press, 2009), 328–344.

——— 'Wadding, Luke [name in religion Francis] (1588–1657)', in Brian Harrison, ed, *Oxford Dictionary of National Biography*, 60 vols (Oxford: Oxford University Press, 2004), vol. 56, 643–649.

——— ed, 'Some Post-Incunabula in St Isidore's College, Rome', *Coll. Hib.*, 44/45 (2002/2003), 7–12.

——— ed, 'An Alphabetical Index for Some Manuscripts in St Isidore's College, Rome', *Coll. Hib.*, 43 (2001), 50–85.

——— ed, 'More Printed Items from the Wadding Papers (FLK MSS D 1–2, and others)', *Coll. Hib.*, 41 (1999), 36–57.

——— ed, 'Printed Items among the Wadding Papers', *Coll. Hib.*, 39/40 (1998), 32–95.

——— ed, 'The 'B' Manuscripts in the Franciscan Library, Killiney', in Benignus Millett and Anthony Lynch, eds, *Dun Mhuire Killiney, 1945–95: Leann agus Seanchas* (Dublin: Lilliput Press, 1995), 150–215.

Fenning, Hugh, 'Some Irish Donors of Books to the Irish College in Rome, 1611–78', in Dáire Keogh and Albert McDonnell, eds, *The Irish College, Rome, and its World* (Dublin: Four Courts Press, 2008), 46–52.

——— ed, 'Irishmen Ordained at Rome, 1572–1697', *Archiv. Hib.*, 59 (2005), 1–36.

——— ed, 'Documents of Irish Interest in the "Fondo Missioni" of the Vatican Archives', *Archiv. Hib.*, 49 (1995), 3–47.

Fernández Álvarez, Manuel, et al., *The University of Salamanca. Eight Centuries of Scholarship* (Salamanca: Ediciones Universidad de Salamanca, 1992).

Fernández Izquierdo, Francisco, *La Orden Militar de Calatrava en el Siglo XVI: Infraestructura Institucional: Sociología y Prosopografía de sus Caballeros* (Madrid, Consejo Superior de Investigaciones Científicas, 1992).

Fidanza, Giovan Battista, *Luke Wadding's Art. Irish Franciscan Patronage in Seventeenth Century Rome* (St Bonaventure University, NY: Franciscan Institute Publications, 2016).

Fidanza, Giovan Battista, 'Being the Court Painter of a Cardinal in Baroque Rome: Chronicle and History of Carlo Maratti for Antonio Barberini the Younger', *Memoirs of the American Academy in Rome*, 69 (2024), 400–464.

Fisquet, Honoré Jean Pierre, 'Oderic de Pordenone', in *Nouvelle biographie universelle depuis les temps les plus reculés jusqu'a nos jours* (Paris: Firmin-Didot Frères, 1862), vol. 38 (Nicolle-Ozerof), col. 469–471.

Flavin, Susan, *Consumption and Culture in Sixteenth-century Ireland: Saffron, Stockings and Silk* (Woodbridge: Boydell, 2014).

Flynn, Thomas, *The Irish Dominicans* (Dublin: Four Courts Press, 1993).

Ford, Alan, ''Firm Catholics' or 'Loyal Subjects'? Religious and Political Allegiance in Early Seventeenth-Century Ireland', in D. G. Boyce, Robert Eccleshall and Vincent Geoghegan, eds, *Political Discourse in Seventeenth- and Eighteenth-century Ireland* (Basingstoke: Palgrave Macmillan, 2001), 1–31.

——— 'The Irish Historical Renaissance and the Shaping of Protestant History', in Alan Ford and John McCafferty, eds, *The Origins of Sectarianism in Early Modern Ireland* (Cambridge: Cambridge University Press, 2005), 127–157.

Forrestal, Alison, *Fathers, Pastors and Kings: Visions of the Episcopacy in Seventeenth-Century France* (Manchester: Manchester University Press, 2004).

Franciscan Fathers, eds, *Father Luke Wadding Commemorative Volume* (Dublin: Clonmore & Reynolds, 1957).

François, Wim, and Violet Soen, eds, *Council of Trent. Reform and Controversy in Europe and Beyond (1545–1700)*, 3 vols (Göttingen: Vandenhoeck & Ruprecht, 2018).

Gajda, Alexandra, 'War, Peace, Commerce and the Treaty of London (1604)', in *Historical Research*, 96 (2023), 459–72. <https://doi.org/10.1093/hisres/htad011>

Galassi Paluzzi, Carlo, and Carlo Pietrangeli, eds, *Le Chiese di Roma illustrate. Collana di monografie* (Rome: Marietti, 1971).

García Cueto, David, *'Seicento' Boloñés y Siglo de Oro Español: El Arte, la Época, los Protagonistas* (Madrid, Centro de Estudios Europa Hispánica, 2006).

García Hernán, Enrique, 'La Misión de Irlanda (1610–1628). Aproximación a una Nueva Investigación', in Marcos Martín, Alberto, ed, *Hacer Historia desde Simancas. Homenaje a José Luis Rodríguez de Diego* (Valladolid, Junta de Castilla y León, 2011), 339–64.

——— *Ireland and Spain in the Reign of Philip II* (Dublin: Four Courts Press, 2009).

——— 'Irish clerics in Madrid, 1598–1665', in Thomas O'Connor and Mary Ann Lyons, eds, *Irish communities in early-modern Europe* (Dublin: Four Courts, 2006), 267–293.

——— 'Philip II's Forgotten Armada', in Hiram Morgan, ed, *The Battle of Kinsale* (Dublin: Wordwell, 2004), 45–58.

García Oro, José, 'Sosa, Francisco de', *DBe*, 50 vols (Madrid: Real Academia de la Historia, 2009–13), 47. <https://dbe.rah.es/biografias/30662/francisco-de-sosa>

——— 'Cuándo San Antonio llega a España', *Verdad y vida*, 53 (1995), 425–43.

——— 'Francisco de Asís en la España Medieval', *Liceo franciscano*, 41, *Francisco de Asís en la España Medieval* (1988), 1–558.

García Oro, José, and María José Porteia Silva, 'Felipe II y la Universidad de Salamanca', in Manuel de Castro ed, *San Francisco de Salamanca y su Studium Generale* (Santiago de Compostela, Imprenta Aldecoa de Burgos, 1998), 337–340.

García Rodríguez, Ceferino, 'El Ilmo Fr. Angel Manrique', *Collectanea Ord. Cist. Ref.*, 12 (1950), 195–207; 13 (1951), 128–39.

——— 'Rememorando al Ilmo. Fr. Ángel Manrique, Obispo de Badajoz (1645–9)', *Cistercium*, 1 (1949), 54–57.

García Villada, Zacarías, *Historia eclesiástica de España*, 3 vols (Madrid: Compañía Ibero-americana de Publicaciones, 1929–1936).

Gentle, Judith, and Robert Fastiggi, eds, *De Maria Numquam Satis. The Significance of the Catholic Doctrines on the Blessed Virgin Mary for All People* (Washington DC: Catholic University of America Press, 2009).

Giblin, Cathaldus, 'Hugh McCaghwell OFM, Archbishop of Armagh (†1626): Aspects of his Life', *Seanchas Ard Mhacha*, 11 (1985), 258–290; reprinted in Benignus Millett and Anthony Lynch, eds, *Dún Mhuire, Killiney, 1945–1995: Léann agus Seanchas* (Dublin: Lilliput, 1995), 63–94.

——'Hugh MacCaghwell OFM and Scotism at St Anthony's College, Louvain', in *De doctrina Ioannis Duns Scoti. Acta Congressus Scotistici Internationalis Oxonii et Edimburgi 11–17 Septembris 1966 celebrati, cura Commissionis Scotisticae*, 4 vols (Rome: Societas Internationalis Scotistica, 1968), vol. 4, *Scotismus decursu saeculorum*, 375–397.

——ed, 'Catalogue of Material of Irish Interest in the Collection "Nunziatura di Fiandra", Vatican Archives: Part 1, Vols. 1–50', *Coll. Hib.*, 1 (1958), 7–136.

—— 'The *Processus Datariae* and the Appointment of Irish Bishops in the Seventeenth Century', in Franciscan Fathers, eds, *Father Luke Wadding Commemorative Volume* (Dublin: Clonmore & Reynolds, 1957), 508–616.

——'A Seventeenth-Century Idea: Two Franciscan Provinces in Ireland', *Franciscan College Annual* (Multyfarnham, 1951), 55–67.

Gillespie, Raymond, 'Review: Matteo Binasco, ed, *Luke Wadding, the Irish Franciscans and Global Catholicism* (Abingdon: Routledge, 2020)', *BCH*, 35 (2021), 489–491.

——*Reading Ireland: Print, Reading and Social Change in Early Modern Ireland* (Manchester: Manchester University Press, 2012).

——'Contrasting Communities: A Comparative Approach to Irish Communities in Baroque Europe', in Thomas O'Connor and Mary Ann Lyons, eds, *The Ulster Earls and Baroque Europe. Refashioning Irish Identities, 1600–1800* (Dublin: Four Courts Press, 2010), 166–82.

——'The Irish Franciscans, 1600–1700', in Edel Bhreathnach, Joseph MacMahon and John McCafferty, eds, *The Irish Franciscans, 1534–1990* (Dublin: Four Courts Press, 2009), 45–76.

——'The Historical Manuscripts Commission and the Franciscan Manuscripts', *Irish Archives*, 14 (2007), 22–32.

——— 'The Irish Economy at War, 1641–52', in Ohlmeyer, ed, *Ireland from Independence to Occupation* (Cambridge: Cambridge University Press, 2002), 160–180.

——— 'The Social Thought of Richard Bellings', in Micheál Ó Siochrú, ed, *Kingdoms in Crisis: Ireland in the 1640s* (Dublin: Four Courts Press, 2001), 212–28.

Gillett, Christopher, 'Political Theology', in James E. Kelly and John McCafferty, eds, *The Oxford History of British and Irish Catholicism*, 5 vols (Oxford: Oxford University Press, 2023), vol. 2, *Uncertainty and Change, 1641–1745*, 189–208.

Giordano, Silvano, *Istruzioni di Filippo III ai suoi Ambasciatori a Roma: 1598–1621* (Rome: Istituto Poligrafico e Zecca dello Stato-Archivi di Stato, 2006).

——— 'Uomini e apparati della politica internazionale del papato', in Maria Antonietta Visceglia, ed, *Papato e politica internazionale nella prima età moderna* (Rome: Viella, 2013), 131–48.

Girard, Aurélien, 'Comment reconnaître un chrétien oriental vraiment catholique? Élaboration et usages de la profession de foi', in Marie-Hélène Blanchet and Frédéric Gabriel, eds, *L'union à l'épreuve du formulaire. Professions de foi entre Églises d'Orient et d'Occident (XIIIe-XVIIIe siècle)* (Leuven: Peeters, 2016), 235–58.

Godman, Peter, *The Saint as Censor: Robert Bellarmine between Inquisition and Index* (Leiden: Brill, 2000).

Gomes Teixeira, Vítor, *O Movimento da Observância Franciscana em Portugal (1392–1517). História, Património e Cultura de Uma Experiência de Reforma Religiosa* (Porto: Centro de Estudos Franciscanos – Editorial Franciscana, 2010).

Graffius, Jan, ''Bullworks against the Furie of Heresie': Identity, Education, and Mission in the English Jesuit College of St Omers', in Liam Chambers and Thomas O'Connor, eds, *Forming Catholic Communities: Irish, Scots and English College Networks in Europe, 1568–1918* (Leiden: Brill, 2018), 93–115. <https://doi.org/10.1163/9789004354364_006>

Guibovich Pérez, Pedro Manuel, 'Martín de Azpilcueta in the Andes (16th-17th centuries)', in Manuela Bragagnolo, ed, *The Production of Knowledge of Normativity in the Age of the Printing Press. Martín de Azpilcueta's Manual de Confessores from a Global Perspective* (Leiden: Brill, 2024).

Guidelli, Taddeo, *Thaddaei Perusini OSA Registrum viatorium, 1577–81* (Rome: Institutum historicum Augustinianum, 2007).

Guidi, Simone, 'Separated Soul and its Nature: Francisco Suárez in the Scholastic Debate', in Juan Antonio Senent de Frutos and Robert Maryks, eds, *Francisco*

Suárez (1548–1617): Jesuits and the Complexities of Modernity (Leiden: Brill, 2019), 351–377.

Gutiérrez, Constancio, 'España por el dogma de la Inmaculada: la embajada a Roma de 1659 y la bula Sollicitudo de Alejandro VII', *Miscelánea Comillas*, 24 (1955), 13–480.

Gutiérrez, David, *Storia dell'ordine di Sant'Agostino: Gli Agostiniani dal protestantesimo alla riforma cattolica* (Rome: Institutum Historicum Ordinis Fratrum S. Augustini, 1972).

Gwynn, Aubrey, 'Archbishop Ussher and Father Brendan O Conor', in Franciscan Fathers, eds, *Luke Wadding Commemorative Volume* (Dublin: Clonmore & Reynolds, 1957), 263–283.

Hagedorn, Lea, 'Minerva in the Printshop: Publisher's Advertising in Frontispieces and the Media Presence of Early Modern Printer-Publishers', in Gitta Bertram, Nils Büttner and Claus Zittel, eds, *Gateways to the Book: Frontispieces and Title Pages in Early Modern Europe* (Leiden: Brill, 2021), 92–123.

Hanly, John, ed, 'Records of the Irish College, Rome, under Jesuit administration', in *Archiv. Hib.*, 27 (1964), 13–75.

Harden Weaver, Rebecca, *Divine Grace and Human Agency. A Study of the Semi-Pelagian Controversy* (Washington DC: Catholic University of America Press, 1998).

Harris, Jason, 'Catholicism', in Sarah Knight and Stefan Tilg, eds, *The Oxford Handbook of Neo-Latin* (Oxford: Oxford University Press, 2015), 313–328.

Harris, Walter, ed and trans, *The Whole Works of Sir James Ware concerning Ireland, Revised and improved. The Writers of Ireland in two books [...] Written in Latin by Sir James Ware, Knight; Now Newly Translated into English* (Dublin: Reilly, 1746).

Haskell, Francis, *Patrons and Painters: A Study in the Relations between Italian Art and Society in the Age of the Baroque* (New Haven: Yale University Press, 1980).

Hauréau, Jean-Barthélemy, 'Occam ou Ockam (Guillaume d')', in *Nouvelle biographie universelle depuis les temps les plus reculés jusqu'a nos jours* (Paris: Firmin-Didot Frères, 1862), vol. 38 (Nicolle-Ozerof), col. 423–424.

Haworth, Richard, 'The Site of St Olave's Church, Dublin', in John Bradley, ed, *Settlement and Society in Medieval Ireland: Studies presented to F. X. Martin, OSA* (Kilkenny: Boethius Press, 1988), 177–192.

Hayes-McCoy, Gerard, *Irish Battles* (Belfast: Appletree Press, 1990).

Hazard, Benjamin, *Faith and Patronage: the Political Career of Flaithrí Ó Maolchonaire, c.1560–1629*. Royal Irish Academy New Directions in Irish History Series (Dublin: Irish Academic Press, 2010).

———'Richard Wadding & Son: Catholic Lawyers and Men of Politics, 1594–1656' in *Decies* 80 (2024), 5–24.

———ed, 'Thomas Wadding's Title to Lands at Knockmaon, Co. Waterford, May 1587', ed, *Arch. Hib.*, 76 (2023), 7–12.

———'Thomas Wadding, Waterford Landowner and Lawyer of Gray's Inn, 1562–1613', *Decies*, 77 (2021), 17–42.

———'Irish Franciscans and the Santiago Province of Spain', in Matteo Binasco, ed, *Luke Wadding, the Franciscans, and Global Catholicism* (Abingdon: Routledge, 2020), 19–38.

———'Illustration and Ornamentation in the Works of Luke Wadding, Seventeenth-Century Historian and Theologian', in Alexander Wilkinson and Alejandra Ulla Lorenzo, eds, *Typography, Illustration and Ornamentation in the Early Modern Iberian Book World* (Leiden: Brill, 2020), 350–371.

———'On mission to Mexico: Michael Wadding SJ of Waterford (1587–1644),' in Salvador Ryan ed, *Treasures of Irish Christianity: to the ends of the earth* (Dublin: Veritas, 2015), 70–72.

———'Luke Wadding and the Breviary of Urban VIII: A Study of the Book Trade between Rome, the Low Countries and the Spanish Empire', *Studia Hib.*, 39 (2014), 87–101.

———'Saint Isidore's Franciscan College, Rome: From Centre of Influence to Site of Memory', in Enrique García Hernán and Óscar Recio Morales, eds, *Redes y espacios de poder de la comunidad irlandesa en España y la América Española, 1600–1825. Power Strategies: Spain and Ireland, 1600–1825* (Valencia: Albatros Ediciones, 2012), 103–114.

———"A New Company of Crusaders Like that of St John Capistran': Interaction Between Irish Military Units and Franciscan Chaplains, 1579–1654', in Óscar Recio Morales and Enrique García Hernán, eds, *Extranjeros en el ejército: Militares irlandeses en la sociedad española, 1580–1818 = Essays on The Irish Military Presence in Early Modern Spain, 1580–1818* (Madrid: Ministerio de Defensa, 2007), 181–97.

Heider, Daniel, and Claus Andersen, eds, *Cognitive Issues in the Long Scotist Tradition* (Basel: Schwabe Verlag, 2022).

Herrero Sánchez, Manuel, 'La perduración de la cuestión irlandesa. Un obstáculo en las relaciones anglo-españolas durante la segunda mitad del siglo XVII', in Óscar Recio Morales, Bernardo José García García, Miguel Ángel de Bunes Ibarra, Enrique García Hernán, eds, *Irlanda y la Monarquía Hispánica. Kinsale 1601–2001: Guerra, Política, Exilio y Religión* (Madrid: CSIC, 2002), 401–22.

Henryot, Fabienne, 'Les Lyonnais et Saint Bonaventure (fin du XVe-XVIIIe siècles)', *Revue Historique*, 682 (2017), 267–296.

Hernández, Rosilie, *Immaculate Conceptions: The Power of the Religious Imagination in Early Modern Spain* (Toronto: Toronto University Press, 2019).

Hernández, Santiago Manuel, 'Don Manuel de Moura Corte Real, Marqués de Castelo Rodrigo: Propaganda, Mecenazgo y Representación en la Monarquía Hispánica de Felipe IV', in Olivier Noble Wood, Jeremy Lawrance and Jeremy Roe, eds, *Poder y Saber Bibliotecas y Bibliofilia en la Época del Conde-Duque de Olivares* (Madrid: Olivier Centro de Estudios Europa Hispánica, 2011), 97–120.

Heullant-Donat, Isabelle, 'Martyrdom and Identity in the Franciscan Order (Thirteenth and Fourteenth Centuries)', *Franciscan Studies*, 70 (2012), 429–453.

Higueras Rodríguez, D., and M. P. San Pío Aladrén, 'Irish Wrecks of the Great Armada', in Don Cruickshank, Patrick Gallagher, eds, *God's Obvious Design: Papers for the Spanish Armada Symposium, Sligo, 1988: with an Edition and Translation of the Account of Francisco de Cuéllar* (London: Tamesis, 1990), 143–166.

Hill, Christopher, *The Century of Revolution, 1603–1714* (Abingdon: Routledge, 1974).

Hofer, Philip, *Baroque Book Illustration: A Short Survey from the Collection in the Department of Graphic Arts* (Cambridge, MA: Harvard College Library, 1951).

Hollingsworth, Mary, Miles Pattenden and Arnold Witte, eds, *A Companion to the Early Modern Cardinal* (Leiden: Brill, 2017).

Holzapfel, Heribert, *History of the Franciscan Order*. Translated into English by Antonine Tibesar and Gervase Brinkmann, with an introduction by Noel Muscat. <https://franciscanstudies.com/wp-content/uploads/2018/10/hol_hist_final.pdf>

Hopkins, Andrew, *Italian Architecture: From Michelangelo to Borromini* (London: Thames and Hudson, 2002).

Humphreys, K. W., *The Friars' Libraries* (London: British Library, 1990).

Hynes, Michael, *The Mission of Rinuccini, Nuncio Extraordinary to Ireland, 1645–49* (Dublin: Browne & Nolan, 1932).

Ingham, Mary Beth, *The Harmony of Goodness: Mutuality and Moral Living according to John Duns Scotus* (New York: Franciscan Publications, 1996).

Iriarte, Lázaro, *Historia franciscana. Nueva edición* (Valencia: Editorial Asis, 1979).

Israel, Jonathan, *Dutch Primacy in World Trade, 1585–1740* (Oxford: Oxford University Press, 1989).

Jalland, Trevor, *The Church and the Papacy* (repr. London: SPCK, 1946).

Jedin, Hubert, and J. P. Dolan, *History of the Church: Reformation and Counter Reformation*, translated by Anselm Briggs and Peter W. Becker (London: Burns & Oates, 1980).

Jedin, Hubert, *A History of the Council of Trent*, translated by Ernest Graf, 2 vols (St Louis, MO: Herder Book Co., 1957–61).

Jefferies, Henry, 'Why the Reformation Failed in Ireland,' *IHS*, 40 (2016), 151–70.

Jennings, Brendan, ed, *'Acta Sacrae Congregationis de Propaganda Fide, 1622–50'*, *Archiv. Hib.*, 22 (1959), 28–139.

Johnson, Timothy, 'Preaching and Praying on the Seine: Minorite Theology and the Prothemes in Bonaventure's *Sermones dominicales*', *The Cord*, 55 (2005), 2–9.

Jones, Pamela M., *Federico Borromeo and the Ambrosiana. Art Patronage and Reform in Seventeenth-Century Milan* (Cambridge: Cambridge University Press, 1993).

Judson, J. Richard, and Carl Van de Velde, *Book Illustrations and Title Pages* (Corpus Rubenianum Ludwig Burchard, XXI), I–II (London: Miller/ Philadelphia: Heyden, 1978).

Kagan, Richard, *Clio and the Crown: The Politics of History in Medieval and Early Modern Spain* (Baltimore MD: The Johns Hopkins University Press, 2009).

Karris, Robert, *The Admonitions of St Francis. Sources and Meanings* (St Bonaventure, NY: Franciscan Institute Publications, 1999).

Keech, Dominic, *The Anti-Pelagian Christology of Augustine of Hippo, 396–430* (Oxford: Oxford University Press, 2012).

Kelly, Francis, *Captain Francisco de Cuéllar: The Armada, Ireland, and the Wars of the Spanish monarchy, 1578–1606* (Dublin: Four Courts Press, 2020).

Kelly, James E., and John McCafferty, eds, *The Oxford History of British and Irish Catholicism*, 5 vols (Oxford: Oxford University Press, 2023).

———'Introduction', in James E. Kelly and John McCafferty, eds, *The Oxford History of British and Irish Catholicism*, vol. 1, *Endings and New Beginnings, 1530–1640* (Oxford: Oxford University Press, 2023), 1–11.

Kerrigan, Paul, 'The Fortifications of Waterford, Passage and Duncannon, 1495–1690', *Decies*, 29 (1985), 12–23.

Kesselring, K. J., *To Pardon and to Punish: Mercy and Authority in Tudor England* (Cambridge: Cambridge University Press, 2000).

Kiliańczyk-Zięba, Justyna, and Magdalena Komorowska, eds, *Early Modern Catholicism and the Printed Book. Agents-Networks-Responses* (Leiden: Brill, 2024).

Kingdon, Robert, 'Patronage, Piety and Printing in Sixteenth-Century Europe', in David Pinkney and Theodor Ropp, eds, *A Festschrift for Frederick B. Artz* (Durham NC: Duke University Press, 1964), 19–36.

Koenigsberger, H. G., *The Habsburgs and Europe, 1516–1660* (Ithaca, NY: Cornell University Press, 1971).

Lantigua, David, *Infidels and Empires in a New World Order. Early Modern Spanish Contributions to International Legal Thought* (Cambridge: Cambridge University Press, 2020).

Lanza, Lidia, and Marco Toste, 'The Sentences in Sixteenth-century Iberian Scholasticism', in Philipp Rosemann, ed, *Mediaeval commentaries on the Sentences of Peter Lombard*, 3 vols (Leiden: Brill, 2002–15), vol. 3, 416–503.

Lapeyre, Henri, *Une Famille de Marchands: les Ruiz. Contribution à l'Étude du Commerce entre la France et l'Espagne au Temps de Philippe II* (Paris: Armand Colin, 1955).

Larkins, Jeremy, *From Hierarchy to Anarchy: Territory and Politics before Westphalia* (Basingstoke: Palgrave, 2010).

Lavenia, Vincenzo, 'Bishops', in Nelson Minnich, ed, *The Cambridge Companion to the Council of Trent* (Cambridge: Cambridge University Press, 2023), 180–208.

Le Goff, Jacques, 'Le roi dans l'Occident médiéval: caractères originaux', in Anne Duggan, ed, *Kings and Kingship in Medieval Europe* (London: Centre for Late Antique and Medieval Studies, 1993), 1–40.

Legrand, Catherine, 'Some Drawings by Carlo Maratti', *The Burlington Magazine*, 136 (1994), 348–356.

Leinsle, Ulrich, *Introduction to Scholastic Theology*, translated by Michael J. Miller (Washington DC: Catholic University of America Press, 2010).

Lemaitre, Nicole, 'L'idéal pastoral de réforme et le Concile de Trente (XIVe–XVIe siècle)', in Wim François and Violet Soen, eds, *Council of Trent. Reform and Controversy in Europe and Beyond (1545–1700)*, 3 vols (Göttingen: Vandenhoeck & Ruprecht, 2018), vol. 2, 9–32.

Lenihan, Pádraig, *Confederate Catholics at War, 1641–49* (Cork: Cork University Press, 2001).

Lennon, Colm, 'Education and Religious Identity in Early Modern Ireland', *Paedagogica Historica*, 35 (1999), 57–75.

——— *Sixteenth-Century Ireland: The Incomplete Conquest* (Dublin: Gill & Macmillan 1994).

Lignereux, Yann, *Lyon et le roi de la bonne ville à l'absolutisme municipal, 1594–1654* (Seyssel: Champ Vallon, 2003).

Little, A. G., *The Grey Friars in Oxford*. Part I: *A History of the Convent*, Part II: *Biographical Notices of the Friars, Together with Appendices of Original Documents* (Oxford: Clarendon Press, 1892).

Logan, Patrick, 'Medical History of Father Luke Wadding', *Journal of the Irish Medical Association*, 40 (1957), 175–178.

Lopes, Félix Fernando, 'As doutrinas escostitas na cultura e escolas de Portugal', in *Revista Portuguese de Filosofia*, 23 (1967), 17–45.

——— 'O ensino das doutrinas de Escoto na Universidade de Coimbra', in *Itinerarium*, 12 (1966), 193–264.

Lyons, Mary Ann, 'Foreign Language Books, 1550–1700', in Raymond Gillespie and Andrew Hadfield, eds, *The History of the Irish Book*, vol. 3: *The Irish Book in English, 1550–1800* (Oxford: Oxford University Press, 2005), 347–367.

——— 'The Role of St Anthony's College, Louvain in Establishing the Irish Franciscan Network, 1607–60', in Edel Bhreathnach, Joseph MacMahon and John McCafferty, eds, *The Irish Franciscans, 1534–1990* (Dublin: Four Courts Press, 2009), 27–44.

Mac Craith, Mícheál, 'Wadding and the Irish Tombs in San Pietro in Montorio', in Matteo Binasco, ed, *Luke Wadding, the Irish Franciscans and Global Catholicism* (Abingdon: Routledge, 2020), 167–84.

——— 'The Franciscan Continental Colleges and the Doctrine of the Immaculate Conception', in Matteo Binasco, ed, *Rome and Irish Catholicism in the Atlantic World* (Basingstoke: Palgrave MacMillan, 2019), 137–165.

——— 'Seraphic Sparks: The Irish Franciscan and Capuchin Colleges on the Continent', in Liam Chambers and Thomas O'Connor, eds, *Forming Catholic Communities: Irish, Scots and English College Networks in Europe, 1568–1918* (Leiden: Brill, 2017), 39–61.

Mac Cuarta, Brian, ed, *Ulster 1641: Aspects of the Rising* (Belfast: Institute for Irish Studies, 1997).

——— *Catholic Revival in the North of Ireland, 1603–41* (Dublin: Four Courts Press, 2007).

Macinnes, Allan, 'Covenanting Ideology in Seventeenth-Century Scotland', in Ohlmeyer, ed, *Political Thought in Seventeenth-Century Ireland*, 191–220.

Macintyre, Alasdair, *God, Philosophy, Universities: A Selective History of Catholic Philosophical Tradition* (Lanham MD: Rowman and Littlefield, 2009).

Maclean, Ian, *Scholarship, Commerce, Religion: The Learned Book in the Age of Confessions, 1560–1630* (Cambridge MA: Harvard University Press, 2012).

MacLeod, Caitríona, 'A Carved Oak Nursing Madonna from Askeaton, Co. Limerick', in Étienne Rynne, ed, *Figures from the Past: Studies on Figurative Art in Christian Ireland in Honour of Helen M. Roe* (Dún Laoghaire: The Glendale Press for The Royal Society of Antiquaries of Ireland, 1987), 249–257.

——— 'Mediaeval Figure Sculpture in Ireland Statues in the Holy Ghost Hospital, Waterford', *JRSAI*, 76 (1946), 89–100.

MacMahon, Joseph, 'Irish Franciscan Scotists of the Seventeenth Century', in Jens Röhrkasten, ed, *Canterbury Studies in Franciscan History*, 2 (2009), 85–112.

——— 'The Silent Century, 1698–1829', in Edel Bhreathnach, Joseph MacMahon and John McCafferty, eds, *The Irish Franciscans 1534–1990* (Dublin: Four Courts, 2009), 77–101.

MacMahon, Joseph, and John McCafferty, 'The Wadding Library of Saint Isidore's College, Rome, 1622–1700', *AFH*, 106 (2013), 97–118.

Marcos de Dios, Ángel, *Portugueses en la Universidad de Salamanca de la Edad Moderna*, in Luis Enrique Rodríguez-San Pedro Bezares, ed, *Historia de la Universidad de Salamanca*, vol. 3, tome 2, *Saberes y Confluencias* (Salamanca: Universidad de Salamanca, 2004), 1101–28.

Marshall, Peter, 'The Break with Rome and the Early Reformation', in James E. Kelly and John McCafferty, eds, *Oxford History of British and Irish Catholicism*, vol. 1, *Endings and New Beginnings, 1530–1640* (Oxford: Oxford University Press, 2023), 12–30.

Martin, F. X., *Friar Nugent: A Study of Francis Lavalin Nugent, 1569–1635. Agent of the Counter-Reformation*, Bibliotheca Seraphico-Capuccina (Rome: Capuchin Historical Institute; London: Methuen, 1962).

Martin, Henri-Jean, *Livre, pouvoirs et société à Paris au XVIIe siècle: 1598–1701*, 2 vols (Geneva: Librairie Droz, 1999).

Martínez, Lope Pascual, 'La Embajada a Roma de Fray Antonio de Trejo, Obispo de Cartagena', *Anales de la Universidad de Murcia. Filosofía y letra*, 32 (1973), 21–42.

Martínez Shaw, Carlos, ed, *Arte y Saber: la cultura en tiempos de Felipe III y Felipe IV.* Museo Nacional de Escultura, Palacio Villena, Valladolid (Madrid: Ministerio de Educación y Cultura Dirección General de Bellas Artes y Bienes Culturales, 1999).

Maryks, Robert, 'Jesuits of Jewish Ancestry under Francisco de Borja's Generalate', in Enrique García Hernán and María del Pilar Ryan, eds, *Francisco de Borja y su tiempo: Política, religion y cultura en la Edad Moderna* (Valencia: Albatros Ediciones; Rome: Institutum Historicum Societatis Iesu, 2011), 189–98.

McCafferty, John, 'Recycling an Island's Past for a Global Catholicism: Irish Franciscans in the Seventeenth Century', in Cormac Begadon and James E. Kelly, eds, *British and Irish Religious Orders in Europe, 1560–1800: Conventuals, Mendicants and Monastics in Motion* (Woodbridge: Boydell, 2022), 60–80.

——— 'A Life in and for Books', in Matteo Binasco, ed, *Luke Wadding, the Irish Franciscans and Global Catholicism* (Abingdon: Routledge, 2020), 108–22.

———'*A mundo valde alieni*: Irish Franciscan Responses to the Dissolution of the Monasteries, 1540–1640', *Reformation and Renaissance Review*, 19 (2017), 50–63.

——— 'Franciscan Rules Printed in the Spanish Netherlands in the Seventeenth Century', *Canterbury Studies in Franciscan History*, 3 (2011), 199–226.

——— *The Reconstruction of the Church of Ireland: Bishop Bramhall and the Laudian Reforms, 1633–41* (Cambridge: Cambridge University Press, 2007).

———'The Communion of Saints and Catholic Reformation in Early Seventeenth-Century Ireland', in Tadhg Ó hAnnracháin and Robert Armstrong, eds, *Community in Early Modern Ireland* (Dublin: Four Courts Press, 2006), 199–214.

McCafferty, John, and Bernadette Cunningham, '*De Oculo Morali* - a Moral Treatise on the Eye', in Edel Bhreathnach and Bernadette Cunningham, eds, *Writing Irish History: The Four Masters and Their World* (Dublin: Wordwell, 2007), 125.

McCarthy Morrogh, Michael, *The Munster Plantation: English Migration to Southern Ireland, 1583–1641* (Oxford: Clarendon Press, 1986).

McCarthy, Pat, ''Waterford and Wexford Swarm with Dunkirkers': Waterford and the War at Sea, 1642–1650', *Decies*, 71 (2017), 1–12.

McCoog, Thomas, 'Mission or Church, 1570–1640?', in James E. Kelly and John McCafferty, eds, *The Oxford History of British and Irish Catholicism*, vol. 1, *Endings and New Beginnings, 1530–1640* (Oxford: Oxford University Press, 2023), 107–126.

McCormack, Anthony, *The Earldom of Desmond, 1463–1583: the Decline and Crisis of a Feudal Lordship* (Dublin: Four Courts Press, 2005).

McGettigan, Darren, *Richard II and the Irish Kings* (Dublin: Four Courts Press, 2016).

McGuinne, Dermot, 'Irish Types in Europe', *Gutenburg Jahrbuch,* 82 (2007), 167–176.

McHugh, John A., and Charles Callan, eds, *Catechism of the Council of Trent for Parish Priests Issued by Order of Pius V*, translated into English with notes (New York: Joseph Wagner, 1936).

McMichael, Steven, and Katie Wrisley Shelby, eds, *Medieval Franciscan Approaches to the Virgin Mary: Mater Misericordiae Sanctissima et Dolorosa* (Leiden: Brill 2019).

Meehan, Charles, *The Confederation of Kilkenny* (Dublin: James Duffy, 1846).

——— *The Rise and Fall of the Irish Franciscan Monasteries and Memoirs of the Irish Hierarchy in the Seventeenth Century* (3rd edn, Dublin: James Duffy, 1870).

Mendes Drummond Braga, Isabel, 'Poor Relief in Counter Reformation Portugal: The Case of the *Misericórdias*', in Andrew Cunningham, Jon Arrizabalaga and Ole Peter Grell, eds, *Health Care and Poor Relief in Counter-Reformation Europe* (Abingdon: Routledge, 2005), 201–14.

Menéndez Pidal, Ramón, *The Spaniards in Their History* (New York: Norton, 1955).

Mertens, Benedikt, 'Philothea's Pilgrimage to Perfection: Vernacular Franciscan Spirituality in a 17th-Century Retreat Manual Written by John Cross', in Michael F. Cusato and Steven McMichael, *"Non enim fuerat Evangelii surdus auditor..." (1 Celano 22): Essays in Honor of Michael W. Blastic OFM on the Occasion of his 70th Birthday* (Leiden: Brill, 2020), 258–280.

Messa, Pietro, 'Le feste mariane nel Breviarium sancti Francisci', in Stefano Cecchin, ed, *La "Scuola Francescana" e l'Immacolata Concezione: atti del congresso mariologico francescano, S. Maria degli Angeli, Assisi, 4–8 dicembre 2003* (Città del Vaticano: Pontificia Academia Mariana 2005), 55–85.

——— 'L'Officium mortuorum e l'Officium beate Marie virginis nel Breviarium sancti Francisci', *Franciscana*, 4 (2002), 111–149.

Miller, R. W. H., *One Firm Anchor: The Church and the Merchant Seafarer, an Introductory History* (Cambridge: Lutterworth Press, 2012).

Millett, Benignus, 'Luke Wadding, (1588–1657), Franciscan Priest, Scholar, and Churchman', in James McGuire and James Quinn, eds, *Dictionary of Irish Biography* (Cambridge: Cambridge University Press, 2009), vol. 9, 680–85.

——— ed, 'Copies of Some Decisions from the Missing Discretorial Registers of St Isidore's College, Rome, 1652–1739', *Coll. Hib.*, 43 (2001), 86–111.

——— 'Heber MacMahon, Bishop of Clogher (d.1650)', *Clogher Record*, 16 (1997), 136–144.

——— 'The Archives of St Isidore's College, Rome', *Archiv. Hib.*, 40 (1985), 1–13.

——— 'Irish Literature in Latin, 1550–1700', in T. W. Moody, F. X. Martin and F. J. Byrne, eds, *A New History of Ireland* (Oxford, 1976; reprinted with bibliographical supplement, 2009), vol. 3, *Early Modern Ireland, 1534–1691*, 561–586.

——— ed, 'Calendar of Volume 2 (1669–71) of the "Scritture riferite nei congressi, Irlanda", in Propaganda Archives: Part 1, ff. 1–401', *Coll. Hib.*, 16 (1973), 7–47.

——— ed, 'Catalogue of Irish Material in Vols. 132–139 of the "Scritture originali riferite nelle congregazioni generali" in Propaganda Archives', *Coll. Hib.*, 12 (1969), 7–44.

——— 'Irish Scotists at St Isidore's College, Rome, in the Seventeenth Century', in *De doctrina Ioannis Duns Scoti, Acta Congressus Scotistici Internationalis Oxonii et Edimburgi 11–17 Septembris 1966 celebrati, cura Commissionis Scotisticae*, 4 vols (Rome: Societas Internationalis Scotistica, 1968), vol. 4, *Scotismus decursu saeculorum*, 399–419.

——— ed, 'Catalogue of Volume 294 of the "Scritture originali riferite nelle congregazioni generali" in Propaganda Archives', *Coll. Hib.*, 8 (1965), 7–37.

——— *The Irish Franciscans, 1651–65*, Analecta Gregoriana, 129 (Rome: Gregorian University Press, 1964).

——— 'Guide to Material for a Biography of Father Luke Wadding', in Franciscan Fathers, eds, *Father Luke Wadding Commemorative Volume* (Dublin: Clonmore & Reynolds, 1957), 229–262.

——— 'Bonaventure Barron OFM, *Hibernus Clonmeliensis*', in Philip O'Connell and W. C. Darmody, eds, *Siege of Clonmel Commemoration: Tercentenary Souvenir Record* (Clonmel: Nationalist Newspaper Co., 1950), 41–46.

Montes Moreira, António, 'Implantação e Desenvolvimento da Ordem Franciscana em Portugal – Séculos XIII-XVI', in *I-II Seminário: O Franciscanismo em Portugal* (Lisbon: Fundação Oriente, 1996), 13–27.

Mooney, Canice, 'Father Luke Wadding – The Last Years', *Assisi*, 19 (1957), 89–91.

——— 'Father Francis Magruairk, OFM', *Seanchas Ard Mhacha*, 2 (1957), 202–228.

——— 'The Writings of Father Luke Wadding OFM', *Franciscan Studies*, 18 (1958), 225–39.

——— 'The Letters of Luke Wadding', *IER*, 5th series, 88 (1957), 396–409.

——— 'Was Luke Wadding a Patriotic Irishman?', in Franciscan Fathers, eds, *Father Luke Wadding Commemorative Volume* (Dublin: Clonmore & Reynolds, 1957), 15–92.

——— 'The Golden Age of the Irish Franciscans, 1615–50', in Sylvester O'Brien, ed, *Measgra i gcuimhne Mhichíl Uí Chléirigh .i. Miscellany of Historical and Linguistic Studies in Honour of Brother Michael Ó Cléirigh OFM, Chief of the Four Masters, 1643–1943* (Dublin: Assisi Press, 1944), 21–33.

Moorman, John R. H., *A History of the Franciscan Order from its Origins to the Year 1517* (Oxford: Clarendon Press, 1968).

——— *The Sources for the Life of S. Francis of Assisi* with a foreword by A. G. Little (Manchester: Manchester University Press, 1940).

Morales Barrero, Consolación, *La imprenta real de Madrid desde su fundación hasta fines del siglo XVII* (Madrid: Artes Gráficas Municipales, 1976).

More, Alison, 'Canonical Change and the Orders of the Franciscan Tertiaries', in Bert Roest and Johanneke Uphoeff, eds, *Religious Orders and Religious Identity Formation, ca.1420– 1620: Discourses and Strategies of Observance and Pastoral Engagement* (Leiden: Brill, 2016), 69–85.

Morello, Giovanni, Vincenzo Francia and Roberto Fusco, eds, *Una Donna vestita di Sole: l'Immacolata Concezione nelle Opere dei Grandi Maestri* (Milan: Motta, 2005).

Morford, Mark, *Stoics and Neostoics: Rubens and the Circle of Lipsius* (Princeton: Princeton University Press, 2017).

Morgan, Hiram, 'Policy and Propaganda in Hugh O'Neill's Connection with Europe', in O'Connor and Lyons, eds, *The Ulster Earls and Baroque Europe: Refashioning Irish Identities* (Dublin: Four Courts Press, 2010), 18–52.

Morrill, John, 'An Irish Protestation? Oaths and the Confederation of Kilkenny', in Michael Braddick and Phil Whithington, eds, *Popular Culture and Political Agency in Early Modern England* (Manchester: Manchester University Press, 2006), 181–195.

———'Civil Wars and Interregnum', in James E. Kelly and John McCafferty, eds, *The Oxford History of British and Irish Catholicism*, 5 vols (Oxford: Oxford University Press, 2023), vol. 2, *Uncertainty and Change, 1641–1745*, 10–34.

——— 'The Covenant in its British Context', in idem, ed, *The Scottish National Covenant in its British Context* (Edinburgh: Edinburgh University Press, 1990), 1–30.

Morrill, John, and Liam Temple, 'Introduction', in James E. Kelly and John McCafferty, eds, *Oxford History of British and Irish Catholicism*, vol. 2, *Uncertainty and Change, 1641–1745* (Oxford: Oxford University Press, 2023), 1–9.

Morrissey, Thomas, 'Review: *A New History of Ireland, Vol. III: Early Modern Ireland, 1534–1691*', edited by T. W. Moody, F. X. Martin, F. J. Byrne, *Studies*, 65 (1976), 349–354.

Mouchel, Christian, *Rome franciscaine: essai sur l'histoire de l'éloquence dans l'Ordre des Frères Mineurs au XVIe siècle* (Paris: Champion, 2001).

Müller, Anne, 'Conflicting Loyalties: The Irish Franciscans and the English Crown in the High Middle Ages', *RIA Proc.*, 107C (2007), 87–106.

Mullett, Michael, *The Catholic Reformation* (repr. Abingdon: Routledge, 2023).

Murphy, Elaine, *Ireland and the War at Sea, 1641–1653* (Woodbridge: Boydell & Brewer, 2012).

Murray, James, *Enforcing the English Reformation in Ireland: Clerical Resistance and Political Conflict in the Diocese of Dublin, 1534–90* (Cambridge: Cambridge University Press, 2011).

Muscat, Noel, 'The Life of Saint Francis in the Light of Saint Bonaventure's Theology on the *Verbum crucifixium*', *Studia Antoniana cura Pontificii Athenei Antoniani edita*, 33 (Floriana, Malta: Edizzjoni Tau, 1989).

Nadal Iniesta, Javier, 'Fray Antonio de Trejo: el primer principe contrarreformista de la diócesis de Cartagena', in María Concepción de la Peña Velasco, et al., eds, *Congreso Internacional Imagen Apariencia*, November 2008 (Murcia: Universidad de Murcia, 2009). <https://digitum.um.es/digitum/bitstream/10201/44224/1/CongresoImagen125.pdf>

Nexon, Daniel, *The Struggle for Power in Early Modern Europe: Religious Conflict, Dynastic Empires, and International Change* (Princeton: Princeton University Press, 2009).

Ní Chinnéide, Síle, 'Luke Wadding, 1588–1657: Tercentenary Lecture', *JGAHS* 26 (1955), 81–93.

Nicholls, Kenneth, 'A List of the Monasteries in Connacht, 1577', *JGAHS*, 33 (1972–73), 28–43.

Nilis, Jeroen, ed, 'Irish Students at Leuven University, 1548–1797 (with index)', *Archiv. Hib.*, 60 (2006/2007), 1–304.

Nora, Pierre, *Realms of Memory*, translated by Arthur Goldhammer, edited and with a foreword Lawrence Kritzman, 3 vols (New York: Columbia University Press, 1996–98).

——— 'Between Memory and History: *Les Lieux de Mémoire*', *Representations*, 26 (1989), 7–24.

Ó Clabaigh, Colmán, *The Friars in Ireland, 1224–1540* (Dublin: Four Courts Press, 2012).

——— 'Harold, Francis (*c.*1617–85), Franciscan Priest and Historian', in James McGuire and James Quinn, eds, *Dictionary of Irish Biography*, 9 vols (Cambridge: Cambridge University Press, 2009), vol. 4, 469–470.

——— 'Review: Benedict O'Sullivan OP, edited by Hugh Fenning OP, *Medieval Irish Dominican Studies* (2009)', *JRSAI*, 139 (2009), 135–136.

——— *The Franciscans in Ireland: From Reform to Reformation* (Dublin: Four Courts Press, 2002).

Ó Conbhuidhe, Colmcille, *The Cistercian Abbeys of Tipperary* (Dublin: Four Courts Press, 1999).

——— *Studies in Irish Cistercian History*, edited by Finbarr Donovan and with a foreword by Roger Stalley (Dublin: Four Courts Press, 1998).

O Connell, Patricia, *The Irish College at Lisbon, 1580–1834* (Dublin: Four Courts Press, 2001).

Ó hAnnracháin, Tadhg, 'The Early Stuarts', in James E. Kelly and John McCafferty, eds, *Oxford History of British and Irish Catholicism* (Oxford: Oxford University Press, 2023), vol. 1, *Endings and New Beginnings, 1530–1640*, 89–106.

——— 'The Regular Clergy and the Episcopate in Ireland, 1600–50', in Cormac Begadon and James E. Kelly, eds, *British and Irish Religious Orders in Europe, 1560–1800: Conventuals, Mendicants and Monastics in Motion* (Woodbridge: Boydell & Brewer, 2022), 43–59.

——— *Confessionalism and Mobility in Early Modern Ireland* (Oxford: Oxford University Press, 2021).

——— 'Conflicting Loyalties, Conflicted Rebels: Political and Religious Allegiance among the Confederate Catholics of Ireland', *EHR*, 119 (2004), 851–872.

——— *Catholic Reformation in Ireland: The Mission of Rinuccini, 1645–1649* (Oxford: Oxford University Press, 2002).

——— 'Disrupted and Disruptive: Continental Influence on the Confederate Catholics of Ireland' in Allan Macinnes and Jane Ohlmeyer, eds, *The Stuart Kingdoms in the Seventeenth Century* (Dublin: Four Courts Press, 2002), 135–146.

——— 'Vatican Diplomacy and the Mission of Rinuccini to Ireland', *Archiv. Hib.*, 47 (1993), 78–88.

Ó Mórdha, Séamus, 'Heber MacMahon, Soldier-Bishop of the Confederation of Kilkenny', *Clogher Record: A Diocesan History*, 3 (1975), 41–62.

Ó Siochrú, 'Barron (Baron), Geoffrey, (1606–51), Lawyer, Politician and Diplomat', in James McGuire and James Quinn, eds, *Dictionary of Irish Biography*, 9 vols (Cambridge: Cambridge University Press, 2009), vol. 1, 315–316.

——— 'O'Neill, Owen Roe (Ó Néill, Eoghan Rua)', in James McGuire and James Quinn, eds, *Dictionary of Irish Biography*, 9 vols (Cambridge: Cambridge University Press, 2009), vol. 7, 786–792.

——— 'The Duke of Lorraine and the International Struggle for Ireland, 1649–53', *HJ*, 48 (2005), 905–32.

——— *Confederate Ireland, 1642–1649: A Constitutional and Political Analysis* (Dublin: Four Courts Press, 2005).

O'Connor, Thomas, 'Exile Movement: Male Institutions, 1568–1640', in James E. Kelly and John McCafferty, eds, *The Oxford History of British and Irish Catholicism*, vol. 1: *Endings and New Beginnings, 1530–1640* (Oxford: Oxford University Press, 2023), 203–222.

——— 'Domestic Grammar Schools and Overseas Colleges in the Formation of Irish Catholic Clergy (1560–1620)', in Anja-Silvia Goeing, Glyn Parry and Mordechai Feingold, eds, *Early Modern Universities: Networks of Higher Learning* (Leiden: Brill, 2021), 208–224.

——— 'Prequels: The Irish European Diaspora', in Bettina Migge and Gisela Holfter, eds, *Ireland in the European Eye* (Dublin: Royal Irish Academy, 2019), 3–19. <https://doi.org/10.2307/j.ctvkwnn86>

——— *Irish Voices from the Spanish Inquisition: Migrants, Converts and Brokers in Early Modern Iberia* (Basingstoke: Palgrave Macmillan, 2016).

——— *Irish Jansenists, 1600–70: Religion and Politics in Flanders, France, Ireland and Rome* (Dublin: Four Courts Press, 2008).

——— 'Luke Wadding's Networks at Home and Abroad', in Dáire Keogh and Albert McDonnell, eds, *The Irish College, Rome and its World* (Dublin: Four Courts Press, 2008), 14–23.

——— *An Irish Jansenist in Seventeenth-Century France: John Callaghan, 1605–54*. The O'Donnell Lecture 2004 (Dublin: National University of Ireland, 2005).

——— 'Marsh's Library and the Irish Catholic Tradition', in Muriel McCarthy and Ann Simmons, eds, *The Making of Marsh's Library: Learning, Politics and Religion in Ireland, 1650–1750* (Dublin: Four Courts Press, 2004), 235–55.

——— 'The Irish College, Rome, in the Age of Religious Renewal, 1625–90', in John Hanly, ed, *Collegium Hibernorum de Urbe, 1628–78. An Early Manuscript Account of the Foundation and Development of the Ludovisian College of the Irish in Rome* (Rome: Pontificio Collegio Irlandese, 2003), 13–32.

——— ed, *The Irish in Europe, 1580–1815* (Dublin: Four Courts Press, 2001).

——— 'Thomas Messingham (*c.*1575–1638?) and the Seventeenth-Century Church', *Riocht na Midhe*, 11 (2000), 88–105.

O'Connor, Thomas, and Mary Ann Lyons, eds, *Irish Migrants in Europe after Kinsale, 1602–1820* (Dublin: Four Courts Press, 2003).

——— eds, *Irish Communities in Early-Modern Europe* (Dublin: Four Courts Press, 2006).

——— *Strangers to Citizens: the Irish in Europe, 1600–1800* (Dublin: National Library of Ireland, 2008).

——— eds, *The Ulster Earls and Baroque Europe: Refashioning Irish Identities, 1600–1800* (Dublin: Four Courts Press, 2009).

O'Doherty, Denis, ed, 'Students of the Irish College Salamanca (1595–1619)', *Archiv. Hib.*, 2 (1913), 13–33.

O'Malley, John W., Gauvin Alexander Bailey and Steven J. Harris, eds, *The Jesuits: Cultures, Sciences, and the Arts*, 2 vols (Toronto: University of Toronto Press, 1999–2006).

O'Malley, John W., *Trent: What Happened at the Council* (Cambridge MA: Harvard University Press, 2013).

——— *The First Jesuits* (Cambridge MA: Harvard University Press, 1995).

——— 'Priesthood, Ministry, and Religious Life: Some Historical and Historiographical Considerations', *Theological Studies*, 49 (1988), 223–257.

——— 'Preaching for the Popes', in Charles Trinkaus and Heiko Oberman, eds, *The Pursuit of Holiness in Late Medieval and Renaissance Religion* (Leiden: Brill, 1974), 408–440.

O'Neill, Charles and José María Domínguez, eds, *Diccionario Histórico de la Compañía de Jesús*, 4 vols (Rome: Institutum Historicum Societatis Iesu–Madrid: Universidad Pontificia de Comillas, 2001).

O'Neill, James, *The Nine Years War, 1593–1603: O'Neill, Mountjoy and the Military Revolution* (Dublin: Four Courts Press, 2018).

O'Reilly, Thomas, 'Manuscripta Franciscana Archivi Conventus Dublinensis OFM', *AFH*, 7 (1914), 749–59.

O'Scea, Ciaran, 'From Convents to Chapels of Ease: Irish Burial and Funerary Practices in Early Modern Madrid, 1600–80', in Benjamin Hazard, ed, *Path to Salvation: Temporal and Spiritual Journeys by the Mendicant Orders, c.1370–1740* (Lausanne: Peter Lang, 2023), 145–164.

O'Shea, Joseph, *The Life of Father Luke Wadding: Founder of St Isidore's College, Rome* (Dublin: M. H. Gill, 1885).

O'Sullivan, Mary D., *Italian Merchant Bankers in Ireland in the Thirteenth Century: A Study in the Social and Economic History of Medieval Ireland* (Dublin: Figgis, 1962).

Ohlmeyer, Jane, 'Introduction', in idem, ed, *Ireland from Independence to Occupation, 1641–60* (Cambridge: Cambridge University Press, 2002), 1–23.

——— *Civil War and Restoration in the Three Stuart Kingdoms: the Career of Randal MacDonnell, Marquis of Antrim* (Dublin: Four Courts Press, 2001).

——— 'The Civil Wars in Ireland', in Peter Kenyon and Jane Ohlmeyer, eds, *The Civil Wars, a Military History of England, Scotland and Ireland, 1638–1660* (Oxford: Oxford University Press, 1998), 73–102.

——— 'Irish Privateers during the Civil War, 1642–50', *Mariner's Mirror*, 76 (1990), 119–34.

——— 'The Dunkirk of Ireland: Wexford Privateers during the 1640s', *Journal of the Wexford Historical Society*, 12 (1988–89), 23–48.

Olden, Michael, ed, *The Life and Times of Patrick Comerford OSA (1586–1652): Counter-Reformation Bishop of Waterford and Lismore, 1629–52* (Waterford: Intacta, 2013).

Oliger, Livarius, 'De nova Lucae Waddingi Annalium Minorum editione', *AFH*, 24 (1931), 402–404.

Oliveira, Maria Gabriela, 'A reedição dos 'Annales Minorum' de Lucas Wadding e a figura de Fr. Joseph Maria da Fonseca e Évora', in José Adriano Moreira de Freitas Carvalho, ed, *Frei Marcos de Lisboa: cronista franciscano bispo de Lisboa. Actas do Colóquio patrocinado por la Faculdade de Letras do Porto* (Porto: Faculdade de Letras do Porto, 2002), 93–104.

Orschel, Vera, and John Hanly, eds, 'Calendar of Seventeenth- and Eighteenth-Century Documents at the Archives of the Irish College, Rome (with Index)', *Archiv. Hib.*, 63 (2010), 7–263.

Osório da Gama e Castro, José, *Diocese e districto da Guarda: serie de apontamentos históricos e tradicionaes sobre as suas antiguidades, algumas observações respeitantes à actualidade e notas referentes à cathedral egitaniense e respectivos prelados* (Porto: Typographia Universal, 1902).

Pandžić, Basilio, 'Gli «Annales Minorum» di Luca Wadding', *AFH*, 70 (1977), 656–66.

Pařez, Jan, and Hedvika Kuchařová, *The Irish Franciscans in Prague, 1629–1786. History of the Franciscan College of the Immaculate Conception of the Virgin Mary in Prague* (Prague: Karolinum Press, 2015).

Parker, Geoffrey, *Spain and the Netherlands, 1559–1659: Ten Studies* (London: Collins, 1979).

——— *The Dutch Revolt* (London: Allen Lane, 1977).

Parrott, David, *Richelieu's Army: War, Government and Society in France 1624–42* (Cambridge: Cambridge University Press, 2001).

Pasiecznik, Marcellus, 'John de Bassolis OFM', *Franciscan Studies*, 13 (1953), 59–77.

Pasztor, Edith, 'Luca Wadding, editore della «Vita Anselmi episcopi Lucensis»', *AFH*, 54 (1961), 303–328.

Pattenden, Miles, *Pius V and the Fall of the Carafa: Nepotism and Papal Authority in Counter-Reformation Rome* (Oxford: Oxford University Press, 2013).

Péligry, Christian, 'La oficina Plantiniana, el monasterio de El Escorial y los libros litúrgicos en España durante el siglo XVII', *Cuadernos bibliográficos,* 37 (1978), 465–473.

Pérez Martínez, Llorenç, 'Fray Lucas Wadding, postulador de la causa de Beatificación de Ramón Llull (1638)', *Studia Lulliana*, 1 (1957), 262–68.

Pérez Pastor, Cristóbal, 'Impresores y libreros de Madrid. Documentos referentes a ellos', *Memorias de la Real Academia Española* (1926), 191–412.

Pérez Tostado, Igor, '"Learned, Attached and Reliable': Luke Wadding, Agent of the Spanish Monarchy', in Matteo Binasco, ed, *Luke Wadding, the Irish Franciscans and Global Catholicism* (Abingdon: Routledge, 2020), 39–48.

——— *Irish Influence at the Court of Spain in the Seventeenth Century* (Dublin: Four Courts Press, 2008).

Pettas, William, *A History and Bibliography of the Giunti (Junta) Printing Family in Spain 1526–1628* (New Castle DE: Oak Knoll Press, 2005).

Pettegree, Andrew, *The French Book and the European Book World* (Leiden: Brill, 2007).

Pinto Costa, Paula, and Renata Cristina de Sousa Nascimento, *A visibilidade do sagrado: relíquias cristãs na Idade Média* (2nd edn. Curitiba: Editora Appris, 2022).

Po-chia Hsia, Ronnie, *The World of Catholic Renewal, 1540–1770* (Cambridge: Cambridge University Press, 1998).

Poole, Stafford, 'The Politics of *Limpieza de Sangre:* Juan de Ovando and his Circle in the Reign of Philip II', *Americas*, 55 (1999), 359–389.

Pou y Martí, José-Maríá, 'Embajadas de Felipe III a Roma, pidiendo la definición de la Inmaculada Concepción de María' *Archivo Ibero-americano*, 34 (1931), 371–417, 508–534; 35 (1932), 72–88, 424–434, 481–525; 36 (1933), 5–48.

Power, Patrick, *The Place Names of Decies* (London: David Nutt, 1907, repr. Cork: Cork University Press, 1952).

——— *Waterford and Lismore: A Compendious History of the United Dioceses* (Cork: Cork University Press, 1937).

——— *Waterford Saints and Scholars (17th century)* (Waterford: Waterford Press, 1920).

Prosperi, Adriano, *Il Concilio di Trento: una introduzione storica* (Turin: Einaudi, 2001).

Quane, Michael, 'Waterford Corporation Free School', *Cork Hist. Soc. Jn.*, 65 (1959), 82–103.

Quigley, E. J., *The Divine Office: A Study of the Roman Breviary* (Dublin: Gill, 1920).

Quinn, Hubert, *Saint Isidore's Church and College of the Irish Franciscans, Rome* (Rome: Tipografia Poliglotta Vaticana, 1948).

Ratzinger, Joseph, *The Theology of History in St Bonaventure*, translated by Zachary Hayes OFM (repr. Chicago: Franciscan Herald Press, 1989).

Recio Morales, Óscar, *Ireland and the Spanish Empire, 1600–1825*, translated by Michael White (Dublin: Four Cours Press, 2010).

——— ed, *La Presencia Irlandesa en los Ejércitos de la Monarquía Hispánica, 1580–1818*, CD-ROM (Madrid: Ministerio de Defensa, 2007).

Rial Costas, Benito, ed, *Print Culture and Peripheries in Early Modern Europe: A Contribution to the History of Printing and the Book Trade in Small European and Spanish Cities* (Leiden: Brill, 2012).

Rietbergen, Peter, *Power and Religion in Baroque Rome: Barberini* (Leiden: Brill, 2006).

Robinson, Paschal, *The Writings of Saint Francis of Assisi* (Philadelphia: Dolphin Press, 1905).

Robson, Michael, 'The Commemoration of the Living and the Dead at the Friars Minor of Cambridge', in John Lee and Christian Steer, eds, *Commemoration in Medieval Cambridge*. History of the University of Cambridge Series (Woodbridge: Boydell, 2018).

Rocciolo, Domenico, 'Cum suspicione morbi contagiosi obierunt. Società, religione e peste a Roma nel 1656–57', in Irene Fosi, ed, *La peste a Roma* (Rome: Università Roma Tre-CROMA, 2006), 111–34.

Rodríguez Cruz, Águeda, *Historia de la Universidad de Salamanca* (Salamanca: Fundación Ramón Areces y Congregación de Santo Domingo, 1990).

Rodríguez de la Torre, Fernando, 'Pérez García, Julián. Iniesta (Cuenca), 31.I.1598 – Murcia, 4.III.1657', *DBe*. <https://dbe.rah.es/biografias/66296/julian-perez-garcia>

Rodríguez Pazos, Manuel, *Los Estudios en la Provincia Franciscana de Santiago-Tratado Histórico* (Madrid: Escuelas Profesionales Sagrado Corazón de Jesús, 1967).

——— 'Las bibliotecas en la Provincia de Santiago', *Archivo Ibero-Americano*, 14 (1954), 456–480.

Rodríguez-San Pedro Bezares, Luis Enrique, *Estudiantes de Salamanca* (Salamanca: Ediciones Universidad de Salamanca, 2001).

Roest, Bert, *Order and Disorder: The Poor Clares Between Foundation and Reform* (Leiden: Brill, 2013).

——— *A History of Franciscan Education, c.1210–1517* (Leiden: Brill, 2000).

Rosa, Mario, *La curia romana nell'età moderna. Instituzioni, cultura, carriere* (Rome: Viella, 2013).

Rudolph, Stella, 'Carlo Maratti e l'Inghilterra', in Liliana Barroero, Simonetta Prosperi, Valenti Rodinò and Sebastian Schütze, eds, *Maratti e l'Europa* (Rome: Campisano, 2015), 127–43.

Rui Gomes Teixeira, Vítor, 'Os Frades Menores em Portugal desde 1217', *Archivo Ibero-Americano*, 77 (2017), 161–220.

Rummel, Erika, *Jiménez de Cisneros: On the Threshold of Spain's Golden Age* (Tempe AZ: Arizona Center for Medieval and Renaissance Studies, 1999).

Ryan, Salvador, 'Reconstructing Irish Catholic History after the Reformation', in Katherine Van Liere, Simon Ditchfield and Howard Louthan, eds, *Sacred History: Uses of the Christian Past in the Renaissance* (Oxford: Oxford University Press, 2012), 186–205.

——— 'Steadfast Saints or Malleable Models? Seventeenth-century Irish Hagiography Revisited', *CHR*, 91 (2005), 251–277.

Ryland, R. H., *The History, Topography & Antiquities of Waterford* (London: Murray, 1824).

Sabatier, Paul, *Life of St Francis* (New York: Charles Scribner, 1894).

Sallman, Jean-Michel, *Naples et ses saints à l'âge baroque, 1540–1750* (Paris: Presses universitaires de France, 1994).

Sánchez y Sánchez, Daniel, 'Metodología didáctica en la Universidad de Salamanca durante el siglo XVI', paper presented at *15th International Congress of Historical Sciences, Bucharest, 1980. Documents, Information, Testimonies*, 3 vols (1980), vol. 3, 409–52.

Sánchez, Magdalena, 'Where Palace and Convent met: the Descalzas Reales in Madrid', *Sixteenth Century Journal*, 46 (2015), 53–82.

Schatz, Klaus, *Papal Primacy: From Its Origins to the Present* (Collegeville MN: Liturgical Press, 1996).

Schaub, Jean Frédéric, 'Maritime Archipelago, Political Archipelago: The Azores under the Habsburgs (1581–1640)', in Pedro Cardim et al., eds, *Polycentric Monarchies: How did Early Modern Spain and Portugal achieve and maintain a global hegemony?* (Eastbourne: Sussex Academic Press, 2012), 11–26.

——— *Portugal na Monarquia Hispânica, 1560–1640* (Lisbon: Livraria Horizonte, 2001).

Schilling, Heinz, 'Christliche und Jüdische Minderheitengemeinden im Vergleich: Calvinistische Exulanten und westliche Diaspora der Sephardim im 16. und 17. Jahrhundert', *Zeitschrift für Historische Forschung*, 36 (2009), 407–44.

——— *Early Modern European Civilization and its Political and Cultural Dynamism* (Waltham MA: Brandeis University Press, 2008).

Schmitt, Clement, 'Manuscrits de la "Franciscan Library", Killiney', *AFH*, 57 (1964), 165–90.

Schmutz, Jacob, 'Bellum scholasticum. Thomisme et antithomisme dans les débats doctrinaux modernes', *Revue thomiste*, 108 (2008), 131–182.

Schüller, Karin, 'Special Conditions of the Irish-Iberian Trade during the Spanish-English War, 1585–1604', in Óscar Recio Morales, Bernardo García García, Miguel Ángel de Bunes Ibarra, Enrique García Hernán, eds, *Irlanda y la Monarquía Hispánica. Kinsale 1601–2001: Guerra, Política, Exilio y Religion* (Madrid: CSIC, 2002), 447–68.

Scott, A. B., 'Latin Learning and Literature in Ireland, 1169–1500', in Dáibhí Ó Cróinín, ed, *A New History of Ireland*. Vol. 1, *Prehistoric and Early Ireland* (Oxford: Oxford University Press, 2005), 934–95.

Shagan, Ethan, 'Early Modern Violence from Memory to History: A Historiographical Essay', in Micheál Ó Siochrú and Jane Ohlmeyer, eds, *Ireland: 1641. Contexts and Reactions* (Manchester: Manchester University Press, 2013), 17–36.

Sheehan, Anthony, 'Irish Towns in a Period of Change, 1558–1625', in Ciaran Brady and Raymond Gillespie, eds, *Natives and Newcomers: Essays on the Making of Irish Colonial Society* (Dublin: Irish Academic Press, 1986), 93–119.

Short, William J., 'Early Franciscan Sources and Joachite Prophetic Sources in the Book of Conformities', in Michael F. Cusato, Timothy Johnson, Steven McMichael, eds, *Ordo et Sanctitas: The Franciscan Spiritual Journey in Theology and Hagiography: A Festschrift in Honor of J. A. Wayne Hellmann, OFM Conv.* (Leiden: Brill, 2017), 251–71.

Sicari, Antonio, *Il Grande Libro dei Ritratti di Santi* (Milan: Jaca, 1997).

Silke, J. J., 'Irish Scholarship and the Renaissance, 1580–1673', *Studies in the Renaissance*, 20 (1973), 169–206.

——— 'The Irish Abroad, 1534–1691', in T. W. Moody, F. X. Martin and F. J. Byrne, eds, *A New History of Ireland* (Oxford, 1976; reprinted with bibliographical supplement, 2009), vol. 3, *Early Modern Ireland, 1534–1691*, 587–632.

Simons, Ludo, and Pierre Delsaerdt, *Plantin and the Typographical Tradition in Flanders* (London: Wynkyn De Worde Society, 2001).

Smith, Charles, *The Ancient and Present State of the County and City of Waterford* (Dublin: A. Reilly, 1746).

Smith, Frederick, 'The Origins of Recusancy in Elizabethan England Reconsidered', *HJ*, 60 (2017), 301–32.

Sommerfeldt, J. R., ed, *Cistercian Ideals and Reality* (Kalamazoo: Cistercian Publishing, 1978).

Sommervogel, Carlos, ed, *Bibliotheque de la Compagnie de Jésus*, 12 vols; 1–10 vols (Brussels: Schepens, 1890–1909; repr. Louvain: Éditions de la Bibliothèque S. J., 1960); vol. 11 (Paris: Picard, 1932); vol. 12 (Louvain: Éditions de la Bibliothèque S. J., 1960).

Spiertz, Mathieu G., 'Anti-jansenisme en jansenisme in de Nederlanden in de achttiende en negentiende eeuw', *Trajecta*, 1 (1992), 233–51.

Spoltore, Giulia, 'Carlo Maratti, Giovan Pietro Bellori, Luke Wadding e Ilarione Rancati: dibattito teologico e strategie politiche a Roma negli anni di discussion dell'Augustinus di Giansenio', in Francesco Carta, Silvia Omenetto and Giulia Spoltore, eds, *Itinera, Uomini, oggetti e idee in movimento* (Rome: Edizioni Efesto, 2023), 131–162.

——— 'Luke Wadding and Scholars for the Arts in Seventeenth-century Rome', in Matteo Binasco, ed, *Luke Wadding, the Irish Franciscans, and Global Catholicism* (Abingdon: Routledge, 2020), 123–144.

——— 'Luke Wadding e l'Eredità di Cesare Baronio: Storiografia e Arte nel Seicento a Roma', *Annales Oratorii*, 17 (2019), 41–60.

Springhetti, Aemilius, 'Urbanus VIII PM poeta latinus et hymnorum Brevarii emendator', *AHP*, 6 (1968), 163–90.

Stalley, Roger, 'Sailing to Santiago: Medieval Pilgrimage to Santiago de Compostela and its Artistic Influence in Ireland', in John Bradley, ed, *Settlement and Society in Medieval Ireland: Studies presented to F. X. Martin OSA* (Kilkenny: Boethius Press, 1988), 397–420.

Stella, Pietro, *Il giansenismo in Italia*, 3 vols (Rome: Edizioni di storia e letteratura, 2006).

Stevenson, David, *Scottish Covenanters and Irish Confederates: Scottish-Irish Relations in the Mid-Seventeenth Century* (Belfast: Ulster Historical Foundation, 1981; repr. 2004).

Stradling, Robert, *The Spanish Monarchy and Irish Mercenaries: The Wild Geese in Spain, 1618–68* (Dublin: Irish Academic Press, 1994).

——— *The Armada of Flanders: Spanish Maritime Policy and European War, 1568–1668* (Cambridge: Cambridge University Press, 1992).

Stratton, Suzanne, *The Immaculate Conception in Spanish Art* (Cambridge: Cambridge University Press, 1994).

Swanson, Robert, *Religion and Devotion in Europe, c.1215–c.1515* (Cambridge: Cambridge University Press, 1995).

Tellechea Idígoras, José Ignacio, *El obispo ideal en el siglo de la Reforma* (Rome: Instituto Español de Historia Eclesiástica, 1963).

Thompson, Augustine, *Francis of Assisi. The Life* (Ithaca, NY: Cornell University Press, 2013).

Thornton, Ryan, *Franciscan Poverty and Franciscan Economic Thought, 1209–1348* (Leiden: Brill, 2023).

Tjoelker, Nienke, and Ian Campbell, 'Transcription and Translation of London version of Richard O'Ferrall's Report to Propaganda Fide (1658)', *Archiv. Hib.*, 61 (2008), 7–61.

Trasselli, Franca, 'Ilarione Rancati "milanese dell ordine cisterciense", il collegio di studi e la biblioteca Romana di S. Croce in Gerusalemme', *Aevum*, 81 (2007), 793–876.

Tuck, Steven, *A History of Roman Art* (2nd edn. Hoboken NJ: Wiley, 2021).

Turchi, Nicola, 'Wadding, Luca, Teologo e storico francescano', *Enciclopedia Italiana di scienze, lettere ed arti* (Rome: Treccani, 1937). <http://156.54.191.164/enciclopedia/luca-wadding_%28Enciclopedia-Italiana%29/>

Turchini, Angelo, 'La nascita del sacerdozio come professione', in Paolo Prodi, ed, *Disciplina dell'anima, disciplina del corpo e disciplina della società tra medioevo ed età moderna* (Bologna: Il Mulino, 1994), 225–256.

Tutino, Stefania, *Uncertainty in Post-Reformation Catholicism. A History of Probabilism* (Oxford: Oxford University Press, 2018).

Úbeda de Los Cobos, Andrés, 'The Pictorial Decoration of the Buen Retiro Palace', in idem, ed, *Paintings for the Planet King, Philip IV and the Buen Retiro Palace* (Madrid: Museo Nacional del Prado, 2005), 15–28.

Underwood, Lucy, *Childhood, Youth and Religious Dissent in Post-Reformation England* (Basingstoke: Palgrave Macmillan, 2014).

Van Dijk, S. J. P., and J. Hazleden Walker, *The Origins of the Modern Roman Liturgy: The Liturgy of the Papal Court and the Franciscans in the Thirteenth Century* (London: Newman Press, 1960).

Van Rossem, Stijn, 'The Bookshop of the Counter-Reformation Revisited: the Verdussen Company and the Trade in Catholic Publications, Antwerp, 1585–1648', *Quaerendo*, 38 (2008), 306–321.

Varela Gomes, Paolo, 'Damnatio Memoriae. A arquitectura dos marqueses de Castelo Rodrigo', in José Luis Colomer, ed, *Arte y Diplomacia de la Monarquía Hispánica en el Siglo XVII* (Madrid: Fernando Villaverde Ediciones, 2003), 351–376.

Vauchez, André, *Francis of Assisi: The Life and Afterlife of a Medieval Saint*, translated by Michael F. Cusato (New Haven CT: Yale University Press).

Vázquez Janeiro, Isaac, 'La enseñanza del escotismo en España', in *De doctrina Ioannis Duns Scoti*, 4 vols (Rome: Societas Internationalis Scotistica, 1968), vol. 4, *Scotismus decursu saeculorum*, 191–220.

Velasco López, María del Henar, 'Divus Iacobus in Ibernia', in Jesús María Nieto Ibañez, ed, *Lógos Hellenikós: Homeaje al Profesor Gaspar Morocho Gayo*, 2 vols (León: Universidad de León, 2003), vol. 2, 783–95.

Villari, Rosario, and Lydia Cochrane, eds, *Baroque Personae* (Chicago: University of Chicago Press, 1995).

Voet, León, 'The Moretuses', *Antwerp's Golden Age: The Metropolis of the West in the Sixteenth and Seventeenth Centuries* (Washington: Smithsonian Institute, 1973).

Von Pastor, Ludwig, *History of the Popes from the Close of the Middle Ages drawn from the Secret Archives of the Vatican and Other Original Sources*, 40 vols, translated and edited by Frederick Ignatius Antrobus and Francis Kerr, Francis (repr. Wilmington NC: Consortium, 1978), vols 28 and 31.

Vos, Antonie, *The Theology of John Duns Scotus* (Leiden: Brill, 2018).

Walton, Julian, 'Age of Faith', in Eamonn McEneaney, ed, *A History of Waterford and its Mayors from the Twelfth to the Twentieth Century* (Waterford: Waterford Corporation, 1995), 81–103.

———'Church, Crown and Corporation in Waterford City, 1520–1620', in William Nolan and Thomas Power, eds, *Waterford: History and Society. Interdisciplinary Essays on the History of an Irish County*, associate editor Des Cowman (Dublin: Geography Publications, 1992), 177–98.

———ed, 'The Freemen of Waterford, 1542–1650', *Irish Genealogist*, 5 (1978), 560–572.

Weinheimer, James, 'Finding Calasio: Princeton's Library Catalogs, 1760–1966', *PULC*, 58 (1996), 32–56.

Welch, Anna, *Liturgy, Books and Franciscan Identity in Medieval Umbria* (Leiden: Brill, 2015).

Welwei, Karl-Wilhelm, 'Presbeia, Presbeis', *Brill's New Pauly, Antiquity volumes*, ed, Hubert Cancik and Helmuth Schneider, English edition by Christine Salazar, *Classical Tradition* volumes edited by Manfred Landfester, English edition by Francis Gentry. <http://dx.doi.org/10.1163/1574-9347_bnp_e1008130>

Weruaga Prieto, Ángel, *Los universitarios y el libro en la Salamanca clásica (ss. XVI-XVIII). Estado de la cuestión, fuentes, retos. «Fuentes, archivos y bibliotecas para una historia de las universidades hispánicas»* (Salamanca: Ediciones Universidad de Salamanca, 2016).

Wilkinson, Alexander, and Alejandra Ulla Lorenzo, eds, *A Maturing Market: The Iberian Book World in the First Half of the Seventeenth Century* (Leiden: Brill, 2017).

——— eds, *Iberian Books Volumes II & III / Libros Ibéricos Volúmenes II y III: Books published in Spain, Portugal and the New World or elsewhere in Spanish or Portuguese between 1601 and 1650 / Libros publicados en España, Portugal y el Nuevo Mundo o impresos en otros lugares en español o portugués entre 1601 y 1650* (Leiden, Brill, 2015).

Wilkinson, Alexander, ed, *Iberian Books / Libros Ibéricos (IB): Books published in Spanish or Portuguese or on the Iberian Peninsula Before 1601 / Libros publicados en español o portugués o en la Península Ibérica antes de 1601* (Leiden: Brill, 2010).

Williams, Patrick, *Philip II* (Basingstoke: Palgrave Macmillan, 2017).

Williams, Thomas, 'Introduction: The Life and Works of John Duns the Scot', in idem, ed, *The Cambridge Companion to Duns Scotus* (Cambridge: Cambridge University Press, 2003), 1–14.

Wilson, Peter, *Thirty Years War: Europe's Tragedy* (Cambridge MA: Belknap Press, 2011).

Wolter, Allan, *John Duns Scotus' Political and Economic Philosophy* (New York: Franciscan Institute, St Bonaventure University, 2001).

Wright, A. D., *The Counter-Reformation: Catholic Europe and the Non-Christian World* (Farnham: Ashgate, 2005).

——— *Catholicism and Spanish Society under the Reign of Philip II, 1555–1598, and Philip III, 1598–1621* (Lampeter: Edwin Mellen Press, 1991).

Zuccari, Alessandro, 'L'Immacolata a Roma dal Quattrocento al Settecento', in Giovanni Morello, Vincenzo Francia and Roberto Fusco, eds, *Una Donna vestita di Sole: l'Immacolata Concezione nelle Opere dei Grandi Maestri* (Milan: Motta 2005), 65–77.

Unpublished Theses

Edwards, David, *The Ormond Lordship in County Kilkenny, 1515–1642* (Unpublished PhD thesis, Trinity College Dublin, 1998).

Gagliardi, Elena Maria, 'Giovanni Pietro Puricelli e l'erudizione ecclesiastica nella Milano del Seicento' (Unpublished Doctoral thesis, Università Cattolica del Sacro Cuore, 2010).

Mazza, Monica, 'Giovanni Pietro Puricelli storico degli Umiliati, tesi di laurea discussa presso la facoltà di Lettere e Filosofia dell'Università Cattolica del Sacro Cuore di Milano' (Unpublished MA thesis, Università Cattolica del Sacro Cuore, 1989/90).

Vander Vennet, Matthew T., 'An Early Defender of the Immaculate Conception of the Blessed Virgin Mary: Fr. Luke Wadding, OFM'. (Unpublished PhD thesis: The Catholic University of America, 2023).

Electronic Sources

Busolini, Dario, 'Franciotti, Marco Antonio', in *Dizionario biografico degli italiani* (Rome: Istituto dell'Enciclopedia Italiana, 1960–2020). <https://www.treccani.it/enciclopedia/marco-antonio-franciotti_(Dizionario-Biografico)/>

Cagnetti, Francesco, 'Benigno da Genova (al secolo Agostino Rosso)', in *Dizionario biografico degli italiani* (Rome: Istituto dell'Enciclopedia Italiana, 1960–2020). <https://www.treccani.it/enciclopedia/benigno-da-genova_(Dizionario-Biografico)/>

García Oro, José, 'Sosa, Francisco de', in *Diccionario Biográfico electrónico de la Real Academia de la Historia* (Madrid: Real Academia de la Historia, 2009–13). <https://dbe.rah.es/biografias/30662/francisco-de-sosa>

Luke Wadding Papers: Correspondence relating to Fr Luke Wadding OFM and the Irish Friars Minor at St Isidore's College. < https://www.ucd.ie/mocleirigh/research/thewaddingpapers/>

Monticone, Alberto, 'Albizzi, Francesco', in *Dizionario biografico degli italiani* (Rome: Istituto dell'Enciclopedia Italiana, 1960–2020). <https://www.treccani.it/enciclopedia/francesco-albizzi_%28Dizionario-Biografico%29/>

Psalterivm Davidis, cum canticis sacris & selectis aliquot orationibvs (Antverpiæ: ex officina Plantiniana Balthasaris Moreti, 1657). <http://www.vlaamse-erfgoedbibliotheek.be/en/database/stcv>

Rodríguez de la Torre, Fernando, 'Pérez García, Julián. Iniesta (Cuenca), 31.I.1598 – Murcia, 4.III.1657. Religioso franciscano (OFM)', in *Diccionario Biográfico electrónico de la Real Academia de la Historia* (Madrid: Real Academia de la Historia, 2009–13). <https://dbe.rah.es/biografias/66296/julian-perez-garcia>

Tribulationes Ordinis Fratrum Miroum Capuccinorum primis annis Pontificatus Pauli III (1534–1541). Haec Brevis Illustratio Monumentorum, editorum vel ineditorum, quae ad dicti Ordinis historiam spectant, correcta et ampliata secundo prodit, cura P. Eduardi Alenconiensis, Romae, Apud Curiam Generalitiam O.M.Cap. cura P. Eduardi Alenconiensis (Romae: apud Curiam generalitiam O.M.Cap., 1914). <https://www.capdox.capuchin.org.au/studies/edoardo-dalencon-troubles-of-capuchins-under-paul-iii/>

Index [1]

1 References to figures and tables are italicized.

Printed by
CPI books GmbH, Leck